# Napoleon and the Struggle for Germany

## VOLUME I

This is the first comprehensive history of the campaign that determined control of Germany following Napoleon's catastrophic defeat in Russia. Michael V. Leggiere reveals how, in the spring of 1813, Prussia, the weakest of the great powers, led the struggle against Napoleon as a war of national liberation. Using German, French, British, Russian, Austrian, and Swedish sources, he provides a panoramic history that covers the full sweep of the battle for Germany from the mobilization of the belligerents, strategy, and operations to coalition warfare, diplomacy, and civil–military relations. He shows how Russian war weariness conflicted with Prussian impetuosity, resulting in the crisis that almost ended the Sixth Coalition in early June. In a single campaign, Napoleon drove the Russo-Prussian army from the banks of the Saale to the banks of the Oder. The Russo-Prussian alliance was perilously close to imploding, only to be saved at the eleventh hour by an armistice.

**Michael V. Leggiere** is Professor of History and Deputy Director of the Military History Center at the University of North Texas.

# CAMBRIDGE MILITARY HISTORIES

*Edited by*

HEW STRACHAN, Chichele Professor of the History of War, University of
  Oxford, and Fellow of All Souls College, Oxford
GEOFFREY WAWRO, Professor of Military History and Director of the
  Military History Center, University of North Texas

The aim of this series is to publish outstanding works of research on warfare
throughout the ages and throughout the world. Books in the series take a
broad approach to military history, examining war in all its military, strategic, political, and economic aspects. The series complements Studies in the
Social and Cultural History of Modern Warfare by focusing on the "hard"
military history of armies, tactics, strategy, and warfare. Books in the series
consist mainly of single-author works – academically rigorous and ground-
breaking – which are accessible to both academics and the interested general
reader.

A full list of titles in the series can be found at: www.cambridge.org/
militaryhistories

# Napoleon and the Struggle for Germany: The Franco-Prussian War of 1813

## Volume I

### The War of Liberation, Spring 1813

MICHAEL V. LEGGIERE

*University of North Texas*

# CAMBRIDGE
## UNIVERSITY PRESS

University Printing House, Cambridge CB2 8BS, United Kingdom

Cambridge University Press is part of the University of Cambridge.

It furthers the University's mission by disseminating knowledge in the pursuit of education, learning and research at the highest international levels of excellence.

www.cambridge.org
Information on this title: www.cambridge.org/9781107080515

First published 2015
Reprinted 2015

Printed in the United Kingdom by TJ International Ltd. Padstow Cornwall

*A catalogue record for this publication is available from the British Library*

*Library of Congress Cataloguing in Publication data*
Leggiere, Michael V., 1969–
Napoleon and the struggle for Germany: The Franco-Prussian War of 1813; The War of Liberation, Spring 1813 / Michael V. Leggiere, University of North Texas.
page  cm. –  (Cambridge military histories)  ISBN 978-1-107-08051-5 (Hardback) – ISBN 978-1-107-43973-3 (paperback) 1.  Napoleonic Wars, 1800–1815–Campaigns– Germany. 2.  Wars of Liberation, 1813–1814–Campaigns–Germany. 3.  Napoleon I, Emperor of the French, 1769–1821–Military leadership. 4.  France. Armée. Grande Armée– History. 5.  France–History, Military–1789–1815. I.  Title.
DC236.L443 2015
940.2'740943–dc23
2014022386

ISBN 978-1-107-08051-5 Hardback
ISBN 978-1-107-43973-3 Paperback

For my little girl,
Jordyn Elise Leggiere

# Contents

| | |
|---|---|
| *List of figures* | *page* viii |
| *List of maps* | ix |
| *Preface* | xi |
| Introduction | 1 |
| 1 Odd man out | 21 |
| 2 A new Coalition | 70 |
| 3 Saxony | 120 |
| 4 The Saale | 175 |
| 5 Großgörschen | 226 |
| 6 The Elbe | 268 |
| 7 Bautzen | 298 |
| 8 The Prussian Thermopylae | 336 |
| 9 Silesia | 382 |
| Assessment | 429 |
| *Bibliography* | 456 |
| *Index* | 465 |

# Figures

1 Napoleon I, 1769–1821       *page* 22
2 Frederick William III, 1770–1840       22
3 Alexander I, 1777–1825       23
4 General Gerhard Johann David Waitz von Scharnhorst, 1755–1813    38
5 General August Wilhelm Antonius Neidhardt von Gneisenau, 1760–1831       47
6 Jean-Baptiste Bernadotte, Charles XIV John of Sweden, 1763–1844    62
7 Alexander and Frederick William reviewing the troops       104
8 General William Schaw Cathcart, 1755–1843       109
9 General Sir Charles Stewart, 1778–1854       110
10 General Gebhard Leberecht von Blücher, 1742–1819       121
11 General Ludwig Adolph Peter zu Wittgenstein, 1769–1843       200
12 Napoleon at the battle of Großgörschen, 2 May 1813       243
13 The charge of the West Prussian Infantry Regiment at Großgörschen    245
14 The Allied left wing at Großgörschen       248
15 Napoleon observing his troops crossing the Elbe at Dresden, 10 May 1813       291
16 The Grande Armée crossing the Elbe at Dresden, 14 May 1813       313
17 Napoleon directing the crossing of the Spree at Bautzen, 20 May 1813       338
18 The Kolberg Infantry Regiment at the battle of Bautzen, 21 May 1813       351
19 The death of General Géraud Christophe Michel Duroc, 22 May 1813       364

*All illustrations reproduced courtesy of the Anne S. K. Brown Military Collection, Brown University Library.*

# Maps

1 The North German and Polish theater of war, 1812–1813  *page* 10
2 The German theater of war, 1813                        11
3 Region between the Unstrut and the Elster Rivers        12
4 Lützen and surrounding area                            13
5 Region between the Elster and the Spree Rivers          14
6 Bautzen and surrounding area                           15
7 Region between the Bober and the Katzbach Rivers        16
8 Prussia in 1806                                        24
9 Prussia after the Treaty of Tilsit                     25
10 Central Europe in 1810                                33
11 Russian advance from the Niemen to the Vistula         74
12 Hamburg and surrounding area                          144
13 Allied advance from the Vistula to the Saale          146
14 French and Allied concentration along the Saale       192
15 Battle of Lützen, 2 May 1813, situation at 12:00 P.M.  234
16 Battle of Lützen, 2 May 1813, situation at 2:00 P.M.   241
17 From Lützen to Bautzen                                299
18 Combat of Königswartha, 19 May 1813                   326
19 Battle of Bautzen, 20 May 1813                        339
20 Battle of Bautzen, 21 May 1813                        350
21 Region between the Spree and the Neiße Rivers         363
22 Region between the Neiße and the Bober Rivers         367
23 Combat at Haynau, 25 May 1813                         386
24 Region between the Katzbach and the Oder Rivers       403
25 Allied retreat to the Oder River                      411
26 The neutral zone in Silesia                           420

# Preface

This seven-year project has been greatly assisted by many dear friends and colleagues who gave limitless support, shared their research, and focused early drafts. Alexander Mikaberidze is a friend like no other: for years he has not merely graciously provided me with Russian sources, but he also translates them; I am deeply indebted to Alex. His help in canvassing Russia's archival collection as well as his insight have greatly improved this work. Other dear friends such as Rick Schneid, Huw Davies, Jack Gill, Dennis Showalter, Jeremy Black, Chuck White, and Peter Hofschröer have provided endless support, inspiration, and assistance. I must also convey my deepest appreciation to Peter Harrington of the Anne S. K. Brown Military Collection at Brown University for providing all the artwork that accompanies the text on the shortest notice. At Cambridge University Press, I wish to thank Hew Strachan for his support, Michael Watson for his patience and understanding, and especially for granting me the opportunity to present the 1813 campaign in two volumes, and Rosalyn Scott for seeing the manuscript through production. At the University of North Texas, I am indebted to the Department of History, the Military History Center, and the College of Arts and Sciences for their generous financial support. Behind all three is my chairman, colleague, and friend, Rick McCaslin, who has been a steady source of support and encouragement. I am fortunate to have worked with two of the foremost military historians in the world: Geoff Wawro and Rob Citino. Both set the standard extremely high but their steadfast advice and encouragement are boundless. I especially want to thank Geoff for his friendship, confidence, and support. Last but not least, I thank my graduate students for their patience when they found the door to my office closed: Jon Abel, Chad Tomaselli, Jordan Hayworth, Nate Jarrett, Casey Baker, and Eric Smith.

I must thank the Sixth Count Bülow von Dennewitz, Hasso, for providing a constant stream of documents and information. I offer special thanks to

Bertrand Fonck as well as the staff of the Service historique de l'armée de terre at Vincennes for patiently handling my requests to exceed the daily limit of cartons. I also express my gratitude to the helpful staff of Berlin's Geheimes Staatsarchiv Preußischer Kulturbesitz for producing repositorium from the former German General Staff archive previously thought to have been lost during the Second World War. I express my sincere gratitude to my mentor, Donald D. Horward, for seeing the potential in me, releasing it, and stopping me from making the mistake of attending law school. My wife of sixteen years and companion of more than twenty, Michele, has always been my source of strength. Our beautiful children, Jordyn and Nicholas, have likewise endured countless hours of having to entertain themselves while I was writing. Finally, I wish to thank my mother, Rosalie, who is always a source of solid support. Many others have contributed in many ways. To them: thanks and an apology for any omission. Whatever merits this work has are due in part to their contributions; whatever faults may lie here are those of the author.

Maps that are required for more than one chapter appear in the Introduction, pp. 10–16. In the text, I employ native, modern spellings of villages, towns, smaller cities, and geographic features as much as possible. Larger cities, capitals, and rivers are Anglicized. I also provide at first mention the modern Polish, Russian, Lithuanian, and Czech names of population centers and geographic features in regions that once belonged to Prussia or Austria. Names of persons are likewise native, except for monarchs, whose names are Anglicized. To avoid confusion, all general officers are referred to simply as "general." Lastly, I use "imperials" to refer to the French and their allies after 1804.

# Introduction

On 2 December 1804, Napoleon Bonaparte crowned himself emperor of the French. Three days later, he held an elaborate ceremony on the Champ de Mars in Paris. In front of the École Militaire, the academy where Napoleon had received his formal training to become an officer in the French army, workers erected an elaborate pavilion modeled on the headquarters of a Roman emperor. On a dais in the center rose the throne of the new Caesar. As a self-made man lacking dynastic legitimacy, Napoleon engineered this spectacle to align his regime with the military ethos and traditions of the Roman Empire. On his signal, deputations from the regiments of his army approached the throne. Napoleon rose and issued orders for the distribution of new battle standards and regimental colors to replace those of the republic that he had toppled. Atop each blue regimental flagpole perched a bronze eagle with outstretched wings and head turned to the left. Again borrowing from ancient tradition, Napoleon modeled his Eagles after the *aquila*, or eagle – the symbol of Rome's legions dating back to 104 BC. Likewise having outstretched wings, the Roman *aquila* looked to its right. After distributing the Eagles, Napoleon spoke to his warriors: "Soldiers! Behold your colors! These Eagles will always be your rallying point. They will always be where your emperor will judge necessary for the defense of his throne and his people. Swear to sacrifice your lives for their defense; and, by your courage, to keep them constantly in the path of victory. You swear."[1]

Like Rome's storied legions, those of the French Grande Armée created a vast continental empire. During the conquest, the French vanquished opponents whose dynasties had ruled not for a handful of years but for centuries. Like the upstart Napoleon, the rulers of these venerable dynasties claimed to be the heirs of the glory that was ancient Rome. Their titles alone affirmed the link: the Russian "tsar" and German "kaiser" both derived from the Latin "caesar." Although not bearing eagles atop their standards, the coats of arms for the Habsburgs of Austria and the Romanovs of Russia featured double-headed eagles. On 2 December 1805, the Eagles of the new Rome triumphed over the Austrians and Russians at the battle of Austerlitz. Success allowed the French Imperator to dissolve the 1,000-year First Reich: the Holy Roman Empire. Its ruler, Francis II of Austria, renounced his title of Holy Roman Emperor, yet retained an imperial mandate with the title of Kaiser Francis I of Austria.

Victory drove the ambition of the French god of war. In the wake of shattering the Holy Roman Empire, he reunified Charlemagne's empire by adding Germany and Italy to his Grand Empire. In 1806, his soldiers carried their Eagles into Germany for a showdown with another state whose ruling dynasty used an eagle for its symbol: Hohenzollern Prussia. Relatively new to the exclusive club of great powers that included Britain, France, Austria, and Russia, the Prussian state had recently celebrated its centennial anniversary of becoming a kingdom. For many years the weakest of the powers, Prussia vaulted to military prominence during the reign of Frederick the Great (1740–1786). Although some forty years had passed since Frederick's masterful victories in the Seven Years War, the Prussian army still enjoyed the reputation of being Europe's finest. Many thought the brash French Imperator and his Eagles would receive a hard lesson.

Like so many military institutions throughout history, the Prussians had prepared their army to fight the previous war rather than the next war. Although they had had the best eighteenth-century army on the continent, few Prussians recognized that the French Caesar had pioneered a new era of warfare. At the twin battles of Jena–Auerstedt on 14 October 1806, Napoleon finally laid to rest the army frozen by time. In less than two weeks, the French Eagles paraded through the Brandenburg Gate and into Berlin, the capital of Prussia. King Frederick William III, the grand-nephew of Frederick the Great, fled eastward with his family, including his two young sons: the future King Frederick William IV and Kaiser William I. He halted at Königsberg (Kaliningrad), hoping that the approaching Russian army could save him. Fortunately for the Prussian king, he did not have to witness the looting of Frederick the Great's tomb by Napoleon, who visited his shrine at Potsdam's *Garnisonkirch*. He confiscated Frederick's sword, decorations, sash, and the colors of his Royal Guard, all of which went to Paris as trophies. At Berlin, the Eagles stripped the Prussian capital of its wealth and few treasures, including the Quadriga, which the Prussians had only recently placed atop the Brandenburg Gate: the goddess of victory went to Paris and did not return until 1814. Napoleon could suffer no rival, dead or alive.

After vanquishing the Russian army in June 1807, Napoleon accepted a request from Tsar Alexander I to negotiate. Frederick William did not receive an invitation to the first day of negotiations, when the epic meeting between Napoleon and Alexander took place on the great raft moored in the middle of the Niemen River. Prussia's envoys could not sign the Treaty of Tilsit (Sovetsk) until two days after the Russians had concluded their negotiations with Napoleon – a symbolic act for all of Europe to see. The French dictated peace terms to the Prussian delegation that reflected the totality of Napoleon's military victory. At Tilsit, Napoleon purposefully humiliated the Prussians at every opportunity. The resulting peace treaty left Prussia a tertiary state at the mercy of Napoleon's iron fist.

From the ashes of old Prussia, a cadre of progressive military officers and civil servants such as Heinrich Friedrich Karl vom und zum Stein, Gerhard von Scharnhorst, August von Gneisenau, Hermann von Boyen, and Karl von Hardenberg initiated a reform movement with the king's conditional blessing. They sought to resurrect the state to one day enable the Prussians to wage a war of liberation against the hated French by unleashing the powers of the nation just as the French had done during their Revolution that spanned the decade of 1789–1799. Napoleon's indifference to extending French reforms – Liberty, Equality, and Fraternity – to Prussia left the Prussians free to mold the ideals of the French Revolution into Frederick William's authoritative monarchy. Thus, any reforms granted by the king as a response to French oppression and neonate nationalism earned him the gratitude of his subjects.[2] While falling short of the gains made by the French during their Revolution, the Prussian reformers successfully negotiated the issue of providing top-down social, political, and military change within an absolutist system. In terms of military reform, the Prussian army of 1813 more than matched the French in organizational and tactical proficiency. A combination of social and military reforms elevated the soldier to a position of respect that transformed him into a savior of the "Fatherland" in 1813. Civic responsibility and submission to lawful authority replaced feudal terror as a means of maintaining discipline. A meritocracy opened the officer corps to men of talent while a revamped General Staff provided unity of command and direction. Prussian success in 1813 is testament to the army's complete overhaul and the success, albeit incomplete, of the social and political reform movement.

Five years after Tilsit, Napoleon prepared to lead his legions into Russia to punish Tsar Alexander for breaching the 1807 treaty. By this time, the French emperor so thoroughly controlled Prussia that he forced Frederick William to contribute 20,000 men to the invasion force. Many Prussian officers resigned rather than take up arms against their former allies. In June 1812, Napoleon led the 600,000 men and 1,300 guns of the Grande Armée into Russia. At the end of the year, unbelievable news rocked Europe: the Grande Armée had ceased to exist. Of the original invasion force, only 93,000 men and 250 guns returned from the unforgiving Russian steppes: an unprecedented human tragedy. Napoleon abandoned the wreck of his army in Russia and returned to France with a handful of followers. Meanwhile, Russian armies slowly pursued the survivors toward Prussia's eastern frontier. Some Prussians viewed Napoleon's monumental disaster as an opportunity to begin a *Befreiungskrieg* (war of liberation), while others viewed it as a chance to earn his goodwill by assisting him in his hour of need.

In early 1813, Frederick William faced a difficult choice: honor Napoleon's demands for help or side with the approaching Russians to fight for freedom. Placed in this unenviable situation, the king discovered that one of his generals had signed a neutrality pact with the Russians. Losing control of his army and confronted by increasing anti-French sentiment among his subjects, he allied with the Russians and chose to wage a *Befreiungskrieg*. Mobilization of the regular army then accelerated, augmented by decrees creating a national militia, the Landwehr, and a civic defense force, the Landsturm. To provide time for his army to mobilize, he delayed issuing a formal declaration against France until 16 March 1813.

In the spring of 1813, Frederick William embraced a people's war: a Franco-Prussian war. Anti-French demonstrations decisively influenced public opinion, especially among the intelligentsia. This suggests that the Prussians viewed the war as a struggle between peoples and nations. On 17 March 1813, the king established his own symbol to counter the French Eagle: the Iron Cross. Based on the icon of the Teutonic Knights, Frederick William declared that the decoration would be awarded for acts of bravery and leadership in Prussia's upcoming struggle for freedom. In 1813, the Iron Cross of a resurrected Prussia confronted the Eagles of the new Rome. While the eagle continued to represent the Hohenzollern dynasty, the Iron Cross represented the nation's struggle for liberation. After Prussia emerged victorious, it came to symbolize the glory and might of Prussian arms, a tradition that became transposed onto the newly unified German Empire, or Second Reich, by the Hohenzollerns and the "blood and iron" of the Prussian army. Ever since 1813, the Iron Cross has served as the symbol of Prussia's armed forces, even to the present day. The Iron Cross is the only remnant of the Prusso-German military tradition that survived the Second World War.

The Prussians embraced the new patriotism "not for reform, constitutional liberty, and Prussian and/or German unity, but out of hatred of the foreign invader and a religiously based traditional loyalty to God, king, and country." This made the Prussian movement akin to those in Calabria, Spain, the Tyrol, and Russia. Although falling far short of the Spanish, Calabrian, or Tyrolean uprisings, Prussia's popular revolt helped persuade the king to renounce his alliance with Napoleon. The fact that the army appeared to be pursuing its own agenda also influenced Frederick William. Due to French oppression and the associated hardships of foreign occupation and exploitation, the Prussian people perceived the struggle as their war. Public opinion, especially aided by the events in East Prussia, helped move the cautious king to fight for Prussia's liberation.[3]

After losing 500,000 men in Russia during the failed invasion of 1812, Napoleon needed a brilliant strategy to produce a decisive victory over his enemies. His planning for operations in 1813 suggests that he believed a strategy of maneuver in North Germany could produce this victory. First and foremost, a drive across North Germany to the Vistula (Wisła) River would jeopardize Russian communications that stretched across Silesia and Poland. Napoleon speculated that such a threat would prompt the Russians to withdraw from Central Europe faster than they had come. Moreover, he would be able to expel the Russians from the Grand Duchy of Warsaw, which they had invaded following his setback in Russia. Napoleon also desired to relieve his besieged garrisons on the Oder (Odra) and the Vistula Rivers to augment his armies with these veterans.[4] Control of the plain between the Elbe and Oder Rivers provided another consideration. If he transferred his base of operations northeast to Pomerania or West Prussia, the Elbe and Oder fortresses would protect his right flank while he fell on the Russians.[5] An operation in North Germany would also keep the war far from Austria's borders. Although Napoleon did not believe his father-in-law, Kaiser Francis, would break the Franco-Austrian alliance, he did not want to give the Austrians any cause to do so. Finally, after Frederick William declared war against him, Napoleon sought to cripple Prussia through a morale-breaking conquest of Berlin.[6] He believed an offensive against Berlin would prompt the Prussians to abandon the Russians and race toward their capital. In this case, he would take a central position and crush the Russians and Prussians in turn.[7] Should the Prussians remain united with the Russians, a weakly defended Berlin would fall and presumably disrupt Prussian mobilization. Most commentaries agree that the emperor never relinquished this "master plan."[8]

Napoleon's first plan to confront the Russians envisioned Prussian assistance in a drive across the North German plain to Danzig (Gdańsk) on the Vistula River. Success would reassert Napoleon's dominance over his reluctant Prussian ally and rescue the besieged fortresses along the Oder and Vistula. The emperor noted that, "after conducting demonstrations to convince the enemy that I will march against Dresden and into Silesia, I will probably march to Havelberg, reach Stettin [Szczecin] by forced marches with 300,000 men, and continue the march to Danzig, which I could reach in fifteen days. On the twentieth day of the movement ... I will have relieved that place and be master ... of all the bridges over the lower Vistula."[9] Napoleon planned to lead his new army from the Main River to the Elbe, unite with the forces commanded by his stepson, Eugene, south of Magdeburg, proceed through Pomerania, and move across the lower Oder.

By thus threatening the Russian line of operations, Napoleon would force them to abandon the Oder and retreat to the Vistula, where he would be waiting for them.

Frederick William's decision to break the Franco-Prussian alliance undermined Napoleon's plan. Prussia's defection and the ensuing Russo-Prussian drive across the Elbe to the Saale threatened to destabilize Napoleon's empire. Had Napoleon executed the master plan, he would have achieved the success he desired. The Russians would have retreated, forcing the Prussians to either follow or face Napoleon's wrath alone. Instead, he decided to cross the Saale and seek to overwhelm the Allies in battle. Unable to organize his new army fast enough, he missed the opportunity of taking a central position between the two Allied armies as they converged on the Saale from different directions. The first marched southwest through Königsberg and Berlin while the second advanced northwest through Dresden and Leipzig.

Subordinated to the Russians, the leaders of the new Prussian army – Scharnhorst, Gneisenau, and Gebhard Leberecht von Blücher – soon became frustrated with the slow pace of the Allied war effort. Although the Prussians complained about the Russians, the community of interest that solidified the Russo-Prussian alliance persisted. Had the Prussians abandoned the Russians in Saxony and raced northward to defend Berlin, the alliance most likely would have imploded. Remembering the fate of their armies in the mountains around Zurich in 1799, the Russians might have reacted to such a retrograde movement by the Prussians by withdrawing from the war, just as Tsar Paul I had done during the War of the Second Coalition.[10] Moreover, Russian sacrifices, which included Moscow, had been immense during their own war of liberation the previous year.[11] Fortunately for the Allied war effort, Frederick William remained committed to fighting Napoleon in Saxony; no Prussian units left the theater to participate in the defense of Berlin.[12] Only after the Russians appeared intent on leaving this community of interest – albeit temporarily – by withdrawing to Poland did the Prussians contemplate a separation. Unfortunately for Napoleon, the needs of his army compelled him to accept the Armistice of Pläswitz just when the goal seemed within his grasp. Napoleon's great hope of reliving his 1796 campaign by taking a central position between two enemy armies and defeating each in turn never materialized.

As for the Allies, after reaching the banks of the Saale River in early April, they largely remained idle for the rest of the month. Lack of Russian support stymied their ability to do more than send raiding parties into the heart of Germany. Finally, after Napoleon led his young Eagles across the Saale in late April, the Allies engaged him at Lützen on 2 May 1813. Still the master of operational warfare, Napoleon came within two hours of effecting a double envelopment that would have ended the Sixth Coalition on that day. Fortunately for the Allies, they escaped before the net could close. Although a victory for Napoleon, the struggle cost him double the casualties he inflicted on the Allies. More detrimental to the French cause, Napoleon's lack of cavalry prevented Lützen from becoming another Jena. The Allies retreated from Lützen convinced they had taught the French a hard lesson.

Napoleon realized his weak cavalry arm and inexperienced infantry could not maneuver the Allies into accepting battle under conditions favorable to him. Therefore, he hoped an operation in North Germany would create the strategic opportunities that his army had not been able to produce in Saxony. He emerged from Lützen convinced that the legs of his young conscripts would have to compensate for his lack of cavalry. Thus, he returned to maneuver on the operational level to force the Allies into a second battle. In so doing, the master plan provided the emperor with the guidelines he needed to achieve success. Immediately following Lützen, he directed Marshal Michel Ney to Leipzig with orders to cross the Elbe at Torgau and Wittenberg with almost 85,000 men. Numerically superior French forces would allow Napoleon to place an army in North Germany considerably larger than any units the Allies could muster in opposition, while the army under his personal command still outnumbered the main Russo-Prussian army in Saxony. He believed Ney's movement toward Berlin would induce the Prussians to separate from the Russians and march with all possible speed to cover their capital.[13] Napoleon would then mask the Russians, reunite with Ney, and lead 175,000 men against an estimated 60,000 to 80,000 Prussians as they marched to save Berlin.[14] Should the Russians and Prussians remain united and decide to again confront Napoleon in Saxony, Ney would be within supporting distance. In addition, if the Allies remained united and continued to retreat, Napoleon could drive them out of Saxony, through Silesia, and as far as Poland. After taking Berlin and rolling across North Germany, Ney might reach the Vistula before the Allies, in which case they would be caught between two numerically superior French armies.

After Lützen, inadequate French cavalry and stubborn rearguard actions by the Russians prevented Napoleon from determining whether the Prussians and Russians had separated. Regardless of his uncertainty, he selected three main objectives to achieve by month's end: occupy Berlin; relieve the fortress of Glogau (Głogów) on the Oder; and take Breslau (Wrocław), the provincial capital of Silesia. He held Ney's operation as crucial to the achievement of these goals. On 13 May, he ordered Ney to Luckau, the halfway point between Berlin and Bautzen. From that position, the marshal would either advance against the Prussian capital or support Napoleon in Saxony. Twenty-four hours later, confirmed reports arrived that the entire Allied army stood at Bautzen on the Spree River. Napoleon believed the Allies would continue their retreat eastward perhaps as far as Silesia rather than remain at Bautzen. For this reason, he wanted Ney to continue east, parallel to Napoleon's march, to prevent the Allies from making a stand at the Spree, Neiße (Nysa), Queis (Kwisa), or Bober (Bóbr) Rivers. In addition, Ney could proceed as far as Glogau on the Oder to sever Russian communication through Poland to Russia. Consequently, Ney received orders to divide his army. While he led III and V Corps to within one day's march of Bautzen, Marshal Claude Victor would advance against Berlin with II and VII Corps.

After surrendering the line of the Elbe to Napoleon, the Allies prepared for a second battle at Bautzen some 110 miles east of Lützen. Napoleon welcomed the opportunity. He intended to launch a frontal assault on the Allied position at Bautzen while Marshal Ney moved southeast to completely envelop the enemy's right. Meanwhile, Victor would advance against Berlin. However, an incompetent Ney frustrated the master plan by bringing II and VII Corps with him to Bautzen. Nevertheless, the emperor demonstrated his operational superiority by massing 144,000 soldiers against 96,000 Allied troops. The battle commenced on 20 May and continued on the 21st with Napoleon gaining the advantage. Yet another costly mistake by Ney robbed him of a crushing victory that could have destroyed the Coalition.

After this second indecisive victory, Napoleon pursued the defeated Allies into Silesia. He ordered Marshal Nicolas-Charles Oudinot to conduct a second offensive against Berlin. Oudinot marched his XII Corps northwest toward Berlin while Napoleon followed the Allies southeast into - Silesia. The marshal's subsequent inability to dislodge the Prussians and take their capital did little to undermine Napoleon's belief in the master plan. In Silesia, meanwhile, cooperation between the Russians and Prussians nearly collapsed. Each side blamed the other for continued failure. A change in command did little to assuage the Prussians, as one Russian commander replaced another. Retreating into Silesia, the Prussians hoped to meet Napoleon for a third battle. Instead, they learned that the Russians intended to retreat to Poland for six weeks of rest and reorganization. Frederick William and his army could either follow or face Napoleon alone. As the Russo-Prussian army approached the banks of the Oder River, the choice of separating from the Russians to defend Silesia or following them and abandoning the Prussian heartland confronted the Prussian king. After having retreated almost 270 miles, his generals demanded that they remain in Silesia. Frederick William issued orders for a Prussian Army of Silesia to be formed from his units currently serving with the Russian army. Yet before the separation of the Allied army could occur, he learned that Napoleon had accepted an Austrian-brokered armistice. Thus, Frederick William was saved from having to cross his Rubicon.

My 2002 work, *Napoleon and Berlin: The Franco-Prussian War in North Germany, 1813*, builds on Gordon Craig's assertion that the Prussian military establishment wanted to wage an almost fanatical holy war against the French for emancipation and freedom.[15] While *Napoleon and Berlin* focuses on the Prussian defense of their capital, *Napoleon and the Struggle for Germany: The Franco-Prussian War of 1813* will continue to develop Craig's thesis by exploring the role played by the Prussians in the main theater of war and particularly their relations with the Russians. Prussia's foremost commanders at the start of the war, Scharnhorst, Gneisenau, and Blücher, struggled to fight a different kind of war – a war guided by "mystical nationalism," according to Craig – than their Russian allies, many of whom believed Russia should play only an auxiliary role following the great exertions of 1812. After six years of French occupation, the leaders of the Prussian military establishment labored to restore both national and international honor to their profession, their army, and, most of all, their state. Prussian generals took the initiative to precipitate a rupture with France, and personal feelings translated into political action. Frederick William allowed himself to embrace the nationalistic fervor that it aroused and summon his people to arms. To the Prussians, the war against Napoleon was not a political struggle, but an ideological "fight against evil, a struggle against the anti-Christ and his minions."[16] More so than the Russians and later the Austrians, the Prussians turned their war against Napoleon into a holy crusade, a total war between two peoples: a Franco-Prussian war. Enthusiasm and popular support did vary greatly, yet Prusso-German patriotism permeated the public mind.[17]

The weakest of Napoleon's adversaries, the Prussians managed to field an army of only 65,000 men in March 1813. Nevertheless, the Prussians truly fought a war of liberation, acknowledging that another defeat at Napoleon's hands probably would result in the end of the Prussian state. Although languishing under Russian leadership during the Spring Campaign of 1813, the Prussians willingly shouldered the weight of the conflict and demanded the opportunity to take the war to Napoleon. This volume explains how Russian war weariness conflicted with Prussian impetuosity, resulting in the crisis that almost ended the Sixth Coalition in early June. In a single campaign spanning only one month, Napoleon drove the Russo-Prussian army from the banks of the Saale to the banks of the Oder. On reaching the Oder, the Russo-Prussian alliance came perilously close to imploding, only to be saved by an eleventh-hour armistice.

The hundred years between 1813 and 1913 witnessed the publication of numerous Prusso-German, French, and Russian official General Staff histories of 1813 as well as a plethora of works written by military officers and contemporaries of the period. They borrowed from each other freely but in general the Prusso-German Staff histories were viewed as authoritative.

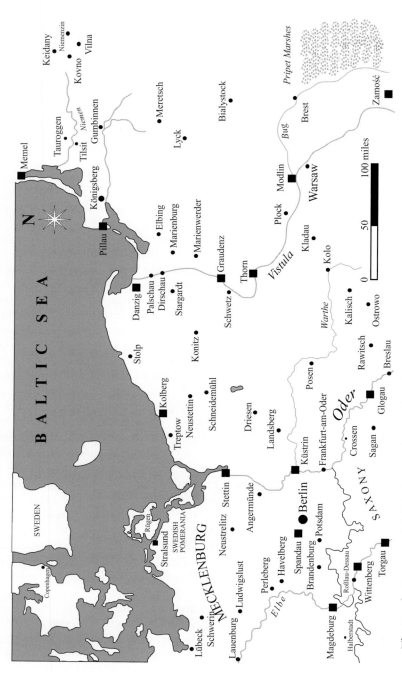

1. The North German and Polish theater of war, 1812–1813

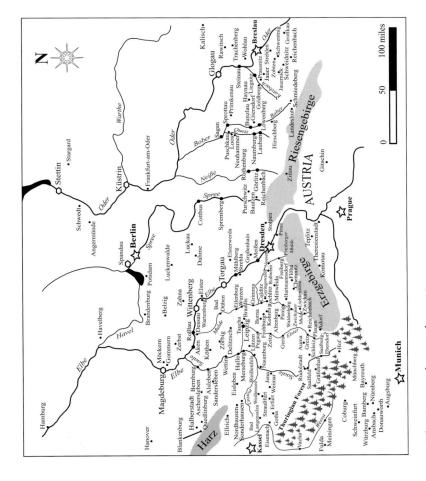

2. The German theater of war, 1813

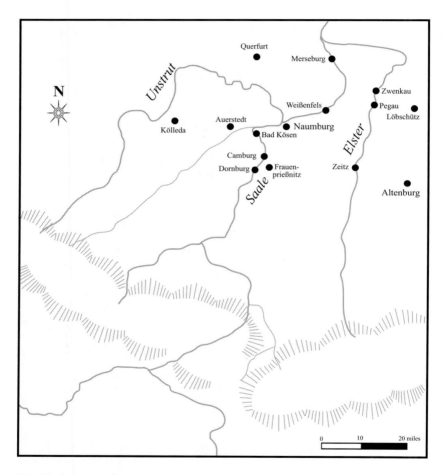

3. Region between the Unstrut and the Elster Rivers

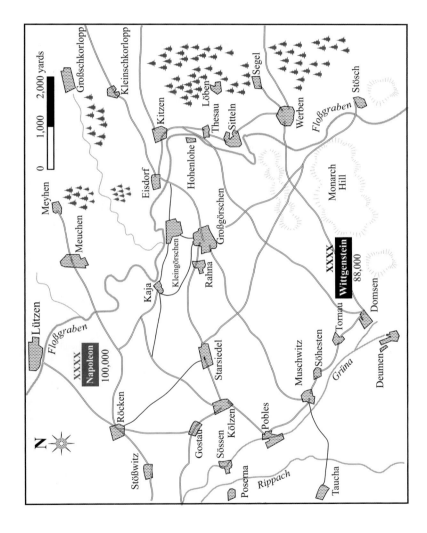

4. Lützen and surrounding area

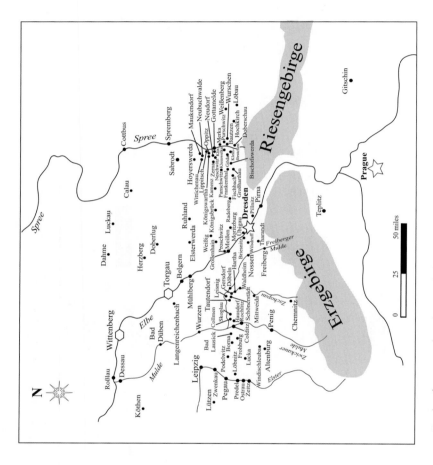

5. Region between the Elster and the Spree Rivers

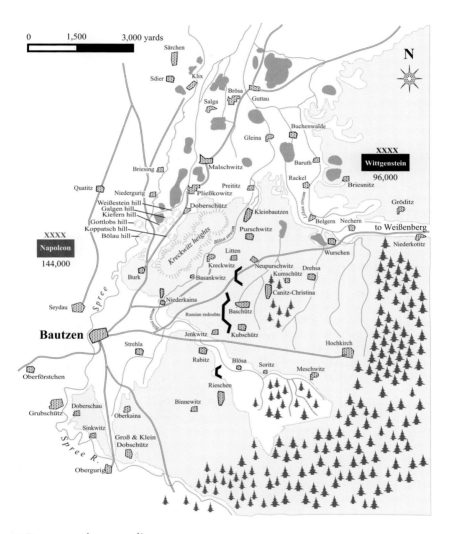

**6.** Bautzen and surrounding area

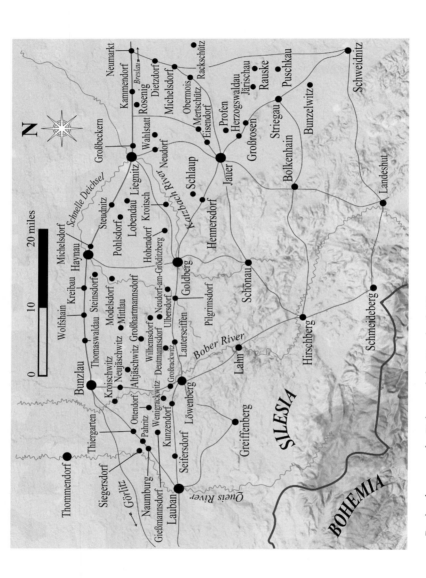

7. Region between the Bober and the Katzbach Rivers

In some cases, whole sections of the Prusso-German histories are reproduced verbatim in the French and Russian studies of the war. Since 1913, few historians have attempted to piece together an operational history of 1813. The destruction of much of the Prusso-German General Staff archives during the Second World War makes the task seem daunting. However, the Geheimes Staatsarchiv Preußischer Kulturbesitz in Berlin still contains much of the documentary record of the Prussian army between 1813 and 1815. Just as crucial, the historians of first the Prussian and then the German General Staff published much of the official correspondence coming from the headquarters of Blücher and Gneisenau during this period in their exhaustive studies. Moreover, thanks to the historiographic war between the German General Staff and Hans Delbrück, this prolific historian likewise published vast quantities of the official correspondence in his massive five-volume biography of Gneisenau. Thus, we have much in terms of primary sources.

Based on German, French, Russian, British, and private archival documents, this book, written from the Coalition's perspective, describes how Napoleon defended his empire against the new coalition that had formed in the wake of his disastrous defeat in Russia. After losing some 500,000 soldiers between June and December 1812, Napoleon miraculously assembled a new army of 200,000 men by April 1813 for a campaign in Germany. While fighting continued in Spain and Italy, Napoleon realized that the fate of his empire depended on his ability to maintain control of Germany. Hoping to stop the pursuing Russians before they could set foot onto German soil, Napoleon looked to his ally, Frederick William, for assistance. With two-thirds of Prussia occupied by Napoleon's forces, Frederick William broke the French alliance and joined the Russians to form the Sixth Coalition. This work is the first unofficial history of the 1813 Spring Campaign in Germany that reconstructs the principal campaigns and operations in Germany to focus on how the Prussians attempted to wage a Franco-Prussian war within the framework of their alliance with the Russians. Like Napoleon, the Prussians believed that decisive battles should settle the war. This often caused friction with their Russian partners. Along with the account of the principal operations, the work also examines the complex diplomacy that led to the formation of the Sixth Coalition. Particular attention is given to the roles of Britain and Sweden in forging a new league to face Napoleon. Despite their fear and hatred of the French, the road to forming a grand alliance against Napoleon was long and bumpy.

The armistice that spanned 4 June to 17 August 1813 provides a clear line dividing the one-dimensional conflict between the French Empire and the Russo-Prussian alliance that ensued during the spring of 1813, and the multidimensional war of a multinational coalition against a French empire dwindling in resources in the autumn of 1813. This volume details the Spring

Campaign during which Napoleon, with an army of 200,000 men, essentially faced a single Russo-Prussian army that numbered barely 100,000 men. To end French hegemony east of the Rhine, the Russians and Prussians hoped to ignite Germany and fan the flames of a people's war based on the Spanish model. Aside from the Russo-Prussian alliance, mutual suspicion and traditional rivalries resulted in nothing more than a series of nonbinding bilateral agreements between the Prussians, Russians, Swedes, and British. The military and political situation changed completely after the armistice. As the subsequent volume will describe, Napoleon faced not one enemy army but three (Army of Silesia, Army of Bohemia, and Army of North Germany), which he opposed with three of his own. Allied forces in Central Europe numbered more than 500,000 men while Napoleon's exceeded 400,000. Austria and Sweden joined the Sixth Coalition. Although a grand treaty of alliance would not be signed until March 1814, the Sixth Coalition was bound by subsidy agreements with Great Britain to continue the war against Napoleon. Metternich was now the prime minister of the Coalition and his tool, Prince Karl zu Schwarzenberg, was named Allied commander in chief. The nature of the conflict changed. Talk of a people's war ended, and Metternich did everything he could to separate British interests from the Russo-Prussian war aims, which he likewise sought to undermine.

## Notes

1  Bourrienne, *Memoirs of Napoleon*, II:221.
2  Rosenberg, *Bureaucracy, Aristocracy, and Autocracy*, 204.
3  Schroeder, *European Politics*, 451–52; Nipperdey, *Germany from Napoleon to Bismarck*, 68.
4  For Napoleon's thoughts on relieving these garrisons as the principal objective of his campaigns, see *La Correspondance de Napoléon Ier* (hereafter cited as *CN*), Nos. 18697, 19721, 20088, and 20281, XXV:61–63, 92–93, 361, 491, and Nos. 20339, 20360, 20365, and 20492, XXVI:13, 34, 39, 153–57. Pelet cites Napoleon's letter of 29 July 1813 to General Jean Rapp, the commander of Danzig. According to this letter, which was not published in the *Correspondance*, Napoleon assured Rapp that as soon as the armistice expired "Our first operation will be to seize Berlin [and] to relieve Küstrin and Stettin. We will promptly establish communications with you": Pelet, *Des principales opérations de la campagne de 1813*, 171; see also Freytag-Loringhoven, *Kriegslehren nach Clausewitz*, 21.
5  Pelet, *Des principales opérations de la campagne de 1813*, 171–72. Pelet notes that, by transferring the theater of war north to the lower Oder and possibly as far as the Vistula, "Napoleon henceforth would not have to be concerned about his flank. He could reconfigure his line of operations by Magdeburg on Koblenz [and] Düsseldorf."
6  Colonel Hugo von Freytag-Loringhoven, chief of Section I of the Military History Department of the Great German General Staff, wrote that the blow to Allied morale that would have been caused by the fall of Berlin cannot be underestimated. Elting and Esposito maintain that "an advance on Berlin would enable him

[Napoleon] to maintain a more central position, [and] would exploit the resources of a hitherto largely unforaged area." Yorck von Wartenburg adds that Napoleon "undoubtedly over-estimated the effect that the capture of Berlin would have produced. He expected results from the capture of this geographical point, which in a war a victory over the enemy's active forces alone gives … Hitherto, the guiding principle of Napoleonic strategy had always been to render all secondary resistance useless and ineffective by a blow against the enemy's main body. But now, Napoleon neglects the main army, at the very moment when … any blow dealt at it might have broken the bond which united the common interests. Yet he permits an operation of secondary importance to take the place of the main operation." Chandler, however, argues that a Berlin offensive "offered palpable advantages." See Chandler, *Campaigns of Napoleon*, 903–06; Elting and Esposito, *A Military History and Atlas of the Napoleonic Wars*, 138; Freytag-Loringhoven, *Kriegslehren nach Clausewitz*, 21; Yorck von Wartenburg, *Napoleon as a General*, II:280–82.

7  *CN*, Nos. 20006 and 20007, XXV:293–94.

8  Pelet refers to this project as "*la grande opération sur Berlin et sur le Bas-Oder.*" Petre adds that "the scheme was never carried out, though we shall find the emperor recurring to modifications of it later on." Maude, when describing Napoleon's plan to launch a fourth offensive against the Prussian capital rather than pursue an Allied army into Bohemia in late August, maintains that "Berlin, on the other hand, held out all the fascination of his original northern plan." See Chandler, *Campaigns of Napoleon*, 875, 878; Maude, *Leipzig Campaign*, 204; Pelet, *Des principales opérations de la campagne de 1813*, 278; Petre, *Napoleon's Last Campaign*, 47–49.

9  *CN*, No. 19697, XXV:61–62. Generalmajor Rudolf Friederich, Chief of Section II of the Military History Department of the Great German General Staff, claims that the emperor's plan "was feasible only with the complete surprise and total inactivity of his adversaries, as well as by the strength of his own army. But why should [Napoleon] base his calculations on the lack of determination, unity, and mobility of the enemy's commanders? Why should it not be based on Napoleon's energy, his ability to urge his French on to extraordinary deeds? In any case, the moral impression of the sudden appearance of a strong French army on the lower Vistula, almost in the rear of the Allies and threatening their line of retreat, would have been completely extraordinary; its consequences would have been completely unpredictable." According to Generalleutnant Rudolf von Caemmerer, Friederich's colleague in the Military History Department of the Great German General Staff, "if Napoleon had accomplished this goal it would have been a fortunate beginning for the campaign." Yorck von Wartenburg claims that this plan "need not fear comparison with his best, either in point of boldness or of brilliancy," while Petre comments that an operation in North Germany "at once strikes one as a deviation from the Emperor's general principle of making his objective the enemy's army." See Caemmerer, *Die Befreiungskriege*, 20; Friederich, *Die Befreiungskriege*, I:188; Petre, *Napoleon's Last Campaign*, 48; Yorck von Wartenburg, *Napoleon as a General*, II:242, 280–82, 307.

10  In the Fall Campaign of 1799, an Austrian army under Archduke Charles marched to Belgium rather than assist the Russians in ousting the French from their stronghold in Switzerland. Consequently, the Second Battle of Zurich

occurred on 26 September 1799 when the French marshal André Massena crushed a Russian holding force of 30,000 men and then continued on to rout another force of 28,000 men commanded by the famed Russian general, A. V. Suvorov.

11 At a council of war in Charlottenburg on 17 August, Russian general Ferdinand von Wintzingerode advised that Berlin be treated like Moscow and that the army covering it should fall back before the advance of enemy forces. This attitude of one Russian general may well have been indicative of the entire Russian high command. See Boyen, *Erinnerungen*, ed. Schmidt, II:620.

12 In *Bernadotte*, 95, historian Franklin Scott claims that "the Prussians likened their capital to a loose woman already so frequently violated that she had no claim to protection."

13 As of 13 May, Napoleon instructed Ney that it was "natural" for the Prussians to separate from the Russians, who were retreating toward Silesia, and advance to Berlin to defend their capital. Pelet adds that "the sovereigns of Prussia and Russia had to choose between two great retreat directions. One for the Prussian states and the lower Oder ... the other, the direction on Dresden, Breslau, and Warsaw, was the great line of communication for the Russian depots and reinforcements." Friederich adds that, "since the Allies had thus far not separated their armed forces, the threat of invading the Mark might succeed in bringing it about." See *CN*, No. 20006, XXV:292–93; Pelet, *Des principales opérations de la campagne de 1813*, 54; Friederich, *Die Befreiungskriege*, I:249.

14 Lanrezac, *Lützen*, 177–78.

15 Craig, "Problems of Coalition Warfare," 42. To avoid repetition, both volumes of *Napoleon and the Struggle for Germany* will focus on the military and diplomatic history of 1813. See *Napoleon and Berlin* for discussions concerning the myths, fabrications, and realities about the origins of Prussian-German nationalism during the war of 1813.

16 Craig, "Problems of Coalition Warfare," 42–43.

17 Nipperdey, *Germany from Napoleon to Bismarck*, 68–69. In *Leyer und Schwert*, 37, Theodore Körner, a Saxon who served in a Prussian volunteer unit – the Lützow *Freikorps* – reflected the mood of the educated and the young when he wrote: "It is not a war of the kind the kings know about; it is a crusade, 'tis a holy war."

# Odd man out

Prussia withdrew from the struggle against Revolutionary France known as the War of the First Coalition (1792–1797) in the year 1795. Declaring neutrality, Berlin followed this course while the other powers again fought France in the War of the Second Coalition (1798–1801). During this conflict, General Bonaparte overthrew the French government and proclaimed himself dictator under the title of First Consul. Citizen Bonaparte led France to victory in that war and concluded peace with Great Britain in 1802. His 1803 reorganization of Germany awarded Prussia generous territorial compensation for Rhineland districts lost to French expansion. Diplomatic relations between France and Prussia remained strong, with Napoleon insinuating that he supported Berlin's goal of organizing North Germany into a Prussian-dominated confederation. Renewed war between France and Britain in 1803 prompted Napoleon to occupy Hanover, a possession of the British crown, with 30,000 French troops. His actions threatened Prussian national security because of Hanover's proximity to Brandenburg. Moreover, the Prussians secretly coveted the Electorate.

Relations between France and Prussia considerably deteriorated two years later during the 1805 War of the Third Coalition. Moved by a November meeting with Tsar Alexander I at Potsdam, Frederick William III agreed to issue an ultimatum to Napoleon that among other stipulations demanded a French withdrawal west of the Rhine. Should Napoleon refuse, the Prussians would join the Third Coalition: Russia, Great Britain, and Austria. After the Prussian foreign minister, Christian von Haugwitz, reached Napoleon's headquarters deep in Bohemia to deliver the ultimatum, the French emperor refused to see him, knowing the reason for his arrival. Shortly after, Napoleon's stunning 2 December 1805 victory over the Austro-Russian army at Austerlitz ended the Third Coalition. Napoleon then summoned Haugwitz. Rather than presenting his ultimatum, Haugwitz received a

1  Napoleon I, 1769–1821

2  Frederick William III, 1770–1840

3 Alexander I, 1777–1825

humiliating Franco-Prussian treaty of alliance. Although the Prussians attempted to escape the trap, their efforts resulted in Napoleon issuing harsher demands. With the victorious Grande Armée stationed in Germany and the Russian army limping home after its drubbing at Austerlitz, Frederick William could do little but accept the treaty or face war with France. As his reward for signing, Frederick William received Hanover. Always ready to give away that which did not belong to him, Napoleon knew well that the Prussians would earn the enmity of the British crown as long as they possessed Hanover. To ensure that Berlin earned London's ire, Napoleon forced the Prussians to close the North German coast to all British commerce. These steps succeeded in prompting the British to declare war on Prussia in April 1806.

During the summer of 1806, Napoleon continued to expand French influence. In particular, his creation of the Rheinbund (Confederation of the Rhine) jolted the Prussians. As its official "Protector," the emperor harnessed the resources of the German states, effectively eliminating Austrian and Prussian influence. In addition to these momentous changes in Germany, Napoleon needed to stabilize southern Italy, where French forces had driven the Bourbons from their Kingdom of Naples in 1805. Fleeing to

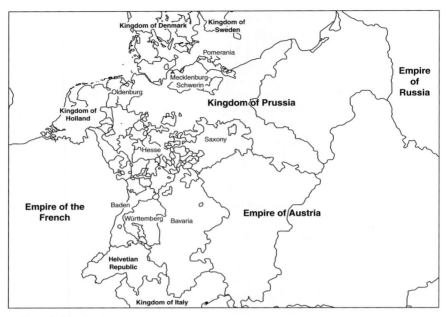

**8.** Prussia in 1806

the island of Sicily, King Ferdinand IV established a government in exile under British protection. As for Naples, Napoleon installed his brother, Joseph, as the new king. From Sicily, the British supported a revolt in Calabria to destabilize Joseph's regime. To ease the pressure on his brother, Napoleon commenced secret negotiations with London during the summer of 1806. Exasperating the Prussians, he offered to return Hanover to King George III if the British withdrew their support for the Neapolitan Bourbons.

Napoleon's duplicity provided the final straw for the Prussians. Frederick William addressed another ultimatum to Napoleon, summoned help from Russia, and healed the rift with Great Britain to form the Fourth Coalition. The next eleven months proved to be a nightmare for the Prussian king. On 14 October, Napoleon destroyed the Prussian army at the twin battles of Jena and Auerstedt. Less than two weeks later, French forces occupied Berlin. During the following month, Prussia's powerful fortresses capitulated, along with the remnant of the field army. Frederick William and the royal family fled first to Königsberg and then to the fortress of Memel (Klaipėda), today in Lithuania. Although Prussian troops assisted the Russians in battling Napoleon to a stalemate in the 7–8 February 1807 battle of Eylau in East Prussia, Frederick William needed a miracle. Spring in

East Prussia brought no such miracle. Although few choices remained for the king but to fight on, Tsar Alexander retained options. After Napoleon smashed his army at the 14 June Battle of Friedland, Alexander requested an armistice that led to the signing of the Franco-Russian and Franco-Prussian treaties at Tilsit on 7 and 9 July 1807 respectively.

Tilsit's draconian terms reduced the Prussian state to a listless rump: Frederick William lost half his kingdom. Although Alexander intervened to save Silesia and Pomerania, fewer than five million subjects remained from Prussia's pre-war population of 9,752,731 inhabitants, while the state's territorial extent of 5,570 square miles had shrunk to 2,877. Napoleon awarded the provinces of New East Prussia and South Prussia to the new Grand Duchy of Warsaw; Danzig on the Baltic Sea became a free city under French authority. Most of Prussia's western possessions, including the Universities of Duisberg, Erlangen, and Halle, went to Jerome Bonaparte's new Kingdom of Westphalia, or Caroline and Joachim Murat's Grand Duchy of Berg. Other conditions stipulated that French troops would occupy all Prussian fortresses, including the great bastions on the Oder River: Stettin, Küstrin (Kostrzyn), and Glogau, with the exception of Kolberg (Kołobrzeg) on the Baltic coast; Graudenz (Grudziądz) and Pillau (Baltiysk) in East Prussia; and Glatz (Kłodzko), Silberberg (Srebrna Góra), and Kosel (Koźle) in Silesia.

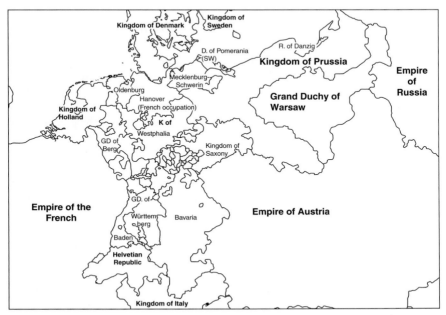

**9.** Prussia after the Treaty of Tilsit

Forced into the Napoleonic state system, Prussia convulsed under the weight of imperial occupation, which would end only after Berlin paid a crippling indemnity. Imperial troops took extensive quarters throughout Prussia to facilitate supply; the strong French presence at Berlin kept the royal family and government in self-imposed exile at Königsberg. The fact that Tilsit tied the withdrawal of French troops from Prussia to an indemnity – the amount of which would be determined at a later date – gave the appearance of endless French martial rule. In addition to the unspecified indemnity, Napoleon insisted that the Prussians cover the cost of provisioning imperial garrisons throughout Prussia and for maintaining the highways he planned to build between the Grand Duchy of Warsaw and the Confederation of the Rhine: an estimated total cost of 216 million francs. Finally, the Prussians found themselves again at war with Great Britain thanks to the conditions that incorporated Prussia into Napoleon's Continental System. Participation in the economic boycott of Great Britain devastated Prussian trade as grain, wood, and wool exports to the British ceased. Other French demands stipulated that Silesian linen could no longer be exported to Italy and Spain. Along with the linen trade, the silk trade fell by 50 percent and grain prices by 70 percent, and the cost of imports such as cotton, sugar, tobacco, and coffee rose sharply.[1]

Tilsit's severe conditions represented a growing trend in Napoleonic statesmanship. On the battlefield, Napoleon's way of war overwhelmed the eighteenth-century military establishments that the French faced in Italy and Germany. Yet in the 1797 Treaty of Campo Formio that ended the War of the First Coalition and the 1801 Treaty of Lunéville that concluded the War of the Second Coalition, he continued the eighteenth-century diplomatic practice of compensation. According to this concept, the peace treaty awarded all parties equitable restitution – usually in the form of land – for the great expenditures that war required. In this way, the principal states that participated in the conflict received a return on their investment in the war, and the gap between victor and vanquished remained narrow. This created a balance of power that prevented the rise of continental hegemons by ensuring that the great powers increased their strength incrementally rather than in radical leaps and bounds. At the same time, the abundance of secondary and tertiary states in Europe allowed predatory cooperation among the primary states, as seen in the three partitions that wiped Poland from the map.

Initially, Napoleon honored the concept of compensation. The Wars of the First and Second Coalitions ended in treaties that awarded Austria – Great Britain's last remaining coalition partner in each conflict – the territory of a third party, in both cases the Republic of Venice. Napoleon negotiated both Campo Formio and Lunéville as well as the 1802 Treaty of Amiens with Great Britain, which even allowed London to maintain control over former French colonies. After his victory over the Third

Coalition, Napoleon imposed the devastatingly harsh Treaty of Pressburg on Austria, the first of the coalition powers to surrender. While Pressburg stripped Vienna of one-sixth of its territory and three million subjects, Kaiser Francis received the paltry compensation of the Electorate of Salzburg. Napoleon's victory over the Prussians in the War of the Fourth Coalition ended his experiments with compensation. Victory would be decided on the battlefield and *all* spoils would go to the victor: he extended his strategy of annihilation to the peace table. Various explanations can be offered to interpret this policy change, but all relate to Napoleon's evolution from general to emperor as well as the genesis of the Napoleonic state system that emerged in 1805 and continued to expand until 1812.

A Franco-Spanish invasion of Portugal in October 1807 resulted in the massive escalation of French forces in Spain after Napoleon decided to oust the Spanish Bourbons. Yet before he could effect the regime change, the people of Madrid revolted against French forces in the heroic Dos de Mayo uprising. Although Napoleon's brother-in-law, Joachim Murat, savagely crushed the Spaniards, the insurrection spread. To the conquered peoples of the French Empire, the struggle in Spain appeared to be a war of liberation. Many Prussian patriots discussed exploiting Napoleon's situation to Prussia's advantage. After news spread that a war party had formed at the Austrian court to agitate for another confrontation with France, Prussian patriots wasted no time in sending war plans to the king at Königsberg. Frederick William knew better: neither his army nor his finances could wage war. Thus, any thoughts of siding with the Austrians should they make a move against France terrified Frederick William. After meeting with the king, Scharnhorst wrote to Stein on 23 August 1808:

> First, I gather that he [Frederick William] expects Russia to guarantee his crown and his state and not the outcome of the war between France and Austria; and, second, that he thus does not believe starting the war in unison with Austria would be good because he fears Austria will not win. These views lead to half-measures, as in the year 1805. The result of this is easy to foresee. The king must provide a yes or no answer to the question of whether he will lead all forces against France in unison with Austria as soon as war breaks out between France and Austria. In the affirmative case, our preparations and measures will continue; but in the opposite case nothing must occur – otherwise it is risking people's lives and compromising the state without sufficient cause. In this case the king must completely side with the French party and remove the people who the world knows are against Napoleon and the French. This, I believe, is what we must say to the king.[2]

Like a blacksmith pounding hot iron, Napoleon molded his empire into the form conceived by his restless mind. In September 1808, the emperor's hammer again fell on the Prussians as a result of his growing commitment in Spain. The arrest in Berlin of a Prussian agent bearing an imprudent letter authored by Stein, Prussia's Chief Minister of Domestic and Foreign Affairs, caught Napoleon's attention. Stein's letter, addressed to Prince Wilhelm Ludwig Georg zu Sayn-Wittgenstein, a Prussian envoy to the British government, called for a Spanish-style insurrection throughout Germany. "The exasperation of Germany daily increases," wrote the Prussian minister; "we must cultivate it and try to influence the people. I want to keep ready contacts in Hesse and Westphalia for any events ... Affairs in Spain are making a lively impression. It would be very useful to prudently spread this news because it shows ... what a nation that has strength and courage can do." Napoleon read the intercepted documents on 3 September. This gift gave him pretext to tighten his choke-hold on Prussia as the expanding war in Iberia forced him to withdraw troops from Germany. Stein's letter handed the Imperator a golden opportunity to substitute diplomatic force for military might.[3]

On the same day that Napoleon read the letter, 3 September, his foreign minister, Jean-Baptiste de Champagny, summoned the king's brother, Prince William, who had joined Prussia's diplomatic mission at Paris, and the Prussian ambassador, Karl Christian von Brockhausen, for a meeting. Champagny presented a new treaty, telling William he needed to accept its terms within twenty-four hours. William's refusal prompted Champagny to produce Stein's letter. Brockhausen immediately rejected it as a fraud but the savvy foreign minister presented other letters signed by Stein for comparison, thus silencing the ambassador. William received an extension but he could not consult his brother. Fearing harsher terms if he did not agree, William signed the Treaty of Paris on 8 September 1808.

The best-known article of the treaty limited the size of the Prussian army to 42,000 men for a period of ten years, effective 1 January 1809. According to the specific terms, the Prussian army would consist of 10 infantry regiments totaling no more than 22,000 men; 8 regiments or 32 squadrons of cavalry not surpassing 8,000 troopers; a corps of gunners, miners, and sappers totaling no more than 6,000 men; and a royal guard of infantry, cavalry, and artillery that did not exceed 6,000 men. "At the expiration of the ten years," stated the agreement, "His Majesty the King of Prussia shall reenter into the common right and shall maintain the number of troops that appears suitable to him according to circumstances." In addition, the treaty prohibited conscription, a militia, and a national guard, thus strictly forbidding any measure to increase the size of the army.

Moreover, Napoleon finally set the amount of the indemnity at 140,000,000 francs, half of which would be paid to the French army within twenty days of the treaty's ratification "in ready money or in good and acceptable bills of exchange" guaranteed by the Prussian treasury. The other half would be financed by mortgages on royal domains reimbursable within twelve to eighteen months of ratification. Glogau, Stettin, and Küstrin would remain occupied until the Prussians completed payment. Frederick William also would officially recognize Napoleon's most recent regime changes: Joseph-Napoleon Bonaparte as the king of Spain and the Indies and Joachim-Napoleon Murat as the king of Naples. In return for the emperor's "friendship," Frederick William had to promise "to make common cause" with Napoleon in case of war between France and Austria within the next ten years and provide a division of 16,000 infantry, cavalry, and artillery for use against the Austrians. Frederick William would not have to provide a contingent if the war began in 1808. Moreover, if a Franco-Austrian war should come in 1809, the size of the Prussian contingent would be only 12,000 infantry and cavalry. Starting in 1810, the Prussians would be responsible for providing the full 16,000-man contingent.[4]

At the least, the terms of the 8 September 1808 Treaty of Paris implied that much of the 200,000-man imperial occupation force would leave Prussia, with only garrisons remaining behind to guarantee the payment of reparations. Few patriots viewed this latest humiliation in such an optimistic light, particularly in view of Stein's fate. Forced by Napoleon to resign and flee to Austria in late 1808, Stein departed before he could finish his great task of reforming Prussia. Regardless, although his reforms fell short of those achieved by the French Revolution, they successfully altered the social fabric of Prussia by accelerating the evolutionary transformation of subject to citizen within an absolutist framework. Frederick William wanted to appoint Hardenberg – himself forced out of his office of foreign minister by the Treaty of Tilsit – as Stein's successor, but Napoleon refused. Despite this setback, Hardenberg remained active behind the scenes, securing the appointment of his protégé, Karl vom Stein zu Altenstein, who co-administered the government with the minister of the interior, Count Friedrich Ferdinand zu Dohna-Schlobitten. Other than promoting the establishment of the new Berlin university, the Altenstein–Dohna ministry could not overcome Prussia's economic crisis. To pay the indemnity, Altenstein proposed ceding Silesia to France. This unpopular idea so weakened Altenstein's position that he resigned on 4 June 1810. This opened the door for Hardenberg to return to office, and this time Napoleon did not interfere. Frederick William not only recalled Hardenberg, but handed him full control of the government under the new title of Staatskanzler (state chancellor). The seemingly unassailable position in Central Europe that Napoleon had created after 1807 may explain his acceptance of Hardenberg's appointment.

Military setbacks in Iberia indirectly accounted for the solidification of French hegemony between the Rhine and the Russian frontier. After a British army chased his brother from Madrid, Napoleon decided to go to Spain and personally oversee military operations. Concerned that the

Austrians would take advantage of his absence to commence the anticipated war, he wanted to meet with Tsar Alexander to reaffirm their alliance. This desire led to the meeting of all crowned heads of Europe in the ostentatious Congress of Erfurt between 27 September and 14 October 1808. Napoleon primarily sought Alexander's assurance to maintain the status quo in Central Europe but the tsar provided only a vague promise of supporting French interests in the case of an Austrian declaration of war. He did persuade Napoleon to reduce the Prussian indemnity by 20,000,000 francs.

Despite the Congress or perhaps because of it, war erupted between France and Austria on 9 April 1809. This Franco-Austrian conflict became part of the wider War of the Fifth Coalition. After having been mauled militarily and diplomatically by Napoleon in the Wars of the First, Second, and Third Coalitions, Kaiser Francis hoped to take advantage of French reverses in Spain and Napoleon's increasing military commitment to the Iberian theater. The Austrians believed they had finally found the answers to beat the French. First, the kaiser's younger brother and Austrian commander in chief, Archduke Charles, attempted to reorganize the Austrian army based on the French corps system. Although still tweaking the new system when his brother declared war, Charles led a much improved Austrian army into the field. Second, Austrian propaganda attempted to portray the struggle as a war of liberation against French rule. Vienna hoped all Germans would rise up, fight foreign tyranny, and cast off the "yoke" of French oppression. Austria itself experimented with the idea of a people's struggle within the context of an absolutist system by organizing a Landwehr (militia). Certainly, the Austrians could not depend solely on patriotic songs, incendiary pamphlets, and overweight middle-class burghers drilling on the town square: Vienna needed allies. London answered the call but St. Petersburg remained neutral, which in itself should be viewed as a victory for Austria, considering Alexander's alliance with Napoleon. Austrian thoughts turned to their Spartan rivals in North Germany: would the Prussians answer the call with their small army of 45,897 men?[5]

At the outset of the struggle, Frederick William appeared more inclined to side with the Austrians. Although Napoleon returned Berlin to Prussian control, the royals remained at Königsberg, where cautious advisors eventually mastered the king. Patriotic war hawks did all they could to convince the monarch to support Austria. Major Karl Friedrich von dem Knesebeck, the Prussian liaison at Austrian headquarters, reported to Frederick William that Archduke Charles and his army remained determined to defeat Napoleon, even after suffering reverses at Regensburg and Abensberg. He suggested that the king dispatch an envoy to judge the feasibility of combined operations with the Austrians. Receiving this task himself, Knesebeck recommended Prussia's direct participation in the war as well as its leadership in raising North Germany against the French. Frederick William viewed such advice with skepticism.

Had Frederick William returned to Berlin in the spring of 1809, the anti-French sentiment that reigned in the capital probably would not have sufficed to convince him to take a decisive step. At the least, the 8 September 1808 Treaty of Paris reinforced the lesson he had so clearly learned in 1805 and 1807: Napoleon did not suffer betrayal. Only a guarantee of success could induce the king to join the Fifth Coalition, and none could be found. Should Prussia suffer another defeat, what would stop Napoleon from settling Prussia's fate the same way he had sealed the fate of other ruling dynasties? Napoleon deposed Hessian Elector William I for supporting Prussia in the War of the Fourth Coalition. William's capital, Kassel, became the capital of Jerome's Kingdom of Westphalia. Like Hesse, Brunswick also became part of Westphalia, with the duke of Brunswick's son and heir, Frederick William, nicknamed "the Black Duke," eventually fleeing to Britain and entering the service of his uncle, King George III. If Napoleon again defeated Prussia, who would stop him from dismembering the state and declaring the House of Hohenzollern forfeit? In this light, Frederick William and his pro-peace advisors certainly appear justified in their caution and fear of Napoleon. Yet ignoring Austria's invitation entailed a certain degree of risk as well. What if the Austrians actually won? If the Prussians remained idle, they could hardly expect the Austrians to restore Prussia's former frontiers and position as a German power. The debates within the Prussian administrative and military circles continued until Tsar Alexander definitively advised Frederick William against joining the Austrians.

Disregarding the king's decision, elements of the army appeared ready to take matters into their own hands. On 28 April 1809, Major Ferdinand von Schill led his 2nd Brandenburg Hussar Regiment out of Berlin to cross the Elbe and incite insurrection in Jerome's Kingdom of Westphalia. Schill, one of Prussia's few heroes from the War of the Fourth Coalition, enjoyed great popularity in Brandenburg and especially in Berlin. Weeks passed as excitement mounted but Frederick William sternly demanded obedience from his army. Although Blücher, another of Prussia's heroes from the recent war, made plans to lead a corps of 30,000 men against the French, action never replaced talk. After news arrived that Schill's ride had ended with his death on 31 May 1809 at the hands of imperial forces, Prussian patriots still hoped Frederick William would declare a war of liberation.

As for the Franco-Austrian conflict, Napoleon rebounded after suffering the first defeat of his career at Aspern–Essling on 22 May 1809. During the 5–6 July battle of Wagram, he inflicted 41,000 casualties on the Austrian army. Napoleon pursued Charles, catching the Austrians at Zniam on the 10th. Charles held his ground for two days but doubted his army's ability to wage another major battle. On 12 July, he requested and received an armistice. Charles's request for a ceasefire caused the Prussians to consider

Napoleon's next step. What if the king's apparent inability to control the patriots among his army and administration prompted Napoleon to turn north after he concluded his business with the Habsburgs? Based on this fear, Frederick William finally appeared ready to enter the war if Austria resumed the struggle. To be better prepared, he extended the army's maneuvers so it could be quickly concentrated. Regardless, the 14 October 1809 Franco-Austrian Treaty of Schönbrunn ended the War of the Fifth Coalition and any talk of the Prussians launching a war of liberation. Francis agreed to cede territory containing 3.5 million subjects, including 1.5 million Poles, as Napoleon added Austrian Galicia to the Grand Duchy of Warsaw. Austria lost more territory (Carinthia, Carniola, Trieste, and part of Croatia) in the Balkans as well as its remaining coastline along the Adriatic Sea, thus land-locking the empire and making it a de facto partner in Napoleon's Continental System. Salzburg and the Tyrol went to France's ally, Bavaria. Kaiser Francis would have to pay an indemnity of 75,000,000 francs and limit the size of his army to 150,000 men.

Although he smashed another coalition, Napoleon could not end the war that continued to rage in Spain and Portugal. Rather than cross the Pyrenees again, he left the war in Iberia to his marshals and his brother Joseph. Despite the situation in Iberia, Napoleon's control of Central Europe appeared incontestable after 1809. Allied with Russia and tightly controlling Prussia, Napoleon seemed to settle permanently his differences with Austria by marrying Marie Louise, the daughter of Kaiser Francis, on 11 March 1810. One year later, at age nineteen, the young bride bore Napoleon a son, Napoléon François Charles Joseph Bonaparte (1811–1832).

Despite the emperor's great joy, his alliance with Russia unraveled that same year. The events between 1808 and 1811 that culminated in Napoleon's 1812 invasion of Russia are well known. Those that proved particularly egregious to Napoleon included Alexander's cool demeanor at the Congress of Erfurt followed by his less than enthusiastic support of French interests during the War of the Fifth Coalition. Conversely, the lack of French diplomatic pressure on the Ottoman Empire to end its war with Russia as well as Napoleon's ambiguity over his intentions regarding Poland embittered Alexander. The Romanov rejection of an imperial marriage with Napoleon crowned the decline of Franco-Russian relations between autumn 1808 and summer 1810.[6] In the second half of 1810, Napoleon expanded his empire by annexing Holland as well as the Hanseatic cities of Hamburg, Bremen, and Lübeck. As a result of the crippling effects of the Continental System, Alexander issued a decree on 31 December 1810 to tax luxury goods and wines, some of France's largest exports. Moreover, the decree opened Russian ports to neutral ships carrying British exports. British goods soon flooded the markets of Eastern and Central Europe. All of Europe recognized the implications of this act: Napoleon would be compelled to enforce

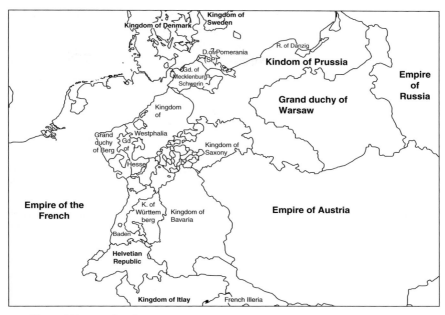

10. Central Europe in 1810

Alexander's participation in the Continental System through war.[7] Continuing to feed his insatiable appetite for territory, Napoleon annexed the Duchy of Oldenburg, east of Hanover in North Germany, on 22 January 1811. Without a word regarding compensation, he dispossessed Duke Peter of Oldenburg, whose younger son, George, was married to the tsar's favorite sister, Grand Duchess Yekaterina Pavlovna. To add insult to injury, Napoleon instructed Foreign Minister Champagny to ignore Alexander's letter of protest. Thus, in 1811, both emperors started preparing for war.

Prussia could not escape the impending crisis between France and Russia. Although paralyzed, the Prussians could hardly hope to remain neutral in the event of war. Frederick William faced the same difficult question he had confronted in the years prior to the disastrous War of the Fourth Coalition: ally with one of the belligerents or remain neutral? In 1811, the option of neutrality hardly seemed possible, forcing the king to choose between Napoleon and Alexander. Either choice presented perilous consequences. By allying with Napoleon, Frederick William could provide the emperor with a secure base from which imperial legions could pour across the Russian frontier. While Napoleon most certainly would strip Prussia of its resources, at least Prussian territory would be spared the devastating consequences of serving as the theater of war. Allying with

Napoleon also offered the slim chance the emperor might reward Frederick William or at least treat him better than a conquered vassal. On the other hand, should Napoleon triumph over Alexander – the sole voice that had spoken on Prussia's behalf – the emperor might extend his reach so far eastward that rear-area security concerns would prompt him to dispossess the Hohenzollerns, partition Prussia, force the state into the Confederation of the Rhine, or all three. Conversely, should Napoleon be defeated, Frederick William certainly would face Alexander's personal wrath. No one could be certain the Russian army would stop at the Niemen River after repulsing the French invader. Already a French client state by virtue of the Treaty of Tilsit, Prussia would emerge in a position that was no better and probably worse if Frederick William found himself on the side of a French defeat.[8]

Allying with Russia meant that Prussia itself would serve as the theater of war. Yet a Russian victory offered the chance of restoring Prussia, albeit on Russian terms. Similar to 1806, no one could answer the difficult but crucial question of how soon the Russian army might arrive. In terms of pros and cons, allying with Russia appeared to be the better of the two options. Many anti-French hawks believed Prussia's salvation lay in an alliance with Russia. Or did it? Certainly a Russian victory would help Prussia's situation but what if Napoleon won? The Russian army's record against the French in no way promised victory, and at this time the Russians found themselves engaged in a fierce struggle with the Turks in the Balkans. Regardless, physical proximity tipped the balance in favor of submission to the French. Imperial forces stood much closer to Prussia than did the Russians: should Frederick William prematurely declare in favor of Russia, Napoleon would destroy Prussia. Thus, timing became essential to the weighty decisions that confronted the Prussian king, who was still reeling from the unexpected death of his 34-year-old wife, Queen Louisa, on 19 July 1810.

In the meantime, Napoleon tightened his hold on Prussia by moving troops eastward and northward, increasing the imperial garrisons that still occupied the Oder fortresses and assembling forces in Poland and on the Elbe. He refused to evacuate the fortress of Glogau even after the Prussians met the conditions for its return to their control. Moreover, the emperor appointed the "Iron Marshal," Louis-Nicolas Davout, commander in chief of all forces in North Germany. On 4 October 1810, Napoleon declared his intention to reinforce Davout's Army of Germany with fifteen infantry and seven cavalry regiments; two days later he set its total strength at forty-eight infantry and twenty-one cavalry regiments.[9]

Throughout the winter of 1810–1811 and into the spring, the danger that Prussia faced became increasingly apparent. According to one contemporary, "the political heavens began to cloud; the outbreak of war appeared unavoidable. [French] troop movements continued."[10] Indeed, imperial forces continuously moved through Prussian territory without providing the required notification. Technically a violation of Prussian sovereignty, the offense did more than wound Prussian pride. The tumultuous events in Spain during 1808 provided a terrifying example of why the movement of imperial armies could not be taken lightly. Under the pretext of reinforcing the French Army of Portugal, more than 90,000 imperial soldiers had crossed the Pyrenees in early 1808, occupying Madrid by 24 March. On 15 June 1808, Napoleon forced the abdication of the Bourbons: King Charles IV and Crown Prince Ferdinand. Shortly afterward, he placed his brother, Joseph, on the throne of Spain. Such transgressions gave the Prussians ample reason to fear that Napoleon intended the same fate for the Hohenzollerns. Nothing seemed to restrain him. After Napoleon extended the empire to Lübeck, the Prussians expected to see imperial legions swarm across Prussia's truncated frontiers at any moment. On top of these fears, the Prussians also found themselves caught between the enforcement of Napoleon's Continental System and the British.

As of August 1810, the Prussian army consisted of 33,857 active soldiers, 10,781 furloughed soldiers, 1,300 garrison troops, 3,300 invalids, and 11,218 soldiers from disbanded regiments who were still capable of service. Normal regimental reserve training made available an additional 9,883 men as replacements for the sick and wounded. The new *Krümper* reserve system provided an extra 3,488 *Beurlaubten* (available trained manpower), meaning additional troops not required for a regiment's normal replacement needs. After the reformers failed to convince the king to adopt the larger program of universal conscription, they settled on the *Krümper* system with the hope of preparing a large, well-trained reserve. According to the system, cavalry squadrons and infantry and foot artillery companies furloughed three to five men each month and replaced them with new recruits who would receive a single month of training. Successfully evading Napoleon's restrictions, the *Krümper* system eventually produced a sizeable reserve of 35,600 trained soldiers, which doubled the size of the field army in 1813.[11]

Other Prussian measures included increasing the Berlin garrison, securing communication between the eight Prussian-controlled fortresses, and building a fortified bridge across the Oder at Schwedt to provide a secure escape route eastward from Berlin. Despite Prussia's financial constraints, Frederick William authorized the construction of entrenched camps at Spandau, Kolberg, and Pillau to serve as rallying points for the units in Brandenburg, Pomerania, and East and West Prussia in case of a French attack. Scharnhorst managed to convince the king that the army needed to be expanded by recalling furloughed soldiers and accelerating the *Krümper* reserve system to train more soldiers. Moreover, the *Krümper* of the Pomeranian and Brandenburg Brigades formed labor units to build and repair fortifications under the supervision of retired officers.

The Prussians knew well that any step they took that Napoleon interpreted as hostile would cost them more than they could afford. Thus, they resorted to secrecy, deception, and passive–aggressive resistance. Gneisenau emerged as the leader of a secret resistance movement. Appealing to London for material assistance in September 1811, his exhortations compelled the British to dispatch "at least 60,000 stand of arms with powder and accoutrements as well as cannon" to the Prussian coast between September and November 1811. A convoy of 4 merchant ships carrying 500 tons of gunpowder and 1,000 tons of lead valued at £90,000, which had been turned away by the Russians as a result of a misunderstanding that same year, also received orders to deliver its cargo to the Prussians. "How much of these war materials were landed is uncertain," notes John Sherwig, "but probably a large portion found their way into Prussian army arsenals."[12]

In late 1810, Tsar Alexander endorsed a plan drafted by his minister of war, General Michael Andreas Barclay de Tolly, to build two lines of fortifications in western Russia that would serve both offensive and defensive operations. For the former, Barclay's lines could provide staging areas and depots for a Russian drive into Central Europe. On the other hand, should Napoleon invade Russia, they could provide strong defensive positions similar to the Lines of Torres Vedras built by Sir Arthur Wellesley, the future duke of Wellington, in Portugal.

While work on the lines commenced, the Russians covertly approached the Poles of the Grand Duchy of Warsaw, hoping to induce them to switch their allegiance to Alexander. Secret talks between Jozef Poniatowski and the tsar's close friend, Prince Adam Czartoryski, ensued. Although Czartoriski sought secrecy, Poniatowski revealed all to Napoleon. By 25 February 1811, Alexander accepted the futility of this attempt and committed himself to an invasion of the Grand Duchy *if* war erupted with France and *if* he decided to take the offensive. To attract allies, the tsar attempted to court Kaiser Francis. He offered a portion of Serbia as well as the Danubian principalities of Moldavia and Wallachia, which Russian forces had recently taken from the Turks, as bargaining chips. Alexander also pledged to support Austria's policy concerning the Italian states. This initiative failed in April 1811 after the Austrians announced their intention to remain neutral in the event of a Franco-Russian conflict.[13]

Well informed concerning the friction between France and Russia, the Prussians viewed Alexander's foreign policy as overly complicated. Consequently, thoughts of a Russian alliance offered Frederick William little comfort, which the complex messages that came from St. Petersburg throughout the first six months of 1811 did not help. On 5 January, Scharnhorst warned the Russian ambassador, Count Christoph Lieven, of Napoleon's apparent preparations to attack Russia and that Prussia could quite possibly be forced to fight on his side. According to his descendant, historian Dominic Lieven, the ambassador was part of a diplomatic corps that kept St. Petersburg "exceptionally well informed about French intentions and preparations. Within Germany the greatest source of intelligence was the Russian mission in Berlin, since January 1810 headed by Christoph Lieven." That same month, Lieven received instructions to inform Frederick William that the tsar considered him to be his best friend and that he would wage war against France to save Prussia. However, on receiving Scharnhorst's warning, the tsar wrote Frederick William a lengthy letter on 19 February stating that, despite Napoleon's preparations, Russia would not give him pretext to attack. Admitting the likelihood of war, Alexander claimed he would be happy to have the Prussians as allies and promised Frederick William compensation for his losses at Tilsit.[14]

In March 1811, Lieven received the task of forwarding to the king, through either the late Prussian queen's 79-year-old *Oberhofmeisterin* (chief lady-in-waiting), Sophie Marie, Countess von Voss, or Frederick William's adjutant, Major August Friedrich von Wrangel, an ultra-confidential letter that presented "the strongest arguments" for Prussia to ally with Russia and not France. That same month, Alexander revealed to the Prussian ambassador, Lieutenant-Colonel Reinhold Otto von Schöler, his plans in the event of a war with France. With some 200,000 men, he would invade the Grand Duchy of Warsaw. He hoped to reach the Oder River before Davout's Army of Germany, which the tsar believed would be numerically inferior to the Russians. Admittedly, a Russian alliance meant Frederick William would be compelled to sacrifice Berlin, albeit temporarily. If Prussian troops concentrated at both Kolberg and Neiße, their presence on the northern and southern extremes of the kingdom would facilitate the movements of the Russian armies by threatening the flanks and rear of the Army of Germany. In Alexander's opinion, the presence of the Prussian army at Kolberg and Neiße would allow the Russians to reach and cross the Elbe. After listening to Russian proposals, an unimpressed Frederick William expressed to Hardenberg on 4 April 1811 that "all of this reminds me of 1805 and 1806, when the tsar's court was seized with the same excitement. I am afraid that the final result again will be an ill-conceived war, bringing misfortune to Russia's friends instead of delivering them from the yoke of oppression."[15]

Some in Prussia wondered if the state could survive another Russian defeat. Many emphatically answered no. Thus, a pro-French party formed based on the idea that the state's salvation lay in a firm union with Napoleon. Blücher derisively referred to the individuals of the pro-French party – Sayn-Wittgenstein, Field-Marshal Friedrich Adolph von Kalckreuth, General Karl Leopold von Köckritz, Foreign Minister August Friedrich von der Goltz, and the royal advisor Johann Peter Ancillon, to name a few – as the *Sicherheitskommissare* (security commissioners). After the unexpected, and for many tragic, passing of the strong-willed, anti-French Queen Louisa in

4  General Gerhard Johann David Waitz von Scharnhorst, 1755–1813

1810, a heart-broken and lonely Frederick William became increasingly susceptible to their arguments. Rumors soon circulated of the projects Napoleon planned to implement based on a Franco-Prussian alliance. Ambassador Lieven asked Hardenberg and Wrangel if the Russian government should be concerned about these rumors. Both assured him on their honor that Prussia was not engaged in secret negotiations with Napoleon. Lieven turned to Scharnhorst, whom he respected and trusted. Scharnhorst confirmed that while no Franco-Prussian alliance treaty aimed at Russia existed, the strong pro-French party sought to convince Frederick William to throw himself into Napoleon's arms. In Scharnhorst's opinion, reported Lieven, the king would have to be forced to sign an alliance with Russia so that he could proceed openly as Alexander's ally, as he had no stomach for covert activity.[16]

Leery of Russia but still willing to explore alliance proposals with Alexander, Hardenberg publicly supported the pro-French party, much to the disappointment of Scharnhorst and Gneisenau. Both chancellor and king felt Prussia should seek a rapprochement with Napoleon. For the Hohenzollern court, the fate of the Spanish Bourbons offered a frightening lesson of the emperor's ruthlessness. In addition, Frederick William could see for himself that Napoleon's mobilization for a war with Russia implied a renewed occupation of Prussia: imperial forces already stood along Prussia's western and southern frontiers. Although Hardenberg did not believe in the immediacy of a Franco-Russian war, he sought a Franco-Prussian alliance in the hope Napoleon would forgive the remainder of the indemnity and allow the Prussian army to expand. Moreover, the revelation contained in Schöler's report of 30 March that upon victory Alexander planned to annex *all* portions of the Grand Duchy of Warsaw meant that Berlin had to view Russia as a potential national security threat. As for Austria, Vienna did not appear reliable, particularly after the Bonaparte–Habsburg marriage. At a ball in February 1811, Frederick William commented to the Russian ambassador, Lieven, that Austria could neither be counted on nor trusted.[17]

To soften Napoleon and establish the groundwork for a Franco-Prussian alliance, Hardenberg sent the extremely pro-French Prince Franz Ludwig von Hatzfeldt to Paris in anticipation of the upcoming birth of Napoleon's child. Typical of the pro-French party, Hatzfeldt believed that Prussia's salvation could be achieved only through an alliance with France. Knowing this, Hardenberg selected Hatzfeldt, confident that the prince would portray him in the same light. In a confidential letter to Hatzfeldt on 31 March 1811, he explained that all talks should be directed toward convincing Napoleon to attach himself to Prussia in a manner that was worthy of his greatness and deserving of the state's gratitude. To demonstrate Prussia's potential value as an ally and to train additional reserves, Frederick William complied with Napoleon's demands to form a coastal defense force to guard against a British landing, presumably while he led the Grande Armée into Russia. On 7 April 1811, the Prussians partially mobilized five of their six brigades to occupy the coast. Prussian strategy in occupying the coast focused on taking positions that obviously allowed them to guard the shore, but more importantly placed them in positions to observe the French and quickly react to their movements.[18]

To Hardenberg, an alliance with Napoleon would reduce and eventually eliminate the threat to Prussia's very existence. The question of whether Napoleon actually intended to destroy Prussia cannot be answered. Yet the idea had been formally presented to him. In his massive study of Russia's struggle against Napoleon, historian Dominic Lieven notes that Russian spies obtained a secret policy memorandum drafted by Champagny and submitted to Napoleon on 16 March 1810. Based on geopolitics and trade, Champagny argued that Russia and Great Britain eventually would become allies in complete violation of the Treaty of Tilsit, which bound Russia to Napoleon's Continental System and thus the French alliance. Concerning Prussia, the foreign minister suggested ceding Silesia to King Frederick Augustus I of Saxony, who, as Napoleon's puppet, likewise served as grand duke of Warsaw. Possession of Silesia would link Saxony and the Grand Duchy, creating a huge Saxon–Polish state along Prussia's southern frontier but more importantly along Austria's northern frontier. A second scenario offered by Champagny called for the complete restoration of Poland after a victorious war against Russia. In exchange for its remaining Polish districts, Austria would receive compensation in the Balkans while Russia would be stripped of its Polish territory, having its western border pushed hundreds of miles eastward. As for Prussia, Champagny's verdict was ominous. Regardless of Napoleon's eastern policy, he suggested partitioning Prussia because it served as an outpost of Russian influence in Europe. Although Alexander himself received copies of Champagny's report, it is not known how much if any of this information he shared with the Prussians. Regardless, such discussions justified Hardenberg's fear for Prussia's survival.[19]

Consequently, Hardenberg predicted disaster if Frederick William bound his fate to Alexander's. Thus, for the moment, the chancellor firmly opposed an alliance with Russia. He would pursue a Russo-Prussian alliance only if Alexander followed a steadfast and unselfish policy. From Hardenberg's perspective, instead of Alexander appearing satisfied with the conquest of Moldavia and Wallachia, the tsar's overtures to the Poles revealed his intentions to unite Poland to Russia. Obviously, this indicated that the districts of Prussian Poland incorporated into the Grand Duchy of Warsaw would not be returned. Moreover, what if the tsar wanted East and West Prussia as well? What of Galicia: would the tsar return Austrian Poland to the Habsburgs? If not, would Vienna remain idle while he created his Polish vassal? In light of these troubling issues, Frederick William wrote to Alexander on 7 April 1811.[20] Subsequent missives to Alexander followed on 12 and 16 April. In these letters, the king explained his difficult position, asking how much he could count on Russian assistance should Napoleon attack Prussia. Frederick William emphasized the urgent need for careful diplomatic preparations – especially with Austria – for war.[21]

Hardenberg likewise continued to press the Russians for definitive answers, especially in regard to the type of direct military support Prussia would receive by way of a Russo-Prussian alliance. He courted Ambassador Lieven but posed tough questions: mainly, would the Russian army immediately cross the frontier to support the Prussians in a war against Napoleon? During a secret meeting between Lieven and Hardenberg on 11 April 1811, the Russian ambassador stated: "You have three courses you can take: you can join us, you can join France, or you can take no risks." Hardenberg immediately responded that the third option would be the worst of all and would expose Frederick William to the same fate as William I of Hesse. He assured Lieven that the king supported the pro-Russian party only. However, the chancellor cautiously informed Lieven that the project of a Russo-Prussian alliance required paramount trust and secrecy. He revealed the plans for the expansion of the Prussian army and assured the Russian ambassador that the Prussian government fully acknowledged the dangers it faced in the event of a Franco-Russian war. Although not specifically stating conditions for Alexander to meet before Frederick William signed a Russo-Prussian agreement, Hardenberg recommended that Lieven urge his government to end its war with the Ottoman Empire and secure Austrian support. A period of acute anxiety followed as Berlin awaited a response from St. Petersburg.

At this point, neither Lieven nor Russian chancellor Nikolai Rumiantsev knew the extent of Hardenberg's double-dealing. The nineteenth-century legal expert and Russian historian Fyodor Martens, whose account of this period is based on Ambassador Lieven's papers, accuses Frederick William and Hardenberg of showing little energy in their pursuit of a Russian alliance. While this is debatable given the situation, the chancellor did not help matters by the way he dealt with his own cabinet, which baffled the Russians more than his entreaties to the French. Hardenberg had a poor working relationship with Goltz, Prussia's foreign minister since 1808. Lieven described Goltz as being completely shallow and totally under the influence of his wife. Although despising Goltz, Hardenberg retained him because he enjoyed a degree of credibility among the French. At the end of the 11 April 1811 meeting with Lieven, the chancellor allegedly stated: "Now you know the secret of the king and his cabinet, and the fate of the state depends on the maintenance of this secrecy. It is necessary to hide our true intentions because Count Goltz himself and the entire Ministry of Foreign Affairs are completely unaware of our views; we believe in principles they strongly oppose." Despite this bizarre revelation, Lieven reported that Hardenberg's measures bore the stamp of "genuine prudence and wisdom." Moreover, the Russian ambassador described Prussia as Russia's first barrier against France and that all anti-French parties in Germany turned their eyes to the Prussian government.[22]

Lieven's opinion changed just one month later, after he became convinced that both Hardenberg and Frederick William would make considerable concessions to France, despite the chancellor's solemn assurances that Prussia would never work against Russia. Conversely, St. Petersburg attempted to downplay the growing crisis with France. In May, Alexander notified Schöler that he had no intention of provoking a new war in Europe; that his military measures along the frontier were purely defensive in nature; that he regarded the alliance between Russia and France as very beneficial to both empires; and that his relations with Napoleon "were indeed very intimate and very good." Regardless, compelling evidence convinced the Prussians of Napoleon's preparations for an immediate war with Russia. With Prussia serving as a buffer between the two empires, its survival as an independent state appeared unlikely. At the least, imperial forces would occupy the state and force the Prussians to participate in the war against Russia. At worst, with Portugal and Spain as the most recent examples, the state would be partitioned, the Hohenzollerns dethroned, and the army dissolved except for the best units, which would be sent as tribute to the emperor. Frederick William's situation became critical after Napoleon refused to respond to Hardenberg's request for a Franco-Prussian alliance that would have provided the state a degree of protection against such scenarios.[23]

From the start, Hatzfeldt's mission experienced difficulty. Finally, after waiting four months, he gained an audience with the emperor. On 14 May 1811, Ambassador Friedrich Wilhelm von Krusemarck officially submitted an alliance proposal to Napoleon on Hardenberg's behalf. Accordingly, if Napoleon became embroiled in a war near the Prussian frontier, Frederick William would provide an auxiliary force by forming an all-Prussian corps commanded by a Prussian general under the overall command of Napoleon or one of his lieutenants. In return, the emperor would guarantee Prussia's territorial integrity and independence. Because such a relationship should be based on trust, Frederick William expected the return of Glogau, particularly as he had already paid half of the indemnity and thus satisfied Napoleon's conditions. Should Prussia fight under the French Eagle, the king requested the renunciation of the remainder of the indemnity because he could not fund a war and pay reparations at the same time. Hardenberg requested that Napoleon repeal the 1808 limits placed on the Prussian army, especially because its expansion would be imperative for participation in a war. The king asked nothing in return for this participation and would leave the issue of a reward to the emperor's discretion. Finally, as the sole precondition, Frederick William requested that the emperor declare the portion of Silesia near the Austrian frontier to be neutral so that it could serve as an asylum for him and his family during the war.[24]

Six weeks after Krusemarck submitted this alliance proposal, the Prussians found themselves in dire straits. Aside from a 4 June 1811 agreement that granted imperial forces access to all of Prussia's military roads, the Prussian legation at Paris still had not received an answer to the alliance proposal.[25] They expected Napoleon to convey his opinion to Hatzfeldt, who was working with Krusemarck on the project. Hatzfeldt had his farewell audience with the emperor on 28 June 1811. Napoleon expressed his satisfaction with Frederick William's political attitude as well as with Hardenberg, whom he had previously detested. He assured Hatzfeldt that France desired nothing from Prussia and that the situation with Russia prompted the increase of imperial forces between the Elbe and the Vistula. Yet the emperor claimed that the situation had already changed so much that he no longer feared a war with Russia. Napoleon did not mention one word regarding the alliance and the conditions Hardenberg requested. The new French foreign minister, Hugues-Bernard Maret, explained that to prevent offending the tsar the emperor could not discuss an alliance with Prussia until he resolved the situation with Russia.

Hatzfeldt's last report, dated 28 June, reached Berlin on 9 July. A predicament indeed! Hardenberg counted on Napoleon needing Prussia for his imminent war against Russia; now he learned that the French would not negotiate with him until the crisis with Russia passed. Napoleon's silence on the issue of a Franco-Prussian alliance made a negative impression on both the chancellor and the king. The evidence pointing to war could no longer be ignored, regardless of Napoleon's optimism. Despite the treaty stipulations, Napoleon steadfastly refused to return the fortress of Glogau to Prussian control. Moreover, he issued orders in March 1811 for preparations to occupy Prussia's remaining fortresses. Reinforcements increased the garrisons of the Oder fortresses to 17,173 men, thus surpassing the stipulated 10,000 men; Danzig's garrison reached 16,000 men. At the end of June, approximately 37,500 imperial troops held positions on Prussian territory between the Elbe and the Oder, with a further 27,000 along the left bank of the Elbe. Napoleon's intentions became obvious to the Prussians: he planned to take a strong stand against Russia and create an unassailable bastion to wage war against Alexander. Prussia would be an integral part of that position. Based on this strategy, he could not destroy Prussia or further diminish the state. Instead, he wanted to render the Prussians helpless so that he could exploit them for his own purposes. Frederick William feared the worst, insisting that Napoleon's intentions remained the same: to end Prussia's existence.[26]

Although the pro-French party was still attempting to sway the king, Hardenberg recognized the steps that needed to be taken. "Rarely has a statesman changed [policy] as quickly as the Prussian chancellor did in those July days of 1811," notes historian Max Lehmann. Napoleon's intentions finally became clear to Hardenberg. Yet salvation briefly appeared within reach. In response to letters written by Frederick William in April 1811, Tsar Alexander responded on 26 May that he would consider a French attack on Prussia as a declaration of war on Russia. This news opened the door for further Russo-Prussian negotiations. Regardless, Hardenberg's duplicitous foreign policy rightly concerned the Russians. Aware of Prussia's quest for a Franco-Prussian alliance, Alexander realized he had few friends left in Europe and so turned inward. Although the Russians kept communication open, Hardenberg's confusing foreign policy prompted them to forgo their military plans to assist Prussia.[27]

In May 1811, the tsar fully (but not officially) approved the defensive aspects of Barclay's lines and accepted General Karl Ludwig von Phull's defensive plan to counter a French offensive. Instead of advancing to meet Napoleon's legions, Russian forces would withdraw to the interior and utilize Barclay's lines of defense. In August 1811, the tsar himself told the Austrian ambassador that if Napoleon invaded the Russians would retreat and render the land a barren desert. Although Prussia would be inundated by French forces, Alexander insisted that the state would not collapse. His letter of 26 May 1811 assured Frederick William that "Russia's political interests imperatively demand the preservation of Prussia." He advised the king to build entrenched camps at Kolberg, Pillau, and Neiße to detain large portions of the French army. After drawing Napoleon into Russia and defeating him, Alexander would liberate Prussia. In fact, Prussia would assume the role of Spain and thus initiate a national uprising throughout North Germany that would tie down considerable French forces. Meanwhile, Russia would fill the role of Portugal, sucking in the French and defeating them, just as Wellesley had done in 1810. Based on this strategy, after his armies defeated the French invader, Alexander would drive them from Prussia.[28]

After changing his view of the situation, Scharnhorst shared similar ideas. In 1808–1809, he had doubted that an insurgency could defeat Napoleon and deliver Prussia. Instead, he had preferred to resurrect the army and confront the battle-hardened French. If the new Prussian army could not challenge the French on its own, he looked to bolster it with a national militia that would be energized by patriotic and nationalistic enthusiasm. Scharnhorst hoped to combine the strength and discipline of the army with the zeal of a national militia led by regular officers. However, the enormous indemnity and painfully slow growth of its army rendered Prussia militarily impotent compared to the French Empire. The enormous resources of time and money required to create a large, powerful army particularly thwarted Scharnhorst's efforts. Acknowledging the political and economic obstacles that prevented the rapid regeneration of the regular army, Scharnhorst changed his position in 1811. Many other reformers and members of the anti-French party such as Gneisenau and Blücher agreed and turned to the idea of a national revolt. Scharnhorst and his close assistant, Boyen, who now served as the king's adjutant-general, believed a popular insurrection offered the only hope of saving Prussia. A national uprising combined with intense fighting around Prussia's fortresses would occupy French forces long enough for Prussia to attract the support of allies.[29]

From the moment a new war with France appeared likely, Scharnhorst argued against pitched battles. Rather than wage a conventional war, he suggested basing Prussian operations on the eight remaining fortresses as well as three entrenched camps that would be built. To Scharnhorst, the examples provided by the Spanish in their defense of fortresses such as Badajoz, Elvas, and Abrantès offered the model for the Prussian war effort. Despite the capitulations of 1806, he remained confident in the strength of Prussia's fortresses. Moreover, he counted on the people's patriotic wrath manifesting in a brutal guerrilla war against the French conqueror. Although Scharnhorst embraced a national uprising, he still recognized that Prussia needed direct military assistance from the Russians. Unfortunately for him, glaring differences separated his plan from that proposed by Phull. Scharn-horst envisioned a Russian offensive to the Oder while Phull advocated withdrawing the Russian army deep into Russia. In Scharnhorst's opinion, Phull's plan would bring about the capitulation of Prussia's fortresses.[30]

Napoleon's silence regarding the Franco-Prussian alliance proposal forced Frederick William to pursue Alexander's offer to consider a French invasion of Prussia as a declaration of war. Although his 16 July letter to Alexander marked the end of the *"franzosenfreundliche"* (pro-French) period of Prussian politics, Frederick William remained wary. In his letter, he delicately pressed Alexander on the issue of effectively aiding Prussia and not abandoning him. "But I count on you, Sire. You will consider everything with wisdom and make the best decisions. Confident of this, I voluntarily pledge not to side with any party other than yours in the event of a war between Russia and France." Frederick William also requested that the tsar comment on Scharnhorst's campaign plan, which Schöler would deliver, and asked whether it would be possible to arrange a secret rendezvous between a Russian officer, Scharnhorst, and Schöler to conclude an agreement.[31]

In the meantime, Hardenberg met with Lieven on 12 and 17 July. Now attempting to be transparent, he opened the conversation on the 12th by reading Goltz's instructions to Hatzfeldt regarding his mission to attract Napoleon to the idea of a Franco-Prussian alliance. Accordingly, Prussia "found itself forced" by national security concerns "to fully embrace the French party and follow blindly." The chancellor then hastened to assure Lieven that Goltz knew absolutely nothing of the king's true intentions. Instead, he purposefully deceived both Goltz and Ambassador Krusemarck into believing that Prussia would ally with France. Hardenberg insisted that the need to better prepare for war against Napoleon prompted him to mislead his own foreign office. He also informed the Russian ambassador that Frederick William "firmly resolved to act in concert with Tsar Alexander and that he had not deviated from this principle for one moment. He would persevere with all the affection he has for His Imperial Majesty and the conviction that the welfare of his state as well as his personal safety require their unity of interests." At the conclusion of the interview, Hardenberg suggested to Lieven that they needed to meet more often but in secret and with the utmost "caution."

During the 17 July meeting, Hardenberg revealed the king's decision to send Scharnhorst to St. Petersburg to define the military relationship between Russia and Prussia. The chancellor relayed his hope that the tsar would view Scharnhorst's mission as proof of Frederick William's desire to ally with his powerful friend. Lieven echoed these sentiments in his 23 July report to Rumiantsev:

> I have received a fair hope for the sincere cooperation of Prussia ... and the choice of the man who will negotiate the common cause between Russia and

Prussia and to prepare for success speaks enough of the complete abandon of
the king, of his unbound confidence in the friendship of our august master,
and of his irrevocable resolution to remain faithful. General Scharnhorst is
known to the king as a man of the strictest integrity, opposed in principle to
the new system that oppresses Europe, devoted to Russia, and above all
deserving of an opportunity to free the sovereign whom he serves from the
yoke he is obliged to bear.

Lieven also forwarded Scharnhorst's recommendation for a "system of
temporization" in Franco-Russian relations that would provide Prussia with
more time to prepare for war.[32]

Frederick William finally realized that compliance with Napoleon's
demands would not produce any guarantee of restoring Prussia's independence. He ultimately agreed with the anti-French party by preferring
a desperate but honorable struggle for survival as opposed to hopeless,
voluntary subjugation. Certainly not a stupid man, Frederick William
perhaps realized that desperate but honorable offered a slim chance of
success while hopeless eventually would lead to the end of Hohenzollern
Prussia. To stay on the side of desperate and honorable while avoiding hopeless, the king needed allies. After Hatzfeldt returned from Paris, Frederick
William tasked Scharnhorst with the secret journey to St. Petersburg for the
sole purpose of drafting war plans with the Russians. Thus, the king
wanted to know not *if* the Russians would help, but *how* they would help.
Frederick William's letters along with Lieven's support helped launch the
Scharnhorst mission with relatively solid prospects for success. In a report
dated 14 August 1811 that reached Hardenberg on the 27th, Schöler
conveyed Alexander's "joy" over Scharnhorst's mission. Berlin responded
by authorizing Scharnhorst to cross the frontier. It would be his task
to persuade the tsar to reject Phull's defensive and adopt – preferably in a
formal military convention – a Prussian proposal for an immediate offensive beyond the Russian frontier.[33]

Following Scharnhorst's departure, the government's resolve to prepare
for war stiffened. On 22 August 1811, Hardenberg received Ambassador
Krusemarck's latest report from Paris. During a 15 August reception at the
Tuileries to celebrate Napoleon's forty-second birthday, the emperor
berated the Russian ambassador, Aleksandr Kurakin, and severely criticized
Alexander. In addition, Krusemarck reported that Napoleon had again
rejected his request for the return of Glogau. To the Prussians, Kurakin's
public humiliation – a calculated provocation – and the retention of Glogau
signaled the imminence of a Franco-Russian war. Although Scharnhorst had
yet to step foot on Russian soil, Frederick William needed to act fast. In
response to Krusemarck's report, he appointed a committee to oversee a
rapid expansion of the army, which already numbered 74,553 men, to
120,000 men. Chaired by Hardenberg, the committee consisted of

5 General August Wilhelm Antonius Neidhardt von Gneisenau, 1760–1831

Gneisenau, Boyen, Privy Councilor and President of Pomerania Johann August Sack, and Colonel Georg Ernst Karl von Hake. A few days later, Frederick William ordered the infantry companies increased to full combat strength as well as the formation of forty reserve and eleven depot battalions from surplus *Krümper*.

To provide weapons, Gneisenau and Hardenberg initiated negotiations with London. In addition, Colonel Wilhelm Kasper von Dörnberg secretly arrived at Kolberg on a diplomatic mission for the British government to evaluate the mood of the Prussians. Although the British instructed Dörnberg not to discuss the possibility of subsidies, Gneisenau used the opportunity to raise the issue of forming a British-financed Prusso-German legion. According to Dörnberg, a British convoy carrying 10,000 muskets, 2,000,000 cartridges, and 3,000 barrels of powder sent by the prince-regent on Gneisenau's request would soon reach the Baltic.[34]

At the end of August, Lieven conveyed his firm belief to Rumiantsev that, while Russia could count on Prussia as an ally, he could not foresee how Napoleon's threats would influence the king's final decision. To soften Lieven's attitude, Hardenberg strove to impress upon him the gravity of Prussia's situation. He also expressed the necessity for Frederick William to know "with absolute accuracy the real intentions" of the tsar in the event of a Franco-Russian war: meaning, would Russia's legions take the offensive or fall back into the vast Russian heartland? News arrived from Russia, but not from Scharnhorst and not the answer that Hardenberg and Frederick

William craved. As Scharnhorst crossed the Russian steppe, a courier hastily made his way west from St. Petersburg to Berlin to deliver Schöler's late-August report to Hardenberg. On 12 September 1811, the chancellor received the dispatch: Alexander reiterated his assurance that he would equate an attack on Prussia with an attack on Russia. Moreover, he would utilize all his forces to wage war against France and would conclude peace only if it guaranteed Prussia's independence. Again the king received the answer regarding the question of *if* Russia would help, yet the question of *how* Russia would help remained unanswered. Hardenberg warned Lieven of increasing French suspicion of Prussia's mobilization: Napoleon demanded an explanation. The chancellor could no longer guarantee that Frederick William could resist French pressure. On 23 September, Lieven explained to his superiors that, if the king knew Alexander's precise intentions, he could reject French demands, despite the consequences.[35]

Regarding Scharnhorst's mission, the Prussians created an elaborate smokescreen to deceive French spies. After he had inspected the Silesian fortresses in 1810, his departure from Berlin on 29 July 1811 received official billing as an inspection tour of the Pomeranian and Prussian fortresses (Kolberg, Graudenz, and Pillau). To further deceive the French, Scharnhorst received a three-week vacation at the end of his inspection to visit a spa in either Silesia or Bohemia. The pass that he carried to the Russian frontier stated that he was a district magistrate from the Prussian portion of Magdeburg. After completing his inspections of Kolberg, Graudenz, and Pillau on 21 August, he waited at his East Prussian estate of Dollstädt (Krasnoznamenskoye) near Elbing (Elbląg) for permission to cross the Russian frontier. After receiving news that Alexander approved his mission, Scharnhorst awaited the arrival from St. Petersburg of his Prussian escort, Captain Bornstedt, the officer entrusted with delivering the king's 16 July 1811 letter to Alexander. After illness had detained him, he finally reached Dollstädt on the evening of 9 September. Using side roads for the sake of secrecy, Scharnhorst reached the Russian frontier, where he met one of the tsar's adjutants. Traveling as a Russian colonel named Menin, Scharnhorst reached Tsarskoye Selo on 24 September, where the general met Schöler and several high-ranking Russian officers including Barclay, Phull, and Minister of War Aleksey Arakcheyev.

Scharnhorst negotiated with the Russians from late September until the middle of October but the tsar did not receive him until 4 October. Unfortunately for the Prussian envoy, Russian ardor cooled due to news from Lieven that Hardenberg appeared to be buckling under French pressure. This accurate report led Alexander to believe that Frederick William would ultimately embrace the French party. Berlin's waffling, which had already cost the Prussians a firm commitment from the tsar, threatened to ruin Scharnhorst's chances of securing Russian support. His first meeting with

Alexander and Barclay on 4 October did not produce much progress. Scharnhorst stated Prussia's needs: a Russian corps posted close to the border of East Prussia, with the rest of the Russian army poised to cross the Vistula as soon as the French invaded Prussia. Repeated requests from both Schöler and Scharnhorst prompted a second audience with the tsar on the 10th. Alexander opened the discussion by presenting his draft of a Russo-Prussian defensive alliance that sought to correct the problems that plagued previous coalitions. First, the proposed alliance obliged both states to aid each other with *all* possible forces in the event of a French attack. Second, neither party would make a separate peace with Napoleon. To Schöler, the document appeared more a political entente than a military agreement. He quickly protested on the grounds that Frederick William had authorized him only to negotiate a military accord. Alexander responded that a political agreement would establish the foundation for a military convention. Scharnhorst quickly interceded, insisting that Frederick William first needed to know the tsar's military intentions in the event of war. If Alexander invaded Poland, the Prussians could hope for a successful outcome of the war. However, if the tsar's legions remained on the defensive inside the Russian frontier, the king considered himself as good as lost. Furthermore, the tsar could count on the Prussians to tie down at least 100,000 imperial troops as well as on the fact that concerted Russo-Prussian action would lead to an insurrection in North Germany supported by the British. Should Alexander abandon Frederick William, Napoleon would have three times the combat force, with which he could invade Russia. In addition, Scharnhorst warned that Russian Poland would revolt, the Ottoman Empire would renew its war with more vigor, and the Austrians would either remain neutral or exploit Alexander's situation for their own gain. Based on these arguments, Alexander dropped his opposition to a military convention and tasked Barclay with concluding the negotiations.[36]

Scharnhorst departed Tsarskoye Selo on 18 October, one day after signing the military convention with his Russian counterparts Barclay and Rumiantsev. He also bore the draft of a Russo-Prussian political alliance written by the tsar himself.[37] Despite the great importance of the military convention, Alexander did not intend for it to replace a formal treaty of alliance that would irrevocably bind the fate of Russia and Prussia in the event of war with France. However, per Scharnhorst's instructions, the ratification of the military convention did not depend on the conclusion of a political alliance. According to the convention, "the two sovereigns want peace but the intentions of Napoleon have become increasingly questionable due to persistent breaches of the Treaty of Tilsit, such as the occupation of the Duchy of Oldenburg, the increase of garrisons in the fortresses of Prussia, and his escalating armaments. In view of these circumstances, the parties are required to sign a document providing proof for their peoples and to the whole world that they have directed all their efforts to prevent war and the sole purpose is to define the available mutual defense measures if one of the two powers is attacked."

According to the terms of the military convention, the "High Contracting Parties" declared that they desired nothing more than the preservation of peace on the continent. "If, despite their efforts to achieve this goal, they are attacked jointly or separately, they solemnly promise to come to the aid of each other with all their forces. Any invasion into the states of the High Contracting Parties or march of French troops through Prussia to the Duchy of Warsaw will be regarded by them as a declaration of war." Thus, aside from actual hostilities, "a considerable increase of French troops or their allies on the Vistula" as well as "any occupation of a portion of the Prussian states" would be viewed as a French declaration of war. After the war started, "the High Contracting Parties undertake to lay down their arms in common." Peace proposals from Napoleon that would "invalidate or prevent the execution of this exact act will be rejected and none of the Contracting Powers will hide proposals to detach this alliance." The convention also bound both monarchs to close cooperation if Napoleon continued his mobilization. The Russians sent a copy to Lieven for Frederick William's signature; the signatures of the two sovereigns would serve as ratification of the convention.

In terms of actual military planning, as soon as Frederick William or the governor of East Prussia, General Hans David von Yorck, informed the Russians of a hostile French act as defined by the convention, Russian forces would march as quickly as possible to the Vistula. A Prussian army of 80,000 men would occupy the state's fortresses and entrenched camps, and "through a defensive posture, which will be conducted with the greatest activity, use all means to hinder the enemy's advance to the Vistula." Frederick William would leave Berlin as soon as the French appeared to be closing on the Prussian capital. If the troops in Brandenburg managed to escape across the Oder, they would advance to Graudenz and unite with the Russians. If they could not escape across the Oder, they would retreat northeast to Kolberg, unite with the Pomeranian Brigade, and operate against the enemy's left flank, remaining in Kolberg's entrenched camp only if threatened by superior enemy forces. If imperial forces closed the road to Kolberg, the Brandenburgers would withdraw to Silesia. There, they would be absorbed into the Silesian Army, which would be formed by mobilizing the province. The Russians would send one division to protect Königsberg and East Prussia's rich military stores. If the East and West Prussian Brigades could stop the imperials at the Passarge (Pasłęka) River, the Russians believed this division could reach Königsberg before the French arrived from Danzig. United with these two Prussian brigades, the Russian forces consisting of twelve battalions, eight squadrons, two Cossack divisions, and numerous cannon would defend Königsberg. If the French marched from Danzig to the Grand Duchy of Warsaw, this Russo-Prussian corps would move closer to the five divisions of the main Russian army, which would cross the Grand Duchy of Warsaw's frontier eight days at the most after receiving orders to march. The Russians would then move through the Grand Duchy toward the Vistula. Alexander also pledged to send warships to protect the sea lanes between Memel, Pillau, and Kolberg (see Map 1).

Although Scharnhorst viewed the military convention as the crowning achievement of his labors, he was too late. Time had expired for Frederick William before Scharnhorst had even met with the Russians. Prussia's military preparations did not escape French vigilance. As the mobilization accompanied the failed Hatzfeldt mission, the French became increasingly suspicious. Napoleon demanded an immediate explanation regarding Prussian intentions. Responding on 26 August to Ambassador Antoine St.-Marsan's inquiries, Hardenberg stated that the emperor's apparent rejection of a Franco-Prussian alliance left Frederick William no alternative but to take precautions. Unsure of the fate Napoleon intended for him, the king decided that "it would be better to die with weapon in hand." Should the emperor renounce all hostile intentions toward Prussia and offer an honorable alliance, Frederick William would demobilize. At Paris, Krusemark offered a similar explanation. Hardenberg's argument impressed St.-Marsan, who thanked the chancellor for his frankness. However, Napoleon instructed his ambassador to inform Hardenberg that negotiations under arms violated his sense of honor. On 11 September 1811, St.-Marsan communicated Napoleon's accusation that Berlin had not only violated the 1808 Treaty of Paris by arming without his consent, but had also jeopardized Franco-Russian relations by mobilizing. St.-Marsan reiterated that the emperor had prohibited any step that could precipitate a Franco-Russian crisis. Thus, the Prussians should immediately disarm. Hardenberg urged the king to placate Napoleon by providing satisfactory proof of Prussia's friendship and unlimited trust. On 12 September, St.-Marsan received a handwritten response from the king himself: the orders to raise forty reserve and eleven depot battalions and to increase the companies to a war footing would be rescinded.

Apparently, this step did not satisfy Napoleon. On 20 September, St.-Marsan presented an ultimatum: Prussia would disarm immediately, reduce the army to the 1808 treaty limitations, discharge all recruits and workers, cease all work on fortifications, and immediately inform the Russians of these steps. Under the conditions of this disarmament, the emperor declared himself favorable to concluding a Franco-Prussian alliance. Frederick William received three days to respond. Should he refuse, Marshal Davout would invade Prussia with all imperial forces stationed along the Elbe. Terrorized by Napoleon, still lacking an answer to the crucial question of how Alexander intended to support him, having barely started negotiations with the British, and with the Austrians remaining aloof, Frederick William caved under this pressure. After meeting with St.-Marsan several times, Hardenberg accepted the futility of his position. The king's lack of confidence in himself and in his people, as well as Hardenberg's own doubts concerning the extent of Alexander's support, prompted the chancellor to advise Frederick William to yield. He informed the French ambassador on 21 September 1811 of the king's decision to comply with the emperor's wishes. Frederick William issued orders to halt the mobilization.[38]

Three days later, Hardenberg notified Lieven of the king's decision to accept Napoleon's offer of a Franco-Prussian alliance. Frederick William assumed full responsibility by admitting that his continued negotiations with the French ruined the chances of securing a firm commitment from Alexander. Despite the turn of events, Hardenberg continued to express a desire to bind the fate of Prussia to that of Russia rather than France. He pointedly informed Lieven of the arguments that could influence the king to recognize the need for an alliance with Russia. But Hardenberg asked the impossible. Should Napoleon force the Prussians to accept a "close alliance" with France based on "aggressive views toward Russia," how would the tsar react? Hardenberg wanted Lieven to guarantee that Alexander "would not view such an association with anxiety and consider it as a hostile measure directed against him and a signal for war." Having absolutely no authority to grant this absurd request, Lieven refused. With few options remaining, Hardenberg again insisted on the need to know Alexander's intentions, specifically regarding Prussia, in the event of a Franco-Russian war.[39]

Six years earlier, in 1805, the British Royal Navy had evacuated the Bourbons from the Kingdom of Naples. In 1807, British ships sailed out of Lisbon with the Braganzas of Portugal just as the French entered the city. Now, in 1811, the prince-regent of England offered to rescue the Hohenzollerns from Prussia via the fleet that lay off the coast of Kolberg. Frederick William politely declined. Nevertheless, Gneisenau, Dörnberg, Hardenberg, and Blücher agreed to retaliate if the French abducted the king either through ruse, which had been the fate of the Spanish Bourbons in 1808, or by force, which had been the fate of Pope Pius VI in 1798. If he was apprehended by the French and "forced" to take steps that appeared detrimental to Prussian interests, they planned to take action to save him and the state, despite any orders they received from him. With Great Britain's assistance, they hoped to ignite a German insurrection on the Spanish model. Supported by Prussia's fortresses, especially Kolberg with its entrenched camp and vital sea communications, the Prussians would fight just as desperately as the Spanish.

London moved quickly. In addition to authorizing the shipment of 10,000 muskets to the Baltic on 8 September 1811, the British government issued instructions on 27 September to send an additional 25,000 as well as a large quantity of ammunition. Shortly afterward, on 1 October, the British dispatched twenty-five heavy guns for Prussia's fortresses and enough field guns to form five batteries. Through a fellow Hanoverian, Colonel Christian Friedrich Wilhelm von Ompteda, Gneisenau maintained private corres- pondence with London that reached the desk of the prince-regent himself. On 22 September, Gneisenau informed Hardenberg that the prince-regent sent another British agent, the Austrian general Laval Nugent, to Berlin with instructions to negotiate with Gneisenau. Nugent assured Gneisenau that the British would provide everything Prussia needed in terms of war mater- iel as well as "all possible help."

On 5 October 1811, Ompteda arrived at London with Gneisenau's 10 September letter detailing Prussian plans to implement a Fabian strategy against the French to gain time. Gneisenau noted Prussia's determination to confront Napoleon but expressed the state's dire need for arms and ammu- nition. According to his estimates, the Prussians could raise an army of 300,000 men but could provide only enough muskets, cannon, and ammuni- tion for a force of 124,000 combatants. In response, London doubled its commitment. On 8 October, the British government issued orders for the shipment of an additional 25,000 muskets, 25 siege guns, and 5 field batter- ies; the convoy would be ready to sail by the end of the month. As Great Britain and Prussia remained formally at war, the Prussians never received any of the arms or ammunition.[40]

As noted, time had run out for Frederick William. To honor Napoleon's ultimatum, he issued a cabinet order on 26 September 1811 to discharge all *Krümper* gradually to avoid rendering thousands of men unemployed. Instead, they would be used on public works projects such as improving roads. On 4 October, St.-Marsan again complained to Hardenberg, claiming that the work on the fortifications continued and that the regiments con- tinued to be reinforced. This prompted Hardenberg to advise the king to discharge all civilian workers on the 5th and furlough all *Krümper* on the 8th, thus removing any question concerning the continuation of work on the fortifications.

Regardless, the French continued to pressure the Prussians. To induce Napoleon to *consider* accepting a Franco-Prussian treaty, St.-Marsan insisted that the Prussians first accept additional conditions. For example, on 19 October, he demanded that the army's food supplies be sold, that all work on the fortifications completely cease, and that all soldiers above the number stipulated by the 1808 Treaty of Paris be discharged. St.-Marsan frankly informed Hardenberg that the emperor did not trust the Prussians and did not believe they would disarm. Thus, as a final humiliation, a staffer from the French legation, St.-Marsan's own secretary, Lefebvre, would supervise these final steps and conduct a personal inspection tour to ensure compliance. Hardenberg objected but St.-Marsan firmly told the chancellor that no interference would be tolerated. In fact, the inspections would receive royal authorization, as the French ambassador instructed Hardenberg to issue letters of introduction on Lefebvre's behalf to all fortress command-ants as well as the local authorities. Allegedly, before Hardenberg could notify St.-Marsan of his refusal to allow the inspections, Goltz issued Lefebvre a passport without consulting the king. Thus, Hardenberg could not prevent the inspection tour by refusing to grant a passport. Moreover, the king withdrew his opposition after St.-Marsan informed him that Napoleon had already received notice that the Prussian government had provided the necessary permission and that Lefebvre had started his tour. "I provided Lefebvre with letters of introduction," explained Hardenberg in a 24 October 1811 letter to Lieven, "because the king wanted the military governors to be informed that they must fulfill the desire of the emperor Napoleon, to establish all the more confidence." The tour started at Kolberg, which Lefebvre inspected on 23 October.[41]

Six days later, on 29 October, St.-Marsan informed Hardenberg that the emperor accepted the idea of an alliance with Prussia. According to the French ambassador, Napoleon understood that Prussia sought to recoup some of its losses. However, believing that his forces sufficed in case of a war with Russia, he felt he did not need Prussia's military assistance. Instead of a military convention, he presented Frederick William two choices: either join the Confederation of the Rhine or accept an offensive–defensive alliance with Napoleon. He rejected Hardenberg's condition that the alliance would go into effect only if Napoleon became embroiled in a war near Prussia's borders. Instead, this stipulation would apply to any war in Europe, by land or sea. A Prussian auxiliary corps of 24,000 men – increased from the original 1808 stipulation of 16,000 men – would be required for a war against Austria and 20,000 for a conflict with Russia; the emperor would accept no limita-tions on how he disposed of the troops. This small number of troops made it unnecessary either to forgive the remainder of the indemnity or to expand the size of the Prussian army. Glogau would not be returned to Prussian control because he could not be deprived of this fortress in view of the possibility of a war with Russia. In case of a war with Russia, imperial forces would receive unrestricted access through Prussia and the unlimited right to make requisi-tions in bread, meat, and forage: payment would be settled at a later date. Until war with Russia commenced, Napoleon could not discuss how he intended to reward Frederick William. Furthermore, Prussia would strictly enforce the Continental System, outfit privateers, and provide two ships of the line and one frigate. The only condition Napoleon accepted was the king's request for a neutral zone in Silesia for the security of the royal family.

Shocked, Hardenberg and Goltz expressed their astonishment over Napoleon's apparent mistrust. If Hardenberg still harbored any pro-French sentiments, St.-Marsan's message dispelled them. He belatedly remembered the sad fate of those states Napoleon had befriended in the past such as Portugal, Spain, and Holland. Although no news arrived from Scharnhorst, a 9 October 1811 letter from Alexander himself reached the king sometime between the 20th and 21st. Writing in his own hand, the tsar reiterated that he would view any hostile act against Prussia as a declaration of war; Russia would stop fighting Napoleon only with Prussia's consent. Lieven communicated the news of the Russo-Prussian military convention on 25 October. In the greatest secrecy, he submitted both the convention and the draft of the political treaty to Hardenberg for Frederick William's signature. Schöler's report on the success of Scharnhorst's mission arrived around the 26th. In particular, it outlined the details of Alexander's interpretation of an act committed against Prussia that Russia would view as a declaration of war: the French occupation of any Prussian territory, a considerable French movement to the Vistula, and of course an attack or declaration of war on Prussia.

The hour had arrived for Prussia to choose between France and Russia. In this crisis, Frederick William solicited advice from every conceivable direction. In particular, he turned to the crown prince's tutor, the pro-French Privy Councilor Ancillon. He urged the king to reject the fantasy of a Russo-Prussian victory over Napoleon that the pro-Russian party guaranteed. He argued that Russia's generals lacked talent; that Europe and Prussia had already learned painful lessons concerning the unreliability of Russian assistance; that Alexander's flighty character offered no security; that, because of Russia's remoteness, Alexander could always secure a tolerable peace, while Prussia would be lost if it had to endure a second Tilsit; that a Russian victory would bring no result but their defeat would lead to a rapid peace; and, finally, that the threat posed by the French, notorious for their speed, was close at hand while the help of the languorous Russians remained far away. Ancillon rejected talk of Prussia being another Spain, explaining to Frederick William that the state lacked Spain's advantageous geography and that his people lacked the religious fanaticism of the Spanish. He bluntly told the king not to expect his people to make a pact with poverty to maintain their independence.[42]

Hardenberg tried but failed to break Ancillon's spell over the desperate monarch. In a lengthy 2 November memorandum that Lehmann describes as "probably the most magnificent document ever written by Hardenberg, distinguished equally by dialectic sharpness, manly determination, and beauty of language," the chancellor urged Frederick William to ally with the tsar, leave Berlin, and open negotiations with Austria and Great Britain. A report from Scharnhorst finally arrived on 3 November describing his success. Nevertheless, on the very next day, the king rejected the Russian alliance. On Ancillon's recommendation, Frederick William dispatched

Knesebeck to St. Petersburg with conciliatory messages but mainly urging the tsar to maintain peace with Napoleon. Alexander accepted Frederick William's advice, claiming that he did not want war and would exhaust all means to avoid a struggle:

> You should see how well my intentions are in agreement with yours and, if unfortunately war occurs, it will be only because the Emperor Napoleon so decides, and then all my care to prevent it shall remain powerless. At least I have the consolation of having worked for years with all my power to save us from this scourge of humanity. There will remain nothing more for me to do but to trust in the Almighty ... to defend myself with courage and perseverance against aggression both unfair and without reason, brought only by the insatiable ambition of Napoleon. My tender friendship for you is boundless and will end only with my life. I remain, Sire, Your Majesty's dear brother, friend, and ally.[43]

How did Hardenberg fail? Echoing his earlier sentiments about Russian promises, Frederick William questioned the tsar's resolve to advance with his entire army on the king's summons. As the tsar's assurance did not answer the question of timing, Frederick William's decision is understandable. The "signal" for the Russians to commence an offensive, given by either Frederick William or Yorck, would come after considerable French forces flooded Prussian territory. Thus, the issue of speed would play a paramount role. How fast could the notoriously slow-moving Russian army reach the Oder? Could the Russians reach the Oder before the swift-moving French reached the Vistula? If not, then Prussia would most certainly be forced to assume the role of Spain. And what if the Russians could not get across the Vistula but instead withdrew into their heartland to imitate Wellesley's retreat to the Lines of Torres Vedras? Although no one could answer such questions with any certainty, Frederick William could reference much recent history as well as the tsar's earlier statements regarding his plans for a defensive strategy. In the end, with so many variables in this complex equation, casting his lot with Alexander would have required a boldness that the Prussian king lacked.

Frederick William simply believed that an alliance with Napoleon could best guarantee the survival of his state. According to his instructions, Hardenberg presented counterproposals to St.-Marsan on 6 November. Of the two choices offered by the emperor – becoming a member of the Rheinbund or concluding an offensive–defensive alliance with Napoleon – Frederick William chose the latter. However, the Prussians insisted on being exempt from wars in Iberia, Italy, and Turkey, as the resources of the state could not support the projection of Prussian power to these distant lands. Hardenberg also requested a guarantee that any Prussian auxiliary corps would be placed under the command of a Prussian general. He assured the

French that the Prussian troops would fight bravely as long as they could serve their king as well as the emperor. On the other hand, he recognized the French occupation of Glogau until the conclusion of the war with Russia. The chancellor gratefully received the neutrality of Silesia but also repeated the hope that the emperor would allow the Prussians to share in the spoils of victory. Hardenberg also sent instructions to Krusemarck to work on convincing Napoleon to allow the Prussians to expand their army.[44]

After receiving the Prussian response, Lieven presented to Hardenberg a statutory declaration from the tsar. It noted that Alexander could not be indifferent to the king's decision to sign an alliance with Napoleon "to dissolve the links that for so long united the cabinets of St. Petersburg and Berlin." Hardenberg did all he could in terms of damage control. Although the king decided against signing the Russo-Prussian military convention, he hesitated to authorize Hardenberg to conclude a Franco-Prussian treaty. Hardenberg explained to Lieven that the king continued to base his hopes on Alexander. Hardenberg's explanations convinced Lieven that Frederick William's conduct "bears the mark of his indecision and not his beliefs." He assured Rumiantsev of his own "profound conviction" that the Prussian king's "feelings are in complete agreement with the interests of Russia and that he would never voluntarily ally with France." Only his weak character and sense of fear could force him to submit to the will of Napoleon. After the Prussians had actually participated in the Franco-Russian War of 1812 as Napoleon's ally, the memory of such reports made it easier for Alexander to forgive Frederick William.[45]

To Davout, the Emperor Napoleon expressed his utter disdain for the Prussians and how easy it would be to crush them. Yet General Bonaparte recognized the importance of having Prussian support in a war with Russia. He recalled how Prussian resistance behind his army had slowed progress in 1806 and 1807. Conversely, Napoleon estimated that the Prussians could provide him with as many as 120,000 men. At this time he did not oppose an alliance with Prussia and especially wanted Prussia's continued support in his war with Great Britain. Of course he made it known that, should the Prussians betray him, he would destroy the state. Regardless, on the verge of war with Russia, Prussia's continued enforcement of the Continental System appeared paramount to Napoleon. He accepted the Prussian requests to exempt them from conflicts in Iberia, Italy, and the Ottoman Empire; a special military convention would be concluded in case of a war with Russia. Yet the emperor could no longer abide Blücher's presence in the Prussian army. After accusing the Prussian general of disobedience, he refused to allow him to serve as a general in his new ally's army. On 3 November 1811, Napoleon instructed Maret to inform St.-Marsan to insist on Blücher's dismissal. Eight days later, Blücher received his discharge. Frederick William informed him that "the current circumstances" did not allow him to grant the general a command. Moreover, he desired that Blücher select a residency outside Berlin.[46]

A disgusted Scharnhorst sought early retirement but instead received indefinite leave, retaining the official post of royal advisor. Frederick William tasked him with supervising the fortresses, military schools, and munitions factories at Potsdam and throughout Silesia: the regions of Prussia that the French could not march through. Consequently, Scharnhorst and his adjutants, Carl von Clausewitz and Karl Ludwig von Tiedemann, as well as his son-in-law, Karl Friedrich zu Dohna-Schlobitten, went to Breslau. Boyen, the king's adjutant-general, likewise received orders to depart for Silesia. To lessen Napoleon's suspicion, Frederick William wanted to distance Boyen, a prominent voice among the anti-French party, from court. Blücher joined these outcasts at Breslau.

More humiliation followed. In February 1812, Napoleon forced another Treaty of Paris on the Prussians. Ratified by Frederick William on 5 March, the treaty opened Prussia's frontiers to imperial troops marching east to the Russian border.[47] Moreover, the terms obligated the Prussians to participate in the invasion of Russia by providing Napoleon with an auxiliary corps of 20,842 men, considerable quantities of provisions, and thousands of pack horses and wagons. Aided by Ancillon, Frederick William wrote a somewhat conciliatory letter to Alexander, asking for the tsar's pity rather than his condemnation:

> I am brokenhearted, Sire, when I think of the role that the most irresistible necessity has forced me to choose, but I am even more deeply aggrieved to think of Your Imperial Majesty, who has always done justice to my feelings, and that I could not render the same justice in the present moment. Your letter, Sire, I did understand. To avoid any misinterpretation of my actions, I had asked Colonel Knesebeck to explain to you verbally and in greater detail the motives that have guided me on this occasion. The correctness of these ideas and the strength of their principles were well known to you and I am sorry they have not convinced you of the power of the pressing circumstances to which the most sacred duty has forced me to sacrifice the affections of my heart.
>
> Your Majesty must remember what I explained to you during our last talks in St. Petersburg regarding the situation that I find myself in Berlin surrounded on all sides by foreign troops even in peacetime. By transferring my residence from Königsberg to Berlin, which was in the best interests of my state, and you even advised me that Your Majesty desired the same, I could not disguise from myself that from that moment I would be in complete dependence on France and in the case of a war between France and Russia my political system unfortunately would be decided under such

auspices. When the good understanding between the two empires began to deteriorate, remember, Sire, how many times I wrote to warn you and warned through Count Lieven to make every effort to avoid a war that could begin under the most unfavorable auspices and that, if Austria refused any kind of participation, would place Prussia in the cruel necessity of taking a desperate part and attaching itself to France. Your Majesty believed it was in the best interests to make the most formidable armaments and to be silent about the reasons and purpose of these preparations; I have always been of the idea that it was the surest way to bring about a war. One year ago the simple explanations and caution dictated by the general interest of Europe would have prevented the terrible struggle that will now ensue. Now the two powers are facing each other, and it will be much more difficult to reach an understanding and agreement.

As the crisis approached, my situation became more painful and more alarming. In these urgent circumstances when my states could be invaded at all points, when the forces and resources at my disposal could be separated and cut off from all directions before I could unite them, when Your Majesty, faithful to a system that does not take the offensive, eliminated all hope of an active and prompt rescue, when the destruction of Prussia would serve as the prerequisite of the war against Russia, I had to take the most urgent action and above all else I had to save the monarchy from certain destruction. You must be quite convinced, Sire, that I do not conceal the disastrous consequences this war will have for my states, or the dangers they may still face in the aftermath, but I had the choice of disadvantages; should the peril of the present prevail, and regardless of the outcome of events the future offers me an opportunity to survive of course in the interests of France and Russia and in Your Majesty's precious friendship.

I do not need to tell you, Sire, that it pains me to play this role, but I think I fulfilled my primary duty in sacrificing my most cherished feelings for the conservation of the state and I rest in my conscience. Pity me then, Sire, but do not condemn me; if I may say, if Your Majesty found yourself in the position where you judged with thoroughly reasonable thinking that it would be better to accept cruel circumstances than to perish for pride and glory, it would be devastating for your heart because you see yourself as a generous and noble person. Whatever the turn of events, my inviolable attachment to Your Majesty's person will lose nothing of its vivacity. If war breaks out, we will do no more damage than that which is strictly necessary, we will always remember that we are united, that one day we will be allies, and, while yielding to an irresistible destiny, we retain the freedom and sincerity of our feelings. Yes, Sire, be sure of mine, they remain the same for you in all circumstances, feeling proud that those feelings will remain for life, Sire, for Your Imperial Majesty, my dear brother, friend, and ally of heart and soul.

The next letter Frederick William received from Alexander, dated 10 November 1812, was the last he received that year. Alexander simply explained his current situation as well as his hopes for the future.[48]

For Frederick William, the alliance with France brought some degree of relief after Krusemarck assured him from Paris that the monarch's action had earned Napoleon's trust. Yet his apparent complacency drew sharp criticism from the anti-French war hawks who demanded a struggle for liberation. "The understanding in Prussia of Frederick William's pro-French policy sank to zero," notes Thomas Stamm-Kuhlmann. After five years of oppressive occupation, more than 300 officers – almost one-quarter of the officer corps – resigned in protest rather than serve the French. Many, including Boyen, Clausewitz, and Dohna, went to Russia; some to Spain; and a few to Great Britain. Gneisenau's warning – "we shall receive the fate we deserve. We shall go down in shame, for we dare not conceal from ourselves the truth that a nation is as bad as its government. The king stands ever by the throne on which he has never sat" – aptly captured the mood of many officers.[49]

Elsewhere, the first quarter of 1812 initiated diplomatic realignments against France that did not include Prussia. As usual, Great Britain assumed one of the leading roles. Prior to 1808, the British had contributed to the successive coalition wars against France mainly by providing funds in the form of loans, subsidies, and credits to allies such as Austria and Russia whose armies would shoulder the main burden of fighting the French. Total domination of the seas allowed the British to conduct limited military operations against secondary targets such as Holland and Naples either unilaterally or in conjunction with the Russians. However, London's 1808 decision to commit the British army to the Iberian peninsula marked a monumental policy change for the maritime economic power. Yet this was not enough. Although the British had distracted Napoleon and tied down vital imperial resources in Iberia and the Mediterranean, they realized that Napoleon's hegemony over the continent could be broken only in Central Europe. For this reason, the British could not turn their backs on Austria, Prussia, and Russia even after all three counted among Napoleon's allies following the failed Franco-Austrian War of 1809. London managed to maintain indirect communication with Austria and Prussia despite the state of war that existed between Great Britain and the German powers thanks to Napoleon's Continental System.

Sweden was also impressed into the Continental System, but its position in the Baltic and its maritime aspirations gave Stockholm an independence and importance that the state's size did not warrant. Protected from imperial armies by the Baltic and the British fleet that patrolled its waters, Sweden only nominally adhered to Napoleon's interdiction against British trade. Sweden's role as a conduit for British goods being smuggled into Europe paved the way for official rapprochement between the two states. While communication with the Swedes, Austrians, and Prussians continued, Anglo-Russian relations ceased during the lean years of 1810 and 1811 partly due to anti-British sentiment among the tsar's leading advisors. Although the British recognized that a French victory over Russia could be devastating to their imperial and economic interests, "the collapse of normal diplomatic channels of communication in 1809," notes Sherwig, "left London woefully ignorant of continental affairs. Reports from Hanoverian envoys at Berlin and Vienna and from British agents elsewhere in Europe were of limited value. Incomplete and unreliable as such intelligence was, it was preferable to silence. What little information reached London made clear that when the time came for a rising of the nations against France, Britain would be expected to support it with both arms and money." Thanks to the efforts of British foreign secretary Richard Wellesley in 1810 and 1811, the British "made clear to the northern powers that Britain would support them when they were ready to act." This was the situation inherited by Wellesley's successor, Robert Stewart, Viscount Castlereagh, in March 1813. By that time, London knew that only Russia's masses could break Napoleon's hold over Europe.

With Anglo-Russian relations still on ice during the first half of 1812, the British turned to Stockholm in the aftermath of a diplomatic contest between Alexander and Napoleon over Sweden. After Russia's seizure of Finland from Sweden in 1809, Stockholm looked to Napoleon for protection. The following year, the childless king of Sweden, Charles XIII, adopted French marshal Jean-Baptiste Bernadotte to be his heir. Although Napoleon approved, he soon regretted his decision. An aspiring maritime power, Sweden suffered under Napoleon's Continental System, which the new crown prince promptly repudiated. Despite the souring relations, Napoleon hoped Charles John (Bernadotte's adopted name) would assist him against the Russians in 1812. To entice the crown prince, he offered the return of Finland as the reward for Bernadotte's cooperation. Not to be outdone, Alexander suggested that, instead of Finland, Bernadotte should take Norway from Denmark, a staunch French ally. After imperial forces occupied Swedish Pomerania and the island of Rügen in January 1812, Alexander and Bernadotte made common cause. In Finland on 24 March 1812, Rumiantsev and Swedish general Karl Löwenhjelm signed the Convention of Åbo, which called for a Russo-Swedish force of 30,000 men to retake Swedish Pomerania and Rügen. Additionally, Alexander would aid the Swedes in acquiring Norway through either direct negotiations with Denmark or a combined military operation. After attaining Norway, the Swedes would commence a military operation in North Germany and spark a German uprising against Napoleon. Although London attempted but failed to make diplomatic inroads with the Swedes in 1811, Bernadotte informed the British of his willingness to negotiate an alliance in return for financial and material aid as well as London's support of his territorial ambitions.

6 Jean-Baptiste Bernadotte, Charles XIV John of Sweden, 1763–1844

Expecting Sweden to actively support Russia in the upcoming war with France, London accepted this opportunity to open alliance negotiations with Stockholm in March 1812 partly in the hope of warming relations with the Russians. Provisions in the Convention of Åbo called for efforts by both signatories to convince the British to join the Russo-Swedish alliance, but Bernadotte's intransigence and Russian coolness dogged the proceedings. Castlereagh instructed his envoy to Stockholm, Edward Thornton, to avoid the issue of providing the Swedes with a subsidy. However, any peace between Great Britain and Sweden would result in dragging the Swedes into the war with Napoleon. To be prepared for this conflict, Bernadotte sought a British guarantee of £1,200,000 a year in subsidies. Moreover, Castlereagh hoped a northern alliance of Sweden, Denmark, and Britain would help Alexander by creating a firm block that could threaten Napoleon's rear and flank should he invade Russia. Regardless, Bernadotte pressed his demands for Norway, rendering impossible an alliance that included both Sweden and Denmark.[50]

In addition, Bernadotte wanted his reward up front: if the Danes refused the peaceful cession of Norway, he would conquer it first and then do his part against Napoleon. From the British he requested naval support and military equipment for the conquest of Norway as well as the cession of a West Indian island – a demand that the venerable British diplomatic historian, Charles Webster, refers to as "one of Bernadotte's strange desires."

Predicting that Norway would have to be given to Sweden in return for Bernadotte to assist Russia militarily, the British hoped to find compensation for Denmark in Germany to satisfy Copenhagen. Castlereagh stated his belief that a negotiated arrangement between the Danes and Swedes provided the only chance for the Allies "to command a disposable force for continental operations within the period that will probably decide the fate of the campaign." The British entertained this hope throughout 1812. "If it were possible to gain Denmark to the common cause," speculated the British envoy at Stockholm, Edward Thornton, "and to effect the union of the Danish and Swedish troops, he [Bernadotte] would not, I am confident, wait for the Russian auxiliaries to commence operations; and I really believe, though I will not vouch for it, that if Denmark could be prevailed to join, the prince might be induced to waive the demand of the exchange of Norway, and to conduct himself with an agreement to entertain that proposition of exchange at a future date." As it stood, Bernadotte wanted the same promises from Britain that he had received from Russia via the Convention of Åbo concerning Norway, as well as a pledge of financial assistance before he broke with Napoleon. After negotiations that ensued for much of 1812, Thornton concluded that "the prince royal will have an extreme repugnance to march, or will absolutely refuse it, unless some satisfaction can be given by England on the subject of Norway. This refusal would be extremely deplorable, for there is certainly a greater prospect than has ever yet been presented of restoring the equilibrium of Europe."[51]

Meanwhile, the Russians showed little interest in repairing relations with the British and managed to offend London by suggesting that Britain could assume Russia's estimated debt of £4,500,000 to certain Dutch banks as a sign of good faith. Stalemate ensued until May, when the Russians finally requested the formal reestablishment of diplomatic relations. Napoleon's invasion of Russia in June 1812 accelerated the process. The following month, the British signed peace treaties with the Swedes and Russians at Orebro on 18 July. Nevertheless, the British refused to accept the stipulations of the 12 March Convention of Åbo and provide Bernadotte with another guarantee of his future possession of Norway. According to Webster, the peace treaties "did no more than put an end to the technical state of war. The real negotiation had yet to begin."[52]

Funds for waging the war became the next issue, as the British themselves faced financial difficulties due to their commitment to Iberia and the economic damage caused by Napoleon's Continental System. While promising the Swedes £500,000 in material aid on 18 July, London would not provide any subsidy as long as the conquest of Norway remained Bernadotte's initial objective. Should he first direct his efforts against Napoleon, British gold *could* be the reward. Bernadotte now found himself in a predicament. Unable to finance his own mobilization, he needed British funds to arm and equip his troops. Desiring to secure public support for the war and thus for his dynasty, he hoped to present Norway to his new subjects and then lead them into the struggle on the continent. Now he could do neither. Regarding subsidies for the Russians, the new British ambassador to Russia, General William Cathcart, sailed from England in late July with authorization to provide to Sweden and the Russians the rather paltry amount of £500,000 should either be in dire financial straits.[53] He would first make for Sweden to meet with Thornton and then proceed to Russia. On 25 July the British decided to send 23,000 muskets and 23 guns to Sweden; Bernadotte's purchasing agents in London received credit to buy gunpowder. The first shipment of arms reached Sweden in September 1812. The £500,000 eventually was divided so that £300,000 was given in materiel while Thornton made small advances to the Swedish treasury that amounted to £200,000 by the end of 1812. Other aid came in the form of a British convoy carrying 50,000 muskets and a half ton of "Peruvian" or "Jesuit's" Bark that contained natural quinine for medicinal purposes being dispatched to Russia in August 1812. In addition, British warships operating in the eastern Baltic contributed to the successful defense of Riga by the Russians later in the year.

London still maintained that the best method of aiding Russia centered on the Swedes opening a second front in North Germany and enlisting Prussia and Austria. For this reason, Cathcart received broad authority to negotiate with Stockholm, Berlin, and Vienna. Bowing to Bernadotte's Denmark-first demand, Castlereagh instructed Cathcart on 3 July 1812 to encourage the Swedes to attack the Danes as soon as possible in the hope that the crown prince could conclude his affairs in Scandinavia in time to land in Germany before the end of 1812. To assist the Swedes in their operation against Zealand – the largest of the Danish isles and the home to Copenhagen – the British would provide naval support and siege artillery. A meeting with Bernadotte convinced Cathcart that the abysmal state of the Swedish army would not allow it to make an impact on the continent without Russian auxiliaries and more British gold. Cathcart then attended a September meeting at Åbo between Alexander and Bernadotte, in which the tsar pledged 20,000 Russians to support the Swedish attack on Zealand. Unfounded optimism helped produce a strong personal friendship between Alexander and Bernadotte that led the former to pronounce his support for the latter's becoming king of France after Napoleon's overthrow. Yet it became apparent that the Swedes would not be able to play a role in the war against Napoleon in 1812. Consequently, Castlereagh resolved not to assent to the stipulations of the 12 March Convention of Åbo while the Swedes remained uncommitted to war against Napoleon on the continent.

At Åbo, Rumiantsev had spared Cathcart from discussing a formal alliance or subsidy treaty. The current Anglo-Russian relationship appeared satisfactory to the Russians after Cathcart accompanied the imperial suite back to St. Petersburg. In fact, the British envoy did not have to embarrass himself by making the meager subsidy offer of £500,000 because the Russians did not request financing. Alexander's indifference to British gold impressed Cathcart and "continued to amaze him in the months that followed." Yet Cathcart misread the signs. Russian financial problems became so acute in late 1812 that a special finance committee led by Swiss native Francis d'Ivernois informed the tsar that he would have to make peace with Napoleon unless he received massive British financial assistance. By the end of 1812, Ivernois's committee, which included Stein, was seeking a way for Britain to provide financial aid to Russia without bankrupting itself. Despite the onset of the Russian winter, Anglo-Russian relations warmed, especially after the Russian Baltic fleet sailed in November to winter in British waters. Still, neither party moved toward negotiating a firm treaty of alliance to create another coalition. As for the tsar, he departed St. Petersburg in December to join the army, leaving behind the diplomatic corps. Alexander did not need the British to convince him of the necessity of continuing the war against Napoleon, even after Moscow fell. Resolved not only to liberate Russia but also to carry the war into Central Europe, Alexander himself became the catalyst for the formation of the Sixth Coalition.[54]

## Notes

1 Shanahan, *Prussian Military Reforms*, 98; Jany, *Preußische Armee*, IV:9; Vaupel, *Die Reorganisation des Preußischen Staates*, 164–69; De Clercq and De Clercq, *Recueil des traités de la France*, II:272–73; Richie, *Faust's Metropolis*, 92; Kitchen, *Military History of Germany*, 38.
2 Scharnhorst to Stein, Königsberg, 23 August 1808, Scharnhorst, *Private und dienstliche Schriften*, Nr. 139, V:230–31.
3 Seeley, *Stein*, II:138–39; Grunwald, *Baron Stein*, 163–66.
4 De Clercq and De Clercq, *Recueil des traités de la France*, II:270–72.
5 Jany, *Preußische Armee*, IV:24; Shanahan, *Prussian Military Reforms*, 176. This number exceeded Napoleon's stipulations due to the ongoing reorganization of the Upper Silesian Brigade.
6 According to historian Dominic Lieven, the Russians did not reject outright the marriage of Alexander's last unwed sister, 16-year-old Anna, to Napoleon, but stipulated that she could not marry until she turned 18. By the time this news reached Paris in February 1810, Napoleon had already decided to marry Marie Louise. Regarding Poland, the Russians feared Napoleon intended to restore an independent Polish kingdom. They waited suspiciously to see if Napoleon would force Francis to cede all of Galicia to the Grand Duchy of Warsaw. In addition, Napoleon refused to sign a Russian-authored convention of 4 January 1810 that barred the restoration of Poland and even the use of the name "Poland" for any political entity. See Lieven, *Russia Against Napoleon*, 77–78.

7 Mikaberidze, *Borodino*, 2.

8 Stamm-Kuhlmann, *König in Preußens großer Zeit*, 357.

9 *CN*, Nos. 16960, 16987, 16988, 16994, and 16995, XXI:151–52, 172–74, 178–79. Hamburg served as Davout's headquarters.

10 The Bülow Family Archive contains the unpublished memoirs of Friederike von Auer, entitled "Erinnerungen aus der Jugendzeit für meine Kinder." Auer was Friedrich Wilhelm von Bülow's sister-in-law through her marriage to his wife's brother, Ludwig. Friederike recorded events from 1806 until 1816, living with Bülow's wife during the 1813–1815 campaigns. Her two handwritten journals remain in the possession of the Bülow von Dennewitz family. Pertinent copies have kindly been provided for the author's use.

11 Wigger, *Blücher*, 103; Unger, *Blücher*, I:359–60; Jany, *Preußische Armee*, IV:40; Shanahan, *Prussian Military Reforms*, 159–76.

12 Sherwig, *Guineas and Gunpowder*, 273–74.

13 Alexander wrote to Francis on 8 February 1811. See Martens, *Recueil des traités et conventions*, III:78; Lehman, *Scharnhorst*, II:362, 378–79, 397.

14 Lieven, *Russia Against Napoleon*, 82; Alexander to Frederick William, St. Petersburg, 19 February 1811, Bailleu, *Briefwechsel*, Nr. 194, 206–10.

15 Quoted in Seeley, *Stein*, II:442; Martens, *Recueil des traités et conventions*, VII:14–16; Lehmann, *Scharnhorst*, II:345, 347, 407.

16 Martens utilized Lieven's reports from 6 March and 23 April: Martens, *Recueil des traités et conventions*, VII:18; Unger, *Blücher*, I:359.

17 Martens, *Recueil des traités et conventions*, VII:15.

18 Lehmann, *Scharnhorst*, II:351; Shanahan, *Prussian Military Reforms*, 172–73.

19 Lieven, *Russia Against Napoleon*, 82–83.

20 After Hardenberg made revisions, the date of the letter was changed to 9 April 1811.

21 Frederick William to Alexander, Berlin and Potsdam, 7, 12, and 16 April 1811, Bailleu, *Briefwechsel*, Nr. 195, 210–14; Lehmann, *Scharnhorst*, II:361–62, 376.

22 Ranke, *Hardenberg*, III:192–95; Martens, *Recueil des traités et conventions*, VII:16. Lieven's report of 11 April 1811 is quoted *ibid.*, VII:17–18.

23 Rumiantsev to Lieven, St. Petersburg, 31 May 1811, in Martens, *Recueil des traités et conventions*, VII:15–16, 18.

24 Ranke, *Hardenberg*, III:192–93.

25 Martens, *Recueil des traités et conventions*, VII:18, refers to this as an "alliance agreement," which was negotiated in great secrecy. Prusso-German sources make no reference to this agreement.

26 *CN*, No. 17454, 20:465–66; Lehmann, *Scharnhorst*, II:375; Ranke, *Hardenberg*, III:194–96.

27 Alexander to Frederick William, St. Petersburg, 26 May 1811, Bailleu, *Briefwechsel*, Nr. 198, 221; Martens, *Recueil des traités et conventions*, VII:20; Lehmann, *Scharnhorst*, II:397. Ranke disagrees with Lehmann's assessment of Hardenberg, claiming that this transformation took place in early November as a response to Napoleon's counterproposals for a Franco-Prussian alliance. He cites Hardenberg's memo of 2 November 1811 as the actual turning point. According to Ranke's view, Napoleon's refusal to respond prompted the Prussians to accelerate the mobilization in July. See Ranke, *Hardenberg*, III:201.

28 Lieven, *Russia Against Napoleon*, 92; Alexander to Frederick William, St. Petersburg, 26 May 1811, Bailleu, *Briefwechsel*, Nr. 194, 221.

29 Shanahan, *Prussian Military Reforms*, 185–87; Boyen, *Erinnerungen*, ed. Nippold, II:102–03, 179–80.

30 Scharnhorst pointed to the capitulations of Barcelona and Tarragona in Spain as examples. See Lehmann, *Scharnhorst*, II:403, 409; Shanahan, *Prussian Military Reforms*, 187–88.

31 Frederick William to Alexander, Charlottenburg, 16 July 1811, Bailleu, *Briefwechsel*, Nr. 201, 228–29.

32 Quoted in Martens, *Recueil des traités et conventions*, VII:18–20.

33 Lehmann, *Scharnhorst*, II:397, 401.

34 Gneisenau to Hardenberg, Berlin, 22 September and 12 October 1811, Geheimes Staatsarchiv Preußischer Kulturbesitz (hereafter cited as GStA PK), VI HA Rep. 92 Nl. Gneisenau, Nr. 20b; Ranke, *Hardenberg*, III:199; Wigger, *Blücher*, 109–10; Lehmann, *Scharnhorst*, II:422; Muir, *Britain and the Defeat of Napoleon*, 185–86.

35 Lehmann, *Scharnhorst*, II:415; Martens, *Recueil des traités et conventions*, VII:20.

36 Sources disagree over how many times Scharnhorst actually met with Alexander. Martens claims that they had "several interviews." See Martens, *Recueil des traités et conventions*, VII:23; Lehmann, *Scharnhorst*, II:385, 401; Ranke, *Hardenberg*, III:204.

37 Again, disagreement exists over the actual author. Lehmann, in *Scharnhorst*, II:412, claims that Schöler drafted the military convention while Alexander authored the political alliance. Martens, in *Recueil des traités et conventions*, VII:23, states that Alexander drafted the military convention.

38 Ranke, *Hardenberg*, III:199; Wigger, *Blücher*, 111–12; Lehmann, *Scharnhorst*, II:412–17; Blasendorff, *Blücher*, 172; Unger, *Blücher*, I:370, 375; Martens, *Recueil des traités et conventions*, VII:20–24.

39 For Lieven's reports of 24 September and 6 October 1811, see Martens, *Recueil des traités et conventions*, VII:21.

40 Gneisenau to Münster, Berlin, 19 and 22 September 1811, GStA PK, VI HA Rep. 92 Nl. Gneisenau, Nr. 20b; Muir, *Britain and the Defeat of Napoleon*, 189.

41 For Lieven's report of 22 October 1811, see Martens, *Recueil des traités et conventions*, VII:21–22; Wigger, *Blücher*, 117; Unger, *Blücher*, I:377.

42 Lehmann, *Scharnhorst*, II:420–21; Wigger, *Blücher*, 117; Seeley, *Stein*, II:448–49; Ranke, *Hardenberg*, III:200–04. The British colonel Hudson Lowe later agreed with this opinion, inferring that the Prussians would not make good partisans or guerrillas because "the young men seem to consider it necessary that they should be dressed in a uniform manner and learn their exercises before they can be called soldiers": British Library Additional Manuscripts (hereafter cited as Add MSS) 37051, 12: Lowe to Bunbury, Bautzen, 18 May 1813.

43 Ranke, *Hardenberg*, III:203; Lehmann, *Scharnhorst*, II:422; Frederick William to Hardenberg, 4 November 1811, in Duncker, *Aus der Zeit Friedrichs des Großen und Friedrich Wilhelms III*, 403; Frederick William to Alexander, Berlin, 31 January 1812, Bailleu, *Briefwechsel*, Nr. 205, 235–36; Alexander to Frederick William, St. Petersburg, 5 March 1812, *ibid.*, Nr. 206, 236.

44  Ranke, *Hardenberg*, III:204–07.

45  For Lieven's report of 22 November, see Martens, *Recueil des traités et conventions*, VII:22.

46  *CN*, No. 18139, XXII:485–86; Ranke, *Hardenberg*, III:206–08; Wigger, *Blücher*, 118; Unger, *Blücher*, I:377.

47  Napoleon's mobilization had profound repercussions on his war effort in Iberia. Prior to the invasion of Russia, French forces in Spain had gained the upper hand over the deadly insurrection that had started in 1808. Strong evidence suggests that, had Napoleon not recalled forces from Spain during his build-up for the Russian campaign, the French would have pacified Iberia. Although in 1810 General Sir Arthur Wellesley had famously beaten back a third French invasion of Portugal, his offensive into Spain in 1811, which took him to Madrid in August 1812, fizzled under the pressure of French counteroffensives, thus prompting the British commander to retreat to Portugal in autumn 1812.

48  Frederick William to Alexander, Potsdam, 31 March 1812, Bailleu, *Briefwechsel*, Nr. 208, 238–39; Alexander to Frederick William, 10 November 1812, *ibid.*, Nr. 209, 240.

49  Quoted in Craig, "Problems of Coalition Warfare," 41; Krusemarck to Frederick William, Paris, 3 April 1812, GStA PK, VI HA Rep. 92 Nl. Albrecht, Nr. 18; Stamm-Kuhlmann, *König in Preußens großer Zeit*, 359; Craig, *The Politics of the Prussian Army*, 58–59. It was not uncommon for monarchs to lose the respect of their officers due to perceived mistakes in foreign policy. Louis XVI of France lost the respect of many of his officers after state finances prevented him from intervening in the Dutch Revolt of 1787.

50  Sherwig, *Guineas and Gunpowder*, 272–75; Webster, *The Foreign Policy of Castlereagh*, I:92; Muir, *Britain and the Defeat of Napoleon*, 176–82; Scott, *Bernadotte*, 13.

51  Castlereagh to Thornton, 13 March 1812, quoted in Webster, *The Foreign Policy of Castlereagh*, I:94; Thornton to Castlereagh, 8 and 30 December 1812, *Correspondence of Viscount Castlereagh* (hereafter cited as *CVC*), VIII:283–84, 295.

52  Webster, *The Foreign Policy of Castlereagh*, I:93–96; Sherwig, *Guineas and Gunpowder*, 275.

53  Born in 1755, Cathcart went to St. Petersburg in 1771 where his father, Charles Cathcart, 9th Lord Cathcart, a general in the army, served as the British ambassador. From 1773 to 1777 he studied law, but after succeeding to the lordship of Parliament in 1776 he obtained a commission in the 7th Dragoons. Serving in the American Revolutionary War in 1777, before the end of that year he had twice won promotion on the field of battle. In 1778, he further distinguished himself in outpost work, and at the battle of Monmouth commanded an irregular corps, the British Legion, with success. Returning home in 1780, he rose through the officer ranks, becoming colonel in 1792. He served with distinction in the Low Countries during the War of the First Coalition, being promoted to general. Starting in 1803, he served as commander in chief in Ireland until William Pitt the Younger placed him in command of the British expedition to Hanover in 1805. With 14,000 men, he occupied Hanover on 14 December but had to withdraw in February 1806 after the Franco-Prussian Treaty of Paris awarded

Hanover to Prussia. In 1807, Cathcart commanded the expedition to Copenhagen, which surrendered to him on 6 September. He served as London's ambassador to Russia from 1812 to 1820 and British military commissioner to the Allied armies from 1813 to 1814.

54 Sherwig, *Guineas and Gunpowder*, 277–82; Muir, *Britain and the Defeat of Napoleon*, 226–29, 243–45. Webster's summary of the situation in early 1813 indicates that the tsar's steadfastness laid the groundwork for the Sixth Coalition: "The situation from Castlereagh's point of view was full of hazard and uncertainty. The war with the United States remained as an irksome and indefinite charge on British energies at this moment of supreme crisis in Europe. Wellington had been forced to retire to Portugal with serious loss of men and prestige ... Bernadotte could only be won by a large subsidy and an engagement about Norway ... The attitude of Prussia was vacillating and uncertain while Austria seemed about to play the part in 1813 that Prussia had played in 1805. The elements of a great coalition were there as a result of Napoleon's disaster, the magnitude of which every report tended to increase. But would the jealousies of the three great powers prevent it from being formed? Fortunately every report showed that the tsar was standing firm." See Webster, *The Foreign Policy of Castlereagh*, I:98–99, 114–15.

# A new Coalition

More than 300,000 imperial troops moved east through Prussia as part of Napoleon's massive 600,000-man army for the invasion of Russia. The orderly requisition of Prussian goods and provisions soon collapsed under the strain, prompting the French to loot indiscriminately. Words fail to describe the devastation of the Prussian provinces, especially East Prussia. Atrocities that accompanied the rape of the land by Prussia's "ally" rivaled the human disaster of the Thirty Years War. The Hanoverian minister Ludwig von Ompteda noted that the French had left the Prussian peasants with "nothing but eyes to weep with in their misery." The French also carried off the 20,842 soldiers who formed the Prussian contingent of the Grande Armée of 1812. Commanded by General Julius August von Grawert, the Prussian corps consisted of the best units drawn from the six brigades of the Prussian army, with the East Prussian regiments providing the largest contribution because their depots stood closest to the staging areas of the imperial army. Napoleon forced Frederick William to demobilize the rest of the Prussian army in accordance with the 42,000-man limit of the 1808 treaty. Thus, approximately 22,000 troops remained in Prussia, backed by a trained reserve of 36,424.[1]

On the evening of 22 June 1812, the Grande Armée commenced the invasion of Russia. Poor health forced Grawert to turn over command to General Yorck. As the 27th Infantry Division of the Grande Armée, the Prussians served in Marshal Jacques-Étienne Macdonald's X Corps. While X Corps marched toward Riga, Napoleon led the main body of the Grande Armée in pursuit of the Russians, who implemented the defensive plans drafted by Phull and Barclay de Tolly. Although failing to destroy the Russian army at Borodino on 7 September, Napoleon reached an evacuated Moscow one week later. Not only did the tsar refuse to negotiate, but the Russians also had burned the city. Having to choose between remaining at Moscow – 1,200 miles from Paris – for the winter or withdrawing, the emperor chose the latter. On 19 October, a much smaller Grande Armée commenced the retreat. On 3 November, the first snows fell; by the end of the month, Napoleon commanded no more than 40,000 walking dead. At 10:00 P.M. on the night of 5 December, he departed for Paris. Of the 655,000 men who had crossed the Russian frontier in 1812, Napoleon lost approximately 570,000 soldiers, with as many as 370,000 dead. Along with elements of XI Corps, which had not crossed the Russian frontier, approximately 93,000 men, including 40,000 Austrians, now held the eastern frontier of Napoleon's empire. Russian casualties have been estimated to be as high as 450,000 with two-thirds dead.[2]

On 14 December 1812, the emperor passed through Glogau en route to Paris. His flight, along with confirmed reports of the destruction of the Grande Armée, excited Prussian patriots, who wanted the people to rise against the French. Yet the reports from Königsberg that described the haggard remains of the imperial army did little to dispel Frederick William's caution. He saw an opportunity for Prussia, but the wrong move could be disastrous. Not one of his advisors could explain the consequences that this monumental human tragedy would have for Prussia. Indeed, the Russians had won but would Alexander pursue Napoleon? Could and would the tsar's mauled army emerge from the Russian heartland to fight for the liberation of Prussia and perhaps all of Germany? Frederick William had reason to suspect Alexander's intentions after the terms of the March 1812 Convention of Åbo claimed the Vistula as Russia's future frontier. This caused concern in Berlin over the fate of East Prussia and Silesia. Technically at war with Great Britain and Russia, and still wary of Alexander, the king embraced prudence. For the moment, he would remain Napoleon's loyal ally and work to improve Prussia's political situation.[3]

Frederick William limited his actions to issuing orders on 20 December to prevent the military stores and men eligible for service from falling into Russian hands. According to his instructions, a reserve corps commanded by General Friedrich Wilhelm von Bülow would assemble at the fortress of Graudenz on the Vistula River. Yet pressure mounted. General Ludwig Adolph zu Wittgenstein, commander of the Russian right wing, issued a proclamation on 14 December summoning the Prussians to end their alliance with the French. At Königsberg some 200 miles west of the tsar's headquarters at Vilna (Vilnius), Bülow observed the wreck of the Grande Armée as it emerged from Russia throughout December. Seventy miles east of Königsberg at Gumbinnen (Gusev), Napoleon's chief of staff, Marshal Alexander Berthier, issued orders directing the remains of I and VIII Corps to Thorn (Toruń); II and III Corps to Marienburg (Malbork); IV and IX Corps to Marienwerder (Kwidzyn); V Corps to Warsaw; VI Corps to Plock (Płock); the depots of the Guard Cavalry to Elbing; all gunners and engineers to Danzig; and all dismounted troopers as well as two infantry divisions to Königsberg. As the senior Prussian commander in East Prussia, Bülow labored to protect the province's remaining military resources from both the French and the Russians. In mid December, Bülow halted all supplies and reinforcements en route to Yorck's corps. He then assembled all reserves, furloughed soldiers, recruits, horses, and supplies from both East and West Prussia at Graudenz, explaining to the French the need of such measures to safeguard the men and materiel from the Russians. Bülow also summoned several depots to Königsberg and recalled cavalry patrols from the Baltic coast. Men and horses moved to Königsberg while military supplies and equipment went to Graudenz (see Map 1).[4]

Desperate to hold back the Russians, the French naturally demanded access to Bülow's resources. The cat-and-mouse game became interesting after the commander in chief of the Grande Armée, Napoleon's brother-in-law, Murat, established his headquarters at Königsberg on the 19th. According to a report made on 21 December, imperial personnel at Königsberg numbered 255 generals, 699 colonels, 4,412 captains and lieutenants, and 26,590 noncommissioned officers and men. Despite these numbers, most of the men could not bear arms due to their exhausted condition. With an additional 6,000 soldiers of all ranks in the hospitals, Murat demanded Prussian support. Bülow stalled for six days, claiming he commanded nothing but unarmed and ill-trained recruits. Finally, on 24 December, he received Frederick William's instructions to form a reserve corps. Fortunately for the Prussians, Murat also received notification that Frederick William would form a second corps to comply with the emperor's demands. On Christmas Day, Bülow informed Murat that he would assemble his men and materiel 130 miles southwest of Königsberg at Graudenz. Not offering a response, Murat departed Königsberg before Bülow's convoys left the provincial capital for Graudenz on 1 January 1813.

On the Russian side, Alexander's decision to pursue the French beyond the sacred soil of Mother Russia did not sit well with many of his senior officers. Despite the tsar's claim that the Russian army continued to pursue the imperials, most of the Russian units that reached Vilna and the Bug River at the end of 1812 halted. The commander of the Russian army, Field-Marshal Prince Mikhail Kutuzov, established his headquarters at the former. Alexander's arrival at Vilna on 23 December did not change the situation of a headquarters that has been described as "very dysfunctional." Pyotr Konovnitsyn served as the army's chief of staff. According to Dominic Lieven, "both Kutuzov and Konovnitsyn were lazy and inefficient administrators. Key documents went unsigned and unattended for days." Past his prime, the 68-year-old "short and corpulent Kutuzov more resembled a good-natured, cheerful German burgher than a field commander."[5]

Another personality with considerable influence at Russian headquarters was Kutuzov's protégé, General Karl von Toll, on whom the old commander bestowed the exalted title of Quartermaster-General of the Russian Army. Kutuzov, whom Alexander proclaimed to be the savior of the Russian Empire, considered Russia's part in the war to be over and became the leader of the peace party. He hoped his master would focus on digesting the Grand Duchy of Warsaw as an indemnification for the war. The other states of Europe should be left to liberate themselves, just as Russia had done the previous year. In late January, Kutuzov tasked Toll with drafting a plan to delegate the main burden of the struggle against Napoleon to the British, Prussians, and Austrians, with Russia merely providing an auxiliary corps for the war effort. Alexander correctly rejected Toll's plan, believing that continuing the war best served Russia's national security. In early 1813, the tsar hoped to end French control of Central Europe and confine France to its natural borders of the Rhine, Alps, Pyrenees, and the Scheldt. No talk was made at this time of regime change in France.[6]

Unwilling to disgrace Kutuzov, the tsar found himself in the difficult position of having to contend with the hero's contrary advice and passive–aggressive rejection of his policies. Yet Alexander foresaw the difficulties that the aging prince "general field-marshal" would pose to his plans and took steps to minimize the interference. Already unhappy with Kutuzov's dilatory pursuit of Napoleon, the tsar resolved to assert greater control over military operations. After Konovnitsyn took extended sick leave, Alexander replaced him with the efficient Prince Pyotr Volkonsky, one of the tsar's confidants. Kutuzov would remain the commander and continue to take the lead in formulating strategy, "but he would do so under the close eye of the emperor and his most trusted lieutenant." The tsar "intervened frequently in military matters but he lacked the confidence to take over command or play the leading role in military operations himself."[7]

Despite Kutuzov's torpor, Wittgenstein continued to advance with the Russian right wing. Fourteen miles north of Vilna, he departed Niemenzin (Nemenčinė) with just under 35,000 men and 191 guns on 17 December. Wittgenstein directed his soldiers seventy miles northwest through Keidany (Kėdainiai) toward the lower Niemen. Four days and 100 miles later, his vanguard of 600 Cossacks commanded by Colonel Friedrich Karl von Tettenborn crossed the Prussian frontier and reached Tilsit. Northeast of Wittgenstein, the Russian governor-general of Riga, the Italian-born General Philippe Paulucci, marched 160 miles southwest to occupy Memel with 2,213 men on 27 December; Memel's Prussian garrison was taken prisoner. East of Wittgenstein and Paulucci, Admiral Pavel Chichagov led the Russian Third Western Army of 15,500 men and 130 guns supported by General Matvei Platov's 6,600 Don Cossacks west from Kovno (Kaunas) on 29 December toward the lower Vistula.

In the center of Kutuzov's position, the three corps that constituted the Russian main army quartered around Vilna: General Aleksandr Tormasov's 17,000 men and 112 guns; an advance corps of 16,000 men and 96 guns

11. Russian advance from the Niemen to the Vistula

under the Hessian-born General Ferdinand von Wintzingerode; and General Mikhail Miloradovich's corps of 11,800 men and 96 guns. From Bialystok (Białystok), Russian cavalry and Cossacks observed the 42,000 men of the fairly intact right wing of the Grande Armée: General Karl zu Schwarzenberg's Austrian Auxiliary Corps, Prince Josef Anton Poniatowski's V Corps (Poles), and General Jean-Louis Reynier's VII

Corps (Saxons). On Kutuzov's left stood General Fabian Gottlieb von der Osten-Sacken's corps of 19,345 men and 92 guns echeloned southwest from Brest on the Bug. Sacken awaited the arrival of reinforcements in the form of General Pyotr Essen III's corps of 9,139 men and 45 guns from the Pripet Marshes (Prypiackija baloty).[8]

The extraction of East Prussia's military resources appeared to go well thanks to the façade of official approval, yet Frederick William's determination to keep a firm grasp on the situation received a potentially fatal blow on 30 December. The story of General Yorck's defection and the Convention of Tauroggen (Tauragè) is shrouded in conjectures and assumptions to such an extent that the truth may never be known. After reaching Riga in October, the Prussian corps did little aside from infrequent skirmishing with the Russians, based on an alleged tacit agreement between the two sides for the Prussians to do only what honor demanded. With the lines of communication open, the Russians did not miss the opportunity to flood Yorck's headquarters with calls for the Prussians to defect. Paulucci even proposed that he and Yorck combine forces and arrest Macdonald. Yorck informed the king of the Russian overtures but received no instructions from Berlin. If Wrangel's memoirs are true, then the fact that Yorck did not receive directions in December is understandable. Published in 1830, Wrangel's account claims that, as one of the king's trusted favorites, he delivered Frederick William's secret verbal message to Yorck in August 1812. According to these instructions, Yorck received authorization to separate from Macdonald and withdraw to Graudenz in the case of a general French retreat. Wrangel also informed Yorck that the king likewise wanted the Prussians to provide the French with only enough service to maintain their honor.[9]

With Russians commanded by the Prussian-born General Johann von Diebitsch threatening his line of retreat, Yorck commenced the march west toward Prussia in December. Diebitsch observed the march and did not attack but kept Yorck fully appraised of the destruction of Napoleon's main army to the south. Diebitsch continued where Paulucci had left off with calls for the Prussians to desert the French, but Yorck refused to tarnish his reputation. He sent his adjutant, Major Anton Friedrich von Seydlitz, to Berlin with an explicit request for precise instructions. Just before Yorck reached the Prussian frontier, Diebitsch cut off his rearguard and requested negotiations. On the morning of 25 December, Scharnhorst's son-in-law, Dohna, now in Russian service, arrived at Yorck's headquarters. Sent by Paulucci, he delivered a letter from Tsar Alexander dated 6 December. According to it, Russia would continue the war to restore Prussia as a great power. Yorck's biographer, Gustav Droysen, claims that this letter, combined with the exhaustion of his troops, deep snow, and bitter cold, persuaded Yorck to open negotiations with Diebitsch. Late on the evening of 25 December, Yorck met with Diebitsch and his adjutant, Clausewitz, also in Russian service. The meeting did not lead to a Christmas miracle as Yorck hesitated to take any unauthorized step, and Diebitsch merely requested some ammunition and artillery as the price for opening the road to the Prussian rearguard. Clausewitz's presence proved detrimental as he and Yorck disliked each other. Although Diebitsch spoke of guns and ammunition, Yorck understood his true request. Paulucci first expressed it in his letter to Yorck: if the Prussian commander did not want to defect, he could declare neutrality.

Yorck stalled, hoping orders would arrive from Berlin that would lift the responsibility from his shoulders. On the 29th, Diebitsch's force of only 1,200 cavalry, 120 Jäger, and 4 guns stood between Yorck at Tauroggen and Macdonald at Tilsit. That same day, Seydlitz returned, bearing verbal instructions that authorized Yorck to act according to circumstances; as Droysen states: "nonspecific instructions [and] no response to the Russian overtures." Seydlitz also informed Yorck of impending negotiations with the Austrian court. Yorck then received a 27 December letter from Diebitsch's superior, Wittgenstein. According to Wittgenstein, he had reached the Niemen with 50,000 men and planned to continue the pursuit of the French. His master, Tsar Alexander, knew of only one enemy: the French. He explained that the tsar's generous nature would be offended if circumstances forced the Russians to occupy Prussian territory as an enemy. Armed with two more letters for Yorck to read, Clausewitz went to Prussian headquarters at Tauroggen, approximately forty miles from Tilsit, around nightfall on the 29th to seek another meeting. The first letter was an intercepted communiqué from Macdonald dated 10 December stating that Yorck could no longer be trusted. The second letter, written to Diebitsch by Wittgenstein's chief of staff, General Frédéric Anton d'Auvray, explained that the main body of the Russian right wing would be in position on the 31st to completely separate Yorck's division from Macdonald's corps.[10]

Yorck initially refused to receive Clausewitz. "Stay away from me," he shouted; "I will have nothing more to do with you." Clausewitz begged Yorck to read the letters; the general relented. After remaining silent for several minutes, he extended his hand to Clausewitz, not in friendship but in the submissive position of a chess player who finally accepted being placed in check-mate. "You have me," stated the general. "Tell General Diebitsch that early tomorrow morning I will be at the Russian outpost at a time and place that he decides." Clausewitz and Dohna left to inform Diebitsch; the former returned around midnight with instructions for Yorck to meet Diebitsch on Wednesday, 30 December at 8:00 A.M. at the Prussian outpost near the mill at Poscherun (Požerūnai), four miles west of Tauroggen.[11]

Accompanied by Clausewitz and Dohna, Diebitsch arrived on time; Yorck made them wait for more than an hour. Yorck finally arrived, measured and aloof, accompanied by Seydlitz and another staff officer. Seydlitz recorded the seven articles that the two sides verbally concluded in a tense atmosphere and not without sharp differences. According to the Convention of Tauroggen, Yorck's troops immediately separated from Macdonald's command and became neutral. The first article stipulated that the Prussian corps would occupy an area between Memel, Tilsit, and the Baltic coast. This area would remain completely neutral while Yorck's corps occupied it with the caveat that Russian troops could pass through en route to Tilsit and from Tilsit to Königsberg, which thus opened the frontier of East Prussia to the approaching Russians. Article two stated that Yorck's corps would become neutral, but if the king of Prussia ordered Yorck to return to French control his troops could not be employed against the Russians until 1 March. The third article established that, if either the king or the tsar repudiated the convention, the Prussian corps could march unhindered on the closest road to any point ordered by Frederick William. Article four promised the return of all transport personnel and supplies that had been cut off from the corps and/or captured by the Russians. According to the fifth and sixth articles, the convention would apply to all Prussian troops posted along the Russo-Prussian frontier. Finally, article seven guaranteed the continued supply of the Prussian corps even if the Russians replaced the local Prussian government. After signing, the two generals embraced.[12]

The exact wording of the verbal orders delivered by Wrangel and Seydlitz has puzzled historians for almost 200 years. Conflicting eyewitness testimonies do not help. A sober assessment of the situation practically rules out the king's complicity. At Potsdam, Frederick William received the news while strolling in the gardens of Sans Souci. Furious, he issued orders for Yorck's dismissal. Despite the stories that later circulated regarding the king's collusion, it is hard to believe that this cautious man would leave the fate of his kingdom in the hands of a general. The manner in which the army and the people – not to mention the advancing Russian army – eventually forced Frederick William to break his alliance with Napoleon renders such subterfuge doubtful. Moreover, comments made by Yorck to his officers after signing the convention likewise do not suggest that he acted on royal authority: "Gentlemen, I do not know what I shall say to the king about my action. Perhaps he will call it treason. Then I shall bear the consequences. I will put my grey head willingly at the feet of His Majesty and gladly die knowing that I have not failed as a faithful subject and a true Prussian."[13]

Almost fifty-six years later, in 1869, King William I of Prussia claimed to have been with his father at the moment the king's adjutant, Henckel von Donnersmarck, returned to Sans Souci from Yorck's headquarters at 3:30 P.M. on 2 January 1813. According to the future German emperor, his father chatted in private with Henckel for almost thirty minutes. Frederick William then returned with "an expression of satisfaction that we had not seen in a long time, but which seemed quite out of harmony with the little speech he made to the assembled group, among whom were our respective adjutants and governors. 'Count Henckel has brought me bad news. Yorck has capitulated with his corps to the Russians; apparently, the times of 1806 are about to be repeated.'"[14]

The problem with this account is that Henckel left Yorck's headquarters on 27 December – three days prior to the signing of the convention – with news that the Russians had separated the Prussians from the French and that Yorck required instructions. Yorck provided Henckel with Paulucci's letters that sought to persuade him to renounce the French alliance. According to Henckel, Yorck explicitly instructed him to verbally explain the situation to Frederick William because it would be too dangerous for Yorck to state his intentions in writing. Henckel is not clear on the details of Yorck's explanation, but apparently the passage of time influenced Henckel's memoirs, which were published in 1846. According to Henckel, he himself informed the king that Macdonald had abandoned Yorck. Cut off by the Russians, Yorck probably would negotiate with them. Henckel explains that the king "was very surprised by my report." With the French occupying Berlin, he claims that the king recognized the dire need for caution, and so immediately dispatched his wing-adjutant, Major Oldwig Anton von Natzmer, to Yorck's headquarters. Natzmer carried orders relieving Yorck of his command and notifying him of an impending court-martial. Unable to get past the Russians to reach the general, Natzmer eventually returned to Berlin and Yorck retained his command. One historian views Natzmer's failed mission as a farce that "of course had been contrived beforehand." According to this version of the story, Natzmer passed through the Russian lines to deliver a letter from Frederick William to the tsar stating the former's approval of Tauroggen. At the moment, he could not risk an open break with Napoleon by publicly ratifying the convention. Yet, if the Russian army crossed the Vistula and reached the Oder, Frederick William pledged to conclude an offensive and defensive alliance with Alexander. Natzmer returned to Potsdam during the night of 19/20 January "with a most favorable answer to the king's proposal." Alexander accepted Frederick William's conditions for an offensive and defensive alliance: the Russian army would advance toward the Oder and continue the war.[15]

Meanwhile, Yorck sent Major Ludwig Gustav von Thile to Berlin on 30 December with tidings of the convention. In a letter written to historian Johann Gustav Droysen on 18 September 1851, Thile claimed that the convention actually pleased Frederick William. Nevertheless, Yorck's justification of his actions earned the monarch's wrath. As Yorck's explanation took a political rather than a military tone, the king felt that his proceedings compromised the virtually defenseless state. Boyen's assessment appears the most probable:

At the first report of this event, the king was extremely outraged at Yorck; the orders to relieve him of command and the investigation into the conduct of the general were measures not taken just to appease Napoleon, but taken by the king with full seriousness; his anger at the moment was not concealed. The king, who, in his manner of thinking and acting, demanded mechanical obedience even in one's thoughts, and never considered the causes and consequences of an action that was taken based on the assessment of the variety of circumstances, viewed this as nothing less than a direct rebellion against his authority by General Yorck.

Regardless of whether Yorck acted with or without royal authorization, he started a chain reaction that led to Prussia's official alliance with Russia and declaration of war against France three months later. As an immediate result, Macdonald could not halt at Tilsit and defend the Niemen but instead withdrew to Königsberg and from there to Danzig. In general, the wreck of the Grande Armée continued to retreat, evacuating the lower Vistula and abandoning the large garrison at Danzig. Without Yorck's relatively fresh 20,000 men, Murat did not believe he could hold Wittgenstein at the Prussian frontier.[16]

Frederick William again found himself in the midst of intense factional strife. The pro-French party struggled to convince him that the state's salvation lay only with Napoleon. It emphasized the vast military resources at the emperor's disposal, the Russian army's dismal condition at the end of the bitter campaign, and Alexander's own personal shortcomings. While Hardenberg hoped to leverage Napoleon's disaster to improve Prussia's position within the French imperium, Scharnhorst lobbied for a Russian alliance. Although the two pursued opposite agendas, both cautioned Frederick William against making a rash decision. Instead, the circumstances required the king to patiently allow the situation to unfold to achieve maximum benefit for the state as an ally of either France or Russia. Still another faction called for the Prussians to lead a North German war of liberation. The rabid hawks demanded that the army prevent the French from provisioning the fortresses they occupied and advised launching a rapid strike to destroy the remains of the Grande Armée. Then, they wanted all available troops to cross the Elbe and take positions in Saxony while partisans inflamed Germany with anti-French fervor.

In this precarious time, Frederick William looked to Austria. Knesebeck arrived at Vienna on 12 January hoping to discuss an Austro-Prussian partnership first proposed in October 1812 by Austrian foreign minister Klemens von Metternich. Metternich's plan included a French withdrawal behind the Rhine and Pyrenees as well as the end of Napoleon's control over the Confederation of the Rhine. Instead of French hegemony, Prussia and Austria would guarantee the independence of the Third Germany. Knesebeck also had instructions to request that Austria join Prussia in a league of armed neutrality designed to force France and Russia to the peace table. Should the Austrians refuse, Knesebeck would then seek Austrian approval of a Russo-Prussian alliance. Metternich rejected the idea of the Austro-Prussian partnership that would serve to encourage the Prussian peace party and frustrate his own plans to mediate a peace. Knowing that Frederick William would soon be forced to side with Napoleon or Alexander, he also withheld Austria's official approval of a Russo-Prussian alliance. Instead, Metternich offered verbal encouragement for the Russo-Prussian alliance.[17]

With Russian forces moving across the Niemen, the French demanded that the Prussians defend their frontiers. In response, Frederick William instructed Krusemarck to request territorial restitution and the payment of 98,000,000 francs for military supplies in return for Prussia's continued support. Despite this diplomatic hectoring, the pro-war patriotism that spread west from East Prussia threatened to carry the state into a war against France with or without the king. Napoleon's refusal brought Hardenberg to the realization that the moment had arrived to sever ties with the French. Napoleon's demand for a second Prussian corps to replace Yorck's allowed the Prussians to mobilize under the façade of remaining a faithful ally. However, the events at Königsberg in early February jeopardized Frederick William's credibility with the emperor. Rejected by the Austrians and suspected of duplicity by the French, the king turned to the Russians. With Boyen serving as the chief liaison, Alexander accepted Frederick William's excuse of being forced into the war. Although in a position to forgive the king, Alexander needed Prussian support to continue the war. The condition of the Russian army and the tsar's own goodwill toward the Prussians elevated Frederick William to the status of a junior partner. Being a junior partner to the Russians appeared to offer greater salvation for Prussia than serving as Napoleon's client. After Knesebeck's mission to Vienna failed, the Prussians turned to Tsar Alexander in the hope of securing fair alliance terms.[18]

For the present, Frederick William officially repudiated the Convention of Tauroggen and issued orders for Friedrich Heinrich von Kleist to replace Yorck, but the royal couriers never reached the general. Instead, Yorck arrived at Königsberg on 8 January; he learned of the king's decision by way of the 10 January edition of the Berlin newspaper. Regardless, as military governor of East Prussia, he took immediate action to defend the province from both French and Russian transgressions. After Bülow had transferred the majority of service-eligible males to Graudenz, perhaps 1,200 untrained recruits remained at Yorck's disposal. Due to the shortage of manpower, he turned to the idea of a Landwehr (militia), which the East Prussians had raised in 1757 for defense against the Russians during the Seven Years War.

Russian troops reached Königsberg on 6 January. Stein as well as Clausewitz soon arrived, both in Russian service, the former as the tsar's governor-general of East Prussia. Alexander hoped Stein could mobilize the province's resources without alienating the Prussian people or scaring Frederick William. For this purpose, Russian headquarters demanded excellent behavior from the troops toward the Prussian civilians. Historian Dominic Lieven claims that, despite the exhaustion of the Russian soldiers, they "responded well and maintained their discipline." One of Stein's more important tasks was the reopening of the port of Königsberg. "Baron Stein is the person most spoken of in this part of the world," wrote British commissioner Colonel Hudson Lowe. "Everything in Prussia is attributed to his exertions."[19]

Not at all friends, the progressive Stein and the reactionary Yorck managed to put aside their personal differences to work for a larger cause. For Yorck, this meant harnessing all available resources to defend East Prussia. For Stein, this meant generating the spark that would cause a mass German uprising against Napoleon. Both men hoped their decisive action in East Prussia would force Frederick William to abandon his alliance with the French emperor and come to terms with Alexander. They tasked Clausewitz with drafting the guidelines for a universally conscripted Landwehr. In early February, Yorck and Stein – a general in disgrace and a former minister now in the service of the enemy – convened the East Prussian Landtag (provincial assembly) at Königsberg. As only the king could summon the Landtag, its members met under a dubious and downright illegal cloud. Nevertheless, the assembly accepted Clausewitz's draft and on 7 February 1813 decreed the creation of a 20,000-man Landwehr as well as a Landsturm (civil defense force).[20] The success of Yorck and Stein can be directly attributed to the bitter resentment the East Prussian people felt after the French ravaged the land in 1812.[21] "At Memel," added Lowe, "the arrival of an English officer was almost an occasion of public rejoicing. The magistrates came to the inn the moment they heard one had arrived there. It is difficult to describe to you the apparent feelings of these persons – they contemplate the favorable prospects open to them like a redemption from slavery. Napoleon passed six days in this town on his march to Russia. The splendor of his French and Italian Guards could only be equaled by their pride and insolence."[22]

As for the French, Murat struggled to rally the wreck of the Grande Armée. In late December, its remains crossed the Niemen and reached the lower Vistula. On 3 January 1813, Macdonald's X Corps marched into Königsberg, from where it further retreated to Danzig. After transferring his headquarters seventy-five miles southwest from Königsberg to Elbing on 1 January, Murat learned of the Convention of Tauroggen and decided to evacuate the line of the lower Vistula. Meanwhile, Wittgenstein and Platov advanced west toward Elbing and Thorn, detaching some 12,300 men and

128 guns under Chichagov to besiege the latter. The unexpected Russian advance prompted Murat to withdraw more than 180 miles southwest to a central position at Posen (Poznań) with 12,000 men, leaving a garrison of 30,000 to hold Danzig and approximately 7,000 men total to defend Thorn and Modlin (Nowy Dwór Mazowiecki). He evacuated Elbing on 11 January, sending one column northwest to Danzig and a second through Stargard (Starogard Gdański) to Konitz (Chojnice). From there, Murat directed the remains of II and III Corps to Küstrin; IV Corps to Glogau; the Guard, IX and VIII Corps to Posen; I Corps to Stettin; and VI Corps to Gnesen (Gniezno). Forty miles south-southwest from Elbing, ten of Platov's Cossack Regiments commanded by General Aleksandr Chernishev attacked Marienwerder on the night of 12 January. Napoleon's stepson and viceroy of Italy, Eugene de Beauharnais, along with Marshal Claude Victor and four French generals, barely managed to escape across the frozen Vistula. Fifteen guns and some 100 prisoners fell into Russian hands. On that same day, the Russians caught Macdonald's rearguard at Palschau (Palczewo) after X - Corps crossed the Vistula in its attempt to reach Danzig. Thanks to General Gilbert-Désiré Bachelu's bold counterattack during the night of 12/13 January, the imperials safely entered the fortress. Wittgenstein continued his advance, crossing the Vistula at Dirschau (Tczew) on 2 February. Six days later, the French evacuated Pillau but left behind a small garrison that surrendered to the Russians on the condition of free passage across the Oder. After detaching General Friedrich Löwis von Menar to blockade Danzig with some 11,800 men, Wittgenstein moved to Stargard, where he remained until 13 February (see Map 1).

Southeast of Wittgenstein, Tormasov led the Russian main army across the Niemen at Meretsch (Merkine) on 13 January; six days later the Russians crossed the Prussian frontier. Russian operations during the second half of January sought to destroy any imperial forces that remained east of the Vistula. By reaching the left bank of this river, the Russians hoped to accelerate direct cooperation with the Prussians while at the same time operating against Schwarzenberg, Poniatowski, and Reynier. On 30 January, Miloradovich concluded an armistice with Schwarzenberg. In its aftermath, the Austrians abandoned the defense of the Grand Duchy of Warsaw and retreated southwest to Kraków rather than to Kalisch (Kalisz) as ordered by the French. Schwarzenberg carried off Poniatowski and his Poles, who remained in Austria until the June armistice, but Reynier's VII Corps separated from the Austrians and made for Kalisch. On 5 February 1813, Tormasov's corps united with the tsar and Kutuzov at Płock, sixty-five miles northwest of Warsaw. Miloradovich occupied Warsaw three days later, while Wintzingerode commenced the pursuit of Reynier that same day.[23]

At Potsdam, security concerns finally prompted Frederick William to flee to Silesia, which Napoleon had guaranteed would remain neutral.

Suspicious movements by French troops on 15 and 17 January alarmed Hardenberg. Following a large dinner party at his Berlin residence on the 17th, the state chancellor sped to Potsdam by means of a coach-and-six. Evidently armed with vital intelligence, he met with Frederick William that night. Still on the same night, the Potsdam garrison received ammunition as general fear of a violent attempt on the king's person spread like wildfire. After 18-year-old Crown Prince Frederick William's confirmation on the 20th and his first communion on the 21st, the king departed Potsdam on 22 January. Traveling through Sagan (Żagań), he reached Breslau on the 25th. Remarking that at Breslau the king "will be quite another man than he is here," Chancellor Hardenberg as well as his staff and the royal family arrived two days later. The entire court and many others, including French ambassador St.-Marsan, likewise went to Breslau.[24]

On 28 January, the king received two uplifting letters from Alexander, dated 6 and 21 January. The first, written from Vilna, reached Breslau by way of Yorck and states:

> I have, Sire, the first favorable opportunity to reiterate to Your Majesty the expression of this old and sincere friendship that no circumstance could shake me from. Believe me, Sire, that despite the painful events that occurred during this year my attachment to you has remained the same, and, since Divine Providence has allowed the affairs to take such a favorable turn, one of my most ardent desires is to convince you how much I have your interests and those of your monarchy at heart. According to my religion, my principles, I like to repay the bad by doing good and I will not be satisfied until Prussia has resumed all its splendor and power. To achieve this goal, I pledge to Your Majesty not to lay down arms until this great goal is reached. But we need Your Majesty to openly join with me. Never has there been a more favorable moment. The French Grande Armée was largely destroyed and its weak remains are completely disorganized. Your Majesty must have been informed that, following these events, General Yorck's corps has been separated from Macdonald's. I hope that by accepting the agreement that I proposed to him, General Yorck acted according to Your Majesty's intentions. Sire, I have great pleasure in thinking that my troops no longer have to fight yours; but at the same time I am compelled to say that this event seems to me to strengthen all the other reasons why you must play a strong role against the oppressor of humanity. You must feel that Your Majesty has everything to fear from the vengeance of this man. By seizing this unique moment, Your Majesty will earn immortal glory for saving Europe and returning Prussia to its former power. For my part, I am happy to contribute and thereby fulfill a vow I made long ago. I implore Your Majesty to carefully consider all that I have just stated. Never was a decision more important than that which you will make. It may save Europe or lose it forever. Accept, Sire, the expression of feelings of the most inviolable friendship that are dedicated to you for life. I remain Your Majesty's good friend and brother.

Alexander's second letter, written from Lyck (Ełk) and dated 21 January states:

> Having set foot in your states, Sire, it is impossible not to send these lines to express the emotion I feel in a country where each time I have been given the most flattering signs of affection by its sovereign and have been received as a true friend. It is still under this title that I return this time, and I hope Divine Providence will allow me to quite happily give you compelling evidence of this. I wrote to Your Majesty from Vilna requesting that General Yorck have a trusted officer deliver it to you. I do not know if it reached Your Majesty. I enclose a copy. I also believe that it is my duty to tell you, Sire, that, according to the line of scrupulous conduct that I must draw in your states, I have vested my full powers in a Russian dignitary, but one who is the most loyal of Your Majesty's subjects: Baron Stein. I hope this will provide proof to Your Majesty of how the conservation of your states and their legitimate sovereign is so dear to my heart. I beg you to believe in the unalterable attachment to you that I have vowed to endure forever. I remain Your Majesty's good brother, friend and shortly, I hope, sincere ally.[25]

These letters, along with the measures taken by the East Prussian Landtag, liberated Frederick William from Ancillon's paralyzing influence and moved him to side with the anti-French party. To oversee the mobilization and expansion of the army, he formed the Armaments Commission, consisting of Hardenberg and Scharnhorst among others, on 28 January. That same day, Scharnhorst resumed his position as head of the War Department. Action could not have come any faster. The following day, 1 February, the king issued a cabinet order to increase the army by 37,000 men and double the number of battalions. News from Vienna arrived two days later. According to Knesebeck, now a colonel as well as the king's adjutant-general and chief military advisor, the Austrian court supported the formation of a Russo-Prussian alliance against France. With this penultimate diplomatic obstacle cleared, Frederick William moved forward with his military preparations. On the urging of the Armaments Commission, he issued the 9 February universal conscription law to provide the 37,000 recruits promised by the 1 February decree. According to initial plans, the concentration of the field army would occur on 12 February, but the king delayed it until an agreement with the Russians could be reached.[26]

On this same day, 9 February, Knesebeck departed Breslau to conclude an alliance with the Russians. He bore Frederick William's response to Alexander's letter of 6 January:

> Sire, it is impossible for me to provide evidence to Your Majesty of how strong I feel, and my appreciation of the feelings that you have preserved for me and the joy that I have of reuniting with you, with a system, and with its

measures that only the most compelling circumstances forced me to separate from for the moment. You cannot question the sincere friendship that I have devoted to you and nothing can change it, considering how precious it was to my heart to regain it based on your 6 January letter from Vilna ... I have provided him [Knesebeck] with the full authority necessary to conclude with those whom you appoint for this purpose a treaty of friendship and alliance that unites our states, I hope, forever, as we are one and the same in heart and feelings. He will reveal to you my best wishes and intentions, Sire, and he will tell you how much I appreciate what you have done for me. Deign to listen and give your trust and rely on my most inviolable attachment and feelings that I have vowed to you for life. I remain Your Majesty's good brother and friend – I cannot wait to add "and faithful ally."

Frederick William also shared the results of Knesebeck's mission to Vienna. Although failing to convince the Austrians to break their alliance with Napoleon, the king did not describe the situation as "hopeless." "It will probably be very beneficial to employ all our means to eliminate issues that could be of concern to Austria," he suggested. Knesebeck would provide the Russians with "reliable information about the views and intentions of Austria."[27]

As for the Austrians, Vienna had rejected a British offer for £500,000 to declare war on Napoleon in the autumn of 1812. Metternich informed London that Vienna's only action would be to persuade the belligerents to negotiate a general peace. With Prussia and Austria adhering to the alliances with France, Sweden attracted far greater British attention than the state's resources warranted. According to Sherwig, "By the opening of 1813 British war diplomacy had identified three major goals. First, the Peninsular War must be given all the support needed to guarantee Wellington's success. Second, a major army must be created in North Germany to aid the Russians. Swedish intervention would go a long way toward attaining this goal. Finally, some firm agreement would have to be reached with the tsar in order to guarantee his continued participation in the war." Although Bernadotte disappointed London by failing to participate in the Campaign of 1812, the British did not question his hostility to Napoleon. "Sweden may be considered in a state of war against France," reported Thornton on 30 December. "The crown prince, I most firmly believe, will follow it up by acts of hostility, the moment he shall be enabled to display a sufficient force by the junction of the Russian auxiliary forces, stipulated by the treaty."[28]

Like the French emperor, Bernadotte tied his popularity to the success of his foreign policy. However, as early as 2 January, the British viewed the negotiations over Norway between Sweden and Denmark as hopeless. Castlereagh's half-brother, General Sir Charles Stewart, described King Frederick VI of Denmark as "determined to hold Norway to the last." With Bernadotte "backed by existing treaties," Stewart predicted that neither would yield and that the issue would have to be settled by a war fought in

Holstein. This, according to Stewart, would require a large army and probably last through the spring. Referring to Bernadotte, Stewart informed Castlereagh that "I feel much surprise and alarm that his Royal Highness does not seem to be considering the magnitude of the enterprise in the manner that becomes a great military mind. He has no efficient siege apparatus, and there is a great want of arrangement throughout his present undertakings. His *état-major* seems to be dispersed in every quarter. From all I witnessed when in Holstein, I cannot help but entertain considerable anxiety for the result of His Royal Highness's campaign." Stewart also expressed the concern that any attempt by the British to restrain Bernadotte would be interpreted as Great Britain deserting him. He concluded his report by describing Bernadotte as "by no means an easy character to act with. But to find such a remedy at such a crisis is not so easy. Great decisions must be made by the great Allied powers at headquarters. To soften differences and to make the machine go on as well as we are able, notwithstanding all the impediments that arise, must be the duty of all."[29]

Written to Britain's undersecretary for war and the colonies, Henry Bunbury, on 29 January 1813 aboard the HMS *Daphne* while en route to Stockholm, a report by Lowe extrapolated London's concerns over Sweden and Bernadotte: "The natural ambition of every sovereign is to render his nation powerful and independent. By losing Finland, Sweden has suffered in both these points – but more in the former, than the latter, for the contiguity of that country to Russia left it constantly exposed to attack and Sweden herself dependent on the caprices of another power for her own repose and tranquility." Although Lowe reasoned that the natural border formed by the Baltic between Sweden and Finland would give Russia "no just cause for further encroachment," he conceded that, unable to resist further Russian aggrandizement, "Sweden naturally would look to power, strength, and resources in another quarter. These could be acquired only on the side of Norway and the Danish Isles. The former, an integral part of the Swedish peninsula, and the latter, sufficiently near to justify the desire of holding them without any other motive than their geographic position."

To attain Norway, Sweden would need France's approval. Although allied to Denmark, Lowe speculated that Napoleon could see the logic in allowing Sweden "to attack and become the master of that country." Lowe explained that "as it is the interest of France to render the maritime position of the Danish Isles and of Norway as subservient as possible to her views against Russia, as well as against England," Napoleon could accomplish this by allowing Sweden to conquer the Danish isles and Norway. "For once this is established, Sweden must become the natural rival of Russia and the enemy, as a great maritime power, of England." Lowe speculated that Napoleon could seize the continental portion of Denmark and thus "obtain a vast outstretching flank for the security" of his other continental possessions. According to Lowe, Napoleon could justify abandoning Denmark:

> I would suppose Napoleon might then argue: "Bernadotte will not assist me in my operations against Russia by making a diversion in Finland because it is not in the interest of Sweden that I should assume such an ascendancy on the shores of the Baltic. By subduing Russia, I may prove fatal to her own views of power and security. It is in her interest to become a great maritime state. I have no objection, as she will then be more able to assist me in my future views against England, but to become one she must possess both Norway and the Danish Isles. In this point, I cannot at present assist her. Bernadotte therefore must endeavor to do it with the aid of Russia and England. Let him therefore throw himself into their hands. In pursuing his own interests, he strengthens mine. The moment he seizes Zealand, I lay hold of Holstein and Jutland. We shall then be closer to each other, and I will descend on making it his interest to join with me in humbling Russia and in attacking England."

Lowe discounted the existence of an existing secret agreement between Bernadotte and Napoleon but cautioned that a future Franco-Swedish alliance could be devastating to British interests: "I do conceive that on any future occasion, after having rendered himself powerful, Bernadotte would have no difficulty in justifying his conduct to Napoleon. I cannot imagine a more formidable coalition to be formed against Great Britain than that of Sweden, thus aggrandized, acting in conjunction with France. The maritime means of France extending from the coasts of the Mediterranean to the mouth of the Baltic and forming a hostile circle of such extent, would require greater exertions than any we have ever yet been called upon to make." To avoid "gloomy speculations so wholly misplaced in the present truly cheerful aspect of public affairs," Lowe suggested that London quickly determine "how to draw the greatest advantages from the present favorable disposition of Bernadotte and the government of Sweden."

Supposing Bernadotte sought only to obtain Norway, Lowe still advised London to be cautious in aiding him in exchange "for his exertions in our favor with a Swedish army on the continent." Thus, Lowe mused over the perplexing question of how to obtain Bernadotte's cooperation. "I must confess," he advised, "I see no other way than to hold forth to Bernadotte the prospect of personal fame, glory, and aggrandizement for himself on becoming the Liberator of Europe without any particular advantage to Sweden beyond the recovery of Pomerania and the Isle of Rügen and the restoration of the Åland Islands by the Russians, with the acquirement of some colonial or transatlantic possession that might be in our power to obtain for her." Lowe then demonstrated the extent to which some British diplomats were ignorant of the interests of the Eastern powers whose alliance against Napoleon London now sought. To protect British maritime superiority, he suggested reestablishing the Kingdom of Poland with Bernadotte as its king and "totally independent of any claim on the crown of Sweden." It is hard to imagine Russia, Austria, and Prussia dropping their national security considerations regarding Poland in order to prevent Bernadotte from becoming king of a Sweden that he would transform into Great Britain's maritime rival as well as Napoleon's ally.

Returning to the issue at hand, Lowe considered that "as Norway really forms an integral part of the Swedish peninsula, it is so natural for Sweden to desire the subjugation of it, that it may appear hardly justifiable, from the idea of any future combination against ourselves, to disrupt her proceeding, nor would Bernadotte or the Swedes perhaps readily admit the justice of any reason we could adduce to that effect." Therefore, he contended that Denmark, which he described as "a natural ally of Great Britain," should receive Pomerania and the Isle of Rügen in exchange for Norway. He suggested that, by ceding Norway to Sweden and awarding Stockholm "some colonial advantages," Bernadotte "would be rendered sufficiently powerful and independent, and receive sufficient indemnification" for any exertions he should make against Napoleon. As for Swedish Pomerania, the British officer maintained that it "is no more necessary to her [Sweden] than any part of the continent of Europe is to Great Britain, except as a friend and an ally."

As for the balance in the Baltic, Lowe argued that breaking Denmark free of Napoleon's grip and restoring Prussia to its pre-1806 material strength would transform Sweden into the honest broker of North Europe. In this way, there would be "no power whose more true interest it would be to preserve the balance of power in Europe on a proper footing than Sweden, who, by suffering either France or Russia to encroach too much on their intermediate neighbors, would lend a hand to the ruin of her own preponderance on the shores of the Baltic and to the loss of that commercial influence which as a maritime power of the first class, she will naturally make it an object of her greatest ambition to acquire and to maintain." Lowe hoped London could gain Bernadotte as an ally without having to promise the cession of Norway to Sweden, "but if it must take place, better it appears to me by the way of negotiation, according to the views I have suggested, than by conquest, which would only inflame animosities, give rise to further encroachments on the part of the conqueror, and sow the seeds of future wars. *England, by yielding to the requisition of Norway by Sweden, gives* a most unequivocal proof of her disinterestedness and *her disregard of every consideration,* by which the *maritime and commercial superiority she now possesses* might in [the] *future* be affected."[30]

Despite considerations such as these, Castlereagh remained determined to employ Sweden in the raising of North Germany due to the uncertainty over Prussia's position. He hoped Bernadotte's Swedes, reinforced by the North Germans, would strike Napoleon's flank while the Russians attacked his front. With Thornton too easily swayed by the crown prince's gasconades, the British dispatched General Alexander Hope to Sweden in January as a special envoy to negotiate an Anglo-Swedish alliance. Making clear that the main objective of this alliance was to obtain Swedish military assistance in North Germany for Russia, Castlereagh authorized Hope to offer a subsidy of £1,000,000 for a Swedish army to fight on the continent in 1813 and another £1,000,000 to fund a legion created from German deserters and prisoners taken by the Russians in 1812. Formed by the Russians under the leadership of Duke Peter of Oldenburg, this "German Legion" would fall under Bernadotte's command. The British also pledged to support Stockholm's claim to Norway and discussed the possibility of Sweden's acquisition of the wealthy Caribbean island of Guadeloupe. Despite these generous offers, negotiations dragged on for two months due in part to Bernadotte's demand for a larger subsidy, itself attributed to the economic repercussions caused by the near failure of the 1812 grain harvest.[31]

Meanwhile, uncertainty about French and Prussian intentions limited Kutuzov's ability and desire to plan his next move. In fact, with his army exhausted and extremely weakened, with no official allies on the continent, and with imperial reinforcements assuredly mustering in Germany, the Russian field-marshal conceded the military initiative to the French. Writing to Wittgenstein on 2 February, he noted that:

> Warsaw, Modlin, and Thorn are still not in our hands; it is not certain where General Reynier will turn after he crosses the Vistula; also, we do not know why the enemy established his headquarters at Posen: will he move up from the Oder and concentrate all available reinforcements to operate from Thorn, Modlin, and the other fortresses or, at Reynier's approach, will he withdraw the French and imperial troops to the Oder and establish a defensive line there? All of this is still shrouded in such darkness that I, as you can see from my orders, cannot prescribe anything categorically for you, but will wait until the time – which will certainly be soon – when the enemy will reveal his intentions to us.[32]

Eugene retreated 100 miles southwest through Schwetz (Świecie) to reach Posen on the 16th. Concern about his own Kingdom of Naples prompted Murat to transfer command to Eugene the following day, a decision the emperor endorsed on 22 January. Napoleon instructed his stepson to buy time for the creation of a new imperial army and to hold as much territory as possible – a task that would have challenged any of Napoleon's generals. After finding Posen indefensible, the viceroy withdrew to Frankfurt-am-Oder, where he rallied 30,000 men and received reinforcements. Napoleon envisioned Eugene's force – the Army of the Elbe – holding this river from

Hamburg to the Austrian frontier. He emphasized the importance of defending Hamburg; establishing bridgeheads over the Elbe at Torgau, Wittenberg, and Dessau; and having Reynier's VII Corps remain master of the upper Elbe. From these positions, the emperor believed Eugene could repulse any Russian attack. Behind the Army of the Elbe, the emperor planned to form his new force: the Army of the Main. Napoleon hoped to mobilize 656,000 men by June of 1813. Calling up the class of 1813 the previous autumn had made for a solid start. With some 137,000 recruits from this class already nearing the completion of their training, Napoleon summoned 80,000 National Guardsmen to the colors on 11 January. For leadership, the emperor transferred experienced noncommissioned officers from his armies in Spain to the new units. These measures allowed him to field almost 200,000 men by late April, but the Grande Armée of 1813 lacked many of the tactical attributes of previous French armies, which in turn placed strategic and operational limitations on Napoleon.[33]

With the French falling back from the Vistula, Wittgenstein's Russians pressed westward. On 13 February, they took Posen after the French had evacuated the town the day before. This news brought relief to Kutuzov's headquarters especially after intelligence had identified Posen as the rallying point for imperial forces retreating from Russia. Kutuzov's question appeared to be answered: no French counteroffensive would occur in Poland. Seventy-five miles southeast of Posen, Wintzingerode reached Kalisch on 13 February. Reynier's VII Corps had arrived the previous evening after forced marches. Wintzingerode attacked around 1:00 P.M. on the 13th, destroying one of Reynier's two Saxon divisions. Considered the last combat of the Russian campaign, the engagement at Kalisch cost the Russians 670 casualties. Reynier lost approximately 3,000 men on the field and during the pursuit. He eventually outran the Russians to reach Glogau on 19 February (see Map 1).

Alexander boasted to Frederick William that the Russians had captured 1 Saxon general, 6 colonels, 36 officers, 2,000 men, 2 flags, and 7 cannon at Kalisch. Moreover, he pressed for Prussian action:

> The remains of Reynier's corps withdrew in the direction of Ostrowo [Ostrów Wielkopolski] to save itself in Silesia. Your Majesty will recognize how important it is that they do not enter Glogau and increase its garrison. Therefore, I beseech you to immediately invest this place with troops that you may have available in the area and by all means prevent the remains of Reynier's corps from escaping. Although you do not judge it possible, Sire, to publicly declare against France at this time, the fact that Glogau should have been returned to you long ago because you have paid more than the total of all that was in arrears, provides you with the best excuse to seize it and announce that you cannot consent to see a thriving city in the province where you now abide be exposed to the plight of an obstinate siege and be guarded by troops other than those of Your Majesty.

In a few days, my headquarters will be established at Kalisch; therefore, communication between us will be as frequent as our current reports require them.[34] I regret that Colonel Knesebeck has not yet joined us. Your Majesty cannot doubt the impatience with which I await the moment to be able to openly express the feelings that I continue to bear. I remain Your Majesty's good brother and friend. P.S. Forgive me, Sire, if I used a foreign hand to write you this letter, but time ran out for me to do it myself. When I finished my letter, Colonel Knesebeck arrived. I have yet to see him. With all my heart and soul.[35]

In response to this letter, Frederick William forwarded a map to him, stating:

You will find the line that marks the neutral portion of Silesia, through which I can refuse passage to the French and allied troops, and the portion where the passage of troops has been stipulated. I flatter myself that you will order your troops, Sire, to equally respect the first. You can see for yourself that yours can march directly on Glogau along a much shorter path than through the neutral portion of Silesia. My troops, hitherto restricted in the neutral portion, would have arrived too late to prevent the retreating French troops from reinforcing the place [Glogau]. I will protest ... to the Minister of France regarding the issue of neutrality. My impatience to declare myself, Sire, is equal to yours. Please accept the renewed assurances of my sincere friendship and inviolable attachment with which I shall not cease to be Your Majesty's good friend and brother.[36]

Alexander offered no response regarding the king's request that Russian troops respect Silesia's neutral zone. Although Frederick William could not prevent Reynier from reaching Glogau, the general retreat of imperial forces from Posen and Kalisch opened the region between the Vistula and the Oder. This development profoundly influenced Russian planning. Kutuzov ordered Wittgenstein to take a central position at Schneidemühl (Piła) facing Stettin and Küstrin. "Through this position," wrote Kutuzov, "you will also move closer to the main army, whose initial movement will be between Posen and Glogau. You will have Yorck's Prussian corps cross the Vistula and move toward Neustettin [Szczecinek]; no Prussian troops will be used for the blockade of Danzig. Send a detachment across the Oder." Meanwhile, the Russian main army commenced the 100-mile march southwest from Plock to Kalisch on 15 February. Five days later, Miloradovich's vanguard reached Kalisch, followed on the 24th by the tsar and Kutuzov.[37]

Prior to Alexander's arrival at Kalisch, Knesebeck joined his head-quarters at Kladau (Kłodawa) on the evening of 15 February 1813 to begin formal negotiations and military planning. He also delivered a copy of Frederick William's instructions to Krusemarck in Paris that named the king's price for continued cooperation with Napoleon. Fearing that Alexander would react to this apparent duplicity, Frederick William attempted to be transparent:

> Colonel Knesebeck will express my position and my ideas. He knows how I intend to change the system, which is the goal of all my wishes, but he agrees that it is also essential to place Napoleon in the wrong, even before his nation, and not provide him with an excuse to inflame the minds and opinion in France by presenting my conduct as a perfidy. I charged Colonel Knesebeck with showing you, Sire, the orders I gave to General Krusemarck. According to all the notions that came back to me and reports that I received today, Napoleon is far from agreeing to my proposals and satisfying my requests. Therefore, he shall clearly be in the wrong, even in the eyes of the French, and I have acted in a manner consistent with my character. In any case, it will not be long until I declare and I flatter myself that our relationship will be completely secured by the sending of Colonel Knesebeck.[38]

This earned a strong rebuke from the tsar:

> But it is impossible to hide from Your Majesty the painful impression made on me by the information Knesebeck provided regarding the latest instructions given to General Krusemarck in Paris. I would like to think that such would not have been had Your Majesty known that my armies were so advanced and that they would assist you. You also know, Sire, based on my constant friendship for you, not to misinterpret these observations. After the enemy was destroyed, forgetting the past, I rushed forward to meet you because the thought of restoration, even the expansion of Prussia has always been nourished in the privacy of my feelings. The time has come when we can achieve this. We must seize it. A moment lost for us is more than a moment won for the enemy, and it is in this great crisis when the odds seem so favorable that negotiations that would slow us seem completely against the interests of the cause that we, I hope, will support together. Allow me, Sire, to add that you want to place Napoleon in the wrong vis-à-vis his nation; you want to prevent public opinion from becoming inflamed; you want to avoid the reproach of perfidy. I respond to this that before God and men your auxiliary role ended with the destruction of the enemy's main forces because you were allied with a power that wanted to and did place 400,000 combatants against Russia; these forces are destroyed; where are your commitments? As to the charge of treachery, what are the parallels between your behavior and that of a sovereign who has violated each article of the Treaty of Tilsit that concerned you and in a manner most unbelievable? You may have to bend to the force of circumstances, but your right to side with those who come forward in support to free you from an oppressive alliance is undeniable, and even in France how strong will the simple statement of fact be on public opinion? We will agree, Sire, I hope on these points and I trust that we will do the same on all others. Friendship, confidence, perseverance and courage; Providence will do the rest.[39]

Regarding military planning, Kutuzov issued a blueprint for military operations on the 17th from Kolo (Koło). His plan reflected the impact of the events on the 13th at Posen and Kalisch as well as the imminent alliance with the Prussians. On the whole, these developments finally persuaded the field-marshal to take the initiative. "After the destruction of the French army in Russia," Kutuzov explained to Wittgenstein, "Napoleon can hardly reinforce the wreck of his forces through Reynier's corps which, united with [Marshal Pierre] Augereau, does not exceed 17,000 men. If the viceroy of Italy assembles the troops that recently evacuated Poland and retreated to Küstrin, as well as Reynier's troops who withdrew on Glogau after being defeated by Wintzingerode, the entire enemy force on the Oder between Frankfurt and Stettin would number around 40,000 men including barely 1,500 cavalry. The superiority of our forces combined with those that the Prussians have assembled to defeat the common enemy provides us with a convenient opportunity to completely destroy this remainder of the enemy's troops."

After detaching the Russian siege corps at Danzig, Kutuzov estimated Wittgenstein's corps to number between 30,000 and 35,000 combatants. To this figure he added Bülow's 10,000 men and Yorck's 20,000, assuring Wittgenstein that the Prussians "have been placed at your full disposal." He wanted this combined army to advance to the Oder with Bülow on the right, Yorck in the middle, and Wittgenstein on the left. "The direction of all columns must be between Stettin and Küstrin to Landsberg [Gorzów Wielkopolski], which stands on the road to Berlin. The main purpose of this movement is to cut off the enemy army from Magdeburg, while the corps of the main army take the direct road from Kolo through Crossen [Krosno Odrzańskie] to Magdeburg in order to meet the enemy if he, after losing the road to Magdeburg, turns on Dresden or Leipzig, where a Prussian army from Silesia will likewise turn." Kutuzov urged secrecy and speed, advising Wittgenstein that his movement would be successful only "if you win a few concealed marches before the enemy learns that you have crossed the Oder." Wittgenstein's numerous light troops could be used to mask his columns; Kutuzov wanted him to assign to Chernishev's cavalry the task of observing and pinning the French on the Oder for as long as possible (see Map 1).[40]

Kutuzov's attempt to seize the initiative misfired because of the incomplete diplomatic arrangements. Unfortunately for the Allies, this failure soured the Russian commander, whose aversion to the Prussians, general opposition to the war, and rapidly declining health all contributed to the paralysis of future operations. Kutuzov's plan could not be executed because both Yorck and Bülow, although in complete agreement with Wittgenstein's suggestion, refused to follow the Russians across the Vistula without explicit orders from Frederick William. "After receiving the reports that neither Bülow nor Yorck would advance," notes the Russian staff officer and future

military historian Aleksandr Mikhailovsky-Danilevsky, "Kutuzov was convinced of the impossibility of executing his initial intention of seizing
the offensive on the other side of the Oder and thus decided to await the
declaration of war against France by the Prussian cabinet by having the main
army move into cantons in the vicinity of Kalisch. Rest for the army was
completely necessary." Wittgenstein's army would likewise halt for a while
and quarter in the region of Driesen (Drezdenko). Yet Kutuzov did not want
to grant the French a reprieve. "You must dispatch a large number of small
*Streifkorps* [raiding parties] across the Oder to spread fear among the enemy,
not only at Berlin, but all the way to the Elbe," he instructed Wittgenstein
on 21 February. "At the same time, the partisans of the main army will turn
toward Saxony after crossing the Oder between Frankfurt and Glogau.
If the enemy remains on the right bank of the Oder and should Yorck's
corps unite with you, for which he will soon receive the order from his
cabinet, you must immediately attack the enemy and – if the opportunity
presents itself – march to Berlin. It is likely that by the time the Prussian
court declares its friendly sentiments toward us, its troops will be marching
from Breslau to Dresden. In this case, the main army also will depart; it
will serve as the reserve for both you as well as the Prussians."[41]

Kutuzov's proximity to the Russo-Prussian alliance negotiations at
the tsar's headquarters allowed him to predict their successful outcome.
Nevertheless, much diplomatic wrangling occurred within a span of eleven
days. Karl Nesselrode, whom Stein described as "a poor little cipher, 500,000
fathoms beneath his position," marginally served as Alexander's diplomatic
advisor. Rumiantsev remained Alexander's foreign minister in name, but the
tsar left him at St. Petersburg after the minister suffered a stroke in 1812.
Lieven maintains that Rumiantsev "was completely excluded from the
making of foreign policy," which was just what Alexander wanted and
needed as he prepared to launch a crusade against Napoleon. Lieven
describes Alexander as "the true foreign minister, unequivocally in charge
and in 1813 on the whole remarkably skillful and effective."[42]

Although Knesebeck gained a very favorable impression of the tsar's
disposition toward Prussia, he initially rejected the monarch's proposals
because Alexander offered no guarantee on the future of Prussian Poland.
Concerned that precious time would be wasted, Stein traveled the seventy-
three miles from Kalisch to Breslau in the hopes of expediting the process
by negotiating with Frederick William. Alexander, likewise tired of the
delays, sent the seasoned Russian diplomat Baron Johann von Anstedt to
assist Stein; both arrived on 25 February.[43] Stein fell deathly ill with a fever
and could do little. Regardless, Hardenberg and Frederick William, believing
the Prussian army to be nearing combat readiness, finally accepted the tsar's
revised proposal regarding Poland. According to Alexander, "the only way
to square the demands of Polish nationhood and Russian security would be

to unite as many Poles as possible in an autonomous kingdom whose ruler would also be the Russian monarch." The Prussians countered that, without the Polish provinces taken from them at Tilsit, "Prussia could not possess the strength or security essential for a great power." Alexander insisted that, at the conclusion of the war with Napoleon, Prussia would exchange most of the Polish territory acquired in the partitions of 1793 and 1795 for Allied conquests in Germany excluding Hanover. During a conversation between Knesebeck and the tsar on the 18th, the latter offered Saxony, claiming "that Prussia must necessarily be aggrandized." Alexander also pledged to leave Frederick William enough Polish territory to connect West Prussia and Silesia. Thus, Alexander vowed to restore Prussia to its pre-Tilsit stature, but not its pre-Tilsit frontiers. According to the military terms of the convention, a Prussian army of 80,000 men would join a Russian force of 150,000 in the war with France; both states pledged not to make a separate peace with Napoleon. On 26 February, Scharnhorst hurried from Breslau to Kalisch with royal approval to conclude the alliance, signing the Treaty of Kalisch on the 28th.[44]

Meanwhile, Lowe reached Stockholm to assess the attitude of the Swedes and their prince royal. News of Yorck's defection made Bernadotte realize that Prussia could replace Sweden as London's proxy in North Germany and compete with Stockholm for British gold. Lowe read a report submitted to Charles XIII by the Swedish government that "completely removed any doubt I may have had as to the possibility of a secret understanding between Napoleon and the prince royal and has at the same time convinced me that the former has not been so cunning a Machiavellian as I had supposed him to be." In addition, the report convinced him that Britain had nothing to fear of *future* collaboration between France and Sweden. In fact, Lowe concluded that the situation was "now more a quarrel between Bonaparte and Bernadotte than between Sweden and France" and that, should Napoleon fall, the principal obstacle to their reconciliation would be removed. Regardless, Bernadotte could not be counted on to adhere to an Anglo-Russian alliance out of the goodness of his heart. "He will pursue the interest of Sweden so long as he can through the medium of England and Russia and when that ceases his natural affection will revert to the side of France." Lowe also described the acquisition of Norway as well as "the establishment of an independent power in Germany which shall neither fear France or Russia" as being "decidedly" in Bernadotte's interest. This led Lowe to believe that "it is a piece of great good fortune to have him on our side and, so long as the establishment of such a power is our object, I think we may depend on his faithful adherence to the common cause."

Moreover, Lowe cautioned that some would view Bernadotte's "great military character" as reason to place him in command of an army. In his opinion, "at the head of a powerful and successful army," the Swedish prince royal "might not be brought so readily to stop" because aside from his "extravagant ambition," "the power and absolute independence of Sweden herself" would always be his main objective. In such a case, "Holstein, Jutland, and the Danish Isles might eventually become appendages to the possession of Pomerania." Claiming that "Bernadotte is not a man to miss opportunities," Lowe felt that Great Britain had all the more reason to "beware that no future combination of France and Sweden leads to such a result." At the moment, Lowe credited Bernadotte "for the moderation of his present views and the sincerity of his present alliance with us, but considering his military character and on what side his natural affections may possibly turn, it will be our duty as he becomes powerful to watch him." Although only the observations of Lowe rather than the British government's official view, these concerns provide an explanation for the patience the Allies would display toward Bernadotte during the war despite behavior that bordered on malicious duplicity.

Nevertheless, Lowe's interactions with Bernadotte increased the former's conviction that he had misjudged the latter. "Whatever may have been his former relations with France," wrote Lowe on 15 February, "there is no doubt whatever that he is at the present moment most sincere in his engagements with us and though among the most skeptical before I arrived in this country ... everything which I have been able to learn since my arrival here has removed all the doubts I formally entertained on the subject." Regardless, Lowe clearly recognized that Bernadotte held no "affection whatsoever for the English nation. It is the decided interest of his adopted country Sweden to stand well both with Russia and England. The great object of Sweden is Norway. This he cannot acquire without the assistance of Russia and England. France cannot assist him. Hence, his present connections. Russia has, I understand, given her consent." Lowe noted that Russia's approval indicated that St. Petersburg did not view Sweden's ambition to become "a commercial and maritime power" as threatening.

For the remainder of his time at Stockholm, Lowe finalized the details for the creation of the German Legion. Bernadotte hoped the Legion would number 9,000 infantry, 600–700 cavalry, and 300–400 gunners. As of 26 February, some 3,000 men of the Legion reached Narva after marching from Lopukhinka, where more than 600 sick had to be left behind.[45] The remaining troops stood somewhere "on the south side of the Gulf of Finland." Lowe and Bernadotte also discussed the deployment of Swedish and Russian forces to the continent. Including the German Legion, a Russian corps of 30,000 men under General Johann Peter Sukhtelen, and an estimated 40,000 Swedes, Bernadotte expected to command a force of more than 80,000 men. Lowe reported that "there [was] a great deal of apprehension manifested about the danger which the country may run from Danish invasion during the absence of the troops, and a good deal said about the opposition of the nobility in consequence of the withdrawing of so large a force from the country, and as a result the prince royal leaves a considerable organized force in the country to calm any inquietude; but I am inclined to believe that much more is said on the subject than is really felt."[46]

Despite the generous offers delivered by Hope, Bernadotte continued to drag his feet. Finally, after Thornton and Hope advanced £215,000 in bills of exchange to the Swedish treasury to cover the cost of mobilization and offered the prospect of negotiating another subsidy treaty later in the year, the crown prince signed the Treaty of Stockholm on 3 March 1813, creating what Castlereagh referred to as the Triple Alliance between Russia, Sweden, and Great Britain. The Anglo-Swedish portion of the alliance obligated London to provide the Swedes with a total of £1,000,000 by October 1813, at which time a new agreement could be arranged. In return, the British expected Bernadotte to field 30,000 men for the Spring Campaign against Napoleon. The British also received trade privileges in the Baltic. Considering the treaty obligated the Swedes to provide only 30,000 men, the £1,000,000 subsidy amounted to £33 per soldier for eight months of service. Compared to the offer that would be made to the Russians and Prussians of £2,000,000 for 230,000 men, the prince royal received a truly generous deal.

Bernadotte informed Thornton that he planned to personally lead an initial force of 3,000 Swedes and 3,000 Russians to Rügen to seize what he believed to be considerable stores of grain. He hoped his arrival on Rügen would distract the imperials and force Napoleon to increase the garrisons of Stettin and Magdeburg, thus reducing imperial field forces through strategic consumption. Although Swedish troops landed at Stralsund in mid March, only 7,000 had arrived by mid April. The corps reached half of its full complement by mid May, when Bernadotte joined his soldiers. As for the well-equipped German Legion, it marched from Narva to Königsberg between 16 and 30 April. Of the sick, 400 remained in Russia and their return to service was doubtful. Another 240 checked into Königsberg's General Hospital and likewise were not expected to return because of "disorders contracted during the severity of the last campaign." Native Germans made up the majority of the men as well as Dutch, Flemish, Swiss, "and a few men from almost every part of Europe except France, Spain, and Italy."[47]

Although having concluded an agreement with the British, Bernadotte came to the continent jaded and disillusioned with the tsar. Castlereagh sympathized with the prince royal, reminding Cathcart that Bernadotte was "entitled, by his own arrangements with Russia, to be at this moment in Norway, with all his own, and 35,000 of her troops. He is now on the continent ... at the instance of Great Britain."[48] Alexander attempted to appease him by continuing to promise a Russian corps and conveying the hope of adding a Prussian corps as soon as Bernadotte reached the

German theater, but the damage was done. In addition, a failed Russian diplomatic effort aimed at inducing Denmark to abandon Napoleon by hinting that the Danes could keep Norway truly soured the native French-man. Moreover, the Russian envoy to Copenhagen claimed that the tsar would not give Bernadotte a single man because 35,000 Russians under his command would make him too strong in Germany and he could not be trusted. All of these reasons combined to keep Bernadotte idle at Stralsund for the entire Spring Campaign of 1813.[49]

Nevertheless, Bernadotte appeared committed to the war against Napoleon. On 13 March, Thornton reported from Stockholm that the French emperor had made overtures to Bernadotte "not in an official or tangible form, but in private letters, written at the instance of Bonaparte by the prince's personal friends," offering money and territory in the form of Finland, but not Norway. "If anything can be called new in these propos-itions, it is the insinuation thrown out in the same manner to tempt the ambition of the prince royal, that Bonaparte would, after putting his armies once more on foot, retire from the military command, and confine himself to the civil concerns of the empire, leaving the military command of all his armies to the prince; and he assures him of his entire confidence in him for the future, as absolutely as if nothing had happened." Thornton guaran-teed Castlereagh that "any sort of reconciliation" between Bernadotte and Napoleon would be impossible.[50]

Frederick William's decision for war required him to appoint a field commander. Scharnhorst made his position clear by insisting that Blücher be named commander in chief of the Prussian army. In his opinion, Blücher alone did not fear Napoleon. Not every military man agreed with this choice, including Knesebeck, who lobbied for General Bogislav Friedrich von Tauentzien, who enjoyed the tsar's favor, as did Field-Marshal Friedrich Adolf von Kalkreuth. Blücher's opponents employed terms such as "old," "sick," and "reckless" to describe him, none of which could be considered untrue. Some of Scharnhorst's intimates likewise expressed concern. Boyen in particular contested the appointment. Basing his objections on Blücher's history of mental illness, Boyen purportedly insisted that the old man once claimed to be pregnant with an elephant. Scharnhorst quickly countered: "And if he has a thousand elephants in his belly, he must lead the army." Boyen maintains that Scharnhorst experienced considerable difficulty per-suading Frederick William. Just prior to his departure for Kalisch, he succeeded in convincing the king to at least appoint Blücher commander of the Prussian troops in Silesia. On 28 February 1813, Frederick William reinstated Blücher and assigned him "command of those troops who will be the first to move into the field."[51]

After Scharnhorst departed Breslau on 26 February, the measures to increase the size of the army slowed. Wanting to keep Napoleon guessing for as long as possible, the king recognized that the creation of a dozen new regiments could not be concealed from the French. He also questioned where the officers would be found to command the new units. Consequently, he not only refrained from issuing a declaration of war, but also refused to take further steps to expand the army until Scharnhorst identified a sufficient number of officers. The patriot party hoped the king would summon the nation to war, but the conservative monarch preferred to wage a conventional war rather than place the fate of his monarchy in the hands of commoners. His alliance agreements with Russia stipulated that Prussia would double its combat strength through the creation of a Landwehr, but he took no steps for this expedient outside East Prussia. With Scharnhorst at Kalisch, the mobilization came to a momentary standstill.

As for the Russians, the main army camped at Kalisch; Wintzingerode's advance corps reached Rawitsch (Rawicz), some sixty miles west of Kalisch and forty miles north of Breslau (see Map 1). The need to besiege or at least blockade the numerous French-held fortresses on the Vistula and throughout the Grand Duchy of Warsaw reduced the Russian main army to approximately 45,000 extremely tired soldiers. Wittgenstein's corps of 20,000 men reached the Oder north of Küstrin and 190 miles west of Kalisch. Bülow and General Karl Ludwig von Borstell completed the mobilization of the Pomeranian, East Prussian, and West Prussian Brigades. During a meeting on the 22nd, Wittgenstein managed to convince Yorck and Bülow to march with him to the Oder. He informed Kutuzov that his army would reach this river by 8 March. As soon as Frederick William declared war on France, Wittgenstein intended to cross the Oder and drive the French from Berlin.[52]

In accordance with Kutuzov's orders, Wittgenstein unleashed three *Streifkorps* (5,000 men total) under Chernishev, Alexander Benckendorff, and Tettenborn that wreaked havoc among the French along the left bank of the Oder. Chernishev and Tettenborn managed to penetrate Berlin on 20 February until French infantry and artillery ejected them. Despite his stepfather's demands to hold the Oder, Eugene withdrew to Berlin. Convinced that his troops could not hold the Prussian capital for long because he believed Wittgenstein's army already to be across the Oder, the viceroy evacuated Berlin on 4 March; Chernishev's Cossacks entered that same day. Eugene's forces retreated to the Elbe in two columns: the first turned to Wittenberg, the other to Magdeburg. Chernishev and Benckendorff hurried after them while Tettenborn proceeded to Hamburg. French garrisons still held the key Oder fortresses of Stettin, Küstrin, and Glogau, but the Prussian heartland was free: a vital prerequisite for Prussian mobilization.[53]

Scharnhorst did not have an easy task at Russian headquarters, despite enjoying the unparalleled respect of his new allies. "Up until the end of his life," asserts Mikhailovsky-Danilevsky, "he was the intermediary between the Russian and Prussian armies; he gained universal love through his noble qualities and strove to maintain friendly relations between the armies of both powers." Regardless, Kutuzov remained indifferent to his Prussian allies. Judging their quality by their performance in the War of the Fourth Coalition, the Russian commander in chief viewed them as more of a liability than an asset. "Blücher was of course highly respected as a courageous warrior and brave partisan," notes the Russian general and historian Mikhail Bogdanovich, "but no one considered him a field commander who could engage in a struggle with an equally strong army, let alone an army commanded by Napoleon himself." Moreover, Kutuzov either knew little of the tsar's plans to materially restore Prussia or cared little to support it. Despite Scharnhorst's efforts, he could not make Kutuzov more favorably disposed to Prussia.[54]

Nevertheless, Alexander needed the Prussians if he wished to secure his military and political objectives. In order for the Prussians to provide an effective army that could shoulder the burden until Russia's reserves reached Central Europe, the Russian army needed to advance beyond the Vistula. If not, the Prussian heartland would remain in French hands, thus critically impeding the mobilization of Frederick William's army. Moreover, the Russians could not concede the Oder to Napoleon: allowing him to begin the next campaign from this river would place the emperor too close to the Poles and the Allies too far from the Austrians. An advance into Saxony offered the prospect of electrifying the South Germans and convincing their princes to abandon Napoleon in his hour of need. From Saxony, the Allies could strike forth in the hope of disrupting Napoleon's mobilization of South Germany and wrecking the timetable of his next offensive. Yet the advantages of advancing further west needed to be weighed against the problems of drawing the exhausted Russians further away from their base of operations on the Niemen and the reinforcements and supplies coming from the Russian heartland. Without Austria or the Poles, many in the Allied camp felt that the Russians could not pass the Vistula. Finally, by continuing to advance, the Russian army would be further reduced by strategic consumption, making the Allies vulnerable to a counteroffensive by larger imperial forces led by Napoleon. General Robert Wilson conceptualizes the Allied dilemma in his journal entry on 5 March 1813: "Our plan of campaign is not yet settled. It certainly would be expedient to advance and to prevent a further concentration of [French] forces upon the Elbe ... [but] we are masters of no fortress on the Vistula or the Oder, and ... the Austrian contingent ... paralyzes Russia and Prussia because Austria will not make a separate treaty of peace."[55]

Despite these complicated considerations as well as Kutuzov's aversion to the war, he and Scharnhorst made several important decisions. Russian leadership of the war effort appeared obvious to all involved, yet the issue of overall command required a formal declaration. According to Mikhailovsky-Danilevsky, the Russians "proposed that the most senior in rank should assume command; Scharnhorst replied that it definitely would be appropriate if a Russian was in command 'because,' he said, 'my countrymen act only as auxiliaries; thus the Russians must, as the main leaders of the war, have the preference'." Kutuzov assumed the role of Allied commander in chief but Blücher received command of a "southern" army consisting of Wintzingerode's corps and most of the Prussian troops assembling in Silesia. Wittgenstein received command of the "northern" army containing corps commanded by Yorck, Bülow, and the Russian general Grigory Berg. With part of the Pomeranian Brigade, Borstell would hold the lower Elbe against the French forces at Stralsund and Hamburg while Tauentzien invested Stettin with the remaining units: 6,000 infantry, 600 cavalry, and 2 batteries supported by two Cossack Regiments. *Streifkorps* under Dörnberg, Tettenborn, and Chernishev as well as the Lützow *Freikorps* (paramilitary partisans) would swarm the enemy's flanks, cut communications, and intercept supplies, arms, reinforcements, and couriers. They would proceed along the left bank of the Elbe through Hanover to Kassel, destroy the Kingdom of Westphalia, and summon the people to rise against the French.[56]

According to Bogdanovich, the Prussians themselves could not agree on a plan of operations and so presented the tsar with two. "Knesebeck," he continues, "who had the reputation of a great strategist, suggested having the united troops of Blücher and Wittgenstein take the direction of Magdeburg against the viceroy to overwhelm him with superior forces, to undertake the investment of the Elbe fortresses, and to send light troops to the former Prussian states and Westphalia to encourage the people to revolt. Yet the absolute confidence the tsar had in Scharnhorst won him approval for his plan of operations." Bearing the unwieldy and ambiguous title of "The Arrangement with the Russians on the Operations of General Scharnhorst," this plan actually sacrificed the initiative to the French. Drafted at Kalisch on 1 or 2 March 1813, the document states that "the movement of the Allied army initially will be determined by that of the enemy, but later the opposite case will most likely arise. The enemy enjoys the advantages of the fortresses and the fortified crossings over the rivers, thus widening for the Allies the theater of war on the Elbe to the right and left and leaving them with no advantageous strategic, dominant position."

The "Arrangement" further indicated that the Russians favored having separate army groups converge on the French along both banks of the Elbe and insisted that operations follow this general outline. Wittgenstein's northern army would advance to Berlin while Blücher's southern army would march on Dresden. With Tormasov's army, Kutuzov would follow three marches behind, "on three to four parallel roads to ease supply" along a front broad enough to support either Wittgenstein or Blücher, whose armies received two tasks. First, the two forward Allied armies should not hesitate to inflict maximum damage on the enemy to keep him off balance. In addition, "the two foremost armies must raid the entire land with detachments to the right and left so that one will be the overall master of the land and the resources of war." Second, the Allied plan did not neglect to calculate the risk of conceding central position to the French. Consequently, Blücher and Wittgenstein would determine the march direction of the main enemy force, jointly advance against it, and avoid the danger of being destroyed individually. If Kutuzov could not arrive in time to directly order their movements, Wittgenstein and Blücher would first agree over the steps to be taken and then coordinate their movements accordingly, uniting if need be, and determining by seniority their command relationship.

The second half of the "Arrangement" provided scenarios of various French operations but offered few guidelines for an Allied offensive. In fact, the document stated only that, after reaching Berlin, Wittgenstein would immediately turn south if the French remained at the Oder, "to bring the enemy between him and Blücher's corps and attack the enemy jointly from two sides." Both parties emphatically agreed on the necessity of flooding Thuringia, North Germany, and Westphalia with irregular forces in the form of *Streifkorps* and *Freikorps* to take advantage of the Coalition's superiority in cavalry. Other than these obvious expedients, the Allies planned to react to the moves of their adversary. If the main French force advanced through Dresden and Torgau in the direction of Warsaw, Wittgenstein and Blücher would unite and operate against it jointly or in unison with Tormasov's army. Conversely, should the French attempt to drive through Saxony between Lusatia and the Bohemian frontier, Blücher would take a defensive position to fix the enemy's front while Wittgenstein attempted a strategic envelopment of the French left and rear, although "time and circumstances" would determine if this plan could be executed. The "Arrangement" did not include provisions for Wittgenstein's next move should he reach Berlin and find that the French had evacuated the Oder. Nor did Blücher receive a task beyond reaching Dresden. "Concerning operations on the other side of the Elbe," concludes Scharnhorst, "nothing can be decided beforehand; it is highly probable that we will soon encounter considerable enemy forces. Operations will be conducted in accordance with the disposition or movements of these forces."[57]

Armchair generals can certainly view the "Arrangement" with skepticism and wonder when the numerous lessons Napoleon had taught his adversaries over the years would be heeded. Conceding the initiative and central position to an adversary who had recently lost 500,000 men on the Russian steppe does not appear to be a blueprint for rapid success. Moreover, 120 miles separate Dresden and Berlin, which served as the respective operational goals for Blücher and Wittgenstein. At such a distance, direct mutual support appeared highly doubtful. Until the armies converged and reduced the gap between them, Wittgenstein could only pose a strategic threat to a French force that took the offensive against Blücher and the same for the Prussian general should the French target Wittgenstein. In addition, the expectations for the Russian main army were laughable. Almost 225 miles separated Kalisch from Dresden, while 230 miles extended between Kalisch and Berlin. As noted, 120 miles would separate the two army groups at Dresden and Berlin. Kutuzov's plan to march along a broad front and serve as a central reserve or even unite with one of the two army groups seems overly optimistic, considering the condition of the Russian army. Thus, the plan established by the "Arrangement" appeared to be a poor imitation of Napoleon's famed *bataillon carré* of 1806.

Nevertheless, numerous concerns demanded caution from both the Russians and the Prussians. As for the former, their exhausted army needed time to rest, reorganize, and resupply, and for its reserves to reach the theater of war. "We were quite expended," explains Wilson's journal entry of 1 March, "we had not 60,000 effectives under arms, and many guns had not *one* artilleryman." According to Boyen, the grueling march to Saxony, the difficulty of moving up replacements, the consequences of strategic consumption to occupy Poland, and the hesitation of the Prussians to make a decision caused a complete standstill in the movements of the Russian main army. Moreover, although Tormasov's army possessed a massive artillery train of 274 guns, it numbered only 32,000 combatants. Visiting the tsar's headquarters at Kalisch in early April, the extremely thin Russian regiments shocked Frederick William. Although the Russians took a page from Napoleon's own manual of deceptive misinformation to loudly claim that reserve armies of 100,000 and 75,000 men would soon reach the theater, they knew better, as time would tell: by May only 20,000 reinforcements had arrived. As for the Prussians, Scharnhorst could hardly plan bold offensive operations from an army he *hoped* would number at least 60,000 men by the time his sovereign declared war. Consequently, a strategic defensive with tactical offensive strikes by irregular forces appeared to offer the best chance of results for the moment. Initial Allied operations needed to liberate and then hold as much of Prussia as possible to complete the mobilization. Equally important, the Russians needed time to complete their reorganization. Finally, given a few extra weeks, Allied diplomacy could succeed in attracting additional friendly forces which would add much needed resources to the Coalition's war effort. Wilson's journal entry of 5 March captures Kutuzov's thoughts: "As the Russians certainly do not have 40,000 disposable men at present and Prussia not even so many, the enemy, in consequence of our dislocation and marches, has many great advantages: indeed if Austria fails us we can make no contest."[58]

7 Alexander and Frederick William reviewing the troops

Prussia's mobilization resumed at a furious pace after Scharnhorst returned to Breslau on 6 March 1813. "Since my entrance into the Prussian territory," remarked Lowe, "I have seen nothing but troops and recruits marching. There has been no declaration on the part of the king, but there is no doubt whatsoever of his intentions." Gneisenau added: "There is a confidence that I cannot justify, yet one can do much with goodwill!" Three days later, Blücher received the royal order appointing him commander of the Prussian II Corps.[59] Manpower remained the most pressing issue. Contrary to the stories that later circulated, the *Krümper* system did not provide 150,000 trained reservists. The numbers produced by the mobilization in Silesia provide the proof. While reservists increased the battalions and squadrons to a war footing, the mobilization produced only an additional five battalions and two squadrons in Silesia. As a result, Blücher's II Corps consisted of 16,800 infantry, 6,000 cavalry, and 100 guns.[60] Regarding organization, the corps contained three combined-arms brigades, each consisting of six to nine battalions, four to eight squadrons, and three batteries. According to Scharnhorst's design, the corps also possessed a cavalry reserve of twenty squadrons and two horse batteries distributed among two brigades as well as an artillery reserve that consisted of a few guns, the ammunition columns, and the two pioneer companies. Including staff and support personnel, Blücher's II Corps accounted for 645 officers and 26,510 men of the 71,382 personnel that constituted the Prussian field army on 16 March. Reserves still mobilizing, garrison troops, and support personnel provided an additional 56,012 men.[61]

Frederick William's 9 March 1813 instructions to Blücher also specified that a portion of the Silesian reserve troops under the command of General Ernst Julius Schuler von Senden would form a siege corps of five battalions, three squadrons, and one and one-half foot batteries to invest Glogau and its garrison of 6,000 men and 80 heavy guns approximately seventy miles north-northeast of Breslau. Like Tauentzien besieging Stettin, Schuler would receive his orders directly from Kutuzov. For rear-area security and to protect the iron works of Upper Silesia from the Poles, the king also ordered the formation of a combined-arms detachment of 800 infantry and the Neumark Dragoon Regiment.[62]

The founding of the Iron Cross occurred on 10 March 1813, the late queen's birthday. On the 11th, Frederick William promoted Scharnhorst to general-lieutenant and named him Quartermaster-General (chief of staff) of the Prussian Army.[63] Two days later, the king declared war on France. Frederick William hosted the Russian monarch for four days at Breslau. On the 15th, the tsar orchestrated his entry into Silesia's capital and inspected the Prussian troops. According to Cathcart: "I have already stated that the Prussian army is in the best state of preparation: nothing can exceed the condition of that part which was assembled at Breslau on the emperor's [Alexander] arrival and it is impossible to exaggerate the enthusiasm which has been exhibited by all ranks of persons throughout the Prussian dominions or the demonstrations of joy with which the emperor was received." "He was expected early in the morning," recalls Henrik Steffens, a physics professor at the University of Breslau, "but we waited in vain; the forenoon passed; we were all tired and hungry. It was almost dark before he arrived: he was received with acclamations by the inhabitants, but the enthusiasm would have been livelier had not everybody been worn out by hunger and impatient waiting."[64]

To summon his subjects to war, Frederick William authorized the famous "An mein Volk" proclamation on 17 March 1813 after much debate among the Prussian leadership. In Gneisenau's opinion, a draft penned by Ancillon failed to capture the needs of the state. "The manifesto," he explained to Hardenberg, "must be submitted to meticulous discussion. If it is French and not German in character, it will not appeal to our nation. Dazzling phrases gleam where feelings, repressed feelings, should be expressed." Evening meetings at Hardenberg's quarters with Scharnhorst, Gneisenau, Thiele, and state councilors Theodor Gottlieb von Hippel and Johann Ludwig von Jordan led to the rejection of Ancillon's draft. Instead, the group presented Frederick William with the "An mein Volk" summons drafted by Hippel with some modification by Hardenberg. After making a few changes himself, Frederick William published the proclamation in the *Schlesische privilegirte Zeitung* on 20 March 1813:

### "To my people"

There is no need to explain to my loyal subjects or to any German the reasons for the war that is about to begin. They lie plainly before the eyes of an awakened Europe.

We succumbed to the superior forces of France. The peace that followed deprived me of my people and, far from bringing us blessings, it inflicted upon us deeper wounds than the war itself, sucking out the very marrow of the country. Our principal fortresses remained in the hands of the enemy, and agriculture, as well as the highly developed industries of our towns, was crippled. The freedom of trade was hampered and thus the sources of commerce and prosperity cut off. The country was left prey to the ravages of destitution.

I had hoped, by the punctilious fulfillment of the engagements I had entered into, to lighten the burdens of my people, and even to convince the French emperor that it would be in his own best interest to leave Prussia its independence. But my purest and best intentions were of no avail against insolence and faithlessness, and it became all too obvious that the emperor's treaties would gradually ruin us even more surely than his wars. The moment has come when we can no longer harbor the slightest illusion regarding our situation.

Brandenburgers, Prussians, Silesians, Pomeranians, Lithuanians! You know what you have borne for the past seven years; you know the sad fate that awaits you if we do not bring this war to an honorable end. Think of the times gone by: of the Great Elector, of the Great Frederick! Remember the blessings for which your forefathers fought under their leadership and which they paid for with their blood: freedom of conscience, national honor, independence, commerce, industry, and education. Look at the great example of our powerful allies, the Russians; look at the Spaniards and the Portuguese. For such objects as these even weaker peoples have gone forth against mightier enemies and returned in triumph. Recall the heroic Swiss and the people of the Netherlands.

Great sacrifices will be demanded from every class of the people, for our undertaking is a great one, and the number and resources of our enemies far from insignificant. But would you rather not make these sacrifices for the Fatherland and for your own rightful king than for a foreign ruler, who, as he has shown by many examples, will use you and your sons and the last ounce of your strength for ends that mean nothing to you? Faith in God, perseverance, and the powerful aid of our allies will bring us victory as the reward of our honest efforts. Whatever sacrifices may be required of us as individuals will be outweighed by the sacred rights for which we make them, and for which we must fight to a victorious end unless we are willing to cease to be Prussians or Germans.

This is the final, decisive struggle; upon it depends our independence, our prosperity, and our existence. There are no other alternatives but an honorable peace or a heroic end. You would willingly face even the latter for honor's sake, for without honor no Prussian or German could live. Yet we can await the outcome with confidence. God and our own firm purpose will bring victory to our cause and with it an assured and glorious peace and the return of happier times.

After reading the proclamation, a smiling St.-Marsan supposedly sneered: "Is this it? I expected them to issue a much stronger justification."[65]

On that same day, the king also authorized the publication of decrees to raise a national Landwehr and issued the "An mein Kriegsheer" proclamation:

### "To my army"

Many times you have expressed the desire to fight for the freedom and independence of the Fatherland. The moment has come! There is not one among the ranks of the people who does not feel this. Youths and young men hurry from all over to voluntarily take up arms. What is voluntary for them is duty for you as members of the army. For you, who are consecrated to defend the Fatherland, this is justified to demand; for them this must be requested.

See how so many sacrifice everything that is most dear to them to give their lives along with you for the cause of the Fatherland. Fulfill your sacred duty doubly. Remember your duty on the day of battle as well as during times of deprivation and hardship, and show your inner strength! The ambitions of each individual, whether he is of the highest or the lowest rank in the army, must disappear in the big picture: if you can feel for the Fatherland you cannot think about yourself. Those who are selfish will earn disgrace; only the common welfare matters. This is all that matters. Victory comes from God! Through obedience and duty demonstrate that you are worthy of his sacred protection. Courage, perseverance, loyalty, and strict discipline will be your glory! Follow the example of your forefathers and you will be worthy of being remembered by your descendants!

Be assured that those who distinguish themselves will be rewarded; but profound shame and punishment will be for those who neglect their duty.

Your king will always be with you; with him the crown prince and the princes of his house. They will fight with you. They and the entire people will fight with you and to our side and our aid as well as Germany's has come a brave people [the Russians], who through noble deeds have won their independence. They trusted their sovereign, their leaders, their strength, and God was with them! So will be the case with you! For we too wage this great struggle for the independence of the Fatherland. Let trust in God, courage, and perseverance be our watchwords![66]

Finally, Frederick William issued instructions to Blücher and Yorck, likewise on 17 March, concerning the punishment for crimes against the security of the army. According to the monarch, he demanded harshness "not because he believed that there could be a traitor to the cause of the country among his people, or in Germany, but for the weak, especially among the civil servants, who are inclined to give in to threats and who are much more likely to commit misdeeds." Hardenberg received a copy with instructions to make the decree a public statute. The king's message was clear: in this war to the death, the shameful capitulations that crowned Prussia's humiliation in 1806 would not be repeated. During a 30 March conversation with Wilson at Crossen, Frederick William gave a short yet interesting summary of how he perceived these steps: "He told me 'that for his own part he had taken his stand; that he was resolved to be an independent sovereign, or lose all but his honor; that he trusted that England would support him, and that, whatever might be the event, he would make a struggle that should cost Bonaparte dear'. He spoke and felt as a man conscious of, and equal to, his difficulties; and I am confident that he will do his duty."[67]

Meanwhile, Alexander remained adamant about bolstering the military convention with a political alliance, to which the Prussians assented on 19 March. Signed by Stein and Nesselrode for the Russians and Hardenberg and Scharnhorst for the Prussians, the Russo-Prussian Treaty of Breslau provided the political supplement to the military alliance forged at Kalisch. According to its terms, the Russians affirmed their agreements to restore Prussia's pre-Tilsit material strength. As stated in the Kalisch convention, Prussia would receive compensation in Germany for the loss of Polish territory to Russia.[68] The British bolstered the alliance by dispatching a convoy to the Baltic carrying 54 cannon as well as 23,000 stand of arms to be shared by the Russians and Prussians.[69] London also undertook to restore official diplomatic relations with Prussia after Frederick William formally declared the abolition of Napoleon's commercial restrictions in North Germany on 20 March. In return, Castlereagh dispatched Charles Stewart as ambassador to Prussia with instructions to offer a sizeable subsidy.[70]

Stewart sailed from Yarmouth aboard the frigate HMS *Nymphe* and eventually joined Cathcart at Allied Headquarters at Dresden in April. The British had numerous official and unofficial envoys accompanying the Allied armies but Cathcart and Stewart held the most sway. "In their capacity of accredited ministers at the headquarters of the armies of the Sovereigns of Russia and Prussia," Cathcart and Stewart were tasked with "making the British government acquainted with all the details of military arrangements and movements, including those of His Royal Highness the Prince Royal of Sweden, to whom Sir Charles Stewart had special letters of authorization as to all matters of a military nature, although the political and diplomatic affairs connected with the court of Stockholm were conducted by Mr. Thornton, who, as British minister at that court, attended the Prince Royal's headquarters." Both envoys received instructions from Castlereagh dated 8 April to reach "a satisfactory arrangement with the two Allied courts [Russia and Prussia]." Castlereagh expected little difficulty in reaching an accord with Russia and Prussia, but gave thought to the bigger picture. "The political arrangement of Europe, in a larger sense, is more difficult at this early moment to decide on. I see many inconveniences in premature conclusions, but we ought not to be unprepared." Thus, "as an outline to reason from," he sent the Pitt Plan, on which was founded the Third Coalition in 1805. To Cathcart he wrote that "while some of the suggestions may now be inapplicable," the Pitt Plan proved to be "so masterly an outline for the restoration of Europe," that he wanted to know if Alexander's thoughts remained the same eight years later.[71]

In France, Napoleon decreed the formation of a new Grande Armée numbering 300,000 men on 12 March 1813. According to his plans, the army would consist of eleven infantry corps composed of thirty-nine divisions.

**8** General William Schaw Cathcart, 1755–1843

9 General Sir Charles Stewart, 1778–1854

The emperor later added two additional corps: XII and XIII. With the exception of IX Corps, the framework for each corps already existed but manpower shortages prevented Napoleon from achieving the numbers he sought. Regardless, the Grande Armée reached 202,000 men by 25 April. The horrendous losses of troopers and horses in 1812 meant that cavalry remained critically insufficient. Organized in three corps, the cavalry of the new army numbered just short of 11,000 officers and men on 1 May. On 26 March, Napoleon officially divided the army into two groups: the Army of the Elbe and the Army of the Main. The former, commanded by Eugene, consisted of XI Corps (three divisions), the Corps of Observation of the Elbe (five divisions), I Corps (two divisions), II Corps (two divisions), VII Corps (two divisions), and I and II Cavalry Corps. On paper, the emperor's own Army of the Main, temporarily commanded by Marshal Ney, included III, IV, and VI Corps, each containing four divisions. In less than three months since the last French units crossed the Niemen, more than 800 cannon and 2,000 caissons were rumbling east on the roads to the Elbe to replace the equipment lost in Russia.[72]

    The Russian disaster did little to shake Napoleon's well-known tendency to exaggerate the size of his own forces while underestimating those of his enemy. "The 300,000 men that compose the four corps of observation are in movement, and the situation will change shortly," he wrote encouragingly to his stepson on 2 March. On the same day, he explained to his brother Jerome that according to the latest reports, all enemy forces – which at this time consisted only of the Russians – appeared to be at Kalisch. Already contemplating a Russian advance on Dresden "to turn the Oder and the Elbe," he informed Jerome that "I have ordered the viceroy to extend his line of operations through Magdeburg, Kassel, and Wesel. If the viceroy is forced to abandon the Elbe, he will defend the Weser and Kassel." Napoleon did not seem very confident that Eugene would be able to hold the Russians, predicting they would cross the Elbe and reach Dresden. Regardless, he did not believe the Russians could achieve much more after gaining the Saxon capital. "You see," continues his letter to Jerome, "the Russian army at Dresden will not harass or threaten anything, because the division in the citadel at Erfurt is well supplied and protected from a *coup de main*. Things being arranged the way they are, when I believe the time has come, I will travel to Mainz, and if the Russians advance, I will arrange the appropriate dispositions, but we badly need to make it to May."[73]

On 5 March 1813, Napoleon drafted general instructions for Eugene. If the Allies forced him to evacuate Berlin, he would retreat to Magdeburg. If driven from the Elbe, he would take a position in the Harz Mountains to protect Kassel and Hanover (see Map 2). If ejected from there, he would defend the line of the Weser. On 6 March, he informed Eugene that the situation would not change much until the beginning of April, at which time Napoleon could move up two observation corps to "support your right and keep in check whatever the enemy wants to send through. But I do not intend to take the offensive until mid May; not counting your army, I will have 200,000 men in hand with suitable cavalry."[74]

Much has been made of Napoleon's anger over Eugene's evacuation of Berlin. Eugene reported the retreat from the Prussian capital on 4 March; Napoleon received his letter on the 9th. While the emperor's biting criticism certainly stung his stepson, Napoleon's instructions placed greater emphasis on defending the 32nd *division militaire*, the heart of Napoleonic Germany. On the 7th, two days *before* he learned that Eugene evacuated Berlin, Napoleon lectured him on the importance of Magdeburg, reiterating his instructions of 5 March: "You must defend Magdeburg, [thus] covering the 32nd Military Division, the Kingdom of Westphalia, Hanover, and Kassel. You will take a good position in front of Magdeburg, occupying Torgau with a good Saxon garrison. If you are forced to quit the Elbe, the Harz Mountains will be your first line, covering Kassel and Hanover; if forced from there, your second line will be between the Harz and Kassel; finally, the Weser."[75]

On 11 March, Napoleon finally revealed his plans for an offensive to Eugene. From Wittenberg, the Army of the Elbe would march through

Havelberg to Stettin, followed by the Army of the Main moving northeast from Leipzig. At this time, Prussia remained France's ally. Thus, the emperor referred to this as "a natural movement that would be easily stolen from the enemy." At Stettin, the combined armies of the Elbe and the Main, some 300,000 men according to Napoleon's estimate, would cross the Oder and march to promptly relieve Danzig, which Napoleon marked as the principal goal of the French army. From there, the French would master the lower Vistula. He figured that this operation would gain him ten marches on the Russians, whom he placed at Dresden, Glogau, and Warsaw. His plans for the defensive remained the same with the principal goal being to protect the 32nd Military Division and Westphalia; he added Hamburg to the list as well.[76] "We can definitely take the offensive at the beginning of May," concluded the emperor. "By this time, Danzig may be besieged, so it will be necessary to arrive at this place and raise the siege before the end of June, which can be done only after deceiving the enemy by debouching from Havelberg."[77]

Three days later, he admitted the likelihood of Prussia declaring against him, using history to encourage his stepson: "It appears that Prussia has not yet decided to take the field against us. However, due to the treason of General Yorck, and the countenance given since, it does not appear that the cabinet of Berlin will remain our ally for long." Napoleon downplayed the number of troops the Prussians could field, reminding Eugene that Prussia's population numbered only four million. Prior to Tilsit, when Frederick William ruled over twice as many subjects, he managed to field only 150,000 men for the Jena Campaign. "Despite all the efforts of the king," continued Napoleon, "he certainly will not have more than 40,000 men for the month of May, of which 25,000 at most will be available as a result of the need to guard Silesia and the fortresses of Graudenz, Kolberg, and Pillau, and having troops to police the country. After the battle of Jena, in the winter campaign that followed, despite all the efforts made by the Prussians, they were never able to field more than 10,000 men. There are many sick in General Yorck's corps." Napoleon also informed Eugene that all information he had thus far receiving concerning Alexander's army indicated that the Russians had many sick as well. "Whatever they say, a large corps is before Danzig," he assured Eugene. "It is true that they have not entered Warsaw, that they have summoned the National Guard to serve, and that they have not established any communication between the city and the army. Is it to hide their situation and to prevent many men from cramming into the city to take refuge against the cold?"[78]

Napoleon's determination to hold Dresden during the Fall Campaign of 1813 is well documented. However, on 15 March, he advised Eugene to sacrifice Dresden in favor of North Germany. The following offers excellent insight regarding the importance Napoleon placed on North Germany as well as the frustration of having so few combat-ready divisions:

> I know the big question is Dresden but it is a question we must ignore. The arrangements you have made up to this the point will not defend this city because if the enemy seriously wants to march on Dresden, what will the 31st Division and the additional six battalions you gave the prince d'Eckmühl [Davout] do? This is nothing. You cannot defend Dresden and you risk failure by jeopardizing this corps if the enemy marches there in strength. In order to defend Dresden, you should move there with all your forces ... *but then Westphalia, Hanover and the 32nd Military Division are exposed: these are the most important points, and I would rather see the enemy at Leipzig, Erfurt, and Gotha instead of Hanover and Bremen.* It is a pity that the 1st and 2nd Corps of Observation of the Rhine and the Corps of Observation of Italy are still not ready to move on Dresden, this is what I will have them do as soon as they can, but I do not want to compromise the whole destiny of the next campaign by sending forward corps whose artillery is not complete and with so few cavalry that they would be exposed to an inglorious defeat.[79]

Wittgenstein's eventual advance to Magdeburg and Blücher's to Leipzig would render Napoleon's offensive project to regain the Vistula unfeasible. Yet the emperor never completely abandoned this "master plan." Following Prussia's betrayal, Napoleon added the capture of Berlin as the first step in this master plan of reaching the Vistula and strategically enveloping the Russian army. For the time being, Napoleon's projected timetable sought to commence offensive operations at the beginning of May. This required Eugene to hold the Elbe against both Wittgenstein and Blücher, with fewer than 50,000 men, for the entire month of April. Such expectations presented the Allies with a golden opportunity to crush the viceroy, reach the German heartland, and ignite a national uprising against the French. Should they fail to defeat or contain Eugene and fall short of reaching the states of the Rheinbund, Napoleon would be free to exact his blood tax. Despite the horrendous losses in Russia, he would force his German allies to again surrender their men to fight for the French Eagle. Would the Allies take advantage of the vacuum in Central Europe created by Napoleon's loss of 500,000 men in Russia?

## Notes

1 Quoted in Clark, *Iron Kingdom*, 356; Jany, *Preußische Armee*, IV:41, 61–62; Shanahan, *Prussian Military Reforms*, 173–78.
2 Chandler, *Campaigns of Napoleon*, 849, 852–53.
3 Schroeder, *European Politics*, 449; Webster, *The Foreign Policy of Castlereagh*, I:86–91.

4 "Aufruf an Preußen," GStA PK, IV. HA, Rep. 15 A, Nr. 66; Seydlitz, *Tagebuch*, 278; Droysen, *Yorck*, I:266; Boyen, *Erinnerungen*, ed. Nippold, II:330; D'Ussel, *La défection de la Prusse*, 146; Holleben and Caemmerer, *Frühjahrsfeldzuges 1813*, I:26. Many documents covering this period can be found in GStA PK, IV HA Rep. 15 A Nr. 147, "Korrespondenz Bülows mit der westpreussischen Regierung über Aushebung von Mannschaften und Pferden sowie Nekleidung und Verpflegung," Rep. 15 A Nr. 48, "Stärke, Ausrüstung, und Formierung der Truppenteile des Korps Bülow," and Rep. 15 A Nr. 154, "Korrespondenz von Bülow mit Major von Krauseneck, Kommandant der Festungen Graudenz, über Einberufung von Krümpern sowie Armierung der Festung beim Herannahen der russischen Truppen."

5 Boyen, *Erinnerungen*, ed. Schmidt, II:552.

6 Bogdanovich, *Geschichte des Krieges*, Ia:14–17; Bernhardi, *Toll*, II:373; Mikhailovsky-Danilevsky, *Denkwürdigkeiten*, 8; Petre, *Napoleon's Last Campaign*, 6; Holleben and Caemmerer, *Frühjahrsfeldzuges 1813*, I:25; Leggiere, *Napoleon and Berlin*, 29–30; Lieven, *Russia Against Napoleon*, 303; see *ibid.*, 287–91, for his analysis of Alexander's reasons for continuing the war against Napoleon.

7 Lieven, *Russia Against Napoleon*, 285.

8 Holleben and Caemmerer, *Frühjahrsfeldzuges 1813*, I:27–28.

9 See Maude, *Leipzig Campaign*, 51.

10 Droysen, *Yorck*, I:350–53, 357; Macdonald to Maret, Stalgen, 10 December 1812, in Clausewitz, *Hinterlassene Werke*, VII:225–26.

11 Quoted in Droysen, *Yorck*, I:362.

12 The best accounts of these events are Droysen, *Yorck*, I:336–77; Clausewitz, *Hinterlassene Werke*, VII:216–33; and Henckel von Donnersmarck, *Erinnerungen*, 163–74. Supporting material can be found in Holleben and Caemmerer, *Frühjahrsfeldzuges 1813*, I:86; H. W. Koch, *A History of Prussia*, 195–96; Maude, *Leipzig Campaign*, 50–52.

13 Droysen does not comment on this statement, which Koch quotes in *A History of Prussia*, 196. Instead, the statement is found almost verbatim in the report Yorck wrote to Frederick William on 30 December and which Droysen, *Yorck*, I:367, reproduces in full.

14 Quoted in Holleben and Caemmerer, *Frühjahrsfeldzuges 1813*, I:86.

15 Henckel von Donnersmarck, *Erinnerungen*, 173–74; Seeley, *Stein*, III:72–73; Bach, *Hippel*, 165.

16 Boyen, *Erinnerungen*, ed. Nippold, II:309; Henckel von Donnersmarck, *Erinnerungen*, 174; Lieven, *Russia Against Napoleon*, 292. Yorck's act, notes Henry Kissinger, "became a symbol of national independence and freedom from foreign bondage." See Kissinger, *A World Restored*, 47.

17 Sherwig, *Guineas and Gunpowder*, 283. See Leggiere, *Napoleon and Berlin*, 28–54, for the details of these diplomatic preparations in the early months of 1813.

18 According to Jomini in *Précis politique et militaire*, I:223, "The spirit that animated this country from the cruel treatment that it had been subjected to after the battle of Jena and by the Treaty of Tilsit was too well known to make it possible to satisfy it through concessions. It was obvious that the king would be carried in spite of himself, and indeed his cabinet already was treating with the Russians." See Schroeder, *European Politics*, 452–66; Lieven, *Russia Against Napoleon*, 290.

19 Add MSS, 20111, 17: Lowe to Bunbury, Königsberg, 13 March 1813; Bogdano-vich, *Geschichte des Krieges*, Ia:11; Lieven, *Russia Against Napoleon*, 292–93; Wilson, *Private Diary*, I:271.

20 The most thorough English-language account of Stein's activities at Königsberg is Seeley, *Stein*, III:39–71. Service in the Landwehr was made obligatory for all men between ages 18 and 45; substitutes could be purchased. Parameters for service in the Landsturm would be established at a later date. See Shanahan, *Prussian Military Reforms*, 190–96, for a thorough discussion of the events in East Prussia.

21 "In Eastern Germany the peasantry had not received at Napoleon's hands those benefits which his rule had brought to Westphalians and Swabians: to them he was only the enemy and the oppressor, the author not of the Code, but of the Continental System": Atkinson, *A History of Germany*, 573.

22 Add MSS, 20111, 16: Lowe to Bunbury, Königsberg, 13 March 1813.

23 Bogdanovich, *Geschichte des Krieges*, Ia:214–17; Mikhailovsky-Danilevsky, *Denkwürdigkeiten*, 8; Petre, *Napoleon's Last Campaign*, 6; Holleben and Caem-merer, *Frühjahrsfeldzuges 1813*, I:47; Lieven, *Russia Against Napoleon*, 303.

24 Bach, *Hippel*, 165; Seeley, *Stein*, III:75.

25 Alexander to Frederick William, 6 and 21 January 1813, Bailleu, *Breifwechsel*, Nrs. 210 and 211, 240–42.

26 Shanahan, *Prussian Military Reforms*, 197–202.

27 Frederick William to Alexander, Breslau, 8 February 1813, Bailleu, *Briefwechsel*, Nr. 212, 242–43.

28 Sherwig, *Guineas and Gunpowder*, 283–84; Thornton to Castlereagh, Stockholm, 30 December 1812, CVC, VIII:283.

29 Stewart to Castlereagh, Hanover, 2 January 1813, CVC, IX:1–3.

30 Add MSS, 20111, 1–4: Lowe to Bunbury, at sea, 29 January 1813.

31 Webster, *The Foreign Policy of Castlereagh*, I:119; Sherwig, *Guineas and Gun-powder*, 285; Muir, *Britain and the Defeat of Napoleon*, 244–45. Duke Peter Frederick Louis of Holstein-Gottorp was descended from a cadet branch of the ruling house of Oldenburg. The younger of Peter's two sons, George, was married to Tsar Alexander's favorite sister, Grand Duchess Catherine Pavlovna.

32 Kutuzov to Wittgenstein, 2 February 1813, Rossiiskii Gosudarstvennyi Voenno-Istoricheskii Arkhiv (hereafter cited as RGVIA), f. VUA, op. 16, d. 3921, ll. 24b–25b.

33 CN, Nos. 19474 and 19500, XXIV:417, 437–40; Chandler, *Campaigns of Napoleon*, 866–67, 869–70. For a discussion of the problems of the Grande Armée of 1813, see *ibid.*, 867–69.

34 Kalisch provided "a central point" from where Alexander could "bring his negotiations with Prussia to a speedy conclusion, communicate with Austria, observe and endeavor to conciliate the Poles, and prepare for the campaign of 1813." See Cathcart, *Commentaries*, 113.

35 Alexander to Frederick William, Kladau, 15 February 1813, Bailleu, *Briefwechsel*, Nr. 214, 244–45.

36 Frederick William to Alexander, Breslau, 17 February 1813, Bailleu, *Briefwechsel*, Nr. 215, 245.

37 Kutuzov to Wittgenstein, Plock, 8 February 1813, RGVIA, f. VUA, op. 16, d. 3921, l. 33b; Mikhailovsky-Danilevsky, *Denkwürdigkeiten*, 22; Bogdanovich, *Geschichte des Krieges*, Ia:18–23.

38  Frederick William to Alexander, Breslau, 17 February 1813, Bailleu, *Briefwechsel*, Nr. 215, 245.
39  Alexander to Frederick William, Zbiersk, 24 February 1813, Bailleu, *Briefwechsel*, Nr. 217, 246–47. Frederick William did not respond to this letter.
40  Kutuzov to Wittgenstein, Plock, 17 February 1813, RGVIA, f. VUA, op. 16, d. 3921, l. 45b.
41  Bogdanovich, *Geschichte des Krieges*, Ia:23–24; Mikhailovsky-Danilevsky, *Denkwürdigkeiten*, 28–29; Kutuzov to Wittgenstein, Plock, 21 February 1813, RGVIA, f. VUA, op. 16, d. 3921, l. 58.
42  Seeley, *Stein*, III:145; Lieven, *Russia Against Napoleon*, 285.
43  Alexander to Frederick William, Zbiersk, 22 and 24 February 1813, Bailleu, *Breifwechsel*, Nrs. 216 and 217, 246–47.
44  Seeley, *Stein*, III:82; Lieven, *Russia Against Napoleon*, 299–300; Frederick William to Alexander, Breslau, 27 February 1813, Bailleu, *Briefwechsel*, Nr. 218, 248.
45  Atkinson points to the Legion's poor recruiting results as testimony that as of yet "there was no approach to disaffection or treachery among the Germans of the Grande Armée. Few of the prisoners enlisted, fewer still deserted the Grande Armée to join the Legion; and even if the privations they had endured may have accounted for their unwillingness to undergo new hardships under new colours, it also shows that the long-suffering Germans were not yet fully roused against Napoleon, or lacked the courage and the determination to risk anything for Germany." Some 150,000 Germans served in the Grande Armée of 1812. See Atkinson, *A History of Germany*, 569.
46  Add MSS, 20111, 5–7, 11–15: Lowe to Bunbury, Stockholm, 13, 15, and 20 February 1813; Lowe to Hope, Åbo, 26 February 1813; and Lowe to Bathurst, Stockholm, 21 February 1813.
47  Stewart, *Narrative*, 7; Thornton to Castlereagh, Stockholm, 3 February 1813, *CVC*, VIII:318; Sherwig, *Guineas and Gunpowder*, 286; Webster, *The Foreign Policy of Castlereagh*, 120; Add MSS, 20111, 23–26: Lowe to Cathcart, Bautzen, 16 May 1813, and Lowe to Bathurst, Bautzen, 16 May 1813.
48  Castlereagh to Cathcart, London, 28 April 1813, *CVC*, VIII:34.
49  Thornton was privy to a letter from Alexander to Bernadotte that gave the tsar's "most cordial assurances of the exertions he will make to fulfill his engagements with Sweden": Thornton to Castlereagh, Stockholm, 26 March 1813, *CVC*, VIII:347; Thornton to Cooke, Stockholm, 18 February 1813, *ibid.*, VIII:326–31; Castlereagh to Cathcart, London, 28 April 1813, *ibid.*, VIII:384; Muir, *Britain and the Defeat of Napoleon*, 244–47.
50  Thornton to Castlereagh, Stockholm, 13 March 1813, *CVC*, VIII:338–40.
51  *Blücher in Briefen*, ed. Colomb, 15; Blasendorff, *Blücher*, 182; Pertz and Delbrück, *Gneisenau*, II:530; Unger, *Blücher*, II:6; Bogdanovich, *Geschichte des Krieges*, Ia:71. Bogdanovich insists that Tauentzien enjoyed "the special good disposition of the tsar" and thus "made strong claims on the main command of the troops."
52  Holleben and Caemmerer, *Frühjahrsfeldzuges 1813*, 162–63; Unger, *Blücher*, II:10.
53  Chernishev to Wittgenstein, 29 February 1813, GStA PK, IV HA Rep. 15 A Nr. 22. Each *Streifkorps* consisted of four to six Don Cossack regiments and two guns. See Bogdanovich, *Geschichte des Krieges*, Ia:217; Mikhailovsky-Danilevsky, *Denkwürdigkeiten*, 31–33.

54 Mikhailovsky-Danilevsky, *Denkwürdigkeiten*, 35; Bogdanovich, *Geschichte des Krieges*, Ia:40; Müffling, *Aus meinem Leben*, 31. Clausewitz sounds a note of bitterness when explaining to his wife that, although the Russians universally "appreciated and loved" Scharnhorst, "naturally the case is completely different at Breslau," where Frederick William still regarded the "Jacobin General" with paranoid caution: Clausewitz to Marie, Dresden, 1 April 1813, in Schwartz, *Clausewitz*, II:72.

55 Lieven, *Russia Against Napoleon*, 308–09; Cathcart, *Commentaries*, 121; Wilson, *Private Diary*, I:300, 331; Wilson served as the British liaison at Kutuzov's headquarters.

56 Mikhailovsky-Danilevsky, *Denkwürdigkeiten*, 35; Pertz and Delbrück, *Gneisenau*, II:530.

57 Bogdanovich, *Geschichte des Krieges*, Ia:70; Holleben and Caemmerer, *Frühjahrs-feldzuges 1813*, 163, 240–41.

58 Boyen, *Erinnerungen*, ed. Nippold, III:16; Holleben and Caemmerer, *Frühjahrs-feldzuges 1813*, I:244, 317; Bernhardi, *Toll*, 404–10; Wilson, *Private Diary*, I:292, 296.

59 At the beginning of 1813, the troops posted in Silesia consisted of twelve battalions, thirty-two squadrons, seven garrison companies, five infantry depots, seventeen and one-half artillery companies, and one company each of artisans and pioneers. After the king left Berlin, four battalions, six squadrons, five garrison companies, one infantry depot, and two companies of foot artillery marched from Brandenburg to Silesia as well as the small depot of the East Prussian Jäger battalion. This produced a total of sixteen battalions, thirty-eight squadrons, one Jäger and six infantry depots, twelve garrison companies, nineteen and one-half artillery companies, and one company each of artisans and pioneers.

60 These figures correspond to the following: 21 battalions of 800 men each; 40 squadrons of 150 men each; and 12 1/2 batteries manned by 13 1/2 artillery companies; 2 pioneer companies totaling 164 men; and 3 park columns staffed by 1,796 support personnel.

61 Add MSS, 20111, 16: Lowe to Bunbury, Königsberg, 13 March 1813; Pertz and Delbrück, *Gneisenau*, II:250; Holleben, *Frühjahrsfeldzuges 1813*, 159–60; Shana-han, *Prussian Military Reforms*, 206; Unger, *Blücher*, II:12.

62 GStA PK, VI HA Rep. 92 Nl. Gneisenau, Nr. 16; GStA PK, IV HA Rep. 15 A Nr. 160 "Mobilmachung der Truppen unter dem General von Blücher in Schlesien." This unit would take positions at Gleiwitz (Gliwice), Beuthen (Bytom), Tarnowitz (Tarnowskie Gory), and Myslowitz (Myslowice) as well as along the border with the Grand Duchy of Warsaw.

63 Frederick William to Scharnhorst, Breslau, 11 March 1813, in Klippel, *Scharn-horst*, 687–88.

64 Add MSS, 20111, 18: Cathcart to Castlereagh, Kalisch, 26 March 1813; Steffens, *Adventures*, 86. Born at Stavanger, Norway, Henrik Steffens (1773–1845) was a Norwegian-born Danish philosopher, scientist, and poet. He received a profes-sorship at the University of Halle in 1804 and from 1811 to 1832 was professor of physics at the University of Breslau, at that time called the Schlesische Friedrich-Wilhelms-Universität zu Breslau. A friend of Scharnhorst and Gneisenau, he

enlisted in the Prussian Army during the mobilization in early 1813 and received the rank of second lieutenant.

65  Quotes from Gneisenau and St.-Marsan are in Pertz and Delbrück, *Gneisenau*, II:520–21.

66  Copies of both royal proclamations are in GStA PK, IV HA Rep. 15 A Nr. 359.

67  Frederick William to Blücher, Breslau, 17 March 1813, GStA PK, VI HA Rep. 92 Nl. Gneisenau, Nr. 18; Wilson, *Private Diary*, I:318.

68  Martens, *Recueil des traités et conventions*, VII:82; Appendix 9 of Holleben and Caemmerer, *Frühjahrsfeldzuges 1813*, 421–22; the full English-language translation is found in Seeley, *Stein*, III:95–97.

69  Although this appears to be a trifling number, despite the heavy demands of the war in Iberia, the British shipped 120,000 muskets to Sweden and Russia before the end of 1812. In February 1813, the first shipment of arms sailed for Russia carrying 50,000 stand of arms. While British gold was important, British material support to the Allies was even more crucial. As Sherwig contends, without the arms and ammunition required to confront the enemy, there might not have been a coalition for the British to create. Shipments in the spring and summer of 1813 amounted to more than 100,000 muskets for the Prussians and 100,000 muskets for the Russians as well as 116 guns and 1,200 tons of ammunition and shells. In the summer of 1813, the Swedes received 40,000 muskets. Stralsund served as the major depot for supplies arriving from Great Britain. In November 1813 Castlereagh reported that nearly 1,000,000 muskets had been sent to Iberia and Central Europe. During the course of 1813, the British provided the following supplies to the Russian, Prussian, and Swedish governments: 218 pieces of ordinance complete with carriages and the necessary stores for the field, rounds of ammunition, and "a suitable quantity" of gunpowder, shot, shells, and caissons; 124,119 stands of arms with 18,231,000 musket cartridges; 23,000 barrels of powder and flints; 34,443 swords, sabers, and lances; 624 drums, trumpets, bugles, and cavalry standards; 150,000 uniforms complete with great-coats, cloaks, pelisses, and overalls; 187,000 yards of cloth of various colors; 175,796 boots and shoes "with a proportionate quantity of leather"; 114,000 blankets; 58,800 linen shirts and pants; 87,190 pairs of gaiters; 69,624 pairs of stockings/socks; 90,000 "sets of accoutrements"; 63,457 knapsacks; 14,820 saddles with blankets; 22,000 forage caps; 14,000 stocks and clasps; 140,600 shoe brushes, combs, and black-balls; 3,000 gloves and bracers; 20,000 great-coat straps, brushes, pickers, and sponges; 5,000 flannel shirts, gowns, caps, and trousers; 14,000 haversacks and canteens; 702,000 pounds of biscuit and flour; 691,360 pounds of beef and pork; 28,625 gallons of brandy and rum; and "marquees, tents, forage carts, and necessary camp equipment; surgical instrument cases, medicines, and all necessary hospital stores." See Sherwig, *Guineas and Gunpowder*, 287; Stewart, *Narrative*, 366.

70  "Fighting Charlie" had served as an aide-de-camp to King George III and four years later became Britain's Undersecretary of State for War and the Colonies. After less than two years in that position, he went to Iberia to command a cavalry brigade during the Corunna Campaign of 1808–1809. In April 1809, he became adjutant-general to Sir Arthur Wellesley, the future duke of Wellington, who commanded British forces fighting in the Peninsular War. Stewart distinguished

himself, particularly at the battles of Busaco and Talavera. From 1810 to 1814, he served as Britain's Envoy Extraordinary and Minister Plenipotentiary to Berlin and starting in 1813 he also held the post of Military Commissioner with the Allied armies. In 1822, he succeeded Castlereagh as 3rd marquess of London-derry, being named the following year Earl Vane and Viscount Seaham. From 1823 he was governor of County Londonderry and was appointed lord lieutenant of Durham in 1842. He was made a Knight of the Garter in 1853.

71 Stewart, *Narrative*, 2–3, 16; Castlereagh to Cathcart, London, 8 April 1813, *CVC*, VIII:356. The Pitt Plan called for reducing France to its 1791 borders, which effectively would strip Paris of all the conquests made during the French Wars since their beginning in 1792.

72 Jomini, *Précis politique et militaire*, I:228; Lanrezac, *Lützen*, 116; *CN*, Nos. 19698 and 19763, XXV:63–65, 124–25. Napoleon started referring to the "Army of the Main" and the "Army of the Elbe" in his dispatches on 11 March; see *CN*, No. 19697, XXV:62. In Napoleon's correspondence, Eugene retains the title of "Commandant en Chef de la Grande Armée" until 11 April. In the next communiqué to him, on 26 April, he is addressed as "Commandant L'Armée de L'Elbe." Ney never received the title of "Commandant L'Armée du Main" and is always referred to as the commandant of III Corps. See *CN*, Nos. 19843 and 19908, XXV:182, 231.

73 *CN*, Nos. 19646 and 19647, XXV:14–17.

74 *CN*, Nos. 19664 and 19675, XXV:29, 39–40.

75 *CN*, Nos. 19687 and 19688, XXV:45–47.

76 "The political consequence of Hamburg as the center of commerce and the focus of all mercantile wealth and resources of North Germany was even greater than its value as a strategic point, although its bridge across the Elbe, so near to the mouth of the river, was of no small military importance": Cathcart, *Commentaries*, 197.

77 *CN*, No. 19697, XXV:62.

78 *CN*, No. 19717, XXV:84–85.

79 *CN*, No. 19721, XXV:90–91, emphasis added.

# 3

# Saxony

On 16 March, the same day that St.-Marsan received official news of the Russo-Prussian alliance along with Frederick William's declaration of war, the vanguard of Blücher's II Corps struck the road to Dresden. The remaining troops followed on the 17th, with the exception of Colonel Friedrich Erhard von Röder's Brandenburg Brigade. Frederick William wanted the Brandenburgers to remain at Breslau due to the presence of Poniatowski's Poles at Tarnowitz, 100 miles southeast of Breslau. However, on Scharnhorst's orders, the brigade followed II Corps on the 24th after Poniatowski continued his forced retreat to Austria. Frederick William would not forget this affront.[1]

With Scharnhorst serving as chief, Blücher's staff represented the very pinnacle of Prussian military thinking and may well have been the greatest staff of all time in terms of intellect, acumen, and collective experience. Majors Karl Wilhelm von Grolman, Johann Wilhelm von Krauseneck, and Otto August Rühle von Lilienstern, joined later by Lieutenant-Colonel Karl Ferdinand von Müffling – all future Chiefs of the General Staff of the Prussian Army – as well as many other majors, captains, and lieutenants, assisted Scharnhorst. Clausewitz, who remained in the tsar's service, accompanied the staff as the Russian liaison. In addition, Prince August, the king's cousin, accompanied headquarters as General Inspector of the Artillery. The seventeen-year-old crown prince, affectionately called "Fritz," the king's brother, Prince William, the king's nephew, Prince Frederick (son of Frederick William's brother, Louis), and the king's brother-in-law, Prince Karl of Mecklenburg-Strelitz, all joined Blücher to earn their spurs. Frederick William remained with the tsar throughout the war.[2]

Blücher departed Breslau on the 18th but Scharnhorst did not join him. He faced the vexing dilemma of not being able to be in two or three places at the same time. With unassailable authority, he directed every facet of the

10  General Gebhard Leberecht von Blücher, 1742–1819

mobilization, making his presence at Breslau indispensable. He described his situation to Gneisenau:

> My sphere of influence gave life to the entire mobilization. I seek to finish it as much as I can before I depart. I arranged the process so it cannot be interrupted – without this the Landwehr cannot come into existence; the other formations probably only in several months. I act as a despot and load many responsibilities onto myself but I believe I have been summoned for this; I set the Brandenburg Brigade in movement on my own accord. In other matters, I have arranged the necessary fortifications, the rearward-lying magazines, and the plan for the siege of Glogau with the necessary resources for it – this is the reason that has kept me from joining you. I will depart tomorrow at 10:00 A.M. Because I will travel by night and day, I hope to soon be with you. Do not delay if the Cossacks have yet to cross the Elbe.[3]

At a time when communications moved only as fast as the courier's horse, Scharnhorst's position as Chief of the General Staff of the Prussian Army required him to campaign with the Prussian field army. The excellent decision made by the Allies to integrate their forces into multinational army groups not only reduced the opportunity for acts of national self-interest but also meant that a homogeneous Prussian army would not take the field as in 1806. Regardless, whether Blücher commanded an all-Prussian army mattered little: Scharnhorst needed to accompany him and serve as his chief of staff. Scharnhorst would provide the brains and Blücher the brawn. Yet Scharnhorst's outstanding rapport with the Russians required his presence at Russian headquarters to coordinate Allied operations. Tsar Alexander sang his praises to Gneisenau at Breslau on 15 March. "Never," exclaimed the Russian monarch, "have I seen such a mind. What strength in reasoning! What great insight!"[4] To avoid the poor planning, misunderstandings, and bad timing that had doomed the operations of five previous coalitions, Scharnhorst correctly viewed his presence at Russian headquarters as his first priority and so returned to Kalisch. In addition, Boyen also reported to Kalisch on the request of the Russians for a staff officer to manage all of Kutuzov's correspondence with Prussian military and civil authorities, to resolve complaints or complications as soon as possible, and to report all developments to Frederick William.[5]

As Scharnhorst would frequently be absent from headquarters, Gneisenau received the post of assistant quartermaster-general, technically assistant chief of staff. Despite his "looking like a god in his general's uniform," according to Clausewitz, this assignment disappointed him. After resisting Hardenberg's request that he go to London to conclude an alliance with the British, Gneisenau hoped to receive a field command. Frederick William informed him on the 11th that he would command a third Prussian corps. This corps would be attached to a multinational army of Russians, British, and Swedes led by Bernadotte. Although Swedish troops had landed on the island of Rügen, this army would not materialize in time to participate in the Spring Campaign. On 15 March, just four days later, Frederick William changed his mind and reassigned Gneisenau to Blücher's staff, assuring him that he would receive command of this third corps at a later time. After Scharnhorst's unexpected death in July, Gneisenau succeeded his colleague as Chief of the General Staff of the Prussian Army, and Bülow eventually received command of the Prussian III Corps.[6]

As for operations, Wintzingerode's corps of 13,136 men and 72 guns marched west from Rawitsch. His vanguard under General Sergey Lanskoy reached Oberwaldau (Wykróty) west of Bunzlau (Bolesławiec) and seventeen miles east of Görlitz on the Saxon frontier on 17 March. As the van of Blücher's army, Wintzingerode's corps continued west through Görlitz, reaching Bautzen on 20 March. Concerning Wintzingerode, Scharnhorst advised Gneisenau: "I believe we will do well if we consider all our steps with Wintzingerode so that an intimate understanding exists between head-quarters and him. Wintzingerode loves and adores Blücher and you, and he is a good patriot; we must cultivate him in our interests." The relationship between Blücher's headquarters and Wintzingerode worked well. "We are very lucky that we are always of the same opinion as your general,"

Scharnhorst later wrote to the Prussian liaison at Wintzingerode's headquarters. The rapport between Blücher and Wittgenstein began in a similarly salubrious manner. Clausewitz, who had served at both headquarters, wrote on 1 April that "the best unity is expected between the two armies, and at both headquarters, as far as I know them, not the slightest seed of intrigue and/or trace of ill will is present. All these people have a heart for the cause and sufficient magnanimity to remove any ulterior motive."[7]

Relations with Kutuzov also appeared to start on a friendly note. Blücher wrote a flattering letter to the Russian prince on the 17th: "The King has entrusted the corps to me and to my sincere joy has subordinated me to Your Highness. I have the double honor of fighting in unison with the victorious Russian army and to be under the orders of a commander who has won the admiration and the gratitude of the peoples. I await your command." Two days later, the Allied commander in chief responded: "With great appreciation I received your letter of 17 March in which you express your feelings toward me. I consider it a special honor to begin the campaign with a general who has long attracted the attention of all of Europe and on whom the Fatherland places so many hopes. Let's hope that the struggle on which we now embark will end successfully because undertaking it is a righteous cause and continuing it a sacred duty."[8]

Behind Wintzingerode, Blücher's Prussian brigades marched from their assembly points west of Breslau toward Dresden along the great east–west highway that ran from Breslau through Görlitz to the iconic city astride the banks of the Elbe. On 19 March, Blücher's headquarters reached Liegnitz (Legnica), 120 miles east of Dresden (see Map 2). That day, Gneisenau wrote that "goodwill and tenacity will do much, and there is such a good spirit among the troops that it needs only mediocre leadership. We have moral superiority while our enemy has lost confidence in himself and his leaders." The patriotic response of Prussia's intelligentsia to the king's call to arms likewise moved him: "It's a great, heart-stirring time. I have seen Eckardt, Jahn, Friesen, Jahnke, and the others in their military uniforms. It was hard for me to hold back the tears when I saw all this magnanimity, this noble German spirit. Your Berliners provided the most inspiring example: seeing the youth of our noble and upper classes arranged in battalions and companies and, disregarding their place in society, attentively listening to the orders of their officers." As Blücher's army marched toward the Saxon frontier, Gneisenau wrote on 22 March that "we approach with the most splendid troops. We bring 7,000 of the best [cavalry] troopers. Hearts are high. My jaunty commander [Blücher] is filled with new enthusiasm. Scharnhorst, our quartermaster-general, leads us. Capable people are at the head of the brigades and regiments; the soldier is ready for combat and is fierce. When our cavalry left Breslau, a swarm of crows flew in the same direction. 'Ha!,' said the soldiers, 'these crows like the taste of French blood; they follow us to feed on more of it.'" Wilson's journal entry of 21 March states: "The Russians are 'brand high [zealous],' and the Prussians seem to have caught the spirit of self-devoting patriotism."⁹

Based on the "Arrangement," Wittgenstein's corps crossed the Oder and continued the march to Berlin with Yorck's corps in tow. Wittgenstein's main body reached the Prussian capital on 11 March while his vanguard under Diebitsch continued toward the French-occupied fortress of Wittenberg on the Elbe. Wittgenstein informed Blücher that his main body would remain in the region of Berlin until he received further orders or special circumstances arose. Behind the Russians, Yorck's soldiers paraded into Berlin on the 17th. On the same day, Bülow's brigade arrived before Stettin; Borstell's units reached Angermünde, forty-five miles south of Stettin. On 19 March, Benckendorff returned to Brandenburg after raiding Dresden with a flying column of 1,700 dragoons, hussars, and Cossacks. Southeast of Wittgenstein, Miloradovich received orders to invest Glogau until relieved by Schuler's Prussians. After subtracting numerous detachments needed to observe the Poles, occupy Warsaw, and invest the fortresses of Modlin and Zamość, Miloradovich's corps numbered 15,687 men and 98 guns (see Map 1). The rest of the Russian main army – 17,100 men and 176 guns – had yet to move from Kalisch, ostensibly awaiting the arrival of reinforcements.¹⁰

At this time, Eugene's army numbered 57,700 soldiers, including some 7,500 men under Davout.¹¹ Napoleon did not want Davout to suffer a defeat defending Dresden or be forced to evacuate the city: "General Reynier retreating from Dresden would not be an inglorious defeat for us or another for Europe. That of the prince d'Eckmühl [Davout] would be an affront; it would show that we wanted to defend Dresden and that we could not."¹² On the 18th, Eugene started assembling his forces at Magdeburg in compliance with Napoleon's directives. That same day, Davout ignored an urgent plea from King Frederick Augustus I of Saxony and blew two arches and one pier of Dresden's bridge, purportedly the most beautiful in Europe. Most sources fail to describe the extent of the damage caused by Davout. Clausewitz provided an eyewitness report shortly after the French blew the bridge: "The beautiful bridge, the most beautiful I have ever seen, is really so blown by the mines (not cannon) that no trace exists of two of the arches and one of the piers." All were shocked by Davout's actions. "Detachments of the Russian army have penetrated to Dresden," Cathcart reported to Castlereagh, "which they now occupy, Marshal Davout having retreated across the Elbe and having destroyed some of the arches of the magnificent bridge at that place." Even Napoleon complained to Eugene about the negative impact Davout's attempt to destroy the bridge had had on the Saxons. Davout then led his troops north to Wittenberg, from where they marched to a position between Magdeburg and Hamburg.[13]

Allied reports indicated that Davout held the Saxon capital with 5,000–6,000 men and that Eugene stood another seventy miles to the west at Leipzig with a corps of 20,000 men. Intelligence gleaned from informants in that city indicated that 80,000 imperial soldiers were marching from Mainz to Erfurt. As the French moved down the Elbe, the Cossacks of Blücher's army followed, establishing posts along the river's right bank from the Bohemian frontier to downstream of Wittenberg. On the 24th, Wintzingerode reached Dresden's *Neustadt* (new city) on the right bank of the Elbe. The pressure of Cossack raiding parties drove the French, Bavarians, and Saxons from Dresden and other crossing points along the Elbe. A Saxon force of fewer than 2,000 troops under General Karl von Lecoq withdrew into Torgau on the 27th, while the French and Bavarians evacuated Dresden. To escape the Cossacks, Frederick Augustus left Dresden on 25 February. Escorted by a small infantry detachment and two cuirassier regiments, the king fled ninety-five miles southwest to Plauen on the Bavarian frontier with his family, treasury, a few ministers, and the French ambassador, Baron Serrat. In March, he took residency in the Bavarian city of Regensburg. On 13 April, he left for Prague, seeking Austrian protection. Regardless of his location, Frederick Augustus remained in communication with Napoleon, proclaimed his continued adherence to the Confederation of the Rhine, and told his people he would return with reinforcements. On the other hand, the king closed the fortresses of Torgau – the assembly point for the Saxon army – to all belligerents, which offered the Allies a glimmer of hope that he would join the Coalition. According to Gneisenau, General Johann von Thielmann, the commandant of Torgau, refused to admit French soldiers into the fortress "and because of his behavior arouses the hope that he has changed sides." Regardless, the Prussians did not think Napoleon would respect any decision made by Frederick Augustus short of absolute compliance with French demands.[14]

From Silesia, Blücher's corps followed Wintzingerode's Russians into Saxony: the two Silesian brigades trooped through Löwenberg (Lwówek Śląski) and Lauban (Lubań) while the Reserve Cavalry and Artillery moved through Bunzlau, both columns making for Görlitz (see Map 2). Blücher expected Scharnhorst to arrive from Kalisch in a few days. Without waiting for Scharnhorst, who undoubtedly would have advised Blücher against involving himself in Allied politics, the general put Gneisenau's gifted quill to work. From Bunzlau on 22 March, Blücher issued a proclamation to the inhabitants of the Cottbus District, which the Prussians had ceded to Saxony as part of the Treaty of Tilsit. The general reclaimed the borough for Prussia, declared the people again to be Frederick William's subjects, and summoned them to the flag:

> Inhabitants of the Cottbus District! An unsavory peace ripped you from us. You accepted your new master, who was thrust upon you, only because you were forced into his vassalage. You belong to the oldest sons of the Prussian monarchy. Your fathers fought bravely in Frederick the Great's battles and you already have spilled your blood for Prussia's independence. Through your devotion to our royal house, you have profoundly justified your right to again belong to us, and we have never ceased in our devotion to you. You are our blood relatives and now you again shall live under our laws. In the name of the King, our master, I again call you his vassals; the eagle, under which you were happy and free, shall again fly in your territory. Those who bore arms for Prussia in the past should again flock to our flags; whoever intends to seize them for our independence should arm and join us.
>
> The distinguished should lead the commoners by noble example; look at your brothers who were separated from you. See how noble enthusiasm is inflaming all hearts, and the sons of the well-to-do and wealthy are renouncing all privileges of birth, all pleasures of life, and are giving up the finest situations to flock to the flag, unconcerned over the rank they receive and content to be with those who fight for the Fatherland. You are no less noble than your brothers, whom fate separated from you. You will do what duty and honor demand of you. Treat with respect and continue to obey the officials of the Saxon government ... as long as they do not tread on the sacred cause of our independence. Supply everything that the royal commissars sent by me demand of you in the name of our Master.[15]

The local Saxon authorities protested to Blücher, claiming that the Treaty of Tilsit had ceded Cottbus to Frederick Augustus as a form of reparations. Blücher's seizure of Cottbus and his claim that the French held Frederick Augustus like a prisoner – when he was at Plauen – alarmed and insulted Saxon officials. "Thus," explained Blücher to Hardenberg, "I answered that we would take what is ours, [and] that if they make common cause with us, I do not know what could prevent them from reclaiming their property. In general, I assured them that we come as neighbors and friends and would remain so until their troops behave in a hostile manner toward us." Blücher felt compelled to claim the Cottbus District to shield it from the hungry Russians, who spared neither friend nor foe. Just a few days earlier, Wintzingerode's troops had ravaged the Wohlau (Wołów)–Steinau (Ścinawa) District of Prussia some thirty miles northwest of Breslau after the local administration failed to supply them (see Map 2). Although the Russians committed excesses against the population, Gneisenau blamed the district authorities, describing the district president as "good-natured, but weak and lacking authority" and the vice-president as "a French sympathizer."

Gneisenau exonerated Wintzingerode for taking the necessary measures in the Wohlau–Steinau District to feed and supply his soldiers, but securing the Cottbus District's military resources for the Prussians received priority. Concerning the Saxon complaints, Blücher simply told Hardenberg to let the eventual peace treaty determine whether Cottbus would be Prussian or Saxon.[16]

This did not satisfy the state chancellor, who chastised the army's leadership, thus straining his relationship with Gneisenau. Scharnhorst informed Gneisenau that "here one [the Russians] is not happy with Blücher's proclamation, mainly that (1) the Cottbus District has been occupied and (2) the king of Saxony is in enemy hands. With regard to the first point, they are incorrect; in regard to the second point, we are wrong. We must make valid the first point but declare the second a mistake." "I cannot conceal from you how upset I am to learn from Scharnhorst that you are not pleased with several of my steps," Gneisenau responded to Hardenberg. To plead his case, the general maintained that in 1807 Blücher had received orders to advance south from Swedish Pomerania and take into possession all former Prussian provinces. Gneisenau claimed that now, in 1813, they were "acting accordingly, analogically speaking." He also asserted that the measure corresponded completely with the Kalisch–Breslau Accords regarding the occupation of former Prussian lands. Similarly to Blücher, Gneisenau argued that the need to shield the inhabitants and resources of Cottbus from Russian reinforcements moving west made necessary the raising of the Prussian eagle. "This will protect the Cottbus District against the advancing Russian troops, who commonly commit great excesses and are not well disposed toward the subjects of Saxony because of the lack of discipline of the Saxon troops in Russia." Finally, he pointed to a practical matter: Prussia's dire need of manpower. Gneisenau estimated that the Prussians could raise as many as 2,000 soldiers from the district. In his rebuttal, he included reports from two military commissars attesting to the inhabitants' satisfaction about the return of Prussian rule.[17]

On the verge of entering Saxon territory, Blücher issued a *Tagesbefehl* (order of the day) at Bunzlau on 23 March 1813 with instructions for his officers to read the proclamation to the troops. Although his commissars would make requisitions of cloth and shoes, Blücher did not want his soldiers ravaging the land and overwhelming the inhabitants. Again authored by Gneisenau, Blücher's order emphasized the need to consider Saxony as a future ally, which the Prussians hoped would shortly be the case. Blücher later ordered his soldiers to be cautious around Saxon troops but treat them well unless they initiated hostilities. In addition, spies informed the Prussians that the attempted destruction of Dresden's bridge had made a very negative impression on the Saxon king and people. "More than any rational argument," wrote Gneisenau to Hardenberg on the 24th, "the danger posed by the French generals may make him [Frederick Augustus] well disposed to our plans." Blücher's order of the day stated:

> Prussians! We cross the frontier of our territory and enter a foreign land not as an enemy but as a liberator. Going to war for the sake of our independence, we do not wish to enslave a neighbor who speaks the same language, who confesses to the same beliefs, who in the past often allowed his troops to fight victoriously with ours, who feels the same hate against foreign oppression, and who only because of the misguided politics of its statesmen – who themselves have been misled by French guile – has been prevented up to now from turning his arms against the myrmidons of foreign tyranny. Be gentle and humane toward these people and consider the Saxons as friends of the sacred cause of German independence for which we have taken up arms; consider them hardy confederates. Saxony's inhabitants will satisfy your fair wishes in an orderly manner. Copy the example of your brothers-in-arms in General Yorck's army corps, who, although standing for a long time on foreign soil [Russia], preserved the honor of the Prussian name through the strictest discipline.
>
> I will not merely recognize as unworthy any among us who desecrate the fame of Prussian honor but will punish his crime with a dishonorable sentence. Soldiers of my army, you know me. You know that I care for you like a father, but you also know that I will not tolerate debauchery and that such conduct will make me a pitiless judge. Act accordingly.

At the same time, the Prussians felt obligated to issue an official statement describing the reasons and intention of the invasion to secure the resources of Saxony through the peaceful cooperation of its inhabitants. Hardenberg had mentioned the possibility of an edict but nothing arrived from Allied Headquarters or either Allied court. Not wanting to wait, the Prussians issued a proclamation to the Saxons, likewise authored by Gneisenau and signed by Blücher, summoning them to participate in the war of liberation. Reminding the Saxons of the sacrifices Napoleon demanded of them, the proclamation encouraged them to raise the flag of resistance against foreign oppression. Thus, Blücher urged the Saxons to act irrespective of their monarch, who no longer enjoyed the freedom of decision. Gneisenau later explained that he imbued the declaration with "somewhat of a poetic vitality because it is meant for the great mass of the people and not just for the upper classes, who through upbringing and egoism have lost the poetic sense; on the other hand, they [the masses] are accustomed to poetic imagery and find favor in the few books that they trust: the Bible and the hymnal":[18]

> Saxons! We Prussians step foot onto your territory, extending you the hand of brotherhood. In Eastern Europe, the Lord God of Hosts rendered a terrible judgment. Through the sword, hunger, and cold, the Angel of Death has devoured 300,000 of those foreigners who in pride and arrogance of their

good fortune endeavored to subject the land to their yoke. Guided and directed by Providence, we are marching forth to fight for the security of time-honored thrones and for the independence of our nation.

We are in the company of a brave people [Russians] who have courageously cast off foreign oppression and who, in full recognition of their own victory, promise liberation to the enslaved nations. We bring you the dawn of a new day. The time has finally come to throw off an odious yoke, which for six years has oppressed us terribly.

An ill-conceived and even worse-concluded war forced the Treaty of Tilsit upon us; however, those harsh treaty articles were not unique to us. Every subsequent treaty escalated the harsh conditions of the previous one. This is why we threw off this most disgraceful yoke and proceed to struggle for our freedom with uplifted hearts.

Saxons! You are a noble, enlightened people. Without independence, you know that all goodness of life for the noble-minded has no worth – that enslavement is the deepest humiliation. You cannot and will not endure slavery any longer; you will no longer tolerate insidious politics that demand the blood of your sons for its very ambitious, rapacious schemes that exhaust the sources of your commerce, paralyze your businesses, destroy your freedom of press, and has now turned your once so prosperous land into a theater of war. Already the vandalism of the oppressive foreigner needlessly and wantonly destroyed your beautiful monument to the art of construction: the bridge at Dresden. Enough! Unite with us, raise the flag of resistance against the foreign oppressor and be free!

Your national army is in foreign service; the freedom of choice has been taken from it. No less than you do we want to get revenge for the deplorable step that has forced it to conform to perfidious politics. For your master, we want to take control of the provinces of your state, which fortune, the superiority of our arms, and the bravery of our troops have placed in our power. Satisfy the meager needs of our warriors and expect from us the strictest discipline. Access to me, the Prussian field commander, is open to anyone who is oppressed; I will listen to any complaint, investigate any accusation, and severely punish any infraction of discipline. Anyone, even the least, can approach me confident that I will warmly receive him.

We shall regard as a brother any friend of German independence; we shall gently lead back to the right path the erring weak; but we shall mercilessly pursue the dishonorable panderer to foreign tyranny as a traitor to the Fatherland.[19]

After crossing the Saxon frontier, Gneisenau reported on the mood of the people. "Here in Saxony we have been received well and friendly," he penned to Hardenberg on the 24th. He repeated the claim on the following day: "We continue to be well received. The mood of the inhabitants is good and thoroughly anti-French." Despite this apparent warm welcome from the

Saxons, the foray into Allied politics cost Blücher. Ironically, the pen rather than the sword landed the general in hot water. Attempting to be proactive, Gneisenau immediately dispatched a courier to Hardenberg with Blücher's declaration. "You expressed to me that you wanted to issue a proclamation to the Saxons," states Gneisenau's cover letter. "Presumably, your overwhelming business caused you to forget about this. At this moment, we are in the process of crossing the border. Therefore, yesterday I felt compelled to draft a proclamation in the name of General Blücher, which just now arrived from the press. It does not miss the meaning you wanted to be included."[20]

Hardenberg responded by scribbling in the margin that the proclamation "should not have been composed without orders, because consequences may emerge from it. It is not my fault that the promised declaration did not materialize; only yesterday I received it from Kalisch and today 500 copies were sent to Blücher." "But you never sent the promised proclamation," countered Gneisenau, "and something needed to be said to the inhabitants of Saxony. In the proclamation I drafted – I have neither the talent nor a knack for such work, as I told you at Breslau – only General Blücher spoke, not the government. If you want this to contain different language, you can still write a proclamation using polished phrases. Here the soldier speaks; there the language of the diplomat would be better. Nothing is irrevocable."

Although a sensible defense of his actions, the subsequent paragraphs of Gneisenau's letter suggest that the issue quickly became much larger in the opinion of Blücher's headquarters:

> I am now forced to consider the sad thought that if your fair, kind, lenient, and enterprising spirit already finds fault in our initial steps, how will it be for us in the future, and what can we expect from those, all of whom lack the so-called initiative, who surround the king and are our enemies? With what bitterness will they censure what we do! What uncertainty will they place in our steps because of this! It is completely impossible to do anything without being censured by one or the other ... Instead of binding fortune to our flags to *achieve* the most that we can, we will only seek to *avoid* another disaster: a condition of constant unrest with the fullest risk of instability. War does not allow for discussion of every issue, and to seek approval; most of the time it is better to do something than nothing at all, even if the result is marginal. If one desires success, one must allow the army commanders complete power according to the general overview. A critic who is too sharp is not acceptable. War is always and overall a state of chance, and fortune will also play its role in it. Thus I go astray in platitudes.[21]

Indeed, Blücher's imperious entry into Saxony produced ill-feelings at Russian headquarters. Kutuzov had tasked his advisors with drafting a proclamation to the German people, "Aufruf an die Deutschen," which he published in the name of Alexander and Frederick William on 25 March. Being preempted by Blücher did not sit well with the Russian commander for several reasons, but especially because the Russians were not specifically named in Blücher's proclamation. In addition, the Saxons issued both formal and informal complaints to the Russian government. They feared that the Prussians had started a war with particular designs on their country. Blücher did not help matters by engaging them in a scathing correspondence in the various Dresden newspapers. They turned for help to Wintzingerode as the ranking Russian officer. He responded "that the tsar's intentions are known all over Europe, and that he desires to restore the freedom of Germany and Saxony." In particular, General Joachim Friedrich Gotthelf von Zezschwitz, a close advisor to Frederick Augustus, requested that Wintzingerode seek clarification of his master's intentions regarding Saxony.

Wintzingerode referred the matter to Kutuzov, who responded that "Blücher acted politically irresponsibly when making his declaration because he was unaware of the intentions of the [Russian] court. He committed a fatal error by not mentioning the tsar of Russia. And, by dismissing the Saxon authorities, he also acted against the wishes of his own court." Kutuzov assured Wintzingerode: "the Central Commission, which shortly will be established at Dresden, will act in such a spirit that it will disperse any clouds that may have gathered as a result of Blucher's most unfortunate proclamation." As for the comments made by Zezschwitz, Kutuzov advised Wintzingerode to reply that "the actions of His Imperial Majesty [Alexander], reflecting his unselfishness, will become increasingly well known in Germany, and princes who join him will not regret their decision. Saxony is no exception to this. I will make just a few comments with respect to the current position of the king of Saxony. He either acts of his own free will or he is subservient to a foreign power. If he is acting freely, he is our enemy."[22]

Allied concern over this issue arose from the challenge posed by authoritarian monarchs calling on the people to fight for their independence against French hegemony. Dominic Lieven explains that Nesselrode convinced Alexander of the folly of inciting a German popular revolt against Napoleonic rule. Thus, "autonomous politics from below – whether led by Jacobin demagogues or by patriotic Prussian generals – would throw Europe into further chaos." Consequently, an aggravated Kutuzov directly scolded Blücher on 5 April, the same day he responded to Wintzingerode. His message resounded loud and clear: no more political statements without his authorization. "To achieve the general coordination of actions between various forces during the current movement of our armies," explained Kutuzov, "it is necessary to adhere to my regulations regarding any published announcements. In my opinion, all proclamations fall into two categories. The first includes announcements related to the various deliveries of requisitions for the troops and lies within the sphere of influence of each commanding general who determines the delivery of required supplies; they can publish such announcements at their own discretion and based on circumstances. The second includes proclamations that have political goals. Such documents first must be reconciled with existing state interests. Therefore, I must ask that, if you find it necessary to publish such a document, you should contact me at once so I can inform you what is required in the current political situation." Kutuzov notified all subordinate commanders that any proclamation published in occupied provinces should be limited to the promise of protection of life and property and to the demand for items needed to supply the troops.[23]

Believing a general had no business issuing a proclamation in the midst of serious political negotiations, Frederick William sided with the Russians. On 9 April, he issued a cabinet order to Blücher concerning his inappropriate conduct, explaining that neither the commanding general nor any other commander could issue proclamations without permission because political considerations remained the exclusive jurisdiction of the Allied courts. As predicted, Blücher reacted coldly. "At Breslau I do not believe they are content with my actions here in Saxony," he wrote, "especially those close to the King: they have their reasons. They mean nothing to me: the end crowns the means. But listen and tell me what is said [at court] over this."[24]

Gneisenau warned Hardenberg against such patronizing treatment, but nothing could be done to save Blücher from a rebuke. The state chancellor did his best at damage control, even falling on his sword over the cabinet order to Blücher. Hardenberg's letter to Gneisenau on 10 April no doubt aimed to assuage any ill feelings at Blücher's headquarters. Regarding the occupation of the Cottbus District, Hardenberg claimed that while the measure appeared "completely correct" and that "everything was initiated appropriately, [Gneisenau] did not know the court's policy regarding former Prussian provinces." Concerning the proclamation to the Saxons, Hardenberg noted that "what you have discussed regarding administration is in complete accordance with the king's opinion, but completely opposite to that of the Russian tsar. Extensive discussions have taken place over this matter." As for the rebuke itself, Hardenberg wrote: "You should not allow yourself to become upset by the disapproval of the proclamations." He explained that "it is one thing to allow the commanding generals a free hand in the military operations," but they could not be allowed to express their own views "without accurate knowledge of the political principles assumed by the courts," regardless of how well they composed their proclamations. He added that proclamations issued by the Russian generals had likewise received the tsar's disapproval.[25] "Unity and results through an outlined system are also completely necessary politically; how can this occur unless it emerges from a central point? In no way is it my fault that the ... proclamation by the tsar and the king, which was issued by Kutuzov in both of their names, did not materialize sooner. I pressed for it incessantly. Incidentally, I do reproach myself over the matter of the cabinet order to General Blücher." After conceding guilt, Gneisenau accepted Hardenberg's argument: "I had the honor to receive your letter of the 10th of this month. It has made me uncommonly happy to again find the dispositions of good-will that you have always bestowed on me. I will never cease to show my worth through my efforts. Also, I will write no more proclamations. The worst is that my old general has suffered a reprimand that I alone deserved."[26]

Aside from these politics, the Russo-Prussian armies continued the advance in two groups. The northern army, commanded by Wittgenstein, numbered 48,000 men. Of this figure, the Prussians provided the majority: Yorck's 13,200 men, Bülow's 11,300, and Borstell's 5,300. Wittgenstein's Russian troops included 12,650 men under Berg and one light corps of 5,000 divided among Tettenborn, Chernishev, and Dörnberg. Positioned in Brandenburg, this northern army faced Eugene to the southwest. In the early weeks of the campaign, Wittgenstein and his chief of staff, Auvray, remained obsessed with defending Berlin and the Prussian heartland. This led to serious friction between them and Kutuzov, who wanted Wittgenstein to advance southeast, cross the Elbe within supporting distance of Blücher, and move into Saxony proper. Kutuzov as well as Volkonsky feared that Napoleon would drive eastward along the Austrian frontier, refuse his left, and with his right sweep behind Wittgenstein, very similar to the emperor's maneuver against the Prussians in 1806. Wittgenstein, however, remained committed to defending Berlin and holding the province of Brandenburg to shield Prussia's mobilization. Wittgenstein failed to see that he could still cover Berlin from the left bank of the Elbe by providing a strategic threat to the flank of any French force marching against the Prussian capital. Consequently, the impasse between the two Russian headquarters resulted from a shortage of troops to cover both southern Saxony and western Brandenburg. "The tension caused by conflicting strategic priorities and inadequate manpower to defend them," explains Lieven, "continued throughout the Spring Campaign."[27]

Blücher's southern army consisted of approximately 26,000 Prussians along with Wintzingerode's 10,500 Russians, one-third of the latter being cavalry. Following Wintzingerode's corps across the Saxon frontier, Blücher's headquarters moved from Görlitz to Löbau on 27 March. Reports claimed that imperial forces had evacuated Dresden that same morning as well as the entire left bank of the Elbe from the Bohemian frontier to Torgau. The

Prussians attributed the French withdrawal from Dresden to the timely activity of Russian cavalry. To confuse the French, 600 troopers from Miloradovich's corps crossed the Elbe not far from Meißen, while some of Wintzingerode's cavalry crossed upstream from Dresden. On this day, Wintzingerode's advance guard occupied Dresden's *Altstadt* (old city) on the left bank of the Elbe after Franco-Bavarian forces withdrew. As a result of the damage done to Dresden's bridge – "the devilry," as Gneisenau called it – Blücher ordered the Russians to throw a pontoon bridge across the Elbe upstream of the Saxon capital. To facilitate the work, Blücher forwarded one of his two pioneer companies in wagons to the point where the Russians planned to assemble the bridge. After news arrived that the French had also destroyed the bridge sixteen miles downstream from Dresden at Meißen, half of the other pioneer company moved there for repair work. Blücher accepted Gneisenau's suggestion to fortify the Schloß at Meißen and build a bridgehead there to provide a secure crossing over the Elbe that would not require a large garrison. An engineer officer accompanied the pioneers to Meißen. Rumors circulated that the Saxon king had ordered all his troops to separate from the French, leading the Prussians to believe that Frederick Augustus would soon join the Coalition. Numerous statements made by General Lecoq during his retreat to Torgau that neither he nor his troops would ever again fight for the French seemed to indicate Saxony's defection from the French alliance.[28]

After passing through Bautzen on the 28th, Blücher covered the next thirty-five miles to reach Dresden's *Neustadt* on the 30th. "I am at Dresden," he informed Hardenberg that same day, "and with God's help I will go further. The disgraceful destruction of the bridge is very bad for Saxony but the move will not stop me." Blücher's brigades remained echeloned eastward to the Silesian border until Wintzingerode could continue his march. This occurred on the 31st, when the Russians finished building the pontoon bridge, and Wintzingerode led the rest of his corps across the Elbe. Blücher moved into Dresden's *Altstadt* on the left bank of the Elbe. Thus far, the Saxons had received him with courtesy. In his monumental biography of Gneisenau, Hans Delbrück claims:

> The corps was greeted with enthusiasm by the inhabitants. Only those who still supported the Napoleonic system remained distant. The excellent discipline and the spirit of the Prussians filled the Saxons with amazement and the wish to join them in the struggle for German freedom. The effect of this sentiment was foiled by the behavior of the Saxon king, who fled and went to Regensburg despite the honest efforts of Frederick William III, who sent General [Levin Karl von] Heister to win him over to the good cause and to convince him to return to his capital.[29] Thus the liberation of Germany ground to a halt and the expectation of the friends of the Fatherland were deceived.

While such passages must be viewed in the political context of nineteenth-century German romantic nationalism, these later movements certainly did not influence Blücher's own words. Although his proclamation failed to persuade Frederick Augustus to join the Allies, the mood of the Saxon capital seemed quite inviting. "I have been nearly overwhelmed with compliments here," wrote Blücher to his wife, "but it appears that these are all that the Saxons are willing to give." His letter to Hardenberg on the 30th was more explicit and frank: "I am very pleased with my reception in Saxony in regards to the nation; but ... the distinguished gentlemen ... find it especially [odious] that we requested some necessities from them; I notified them that we come to them with our allies, as they had gone [to Russia] with theirs [the French], and that we have to provide ours with the necessary food." Nevertheless, Mikhailovsky-Danilevsky claims that, while the Saxons greeted the Russians with "enthusiasm," Blücher's proclamations, "through which he abolished the provisional government that the king of Saxony had established at Dresden upon his departure," resulted in the Prussians being "received with hostile feelings."[30]

Blücher's headquarters demanded requisitions, publishing in Dresden lists of supplies they expected the inhabitants to provide. Yet Scharnhorst criticized this conduct, accusing Blücher's friend and war commissar, Friedrich Wilhelm Ribbentrop, of treating the Saxons no better than the French had treated the Prussians. Scharnhorst explained to Gneisenau that, "while our proceedings must be conducted according to the pressure of the circumstances, I must confess that the requisition of uniforms and boots did not please me, partly because it came too early, partly because it was stated in the tone of a decided enemy. We must show leniency and brotherly love in all our actions; our harshness must be justified by iron necessity. Ribbentrop is a capable man but he acted in the spirit of a French commissar." Scharnhorst requested that Gneisenau regulate "the requisition of clothing based only on the amount of equipment the battalions still lack, which should be very little. With the boots it is a different story; we have a right to them. For the most part, the Saxons are still in the mood of the period of misfortune during and after the Seven Years War; we must treat them in a careful and fatherly manner but not bitterly. The manner in which we treat Saxony will have a great influence on other Germans."[31]

On 6 April 1813, Kutuzov issued a proclamation in the name of Alexander and Frederick William to announce the establishment of a Central Commission for the Occupied German Territories. Chaired by Stein, the Central Commission would coordinate the Allied occupation of Napoleon's former German satellites. The Board would supervise requisitions so the resources of these states could be quickly placed at the disposal of the Allies in an orderly manner that respected the inhabitants. "It is not designed to govern Saxony," Kutuzov explained to Wintzingerode, "but to protect the interests of the German states that have been liberated as well as those that will be freed in the future. The actual governing of the country will be entrusted to Saxon authorities, the appointment of whom, in my opinion, will be the first matter for this commission [to decide]."[32]

Stein went to Dresden, the seat of the Central Commission, to begin this experiment in Allied occupation policy. Meanwhile, the Allied courts bombarded Regensburg with calls for the Saxon king to sever his ties with Napoleon. Both Allied policies failed. Frederick Augustus remained true to the emperor while Stein, like Blücher, could not overcome passive Saxon resistance after his arrival at Dresden on 9 April. The regard for Saxony's inhabitants and resources may have earned the Allies goodwill but in the end their progressive occupation policy achieved little. Ultimately, Allied control of Saxony lasted less than one month before Napoleon launched a counteroffensive that drove the Russians and Prussians 250 miles eastward to the Polish frontier.

Before joining Blücher in early April, Scharnhorst concluded a second round of Allied planning at Kalisch. The meeting, necessitated by the news that the French had evacuated the entire stretch between the Oder and the Elbe, culminated in a 20 March council of war that decided to implement the "Proposed Plan of Action Beyond the Elbe." Kutuzov and his staff based this draft on the news that Erfurt was serving as "the enemy's main point of assembly." According to reports, 40,000 French troops had already arrived and their numbers were "increas[ing] daily." The Russians assumed that a French corps at Leipzig, estimated to be "20,000 men strong," was serving as the vanguard of the army forming seventy miles to the west at Erfurt. An overly cautious Kutuzov deemed that Blücher's 50,000 men would be too weak "to operate from Dresden toward Leipzig against the combined enemy forces … because the enemy forces are continuously being reinforced." Therefore, to offset the enemy's numerical advantage, the "Proposed Plan of Action Beyond the Elbe" required Wittgenstein and Yorck to move south from Berlin along the right bank of the Elbe through Dahme, Elsterwerda, and Großenhain. As soon as he learned that Blücher's army had crossed the Elbe at Dresden, Wittgenstein would lead his army across the river further downstream at a point between Meißen and Dresden. After crossing the river, Wittgenstein would detach part of his troops to blockade Torgau and then unite with Blücher on the left bank of the Elbe; both armies would then proceed to Leipzig. Tormasov's main army would remain at Kalisch awaiting reinforcements. However, Miloradovich's corps would advance from Glogau to Dresden after being relieved by Schuler's siege corps, tentatively scheduled to arrive on 1 April (see Map 2).

Despite growing impatience at Blücher's and Wittgenstein's respective headquarters, intelligence indicating that a new French army would soon be in the field mastered Kutuzov's thoughts. All reports indicated the concentration of large imperial forces at Würzburg under Marshal Ney in addition to the 60,000 men Eugene had purportedly assembled between Erfurt, Leipzig, and Magdeburg. An estimated 40,000 "Italians" filed north from Italy to Augsburg while fresh Bavarian forces concentrated at Hof. Obviously, Eugene's army at Magdeburg posed the immediate threat to Wittgenstein but Kutuzov assumed that, even with 50,000 men, Blücher would be weaker than the enemy's forces at Erfurt, which appeared to be growing steadily. In the cover letter to Wittgenstein that accompanied the "Proposed Plan of Action Beyond the Elbe," Kutuzov cautioned that, although the combined forces of Blücher and Wittgenstein certainly outnumbered the French, any increase in the enemy's forces, even if they simply achieved parity with the Allies, would pose a dangerous threat considering that Tormasov's own army remained two weeks behind. "Our main army stands at Kalisch," explained Kutuzov, "and the distance from this place to Leipzig is very considerable; if the enemy is weaker than we estimate him to be between Leipzig and Erfurt – say only around 60,000 men – your corps and Blücher's corps, together around 90,000 to 100,000 men, are sufficient to operate at a distance [from the Russian main army]. However, he will soon increase his forces and be equal to yours, thus making your operations very risky without reinforcements from the main army, which must remain here for two full weeks." Consequently, Kutuzov implored Wittgenstein to provide reports on the enemy that "are as reliable as possible and to base your distance from Dresden upon them. Yours and Blücher's corps must avoid crossing the Elbe at points that are so far apart from each other that the attack of a strong enemy on your left flank or Blücher's right can prevent you from uniting with this general on the other side of the Elbe, which would have the most pernicious consequences."

To his credit, the Russian commander did not attempt to micromanage the war from Kalisch. He explained that news of French movements would reach Wittgenstein days before the reports arrived at Kalisch. This fact, coupled with the distance between the Russian main army and the two forward armies, warranted Wittgenstein's exercise of independent command. Rather than bind his subordinate to a specific operations plan, Kutuzov instructed Wittgenstein to proceed according to circumstances. Regardless, he concluded his letter with advice meant to discourage Wittgenstein from seizing the offensive: "Basically, wherever you encounter the enemy, as long as he is weaker than you, he will not risk holding his ground and thus you can do no great damage to him; he will fall back on his main force and reinforce himself according to the measures of his retreat." Kutuzov's belief in the futility of attacking the French only increased in the following weeks.[33]

Kutuzov's "Proposed Plan of Action Beyond the Elbe" brought a greater degree of rationality to the original "Arrangement" by providing instructions – the crossing of the Elbe – that at least would create the opportunity for mutual support between Wittgenstein and Blücher by closing the gap between them.[34] Yet such was the respect for French maneuver and speed that the Allies remained concerned that one of the army groups would be caught before the other could reach a supporting distance. Thus, the 20 March council of war had placed even greater emphasis on coordinating movements that would bring Wittgenstein and Blücher across the Elbe within mutual supporting distance. Again, Kutuzov's refusal to move west and thus closer to the theater of war meant that the Allied commander in chief could not direct operations. Nevertheless Blücher, the senior officer, ensured Allied unity of command by declaring that he would accept Wittgenstein's orders unconditionally. Blücher would subordinate himself to the Russians throughout the Spring Campaign of 1813 but he learned a hard lesson, one that he would not forget during the Fall Campaign. After playing the role of dutiful subordinate in April and May, Blücher would listen to no one – neither general, statesman, nor monarch – in August and September.

Wittgenstein received the instructions detailing the necessity of advancing with Yorck directly south from Berlin to cross the Elbe somewhere between Meißen and Dresden. In turn, he ordered Bülow to observe the stretch of the Elbe between Magdeburg and Wittenberg, dispatching *Streifkorps* across the river to disrupt French communication. After posting a blockade corps at Torgau, Wittgenstein planned to cross the Elbe and advance in unison with Blücher toward the Leipzig–Altenburg line.[35] Kutuzov's 20 March instructions estimated the strength of the Allied forward armies to be 25 percent larger than Wittgenstein's headcount, which may have added to the field-marshal's lack of urgency in leading the Russian main army west from Kalisch. Wittgenstein quickly informed his superior of the discrepancy: "In response to your order of 20 March, I have the honor to report that the forces that I have under my command for operations beyond the Elbe are not as considerable as you assume. Instead of 100,000 men, I hardly have between 70,000 and 75,000 men. His Majesty the King [Frederick William] informed me that Blücher's corps consists of 24,000 men, Wintzingerode has up to 15,000; my corps and Yorck's corps are some 35,000 men. From these forces, I must leave Bülow with 10,000 men to blockade Magdeburg, placing no more than 65,000 at my disposal."[36]

Numbers mattered little to Blücher. Remarking on the order to advance, he assured Hardenberg that "if this does not force them [the French] to move away from Leipzig, they will run the risk that I and Wittgenstein will drive them into the sea. I will now cross the Elbe and advance to facilitate the operation of Wittgenstein's corps; I will offer him my hand and we will see what can be done together." Remaining at Berlin until 30 March, Wittgenstein did not move as fast as Blücher desired. According to the plans made on 20 March, Wittgenstein's army should have been prepared to cross the Elbe between Meißen and Dresden at the same time that Blücher crossed the river at Dresden. Yet Wittgenstein informed Blücher on the 26th that he did not intend to follow the Dahme, Elsterwerda, and Großenhain line due south to the Elbe. Instead, he planned to establish his headquarters at Belzig on the 29th, forty-five miles east of Magdeburg and ninety-five miles north-northwest of Meißen, where he would await news of Blücher's arrival at Dresden.

Eugene's presence at Magdeburg and the threat he posed to Berlin eventually compelled Wittgenstein to disregard Kutuzov's instructions altogether. Whether the viceroy commanded 30,000 or 50,000 men mattered little to Wittgenstein. As soon as he distanced himself from the Prussian capital by marching through Dahme to Großenhain, Eugene could take Berlin, relieve Spandau, and reach the Oder to raise the sieges of Küstrin and Stettin (see Map 2). At Belzig, Wittgenstein planned to await Blücher's "arrival at Dresden to be able to cooperate with you and combine our forces. Should the enemy really want to maintain himself at Magdeburg and therefore operate against Berlin and Spandau, I believe a flank movement by your left against Leipzig will undoubtedly force him to abandon Magdeburg with the unessential troops because otherwise he would risk being driven into the sea by you and me." Conversely, Kutuzov rejected his subordinate's concerns over the Prussian capital, arguing that, in the case of a French operation against Berlin, Wittgenstein could easily sever Eugene's line of communication and thus reel in the viceroy. Regardless, Wittgenstein remained committed to his defense of Berlin, thus increasing the gulf between him and Kutuzov.[37]

On Wittgenstein's right, his *Streifkorps* advanced toward the lower Elbe in late February. In addition to General Claude Carra St.-Cyr's 1,000-man garrison at Hamburg, General Joseph Morand's 34th Division of 2,800 French and Saxons supported by 12 guns at Stralsund represented all the forces that constituted Eugene's left wing. On 24 February, anti-French unrest erupted at Hamburg amid rumors concerning the approach of large Allied forces. At Hamburg's Altona Gate, the unusual *Revision* (customs inspection) of a young doctor returning to the local military hospital by the authorities, although a minor incident, prompted a mob to gather and attack the customs house. The agents opened fire and several of the attackers fell, but the mob stormed the building, destroying the guard house and several toll barriers. That same day, serious events occurred at the harbor and in its vicinity. Hamburg's Prefecture Guard, consisting of the sons of the city's elite, had received orders to serve as replacements for Napoleon's Imperial Guard. Although such a measure would violate existing agreements, the empire's needs superseded local arrangements. Before the Guard departed, the customs agents wanted the young men to surrender their cash, but they refused. The pro-French mayor, Dr. Amandus Augustus Abendroth, a native of Hamburg, hurried to the scene, but the angry mob met him with stones. Protestors threw down a French Eagle and trampled it in the streets, while their comrades razed the police commissioner's house and abused the official himself.

Annexed to France in 1810, Hamburg provided Napoleon with one of the strongest fortresses between the Rhine and the Elbe and served as the capital of the Bouches-de-l'Elbe Department. Possession of Hamburg, like the mouths of the Elbe and the Weser Rivers, remained an absolute necessity for Napoleon's Continental System, which sought to close Europe to all British trade and thus destroy Britain financially. Hamburg's merchants served as the middlemen for the distribution of goods and wealth to Central Europe. Napoleon could not claim authorship of either the continental blockade or the closure of the North Sea's coast. Both plans had their origins in the French Revolution. During the Directory period of the Revolution, Emmanuel Joseph Sieyès had referred to the German North Sea coast as "the most important part of the world for France. If one possessed it, one could close all British trade markets and ports on the Continent from Gibraltar to Holstein, even to the North Cape." One historian refers to Hamburg as "the commercial nerve center for half the continent" during the eighteenth century, with wealth built on "a fortuitous combination of commerce and manufacturing. Commerce had always dominated the partnership, but never as thoroughly as it did in the eighteenth century, when Hamburg's seemingly boundless prosperity rested almost entirely on the strength of its position in the world market." Despite closing the continent to British commerce and greatly hampering the ability of neutral states to conduct trade in Europe, Napoleon did not desire the demise of Hanseatic trade. Had he succeeded in his economic war with Britain, Hamburg's trade "would have experienced a new and infinitely grander recovery." In case the Continental System should fail, Napoleon planned to build a canal system linking the Elbe and the Rhine and ultimately Paris with the Baltic Sea.[38]

Although aware of the unrest, Napoleon could not prevent the evacuation of French forces from Hamburg. "Place the prince d'Eckmühl [Davout] with his sixteen battalions on your left," Napoleon instructed Eugene; "this will be very good. He knows Hamburg and is known there, and his proximity to the city will be very useful." Reinforced by the 700 muskets of the 152nd Line, Carra St.-Cyr held Hamburg itself. Help appeared to be on the way. Wittgenstein's push to Berlin, which he reached on 11 March, prompted Morand to evacuate Stralsund on 9 March; Eugene ordered the general to retreat 150 miles southwest to Hamburg. Yet Carra St.-Cyr lost heart after receiving reports of anti-French sentiment manifesting at Lübeck, Lüneburg, and Stade. Despite Napoleon's demand

for St.-Cyr to "show more firmness," he withdrew from Hamburg on
12 March. On learning of the general's retreat, Napoleon informed his minister of war, Henri Clarke, to "tell General St.-Cyr that in all he had acted with
haste and without composure ... that regarding the evacuation of Hamburg,
it was made without reason, without order, and without spirit ... that all the
rumors regarding the Cossacks were exaggerated or false. Tell him he must
hold a position vis-à-vis Hamburg with General Morand and all customs
agents; that 1,500 custom agents will go with him to strengthen the lines;
finally, that thirty battalions under General [Dominique-Joseph] Vandamme
are marching toward the 32nd [Military] Division." Demonstrating his
tendency to undervalue the size of enemy forces in order to shame subordinates for their mistakes, Napoleon also blamed Carra St.-Cyr's immediate
superior, General of Division Jacques-Alexandre Lauriston: "Respond to
General Lauriston that the evacuation of Hamburg, which causes so much
harm to customs and finances and public opinion in the 32nd [Military]
Division, is the result of the wrong instructions he gave to General Carra St.-
Cyr. Instead of stabilizing Hamburg, everything there was alarmed ... but
he took no precautions and 200 Cossacks will seize the region."[39]

Crossing the Elbe, St.-Cyr commenced a march sixty-five miles southwest to Bremen. Consequently, Tettenborn received orders to occupy
Hamburg, summon the inhabitants of the left bank of the lower Elbe to rise
against the French, and destroy all imperial depots and supplies in North
Germany. Crossing the Elbe with 1,300 troopers and 2 horse guns,
he reached Perleberg some ninety miles southeast of Hamburg on 11 March.
Continuing northwest through Ludwigslust and Lauenburg, Tettenborn
encountered Morand's division south of Hamburg at Bergedorf and
Escheburg five days later. While en route from Stralsund, Morand discovered a Danish division blocking the direct route to Hamburg that ran
through the Danish province of Holstein. Its commander, General Johann
Ewald, refused to grant the French passage through the neutral territory.
This forced Morand to make for Zollenspieker south of Hamburg.[40] After
engaging the outnumbered Russians, Morand decided to retreat across
the Elbe in an effort to reach Zollenspieker. Although he left behind six
guns, Morand arrived but continued to Bremen at Carra St.-Cyr's request
after civil unrest erupted there as well.

Instead of continuing the pursuit, Tettenborn turned north and entered
Hamburg on 18 March, to the joy of its inhabitants. He wasted no time
in issuing a general call to arms. The dukes of Mecklenburg-Schwerin and
Mecklenburg-Strelitz issued modest mobilization orders in their respective
states, each calling for 2,000 infantry and 1,000 cavalry. The formation of a
Hanseatic Legion also ensued, and plans were made for the raising of
a Hanoverian Legion. Yorck sent a detachment of 3 officers and 200 men
to Hamburg to assist with the mobilization. Possession of Hamburg

provided the Allies with numerous advantages. The opening of Hamburg – being a bustling port and financial capital – to British trade dealt "the final death blow to the Continental System" and meant increased revenues for the Allied war effort. Strategically, the city formed the gateway to Napoleonic Germany and Napoleon's 32nd Military District.[41] Hamburg also served as a communication hub, particularly between the Allies and Great Britain as well as between Denmark and France. The presence of Allied forces at Hamburg facilitated the landing of 500 British troops seventy miles to the northwest at Cuxhaven. Symbolically, the great port numbered among the other historical cities, such as Rome, Antwerp, and Amsterdam, that belonged to France after Napoleon's annexation in 1810. Thus, by occupying Hamburg, the Allies had invaded the territory of the empire itself.[42]

News of the events at Hamburg aggravated Napoleon and prompted a short letter to Eugene on 17 March: "My son, I am sending you two newsletters from Hamburg; it must be crazy in that region. When you have 80,000 men at Magdeburg, I do not see how we can still have these concerns at Hamburg. These circumstances make the arrival of the prince d'Eckmühl necessary." He noted that reinforcements were en route and ominously reiterated that Davout "knows Hamburg and there he is well known."[43] An angry Napoleon wrote to Eugene again on the 17th. Although unfairly chastising him, Napoleon attempted to educate his stepson by demonstrating that the best defense against a weakened, tired pursuer is to maintain an offensive countenance. More importantly for understanding the 1813 Campaign, Napoleon again offered insight into the importance of North Germany. This goes very far in explaining why he would leave Davout posted at Hamburg during the Fall Campaign when he desperately needed capable commanders to conduct independent operations:

My son, I am sending you a newsletter from Hamburg dated the 12th: you will see that 200 Cossacks are going to seize the entire 32nd Military Division. They cost me millions; they spread the insurrection to all that is behind the line of the Elbe. This is the result of you standing on the defensive behind the left bank; you no longer have any effect on the enemy. I have repeated this; I hope you finally feel the need to occupy a camp before Magdeburg and threaten to cut off all enemy units that attempt to infiltrate from the side of Hamburg, at eighty leagues from the main body of their army. This is even more important because what occurs in the 32nd [Military] Division is likely to attract landings by the English, Swedish, and perhaps even the Russians; and, if the enemy establishes himself on the lower Elbe, you will have nothing to oppose him when he makes a movement in strength against Dresden and you will find yourself without a line of operation. By reuniting your cavalry at a camp before Magdeburg, the enemy would have been forced to keep all of his in check, and you would have protected the return of General Morand from Swedish Pomerania. According to the attached bulletin, his return seems likely to experience many obstacles. Why did this general start his movement on the 11th when you quit Berlin on the 4th?

I have nothing to add to all the letters I wrote to you in the course of this month. The great issue is the 32nd Military Division and Westphalia because Holland is dependent on them: both can be guarded by an offensive position before Magdeburg. All the remounts that are scheduled to occur in the 32nd Division will be lost. Thus, the resources for our cavalry are paralyzed by 200 or 300 men.[44]

On the 18th, Napoleon sharply instructed Eugene to place Davout in command of the viceroy's left wing on the lower Elbe. He reiterated: "The 32nd Military Division and Westphalia are the main objects of my concern. The evacuation of Hamburg cost me many millions and more than one hundred pieces of cannon and it causes your cavalry to be far behind in its organization." Later that same day, he wrote: "As soon as the prince d'Eckmühl arrives on the left, you will give him command of the 1st Division under General Morand, General Vandamme's corps, and all the 32nd Military Division. By his knowledge of the region, this marshal is well suited to restoring order and making severe examples." Even later that day, Napoleon again wrote to Eugene: "Vandamme will move his headquarters to ... Bremen; he will restore the police on the coast; he will reestablish Carra St.-Cyr in Hamburg, and will place everything in order at Lübeck. Tell Morand to keep his gunners and sailors; my intention is to return him to Pomerania with 1st Division as soon as we are on the Oder."[45] As a preliminary step toward repairing the situation, Eugene instructed Morand to depart Bremen and take a position at Lüneburg, a little over thirty miles south of Hamburg.

On 1 April, Morand reached Lüneburg, a town of 10,000 inhabitants. After learning of Morand's advance, Chernishev and Dörnberg led their *Streifkorps* from the area around Lüchow northeast toward Lüneburg. Reinforced by a Prussian fusilier battalion from Pomerania, one half-battery of Prussian horse artillery, and General Aleksandr Benckendorff's detachment, Dörnberg's command numbered 2,000 cavalry, 1,100 infantry, and 6 guns. With infantry, artillery, and a few Cossacks, Dörnberg halted six miles east of Lüneburg at Barendorf on 1 April. Benckendorff led Dörnberg's cavalry to Bienenbüttel some nine miles south of Lüneburg while Chernishev stopped for the night at Bad Bevensen, itself six miles south of Benckendorff's position. Uniting their columns east of Lüneburg, the Allies attacked shortly after 6:00 on the morning of 2 April. Completely surrounded by a wall, Lüneburg was not easy pickings. After a stubborn contest that lasted until 5:00 P.M., a severely wounded Morand ordered the retreat. Morand, who died two days later from his wounds, lost almost his entire

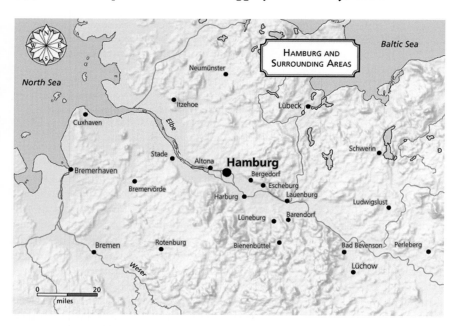

12. Hamburg and surrounding area

division: 2,300 prisoners, 9 guns, and 3 flags fell into Allied hands. Allied losses amounted to 300 killed and wounded including 46 Prussians. This success provided a great morale boost for the Allies. Frederick William awarded the commander of the Pomeranian battalion, Major Karl August von Borcke, the first of the new Iron Cross (2nd Class) decorations for his actions at Lüneburg.

Following the victory at Lüneburg, the British attempted to maintain the momentum in North Germany. Vigorous recruitment in Mecklenburg raised battalions that the British armed and bolstered with 500 seasoned veterans of the King's German Legion, one hussar regiment, and two artillery batteries as well as one rocket battery. A Hanoverian in Russian service, General Ludwig Georg Wallmoden, received command of the motley corps. In addition, the British dispatched the German Legion to the lower Elbe and expected the Swedes to assist Wallmoden, who reached Hamburg on 17 April. Yet time did not favor the Allies. Although reinforced by two Swedish battalions as well as Hanoverian troops, Wallmoden could not maintain his position on the left bank of the Elbe.

Davout began his counteroffensive in late April. Advancing from the southwest, Vandamme took Harburg on 29 April. By early May, the Allies could no longer conduct communication down the lower Elbe. "The state of affairs on the Elbe will not permit us for the present to risk any dispatches of importance by that route," Castlereagh informed Stewart; "and I hope none from your side may fall into the enemy's hands, as we must be aware how great an object it would be either to the Danes or French at this moment to lay hold of an English courier." Vandamme gained possession of the islands formed by the arms of the Elbe south of Hamburg during the second week of May. On 18 May, the Danish garrison three miles west of Hamburg at Altona received orders to support the French as the result of the signing of a Franco-Danish accord. Wallmoden requested assistance from the ranking Swedish commander at Stralsund, General Georg Carl von Döbeln, who responded by dispatching two battalions without first seeking Bernadotte's authorization. After learning of this, Bernadotte recalled the battalions on 28 May. Increased Franco-Danish pressure combined with news of Allied defeats in Saxony prompted the Allies to evacuate Hamburg on 30 May. Nevertheless, they managed to achieve a moral victory by holding Hamburg for almost two months.[46]

Meanwhile, Wittgenstein's caution, although warranted by Eugene's presence at Magdeburg, did not excuse his tardiness, which irked Blücher. "Tomorrow, my troops will cross the river," he informed Hardenberg on 30 March. "I only wish that Wittgenstein's army would likewise press forward; by pushing a corps to Möckern [fifteen miles east of Magdeburg], the French apparently want to deceive us but we will certainly conform to their plans if we allow this to delay us." As the "Arrangement" expressly provided for an agreement between Wittgenstein and Blücher over the measures to be taken if Kutuzov could not personally direct their individual movements, the Russian commander requested a meeting with Scharnhorst at Belzig: "You will endear yourself to me if you instruct Scharnhorst to join me in a few days so we can discuss the operations in detail, because only supreme agreement can bring us closer to our goal," wrote Wittgenstein to Blücher. Perhaps to assuage Blücher, Wittgenstein confidently shared news of Allied success in North Germany: "The affairs on the lower Elbe have had the best results. Tettenborn, who cleared the enemy from Mecklenburg-Strelitz and Mecklenburg-Schwerin as well as Hamburg and Lübeck, stands at Hamburg with his detachment and has sent some troops to the left bank of the Elbe. Both duchies of Mecklenburg have allied with our exalted sovereigns and will supply a corps of 3,000 men. Lübeck will provide 6,000 Reichsthaler for the war; Hamburg is organizing 5,000 men and will give 2,000,000 Reichsthaler. Everyone is excited at Hanover and Brunswick; the people only await the arrival of our troops to join our flags."[47]

Blücher had already ordered the advance of his army to the Grimma–Penig stretch of the Mulde River when he received Wittgenstein's

letter on 26 March indicating that the Russian would move no further than
Belzig until he spoke with Scharnhorst. The Prussian staff chief immediately
departed, reaching Belzig on the 30th. Arriving on the 31st, Wittgenstein
held intensive discussions with Scharnhorst based on the latest intelligence. With the exception of the imperial-controlled fortresses of
Spandau, Magdeburg, Wittenberg, and Torgau, it appeared that the French
had evacuated the region between the Oder and the Elbe from the Danish
to the Austrian frontiers. Thielmann held Torgau with 9,000 Saxons while
Magdeburg and Wittenberg supported Eugene's army of approximately
50,000 men. With the emperor coordinating from Paris, his lieutenants started
assembling the new army at Frankfurt, Würzburg, and Erfurt. Aside from
French recruits and veterans pulled from other theaters, the new legions
continued to reflect the imperial character of the army: Italians marched north
to join German troops from Bavaria, Württemberg, Baden, Darmstadt,
Nassau, and Thuringia.[48]

Four main highways – two each in the north and south – could be
utilized for Allied operations or, if the Coalition delayed, for Napoleon's
counteroffensive. Eugene's army and the fortress of Magdeburg barred the
first of the two northern routes. Although the second, more northern

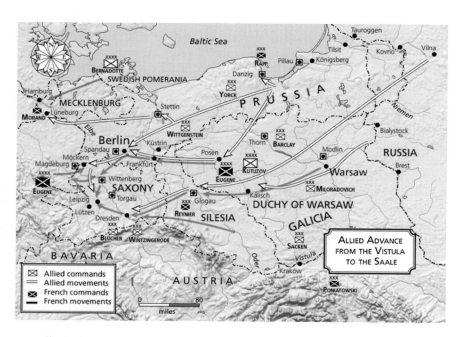

**13.** Allied advance from the Vistula to the Saale

road through Hamburg remained open, Allied combat power did not suffice for significant operations in this direction. As noted, a Swedish corps had landed at Stralsund but remained idle until July. Of the two southern routes, the more southerly ran from Breslau through Dresden, Plauen, and Hof to Bamberg, and figured prominently in Allied planning. At Dresden, the highway formed the Russian main line of communication east through Poland to Russia. West of Dresden, the Allies utilized this artery to maintain communication with Austria, whose importance to the Coalition increased exponentially. Moreover, Napoleon had executed his brilliant maneuver in 1806 by utilizing the portion of the highway that led from Bamberg through Hof and Plauen to strategically envelop the left flank of the Prussian army. Fear that Napoleon would repeat this maneuver kept Allied attention fixed on Hof. The second road ran more than 300 miles southwest from Leipzig through Erfurt, Eisenach, and Würzburg to Frankfurt on the Main River. This route offered Napoleon the advantage of moving his main army close to Eugene and establishing communication with him in the vicinity of the three Elbe fortresses: Magdeburg, Wittenberg, and Torgau. In this way, the emperor could concentrate all his forces for a decisive battle. Although conscious of the threat from Hof, Scharnhorst and Gneisenau correctly predicted that Napoleon would utilize the Frankfurt–Leipzig highway to unite with Eugene. For this reason, the Prussians wanted to attack Eugene before Napoleon could arrive with the new army and unite his forces. Yet, because estimates placed Eugene's army at 50,000 men, Blücher and Wittgenstein first needed to unite if the Allies hoped to defeat the viceroy. Per the "Proposed Plan of Action Beyond the Elbe," Kutuzov resisted plans for a combined attack on Eugene, arguing that such an operation would open the Dresden–Breslau highway, thus exposing the Russian line of communication.[49]

Kutuzov did not dispute the advantages of having Wittgenstein and Blücher gain as much territory as possible to facilitate popular insurrection in Germany. However, he indicated to Wittgenstein on 29 March that this would require the forward armies to extend across the Elster River and thus beyond Leipzig. "Is this advantage," asked the Russian field-marshal, "worth the danger that we will face by weakening ourselves through the extent of our separation, which only serves to reinforce the enemy?" In his opinion, he needed to restrain the land grab to prevent the Allies from dispersing their limited forces: "I thus hold it as absolutely necessary that we go no further than the Elster, which is the extreme line." Kutuzov did admit that together Wittgenstein and Blücher could drive the imperial forces situated around Leipzig and Erfurt to the Rhine. "But one must consider," he added, "that the forces of the French do not consist merely of these troops; instead, they consist also of those that are already en route from the

Rhine or those that soon will be." Kutuzov simply felt that the risks outweighed the benefits. He skillfully concluded his argument by reminding Wittgenstein that warfare consisted of more than winning hearts and minds: "By greatly distancing yourself from the Elbe, you may encounter a superior enemy; thus, your movement beyond this river would have the sole purpose of inflaming the spirit in all of Germany and paralyzing the enemy with uncertainty and inaction. No doubt you will see that this manner of war must change in time, and this change will occur with the approach of our reserves."[50] Regardless, plans for Wittgenstein and Blücher to push west to the Elster received Kutuzov's approval.

Scharnhorst appreciated the need for caution. His ensuing disagreement with Blücher over operations illustrates the necessity of the military marriage between the aggressive field commander and the erudite staff chief. Scharnhorst did not believe the Allies could advance west of the Elbe until Tormasov's army moved up. In fact, without Tormasov, he insisted that an Allied offensive remained out of the question. Poor planning, a rash advance, or movements that lacked support – all mistakes the Prussians committed in 1806 – could lead to an Allied mishap that, aside from the military consequences, would place the Coalition at Austria's mercy. According to the plans coauthored at Belzig by Wittgenstein and Scharnhorst, Blücher would continue his march west, but the concentration of French forces in Franconia and the presence of the Bavarians at Hof required him to slide southwest toward Altenburg, less than thirty miles directly south of Leipzig.

"At Magdeburg," Scharnhorst wrote to Blücher on 1 April from Belzig, "the enemy probably has 40,000–50,000 men including the garrison and another 4,000 men at Wittenberg; he is extended as far as Spandau. We do not have much to fear from this corps as long as no others arrive from Erfurt or Gera." Scharnhorst posed three points for Blücher to consider: "First, the regions around Plauen and Gera must be observed to prevent a superior enemy force from marching on Dresden while your army marches to Leipzig. Second, a bridge must be established as quickly as possible at Mühlberg or Strehla for your army to cross to the right bank of the Elbe without having to utilize the bridge at Dresden. Third, you cannot extend yourself too far west so that you are in danger of being isolated and defeated." For clarification, he explained that thus far the Allies did not intend to bridge the Elbe downstream of Torgau at Wartenburg. "Thus, without a bridge at Mühlberg, we can easily be driven against the Elbe and overwhelmed by superior forces." Scharnhorst advised that the tow and anchor for the Mühlberg bridge be transported night and day. In the spirit of cooperation, Wittgenstein would bypass Eugene's forces at Magdeburg to cross the Elbe seventeen miles downstream of Wittenberg at Roßlau. Yorck would take a position between Zerbst and Zahna while Bülow, who would continue to observe Magdeburg and dispatch *Streifkorps* beyond the Weser River, provided the only line of defense between Eugene and Berlin.[51]

After concluding his meetings with the Russians at Belzig late on 2 April, Scharnhorst rode 100 miles south to rejoin Blücher's headquarters at Penig, where he arrived on the 5th. He delivered news of the precautionary measures demanded by the Russians as the conditions to commence combined operations. As noted, the main point called for the observation of the 35-mile stretch between Gera and Plauen to prevent superior enemy forces from marching on Dresden while Blücher's army advanced to Leipzig. The second point required the rapid construction of a bridge at either Mühlberg or Strehla as well as the repair of the bridge at Meißen. In case of a retreat, these additional bridges would be vital.[52] Third, the Allies could not overextend themselves to the point that they could not unite. This excluded a preemptive strike against French forces presumably assembling at Bayreuth, forty miles southwest of Hof. The plan also acknowledged that any sortie from Magdeburg would be confronted in the field and that Borstell's small brigade would observe Wittenberg and Torgau.[53]

Wintzingerode's Russians entered Leipzig on 3 April. The following day, his main body reached Grimma, twenty miles southeast of Leipzig, while Blücher's vanguard arrived at Penig, twenty-five miles south of Grimma. Blücher's headquarters also reached Penig on the 4th after having departed Dresden two days earlier. With the exception of the Brandenburg Brigade, Blücher's army reached the line of the Mulde River on 5 April. West of his army, *Streifkorps* crossed the Saale. Attempting to cause Eugene concern for his communications and force him to evacuate the stretch between the Elbe and the Weser, they raided toward Halberstadt, Nordhausen, Naumburg, and Jena (see Map 2).[54]

Gneisenau reported that, "except for one member of the Dresden government and some persons attached to the royal family, the inhabitants of Saxony appear to be attuned to our views and everywhere accept us well. One [the Saxons] seeks with desire to obtain our proclamations as well as those of the Russians. Our troops have excellent discipline. The sight of our warrior-like people, especially our numerous cavalry, made an extraordinary impression in Dresden. The troops took three days to march through. It was the most beautiful weather." Municipal officials from Altenburg visited Prussian headquarters and hinted that the inhabitants would not voluntarily arm for the Allied cause. However, they advised the Allies to sternly demand the mobilization. This would provide the people with a pretext to justify their actions to Frederick Augustus. If the Coalition took this step, the Saxon officials claimed the people would willingly obey. Gneisenau suggested that Hardenberg forward this information to Stein, which the state chancellor did, along with a complaint about the foot-dragging of the Central Commission. "It is probably high time that those men who were named by the two monarchs for the administration of the conquered states be immediately directed hither in order to make all of the preparations for the mobilization," carps Gneisenau. "Only a single administrator has been named for the rich region of the land that we have just passed through and of course his jurisdiction is mainly Dresden." Gneisenau described the Allied administrator, a Russian colonel, as "agreeable in the diplomatic mold and very upright, but almost too soft and really inexperienced in the policing and administrative business of his current post. I have sent Ribbentrop there to help him organize his bureau and to instruct him."[55]

At Dresden, Stein commenced the work of the Central Commission. One of his first measures resulted in a decree that prohibited Allied forces from demanding money from the Saxon people. Any funds would come only from the Central Commission. Blücher's headquarters responded by instructing the Prussian troops that they could not issue demands for money. Instead, headquarters would ensure the delivery of food, clothing, and equipment. At the same time, Ribbentrop would procure the best muskets from the countryside for use by the Prussian Landwehr, which was suffering from acute shortages of equipment. While the Prussians certainly enforced the ban on extorting funds, a Russian colonel purportedly seized the state treasury of the Duchy of Gotha and Wintzingerode supposedly collected quite a sum of money at Leipzig.[56]

Regardless of the events behind the army, beautiful spring weather accompanied Blücher's march from Dresden to the Mulde. On 4 April, Clausewitz commented on the feisty mood of the army: "The troops are cheerful and sing '*Auf, auf, Kameraden*' and similar songs, others yodel in perfect tone." All of this served to increase Blücher's confidence. "Already I am here," he wrote from Borna on the 5th, "and in two days I will be at Leipzig. I think I will soon try my strength against my adversary." "Travel to Dresden," he suggested to his wife one week later, "and from there to Leipzig so you can soon follow me to Frankfurt-am-Main. It is the most beautiful time of year and in June you can go to a spa and afterwards visit Münster." Although the Russians and Prussians cleared all of Saxony as far as the line of the Mulde in just two weeks, Blücher's thought of reaching Frankfurt by June certainly indicates his extreme confidence as well as a touch of naïve optimism. His patrols formed an eighty-mile screen west of the Saale River extending from Halle to Saalfeld to monitor the imperial forces assembling at Bayreuth, Erfurt, and Würzburg. Gneisenau's 5 April letter to Hardenberg provides insight into the conclusions being drawn at Blücher's headquarters concerning French preparations: "We have arrived at the Mulde. Enemy troop masses have assembled at Hof, Würzburg, and Erfurt. We are on our guard against them. The army that Napoleon will personally command is probably the one between Magdeburg and Halberstadt. The other troop masses are of poor composition."[57]

Despite Gneisenau's conjecture, the Allies simply did not know whether the emperor would advance through Hof and Plauen or through Würzburg and Erfurt, and whether he intended to gain time or to take Berlin (see Map 2). This uncertainty held Blücher at the Mulde between Dresden and Leipzig, and Wittgenstein at the Elbe between Leipzig and Berlin. Scharnhorst remained cautious. Rumors claimed that Napoleon had reached Gotha (ninety miles west of Leipzig) at the end of March with 30,000–40,000 troops. Scharnhorst assumed the emperor would advance through Franconia toward Dresden to utilize terrain that would protect his infantry from the superior Allied cavalry. He advised Blücher not to move his army too far from the bridges over the Elbe at Dresden and Meißen. "Regarding the enemy," reported Scharnhorst to Volkonsky, "we know that he has significant strength at Würzburg and Erfurt while the Bavarians have a strong force at Hof. It appears the enemy army will assemble at Würzburg and Erfurt while the forces on the Elbe will temporarily concentrate at Magdeburg. We cannot undertake anything decisive against the latter without the concern of our bridges on the upper Elbe being threatened by the enemy at Erfurt and Hof."

In addition, Scharnhorst did not think an advance against Eugene at Magdeburg would produce any measurable success. Like Kutuzov, he figured the viceroy would simply retreat. Scharnhorst further indicated that a French offensive from Hof and Erfurt into Saxony before the Russian main army reached the Elbe would probably force Blücher to retreat across the river. If Wittgenstein crossed the Elbe, he too would be compelled to retreat. If Blücher and Wittgenstein stood their ground, their armies would be compromised by Eugene's threat to the bridges over the Elbe. Consequently, battle would be accepted only under extremely disadvantageous circumstances. "You can see how important it is for the main army under the command of his grace, Prince Kutuzov, to reach the vicinity of the Elbe," concluded Scharnhorst in his letter to Volkonsky, "because then the enemy would have to view any advance to the Elbe as not merely futile but dangerous. Therefore, the unremitting advance of the main army is of the highest importance and I request that you do everything possible to make this happen. I will say only that the enemy at Hof is the same distance to the Elbe as the main army is from Kalisch." Approximately 270 miles separated the Russian main army at Kalisch from the Mulde. Excluding rest days, Kutuzov needed sixteen marches to reach Blücher. Based on these considerations, Scharnhorst advised Blücher to await the enemy's move and not extend beyond the Mulde – advice that frustrated the old hussar.[58]

Yet, on 4 April, Wittgenstein confirmed rumors that had reached the Prussians the previous day concerning an advance by Eugene along the right bank of the Elbe with 30,000 men. Although 135 miles separated Magdeburg from the Saxon capital, the French initiative threatened Blücher's bridges at Dresden and Meißen. Eugene's advance also made clear that the distance between Blücher and Wittgenstein still did not allow mutual support. To achieve the union with Wittgenstein more rapidly, Blücher decided to move north. The cavalry would mask the infantry and determine if the enemy's measures on the right bank of the Elbe presented a serious threat to either Berlin or Dresden, or was just a feint. Blücher's headquarters remained at Penig on the 5th while the troops crossed the Mulde, moving between Chemnitz, Borna, and Mittweida; the cavalry advanced as far as possible in the direction of Leipzig.[59] Meanwhile, Colonel Florenz Ludwig von Dolffs led Blücher's Reserve Cavalry in the opposite direction, taking the road south toward Gera; light cavalry would continue even further, occupying Plauen, Reichenbach, and Greiz on the road to Hof. Patrols and spies disguised as travelers rode toward Erfurt, Gera, and Plauen to reconnoiter the French march (see Map 2). "In this manner," explains Scharnhorst, "we will observe all roads coming from Franconia and the Thuringian Forest; we will threaten the rear of the enemy troops at Magdeburg as well as their communication with those assembling in Thuringia and Franconia. From Nossen, the Brandenburg Brigade will cover our bridges at Dresden."[60]

That evening, reports indicated that, while imperial forces had commenced the 115-mile march south from Erfurt to Würzburg, the number of enemy troops at Hof – ninety miles south of Leipzig – appeared to be increasing. Although incorrect on both accounts, this news caused Blücher's headquarters to rescind the marching orders for the 6th. A postscript in Scharnhorst's report to Volkonsky describes his assumption that the French would assemble considerable forces at Hof and that a large army already could be advancing from there. Until this could be confirmed, the march north would be postponed. Around 11:00 P.M. on 5 April, Scharnhorst issued orders for the troops to remain in their quarters until further notice; only the Brandenburg Brigade marched to Nossen on the 6th, continuing its march west to catch up with the rest of the army. Wintzingerode had already started his march when he received new orders to remain at Wurzen until the enemy's intentions became clear and until he learned that Wittgenstein had crossed the Elbe.[61]

News arrived on the 6th that again altered the situation. Blücher learned that Wittgenstein had successfully attacked Eugene between Möckern and Gommern during the course of the 5th, prompting the viceroy to retreat into Magdeburg on the 6th. During their retreat, the French destroyed the bridges on the roads leading to Berlin, thus reducing the likelihood of Eugene making a serious attempt against the Prussian capital from this direction.[62] To his credit, Eugene's presence at Magdeburg gained time for Napoleon to mobilize the Army of the Main. Although Eugene's "offensive" actually amounted to little more than a large sortie from Magdeburg to secure an extended zone for his troops to forage, its failure provided much fodder for Allied propaganda. In addition, with Eugene confined to Magdeburg, the imperial force at Hof now posed the greater threat to Blücher. Therefore, his headquarters directed the Lower Silesian Brigade to Zwickau and the Reserve Cavalry to Frohburg, Kohren, and Altenburg on the 7th. The Upper Silesian and Brandenburg Brigades remained at Penig and Nossen respectively. From Plauen, which Frederick Augustus had recently departed ignobly, patrols advanced toward Hof while the Reserve Cavalry scouted in the direction of Gera and Zeitz. Blücher's headquarters moved to Rochlitz. Wintzingerode received the task of mastering the terrain between the Elbe and the Saale. While Prussian light cavalry observed the roads coming from Franconia and Thuringia, Wintzingerode's troopers patrolled the region along the left bank of the Elbe from Dessau to Torgau.

Should enemy forces advance from Hof, the three Prussian brigades would offer resistance. However, if the Prussian cavalry and Wintzingerode could not move up in time to enable Blücher to accept battle under favorable conditions, the Prussian corps would gradually withdraw on Dresden and Meißen. During this hypothetical retreat, Wintzingerode and a part of the Prussian cavalry would operate against the enemy's left flank and receive support from Wittgenstein, whom Scharnhorst expected to be astride the Elbe upstream of Magdeburg. In this way, both Allied armies would assume a central position between the imperial forces at Magdeburg and Hof. According to Scharnhorst, they would not be "exposed to mishaps" and could "operate according to circumstances either to continue the offensive against the enemy's left flank ... or to concentrate our force at a point on the right bank of the Elbe and deliver a battle." Again Scharnhorst advocated patience. If a French army did not advance from Hof, he recommended that the Allies "first see from the circumstances and the position of enemy forces which direction we can give to our current offensive movements." With negotiations underway to persuade Vienna to join the Sixth Coalition, Scharnhorst advised giving battle only under the most favorable circumstances.[63]

Blücher accepted Scharnhorst's advice and viewed the union with Wittgenstein as the prerequisite for further operations. He informed Wittgenstein of the situation, expressing concern that the troops marching from Erfurt to Würzburg would cross the Thuringian Forest, unite with the troops at Hof, and advance through Plauen, Zwickau, Chemnitz, and Freiberg against his bridges over the Elbe. He planned to continue to observe all roads leading to the Elbe from Franconia and Thuringia but hoped Wittgenstein would cross the river. He ordered Wintzingerode to establish secure communication with Wittgenstein and to learn where and when he planned to cross the Elbe. To procure further intelligence and sever French communication between Magdeburg and Frankfurt, Scharnhorst and Blücher requested that Wintzingerode send Colonel Victor Prendel with several Cossack regiments and a Prussian staff officer through Naumburg to Weißensee and Bad Langensalza (see Map 2). From there, if possible, they would proceed eighty miles north along the eastern foothills of the Harz Mountains to Nordhausen and Halberstadt while Blücher's light troops proceeded forty miles north from Weimar to Sondershausen and likewise up the eastern edge of the Harz. Both groups would spread word that they served as the vanguard of a large army, arrange flour supplies, and give the appearance of being everywhere.[64]

Scharnhorst remained pessimistic despite the news that the Russian main army had finally departed Kalisch on 7 April after six weeks of rest. Aside from Wintzingerode, cooperation with the Russians seemed to be floundering. In fact, two days earlier, Kutuzov reached the conclusion that, rather than the Elster, the Allies could not distance themselves too far from the Elbe but instead should await the arrival of the Russian reserves. Yet he continued to urge Blücher and Wittgenstein to pursue two goals: facilitating the revolt of the German people and keeping the enemy uncertain and inactive. "Regarding the operations," Scharnhorst wrote to Knesebeck, who remained with the king, "nothing I suggest has been accepted at the headquarters of the prince [Kutuzov] other than Wittgenstein operating in the direction of Magdeburg, Blücher on Dresden, and the main army following three marches behind them." With Kutuzov now sixteen marches behind, Scharnhorst could not conceal his concern about advancing further. "There is no consensus over what will happen next in terms of operations. According to an agreement with me, the crossing of the Elbe before the main army moved up should not have been ordered. Nevertheless, I do not disapprove of the order; the mistake is that the main army has not followed. In the meantime, one cannot undertake anything in war without some risk and we must therefore expose ourselves; it remains our responsibility not to neglect caution and subject ourselves to avoidable danger."[65]

Just as Scharnhorst started to despair, he received a conciliatory letter from Volkonsky. Dated 9 April, the missive claimed that Kutuzov also believed the French force concentrating between Würzburg and Erfurt would advance on the road to Hof. "Therefore," wrote the Russian staff chief, "it is of paramount importance to assemble our forces on the left flank so that by remaining close to the Bohemian mountains we retain the opportunity to defend this position with all our strength." He informed Scharnhorst that the main army's vanguard under Miloradovich had received orders to proceed from Bunzlau through Dresden toward Freiberg. Three days earlier, the main army itself marched with the goal of reaching Dresden by 24 April. "Thus, all the desires you expressed over this matter will be met. Prince Kutuzov shares the opinion that it would be disadvantageous for us to recross the Elbe and abandon Saxony. Your views on the concentration of enemy forces in Saxony are also in complete agreement [with Kutuzov's], as is your opinion regarding the forces deployed on the lower Elbe with the task of operating in North Germany. [Kutuzov] expresses his consent on the further advance of Blücher's corps in the direction of Leipzig. The attached copy of the letter to ... Auvray, which was sent before your letter was received, will reassure you that [Kutuzov's] opinions completely coincide with yours." In addition, Kutuzov approved the concentration of Blücher's corps on the road to Plauen and requested that detachments probe toward Hof to observe imperial movements. Nevertheless, the Russians cautioned Scharnhorst against moving the main body of Blücher's corps too far west before the arrival of the main army.

The last paragraph of Volkonsky's letter makes clear that Kutuzov did not "anticipate a rapid advance of enemy forces because the French do not seem to have gathered superior strength yet. The enemy, suffering from the lack of manpower and with his cavalry clearly demonstrating its weakness, would find himself in a very disadvantageous position if he attempted to march through the Thuringian Forest and into open country. Therefore, for the foreseeable future, we probably should not be concerned about a rapid enemy attack." However, should the French launch an offensive, Kutuzov wanted an immediate concentration of all forces including Wittgenstein's army; Bulow and Borstell "as well as a few thousand Russian troops" would observe Eugene's forces at Magdeburg.[66]

Meanwhile, Blücher's cavalry screen continued to provide intelligence concerning the increase of imperial forces in Germany. A detachment of Prussian hussars and Cossacks that reached Saalfeld on the 7th reported the constant movement of large troop units north from Meiningen to Gotha. According to a reliable spy at Würzburg, the site of Ney's headquarters, new troops arrived daily. After the marshal reorganized the march units, they continued north in the direction of Schweinfurt. The informant stated that Ney's corps would be 30,000 strong and consist of one cavalry and four infantry divisions, three of which had already passed through Würzburg. These divisions included Rheinbund troops from Darmstadt, Baden, and Württemberg. It appeared that Ney's corps would assemble at Meiningen, Gotha, and Erfurt but the marshal had also secured the road to Fulda for the army's use. News arrived from Öttingen, some seventy-five miles south of Würzburg, that 40,000 Italian and French troops had marched from Augsburg and Donauworth toward the Main River. All of this confused Blücher's headquarters over Napoleon's intentions. Some drew a comparison between Ney's corps and the left wing of the Grande Armée in 1806, which Napoleon "refused," while his right wing swept around the

Prussian left. Just like in 1806, those who saw French movements in this light called for an advance to the Thuringian Forest: the difference being that in 1813 the passages across the Elbe would be secured. Others believed the imperials would simply march north to reinforce Eugene at Magdeburg.[67]

After repulsing Eugene, Wittgenstein continued his march south. On 10 April, Yorck's I Corps crossed the Elbe at Roßlau and moved southwest through Dessau to reach Köthen – twenty-one miles north of Wintzingerode's Cossacks at Halle. Wittgenstein reached Dessau on the 8th, where he received a 6 April communiqué from Kutuzov written by Toll. The Allied commander in chief advised against Wittgenstein's plan to cross the Elbe at Roßlau because of the threat posed by the 50,000 imperial troops thirty-five miles downstream at Magdeburg. Although surprised by Wittgenstein's estimate of French forces, Kutuzov did not attempt to alter his subordinate's perception of the situation. Assuming Wittgenstein's intelligence to be correct, Kutuzov speculated on the consequences of an ill-advised crossing of the Elbe at Roßlau rather than between Meißen and Dresden per his instructions. Kutuzov explained that from Magdeburg, Eugene needed to dispatch only 10,000 men along the left bank of the Elbe to Roßlau to stymie Wittgenstein's crossing. Meanwhile, after leaving a substantial garrison upwards of 10,000 men at Magdeburg, the viceroy could advance on Berlin with 30,000 men, brushing aside Bülow's 10,000 troops. Should Wittgenstein manage to reach the left bank of the Elbe, he would be unable either to support Bülow or to close the road to the Prussian capital. By remaining on the right bank of the Elbe, he could support Bülow at any time and deter Eugene from extending too far from his stronghold at Magdeburg.

Fortunately for Blücher, Kutuzov did not instruct Wittgenstein to make an absurd retrograde movement. "Now, because you have probably completed the crossing at Roßlau," speculates Kutuzov, "there is nothing for you to do but to approach the corps of General Blücher, which stand forward [west] of Dresden, as quickly as possible." Indicative of his own mindset, Kutuzov placed no value on speed or initiative: "I must repeat my opinion, mainly, that our rapid advance is completely useless for the main goal of the forthcoming campaign; this belief is based on both the enemy forces that are approaching as well as the troops that we expect to receive." Kutuzov's thoughts are best revealed in his 5 April letter to Wintzingerode:

> I can see from your report that you are moving toward Leipzig. This must be in full agreement with General Blücher. Let me once again comment on the rapidity of your advance. I must start by citing you an excerpt from my letter to Wittgenstein. I know that every mediocrity in Germany is now criticizing the slowness of our movement. They believe that our very advance equates to victory, and every day lost is a defeat. Yet my responsibilities compel me to follow plans and make careful calculations based on the distance of our

reserve troops from the Elbe and the forces that the enemy has at his disposal or that we may encounter in any given theater of war. Minor victories over the small forces that the enemy has deployed in front would produce but one result in forcing them to retreat to the main [enemy] forces and augment them like a snowball. I must always judge the gradual reduction of our forces in rapid offensive movements with the distance from the sources of our strength. This burdens me with a responsibility to explain these dangers to the generals whom His Majesty has entrusted with the command of major forces. You can be assured that the defeat of one of our detachments would immediately destroy the favorable opinion that they now have of us in Germany. I cannot talk so candidly to General Blücher but you must influence him in the same spirit without sharing details.

According to Mikhailovsky-Danilevsky, "such letters provide evidence of the caution with which the field-marshal directed the movements of the armies, a caution that forms a distinct characteristic of great field commanders and at this time was all the more noteworthy since it was in complete contradiction to the views of most of the generals who, basing their judgment on the spirit that had inflamed Germany, wished for a rapid advance of the army."[68] Wittgenstein responded to Kutuzov on 8 April, maintaining that his own estimate of Eugene's strength at Magdeburg "was completely correct." Moreover, he bluntly informed the field-marshal that he had not misread the viceroy's intentions. Wittgenstein took credit for luring Eugene out of Magdeburg and defeating him. Citing the destruction of the bridges over the Elbe in the vicinity of Magdeburg, the Russian general insisted that "for us this maneuver was very convenient and advantageous, because Berlin is now completely secure against Magdeburg."

The second paragraph of Wittgenstein's letter is far less defiant, and assured Kutuzov that his army would move no further from Dessau. Wittgenstein claimed to be "in position to act according to any circumstance. To my rear are two secure crossing points: at Elster [Wartenburg] and Roßlau, of which the latter can in no way be threatened, because the position itself ... is extremely strong. In this position I will await the approach of the main army or the arrival of new orders from you.[69] Until then, I will only conduct the *kleinen Krieg* through partisans." Wittgenstein adhered to his plan to remain at Dessau but did so having little news of the enemy's main army. Meeting with him on 10 April, Wilson recorded the following in his journal: "He had no accounts of the enemy now being at Erfurt, nor anything more than reports of Bonaparte's arrival at Gotha, but he believed that since 1 January 100,000 men had passed the Rhine, so he presumed that a considerable force was now ready for him. He lamented the distance of the Russian [main] army."[70]

Reports confirmed that French forces along the lower Saale from Alsleben to the mouth of the Elbe amounted to 12,000 men under Marshal

Victor, whose headquarters stood at Sandersleben, twenty-one miles west of Köthen. Behind this forward screen, the main imperial force continued to assemble in Franconia and on the lower Main. Although estimates varied, apparently a considerable army camped in the region of Würzburg and an additional 25,000 men assembled west of the Thuringian Forest in the valley of the Werra. All reports likewise indicated that the army of 30,000 to 40,000 Italians would soon reach the German theater. Blücher's staff believed that Napoleon would utilize the shortest line of operations to the Elbe: the road from Hof to Dresden. In addition, the rugged terrain of southwestern Saxony would favor his infantry while obstructing Allied cavalry. If Blücher continued to march north through Leipzig and toward Magdeburg or the Harz Mountains, he risked being strategically enveloped by a French force crossing the 115 miles that separated Hof from Dresden. In this scenario, Blücher would lose his bridges over the Elbe, be cut off from Kutuzov, and find himself caught between Eugene's 50,000 men at Magdeburg and presumably Napoleon's 100,000 troops at Dresden. His only salvation would be to escape north if Wittgenstein could keep Eugene in check at Magdeburg long enough for Blücher to get across the Elbe. Saxony's ambiguous political position did not help. Should Frederick Augustus place his troops at Napoleon's disposal, the threat of 12,000 Saxons advancing forty-five miles downriver from Torgau toward Roßlau would do nothing to ease Blücher's crossing of the Elbe in that region. Again, the absence of the Russian main army severely limited Blücher's options. According to Scharnhorst, had Tormasov remained three days behind Blücher as stipulated in the "Arrangement," or if Miloradovich's corps alone had reached Dresden, "a bold operation" against the viceroy on the left bank of the Elbe up to the foot of the Harz "would be available for execution."[71]

With Eugene apparently anchored to Magdeburg, Blücher wanted to sever the viceroy's communications with the forces assembling in Franconia and along the Main River by dispatching cavalry detachments as far as possible. Taking positions that Scharnhorst described as "the most appropriate according to the circumstances," Prussian light cavalry established a seventy-mile outpost chain west of the Saale River extending south from Naumburg through Jena and Schleiz to Plauen. Small detachments patrolled all roads running through the Thuringian Forest to Magdeburg (see Map 2).[72] Wintzingerode led his corps north-northwest toward the Saale. To maintain communication with him and perhaps impress French spies, Blücher moved the Prussian Guard du Corps Regiment to Leipzig. Scharnhorst summarized the idea behind these movements in a letter to Wittgenstein's chief of staff, Auvray, on 8 April: "We are thus secured against all misfortunes and should the viceroy undertake something against Wittgenstein on the lower Saale we are in position to proceed against his right flank. Finally, we are disrupting the direct communication between the two enemy armies on the Elbe and in Franconia and hope to soon capture couriers who will provide details of the enemy's intentions."[73]

On 9 April, Toll wrote a long letter to Auvray expressing the strategic views of Kutuzov's headquarters. According to Toll, the two forward armies could not cross the Elster while the Russian main army remained so far behind. Should Blücher and Wittgenstein cross the Elster, they risked being enveloped by the French army advancing from the Main Valley through Hof or Gera. Above all, he called for vigilance to prevent Napoleon from surprising the Allies as he had the Prussians in 1806 and executing the same maneuver. The time for further offensive operations would arrive as soon as the Russian main army reached the left bank of the Elbe. In addition, Toll advised suspending Allied operations until General Barclay de Tolly had concluded the siege of Thorn and reached the Elbe. Until then, Toll envisioned three groups of frontline Allied forces all under Wittgenstein's command: Blücher and Wintzingerode; Wittgenstein and Yorck; and Bülow, Borstell, and Russian general Mikhail Vorontsov, who commanded 3,500 men. Bülow, Borstell, and Vorontsov would observe Magdeburg and prevent imperial forces from retaking Berlin. Toll suggested that the Prussian authorities arm the peasants of Brandenburg to assist with the defense of the capital. As soon as Vorontsov united with Bülow and Borstell, Wittgenstein and Yorck should cross the Elbe at Roßlau and proceed to Leipzig while Blücher and Wintzingerode concentrated thirty miles further south at Altenburg. The Russian main army would form the second line of Allied forces and move to within one day's march of Wittgenstein's troops. "For the day of battle, the further approach and union of the [main] army with the various groups can occur according to circumstances." Toll assumulated that the French could delay offensive operations for another six weeks, the amount of time he believed Napoleon needed to finish rebuilding his cavalry arm. At that time, Toll assumed that the Swedes, reinforced by Barclay, could relieve Bülow's group so it could join Wittgenstein at Leipzig. Similar to earlier ideas that had reigned at Kutuzov's headquarters, Toll's plan falls short of prescribing an Allied offensive that would seek battle.[74]

Meanwhile, Napoleon assured Ney and Eugene that the Russians could not have crossed *the Oder* in significant numbers. Only "Allied partisans and vanguards" stood between the Oder and the Elbe: "Wittgenstein could not have reached Berlin with more than 6,000 infantry" as 40,000 Russians stand before Danzig and "one of their divisions blockades Thorn, another is at Warsaw in front of Modlin and 30,000 before the Austrians and Poles." On 29 March, the emperor identified his new goal to be the movement of Ney's army across the Mulde to cover Leipzig. At the least, he wanted the marshal to reach the Saale to cover Weimar. On 5 April, Napoleon backtracked somewhat. Based on the reports he had received concerning the number of Russian forces investing Danzig, facing Schwarzenberg, and blockading the Oder fortresses, he wrote to Ney: "I do not think the Russians are in a position to cross *the Elbe* in great force." Although conceding that the Allies had crossed the Elbe, the next day he insisted that "the enemy does not appear to be in a position to cross the Elbe with large forces. All rumors are exaggerated and false." Three days later, on 9 April, the emperor learned that Blücher had reached Dresden, and that Yorck and part of Wittgenstein's corps opposed Eugene between Brandenburg and Magdeburg. "I do not think the enemy plans to move major forces through Dresden," speculated Napoleon, "or he may do so with no more than 25,000 men." He asked Ney to judge for himself the strength and intentions of the Allies and to seize the crossings of the Saale in conjunction with the viceroy.[75]

As a result of the Allied threat to the headwaters of the Saale and Main Rivers and thus Bavaria, Napoleon accelerated the concentration of the Army of the Main – an estimated 150,000 infantry, 16,000 cavalry, and 330 guns – at Erfurt. He informed his brother, Jerome, on 11 April that he planned to be at Erfurt with 200,000 men – independent of the Army of the Elbe – between the 20th and 22nd of that month and would then attack the enemy. "I do not know what you will do," he wrote to Eugene; "maneuver accordingly." If the Allies continued the advance from Dresden, an opportunity would arise to catch them in an unfavorable position. At the least, the further west they advanced from Dresden, the more they would expose their communications to Eugene.[76]

The master went to work devising a plan to take advantage of any opportunity the Allies offered. He sensed they would stumble: "The enemy is very far from suspecting that a considerable force will concentrate on the Saale." After reaching the Saale and uniting with Eugene, Napoleon intended to cross the river and drive through Leipzig, seizing Dresden and the other crossings over the Elbe to the rear of the Allied army. Thus cut off from Silesia to the east and Brandenburg to the north, the Allies would be forced to fight a battle in which Napoleon's superior generalship and numbers would end the war in one bold stroke. "My intention," he explained, "is to refuse my right and allow the enemy to penetrate toward Bayreuth, thus making a movement that is *the inverse* of the one I executed during the Jena campaign; providing the enemy moves through Bayreuth – the result will be my arrival at Dresden ahead of him, and his severance from Prussia."[77]

As for the Army of the Main, its left wing, formed by VI Corps and the Imperial Guard, would march 165 miles on the great highway from Mainz through Fulda and Gotha to Erfurt. In the center, III Corps would turn north to continue its march from Schweinfurt to Meiningen. On the right, IV Corps would likewise continue north, covering the fifty miles between Ansbach and Bamberg, and then trooping another sixty through

Coburg to Gräfenthal. Napoleon's timetable placed the 60,000 men of Ney's III Corps at Erfurt, seventy-two miles southwest of Leipzig, on the 20th. He expected Marshal Jean-Baptiste Bessières with the Guard Cavalry and Marshal Auguste Frédéric de Marmont's VI Corps, a total of 40,000 men and 10,000 cavalry, to arrive at Eisenach, thirty miles west of Erfurt, between 20 and 22 April (see Map 2).[78]

On 11 April, Eugene's Army of the Elbe stood approximately thirty miles south of Magdeburg around Aschersleben. Meanwhile, the corps belonging to the Army of the Main continued toward the Saale. Almost 160 miles southwest of Aschersleben, the head of Ney's III Corps reached Schweinfurt, with the main body extended sixty miles westward along the highway to Aschaffenburg on the Main River. Marmont's VI Corps assembled seventeen miles downstream of Aschaffenburg at Hanau, with the Imperial Guard still on the Rhine at Mainz. More than 100 miles southwest of Hof, the "Italian Corps of Observation" (40,000 men), which the emperor had divided into IV and XII Corps, started arriving at Ansbach, with the rear of the column extending seventy-five miles south to Augsburg. General Henri-Gatien Bertrand's IV Corps received one division each of Italian, French, and Württemberger troops; Marshal Nicolas-Charles Oudinot's XII Corps consisted of two French divisions and one Bavarian. While Bertrand continued north, Oudinot temporarily remained in Bavaria, with his French divisions posted between Ansbach and Nürnberg, and his Bavarian division at Bayreuth.[79]

Returning to Wittgenstein, reports suggested that Eugene had directed his troops south toward Erfurt. With his right apparently secured by the *Streifkorps* and with Eugene withdrawing from before his center, he briefly considered but then decided against an operation to take Wittenberg. On 12 April, Wittgenstein informed Blücher that Chernishev and Dörnberg would reconnoiter the region between Hanover, Brunswick, and the Harz Mountains in an attempt to ascertain the intentions of both Davout and Eugene. Moreover, Miloradovich would reach Dresden on the 16th, but Tormasov's army would not arrive until 28 April. Wittgenstein communicated his belief that the French would not launch an offensive before this date, citing as evidence Davout's unexplained movements as well as Eugene's withdrawal from Magdeburg. To Wittgenstein, this indicated that the French still lacked the necessary strength to undertake a serious offensive against the two Allied armies. He also cited reports of Napoleon's prolonged stay at Versailles and Paris as confirmation that the French were not prepared for a general offensive. Nevertheless, should a considerable imperial army emerge from Franconia and make for Dresden, he advised Blücher to open the road to the Saxon capital and fall back to Grimma, "where I can likewise be in two or three days so that combined we can force him to accept a battle in his flank."[80]

After learning from Wittgenstein that Eugene had led the majority of his troops south from Magdeburg to unite with reinforcements coming from Erfurt, Blücher prepared for the assumed French offensive to the upper Elbe. "We still have not encountered any significant resistance," Blücher wrote to his wife on the 12th, "but the decisive events will now begin. The French have concentrated strong forces at Erfurt and Würzburg, and we now wait to see what they will do." Wintzingerode received orders to move south through Leipzig on the 11th to reach Borna by the 12th unless good reason prevented his march south. The Guard regiment likewise marched south from Leipzig to Altenburg on the 11th and 12th. Dolffs's Reserve Cavalry reached Lichtenstein, northeast of Zwickau on the 12th. Blücher transferred his headquarters to Chemnitz, sixty-five miles northeast of Hof, on the 12th. On the following day, the 13th, Blücher, Scharnhorst, and Gneisenau conducted reconnaissance in the region of Zwickau to become familiar with the terrain. As a result of the reports on French movements, Blücher's headquarters as well as the Lower Silesian Brigade moved to Zwickau on the 14th and from there to the Pleiße River on the following day. Hardenberg impressed on Scharnhorst and Gneisenau the need for caution as a response to Vienna's repeated claim that Austria would remain neutral if the Allies suffered a defeat. Both staff officers recognized the wisdom of avoiding a setback at the commencement of the campaign. "Thus far we have advanced as far as the current course of events has permitted," wrote Gneisenau; "to proceed further would suit many a troubled soul but a further advance corresponds neither to the strategic situation nor to the political conditions. Things are in the crisis of development, and it would be dangerous to disrupt them too early. In a few days, the situation might be clearer."[81]

Prussian headquarters continued to view Kutuzov's arrival in Saxony as the key to commencing *limited* offensive operations that, in the end, still left the initiative to Napoleon. "The great attention on our left flank ends as soon as the main army is close enough to position itself at Dresden before the enemy army can reach this point," explained Scharnhorst to Wintzingerode, who requested orders to press the offensive. "Because this point in time is no longer far off, we can now operate more freely and aggressively. For the moment, Blücher's corps can move further south and west as soon as Miloradovich's corps reaches Dresden; from the 18th onward, it can operate still freer than up to now if the enemy does not advance any further because starting on this day the enemy no longer will be in a position to reach the Elbe before the main army arrives there. *Our next step must then depend on news of the enemy.*"[82]

Blücher likewise could not see beyond Kutuzov's arrival at Dresden. "When the Russian main army reaches the right bank of the Elbe and Miloradovich's corps reaches the [left] bank ... then it may be time to begin our combined offensive operations if the enemy does not deploy before this," he speculated in a memo to Wittgenstein on the 14th. In the midst of writing this letter, he received his Russian counterpart's dispatch from two days earlier. As a result of the news that Miloradovich would reach Dresden on the 16th, Blücher decided to march the Brandenburg Brigade twenty miles west from Nossen to Mittweida as part of a partial concentration of II Corps. His Reserve Cavalry and headquarters moved to Altenburg while the Upper Silesian and Lower Silesian Brigades maintained their quarters around Penig and Zwickau respectively: a front of thirty-five miles. Wintzingerode would remain close to Leipzig.[83]

Meanwhile, Blücher's light cavalry continued to disrupt French communication and destabilize rear areas. One patrol surprised and captured a battalion of 412 Rheinbund troops from the Duchy of Saxony; Blücher accepted their request to serve in the Prussian army.[84] Documents taken from the Bavarians at Bad Langensalza indicated that 20,000 Italians had joined Ney's corps in Franconia, where Napoleon was expected to arrive soon. On learning that the French envoy to Gotha, Nicolas-Auguste St. Aignan, remained in the city, the Prussian captain who commanded the post at Saalfeld made an attempt to apprehend the French diplomat on the night of 11/12 April. Although the operation failed because St. Aignan hid, the Prussians confiscated his papers and arrested his secretary. The documents contained an accurate assessment of Prussian troop strengths in Silesia as well as reports on the concentration of the French main force between Erfurt and Würzburg. In addition, correspondence indicated that the emperor soon would join the army but was at Paris as of 5 April. News of the raid earned a mixed reaction from Blücher, providing us with insight into the manner in which he balanced regulations and discipline. "I strongly rebuke this officer for his conduct that went against regulations," he wrote to the captain's immediate superior, Lieutenant-Colonel Karl Friedrich von Hobe, "and I task you with informing this officer to remain with his regiment. Yet because his operation had good intentions and appears to have been motivated only by zeal and a misunderstanding of his duties and moreover because among the papers apprehended by him are many notes of importance, there will be no punishment this time. You will send the French secretary, who was left behind ill at Rudolstadt, to Altenburg as soon as he can travel."[85]

At Torgau, negotiations with the Saxon general Thielmann resulted in his agreement to join the first corps of Tormasov's army that reached the Elbe. Thielmann's conditions included maintaining Frederick Augustus on the Saxon throne, the guarantee of Saxony's material status prior to the 11 December 1806 Peace of Posen, the independence of the Saxon army under Thielmann's command, and the continued occupation of Torgau by Saxon troops. In addition to this good news, Blücher's report to Frederick

William stated: "The behavior of Your Majesty's troops under my command is truly exemplary. Nowhere are there complaints. The Saxon Immediate Commission itself, which has not been very friendly toward us, felt compelled by this exemplary behavior as well as the excellent spirit that reigns among the Prussian troops to boast of it in a letter to General Thielmann at Torgau. Also, there are few sick men in my corps."[86]

Regardless of the apparent progress with the Saxons, which eventually came to naught, prudence mastered Blücher's headquarters as Scharnhorst continued to feel paralyzed by Kutuzov's tardiness and inadequate intelligence. "Had the main army reached the Elbe earlier, it is highly probable that we would have defeated the enemy in offensive operations," Scharnhorst reported to the king's headquarters, "but under the circumstances we have not risked extending ourselves too far from the crossings over the Elbe; also we have not received adequate information over the enemy's situation." Napoleon had lost 500,000 men in Russia but not his reputation for speed and maneuver. By the 15th, reports could only confirm the arrival in Germany of the Italian army and that Ney's army concentrated in the valley of the Werra. A combination of verified intelligence and educated assumptions based on the advance of French units from the lower Main strongly suggested that imperial forces in Franconia and Thuringia appeared to be uniting for an offensive that would restore Napoleon's prestige and scare straight the courts of allies and satellites who were contemplating leaving the emperor's fold. Uncertainty over the road that this main force would utilize during its advance from Franconia prompted Scharnhorst's concerns of being isolated and defeated.[87]

Moreover, the haunting memory of past mistakes provided lessons that the Prussians could not ignore. The baby steps attracted criticism, forcing Scharnhorst to respond to his critics. Scharnhorst refused "to engage in operations whose results are not only unsafe, but also could be highly dangerous." He received Blücher's full support and later that of his pupil, Clausewitz:

> This thinking led to the conviction that prior to the arrival of the Russian main army, which would secure the Elbe ... no further offensive operations could be undertaken along this river. In this depiction, I wished to convince my Prussian brothers-in-arms that at no moment did a punishable absence of mind concerning our purpose occur and that our commanders did not for reasons of indecisiveness or inertia fail to utilize a good moment to employ the powers of reason against an unprepared enemy. The momentum of the victories that had been attained on the Moskva had been exhausted on the Elbe. The Russian army, weakened by the immense operations during its historically unprecedented pursuit of the enemy and by the countless fortresses that it had to besiege and storm, would not have been in a condition to remain one moment at the Elbe if it had not found in the military forces of

# DISCOVER MORE ABOUT MILITARY HISTORY

Frontline Books is an imprint of Pen & Sword Books, which has more than 1500 titles in print covering all aspects of military history on land, sea and air. If you would like to receive more information and special offers on your preferred interests from time to time, along with our standard catalogue, please indicate your areas of interest below and return this card (no stamp required in the UK). Alternatively, register online at www.frontline-books.com. Thank you.

**PLEASE NOTE: We do not sell data information to any third party companies**

Mr/Mrs/Ms/Other.................. Name.................................................................

Address. ............................................................................................................

................................................................................... Postcode.........................

Email address. ....................................................................................................

If you wish to receive our email newsletter, please tick here ☐

### PLEASE SELECT YOUR AREAS OF INTEREST

| | | | |
|---|---|---|---|
| Ancient History | ☐ | Medieval History ☐ | English Civil War ☐ |
| Napoleonic | ☐ | Pre World War One ☐ | World War One ☐ |
| World War Two | ☐ | Post World War Two ☐ | Falklands ☐ |
| Aviation | ☐ | Maritime ☐ | Battlefield Guides ☐ |
| Regimental History | ☐ | Military Reference ☐ | Military Biography ☐ |

Website: www.frontline-books.com • Email: info@frontline-books.com

2

Frontline Books
FREEPOST SF5
47 Church Street
BARNSLEY
South Yorkshire
S70 2BR

Prussia a powerful ally. Yet, even if it had been within the means of this ally to aid the Russian army, whose operations by their very nature had to end at the Vistula, as it passed along the path of all the fortresses up to the Elbe, their combined strengths were not sufficient to move the theatre of war another 120 miles forward to the Main. It also betrays a complete lack of general judgment if one can forget for a moment that the enemy's strength increases by moving closer to his sources of support, whereas by the same measure ours decrease.[88]

Blücher's headquarters and the Reserve Cavalry went to Borna on the 16th; his three brigades remained at Zwickau, Penig, and Mittweida. At Leipzig, Wintzingerode served as the link between the Prussians and Wittgenstein. Along the front of Blücher's army, cavalry detachments extended deep into Germany, reaching Plauen, Weimar, and Straußfurt, the last being seventy-five miles west of Borna. Prussian patrols and partisans went even farther, passing through the Thuringian Forest to Gotha as well as crossing the Harz and proceeding to Ellrich. Wintzingerode's Cossacks and light cavalry reached Halberstadt, Blankenburg, and Seesen (see Map 2). Despite the broad coverage, the intelligence provided exaggerated, confusing, and at times completely incorrect reports. The Italian corps received strengths anywhere between 45,000 and 52,000 men while the French army in Germany reached 300,000 soldiers. For the time being, the wealthy lands of western Saxony fed the Allied army while cavalry detachments patrolled and disrupted French communications. "This and the establishment of bridges over the Elbe are all that we can do before hand," wrote Scharnhorst on 15 April. "Now, if the enemy advances through Thuringia on the direct road to the Elbe, we are in a position to take him in the front with both armies and if he comes on the road from Plauen to Dresden he can be taken in the left flank. Now it comes down to exploiting this rich land to establish magazines on the right bank of the Elbe. I have turned to Stein for this. Regarding further operations, we can do nothing until the Russian main army arrives except take possession of the Harz as long as this can be done without great sacrifice."[89]

Like the Austrians in 1809, the Prussians planned for a German uprising to support their war effort to such an extent that Vienna regarded Blücher's headquarters as a nest of Jacobins. Supported by Prussian light and non-conventional forces, a people's war would engulf Germany while the Prussians themselves formed an army with all possible resources.[90] Blücher, Scharnhorst, and Gneisenau envisioned operations that would allow no time for the remains of the French army to recover or receive reinforcements. Both components of this plan failed in March and April. Aside from the sheer speed with which Napoleon formed a new army, causes for this failure can be found in the paucity of manpower that initially characterized the Sixth Coalition. Regarding the expected auxiliary troops, neither the

British nor the Swedes appeared, and the Danes remained indecisive spectators who eventually sided with Napoleon. The Prussian army could barely field 65,000 men. An appeal from Gneisenau to his friend and fellow Hanoverian, Count Ernst Friedrich zu Münster, for British support clearly illustrates Prussia's needs: "Our mobilization continues with zeal and as much as our resources allow, but these are very limited. There is a lack of military hardware, not bodies – these we have in sufficient number – but specifically: cloth, leather equipment, arms, ammunition, and money. If we had this currently, we could double our strength on the go. Our economic arrangements are so splendid that an army of 80,000 men outfitted and placed in the field will cost no more than 400,000–500,000 thalers per month. Please inform the prince-regent of this circumstance. Just a small effort and we are all saved."[91]

Blücher became ill sometime after 12 April but the days passed quietly as he recuperated. Scharnhorst found time to lecture the Prussian crown prince on military affairs; to arrange with Ribbentrop the army's supplies and logistics; and to instruct Major Oppen in the duties of the General Staff. To ease supply and maintain morale, Gneisenau distributed the troops around the region, yet they remained close enough to quickly reach the assembly point as soon as the alarm cannon at the Altenburg Schloß fired the signal. The affection that the inhabitants of Altenburg and the surrounding lands showered on Blücher and his entourage helped him cope with his impatience and illness. One afternoon a letter arrived, addressed to Blücher, that lacked a signature, but the old hussar immediately recognized the author: Duke Karl August of Weimar. The letter concluded with the meaningful words: "Always move forward! Do you want to relive the year 1806?"[92]

## Notes

1   Holleben and Caemmerer, *Frühjahrsfeldzuges 1813*, I:244; Pertz and Delbrück, *Gneisenau*, II:546.
2   Grolman served as General Staff chief from 1814 to 1819, Rühle from 1819 to 1821, Müffling from 1821 to 1829, and Krauseneck from 1829 to 1849. Prince Frederick William Henry Augustus of Prussia (1779–1843) was the son of Frederick the Great's youngest brother, Prince Augustus Ferdinand. Augustus's older brother, Louis Ferdinand, was killed at Saalfeld in 1806. Both Louis Ferdinand and Augustus often are mistakenly referred to as brothers of Frederick William III instead of second cousins. See Unger, *Blücher*, II:11–12.
3   Scharnhorst to Gneisenau, Kalisch, 25 March 1813, GStA PK, VI HA Rep. 92 Nl. Gneisenau, Nr. 23.
4   Alexander made this comment to Gneisenau, which Clausewitz relayed to his wife: Clausewitz to Marie, Penig, 4 April 1813, in Schwartz, *Clausewitz*, II:73. Pertz and Delbrück, *Gneisenau*, II:254, describes Scharnhorst as "the soul of the Allied

army," who "brought about general agreement in the planning through his personal presence in the various headquarters, and at the same time worked with the greatest activity to organize Prussia's armed forces."

5 Boyen, *Erinnerungen*, ed. Nippold, III:13.

6 Clausewitz to Marie, Penig, 4 April 1813, in Schwartz, *Clausewitz*, II:73; Gneisenau to Hardenberg, Breslau, 11 March 1813, GStA PK, VI HA Rep. 92 Nl. Gneisenau, Nr. 20b; Frederick William to Gneisenau, Breslau, 11 March 1813, *ibid.*, Nr. 16; Gneisenau to Eichhorn, Liegnitz, 19 March 1813, *Gneisenau*, ed. Griewank, Nr. 105, 214–15.

7 Bogdanovich, *Geschichte des Krieges*, I:77; Scharnhorst to Gneisenau, Kalisch, 25 March 1813, GStA PK, VI HA Rep. 92 Nl. Gneisenau, Nr. 23; Clausewitz to Marie, Dresden, 1 April 1813, in Schwartz, *Clausewitz*, II:71–72; Holleben and Caemmerer, *Frühjahrsfeldzuges 1813*, I:321.

8 Blücher's letter is quoted in Mikhailovsky-Danilevsky, *Denkwürdigkeiten*, 36; Kutuzov to Blücher, Kalisch, 19 March 1813, RGVIA, f. VUA, op. 16, d. 3921, l. 96.

9 Gneisenau to Eichhorn, Liegnitz, 19 March 1813, *Gneisenau*, ed. Griewank, Nr. 105, 214–15; Gneisenau to Dörnberg, Haynau (Chojnów), 22 March 1813, *ibid.*, Nr. 107, 216; Wilson, *Private Diary*, I:311–12.

10 Holleben and Caemmerer, *Frühjahrsfeldzuges 1813*, I:242–44; Plotho, *Der Krieg*, I:47–49; Bogdanovich, *Geschichte des Krieges*, Ia:240–43; Mikhailovsky-Danilevsky, *Denkwürdigkeiten*, 35–36.

11 Davout's command contained General Joseph von Rechberg's Bavarian division of 2,000 men; Pierre-François Durutte's French division of 2,500; and the remains of I Corps, 3,000 men. Eugene's main army consisted of the 5,000 men of II Corps; 18,000 of XI Corps; 16,000 of V Corps; an ad hoc corps of 6,000 commanded by General Dominique-Joseph Vandamme; 1,800 troopers of I Cavalry Corps; 1,000 of II Cavalry Corps; and 2,400 of François Roguet's Guard Cavalry Division. After retreating from Berlin and crossing the Elbe, Eugene's troops took the following positions: the right wing of 4,500 men commanded by Reynier stood between Dresden and Meißen. The Saxons earmarked for Reynier's VII Corps held Dresden and Torgau. Davout likewise halted at Dresden with 3,000 men, while the 5,000 survivors of Victor's II Corps occupied Wittenberg, Roßlau, and Aken. General Paul Grenier's XI Corps moved to Wittenberg; General Jacques-Alexandre Lauriston's V Corps to Magdeburg; Vandamme with Lauriston's 3rd Division and General Joseph Morand's 34th Division to the lower Elbe. General Marie-Victor Latour-Maubourg's I Cavalry Corps joined V Corps at Magdeburg, while the Guard cavalry escorted Eugene; II Cavalry Corps was forming in Brunswick.

12 *CN*, No. 19721, XXV:90; Bogdanovich, *Geschichte des Krieges*, Ia:78; Vaudoncourt, *Histoire de la guerre*, 49–50.

13 Clausewitz to Marie, Dresden, 1 April 1813, in Schwartz, *Clausewitz*, II:72; Add MSS, 20111, 18: Cathcart to Castlereagh, Kalisch, 26 March 1813; *CN*, No. 19767, XXV:126–27.

14 Holleben and Caemmerer, *Frühjahrsfeldzuges 1813*, I:244–46; Bogdanovich, *Geschichte des Krieges*, Ia:68–69; Pertz and Delbrück, *Gneisenau*, II:530–31; Gneisenau to Hardenberg, Bunzlau, 24 March 1813, *Gneisenau*, ed. Griewank, Nr. 108, 217–18.

15 Proclamation to the inhabitants of the Cottbus District, Bunzlau, 22 March 1813, *Blücher in Briefen*, ed. Colomb, 16–17; Blücher to Eisenhart, Bunzlau, 23 March 1813, *ibid.*, 156.

16 Blücher to Hardenberg, Dresden, 30 March 1813, Blücher, "Aus Blüchers Korrespondenz," ed. Granier, 157–58; Gneisenau to Hardenberg, Liegnitz, 19 March 1813, GStA PK, VI HA Rep. 92 Nl. Albrecht, Nr. 47.

17 Scharnhorst to Gneisenau, Kalisch, 25 March 1813, GStA PK, VI HA Rep. 92 Nl. Gneisenau, Nr. 23; Gneisenau to Hardenberg, Stolpe, 30 March 1813, *ibid.*, Nl. Albrecht, Nr. 47.

18 "Aufruf des Generalfeldmarschalls Fürst Blücher von Wahlstatt an seine Truppen," Bunzlau, 23 March 1813, GStA PK, IV HA Rep. 15 A Nr. 685; Holleben and Caemmerer, *Frühjahrsfeldzuges 1813*, I:319; Gneisenau to Hardenberg, Bunzlau, 24 March 1813, *Gneisenau*, ed. Griewank, Nr. 108, 218.

19 "Aufruf des Generalfeldmarschalls Fürst Blücher von Wahlstatt an Sachsens Einwohner," Bunzlau, 23 March 1813, GStA PK, IV HA Rep. 15 A Nr. 686.

20 Gneisenau to Hardenberg, Loschwitz by Görlitz, 25 March 1813, GStA PK, VI HA Rep. 92 Nl. Albrecht, Nr. 47; Gneisenau to Hardenberg, Bunzlau, 24 March 1813, *Gneisenau*, ed. Griewank, Nr. 108, 217–18.

21 Hardenberg's response is quoted in Pertz and Delbrück, *Gneisenau*, II:534; Gneisenau to Hardenberg, Stolpe, 30 March 1813, GStA PK, VI HA Rep. 92 Nl. Albrecht, Nr. 47, emphasis added.

22 The "Aufruf an die Deutschen" can be found in Boyen, *Erinnerungen*, ed. Nippold, III:271–72; Mikhailovsky-Danilevsky, *Denkwürdigkeiten*, 53; Kutuzov to Wintzingerode, Kalisch, 5 April 1813, RGVIA, f. VUA, op. 16, d. 3921, ll. 133b–134b.

23 For Nesselrode's opposition to Stein's call for a popular revolt to overthrow Napoleon, see Lieven, *Russia Against Napoleon*, 290–91; Mikhailovsky-Danilevsky, *Denkwürdigkeiten*, 53–54; Kutuzov to Blücher, Kalisch, 5 April 1813, RGVIA, f. VUA, op. 16, d. 3921, ll. 135b–136.

24 Blücher to Amalie, Dresden, 31 March 1813, *Blüchers Briefe*, ed. Unger, 158; Holleben and Caemmerer, *Frühjahrsfeldzuges 1813*, I:319.

25 Wittgenstein issued two proclamations, the first, entitled "Deutsche Jünglinge und Männer [German Lads and Men]," on 23 March 1813, the same day as Blücher's missive to the Saxons. Wittgenstein's second came on 30 March and was simply entitled "Saxons." Copies can be found in GStA PK, VI HA Rep. 92 Nl. Gneisenau, Nr. 19.

26 Hardenberg to Gneisenau, Breslau, 10 April 1813, GStA PK, VI HA Rep. 92 Nl. Gneisenau, Nr. 24; Gneisenau to Hardenberg, Altenburg, 18 March 1813, *ibid.*, Nl. Albrecht, Nr. 47.

27 Cathcart reported on 26 March that all three *Streifkorps* probably had crossed the Elbe with Dörnberg advancing on Hanover, Tettenborn on Bremen, and Chernishev on Brunswick. See Add MSS, 20111, 18: Cathcart to Castlereagh, 26 March 1813; Lieven, *Russia Against Napoleon*, 309–10. Bogdanovich, *Geschichte des Krieges*, Ia:79, blames "the inactivity" of Wittgenstein's army after taking Berlin on "the different views of Prince Kutuzov and General Scharnhorst especially over the latter's proposed plan of operations."

28 GStA PK, IV HA Rep. 15 A Nr. 187; Gneisenau to Hardenberg, Bautzen, 27 March 1813, GStA PK, VI HA Rep. 92 Nl. Albrecht, Nr. 47; Holleben and Caemmerer, *Frühjahrsfeldzuges 1813*, I:248; Beitzke, *Geschichte der deutschen Freiheitskriege*, I:163.

29 Napoleon eventually caught wind of Heister's mission, which took the Prussian general to Regensburg in Bavarian territory. On 20 April, the emperor ordered the Bavarians to arrest him as a spy. Heister escaped before the net closed on him. *CN*, No. 19882, XXV:212.

30 Blücher to Amalie, Dresden, 31 March 1813, *Blüchers Briefe*, ed. Unger, 158; Blücher to Hardenberg, Dresden, 30 March 1813, Blücher, "Aus Blüchers Korrespondenz," ed. Granier, 156–58; Pertz and Delbrück, *Gneisenau*, II:545–46; Mikhailovsky-Danilevsky, *Denkwürdigkeiten*, 52–53.

31 Scharnhorst to Gneisenau, Kalisch, 25 March 1813, GStA PK, VI HA Rep. 92 Nl. Gneisenau, Nr. 23. Ribbentrop's requisitions for March and April can be found *ibid.*, Nr. 119. See also Mikhailovsky-Danilevsky, *Denkwürdigkeiten*, 48; Holleben and Caemmerer, *Frühjahrsfeldzuges 1813*, I:318–19; Unger, *Blücher*, II:14.

32 Kutuzov to Wintzingerode, Kalisch, 5 April 1813, RGVIA, f. VUA, op. 16, d. 3921, ll. 133b–134b.

33 Kutuzov to Wittgenstein, Kalisch, 20 March 1813, RGVIA, f. VUA, op. 16, d. 3921, ll. 98–99b.

34 In *Toll*, I:440, Bernhardi states "At the same time, Scharnhorst had drafted a plan of operations that was similar in many respects but in which he of course erroneously presupposed that Kutuzov would really follow Blücher's army in the agreed distance of only a three days' march. Like Toll, he expected the enemy to strike Dresden from Erfurt." Scharnhorst advocated leaving Borstell and Bülow to observe Magdeburg and Wittenberg respectively, while Allied light forces attempted to move around the enemy's left wing on the lower Elbe. He wanted Wittgenstein to cross the Elbe at Elster and advance in unison with Blücher on Leipzig and Altenburg and ultimately further to prevent Napoleon from debouching from the Thuringian Forest. "This plan," continues Bernhardi, "went further than the one prepared in the Russian headquarters and was bolder, because it offered the possibility of attacking the enemy at Erfurt, driving him through the Thuringian Forest, and liberating all of northern Germany, whereas at Kalisch, for now, one only thought of a defense of the terrain between Altenburg and Dresden."

35 This corresponded with Kutuzov's order from 20 March: Kutuzov to Wittgenstein, Kalisch, 20 March 1813, RGVIA, f. VUA, op. 16, d. 3921, ll. 99–99b.

36 Wittgenstein to Kutuzov, Berlin, 26 March 1813, RGVIA, f. VUA, op. 16, d. 3908, ll. 201–201b.

37 Wittgenstein to Blücher, Berlin, 26 March 1813, GStA PK, Rep. 92, Nl. Gneisenau, Nr.18, I; Mikhailovsky-Danilevsky, *Denkwürdigkeiten*, 54–55.

38 Holzhausen, *Davout in Hamburg*, 37–39; Lindemann, *Patriots and Paupers*, 3.

39 *CN*, Nos. 19714, 19718, 19719, 19721, 19737, and 19747, XXV:81, 86–87, 89, 106, 116–17.

40 Bergedorf and Escheburg stand twelve and seventeen miles east-southeast of Hamburg; Zollenspieker is sixteen miles southeast of Hamburg.

41  The 32nd Military Division consisted of three French departments: Bouches-de-l'Elbe, Bouches-du-Weser, and Ems-Supérieur. Hamburg, which served as the headquarters, stood in the Bouches-de-l'Elbe department. That department as well as the Bouches-du-Weser controlled the mouths of the Elbe and the Weser Rivers respectively while the Ems-Supérieur controlled the mouth of the Ems River.

42  Holzhausen, *Davout in Hamburg*, 41; Holleben and Caemmerer, *Frühjahrsfeld-zuges 1813*, I:208–11, 268–69; Muir, *Britain and the Defeat of Napoleon*, 252.

43  "Six battalions are currently moving through Wesel toward Bremen. The twenty-eight 2nd Battalions of I and II Corps are underway: the twenty-eight 4th Battalions are also underway; fifty-six battalions belonging to I and II Corps will be on the lower Elbe in the 32nd Military Division": CN, No. 19727, XXV:100.

44  CN, No. 19728, XXV:100–01.

45  CN, Nos. 19734 and 19735, XXV:103–06. "I sent General [Jean-Louis] Dubreton to command the 4th Division of the Grande Armée, composed of the twelve 2nd Battalions of II Corps, which will assemble at Magdeburg," Napoleon explained to Eugene. "General Morand, who was in Pomerania, commands sixteen battalions of I Corps, forming 1st Division. General [Jean-Baptiste] Dumonceau went to Osnabrück to take command of sixteen 4th Battalions of I Corps, forming 2nd Division. General [François-Marie] Dufour commands the twelve 4th Battalions of II Corps, forming 5th Division. These two divisions will unite at Osnabrück and Bremen, under the command of General Vandamme, and will soon arrive. As a result, the four divisions of I and II Corps will be united between the sea and the lower Elbe. The duc de Bellune [Victor] does not know enough about the 32nd Military Division, neither the men nor the situation, and there he is not known: it is necessary for the prince d'Eckmühl to be in command."

46  Holleben and Caemmerer, *Frühjahrsfeldzuges 1813*, I:268–72; Bogdanovich, *Geschichte des Krieges*, Ia:86–92; Atkinson, *A History of Germany*, 583; Castle-reagh to Stewart, St. James's Square, 4 May 1813, *CVC*, IX:5–6; Gallaher, *The Iron Marshal*, 274–75; Muir, *Britain and the Defeat of Napoleon*, 252. Döbeln was court-martialed, found guilty of insubordination, and sentenced to be executed. Bernadotte later pardoned him. In *Russia Against Napoleon*, 305, Lieven states that blame for the fall of Hamburg was "the first act in the 'Black Legend' created by German nationalists against Bernadotte." Increased Franco-Danish pressure combined with news of Allied defeats in Saxony prompted the Allies to evacuate Hamburg on 30 May.

47  Blücher to Hardenberg, Dresden, 30 March 1813, Blücher, "Aus Blüchers Korrespondenz," ed. Granier, 157–58; Wittgenstein to Blücher, Berlin, 26 March 1813, GStA PK, VI HA Rep. 92, Nl. Gneisenau, Nr. 18, I.

48  Wittgenstein to Blücher, Berlin, 29 March 1813, GStA PK, VI HA Rep. 92, Nl. Gneisenau, Nr. 160.

49  Pertz and Delbrück, *Gneisenau*, II:548–50.

50  Kutuzov to Wittgenstein, Kalisch, 29 March 1813, RGVIA, f. VUA, op. 16, d. 3921, ll. 117b–119.

51  Scharnhorst to his daughter, Belzig, 2 April 1813, *Scharnhorsts Briefe*, No. 350, 464–65; Pertz and Delbrück, *Gneisenau*, II:553; Bernhardi, *Toll*, I:423;

Wittgenstein reported to Kutuzov on 2 April that the enemy had already united an army of 50,000 men in the region of Magdeburg and expressed his concern that Eugene would attempt to regain Berlin.

52 After Gneisenau accelerated the construction and repairs on Dresden's bridge, the pioneers completed the work there on 5 April, which provided the Allies with an additional bridge: Pertz and Delbrück, *Gneisenau*, II:552.

53 Scharnhorst to Blücher, Belzig, 1 April 1813, GStA PK, VI HA Rep. 92 Nl. Gneisenau, Nr. 23; see also Mikhailovsky-Danilevsky, *Denkwürdigkeiten*, 34–35; Pertz and Delbrück, *Gneisenau*, II:699; Holleben and Caemmerer, *Frühjahrsfeldzuges 1813*, I:266, 301–02, 309–10; Bernhardi, *Toll*, I:423; Unger, *Blücher*, II:14.

54 Scharnhorst to Volkonsky, Penig, 5 April 1813, in Pflugk-Harttung, *Das Befreiungsjahr 1813*, Nr. 58, 77; Bogdanovich, *Geschichte des Krieges*, Ia:98–99; Mikhailovsky-Danilevsky, *Denkwürdigkeiten*, 54.

55 Gneisenau to Hardenberg, Penig, 5 April 1813, GStA PK, VI HA Rep. 92 Nl. Albrecht, Nr. 47.

56 Stein to Ribbentrop, Dresden, 17 April 1813, GStA PK, VI HA Rep. 92, Nl. Gneisenau, Nr. 18, I; Pertz and Delbrück, *Gneisenau*, II:559.

57 Clausewitz to Marie, Penig, 4 April 1813, Schwartz, *Clausewitz*, II:73; Blücher to Amalie, Borna, 5 and 12 April 1813, *Blüchers Briefe*, ed. Unger, 158–60; Gneisenau to Hardenberg, Penig, 5 April 1813, GStA PK, VI HA Rep. 92 Nl. Albrecht, Nr. 47. In *Précis politique et militaire*, I:233, 240, Jomini notes that the Allies continued to advance with "*une confiance excessive*" and that they marched "to the Saale with the same self-assurance that had been so fatal to the Prussians in 1806."

58 Wittgenstein to Blücher, Etzdorf, 4 April 1813, GStA PK, VI HA Rep. 92, Nl. Gneisenau, Nr. 160; Scharnhorst to Volkonsky, Penig, 5 April 1813, in Pflugk-Harttung, *Das Befreiungsjahr 1813*, Nr. 58, 77–78; Unger, *Blücher*, II:15–16; Holleben and Caemmerer, *Frühjahrsfeldzuges 1813*, I:316. Clausewitz agreed with Scharnhorst's assessment: "The operations against the viceroy could not occur until the middle of April, because at that time Count Wittgenstein would finish building his bridge across the Elbe and Blücher's army would reach the lower Saale. By the middle of April, however, the majority of the enemy's forces were in Thuringia. Therefore, the whole length of the upper Elbe with all its bridges would have been exposed and abandoned, and one would have had to limit himself to the bridge at Roßlau, itself between the two enemy fortresses [Magdeburg and Wittenberg]. This would have been a very baleful situation. However, one could have risked this disadvantage, if one could have hoped to obtain a decisive advantage against the viceroy. Yet the viceroy, who according to the reports planned to evacuate the Saale and withdraw to Thuringia as soon as more powerful forces advanced against him, would not have stood his ground, and the whole plan was based on marching to change the situation in the theater of war. The Wittgenstein–Blücher army would have had its back against the middle Elbe, and it was precisely the road to the upper Elbe that would have been opened to the enemy. Obviously, this was a poor exchange. Everywhere the shorter routes to the sources of support [Berlin and Dresden] would have been abandoned. This would have allowed the enemy to take a position between us

172 Napoleon and the Struggle for Germany, vol. I

and the Russian main army with two enemy fortresses, Magdeburg and Wittenberg, behind him." In this scenario, Clausewitz is referring to the Allies launching an offensive against Eugene which would have provided Napoleon with the opportunity to execute the same movement that he had executed against the Prussians in 1806, only along the Elbe rather than the Saale. See Clausewitz, *Hinterlassene Werke*, VII:264–65.

59 Plans called for Blücher's headquarters to reach Borna on the 6th, while Wintzingerode concentrated at Eilenburg with the units of the Prussian II Corps echeloned in the following manner: Colonel Wieprecht Hans Karl von Zieten's Upper Silesian Brigade at Colditz, Colonel Joseph Friedrich Karl von Klüx's Lower Silesian Brigade at Grimma, and General Friedrich Erhard von Röder's Brandenburg Brigade at Nossen.

60 Wittgenstein to Blücher, Etzdorf, 4 April 1813, GStA PK, VI HA Rep. 92 Nl. Gneisenau, Nr. 160; Gneisenau to Hardenberg, Penig, 5 April 1813, *ibid.*, Nl. Albrecht, Nr. 47; Scharnhorst to Volkonsky, Penig, 6 April 1813, is outlined in Volkonsky to Scharnhorst, 9 April 1813, RGVIA, f. VUA, op. 16, d. 3921, ll. 150–151b; Holleben and Caemmerer, *Frühjahrsfeldzuges 1813*, I:311.

61 GStA PK, IV HA Rep. 15 A Nr. 187; Scharnhorst to Volkonsky, Penig, 5 April 1813, in Pflugk-Harttung, *Das Befreiungsjahr 1813*, Nr. 58, 79–80.

62 Clausewitz, *Hinterlassene Werke*, VII:267–68. See also Leggiere, *Napoleon and Berlin*, 49; Holleben and Caemmerer, *Frühjahrsfeldzuges 1813*, 284–301.

63 Scharnhorst to Volkonsky, Penig, 6 April 1813, is outlined in Volkonsky to Scharnhorst, 9 April 1813, RGVIA, f. VUA, op. 16, d. 3921, ll. 150–151b.

64 Blücher to Wittgenstein, Penig, 6 April 1813, in Appendix 18 of Holleben and Caemmerer, *Frühjahrsfeldzuges 1813*, 447; Pertz and Delbrück, *Gneisenau*, II:558.

65 Kutuzov to Wittgenstein, Kalisch, 5 April 1813, f. VUA, op. 16, d. 3921, ll. 132–33; Scharnhorst to Knesebeck, Penig, 6 April 1813, in Klippel, *Scharnhorst*, 700.

66 Volkonsky to Scharnhorst, 9 April 1813, RGVIA, f. VUA, op. 16, d. 3921, ll. 150–151b.

67 GStA PK, IV HA Rep. 15 A Nr. 187. Summaries of French troop movements also can be found in GStA PK, VI HA Rep. 92 Nl. Gneisenau, Nr. 18, I; Holleben and Caemmerer, *Frühjahrsfeldzuges 1813*, I:368.

68 Kutuzov to Wintzingerode, Kalisch, 5 and 6 April 1813, RGVIA, f. VUA, op. 16, d. 3921, ll. 133b–34b; 136b–38; Bernhardi, *Toll*, I:423; Mikhailovsky-Danilevsky, *Denkwürdigkeiten*, 43.

69 Wittgenstein based this claim on the position of Allied forces: "Blücher's corps around Zwickau, Penig, and Nossen, Wintzingerode's at Leipzig with his light troops raiding toward Halberstadt and Weimar, Yorck's corps at Köthen with outposts on the Saale, Kleist blockading Wittenberg, and Berg's corps guarding the bridge at Roßlau." See Wittgenstein to Kutuzov, Dessau, 8 April 1813, in Mikhailovsky-Danilevsky, *Denkwürdigkeiten*, 58–59.

70 Wilson, *Private Diary*, I:325–26.

71 GStA PK, IV HA Rep. 15 A Nr. 187; Intelligence Summary; Wittgenstein to Blücher, Dessau, 11 April 1813, *ibid.*, VI HA Rep. 92 Nl. Gneisenau, Nr. 18, I; Scharnhorst to Auvray, Rochlitz, 8 April 1813, RGVIA, f. VUA, op. 16, d. 3904, ll. 337–338; Holleben and Caemmerer, *Frühjahrsfeldzuges 1813*, I:308.

72 Behind the light cavalry, Klüx's Lower Silesian Brigade occupied Zwickau to monitor southwestern Saxony as far as the Bohemian frontier, Zieten's Upper Silesian Brigade camped twenty-two miles to the northeast at Penig, Dolffs's Reserve Cavalry stood ten miles northwest of Penig at Kohren, and Röder's Brandenburg Brigade remained thirty-five miles east of Penig at Nossen.

73 Scharnhorst to Auvray, Rochlitz, 8 April 1813, RGVIA, f. VUA, op. 16, d. 3904, ll. 337–338.

74 The letter is in Bernhardi, *Toll*, I:425–28.

75 *CN*, Nos. 19778, 19782, 19788, 19809, 19818, and 19833, XXV:140–41, 148–49, 162–63, 166–67, 176–77, emphasis added.

76 *CN*, Nos. 19839, 19843, and 19845, XXV:178, 182, 184.

77 *CN*, No. 19852, XXV:189, emphasis added; Chandler, *Campaigns of Napoleon*, 878.

78 *CN*, No. 19852, XXV:189; Maude, *Leipzig Campaign*, 90–91; Petre, *Napoleon's Last Campaign*, 50–54.

79 *CN*, No. 19900, XXV:223.

80 Wittgenstein to Blücher, Dessau, 8 and 12 April 1813, GStA PK, VI HA Rep. 92 Nl. Gneisenau, Nr. 18, I; Holleben and Caemmerer, *Frühjahrsfeldzuges 1813*, I:323.

81 Blücher to Amalie, Colditz, 12 April 1813, GStA PK, VI HA Rep. 92, Nl. Blücher von Wahlstatt; Blücher to Wittgenstein, 10 April 1813, *Briefe des Generals Neithardt von Gneisenau*, ed. Pflugk-Harttung, Nr. 137, 179; Gneisenau is quoted in Holleben and Caemmerer, *Frühjahrsfeldzuges 1813*, I:323–24, 327.

82 Scharnhorst to Wintzingerode, Chemnitz, 13 April 1813, in Holleben and Caemmerer, *Frühjahrsfeldzuges 1813*, 325, emphasis added; "Wallmoden and Wintzingerode want to operate completely on the offensive": Scharnhorst to Knesebeck, Zwickau, 15 April 1813, in Klippel, *Scharnhorst*, 701.

83 Blücher to Wittgenstein, 14 April 1813, Zwickau, GStA PK, VI HA Rep. 92 Nl. Gneisenau, Nr. 16.

84 An extensive report on this event is contained in GStA PK, VI HA Rep. 92 Nl. Gneisenau, Nr. 18. See also Scharnhorst to Boyen, Altenburg, 18 April 1813, in Boyen, *Erinnerungen*, ed. Nippold, III:297.

85 GStA PK, IV HA Rep. 15 A Nr. 187. See also Blücher to Frederick William, Altenburg, 15 April 1813, GStA PK, VI HA Rep. 92 Nl. Gneisenau, Nr. 16; Blücher to Hobe, Altenburg, 15 April 1813, in Holleben and Caemmerer, *Frühjahrsfeldzuges 1813*, I:330.

86 Blücher to Frederick William, Altenburg, 15 April 1813, GStA PK, VI HA Rep. 92 Nl Gneisenau, Nr. 16.

87 Scharnhorst to Knesebeck, Altenburg 16 April 1813, in Holleben and Caemmerer, *Frühjahrsfeldzuges 1813*, 359; Wittgenstein to Bülow, Nedlitz, 15 April 1813, GStA PK, IV HA Rep. 15 A Nr. 248.

88 Scharnhorst wrote on 14 April: "Should Blücher advance through Hof to Franconia while a part of the enemy troops from the Werra Valley unite with what remains at Kassel to sever his communication? Should Wittgenstein prevent this, or should he cover the Elbe or the bridges against the troops at Magdeburg? In 1806 we advanced toward the Thuringian Forest without having covered the

passages of the Elbe and paid dearly for this. Now, when the [Russian] main army is marching to the Elbe, a protected line across the river soon will be established for us, why should we get involved in operations, the outcome of which, if negative, would rob us of Austria's help – in which lies the surest guarantee of success in the duration of the war? No responsibility for the Fatherland? Winning a stretch of land does not matter, but defeating the enemy does. Frederick II gained nothing in 1757 until he withdrew from Kolin. Had he not correctly judged his forces and had he wanted to defend Prussia at the Niemen or the Pregel, he probably would have perished." See Scharnhorst to Röder, 14 April 1813, in Holleben and Caemmerer, *Frühjahrsfeldzuges 1813*, I:453; Clausewitz, *Hinterlassene Werke*, VII:265–67.

89 Gneisenau to Wittgenstein, Zwickau, 15 April 1813, GStA PK, VI HA Rep. 92 Nl. Gneisenau, Nr. 16; Scharnhorst to Knesebeck, Zwickau, 15 April 1813, in Klippel, *Scharnhorst*, 701–02.

90 In *Précis politique et militaire*, I:231, Jomini confirms that "secret societies were working on the people of Bavaria, Saxony and Westphalia, and agents of the coalition roamed Germany in all directions to preach a crusade against him [Napoleon]."

91 Seeley, *Stein*, III:136; Gneisenau to Münster, 1 April 1813, GStA PK, VI HA Rep. 92 Nl. Gneisenau, Nr. 20b.

92 Blasendorff, *Blücher*, 186; Unger, *Blücher*, II:18.

# 4

# The Saale

"At this moment, I am leaving for Mainz," Napoleon informed his father-in-law, Kaiser Francis, on 13 April 1813. "I had no plans to do so before the 20th but the news I received of enemy movements on the left bank of the Elbe has prompted me to hasten my departure by several days. I will be at Mainz between the 15th and 16th." From Mainz, he informed Jerome on the 18th that Marshals Bessières and Marmont had reached Eisenach with "a corps of 50,000 men, all French," that Ney had arrived at Erfurt with 60,000 men, and that Bertrand had started his march from Bamberg to Coburg "with 60,000 men, two-thirds French, one-third Italian." According to the latest report Napoleon received from Eugene, dated the 16th, the left wing of Army of the Elbe extended to the Elbe west of its confluence with the Saale while the right reached the foothills of the Harz. Napoleon anxiously sought to push his Army of the Main to the Saale just south of Eugene. His chief of staff, Marshal Louis-Alexandre Berthier, explained to Ney that "this movement requires some caution and, once completed, IV, III, VI Corps, and the Guard will be on the line of the Saale on the same battlefield."

On the 19th, Berthier issued Napoleon's orders for Bertrand to secure the bridge over the Saale at Saalburg-Ebersdorf with the main body of IV Corps and take a position there to "dominate the Saale." From there, the emperor wanted Bertrand to send patrols across the Saale to Schleiz, seven miles to the northeast and seventeen miles northwest of Blücher's outpost at Plauen. Bertrand also received orders to take the bridge over the Saale at Saalfeld, the site of the beginning of the end of the old Prussian army in 1806. "It is particularly important to know the width of the river, the posts and villages that have walls to protect them from a *coup de main* by the enemy," added the ever diligent chief of staff. To Ney, the emperor warned that "until we have taken the line of the Saale and have driven the enemy to the right bank of the river, there is concern that we will be harassed by his light cavalry." Bessières received the task of taking "*les plus grandes mesures*" to secure communication between Gotha and Erfurt. Orders stipulated that large escorts be assigned to all convoys of artillery and military equipment.

Intelligence indicated that Wittgenstein's corps, estimated to be 10,000 bayonets, along with Wintzingerode's corps of 6,000 men, Yorck's 15,000 Prussians, and Blücher's corps, which Napoleon assumed likewise to number 15,000 troops, had already crossed the Elbe. This led him to believe that 60,000 to 70,000 Allied soldiers stood on the right bank of that river. He knew that their "Grand Headquarters" remained east of the Elbe, and that the Allies had diverted considerable numbers of troops to mask the French-held fortresses on the Vistula and the Oder, and to observe the Austrians. Regardless, Napoleon sensed that the time for battle was fast approaching. On 21 April, Ney received orders to locate a favorable position to unite the army and accept battle.[1]

As for the Allies, the Prussians believed that the arrival of Miloradovich's 15,000 men at Dresden would change the situation and provide a broader range of options for operations. By securing Dresden and the local bridges over the Elbe, Miloradovich would eliminate the threat of Napoleon enveloping Blücher's left and reaching the Saxon capital.[2] In turn, this would afford the Allied armies greater freedom by placing them in a position to seize the offensive if they acted quickly. Because they knew that the Italian corps had reached the German theater and that Ney's army had started its advance, speed became essential. Blücher and his staff decided to accept battle but only with the full support of Wittgenstein's army. Uniting with the 20,000 men under Wittgenstein, Yorck, and Berg, Blücher could muster some 65,000 men. To defend the flank and rear of the combined Allied armies from the French forces that remained at Magdeburg, the Prussians hoped Borstell and Bülow would take positions astride the Elbe in the region of Roßlau–Dessau. Wintzingerode received orders on the 16th to move twenty-seven miles south from Leipzig to Colditz, which lay sixteen miles east of Blücher's position at Borna. However, at 3:00 A.M. on the 17th, Scharnhorst issued counterorders to Wintzingerode, thus demonstrating the combination of uncertainty and caution that reigned at Prussian headquarters. Instead of marching south to Borna, Scharnhorst wanted Wintzingerode to move west and pressure Eugene, who appeared to be attempting to move closer to Ney's army.[3]

During the course of the 17th, Blücher received intercepted imperial dispatches dating back to the 13th that finally shed adequate light on the situation. A preliminary examination of these documents indicated that a French offensive did not appear likely any time soon. According to the reports, Eugene would not retreat toward Erfurt but instead had assumed a position with his right wing anchored on the Harz Mountains, his left on the Saale, and his headquarters at Aschersleben, fifty-five miles northeast of Leipzig. One intercepted dispatch placed the strength of his army at 38,000 infantry and 2,500 cavalry. Because of his shortage of cavalry, he did not intend "to undertake anything" until the emperor arrived, except to defend his position between the Harz and the Saale. "There was no mention of a union with Ney," commented Scharnhorst in a letter to Boyen concerning the intercepted dispatches, "and the news coming from Wittgenstein's headquarters of the departure of the viceroy's army to Halberstadt and Quedlinburg appears to be incorrect. All arguments based on this automatically fall to the wayside."

As for Ney, reports confirmed the march of imperial forces from Eisenach and Meiningen to Gotha, and that the marshal "is also proceeding there. It is probable that the troops of Ney's army will turn to Gotha and Erfurt, and there unite with the troops from Frankfurt and Kassel. Today talk could be heard in Leipzig that the emperor had joined the army." In a second letter to Boyen, Scharnhorst expressed his belief that Ney would advance to Erfurt and "after uniting with the viceroy will turn against us. That is when Napoleon probably will arrive." Always thinking ahead and perhaps overly cautious, he conveyed his disagreement over making Dresden Allied Headquarters "because, should we be forced to withdraw across the Elbe, Headquarters would have to be moved, thus causing a negative impact on morale."[4]

The intercepted communiqués provided the Prussians with enough information to propose an offensive to Wittgenstein. "Based on the letters intercepted from the viceroy's army," wrote Blücher, "we have an accurate view of the situation of the French army. According to the intelligence, the enemy currently is not in the process of acting offensively, as I had earlier believed, but instead seems to fear an offensive by us." Blücher then reasoned that, because Miloradovich had reached the Elbe and Tormasov had followed a few days behind, "we can do something offensively if we do not want to await the imminent French offensive." He continued by expressing his concern over the difficulty of operating against Eugene "because he would probably withdraw behind the Harz toward, for example, Kassel, so that we would waste our time and distance ourselves from our proper theater of war, where we have our crossings over the Elbe. Therefore, we must fall on Ney's army in Thuringia." To attack Ney, Blücher suggested that Wittgenstein direct a part of his army to Erfurt while Blücher's army assembled along the Plauen–Saalfeld line. "The enemy in Franconia and Thuringia is probably no more than 50,000–60,000 men strong. If you can provide 15,000–20,000 men for this offensive, together with my army we would be at least just as strong numerically as the enemy. At the same time, we would have Miloradovich behind us with 10,000, perhaps even 20,000, men." Blücher assumed that Eugene would not attempt to counter this movement by advancing against the Allied right "because we see from the letters that in the case of our offensive he should seek to unite with the force in Franconia; also the [Russian] main army will make any operation against our rear impossible. Therefore, based on sound military reasoning, it appears to me that a determined, rapidly executed attack on the enemy in the Thuringian Forest thoroughly corresponds to logic and to all of the rules of war, especially when we consider the moral superiority of our troops."

To conclude, Blücher turned to the issue of politics. Apparently, Allied Headquarters wanted to delay a battle for as long as possible to give Austria time to mobilize and declare for the Coalition. Although Blücher never feared being defeated, the implications of a defeat on the course of Allied politics demanded his attention. "To judge the situation politically is another story," he concedes. "Someone who knows the situation well has urgently warned me that we must avoid repeating the example of 1805. A lost battle would make a very bad impression on the kaiser. This makes me dubious, which is prudent, of using this favorable opportunity ... [and] in regard to Austria, of avoiding the decision for as long as possible." He cautioned that Vienna could change policy at any time, especially if the Allies suffered a defeat.[5]

We can only speculate on whether Blücher's offensive through Thuringia and Franconia to strike the French before Napoleon completed his mobilization would have worked. According to Clausewitz:

> A calm consideration and comparison of forces will show that this was utterly impossible. Therefore, it would have been unconscionable to start operations due to simple restlessness and vanity and place oneself in an even more disadvantageous position than one was in already. Along the entire Elbe, we did not have one protected point. Moreover, because of Magdeburg, Wittenberg, and Torgau, the river was in the hands of the enemy. In addition, the viceroy was much stronger than Count Wittgenstein ... It was clear to him from the previous history of the war that against the emperor Napoleon such a situation could lead to decisive defeats and horrific consequences. No person could justify placing the hopes of Europe on such a reckless undertaking before himself or others.

Writing in the early twentieth century, General Albert von Holleben of the German General Staff viewed this letter as one of Blücher's few strategic studies but criticizes it for providing Wittgenstein with information "only for the drive forward. The underestimation of enemy forces is therefore a very important point." We do not know if Wittgenstein responded and Blücher certainly did not receive authorization to commence an offensive through Thuringia and into Franconia.[6]

Allied intelligence on French movements proved more accurate than their estimations of imperial troop strengths. According to reports, the lead units of General Joseph Souham's division from Ney's corps reached Weimar on 18 April; Ney himself arrived at Erfurt on the 19th. This news confirmed a report from an agent at Coburg, approximately 100 miles southwest of Altenburg, which stated that the "army" under Ney – now 6 divisions totaling 70,000 men – was advancing through Gotha and Erfurt toward Weimar. According to this report, the lead division (Souham's) left Meiningen on the 15th and headed for Erfurt. In addition, an Italian corps of 25,000 men would unite with 10,000 Bavarians between Coburg and Hof. Spies at various imperial headquarters obtained much information from the carefree chatter of French officers. According to their reports, Napoleon reached Mainz on the 14th and intended to deliver a decisive battle in the east. Further confirmation of this news soon followed, including the report that Ney had reached Erfurt with 25,000 French soldiers and would continue to Naumburg on the 19th, while a second large body of troops was expected at Eisenach, thirty-five miles west of Erfurt. From his son, Major Franz von Blücher, who reported from Weimar on the 16th and 17th, Blücher learned of the march of another French corps, Marmont's VI (18,000 men), northwest through Vacha toward Eisenach, thirty-five miles west of Erfurt.[7]

Scharnhorst immediately grasped the meaning of these movements. Ney would unite with Eugene behind the Saale and then operate against the Allies. "My dear Boyen, the enemy approaches, either we must fight or retreat across the Elbe," he solemnly declared. In addition, the movement of imperial forces north toward Erfurt and Weimar thus reduced the threat of a French advance toward Dresden from Hof. In fact, a Prussian patrol found both Hof and Münchberg evacuated on the 17th after the Bavarians had marched to Coburg on the previous day. Still wary of the cover that the Thuringian Forest provided to the French, Blücher directed two squadrons to Schleiz on the 18th to observe the roads coming from Hof and Saalfeld, where Prussian detachments would be posted. Cavalry moved from the Harz to the edge of the Thuringian Forest to observe the roads leading through both. "I will concentrate my army corps where I am in the best position to observe the enemy's steps while I await further orders from Prince Kutuzov or Count Wittgenstein," Blücher reported to the king. "If I was the commander in chief of the armies," wrote Scharnhorst, "I would march on Halle today with everything that I had, dislodge the viceroy, and from there turn against the approaching army, but everything that we do will probably be too late."[8]

With Napoleon's Army of the Main approaching the Saale, Blücher ordered the Reserve Cavalry to take security measures against a surprise attack. Posts of one officer and thirty sabers occupied Naumburg and

Weißenfels while a detachment of one officer and twenty troopers rode to Jena on the 19th. Aside from these forward posts, the Prussians cleared the roads coming east from Weimar and Erfurt, and the Reserve Cavalry took a frontline position at Altenburg with no other troops west of it. In the midst of this work, orders arrived announcing the 17 April change from regional to numerical designations for the brigades. To enable the corps to concentrate for any contingency, Blücher pulled back Klüx's 1st (Lower Silesian) Brigade twenty-two miles northeast from Zwickau to the region of Hartmannsdorf on the Chemnitz–Penig road; Zieten's 2nd (Upper Silesian) Brigade moved twelve miles north from Penig to Rochlitz; Röder's Reserve (Brandenburg) Brigade assembled eleven miles east of Rochlitz at Mittweida; and the majority of the Reserve Cavalry remained at Altenburg.[9]

Blücher's headquarters carefully assessed the situation. It appeared that French magazines stood at Würzburg, Kassel, Erfurt, and Magdeburg. If Napoleon intended to unite his main army with Eugene's forces at Magdeburg, the Prussians believed such a huge mass would exhaust the fortress's supplies in a matter of days. Moreover, lack of cavalry would prevent the imperials from procuring foodstuffs from the wider periphery. If Napoleon managed to miraculously rebuild this arm, the Prussians felt that the Allied cavalry would still enjoy a threefold advantage: in numbers, quality, and self-confidence. They also speculated that, if the emperor decided to conduct a war of maneuver rather than march to Magdeburg, he would be obliged to deposit at least 20,000 men at the fortress to cover his flank and rear.

Regarding a war of maneuver, Blücher and his staff assumed that the entire region between the Elbe, Weser, and Thuringian Forest could support an army of 60,000 men for three days only, especially because the Allied cavalry had already utilized part of the region for sustenance. By dispatching strong detachments to the rear and flanks of the French army, the Prussians calculated that they could limit Napoleon's range for foraging to perhaps half of the region between the Elbe, Weser, and Thuringian Forest. Popular resistance figured in their plans. Because of the proximity of Coalition forces, Gneisenau hoped the German peasants would be encouraged "to refuse the requisitions, and so we could force him [Napoleon] to move quickly, and through this provide ourselves with a favorable opportunity for battle, be it rearwards, be it forwards. If the former, we will repeat the same process so that he will be restricted to an even more confined area. Our superior cavalry will allow us to follow this system without depriving us of its use on the day of battle."[10]

According to Delbrück, Gneisenau argued in favor of the offensive, an "*Angriffskrieg* ... as the purpose of this war, whose success depended on the destruction of the enemy's power." In a letter to Hardenberg dated 18 April, Gneisenau provided insight into the thought process at Blücher's headquarters. He began by assuring the chancellor that Blücher and his staff heeded Hardenberg's warning to be cautious. "We moved across the Elbe because few enemy forces were present and we could maintain ourselves in a rich land at foreign cost. We advanced but not beyond this land so that we did not distance ourselves from the Hof–Dresden road and as a result perhaps give a bold opponent the opportunity to undertake something against our few bridges before the Russian main army could arrive. We now have five bridges (not counting Wittgenstein's) and three bridgeheads." However, in his opinion, the situation changed drastically due to Miloradovich's crossing of the Elbe at Dresden, which occurred between the 16th and 19th, and the approach of Tormasov's army. "All along we have adhered to three principles: (a) the protection of our bridges; (b) the reinforcement of our combat power from the interior; (c) [getting] the Austrians [on our side]. The first has been secured; the second achieves fruition daily. The third remains a concern but we cannot postpone further operations on their account." With the French advancing toward the Saale, Gneisenau explained that he urged a bold offensive. "It must come down to a battle. A victory will carry Austria. Because of our great superiority in cavalry, we will never suffer a decisive defeat while a victory most likely will purge the enemy from all of Germany. According to the intercepted dispatches, the enemy needs time. Never have so many reasons supported a battle." Nevertheless, Gneisenau implied that disagreement may have existed among the Prussians. "I do not know if General Scharnhorst accepts my reasons as fully valid. Up to now he has placed the highest concern on the prevailing political situation while my reasons are more military and psychological in nature." As for seeking battle, he claimed that "Scharnhorst is also for this but believes that he cannot take on the responsibility for such. We are dependent on Kutuzov and Wittgenstein. If they could be attuned to our plans, I would view the fate of the war as decided."[11]

Blücher appears to have unconditionally supported Gneisenau's call for a general offensive. Wilson arrived at Altenberg on the 17th; his journal entry for 19 April reveals Blücher's frame of mind: "with pain I saw that Blücher did not hold his enemy in sufficient estimation, that he thought he was already in retreat, and that Bonaparte himself could not leave Paris: in short, he entertained all those illusions that have been the cause of so much military error and such national misfortune." Wilson's dour observation fails to take into consideration the role that Blücher preferred to play. He did not pretend to be a strategist but instead stood as the leader. As such, he needed to inspire his officers and men, not cower behind a map. Scharnhorst's General Staff system ideally suited Blücher's desire to play this role and represents a tremendous example of institutional change and adaptation. In 1806, Scharnhorst had served as a mere secretary to the duke of Brunswick. Now, in 1813, he formulated strategy with his staff and the commander's input. Throughout the 1813 Campaign, Blücher's contribution took the form of inspirational, optimistic, and unwavering leadership to get the most from his officers and men. Blücher willingly conceded to Scharnhorst and later Gneisenau the task of planning but, as a natural leader of men, he bore the burden of leading through word of mouth and example.[12]

Despite Gneisenau's statement concerning Scharnhorst's agreement, the overall picture still did not please the staff chief. With Napoleon's main army approaching, Scharnhorst hinted at the ever increasing dissatisfaction in Blücher's headquarters over Russian leadership. "Our current situation demands a firm resolution for the next operation," he wrote Knesebeck on 18 April, hoping the content of his letter would reach the eyes or ears of the king. "We must now fight or evade Napoleon's main army without yielding all advantages for the future."[13] Should the Russians decide to confront Napoleon, Scharnhorst insisted that the Russian main army unite with Blücher on the left bank of the Elbe. If Kutuzov refused, Scharnhorst did not recommend a general retreat for Blücher and Wittgenstein. Instead, he suggested that they move around Napoleon's left flank. "If one [Kutuzov] does not want to cross the Elbe with the main army, I have a plan for falling on the viceroy and then taking the Grande Armée in the left flank. True, this operation is very dangerous but what isn't in an emergency? Yet I fear that in a few more days no more time will be left to adopt it. The best [plan] would be if the main army crossed to the left bank, united with us, and accepted a battle here."[14]

Although writing after the fact, Clausewitz provides insight into Scharnhorst's thought process:

> The strength of French forces was known fairly accurately: what had arrived from Würzburg via the Thuringian Forest could be estimated at 60,000 to 70,000 men. The Italian divisions under General Bertrand could number around 30,000 men. Yet it was not clear if they would all be called on, since, according to previous plans, two were to remain on the Danube. However, the exact strength of the viceroy's army was known. Excluding the Magdeburg garrison but including Marshal Davout's force, it numbered 38,000 men. Of this number, Marshal Davout had 12,000 men with him. Therefore, it was thought that the viceroy with 20,000 men strong would unite with the main army. After adding everything together, this totaled a force of 120,000 men. The combined armies of General Blücher and Count Wittgenstein, after accounting for the requisite numbers left behind at Wittenberg, the bridgehead at Dessau, and along the lower Saale, numbered 55,000 men. The Russian main army amounted to 30,000, the total numbering 85,000 men. Therefore, as could have been predicted, one was not in a position to confront the enemy in Saxony with an equal force. There was only a choice between two options: either leave Saxony without striking a

blow to establish positions behind [east of] the Elbe to defend this river or attack the enemy as soon as he crossed the Saale. The defense of the Elbe would not have delayed the enemy for long. As he possessed Wittenberg and, in the case of an Allied withdrawal across the Elbe, he certainly would have had Torgau at his disposal as well, the crossing of such a narrow river in any regard would not have presented any great difficulties. Thus, it appeared that the Allied army would be placed in a dangerous defensive position. As was already clearly seen at the time, it would have been impossible to gain enough time for the Austrians to help. To take the retreat all the way to Lusatia and Silesia in order to gain time for the Austrian contribution was even less feasible, as it was foreseeable that this would have brought the Allies to the border of Poland and beyond. Therefore, a battle had to be attempted, and it seemed to be more advantageous to avoid voluntarily submitting to the unpleasant impression that a withdrawal would have made on Germany and the army and instead to boldly attack the enemy rather than accept battle from a defensive position taken on the retreat.[15]

Knowing he himself enjoyed the confidence of Russian headquarters, Scharnhorst wrote to Volkonsky on the 18th. Based on the intelligence summaries of that day, he speculated that a French army of 105,000 men was advancing through the Thuringian Forest. Allowing for exaggerated accounts of French troop strength, Scharnhorst hypothetically placed this main French army at 90,000 men. Combined with Eugene's troops, cautiously estimated at 25,000 men, the French could cross the Saale with 115,000 men. Owing to strategic consumption, Wittgenstein would not be able to provide more than 20,000 men while Blücher's troops numbered fewer than 40,000. Without Miloradovich, the Allies would be hopelessly outnumbered and forced to "deliver a battle only under unfavorable circumstances."

Scharnhorst viewed a withdrawal across the Elbe as providing an opportunity to cooperate with Kutuzov but such a drastic retrograde movement would reinvigorate the French troops and damage Allied prestige in the battle for German hearts and minds. He recognized the danger that would result from an Allied retreat across the Elbe: Napoleon would halt at the river, refuse his right, and operate with his left against Berlin. "If the [Russian] main army does not cross the Elbe and unite with Wittgenstein's and Blücher's corps to deliver a battle, then nothing else will remain but to have the main army defend the Elbe while Blücher's corps marches to the right [north], unites with Wittgenstein, and advances through Halle against the viceroy." The Allies would attack Eugene wherever they found him "and the attempt made to destroy him so he cannot seek protection in Magdeburg."

Following Eugene's destruction, Scharnhorst suggested having Blücher and Wittgenstein circumnavigate the Harz and advance toward Eisenach.

Miloradovich, Bülow, and Borstell would remain at the Elbe to defend the crossings. Scharnhorst believed that such an operation would cause Napoleon to terminate his offensive at the Elbe. Based on his experience in Russia, he would realize that the Russian main army did not have to accept battle under his conditions, but instead could fall back to the Oder and thus be closer to its reinforcements. If Napoleon chose to pursue Kutuzov, he would leave the 60,000-man combined army of Blücher and Wittgenstein to his rear as well as a Germany on the verge of insurrection. Viewing operations as Napoleon himself would, Scharnhorst assumed that "Wittgenstein and Blücher could abandon their communication with the upper Elbe, throw bridges downstream of Magdeburg, having Dörnberg, Chernishev, and Tettenborn operate on the right wing. They would have extensive provinces, the Swedes, possibly the Danes, and the sea behind them, which would minimize the dangers of their detached position. The possession of numerous cavalry supports this plan." Scharnhorst also wrote to Hardenberg: "For several reasons, please inform me of the political situation with Austria, Denmark, and Sweden. If we cannot count on Austria, or if we should lose a battle, the situation still would not be all that bad if Denmark declares against France or concludes [an alliance] with England. We would then avoid Napoleon in the front and go around his left, operating from the lower Elbe and the Weser upriver against France. From this, you see that our operations would take on a second line of direction with Denmark's accession."[16]

On this day, 18 April, Müffling joined Blücher's staff at Altenburg. He found Scharnhorst very dejected over Kutuzov's opposition to his plans. Unable to rest his mind, Scharnhorst left Altenburg late that same day and traveled to Wintzingerode's headquarters at Leipzig. Wittgenstein joined him on the 19th to discuss operations. The Russian commander suspected that Napoleon intended to advance to the lower Saale, unite with Eugene, and together drive a wedge between the two Allied armies. For this reason, Wittgenstein decided on the evening of the 19th to move closer to Blücher.[17] During his meeting with Scharnhorst, Wittgenstein expressed the need to concentrate and unite all Allied forces. However, he noted that circumstances would compel them to await the enemy's further advance and then quickly fall on one of his columns. Scharnhorst apparently agreed. Returning to Blücher's headquarters on the 20th, he notified Volkonsky that, according to his meeting with Wittgenstein, the Allies would form an 85-mile front extending south from Zörbig to Chemnitz.[18] If Kutuzov moved his army across the Elbe, the Allies believed they could hold their ground defensively until the French emerged onto the plains of Leipzig. On this open terrain that would favor their superior cavalry, the Allies would seize the offensive.[19]

As of 20 April, Blücher's headquarters still attempted to piece together intelligence to divine French operations and intentions. An army consisting of one Guard and five infantry divisions marched from Würzburg and Frankfurt to the region of Gotha and Erfurt with the intention of concentrating at the latter. It had already pushed a vanguard of 5,000–6,000 men toward Weimar. Ney commanded the army but all expected Napoleon's arrival shortly. Again, estimates of strength varied between 50,000 and 90,000 men, yet the Prussians figured that at most it possessed only 2,000 cavalry. Although Badeners and other Rheinbund troops served in Ney's army, the Prussians had received no clear news regarding the Württembergers and Bavarians. Of the Italian units that formed Bertrand's IV Corps, two divisions and a cavalry reserve reached Nürnberg and Ansbach on 10 April. Estimated to be 25,000 men, the Prussians learned that IV Corps would operate with Ney's army but they did not know which road the Italians would take to reach the theater. Estimates still placed Eugene, Davout, and Victor at 50,000 men altogether. Two days later, reports confirmed the march of Marmont's VI Corps to Fulda and the concentration of the Italian units of IV Corps at Coburg; an Italian vanguard of 2,200 men reached Saalfeld, forty miles northeast of Coburg. Imperial forces quickly filled the gap between Weimar and the Thuringian Forest (see Map 2).

On 21 April, Blücher's 1st and 2nd Brigades held a ten-mile line extending south from Borna through Frohburg to Kohren. The Reserve Brigade took post twelve miles to the east at Rochlitz, while the Reserve Cavalry remained at Altenburg, less than nine miles west of Kohren. To keep spirits high, Blücher instructed his officers to tell the troops of Miloradovich's approach from Dresden. Nevertheless, pressure mounted in Blücher's headquarters, fueled by aggravation with the Russians and the feeling that the army's inactivity hurt morale on the home front. "The impatience that consumes those in Berlin is very understandable to me," Clausewitz explained to his wife, "but I can assure you that if up to now nothing decisive has happened, there are no special circumstances that are the cause but instead it is the nature of things. *The fact that we know what we are doing is probably the most you can expect from us. We are certainly not our own master but are under Wittgenstein followed by Kutuzov.*"[20]

With the prospect of battle approaching, Gneisenau recalled the ammunition shortages that had impacted Russian operations in 1807. As the army's quartermaster, he repeatedly requested a status report on Wintzingerode's available ammunition supply. Never receiving the requested information, he reiterated the request on the 21st in a letter to the Prussian liaison officer at Wintzingerode's headquarters. Gneisenau wanted the Russian corps to be equipped with ammunition for two battles but remained concerned about the considerable distance that separated the Russians from their depots. Shortages would be replenished as soon as possible by Saxon powder mills at Bautzen and Dresden, where Allied representatives had already signed contracts. Yet the process of casting shot would be unduly problematical and thus lengthy due to the various calibers used by the Russians. Gneisenau urged haste in the completion of this fact-finding assignment. "If Wintzingerode's corps is supplied with ammunition for two battles and especially with much pocket ammunition [cartridges], I will indeed feel better about this matter. But if this is not the case – and based on history I must conclude it is not – it is urgently necessary to inform us of the shortages so we can see to the production of the ammunition. The circumstance that the calibers are not uniform complicates the purchase of molds to cast the lead balls." Gneisenau's concern about Russian ammunition shortages proved prophetic not only for Wintzingerode's corps but for Wittgenstein's as well. On 22 April, Wittgenstein informed Yorck that the Russians would soon exhaust their supply of cartridges because the parks remained too distant to resupply the men. He hoped cartridges could be manufactured in Berlin and requested that an artillery company be sent there from Kolberg to do the work. Yorck forwarded the request to the king while Gneisenau scrambled to resupply Wintzingerode's corps.[21]

Meanwhile, Blücher instructed his light cavalry "to cause the enemy alarm" so that the imperial troops "could not take one step without you knowing of it and me through you." This resulted in several successful raids east of the Saale between the Harz and the Thuringian Forest.[22] Other squadrons and patrols encountered various enemy detachments, taking numerous prisoners and artillery, routing one Thuringian battalion, capturing 100 Bavarians and a few guns, and dispersing a Westphalian cavalry regiment. On the night of 17/18 April, "Captain Helwig with one squadron surprised a post of 1,800 men at Tennstädt by Bad Langensalza, cut down many, and captured five cannon, which I have just seen," the usually calm Scharnhorst excitedly wrote to Boyen. Blücher wrote: "My Cossacks have captured one lieutenant-colonel ... and his entire squadron; shortly after that he defected to us, certainly not out of goodwill but out of necessity. I saw him for only a moment and you can imagine how I gave him the business; today I sent him to Russian headquarters. I despise these chaps with all my heart."[23]

Conversely, the situation on the opposite bank of the Saale remained a mystery to Napoleon. Berthier expressed the emperor's frustration by snapping at Ney: "Your letters from the 21st do not provide us with any news of the enemy." As a result of the paucity of intelligence, Ney received orders to conduct reconnaissance on the 22nd with a detachment of three battalions. Berthier cautioned the fiery marshal not to sacrifice these troops: "if you are concerned about the news that you receive of the enemy, do not hesitate to withdraw them so they are not compromised." On the 22nd, Napoleon decided to occupy the left bank of the Saale to prevent Allied units from crossing the river and harassing his communications as well as to place his cavalry in a position to obtain news of the enemy's movements.

Berthier instructed Ney to keep marching west from Weimar to occupy Jena and Naumburg, both on the Saale. In accordance with Napoleon's intention to occupy the left bank of the Saale, Eugene received orders to fortify Halle and Merseburg as bridgeheads, using palisades to close every gate to the Cossacks. Downstream, Napoleon wanted the bridges over the Saale near Wettin destroyed. The viceroy needed to remain "on high alert" and ready to march immediately if the Allies launched an offensive through Jena and Naumburg.[24]

"I have no news of the enemy," a frustrated Napoleon wrote directly to Bertrand on the morning of 23 April. Still at Mainz – 178 miles southwest of Weimar – Ney's courier had yet to reach Imperial Headquarters with the results of the reconnaissance he had conducted on the 22nd. After he arrived just before 10:00 on the morning of the 24th, the emperor learned to his chagrin that Ney's patrols had found little to report. This in part prompted another missive from Berthier to Bertrand: "Above all provide news of the enemy. Have you sent out spies? Have you questioned everyone in Coburg who could be a spy?" From the lower Saale, Eugene at least provided some useful information: Wittgenstein had considerably reduced the forces facing him and appeared to be heading for the bridges over the Elbe and Mulde at Roßlau–Dessau. Lacking specific news of the enemy's movements and intentions forced Napoleon to make very general plans to attack in succession the enemy forces he encountered at the Saale, the Mulde, and the Elbe. "The first goal of my operations is to repulse the enemy on the right bank of the Saale," he explained to King Frederick of Württemberg on the 24th, "on the right bank of the Mulde, and on the right bank of the Elbe. I tell this to Your Majesty for your peace of mind."[25] Perhaps such a plan calmed Frederick's anxiety but its emptiness reveals the emperor's unease.

As Napoleon contemplated his next move, the Army of the Main continued its advance to the Saale. Ney's III Corps reached Weimar on the 24th with the Imperial Guard following. Further west, Marmont's VI Corps stretched across the forty miles of road between Vacha and Gotha. Forty miles south of Weimar, the head of Bertrand's IV Corps reached Gräfenthal, itself twelve miles south of Saalfeld, with the main body between Coburg and Ansbach. On the extreme right, General Clemens von Raglowich's Bavarian division (8,000 men) of Oudinot's XII Corps stood at Bayreuth, some fifty miles southwest of the Allied post at Zwickau; Napoleon expected all of XII Corps to join IV Corps at Saalfeld by the 26th. On the opposite end of a front that extended 140 miles, Eugene's army maintained its positions between the Harz and the Saale (see Map 2).

According to the early twentieth-century historian Colonel F. N. Maude of the British General Staff, Ney confounded the emperor's timetable by taking the wrong road to Erfurt, thus delaying the progress of the Guard and VI Corps. Had Ney stuck to his appointed route, Maude maintains that the French could have crossed the sixty miles between Weimar and Leipzig before the end of April. The documentary evidence simply does not support this conclusion, but the basis of it – the question of why Napoleon did not cross the Saale sooner – needs to be addressed. First, we must recall Napoleon's plan of 12 April "to refuse my right and allow the enemy to penetrate toward Bayreuth, thus making a movement that is *the inverse* of that which I executed during the Jena campaign; providing the enemy moves through Bayreuth – the result will be my arrival at Dresden ahead of him, and his severance from Prussia." Despite his correct estimate of the relative weakness of the Allied armies in Saxony, Napoleon hoped Wittgenstein would initiate an offensive. Such an operation would play right into his hands by providing him with an enemy army to defeat: a circumstance that had eluded him for much of the Russian campaign.[26]

Aside from the hope that Allied strategy and operations would conform to his wishes, Napoleon's correspondence reveals uncertainty, hesitation, frustration, and apprehension. To be fair, he sorely missed his cavalry arm, assuring King Frederick that an additional 15,000 cavalry would enable him to "promptly end the affair." Nevertheless, we see a General Bonaparte concerned with securing a river line against Cossacks and light cavalry. After correctly estimating the size of the Blücher–Wittgenstein army on the other side of the Saale, Napoleon could have crossed the river with only Ney's corps and Eugene's army and still outnumbered the Allies. Yet on the 24th, Berthier informed Ney that "the arrival of Bertrand's two divisions as well as that of General Jean-Gabriel Marchand appears necessary before we commence our movement. The intention of the emperor is that we first take Jena, then, by marching on Naumburg, we take possession of the bridge and debouches [across the Saale] at the same time that the viceroy takes Halle and Merseburg; this would complete the occupation of the Saale. If possible, building a redoubt for one battalion on the heights of Jena to protect against the Cossacks would be beneficial for this operation."[27]

We are left wondering why the master of war appeared obsessed with a river line and Cossacks rather than finding and destroying the enemy's army. General Bonaparte never allowed the Po, the Vistula, the Danube, or the mighty Alps to get in his way. While Ney can be blamed for foiling not a few of the emperor's plans, the march to the Saale does not fall into this category. Instead, Napoleon, for a brief instant, perceived his mortality and acknowledged the gravity of his situation. More so than any previous campaign since his miracle at Austerlitz, the fate of his empire rested on his every move. Many questions weighed heavily on him. Without a cavalry arm, what would provide the eyes and ears of his own army as well as the shield that masked its movements? What of his raw conscripts, many of whom had finished their basic training while marching to the Saale: would they perform under fire and could they sustain the harsh demands of campaigning?

Moreover, could he depend on the Germans and Italians to provide manpower? The disaster in Russia, Prussia's defection, and the ongoing setbacks in Iberia all combined to send shock waves through the allied, satellite, and client states of the empire. What if the South Germans followed Prussia's example? Perhaps the biggest question on Napoleon's mind was: what of Austria? Would his father-in-law betray him? "All possible calculations lead me to believe that Austria will persist in its system or will be neutral," concludes his letter to Frederick. "However, if she declares against me, I think, in the month of July, the period which would be necessary for her to prepare, I will be able to cope with this increase of forces against me."[28]

Thus, we find our answers: without cavalry to mask his approach, Napoleon intended to use the Saale to conceal his movements. Describing the river as a "curtain," he insisted on all movements being completed on the left bank and none on the right. In this way, he could burst across the Saale and take the Allies by surprise. Because of his raw, untested troops, Napoleon needed mass. Simply outnumbering the Allies did not suffice; he wanted all "300,000" of his men available on the day of battle. "You know my principle is to debouch en masse," he explained to Eugene. "It is therefore en masse that I wish to cross the Saale River with 300,000 men." These 300,000 men, according to his estimation, would not be ready to take the offensive until early May. Napoleon needed overwhelming mass to achieve a decisive victory, particularly because he lacked cavalry to exploit a pursuit. In addition, he needed to end the undercurrents of defeatism, disloyalty, and sedition that had spread like a disease through the arteries of his empire. Emperor Napoleon needed to restore his image, aura, and reputation. His vassals, including the emperor of Austria, had to be overwhelmed by his greatness and power. First impressions are always the strongest, and Napoleon needed to make a great impression following the debacle in Russia. This could be done only through a crushing, decisive victory over the Russians and Prussians. Thus, every detail needed to be carefully arranged. For Emperor Napoleon, the stakes had increased exponentially since he had rashly and prematurely pushed his army across the Danube almost four years earlier at Aspern–Essling. Thus, until all of his new army reached the Saale, Emperor Napoleon kept a tight leash on General Bonaparte.[29]

While French forces converged on the Saale, Tormasov's army plodded west toward Dresden and the Elbe. Through Boyen, the Prussian liaison at Kutuzov's headquarters, Blücher sought to influence Russian decision-making and accelerate Tormasov's march. "Well, my old Boyen," wrote Blücher, "now we will resume our friendly relationship. I am very happy to know you are so close. Now cross the water [Elbe]! A main blow must occur. The advantage is on our side. A beautiful and superior cavalry, animated by the best will, promises us much success. Everything goes well here; my people fight splendidly and are constantly in close contact with the enemy."[30]

Kutuzov still thought in defensive terms. News concerning the concentration of imperial forces at Erfurt reached him on a daily basis. This convinced the commander in chief that Napoleon intended to envelop the Allied left by advancing through Hof, thus repeating the exact maneuver he had executed against the Prussian army seven years earlier. As usual, the emperor remained one step ahead of his opponents. Regardless, Kutuzov resolved to block this operation by ordering Wittgenstein and Blücher to remain as close to each other as possible for as long as possible. He directed his two subordinates to concentrate along a thirty-mile front between Chemnitz and Borna, a position he believed would grant sufficient freedom to act either offensively or defensively. After the imperials crossed the Saale and thus signaled their intent to begin an offensive, Kutuzov planned to dispatch Miloradovich to Chemnitz to reinforce Blücher. Kutuzov based his plans on the need to maintain the crossings over the Elbe between Mühlberg and Dresden, which would facilitate the retreat of Wittgenstein and Blücher should they be defeated. Preserving his line of communication, which ran from Dresden through Görlitz, Bunzlau, Breslau, and Kalisch to Russia, understandably remained his ultimate concern.

Kutuzov also envisioned Eugene making a diversion against Berlin as soon as the French main army advanced from Erfurt toward Dresden. "You must pay no attention to this movement," he instructed Wittgenstein on the 18th, the last order he signed before his death. "Your only concern should be your union with Blücher and with our main army. If you distance yourself from Dresden, then our forces there will be so weak that the enemy will be in a position to force the passage of the Elbe and establish communication with the Duchy of Warsaw. However, if we leave Berlin in the wind, we thus maintain our main line of operation. The Prussian court likewise sees this as a necessity." Although Wittgenstein did not agree with this plan, he obeyed the field-marshal.[31]

Alexander and Kutuzov reached Bunzlau on 18 April; two days later a sense of urgency unexpectedly seized Russian headquarters. Boyen informed Knesebeck, who returned to Breslau with the king on the 16th, that Blücher's reports of the start of a French offensive had prompted Kutuzov to unite all Allied forces along the left bank of the Elbe near the Freiberger Mulde (see Map 2). If necessary, he would accept a battle in that position. Despite this, Holleben criticizes the attitude behind Kutuzov's decision: "You can see the reluctance to energetically employ his forces wherever the opportunity arises. If there was no other way out, he could be forced to fight." Holleben rejects the idea of seeking battle based on defensive principles: "If one seeks battle, it must be shared with the offensive as the primary goal." Regardless, the idea of delivering a battle quickly increased among the Russians. In fact, Tsar Alexander, who left Kutuzov at Bunzlau on the 21st and headed for Dresden, convened a council of war at Bautzen on the 23rd to debate the issue. A unanimous vote in favor of not merely accepting battle between the Saale and Elbe, but seeking it, strongly suggests that the mood at Russian headquarters had changed. In part, this can be attributed to Kutuzov's absence. Too ill to follow Alexander, the Allied commander in chief remained at Bunzlau. Purportedly, he communicated with the tsar over reports and answered questions from Volkonsky until his death on 28 April.[32]

The reports Blücher received on the 23rd indicated that several thousand Italian troops had reached Saalfeld and would continue east. That night (23/24 April), "the enemy pressed forward in great number on the highway from Weimar to Jena. For this he set off flares. Since then he has gone back." West of the Saale, the emperor pushed his new legions toward this river. His own Army of the Main marched to Jena and Naumburg while Eugene's Army of the Elbe moved up the Saale to Halle and Merseburg. The rapid escalation of French forces facing the Saale left Blücher scurrying to defend its points of passage. He requested that Wintzingerode send 2,000 cavalry as well as horse artillery toward Naumburg while Prussian light forces moved to the Saale crossings at Camburg, Dornburg, and Bad Kösen (see Map 3). Blücher instructed Wintzingerode to employ cavalry and horse artillery to prevent the French from advancing on Leipzig from Naumburg or Weißenfels for as long possible. As soon as Wittgenstein's troops reached Leipzig, Wintzingerode's corps would slide twenty miles south to Borna.[33]

After leaving Kutuzov's side, Toll rejoined Alexander at Bautzen on the 23rd in time for the tsar's council of war. Toll managed to convince him of the need to concentrate all Allied forces around Altenburg. Toll did not believe the French would be ready to attack until the end of May, by which time Austria's entry into the Coalition would completely alter the situation. Having studied Henri Jomini's writings on the use of lines of operation, he believed that the 1806 campaign had been decided by Napoleon's axis of operations. Because the current situation appeared very similar, Toll expected a repeat of the 1806 maneuver. He recommended treating the advance of French columns toward the Allied left wing as Napoleon's main attack. To counter this threat, Toll suggested that the Allies immediately attack these approaching columns.[34]

After Alexander accepted this plan, Toll expected the Allies to proceed from the region of Altenburg toward the Naumburg–Leipzig road, thus advancing against the enemy's strategic flank, a maneuver expected to produce a decisive effect. Allied Headquarters moved to Dresden on the 24th while Toll went to Wittgenstein's headquarters to deliver the news of

14. French and Allied concentration along the Saale

the tsar's decision. That same day, 24 April, Scharnhorst arrived at Dresden to deliver a plan for offensive operations. Encountering Wilson on the road to the Saxon capital, "Charnhotzh" (Scharnhorst) informed the British general that Napoleon "occupied the line of the Saale with 110,000 men, exclusive of Beauharnais's 40,000. He was convinced that they would advance immediately, and move by Leipzig on Wittenberg and Glogau." Wilson claims that Scharnhorst agreed with him that the Allies "had no alternative but the desperate one of meeting and giving battle before the enemy marched, or retiring. In the former case, energy must supply the want of numbers, and activity must prevent the seizure and use of more advantageous positions; in the latter case, we must clear a way to the rear, resist with detached corps as much as possible the progress of the enemy."[35] Even after Napoleon had lost 500,000 men in Russia, and with the French still waging war in Iberia against the British, Portuguese, and Spanish, the Eastern Allies recognized that the emperor still outnumbered them.

Scharnhorst went to Dresden armed with a plan that he and Gneisenau had drafted and Blücher had approved. "It covers every scenario," boasted Gneisenau to Hardenberg on 23 April, "and through absolute boldness will provide the surest result, a result that will decide the entire course of the war. The enemy will not expect it and it is calculated to bring him to despair.

Those who have a typical view of war will certainly reject it but that is its advantage." Two days later he again wrote to the chancellor, "I include it so that when you have fifteen minutes of free time you can look it over and judge for yourself. If you alone judge it, and you do not consult a military man over it, I am certain it will receive your approval. It is also being sent to you with the intent that if we should suffer a misfortune, the future will know that we suggested something better."[36]

Calculating the total strength of French forces to be 129,000 men and allotting the Allies a maximum of 94,000 men, the Prussian plan presented the Allies with a choice.[37] They could either *accept* a defensive battle between the Mulde and the Elbe or take the offensive and *seek* battle between the Elster and the Saale. The Prussian plan placed considerable emphasis on the likelihood of Napoleon directing his main force on the highway from Erfurt. Moving east from Erfurt, this main body would form the emperor's center and would make for either Leipzig or Altenburg. As Napoleon's left wing, Eugene's army would advance through Eisleben toward Leipzig while the emperor's right wing pushed through Saalfeld and Schleiz either to Zwickau or Altenburg (see Map 2). "Therefore, the enemy force probably will strategically march between Leipzig and Zwickau. If we stand against this force and accept battle, it can take place between the Mulde and the Elbe or further forward between the Elster and the Saale." The wording of the plan makes clear that the Prussians rejected the former. Awaiting Napoleon's attack in a defensive position on the left bank of the Elbe posed obvious disadvantages that Scharnhorst did not fail to emphasize. Aside from surrendering the initiative, Allied dispositions would be dependent on protecting the crossings over the Elbe. Such prerequisites would paralyze their forces and provide little chance of success.[38]

For the offensive between the Elster and the Saale, which the Prussians favored, Scharnhorst argued against granting Napoleon time to unite his columns. Instead, all Allied forces should be directed against one of the French columns before Napoleon could concentrate his army. "In this second case," states the Prussian plan, "the battle must be offensive. Thus, because the enemy's columns are still not united, it would be extremely foolish to await their union while we take a defensive position. Second, the columns on the right and the left would bar us from our points of retreat; they will march so far around us that they will sever all of the roads and then attack us jointly. In this case, a victory would only be possible because of our moral superiority and the superiority of our cavalry." With the crossings over the Elbe at Dresden, Meißen, and Mühlberg secure and in view of the numerical advantage Coalition forces possessed in cavalry, the Prussian plan asserted that the Allies could gamble everything on this battle. Scharnhorst again suggested attacking the imperial army on the plains of Leipzig, between the Mulde and the Elster: "First, because of our cavalry and second, in order to be as far from the Elbe as possible. The difficult crossings of the Elster and the Saale do not permit a further advance."

Although Scharnhorst identified an offensive engagement with Napoleon as the primary Allied objective, Russian resolve concerned him. If the Russians rejected the idea of attacking Napoleon's main army or should Tormasov's army not cross the Elbe, he resurrected the plan for Blücher and Wittgenstein to overwhelm Eugene and envelop the emperor's left wing. "Of a completely different nature is a great flanking operation, thus an offensive in the flank of the enemy's theater of war. We cannot select the right flank because the neutral line of Bohemia makes this ineffective, and Bavaria – a hostile state – will fall on the rear of this movement. The left flank presents a different case. There we will obtain space for our cause to inspire North Germany with enthusiasm, namely the provinces from the Elbe to the Weser and to the Rhine, and we will find reserves in the Swedes, Danes, etc. The following operation would suffice: the moment that the enemy's main army advances from Erfurt toward the middle Saale and arrives at this river, Blücher will march to the right [north], unite with Wintzingerode [and] with Wittgenstein, and fall on the viceroy, defeat him, destroy him, and march between Magdeburg and the Harz, then turn left [south] and take the Eisenach–Frankfurt road. Meanwhile, Miloradovich will move [east], if he is pressed, behind the Elbe, and the main army will defend this river from Mühlberg to Dresden."

The Prussians maintained that, as long as Napoleon's main army did not cross the Saale, nothing could hinder Blücher and Wittgenstein from uniting and attacking Eugene. To prevent the emperor from executing a rapid march to thwart the offensive against his stepson, Blücher and Wittgenstein would leave behind a portion of their cavalry to slow Napoleon's advance. "The battle against the viceroy in any region cannot be doubted due to the superiority of our troops generally and the cavalry specifically. Moreover, we must accept the destruction of this army as certain, if not – which is unlikely – its flight into Magdeburg. However, if we cannot intercept this army, it cannot do anything to hinder our march."

In terms of results, the Prussian plan claimed that the "great flanking operation" would force Napoleon to immediately halt his advance to the upper Elbe to strike the Russian main army. If the emperor did continue his offensive, "the Russian main army in the worst case could fall back toward Silesia and its reinforcements. But, in general, he cannot operate on the upper Elbe while an army of 60,000–70,000 men stands on his line of communication through Eisenach. Therefore, the emperor will be forced to turn left with a portion of his forces to follow us, while the remainder observes the Russians at the Elbe." The document identifies no fewer than six points as the direct advantages of this operation: "First, we will win a great battle against the viceroy. Second, we could delay a decisive engagement until the other forces appear in the theater of war. Third, we can promote the organization of North Germany. Fourth, we will force the emperor to divide his main force in two, and he can command only one of them. Fifth, by way of the battle and the unexpected advance, we will impact the mood of the [Allied] army. In the emperor's army, the retrograde march with which he will be forced to begin the campaign will produce a very adverse impression and completely shatter its already extremely shaky confidence. Sixth, we will shift the war from Saxony to the Main, because it is very unlikely that the [imperial] forces that remain behind in Saxony will resist the Russian main army if it does not retreat."

The proposed operation would be jeopardized if the viceroy withdrew and Napoleon closed on the pursuing Blücher and Wittgenstein. Their worst scenario would be getting caught by Napoleon while pursuing Eugene: the emperor would be able to achieve a numerical advantage of at least two to one. "The situation would come to a decision between Kassel and Eisenach. [But] it would be too dangerous for Wittgenstein to commit himself to a battle and so it would remain ... to win time to move up the cavalry detachments of 6,000–7,000 troopers and the new units of 10,000–12,000 men; to await the Swedes and the Danes; and await the Austrian declaration," which again appeared probable. Stewart reported favorable signs on Austria's part: "The emperor of Austria has just determined on permitting the sale of saltpetre at any amount to Prussia, never having furnished or permitted supplies of any kind to be granted to the French army on its retreat. Also, a very rich merchant of this town [Dresden] affirms that the Austrian government has taken measures for an immediate issue of paper money, which, with them, is as decisive as the march of troops, or the collecting of forces."[39] At Dresden, Scharnhorst learned that the Prussian envoy to Vienna, Wilhelm von Humboldt, had reported that the Austrians had decided to join the Coalition and would have 190,000 men ready for battle by 20 May. Although encouraging, this development would take three months rather than one to reach fruition.

One consideration the Prussian plan failed to make concerned the danger of allowing Napoleon to take a central position between the Blücher–Wittgenstein army and the Russian main army, which outweighed the advantages of Scharnhorst's proposed *manoeuvre sur les derrières*. The plan does include other considerations, probably influenced by the Russian officers attached to Blücher's headquarters: "The success of a battle on the Elbe is obviously uncertain; at the least, it is not comparable with the probability of success against the viceroy. If a battle on the Elbe is lost, we will leave a great amount of our artillery in the defiles and probably evacuate the region between the Elbe and the Oder. Naturally, this would be a very unfortunate event for the overall success of the war. This operation can be compared with the march to Kaluga. Nothing can prevent Field-Marshal Kutuzov from executing this march; nothing can force him to abandon his new line of operation because he has vast provinces behind him where he can hide and where he can obtain his needs; this is even the case here. Even if the French army at Moscow had not already encountered the seed of its complete dissolution and destruction, the march to Kaluga had in any case forced the emperor to abandon his former line of operation and thus to go where his enemy wanted him. We must also espouse this in our current situation."[40]

Informed by the Russians of Toll's suggestion for a concentration at Altenburg, Scharnhorst objected because the French still had not revealed their intentions: an Allied concentration at Altenburg would be appropriate only to confront an enemy army that had likewise concentrated for battle. In addition, supply problems would not permit the Allied armies to remain concentrated indefinitely. The Prussians feared that hunger would force the Allies to disperse just when a concentration became necessary. Gneisenau wrote in similar terms to Hardenberg: "But what if the enemy does not come and we concentrate too early, before we can deliver a battle? Thus, forced by hunger, we will have to separate our forces at the end of April, and we probably will not be united when we should be. Regardless, I hope Napoleon will see himself forced to deliver a battle before Austria declares itself and in this way our premature concentration will not hurt us."[41]

Scharnhorst did not believe Napoleon intended to immediately cross the Saale but viewed it as probable and recommended preparing for it, but not by concentrating the army. Alexander agreed, yet the measures chosen by the Russians fell far short of Scharnhorst's proposed plan. Although Tormasov's army would be across the Elbe by 28 April, it would advance only to the Nossen–Freiberg line, fifty-five miles southeast of Leipzig. Instead of taking the offensive, the Allies would *accept* a battle on the left bank of the Elbe at the first opportunity. For the time being, Wittgenstein and Blücher would maintain their positions at Leipzig and Altenburg respectively, while Miloradovich advanced to Zwickau and Tormasov led the Russian main army to Chemnitz. After discussing the issue with Frederick William, Scharnhorst departed for Wittgenstein's headquarters to lobby against Toll's proposed concentration at Altenburg. "The misfortune is that General Toll will go to Count Wittgenstein the moment I leave there," he lamented to Gneisenau.[42]

On the morning of the 25th, Blücher notified his Prussian troops that considerable imperial forces had reached the Saale. The firing of three artillery rounds from the Altenburg Schloß would serve as the signal for the brigades to assemble. Reports from the forward patrols arrived, revealing that Hof remained free of enemy forces but that approximately 10,000 French troops had occupied Jena. Another 15,000 bayonets had purportedly reached Auerstedt. Around noon, the enemy crossed the Saale downstream from Jena at Camburg and Dornburg, dispersing the Prussian posts and bivouacking at Frauenprießnitz, forty miles west of Blücher's headquarters at Altenburg (see Map 3). That same day, Toll met with Blücher and Gneisenau; the latter remained unimpressed. "This is a very arrogant person who has only general military knowledge," complained Gneisenau to Hardenberg. "He is very insensitive and incompetent when it comes to grand ideas. That is why he has fought against and rejected Scharnhorst's really ingenious plan of campaign. One should now concentrate and fight. But if Kutuzov and his entourage, like at Borodino, are concerned for their line of retreat and move to it too early, the crossing of the Elbe will involve loss and disorder." Gneisenau's renowned biographer, Hans Delbrück, admonishes him for this unduly harsh criticism, claiming that "the historical critic must give his quiet appreciation" to Toll and that, "despite his theoretical tendencies, Toll possessed the genuine soldierly desire for battle and because of this provided important service during the course of the war." First impressions meant everything, and Gneisenau's first impression of Toll left him little confidence. "I think we are on the eve of great events," he revealed to Hardenberg; "courage will be the decisive factor where brains are lacking."[43]

Toll took advantage of his visits with Wittgenstein and Blücher to acquaint himself with the latest reports of Ney's advance through Weimar toward the Saale and Bertrand's continued march north from Bavaria. Struck by the gravity of the situation, Toll hurried to Dresden, arriving at the same time as the news that Napoleon had reached Erfurt. The rapid pace of events caught Russian headquarters by surprise. In fact, Alexander had departed to visit his sister at Teplitz (Teplice) in Bohemia. To their credit, Toll and Volkonsky recognized the urgent need for haste and assumed responsibility for moving Tormasov closer to Blücher and Miloradovich, the latter having reached Chemnitz on the 24th. According to Toll's instructions that Volkonsky drafted into orders, Tormasov would lead the main army from Dresden in two columns on 27 April so it could reach Roßwein and Freiberg on the 28th; Geringswalde and Mittweida on the 29th; and Frohburg and Kohren on the 30th.

Blücher's troops remained on standby: Wintzingerode's corps maintained its quarters between Leipzig and Borna, while the Prussian infantry did the same in the Borna–Altenburg–Mittweida region. One Russian cavalry brigade pushed west to Merseburg while another went to Weißenfels; the Prussian Reserve Cavalry stood west of Altenburg. Russian *Streifkorps* operated before the front of Eugene's Army of the Elbe while the Prussians patrolled along the front of Napoleon's Army of the Main. For the 27th, Blücher ordered reconnaissance conducted in force on Saalfeld, Jena, Dornburg, Camburg, and Naumburg in unison with 2,000 troopers provided by Wintzingerode. For reasons unknown, the Russians did not comply.[44]

Meanwhile, north of Blücher, Wittgenstein's headquarters likewise prepared for the approaching storm. On the 26th, the Russian commander announced his intention to concentrate all disposable troops at Leipzig. If the French took the offensive by crossing the Saale, he would offer battle at Lützen in cooperation with Blücher. Wittgenstein did not doubt the need to confront Napoleon; the Allies could not evacuate Saxony without a fight. Several considerations promised victory: the quality of the Allied troops, the great mood of the Prussians, Allied superiority in field guns and cavalry, and the inexperience and rawness of Napoleon's troops. Victory offered the end of French control of Germany and Austria's entry into the alliance. But to attain this victory, the Russians and Prussians needed to agree on a plan of action. Thus far, all they could agree on was that a battle had to end with the destruction of the emperor's new army.[45]

In the meantime, Alexander and Frederick William continued their negotiations with the Swedes and British. On 22 April, the Prussians and Swedes finally concluded a treaty of alliance after some disagreement. Again, the issue over Norway as Bernadotte's price for participating in the war against Napoleon proved to be an obstacle. Aside from the cession of Norway, the crown prince wanted 35,000 Russians and 27,000 Prussians – all placed under his command – to join a Swedish force of 18,000 men at Stralsund. To compensate Frederick VI for the loss of Norway, Bernadotte wanted Denmark to annex the Hanseatic cities and other regions of North Germany. Frederick William objected and refused to ratify the treaty; Alexander supported the king's position. This impasse persisted for the remainder of the Spring Campaign. Nevertheless, Castlereagh described the Prussian treaty with Sweden as "highly satisfactory," claiming that it provided "a uniformity to the principles of the alliance at a moment."[46]

Escorted by Tormasov's army, the monarchs established their headquarters at Dresden on 24 April; Stewart arrived on the 25th. While Cathcart met with Nesselrode, Stewart conversed with Hardenberg about the issue of subsidies and loans. The Russian ambassador to Great Britain, Lieven, already had requested financial assistance in the amount of £4,000,000, a figure Castlereagh deemed excessive. London also offered to cover the £500,000 bill for the Russian fleet to winter in British waters. As for Iberia, subsidies to Portugal and Spain in 1813 would amount to at least £3,000,000. If the war unfolded in 1813 according to London's plans and expectations, it could cost the British more than £7,000,000 in subsidies alone. Nevertheless, Castlereagh remained committed to financing the Coalition, as is best seen in a 22 January exhortation to Cathcart "that we must not starve the cause." Consequently, Cathcart and Stewart explained that, despite the commitments to Iberia and Sweden, London could provide £2,000,000 to be shared by the Russians and Prussians with the former taking £1,333,334 or two-thirds and the latter £666,666. The British requested that the majority of this figure be taken in the form of war materiel and supplies rather than cash. In return, the British stipulated that the Russians and Prussians field armies of 200,000 and 100,000 men respectively. Lastly, all parties would agree not to make a separate peace with Napoleon.

Stewart met with Frederick William on the 27th, later claiming that "it was not possible to be received in a more gracious or satisfactory manner. The king, whose courage and prudence had of late shone forth in a manner worthy of the descendant of the great Frederick . . . now came forward . . . to place himself at the head of the greatest national efforts which our, and it may perhaps be said any, age had witnessed." One issue Stewart settled concerned "a tariff of duties at all the Prussian ports of the Baltic, so oppressive in its provisions as to destroy British trade altogether, and especially to put an end to any exportation of corn from the Prussian territories." Stewart's complaints prompted Hardenberg to temporarily suspend the tariff until a commercial treaty could be negotiated. Regarding the subsidy, Frederick William countered that the size of his army at the moment fell far short of the number it would reach in a few months, thus hinting that he required more financial aid. Conversely, Alexander did not feel comfortable agreeing to field more than 150,000 men in light of the great sacrifices made by the Russians in 1812. Consequently, negotiations dragged on throughout May and into June. In fact, a single treaty of alliance against France would not be signed until 1814. For now, the Sixth Coalition existed by virtue of the Convention of Åbo and the bilateral treaties signed by the Russians, Prussians, Swedes, and British. "We have done everything in our power to check jealous feelings," concluded Castlereagh, "and have no doubt you will have done the same. Neither Russia nor Great Britain (were it even politic) can now break with Sweden, without a loss of character, and the only object now is to render the alliance useful to the common cause."[47]

Elsewhere, Kutuzov, now on his deathbed, remained at Bunzlau. "The marshal [Kutuzov] has had a glimpse of the enemy, and has taken ill very *opportunely*," Wilson coldly wrote in his journal entry of 25 April. "Perhaps it is a 'Kamenski stratagem,' to get rid of the responsibility which is about to attach heavily somewhere."[48] Not opportune but fatal, the illness eventually took Kutuzov three days later. Due to the decline in Kutuzov's health, the monarchs had already contemplated the issue of a successor. According to Delbrück, the names of Wittgenstein and Blücher repeatedly surfaced. Blücher withdrew his name, making it easier to secure the agreement of the Russian generals for the appointment of a Russian to the post of Allied commander in chief. To succeed Kutuzov, Alexander appointed the 44-year-old Wittgenstein, whose campaign the previous year on the Dvina River had earned him fame as the savior of St. Petersburg. Compared to Kutuzov's lethargy, Wittgenstein's vigor, recently demonstrated by his liberation of

11 General Ludwig Adolph Peter zu Wittgenstein, 1769–1843

Prussia, appeared absolutely vital for the crucial responsibilities of this post. Moreover, his fluency in French and German enabled him to easily communicate with his allies. His concern for Berlin and defending the Prussian heartland made him popular in Prussian circles.[49]

Despite Wittgenstein's attributes, Alexander managed to confound the situation in part to offset any objections from Blücher, Miloradovich, and Tormasov, all of whom were senior to Wittgenstein. Alexander's choice did indeed infuriate Miloradovich and Tormasov; the latter returned to Russia after the 2 May battle of Lützen claiming illness. Under the pretext of preserving harmony, the tsar used the opportunity to make himself the de facto Allied generalissimo, a role he coveted. The German General Staff historian Rudolf von Caemmerer describes Volkonsky's 27 April letter to Wittgenstein as "a most remarkable document, reflecting the ambiguity that existed in the mind of the task giver over the nature of the task. The inscription named Wittgenstein as 'commander in chief of the Combined Army of the Allied Powers' but the text conferred on him only 'the command of all troop units under Blücher as well as Wintzingerode' and instructed him 'to dispose of these troops according to his judgment.' Nothing is said of the two parts of the Russian main army under Tormasov and Miloradovich." Alexander's headquarters continued to issue orders directly to both, whose physical distance from Wittgenstein could serve as an excuse to ignore directives from him. "If Wittgenstein was elated over the new command structure," continues Caemmerer, "and if he expressed confidence in victory, he would very soon learn the narrow limits of his actual authority." "Wittgenstein's situation was very difficult," adds the Russian General Staff historian Bogdanovich. "Having hardly assumed command of the army, he had to confront Napoleon. Up to now, he had never faced Napoleon. Wittgenstein fought against the French in 1812 with Russian troops only; now he received command of two armies; he knew neither the Prussian troops nor their commanders. In 1812, he had acted completely independently; in 1813, he had to work in the immediate presence of his monarch and the king of Prussia, report his intentions to them, and request their permission to execute his plans. All of this led to delays." Wittgenstein probably should have turned over the direct command of his own army to another and immediately moved to Allied Headquarters. Instead, he avoided it for as long as he could, to maintain his independence. What he failed to realize was that he had no independence to maintain.[50]

Blücher repeatedly stated that he did not have the slightest reservation about serving under a younger man. Moreover, it is relatively safe to assume that he would not have objected to being subordinated to a Russian. Nevertheless, for the sake of preserving unity of command, Frederick William requested that he make a formal statement of his agreement to obey Wittgenstein.[51] On the following day, Blücher responded that, when the king decided for war, he had resolutely declared his willingness to sacrifice all personal considerations for the interests of "Your Royal Majesty, the Fatherland, and the general cause." He assured Frederick William that his actions would prove that he remained true to these "sacred principles." Nevertheless, he wrote Wittgenstein an explicit declaration of his willingness to obey his orders and follow them verbatim. "Today, I have repeated the assurance to Wittgenstein that I place myself under his orders and will follow these punctually," he informed Frederick William. "This is only a small token of the feeling of true devotion and the deepest reverence with which I would die for you."[52]

Scharnhorst's role and the tremendous influence he enjoyed among the tsar's entourage proved more of a hurdle for Wittgenstein than any opposition from Blücher. Alexander, Volkonsky, and Toll recognized Scharnhorst as the foremost Prussian military representative, which corresponded to his position as Chief of the General Staff of the Prussian Army. Their respect allowed him to achieve a level of involvement in Allied planning that far exceeded his nominal position as chief of staff of Blücher's army. As the Russian General Staff system closely resembled that of the French, where the staff chief served as a glorified clerk to the field commander rather than his partner in operational planning, it is not surprising that the extent of Scharnhorst's authority came as somewhat of a surprise and shock to Wittgenstein, who had not been present during the deliberations at Kalisch. In addition, Wittgenstein doubted the combat-effectiveness of the new

Prussian army. Seeking firmer, more direct control over it, he intended to abolish Scharnhorst's combined-arms brigades and incorporate each regiment into the Russian army according to its branch of service. This move would accommodate the Russian system which, largely based on eighteenth-century linear tactics, made little use of combined-arms units. Russian orders of battle typically grouped the infantry in massive waves with the cavalry in the rear. Such a measure would have had a disastrous effect on the success of the organizational and tactical changes the Prussians had made to modernize their army. Fortunately for them, they managed to convince the new commander of the shortsightedness of this plan.[53]

On the very day of his appointment (27 April) and having barely gained an overview of the office assigned to him, Wittgenstein instructed his staff chief, Auvray, to draft a general disposition for the operations of the Russo-Prussian army. Specifically, the new commander in chief wanted to announce his intention to *deliver* a battle in the region of Leipzig. French movements indicating a concentration at Naumburg convinced Wittgenstein that Napoleon intended to advance through Leipzig to Torgau and beyond to sever Russian communications. To counter this threat, Wittgenstein sought to concentrate the Allied armies along an eighteen-mile east–west line between Wurzen and Leipzig. Thus, Auvray issued Wittgenstein's "Instructions," which have received much criticism and not merely because of their awkwardness and prolixity. To his credit, the Russian commander attempted to provide his subordinates with directives for any situation possible. At the least, his desire to deliver a battle clearly emerged, albeit with a mindboggling range of scenarios. The document is worthy of review because of the insight it provides into the dichotomy of the Russo-Prussian coalition.[54]

Wittgenstein began the disposition with the typical positioning of Allied forces. Forming the vanguard of the right wing, the Prussian general Kleist's Russo-Prussian corps of 6,200 men and 32 guns would occupy and defend Halle for as long as possible.[55] Should the French attack with superior numbers, Wittgenstein instructed Kleist to withdraw east to Yorck's position at Schkeuditz. Yorck's main body would remain at Schkeuditz with a strong vanguard posted at Merseburg. If a "very superior" French force advanced into his sector, he would unite with Kleist and withdraw all troops toward Leipzig. Berg would take a position just west of Leipzig to guard the city against any threat from the direction of Weißenfels and to support Yorck's post at Merseburg. Wittgenstein directed Wintzingerode to place all of his cavalry at Lützen; strong posts at Osterfeld and Weißenfels would be supported by Wintzingerode's infantry, which would assemble at Zwenkau. These posts would observe the stretch of the Naumburg–Merseburg road as far as Jena and "never lose sight of the enemy." Blücher's troops likewise would concentrate between Altenburg and Borna, with a strong cavalry detachment at Gera and forward posts extending south from Jena through Auma to Schleiz. Until gaining "precise reports over the enemy's advance toward Leipzig," Miloradovich would remain at Chemnitz with a cavalry detachment at Zwickau to monitor the fifty-mile line extending from Schleiz through Plauen to Adorf near the Bohemian frontier. Should either the French advance on Leipzig or Tormasov move up, Miloradovich would march seventeen miles west to Waldenburg. Wittgenstein concluded the first portion of the disposition by summoning Tormasov to march west from Nossen and Freiberg to Rochlitz (see Map 2).

The second half of the document began with Wittgenstein's avowal to deliver a battle. "According to the current enemy movements, he has concentrated his main force in the region of Naumburg and probably wants to drive through Leipzig toward Torgau to separate the operations line of the lower Oder from that of the Bober [Bóbr] and the Queis [Kwisa], and thus win for himself an interior line of operations. Our position and our disposition must be arranged so that in any situation we can give the enemy battle at any point under favorable conditions." Wittgenstein continued by offering plans to counteract several possible French operations. He based four of his six scenarios on the distinction between a "strong" or general enemy advance compared to that of a "weak" advance, which he fails to define. Two of the cases scripted a response to a "strong" French offensive through either Halle or Merseburg–Naumburg. In both cases, all Allied forces including the Russian main army would concentrate in two marches at Wurzen so that "the enemy offensive against Leipzig will be countered by our combined strength."[56] The Allied reaction to the approach of the French provides the only difference in the instructions for these two scenarios. Should the French advance through Halle, Yorck would support Kleist, who would slowly withdraw toward Leipzig and delay the enemy for forty-eight hours "to provide our main army with the necessary time to unite with Blücher's corps." However, should the French advance through Merseburg–Naumburg, Wintzingerode and Berg along with Yorck's post at Merseburg would delay the enemy's advance on Leipzig for two days. Two scenarios likewise concerned a "weak" enemy advance through either Halle or Merseburg–Naumburg. In the case of the former, Blücher, Miloradovich, and Tormasov would remain in their positions to cover the Allied left while Yorck, Berg, and Wintzingerode delivered an offensive battle between Leipzig and Halle. Should a French advance from Merseburg–Naumburg be considered "weak," Wintzingerode and Berg would hold the enemy at Lützen while Blücher and Yorck rushed there to deliver a battle.

The document's final two scenarios envisioned a French attempt to envelop the Allied left in a repeat of Napoleon's 1806 campaign. The first described the reaction to a French advance through Gera to Altenburg and Colditz. Accordingly, Tormasov, Blücher, and Wintzingerode's infantry would concentrate between Colditz and Rochlitz. Miloradovich would waste no time in operating against the enemy's right wing while Yorck, Berg, and Wintzingerode's cavalry assembled between Leipzig and Grimma to advance against the French left wing and rear. Lastly, if the French advanced through Gera and Plauen in the direction of Zwickau, then Miloradovich, Tormasov, and Blücher's infantry would concentrate at Flöha, eight miles east of Chemnitz. All remaining corps would assemble in two marches between Borna and Altenburg to move against the French left and rear.

Wittgenstein concluded with orders for Bülow to operate along the Saale in the left flank and rear of the viceroy at the commencement of any imperial offensive. In addition, he cautioned the light cavalry against abandoning the forward posts too quickly. In case of a French offensive, the Russian commander instructed the light cavalry to impede "the enemy's further advance by operating as partisans in his flank and rear."[57]

Wittgenstein's 27 April disposition earned immediate criticism from Scharnhorst. Although approving the idea of a battle between Leipzig and Wurzen, he vehemently rejected the distinction between a "strong" and "weak" enemy advance, emphasizing the difficulty of determining the extent of a French movement. Fearing that such a determination could not be made before the speed of the French voided any Allied reaction, he predicted that the "wait and see" approach inherent in Wittgenstein's scenarios would lead either to the Allies being defeated piecemeal or to Napoleon reaching the Elbe with his main force. Moreover, if the French advanced in numerous columns toward several points – which seemed likely for a crossing of the Saale – Scharnhorst found no provisions for an Allied response. Again, the Allies would risk being attacked piecemeal while they attempted to determine not only the objective of the offensive but also which column constituted Napoleon's main force.

Scharnhorst also returned to his original concern over extending west beyond the Elster due to the difficulties posed by crossing that river. He reiterated his 24 April recommendation to take a position between the Elster and the Mulde, citing the favorable terrain for battle. In this position, the entire Allied army could unite and attack an advancing enemy force. Allied cavalry and horse artillery would observe and delay the French until the infantry and artillery arrived. Believing the French would march on either Zeitz or Leipzig, Scharnhorst preferred a position at Brandis, west of the Mulde and the mid-point on Wittgenstein's Leipzig–Wurzen line. "From here we must attack him if he advances further, especially through Leipzig," Scharnhorst wrote a few days later. "This always has been my opinion." Nevertheless, he deferred to Wittgenstein's choice of Wurzen (seven miles east of Brandis and on the opposite bank of the Mulde) as long as the cavalry closely monitored French movements to prevent any threat to the army's line of retreat to Dresden. "If the enemy does not attack through Leipzig, we must then go to where he is. All reports agree that no enemy forces face our left flank and that they move on our right."[58]

On the other side of the Saale, Napoleon left Mainz on 24 April, driving through the night to cover 160 miles and reach Erfurt at 9:00 P.M. the next day. At Erfurt, he found the Guard reorganized. Fourteen miles east of Erfurt, Ney's massive III Corps of 45,000 men assembled around Weimar. Thirty-two miles southeast of Erfurt stood Bertrand's IV Corps (18,000 men) with Oudinot's XI (24,000 men) some sixty miles south of Erfurt at Coburg. Marmont's VI Corps (24,000) brought up the rear at Gotha some fifteen miles west of Erfurt. Eugene's 40,000 men camped under the guns of Magdeburg just over ninety miles north-northeast of Erfurt. At Würzburg, more than 100 miles south-southeast of Erfurt, Augereau worked to form five divisions that would observe Bohemia and insure the Bavarians against Austrian aggression.[59]

Neither Napoleon nor Berthier issued any orders of consequence on the 25th, yet the quills of their secretaries remained busy on the 26th. At 6:00 that morning, the emperor instructed Berthier to move up Marmont's VI Corps. Napoleon wanted its 20th Division, commanded by General Jean-Dominique Compans, to march twenty-two miles northeast from Bad Langensalza to Weißensee, with posts extending to Kölleda (see Map 2). Marmont's other two divisions would be stretched between Gotha and Erfurt with corps headquarters at the former. Although Compans's division would be south of Eugene at Querfurt and west of Ney's III Corps, which received orders to march from Weimar to Naumburg, Napoleon insisted that Compans's men bivouac in a single large square. If artillery could be heard from the direction of Naumburg, the division would march to the sound of the guns. While prudent measures, these orders reflect Napoleon's continued concern about the Cossacks, his uncertainty over Allied positions and intentions, and his assumption that the Allies might launch their own offensive.[60]

Around noon, Berthier issued the emperor's orders for Ney, Bertrand, and Oudinot. The foremost received instructions to move four of his divisions northeast to Naumburg and to guard the bridge over the Saale fourteen miles upstream at Dornburg. Bertrand's IV Corps would move down the Saale from Saalfeld to Jena, relieving Ney's troops there. Thus, III and IV Corps would be stretched twenty-one miles along the left bank of the Saale between Naumburg and Jena. To replace IV Corps at Saalfeld, Berthier directed Oudinot's XII Corps to march as fast as possible to Saalfeld. In addition to these marching orders, Napoleon also finalized the organization of IV and XII Corps. Bertrand received command of the 12th (French), 15th (Italian), and 38th (Württemberger) Divisions while the 13th (French), 14th (French), and 29th (Bavarian) Divisions comprised Oudinot's corps.[61]

At 1:00 on the afternoon of the 26th, Napoleon revealed his thoughts to Ney: "At the moment, my main task is to reunite with the viceroy and occupy all of the Saale from Saalfeld to its junction with the Elbe. It is necessary that Naumburg be secured against the Cossacks." In addition, the emperor informed Ney that the Guard would move into Weimar. On the other hand, he ordered 200,000 rations of biscuit stored at Erfurt "so that in case of a retreat we can find it there." He somewhat explained his ideas in a letter to Eugene, likewise dictated at 1:00 P.M. Napoleon's first goal remained garrisoning the line of the Saale, but he added reoccupying Hamburg as well. "My second operation will be to occupy the Elbe. Please tell me what constitutes the garrison at Magdeburg."[62]

Reports soon arrived indicating that Eugene would occupy Halle and link with Ney during the course of the 27th. Consequently, at 8:00 that morning, Napoleon took some satisfaction in achieving his first goal: "The occupation of Jena, Dornburg, Naumburg, Merseburg, and Halle was my first project. We can also occupy Weißenfels, which has a bridge over the Saale and a road from the left bank." At last, Napoleon prepared to cross the Saale at Weißenfels, a mere nine miles from Ney's position at Naumburg. For the 28th, Eugene received a request for an immediate status report on his army as well as orders to procure enough bread for several days. The restless emperor dictated this communiqué at 3:00 A.M. on the 28th. Thirty minutes later, he wrote directly to Ney: "if it is possible, I desire that we cross [the Saale] from the left bank." Reports indicated that one Russian corps still faced the Austrians and Poles near Kraków and that all of Barclay de Tolly's army remained at Thorn after its Bavarian garrison capitulated on 16 April. "Therefore," he continues, "the Russians are not in a position to seriously dispute the Elbe and, as Wittgenstein is quite daring, by debouching with great masses we can make him suffer consider-able losses. I think the first point is to arrive at Leipzig. The viceroy can debouch from Merseburg. The main business is now the junction; forward this letter to the viceroy."[63]

The master of war selected Leipzig not simply as his first geographic objective, but as the key to reversing the crisis confronting his empire. An advance through Leipzig would sever the Prussians from Berlin and the resources of Brandenburg. Depending on the direction of their retreat, Wittgenstein and Blücher could be driven south and forced to violate Austrian neutrality. If they withdrew east along the Russian line of communication through Dresden to Kalisch, then Napoleon could drive as far as the Oder. Should the Prussians and Russians separate at Leipzig with the former withdrawing on Berlin while the latter fell back along their line of communication, he would defeat each isolated enemy army in turn. Variables existed in the emperor's plan but they arose because he could not predetermine the direction in which the Allies would retreat after he took the initiative by commencing an offensive toward Leipzig. After achieving mass, he no longer intended to await the enemy's move. In fact, news from Vienna indicated the increase of anti-French sentiment at the Austrian court. After retreating to Austria, the Austrians disarmed Poniatowski's Poles: V Corps of the Grande Armée of 1812. Although the Austrians granted the Poles free passage to Saxony or Bavaria, Napoleon viewed the disarming of the troops as a hostile act. Thus, he had to crush the Russians and Prussians before Austria moved against him.

During the course of the 27th, Wittgenstein reduced the gap between himself and Blücher, sending Berg to Leipzig and Yorck to Schkeuditz, nine miles west of Saxony's second city. Just as Wittgenstein slid south, Eugene's Army of the Elbe trooped to the lower Saale, forcing Yorck's Prussians to evacuate the bridgehead at Wettin and destroy the bridge. Regardless, Blücher moved Wintzingerode's infantry south and closer to Borna; he likewise summoned the Reserve Brigade from Mittweida to Rochlitz. After pushing a cavalry brigade to Zwickau, Miloradovich's corps remained at Chemnitz, twenty-seven miles southeast of Blücher's headquarters at Altenburg. On the following day, the 28th, Kleist repulsed an attempt by Lauriston's V Corps to take Halle, but expected the imperials to return in greater force. Yorck remained at Schkeuditz and Berg's corps west of Leipzig. Miloradovich advanced from Chemnitz to Penig and Tormasov's columns moved to Nossen and Freiberg but Blücher made no significant changes in the position of his army.[64]

As the French advanced through the valley of the Saale, small engagements flared across the front of Blücher's army on the 28th. Blücher could not have been more ready to grapple with Napoleon. "I have wished for some time that the enemy would cross the Saale and come in the open field," he wrote Boyen. That morning, Blücher assumed "that the enemy will advance with his force from Naumburg toward Leipzig. We are now ready for this case. Wittgenstein has moved to Leipzig and Wintzingerode has moved closer to me. It would be very desirable if we could deliver a battle on the plain of Leipzig, somewhere near Lützen. The last portion of the Russian main army crosses the Elbe today; its van stands at Zwickau. If we are attacked, the Russians will move closer to us."[65]

Toll returned to Blücher's headquarters at Altenburg on the 29th, symbolizing the bizarre situation atop the Russian high command. Rather than Wittgenstein or Alexander, Toll wanted to meet with Scharnhorst. His arrival handed the Prussians an opportunity to complain about Wittgenstein's disposition, which Toll had yet to see. Although he disagreed with Scharnhorst's call for a concentration at Brandis, he immediately wrote to Wittgenstein, urging him to return to the basic idea of concentrating all Allied forces thirty miles south of Leipzig at Altenburg. He based this suggestion on his opinion that Napoleon would seek to separate

Wittgenstein and Blücher by driving his army like a wedge between Leipzig and Altenburg. In this scenario, the concentration of all forces at Altenburg became imperative, as Toll explains:

> If the enemy advances on Leipzig when our army is united at Altenburg, any offensive movement by him along the Naumburg–Leipzig line will place his line of operations in danger of being lost and we will then drive him against the Elbe between Magdeburg and Wittenberg. On the other hand, if he moves against Altenburg, not only will we have the advantage of favorable terrain, but we will also maintain our entire line of operation with Dresden through the four bridges of Mühlberg, Meißen, and Dresden (where there are two bridges). But, if we concentrate all of our forces at Leipzig, the enemy will maneuver against our left and push us back toward Roßlau, toward the single bridge that will remain available to us, therefore completely away from our line of operation. *You know, general, that when Napoleon seizes the offensive it is like lightning; thus, we must decide quickly.*[66]

Meanwhile, Wittgenstein's disposition also reached the tsar's headquarters on the 29th. The planned concentration at Wurzen received profound disapproval. Alexander also rejected the idea of a battle east of Leipzig. He immediately dispatched Volkonsky to Leipzig to instruct Wittgenstein to situate the army along a twenty-mile north–south line between Leipzig and Borna. By the time Volkonsky arrived, imperial forces had reached Weißenfels and Merseburg. This signaled Napoleon's intention either to march on Leipzig or to drive between Leipzig and Altenburg to separate Wittgenstein and Blücher, just as he had separated the Austrians and Sardinians in 1796. With the situation thus clarified, Wittgenstein ordered the entire Allied army to unite between Leipzig and Borna, cross the Elster, and advance toward Lützen to strike the imperial army in the flank as it marched east.[67]

The Coalition's political situation demanded that a battle be delivered on the left bank of the Elbe. Although sheer numbers probably would favor Napoleon, the superb morale of the Allied troops presumably would negate this advantage. These considerations fueled Wittgenstein's desire to immediately attack Napoleon. Bogdanovich has no doubt that he would have executed this attack on 1 May had his army been united at the Elster. Yet the Russian main army still remained two days behind. According to the march table, it could not participate in a battle until 2 May. Consequently, Wittgenstein believed he could do little except await Napoleon's measures on 30 April and 1 May before determining his own actions.[68]

As noted, the French surged east to Weißenfels and Merseburg on the 29th. Yorck's post at the latter fell back on his main body as XI Corps of Eugene's army occupied the city and its suburb on the right bank of the Saale. Yorck sent reinforcements toward Kleist at Halle, but the Prussian general felt that the loss of Merseburg rendered his position untenable. At midnight, Kleist withdrew toward Schkeuditz; the French moved into Halle the following morning.[69] Further south, Napoleon's Army of the Main pushed across the Saale with 8th Division from Ney's III Corps occupying Weißenfels that evening. Wintzingerode led the mass of his cavalry twelve miles west from Zwenkau to Lützen; his infantry moved to the vicinity of Lützen during the night.

Toll had convinced Blücher to concentrate his corps at Altenburg; the 2nd Brigade had already started the eleven-mile march south from Borna. While in the midst of arranging the concentration at Altenburg, Blücher received directions from Wittgenstein. Issued before Volkonsky's arrival and adhering to the disposition of 27 April, Wittgenstein ordered the concentration at Leipzig. Blücher recalled 2nd Brigade and orchestrated the movements of the other brigades to comply with the new orders. Knowing the French faced him along the Saale from Saalfeld through Halle, Blücher correctly assumed that Napoleon awaited only the arrival of his most rearward troops before he crossed the river. Confidence in the army could not have been higher. "We have daily combats, which turn out well," Blücher wrote to his wife on 29 April. "The great blow is close at hand."[70]

On the 30th, Wittgenstein took the final step in sliding his own troops south and into position for battle. Both Berg and Yorck moved to Zwenkau; Kleist marched from Schkeuditz to Lindenau. Blücher's corps assembled at Borna while Wintzingerode's corps faced the imperial army along the Saale; Tormasov's columns reached Frohburg and Kohren. Miloradovich remained at Penig on the 29th and did not receive any orders to march on the following day. Instead, on the 30th, he received a polite yet thoroughly detailed invitation to join the concentration by immediately moving from Penig to Altenburg. Regardless, Miloradovich spent the entire day idle at Penig. Anticipating this friction, Toll asked Volkonsky to issue firm orders to Miloradovich.

By the evening of the 30th, Kleist held the extreme right wing at Lindenau with his vanguard on the road to Merseburg. In the center, Yorck's corps camped close to Zwenkau with the front facing Lützen; behind it stood Berg's corps. Blücher's corps bivouacked at Borna, eleven miles southeast of Zwenkau. West of the army and on the other side of the Elster, Wintzingerode held Lützen. On left wing, Tormasov reached Frohburg, six miles south of Borna, and Miloradovich remained a further twelve miles south at Penig. If Wittgenstein wanted both Tormasov and Miloradovich to participate in a strike against Napoleon's army, he would have to delay the enemy's march through Lützen for at least twenty-four hours until Sunday, 2 May. That night, Wittgenstein met with Blücher at Rötha, between their respective headquarters of Zwenkau and Borna. Nothing is known of their conversation. Wittgenstein probably wanted to meet with his senior subordinate out of respect and discuss the intelligence received that day. According to his 3 May report to the tsar, he learned "that the greater part of Ney's army, a portion of the Italian troops, and the French Guard had crossed the Saale River near Naumburg. At the same time, rumors claimed that Emperor Napoleon reached the army. It was also noticed that the forces of the viceroy were proceeding on our right. All these factors indicated that the enemy was seeking to concentrate his forces and was probably intent on fighting a general battle."

Indeed, the favorable moment had arrived if the Allies wanted to fall on the advancing imperial army. On 29 April, Ney's lead division of 8,000 men marched from Naumburg to Weißenfels, forcing Wintzingerode's cavalry to retreat. Eugene not only took Merseburg and its crossing over the Saale, but also achieved the union with the Army of the Main. Napoleon's headquarters reached Weißenfels on the following day while Eugene's moved to Merseburg (see Map 3). On 1 May, Ney's III Corps continued the pursuit of Wintzingerode, who received orders to conduct a powerful reconnaissance from Leipzig to Weißenfels. At Rippach, halfway between Lützen and Weißenfels, the Russians and French collided. Wintzingerode launched several cavalry attacks against the raw youths of the imperial army. Ney raved about the steadfastness of his troops, who repulsed successive Russian attacks. Wintzingerode fell back to Lützen but the French forced him from that position as well. Utilizing "a very heavy and destructive cannonade, supported by cavalry," Wintzingerode retreated, assembling his troops at Hohenlohe and Thesau along the right bank of the Floßgraben, a brook that ran nearly parallel to the Elster and supplied the millponds of the numerous villages that dotted the landscape. The Russian commander sent his baggage east to Zwenkau but it became so disordered that it blocked the defiles and passes that Yorck's troops needed to utilize to get through the Elster's marshes. That evening, Souham's 8th Division reached the villages of Großgörschen and Kleingörschen, fifteen minutes from Wintzingerode's Russians. The day's fighting claimed one French marshal: a round shot tore through Bessières at the crossing of the Rippach, an arm of the Saale.[71]

Escorted by two battalions of Old Guard and the Guard Cavalry, Napoleon established his headquarters at Lützen.[72] He did not know just how close Wittgenstein's army – which he expected to be east of Leipzig – stood to him. Regardless, Napoleon intended to attack the Allies wherever he encountered their army. Although Oudinot's XII Corps and one Württemberger division remained two marches to the rear, the emperor knew he could concentrate 145,000 men in less than twelve hours and that the Allies could oppose him with only two-thirds this number. Another early twentieth-century British staff officer turned historian, F. L. Petre, maintains that on the evening of the 1st the emperor learned of a concentration of enemy forces around Zwenkau. According to Petre, his orders over the course of the next twelve hours clearly reflected his hope and expectation that the Allies would cross the Elster and offer battle. This assertion does not stand up under close scrutiny of the documents. As of 7:00 P.M. on 1 May, Imperial Headquarters knew only that Wintzingerode retreated toward Zwenkau and Pegau. At 4:00 A.M. on 2 May, Napoleon directed Eugene's V Corps to Leipzig and XI Corps to Markranstädt, from where they would conduct reconnaissance northeast to Leipzig and southeast to Zwenkau. Ney received instructions to assemble his five divisions at Kaja and dispatch two strong reconnaissance teams, one to Pegau and the other to Zwenkau to link with patrols from XI Corps (see Map 3). Four hours later, at 8:00 A.M., Napoleon ordered Eugene to have XI Corps move into Zwenkau "to cover the occupation of Leipzig by V Corps," and to place the majority of his cavalry in a position to be able to support either V or XI Corps, "if it is necessary."[73]

News of the enemy did reach Imperial Headquarters: Bertrand detected Miloradovich's Russians at Zeitz. In response, Berthier ordered Bertrand to halt at Taucha but send his Italian division to Gleisberg and his Württemberger division to Stößen, both to the southeast. In these positions, IV Corps would be able "to cover Naumburg and Weißenfels, threaten Zeitz, and support at Pegau if the enemy threatens to debouch there. If the enemy debouches from Zeitz, reunite your three divisions and march there." At the same time, 9:00 A.M., Berthier sent a letter to Marmont, explaining Bertrand's directions and ordering VI Corps to march to Pegau. Napoleon likewise wrote to Marmont at 9:00. Aside from reiterating the directives that went to Bertrand as well as the reasoning behind Marmont's new instructions, Napoleon shared the latest intelligence, which had most likely just arrived. "All of the information states that the enemy retreated from Leipzig to Zwenkau; that he has more than one corps at Borna; and that Tsar Alexander is at Rochlitz. If there is nobody or only few people at Pegau, you will [provide] support between Pegau and Zwenkau. Try to arrive at Pegau before 5:00 P.M." Thirty minutes later, Napoleon dictated a letter addressed to Ney, telling the marshal that VI Corps would take a position between Pegau and Zwenkau. "If you hear a cannonade from this direction, be ready to march toward it." Only now, at 9:30 A.M., did the reports Napoleon received confirm "that the enemy is united at Zwenkau and Wittgenstein has been named commander in chief. Let me know the position of your five divisions. All of my Guard will be available to support in that direction."[74]

As we will see, the attack by the audacious Wittgenstein did surprise Napoleon, whose correspondence between 7:00 P.M. on 1 May and 9:30 A.M. on 2 May does not indicate that he expected a major battle. Fortunately for the Allies, Wintzingerode's retreat on Zwenkau attracted his attention and equally important proved to be Bertrand's report on the Russians at

Zeitz. Even so, Napoleon did not proceed from his headquarters at Lützen southeast toward Zwenkau and Pegau, but instead went to review XI Corps and oversee the march of V Corps to Leipzig. Consequently, we can conclude that Napoleon did not suspect that Wittgenstein would cross the Elster and seek battle.[75]

Ney's repulse of Wintzingerode's reconnaissance confirmed that a considerable imperial army – correctly identified by Wittgenstein as the main enemy force – had reached Weißenfels and Lützen. Wittgenstein "assumed" that Eugene had reached a position "somewhere between Leipzig and Halle." Regardless, the reconnaissance clearly revealed Napoleon's intention to take Leipzig. Reports of French movements and the recent combats clearly indicated that he would converge on Leipzig in two groups: Eugene from Magdeburg and Napoleon himself from Weißenfels. "On the evening of the 1st," reported Cathcart, "the enemy appeared to have great masses of his force between Lützen and Weißenfels, and after dark a strong column was seen moving in the direction of Leipzig, to which place there was clear evidence that he intended to move."

At 6:00 P.M. on 1 May, Wittgenstein informed the tsar that "because the enemy has advanced as far as Lützen, I have decided to attack his right wing from Pegau tomorrow at daybreak and in the case of an unfavorable outcome of the battle, God forbid, I will retreat to Altenburg." "It was clear that the enemy intended to occupy Leipzig and give us a battle," he stated in his after-action report. "I decided to anticipate his moves and wreck his plan with a daring attack. Our main intention was to allow a powerful enemy corps to proceed toward Leipzig, attack the weakened enemy forces, and, after delivering a blow, provide our light forces ... with greater freedom to operate." Wittgenstein's plan appeared simple: "turn Napoleon's right between Weißenfels and Lützen while his attention was directed to his left between the latter and Leipzig."[76]

By nightfall, Wintzingerode's corps stood between the Schkorlopp villages and Zwenkau after being forced to retreat by Ney. His Cossacks had reached the rear of an enemy column of 8,000 men advancing east from Weißenfels and captured a few caissons. Inexplicably, the Cossack patrols failed to observe an entire French division take position in the quadrilateral formed by the villages of Kleingörschen, Großgörschen, Rahna, and Kaja, nor did they detect a second French division that had camped a few miles west of Rahna at Starsiedel (see Map 4). Wintzingerode's failure to reconnoiter these five villages lying so close to his front defies explanation. Moreover, a grossly exaggerated Prussian report misled Allied High Command. One of Blücher's patrols claimed that an enemy cavalry detachment reached Droyßig, five miles west of Zeitz. According to the locals, large imperial forces occupied all of the villages west of Droyßig. We will see how this mistake impacted Miloradovich shortly. Meanwhile, Blücher's corps moved from Borna to Rötha, behind Yorck and Berg.

Tormasov moved closer to Blücher's left by converging on Borna. Miloradovich reached Altenburg, where he received a communiqué from Volkonsky explaining the intention to attack Napoleon as his army marched to Leipzig on the 2nd. To cooperate, Miloradovich was to lead his corps to Predel (five miles south of Pegau) and be ready "to participate in the operations of the army."[77]

A chain of gentle hills running southwest to northeast between the banks of the Saale and the Elster provided the scene for the first clash between the Allies and Napoleon. Across this hill chain, the imperial army marched along the highway from Weißenfels through Rippach, Lützen, Markranstädt, and Lindenau toward Leipzig (see Map 3). Although ultimately enclosed by the Saale and the Elster and its arms, the sector where the battle would be fought on 2 May was bordered to the west by the Grüna brook, an arm of the Rippach that converged with this stream near the village of Rippach and then discharged into the Saale northeast of Weißenfels. The Grünabach (Grüna brook) rarely appears on modern maps. The Floßgraben, a large irrigation canal sufficient "to float timber," formed the eastern edge of the battlefield. Meandering northwest, the Floßgraben passed Lützen to the east and likewise discharged into the Saale. In the event of a retreat, the Allies would have little problem getting across the fordable Floßgraben but the same could not be said of the Elster, which could be crossed only by bridge. Napoleon likewise would have his back to a river: the Saale. Wittgenstein correctly assumed that Napoleon had extended his army in a long column for the march from Naumburg through Weißenfels and Lützen to Leipzig. He planned to attack the right flank of this column and work around to its rear, driving all northeast into the marshes of the Elster near Leipzig.[78]

At Zwenkau, Diebitsch started drafting the battle orders around 10:30 P.M. on 1 May. After one hour of his steady grinding, aides received the final draft to make copies for all subordinates. The plan simply called for attacking the imperial army in the flank and destroying the closest divisions before others could come to their assistance. At first glance, the disposition seemed clear enough, but mistakes typical of the day plagued the directives. Using the inaccurate *Topographic–Military Map of Teutschland* published in 1807 by the Geographic Institute of Weimar, the Russians drafted instructions based on a faulty overview of the region. According to Caemmerer, the characteristic square formed by the villages of Großgörschen, Kleingörschen, Rahna, and Kaja is portrayed on this map as a slender triangle, the villages of Starsiedel, Meuchen, and Meyhen are incorrectly placed, and its scale of approximately 1:170,000 only vaguely outlined the hills. Moreover, the map placed the village of Sitteln on the direct line that led from Werben through Großgörschen to Lützen, therefore west of the Floßgraben, when it actually stood north of Werben and east of Großgörschen on the right or eastern bank of the Floßgraben (see Map 4).

Designating Blücher's corps as the first wave, Diebitsch instructed the Prussians to advance in two columns. Blücher's left wing would cross the Elster at the village of Carsdorf, on the opposite bank from Pegau. Most German accounts simply refer to the crossing as the Pegau bridge but in 1813 the bridge actually stood almost two miles northwest of Pegau, whose urban sprawl eventually absorbed Carsdorf so that it cannot be found on modern maps. This column then would march west from Carsdorf and cross the Floßgraben one mile west of the Elster by 5:30 A.M. Blücher's right wing would cross the Elster at Storkwitz and received one hour to complete the process of getting across the Floßgraben. After both columns crossed the Floßgraben at Werben – and this is where the use of a faulty map came into play – the left wing would march to Sitteln while the right moved "from Werben to Sitteln or Weißenfels." With Sitteln actually located on the eastern bank of the Floßgraben, the orders made little sense, although this could hardly be blamed on Wittgenstein. Fortunately for the Allies, this mistake did not affect the approach march on the 2nd.

After completing this march, Wittgenstein wanted Blücher to slide his left wing west to the Grünabach. "General Blücher must immediately send cavalry and horse artillery across the rivulet in his left flank in order to win the opposite bank and the hills; and, as much as possible, he must refuse his right wing during the battle and have it based on the Floßgraben. From this position we will advance between the two rivulets, the Rippach [actually the Grünabach] and the Floßgraben." Like the march to Sitteln, events on the 2nd did not require Blücher to extend his left wing to the Grünabach and anchor his right to the Floßgraben. This proved fortunate for Wittgenstein because spreading Blücher's corps between these two watercourses would have extended the Prussian front two and one-half miles when his infantry only could have covered a front of less than one and one-half miles. Even if Blücher's Reserve Cavalry and Wintzingerode's squadrons had extended the left wing of the Prussian infantry, the total length of the battle line would have increased to only two miles. Moreover, with the Prussian cavalry being placed directly under Wintzingerode's command rather than Blücher's, the instructions to cross the Rippach probably appeared completely incomprehensible to the Prussians.[79]

As the second wave, the corps of Berg and Yorck would "be immediately behind Blücher's columns likewise around 5:00 A.M.," with Berg's on the road to Storkwitz, Yorck's on the road from Audigast to Pegau. After crossing the Floßgraben, the two corps would unite under Yorck's command with the Russians forming on the right and the Prussians to the left; each wing having its own reserve. "The second line and reserve will directly follow all movements of the first line in a parallel direction," continues the battle orders, "so that it can be reinforced in a timely manner." After posting 1,000 men to guard the defiles of Zwenkau and maintain communication

with Kleist at Leipzig, Wintzingerode's corps needed to reach Werben by
6:00 A.M. to cover Blücher's march. Wittgenstein instructed Wintzingerode
to exchange his twelve-pound batteries for Blücher's Reserve Cavalry. At
the time, Wintzingerode enjoyed the reputation of being a great cavalry
commander, yet Scharnhorst protested against surrendering Blücher's
Reserve Cavalry to the Russians. While the Prussian brigades each contained
cavalry, so that Blücher's infantry would still have mounted support, the
move undoubtedly rekindled the anger over Wittgenstein's earlier plans to
dismantle the Prussian brigades. Although the same orders placed Berg's
Russians under Yorck's command, Scharnhorst objected to handing over
control of the Prussian cavalry to the Russians. Despite the great respect that
Scharnhorst enjoyed among the Russians, Wittgenstein refused to change his
plans. The Allied commander wanted to assemble a great mass of cavalry on
the left wing to deliver the main blow by enveloping and routing the enemy's
right. "It is painful to have to admit," judges Caemmerer, "that this good
idea was opposed especially vigorously by Scharnhorst and that the
Prussians viewed it almost as a matter of honor to oppose it. It is plainly
evident from this example the extent of the difficulties that Wittgenstein
had to endure. If even a Scharnhorst could fall into a narrow particularism,
one thus can see how difficult it is to find the right tone for an alliance."[80]

As for reinforcements and support, Wintzingerode's infantry under
Duke Eugen of Württemberg would serve as the army's first reserve.
Wittgenstein instructed Tormasov to reach Pegau and Storkwitz by 7:00
in the morning. After detaching Prince Andrey Gorchakov's detachment
of 3,000 men and one battery to guard the crossings through the wetlands
between the Floßgraben and the Elster at Werben, Storkwitz, Pegau, and
Stönsch, Tormasov's army would form the main reserve. If the French
advanced in force from Weißenfels against Blücher's left wing, Tormasov
would counter by moving west from Stönsch to threaten the enemy's right.
"The cuirassier divisions and horse artillery can perform excellent service in
the open terrain," instructed Wittgenstein. At Leipzig, Kleist received
orders to march to the sound of the guns if he heard heavy firing or if the
French forces facing him turned against Wittgenstein. Should a superior
French force pressure him, he would retreat to Wurzen, defending "as much
as possible the road to Dresden, ruining its passage as well as the road from
Eilenburg." Should the Allied army be forced to retreat, Wittgenstein chose
Altenburg and Frohburg as the direction. All baggage would go to Borna
and in the case of a retreat would move through Rochlitz to Dresden.
Wounded and prisoners would be sent to Frohburg.

Regarding Miloradovich, the issue over seniority that the tsar foolishly
created combined with the exaggerated Prussian report over large imperial
forces occupying all of the villages west of Droyßig to create a condition
that a lazy general could exploit. First, Volkonsky rather than Wittgenstein

ordered Miloradovich to march on 2 May from Altenburg to Predel, four miles upstream the Elster from Pegau. Second, as noted, on 1 May a Prussian patrol found French cavalry at Droyßig, five miles west of Zeitz (see Map 3). Based on this intelligence, Wittgenstein envisioned the march of a strong French corps from Naumburg through Stößen and Droyßig to Zeitz. A corps taking this direction would threaten the left flank and rear of the Allied army as it drove northwest across the Elster. Thus, believing the army needed a strong flank guard, the disposition ordered Miloradovich to advance to Zeitz, seventeen miles south of Sitteln. In itself, the idea of a flank guard cannot be contested: even Scharnhorst feared a French advance from this direction. However, Miloradovich's cavalry should have been assigned the task of observing this fictitious enemy corps and slowing its march while the Russian infantry marched to the sound of the guns and contributed to the battle. To further complicate the situation, on the 2nd, Miloradovich received a report from his vanguard commander, General Dmitri Yuzefovich, written at Zeitz and dated 11:00 P.M. on 1 May that dismissed the exaggerated news about the strength and extent of a French movement on Zeitz. Instead, Yuzefovich correctly identified the French advance through Weißenfels and reported that the rumors circulating in the French army indicated its objective to be Leipzig. We will see how Miloradovich responded.[81]

"Should the enemy seek to win our right wing, the artillery must operate superbly against him," continues Wittgenstein's disposition for 2 May. "The infantry in battalion columns will move directly behind the artillery and will be supported by cavalry. If the enemy places himself in force, the reserve cavalry and horse artillery must quickly advance, bring him to disorder through caseshot, and charge him with the cavalry. The main goal of all maneuvers must be to win the enemy's right flank and therefore the troops must hold themselves to the left and ready to pivot. The skirmishers must fire as much as possible, especially in the open, and the battalion columns will support them, advancing to the beat of the drums. Cavalry that finds itself within the [French] lines must immediately exploit any disorder among the enemy troops."[82]

Although such instructions have no place in general orders, they are indicative of the tendency among Russian commanders to assign each battalion, each squadron, and each battery its place in the line, thus limiting the initiative of subordinates, the exact opposite of French tactics. "Apparently, one had no idea," comments Caemmerer, "that the French generals commanding corps and divisions received a fair amount of autonomy and that they were granted the benefit of the doubt to adapt to circumstances and locality." General Charles-Louis Lanrezac of the French General Staff, a professor at the French military academy of Saint-Cyr, adds that "practically no independence was left to corps commanders in the battle, which ... Wittgenstein seemed to think could be arranged in advance like a ballet." Finally, Bogdanovich judges that "this rather extensive disposition, which showed the desire to direct the individual commanders in all cases (which is not possible), nevertheless was very unspecific, and gave rise to misunderstandings. Its dispatch to the corps – as eyewitnesses claim – was late and thus it could not be completed in time." While the verbiage and length (1,100 words) of the disposition were unnecessary, such judgments are overly harsh and unfair to Wittgenstein and, more importantly, do not reflect the actual events of the battle.[83]

Diebitsch's arrangements did suffer from the same mistakes that would plague Napoleon's planning on 2 May 1813: too many soldiers – 20,000 men for the Allies – would not reach the battlefield. No doubt remembering the horrors of Friedland, the Russians wisely gave thought to defending the defiles in the rear of the army in case of a retreat, yet the strength of the units allocated to the Elster bridges appears excessively high. Wittgenstein could have employed his mass of Cossacks to protect the flanks and rear of the army from the extremely weak French cavalry and thus reduce the amount of infantry occupying the crossing points. Moreover, the troops that did reach the killing grounds around Großgörschen had been unnecessarily fatigued in part by long night marches caused by faulty planning and in part due to the distance they needed to cover to reach the battle. On top of this, they wasted time preparing to be reviewed by the monarchs instead of resting.[84]

For the battle on 2 May, Wittgenstein could marshal approximately 88,000 men and 552 guns.[85] Napoleon's army of 145,000 men and 372 guns outnumbered the Allies in infantry but faced a threefold superiority in cavalry and almost double the artillery. Although Napoleon had fewer total guns, he possessed more heavy batteries than the Allies, which granted the French artillery the advantage in range and effectiveness.[86] Rather than an encounter battle, Scharnhorst recommended a set battle on the plains of Leipzig, where the Allies could maximize their indisputable advantage in cavalry. In view of the Russian preference for set, mainly defensive battles like Borodino, Wittgenstein's desire for a Napoleonic-style encounter battle represents a partial coming of age for the Russians, albeit at the wrong time and place in Scharnhorst's opinion. Moreover, as we will see, Wittgenstein's reliance on the underlying principles of linear tactics suggests that the Russians still had some way to go before they could be considered practitioners of modern, Napoleonic warfare. Nevertheless, the exceptional morale of the Allied army worked to stifle Scharnhorst's reservations. Neither the Russians nor the Prussians had lost respect for the combat proficiency of the French soldier but the excellent spirit of the army worked like a soothing elixir to overcome any objections to battle especially as the imperials stood so close.

The choice of the battlefield did not please Scharnhorst, particularly because the Allies did not know where they would encounter the French. Regardless, the Allies optimistically speculated that Napoleon might not have all 120,000 men of his army on hand the next day. By rushing to attack him after his forces crossed the Saale, the Allies would force him to fight with his back against the steep valley of the Saale. "In our army," wrote Clausewitz, "there were approximately 25,000 men in the cavalry, whereas the enemy hardly had 5,000 men of this arm. Without doubt, our troops were better than those of the enemy. Perhaps he did not expect us to take the daring decision to attack. Because the emperor and his army had never been in a purely defensive battle, we expected all the more that the enemy would be surprised and not conduct his business as skillfully or with his usual optimism."[87]

At Blücher's headquarters, the Prussians heard the rumble of artillery to the west starting around noon on the 1st. With each moment the intensity seemed to grow. Blücher knew that Wintzingerode stood in combat with Napoleon's advance troops somewhere between Weißenfels and Lützen. Finally, at 6:00 P.M., after several hours of painful idleness, he received Wittgenstein's order to commence the ten-mile march west from Rötha to Pegau, where he would receive detailed instructions for the next day. Around 11:00 P.M., the corps began the march; Blücher joined the column around 2:00 A.M.

The resurrected Prussian army would face its first major test later that day. Scharnhorst used the month in Saxony to improve the organization and cohesion of the Prussian units after the haphazard mobilization. "The bellicose appearance and yet the proper behavior of the Prussian troops arouses a universal and well-deserved sensation," boasted Blücher. "Never have I seen troops influenced by a greater confidence." Clausewitz claimed that "never was an army motivated by a better spirit." A Prussian brigade marching through Borna made the impression on Boyen that "6,000 educated men of honor resolutely went to a duel of life and death." "Never was there a finer army of its number," reported the British commissioner with the Russian army, Colonel Neil Campbell, to Undersecretary of State for War and the Colonies Henry Bunbury. One week earlier, Blücher had thanked the troops for their good conduct, especially toward the inhabitants:

> Soldiers of my army! Your exemplary conduct has undergone no change whatsoever since you left your native provinces and entered the lands of Saxony. You have hitherto made no distinction between the two countries but have held yourselves bound in duty to observe the same excellent discipline. I thank you for this proof of your noble forbearance. Such conduct evinces the true spirit of warriors, and is befitting of us, because we fight for the noblest good: our Fatherland and our freedom.

Through the moderation of your demands and the mildness of your treatment, prove to the inhabitants of the German provinces that we come not as their oppressors, but as their brethren and saviors. Continue to act with this excellent spirit of subordination, and should the fame of your exalted behavior precede you far and wide, you will be received with blessings and open arms wherever you show yourselves and wherever fate may lead you.[88]

Blücher's message certainly indicated his optimism: the Prussians would continue to move west to "prove to the inhabitants of the German provinces that we come not as their oppressors, but as their brethren and saviors." Little did he know that in one month's time he would be begging his king not to follow the Russian retreat across the Oder and into Poland.

## Notes

1 *CN*, Nos. 19872, 19875, 19877, 19883, and 19858, XXV:195, 203, 206–07, 209–10, 212; Service historique de l'armée de terre (hereafter cited as SHAT), C$^{17}$ 176: Berthier to Bertrand, Ney, and Bessières, Mainz, 19 April 1813; Berthier to Ney, Mainz, 21 April 1813; Berthier to Bertrand, Mainz, 22 and 23 April 1813. According to *CN*, No. 19883, Ney reached Erfurt on the 17th and planned to occupy Weimar on the 18th.

2 As of 17 April, the Allies could utilize the restored bridge at Dresden and one pontoon bridge upstream of the capital, one pontoon bridge at Meißen, and one pontoon bridge at Mühlberg. Strong bridgeheads guarded all three pontoon bridges. Although Scharnhorst planned to build a fifth pontoon bridge at Dresden and float it to Mühlberg, the bridge never materialized. See Scharnhorst to Boyen, Altenburg, 17 April 1813, in Boyen, *Erinnerungen*, ed. Nippold, III:296.

3 Pertz and Delbrück, *Gneisenau*, II:564; Gneisenau to Wittgenstein, Altenburg, 15 April 1813, GStA PK, VI HA Rep. 92 Nl. Gneisenau, Nr. 16.

4 Scharnhorst to Boyen, Altenburg, 17 April 1813, in Boyen, *Erinnerungen*, ed. Nippold, III:295–96. Both letters bear the time of 11:00 P.M.

5 GStA PK, IV HA Rep 115, Nr. 13, contains a copy of this letter; Gneisenau to Wittgenstein and Kutuzov, Altenburg, 18 April 1813, GStA PK, VI HA Rep. 92 Nl. Gneisenau, Nr. 16.

6 Clausewitz, *Hinterlassene Werke*, VII:263–65; Holleben and Caemmerer, *Frühjahrsfeldzuges 1813*, I:465.

7 GStA PK, IV HA Rep. 15 A Nr. 187; Gneisenau to Wittgenstein, 18 April 1813 and to Kutuzov, 18 and 19 April 1813, GStA PK, VI HA Rep. 92 Nl. Gneisenau, Nr. 16; Scharnhorst to Boyen, Altenburg, 18 and 20 April 1813, in Boyen, *Erinnerungen*, ed. Nippold, III:297–98.

8 Scharnhorst to Boyen, Altenburg, 17 and 18 April 1813, in Boyen, *Erinnerungen*, ed. Nippold, III:296; Gneisenau to Kutuzov, Altenburg, 18 April 1813, GStA PK, VI HA Rep. 92 Nl. Gneisenau, Nr. 16; Blücher to Frederick William, Altenburg, 18 April 1813, *ibid.*; Pertz and Delbrück, *Gneisenau*, II:564; Scharnhorst to Knesebeck, Altenburg, 18 April 1813, in Holleben and Caemmerer, *Frühjahrsfeldzuges 1813*, I:375.

9 GStA PK, IV HA Rep. 15 A Nr. 187.

10 Gneisenau to Wittgenstein, 18 April 1813 and to Kutuzov, 18 and 19 April 1813, GStA PK, VI HA Rep. 92 Nl. Gneisenau, Nr. 16; Gneisenau to Hardenberg, Altenburg, 18 April 1813, *ibid.*, Nl. Albrecht, Nr. 47; Holleben and Caemmerer, *Frühjahrsfeldzuges 1813*, I:372–73; Pertz and Delbrück, *Gneisenau*, II:565–66.

11 Gneisenau to Hardenberg, Altenburg, 18 April 1813, GStA PK, VI HA Rep. 92 Nl. Albrecht, Nr. 47; Pertz and Delbrück, *Gneisenau*, II:568–70; Bogdanovich, *Geschichte des Krieges*, I:172; Beitzke, *Geschichte der deutschen Freiheitskriege*, I:352.

12 Wilson, *Private Diary*, I:338.

13 Scharnhorst to Knesebeck, Altenburg, 18 April 1813, in Holleben and Caemmerer, *Frühjahrsfeldzuges 1813*, I:375.

14 Scharnhorst to Boyen, Altenburg, 18 April 1813, in Boyen, *Erinnerungen*, ed. Nippold, III:296–97.

15 Clausewitz, *Hinterlassene Werke*, VII:269–70.

16 Scharnhorst to Volkonsky, Altenburg, 18 April 1813, in Holleben and Caemmerer, *Frühjahrsfeldzuges 1813*, I:375; Scharnhorst to Hardenberg, Altenburg, 18 April 1813, GStA PK, VI HA Rep. 92 Nl. Albrecht, Nr. 47.

17 Holleben and Caemmerer, *Frühjahrsfeldzuges 1813*, I:357, 386. According to Wittgenstein's plan, Yorck would evacuate Köthen, observe the Saale only with a detachment of light troops, and march his corps through Zörbig on the 20th to reach Bad Düben by the 21st, where he would be fifty miles north of Leipzig. After posting two battalions to observe Wittenberg, Kleist would advance to Dessau and Roßlau, while Berg marched through Bad Düben to Eilenburg. The Russian general Gothard August von Helfreich would occupy Köthen on the 20th and follow to Zörbig on the 21st. In the case of a serious French offensive, all light troops patrolling the Saale would withdraw on Kleist's position at Dessau. On the 20th, Wittgenstein determined that, because rumors of the French offensive could not be confirmed, Yorck's corps would move into quarters at Zörbig rather than march to Bad Düben, while Berg remained at Delitzsch, Helfreich at Köthen, and Kleist at Dessau: a front of forty miles. Twelve miles south of Delitzsch, Wintzingerode quartered at Gohlis, slightly northwest of Leipzig, with his corps camped between Gohlis and Borna east of the Pleiße. His vanguard held Merseburg while light cavalry patroled toward the Harz.

18 Miloradovich would take a position at Chemnitz with an outpost in Plauen; Blücher would place his left wing at Altenburg and his right at Borna; Wintzingerode's left wing would link with Blücher's right at Borna, his right wing would extend to Leipzig; and Wittgenstein would take a position between Leipzig and Zörbig with his headquarters at Delitzsch.

19 Müffling, *Aus meinem Leben*, 31; Scharnhorst to Volkonsky, Altenburg, 20 April 1813, in Holleben and Caemmerer, *Frühjahrsfeldzuges 1813*, I:376–77.

20 GStA PK, IV HA Rep. 15 A Nr. 187; Scharnhorst to Boyen, Altenburg, 20 April 1813, in Boyen, *Erinnerungen*, ed. Nippold, III:298; Holleben and Caemmerer, *Frühjahrsfeldzuges 1813*, I:373–74, 378–81; Clausewitz to Marie, Altenburg, 22 April 1813, in Schwartz, *Clausewitz*, II:76–77, emphasis added.

21 Holleben and Caemmerer, *Frühjahrsfeldzuges 1813*, I:387.

22 According to French correspondence, General François Garnier de Laboissière, the commander of the light cavalry brigade assigned to III Corps, repulsed 400 Prussians at Weimar, capturing 100 men and 4 officers, of whom one was purported to be Blücher's adjutant. German sources do not mention this incident. Based on Blücher's relationship with his staff and the large amount of literature pertaining to his headquarters, it is difficult to believe that the capture of an adjutant would have been omitted from correspondence, memoirs, and the official account. Nevertheless, Napoleon purportedly interrogated the Prussian officer for hours: SHAT, C$^{17}$ 176: Berthier to Ney and Jerome, Mainz, 21 April 1813.

23 Unger, *Blücher*, II:17; Maude, *Leipzig Campaign*, 94; Scharnhorst to Boyen, Altenburg, 18 April 1813, in Boyen, *Erinnerungen*, ed. Nippold, III:297; Blücher to Amalie, Altenburg, 22 April 1813, GStA PK, VI HA Rep. 92 Nl. Blücher von Wahlstatt.

24 "It appears that Bertrand is the most exposed in the march he is making on Saalfeld. He must be very alert to be able to support where appropriate": SHAT, C$^{17}$ 176: Berthier to Ney, 23 April 1813; Berthier to Eugene, 22 April 1813.

25 *CN*, Nos. 19894 and 19902, XXV:217, 225–26; SHAT, C$^{17}$ 176: Berthier to Bertrand, 24 April 1813; Berthier to Ney, 21 and 22 April 1813; Berthier to Eugene, 22 April 1813.

26 Maude, *Leipzig Campaign*, 92–93; *CN*, No. 19852, XXV:189, emphasis added.

27 *CN*, No. 19902, XXV:226; SHAT, C$^{17}$ 176: Berthier to Ney, 24 April 1813.

28 *CN*, No. 19902, XXV:226.

29 *CN*, Nos. 19912 and 19916, XXV:233, 236.

30 Blücher to Boyen, April 1813, in Boyen, *Erinnerungen*, ed. Nippold, III:303.

31 Kutuzov to Wittgenstein, Bunzlau, 18 April 1813, RGVIA, f. VUA, op. 16, d. 3921, ll. 165b–166; Wittgenstein to Blücher, 20 April 1813, GStA PK, VI HA Rep. 92 Nl. Gneisenau, Nr. 160; Mikhailovsky-Danilevsky, *Denkwürdigkeiten*, 63–64.

32 Holleben and Caemmerer, *Frühjahrsfeldzuges 1813*, I:384–85; Mikhailovsky-Danilevsky, *Denkwürdigkeiten*, 66.

33 GStA PK, IV HA Rep. 15 A Nr. 187; Pertz and Delbrück, *Gneisenau*, II:566–67.

34 See Scharnhorst's memo of 25 April in Holleben and Caemmerer, *Frühjahrsfeldzuges 1813*, II:359; Bernhardi, *Toll*, II:435, 447.

35 Holleben and Caemmerer, *Frühjahrsfeldzuges 1813*, II:25–26; Wilson, *Private Diary*, I:348–49.

36 Gneisenau to Hardenberg, Altenburg, 23 April 1813, is in Pertz and Delbrück, *Gneisenau*, II:571, while his letter of the 25th is in GStA PK, VI HA Rep. 92 Nl. Gneisenau, Nr. 20b.

37 Scharnhorst's figures are based on the following calculations: "(1) The Viceroy of Italy has 38,000 men including Davout; 10,000 men under Victor, etc.; and 6,000 men in Magdeburg for a total of 54,000 men. Of these perhaps 12,000 men under Davout will remain on the lower Elbe and 8,000 men will remain at Magdeburg, so for operations Eugene will have 34,000 men. (2) The army under Ney including the Guard: 70,000 men. The Italians under Bertrand: 25,000 men. Altogether: 129,000 men. Perhaps 10,000 Bavarians must be included, perhaps these 10,000 men already have been included; regardless, we must accept this total. In Saxony,

we have in disposable troops: 20,000 under Wittgenstein and Yorck; 13,000 under Wintzingerode; 30,000 under Blücher; 11,000 under Miloradovich; 20,000 in the Russian main army for a total of 94,000 men. If our numbers are too small, then those of the enemy facing us are too large." See "Über die nächsten Operationen bei Eröffnung des Feldzuges von 1813 in Sachsen," GStA PK, VI HA Rep. 92 Nl. Gneisenau, Nr. 18.

38  "In the first case, we must await the enemy's attack. Then, because we have only certain crossing points on the Elbe, and in this region they are mainly directly behind us, we must position ourselves on the highway. Such a battle would be conducted with paralyzed forces and thus with little to no chance that we can win; if the enemy gains 1,000 paces of terrain in one of our flanks, concern for the [line of] retreat will probably prompt the order to retreat to be given before attempting the last extreme and, without having the last extreme to attempt, we cannot win such a battle. Moreover, under these circumstances we will have to face the combined strength of the enemy." See "Über die nächsten Operationen bei Eröffnung des Feldzuges von 1813 in Sachsen," GStA PK, VI HA Rep. 92 Nl. Gneisenau, Nr. 18.

39  Stewart to Castlereagh, Dresden, 29 April 1813, *CVC*, VIII:387.

40  "Über die nächsten Operationen bei Eröffnung des Feldzuges von 1813 in Sachsen," GStA PK, VI HA Rep. 92 Nl. Gneisenau, Nr. 18.

41  Gneisenau to Hardenberg, Altenburg, 25 April 1813, GStA PK, VI HA Rep. 92 Nl. Gneisenau, Nr. 20b.

42  Scharnhorst to Gneisenau, Dresden, 24 April 1813, GStA PK, VI HA Rep. 92 Nl. Gneisenau, Nr. 23; Pertz and Delbrück, *Gneisenau*, II:578.

43  Gneisenau to Hardenberg, Altenburg, 25 April 1813, GStA PK, VI HA Rep. 92 Nl. Gneisenau, Nr. 20b; Pertz and Delbrück, *Gneisenau*, II:579; Holleben and Caemmerer, *Frühjahrsfeldzuges 1813*, I:396–97, II:25.

44  Mikhailovsky-Danilevsky, *Denkwürdigkeiten*, 72; Holleben and Caemmerer, *Frühjahrsfeldzuges 1813*, II:26–28.

45  Auvray to Gneisenau, Delitzsch, 25 April 1813, GStA PK, VI HA Rep. 92 Nl. Gneisenau, Nr. 160; Wittgenstein to Blücher, Delitzsch, 26 April 1813, *ibid.*; Pertz and Delbrück, *Gneisenau*, II:582. On the 26th, Bülow's forward troops reached the lower Saale; his main body camped between Cöthen and Roßlau. At Zörbig, Yorck stood halfway between Dessau and Halle, with two strong posts at Wettin and Halle, the latter occupied by Kleist's division of twelve battalions, twelve squadrons, and four batteries. Eight miles south of Zörbig, Berg quartered at Landsberg. Cossacks maintained contact with the enemy along the Saale.

46  Castlereagh to Stewart, St. James's Square, 4 May 1813, *CVC*, IX:6.

47  Castlereagh to Cathcart, London, 22 January 1813, *CVC*, VIII:313; Stewart to Castlereagh, Wurschen, 20 May 1813, *ibid.*, IX:15; Castlereagh to Cathcart, London, 28 April 1813, *ibid.*, VIII:382–83; Webster, *The Foreign Policy of Castlereagh*, I:127; Sherwig, *Guineas and Gunpowder*, 282, 284; Stewart, *Narrative*, 13, 15–16.

48  Wilson, *Private Diary*, I:349. The "Kamenski stratagem" is a reference to Count Mikhail Fedotovich Kamensky, who received command of the Russian army facing Napoleon in December 1806 but resigned on the grounds of illness as soon as he saw the severe supply problems affecting the army.

49 Mikhailovsky-Danilevsky, *Denkwürdigkeiten*, 64–70; Bogdanovich, *Geschichte des Krieges*, I:173; Pertz and Delbrück, *Gneisenau*, II:581; Lieven, *Russia Against Napoleon*, 313. None of Blücher's biographers mentions his candidacy as Kutuzov's replacement nor do the historians of the German General Staff.

50 A copy of Volkonsky's letter to Wittgenstein can be found in Volkonsky to Blücher, 28 April 1813, GStA PK, VI HA Rep. 92 Nl. Gneisenau, Nr. 160; Holleben and Caemmerer, *Frühjahrsfeldzuges 1813*, II:24; Bogdanovich, *Geschichte des Krieges*, I:174–75.

51 This letter is reproduced in full in Mikhailovsky-Danilevsky, *Denkwürdigkeiten*, 70.

52 Blücher to Frederick William, Altenburg, 29 April 1813, GStA PK, VI HA Rep. 92 Nl. Gneisenau, Nr. 16; Mikhailovsky-Danilevsky, *Denkwürdigkeiten*, 70.

53 Holleben and Caemmerer, *Frühjahrsfeldzuges 1813*, II:25; Droysen, *Yorck*, II:56; Pertz and Delbrück, *Gneisenau*, II:583.

54 Bogdanovich, *Geschichte des Krieges*, I:175.

55 Kleist's Prussians included 2,200 infantry in 4.5 battalions; 440 cavalry in 4 squadrons; and 2,840 gunners servicing 16 small caliber pieces (one horse battery and a half-battery each of six-pound and three-pound guns). His Russian units amounted to 1,800 infantry in 8 battalions; 560 troopers in 6 squadrons; 800 Cossacks in 3 regiments; and 200 gunners serving 16 guns (1 heavy battery of 10 guns and one half-battery of horse artillery). Holleben and Caemmerer, *Frühjahrsfeldzuges 1813*, II:366–67.

56 In *Geschichte des Krieges*, I:176, Bogdanovich rejects Wurzen as the Allied point of concentration: "In reality, Wittgenstein's plan to concentrate our troops [at Wurzen] placed us in the danger of being driven from the upper Elbe and losing contact both with Silesia and the main line of our resources [through Poland to Russia] as well as with Austria."

57 Auvray to Blücher, Lindenau, 28 April 1813, GStA PK, VI HA Rep. 92 Nl. Gneisenau, Nr. 160. The individual orders are found in RGVIA, f. VUA, op. 16, d. 3922, ll. 40b–42b.

58 Reports from Majors Blücher and Hobe from 26 and 27 April are in GStA PK, VI HA Rep. 92 Nl. Gneisenau, Nr. 18, I, and IV HA Rep. 15 A Nr. 187; Scharnhorst to Boyen, Altenburg, 27 April 1813, in Boyen, *Erinnerungen*, ed. Nippold, III:299; Lehmann, *Scharnhorst*, II:611; Holleben and Caemmerer, *Frühjahrsfeldzuges 1813*, II:32.

59 Jomini, *Précis politique et militaire*, I:237–38.

60 *CN*, No. 19904, XXV:228; SHAT, C¹⁷ 177: Berthier to Marmont, 26 April 1813.

61 SHAT, C¹⁷ 177: Berthier to Ney, Bertrand, and Oudinot, 26 April 1813.

62 *CN*, Nos. 19906 and 19908, XXV:229–31.

63 *CN*, Nos. 19912, 19916, and 19917, XXV:233, 236–37.

64 Auvray to Gneisenau, Lindenau, 28 April 1813, GStA PK, VI HA Rep. 92 Nl. Gneisenau, Nr. 160; Holleben and Caemmerer, *Frühjahrsfeldzuges 1813*, II:27–29, 36.

65 Blücher to Boyen, April 1813, in Boyen, *Erinnerungen*, ed. Nippold, III:303; Blücher to a cavalry officer, Altenburg, 28 April 1813, *Blüchers Briefe*, ed. Unger, 163–64.

66 Toll to Auvray, Altenburg, 29 April 1813, in Bernhardi, *Toll*, I:436–38, emphasis added.

67 Auvray to Gneisenau, Gohlis, 29 and 30 April 1813, GStA PK, VI HA Rep. 92
   Nl. Gneisenau, Nr.160; Bernhardi, *Toll*, II:443–44.

68 Auvray's three letters to Gneisenau on the 29th and one from 30 April, all written
   at Gohlis, can be found in GStA PK, VI HA Rep. 92 Nl. Gneisenau, Nr. 160;
   Bogdanovich, *Geschichte des Krieges*, I:181.

69 Many wondered how the new Prussian army would perform; foreign observers
   and allies were quick to comment. In a report to London, Carthcart notes that
   the Prussians "behaved with great gallantry" at Halle and Merseburg. This was
   important news for the British government because of the huge investment
   being made to subsidize the Coalition. See Add MSS, 20111, 21: Cathcart to
   Castlereagh, Dresden, 6 May 1813.

70 Blücher to Amalie, Altenburg, 29 April 1813, *Blüchers Briefe*, ed. Unger, 164;
   According to Stewart, Napoleon "does not want for men, and he has got great
   supplies of horses for his cavalry. But the miserable deficiency he will experience
   is in the formed material; everything is new levy, conscript, and undisciplined.
   There is no doubt entertained here of a great (and if great it must be decisive)
   action in the course of a few days." Undoubtedly this feeling spread throughout
   the Allied armies. See Stewart to Cooke, Berlin, 22 April 1813, *CVC*, IX:3–4.

71 Wittgenstein to Alexander, 3 May 1813, RGVIA, f. VUA, op. 16, d. 3926, ll.
   77–79b; Jomini, *Précis politique et militaire*, I:241; Droysen, *Yorck*, II:55–56;
   Cathcart, *Commentaries*, 123–24; Bogdanovich, *Geschichte des Krieges*,
   I:180–81; Atteridge, *Ney*, 245–46.

72 By that evening, Eugene's army reached the following positions: the viceroy at
   Ötsch, just north of Lützen; XI Corps north of Markranstädt and Quesitz;
   I Cavalry Corps south of Schladebach; and V Corps between Schladebach and
   Merseburg. The emperor's Army of the Main settled into camps that reflected the
   advance from Weißenfels through Lützen: Ney established III Corps's headquarters at Kaja, with his 8th Division camping in the quadrilateral formed by the
   villages of Kleingörschen, Großgörschen, Rahna, and Kaja. West of 8th Division,
   10th Division passed the night at Starsiedel; 11th, 9th, and 39th Divisions between
   Starsiedel and Lützen. Less than four miles west of Starsiedel, 21st Division
   of Marmont's VI Corps as well as the marshal's headquarters halted at Rippach,
   with 20th Division slightly to the west, and 22nd Division still several miles
   further west at Naumburg. Five miles west of Rippach, two divisions of Guard
   Infantry reached Weißenfels. Some seven miles south of the Guard, the headquarters of Bertrand's IV Corps reached Stößen, with its van – 12th Division – two
   miles further southeast at Pretzsch.

73 *CN*, Nos. 19942, 19944, and 19951, XXV:253–55, 258–62; SHAT, C[17] 177:
   Berthier to Marmont, 1 May 1813; Berthier to Eugene and Ney, 2 May 1813;
   Jomini, *Précis politique et militaire*, I:241; Odeleben, *A Circumstantial Narrative*,
   I:42–43; Petre, *Napoleon's Last Campaign*, 62–63, 71–72.

74 *CN*, Nos. 19446 and 19947, XXV:255–57; SHAT, C[17] 177: Berthier to Bertrand
   and Marmont, 2 May 1813.

75 Jomini simply states that Napoleon "s'attendait si peu à être assailli de ce côté
   [believed an attack from that side to be so unlikely]": Jomini, *Précis politique et
   militaire*, I:243.

76 Mikhailovsky-Danilevsky, *Denkwürdigkeiten*, 73–74; Wittgenstein to Alexander, 3 May 1813, RGVIA, f. VUA, op. 16, d. 3926, ll. 77–79b; Add MSS, 20111, 21–22: Cathcart to Castlereagh, Dresden, 6 May 1813.

77 Volkonsky to Miloradovich, 1 May 1813, RGVIA, f. VUA, op. 16, d. 3921, l. 189b; Holleben and Caemmerer, *Frühjahrsfeldzuges 1813*, II:38–39, 51.

78 Add MSS, 20111, 21: Cathcart to Castlereagh, Dresden, 6 May 1813; Jomini, *Vie politique et militaire de Napoléon*, IV:283.

79 Holleben and Caemmerer, *Frühjahrsfeldzuges 1813*, II:43–44, 48. In *Napoleon's Last Campaign*, 68, Petre repeats Wittgenstein's mistake, referring to the rivulet that flows from Großgrimma to Dehlitz as the Rippach instead of the Grünabach.

80 Holleben and Caemmerer, *Frühjahrsfeldzuges 1813*, II:49; Pertz and Delbrück, *Gneisenau*, II:583.

81 Clausewitz, *Hinterlassene Werke*, VII:272; Holleben and Caemmerer, *Frühjahrsfeldzuges 1813*, II:50–51.

82 "Disposition," Zwenkau, 1 May 1813, RGVIA, f. VUA, op. 16, d. 3909, ll. 324–325b. A beautiful hand-written copy in French can be found in Lowe's papers: Add MSS, 20112, 114–16.

83 Holleben and Caemmerer, *Frühjahrsfeldzuges 1813*, II:47; Lanrezac, *Lützen*, 157; Bogdanovich, *Geschichte des Krieges im Jahre 1813*, I:185.

84 Pertz and Delbrück, *Gneisenau*, II:583; Holleben and Caemmerer, *Frühjahrsfeldzuges 1813*, II:49. Clausewitz claims that "defensive positions were even established on the road coming from Leipzig, in order to drive him, if he were defeated, from Weißenfels and Naumburg completely and against the swampy arms of the united Pleiße and Elster rivers." See Clausewitz, *Hinterlassene Werke*, VII:271.

85 Holleben and Caemmerer, *Frühjahrsfeldzuges 1813*, II:39, Pertz and Delbrück, *Gneisenau*, II:584, and Mikhailovsky-Danilevsky, *Denkwürdigkeiten*, 75, generally agree that the Allied army consisted of 56,240 infantry in 132.5 battalions, 19,340 cavalry in 139 squadrons, 5,000 Cossacks in 18 regiments, 552 guns in 53.5 batteries supported by 7,660 gunners and engineers. The figures provided by Bogdanovich in *Geschichte des Krieges*, I:185, are smaller: 50,000 infantry, 17,000 line and irregular cavalry, and 6,000 gunners servicing 400 pieces. His national breakdown states 40,000 Russians and 33,000 Prussians.

86 "He had an immense quantity of ordnance, of twelve pounders and larger natures, distributed throughout his line and in the villages": Add MSS, 20111, 22: Cathcart to Castlereagh, Dresden, 6 May 1813.

87 Clausewitz, *Hinterlassene Werke*, VII:270–71; Pertz and Delbrück, *Gneisenau*, II:582.

88 Quotes from Blücher, Clausewitz, and Boyen are in Unger, *Blücher*, II:20–21; Campbell to Bunbury, Dresden, 7 May 1813, in Bunbury, *Memoir*, 323. Blücher's proclamation was issued from Altenburg on 24 April 1813 and is in Gneisenau, *Blücher*, 76–77.

# 5

# Großgörschen

In the dark night of 1/2 May, Blücher's corps became strung out on the ten-mile march from Rötha to Pegau. As a result, the head of his column rather than the whole corps reached Audigast late, around 5:00 A.M. With the disposition awaiting him two miles further west at Pegau, Blücher did not know that Yorck's corps would be moving southwest from Zwenkau to strike the Rötha–Pegau road in accordance with Wittgenstein's instructions to be "immediately behind Blücher's columns around 5:00 A.M." Although some discrepancy exists among the sources, it appears that Blücher directed his foremost brigades – Zieten's 2nd and Klüx's 1st – to Storkwitz as the right wing. While marching to Storkwitz, Zieten's brigade collided with the lead unit of Yorck's corps at Audigast (see Map 3). The resulting entanglement and confusion cost the Prussians four precious hours. It did little good that Wittgenstein, who rode up and met with Yorck's staff for a short while, explained how the Corsican, with his back to Berlin, would be forced to accept battle on terms that favored the Allies. The bungled march particularly aggravated General Friedrich Heinrich von Hünerbein, commander of Yorck's 8th Brigade, who sarcastically shouted to Chaplain Schultze that Wittgenstein seemed all too willing to give a consolation sermon. After clearing his troops from the road, Yorck waited for Blücher's brigades to march past. As soon as Dolffs's Reserve Cavalry struck the road to Pegau, Yorck followed. This meant that Blücher's left wing column, Röder's Reserve Brigade, which remained far behind due to the slow march from Rötha, first needed to wait for Yorck and then Berg to pass.

From the position of the Allied army on 1 May, Wittgenstein could have simplified the crossing of the Elster to prevent the collision of Blücher and Yorck, despite the slow march of the former to Pegau. To evenly distribute the various corps to the available crossings, Yorck and Berg should have advanced in a straight line due west from Zwenkau toward Hohenlohe, while Blücher's entire corps marched through Storkwitz, and Tormasov utilized the crossing at Pegau. Because Blücher's corps formed the longest column, Wittgenstein could have directed Dolffs's Reserve Cavalry to the Carsdorf–Pegau crossing. According to a comment in Yorck's journal, the Allies dropped the idea of crossing the Elster at Zwenkau after Wintzingerode's corps withdrew on the evening of 1 May to a position between the Schkorlopp villages and Zwenkau very close to the bridge. Although the advance of Yorck and Berg would have provided immediate support, Wittgenstein apparently wanted to keep open Wintzingerode's line of retreat. Regardless of the reason why Wittgenstein did not want Yorck and Berg to cross the Elster at Zwenkau, he should have sent them both to Storkwitz. Yet because he ordered Yorck to Pegau and instructed Blücher to send one column to Storkwitz, a collision occurred, almost as if planned. This could have been avoided only if Blücher's right column had crossed the Storkwitz passage on the Zwenkau–Pegau road at the same time as Yorck's corps departed Zwenkau. Instead, he received these instructions on reaching Pegau. Theoretically, the fault for these inadequate marching orders can be found in Russian adherence to linear tactics. Although closer to the Elster, the battle orders placed Yorck's corps in the second wave and behind Blücher. If Yorck had advanced through Storkwitz, he would have converged on the battlefield right next to Blücher. Rather than a delay, the Allies would have used speed to achieve mass at the point of attack. Although Wittgenstein's emphasis on deep columns is commendable, speed and mass are much more valuable as force multipliers in an encounter battle.[1]

Wintzingerode led his troops from Großschkorlopp and Kleinschkorlopp to Werben, where the corps arrived at 6:00 A.M. Four hours earlier, at 2:00 A.M., Frederick William and Alexander had departed their quarters at Borna and ridden thirteen miles west, reaching a point between Groitzsch and Pegau at 4:30. There, in the open field not far from Pegau, they planned to observe the troops as they marched to the Elster. Wittgenstein and his entourage rode from Zwickau toward Pegau; the monarchs greeted him with gracious and flattering expressions. Not having seen the general since 1812, the tsar ran to embrace him. That same day, Alexander received news of Kutuzov's death and formally appointed Wittgenstein his successor as Allied commander in chief with authority over the Russian main army as well. Wittgenstein then went to Pegau to observe the passage of the Prussians. Colonel Campbell reported: "On the morning of 2 May, Count Wittgenstein passed along the front of the Prussian troops between Zwenkau and Pegau. They appeared to be fine young men, in high spirits, and well equipped. Recognizing him as the general by whom they were to be led to the expected combat, they cheered him with the most animated huzzas, and in every way testified the greatest ardor."[2]

Enjoying snacks brought to them by the inhabitants of Pegau, the monarchs finally received the salutes of Blücher's Reserve Cavalry, which passed their position around 7:00 A.M, at which time Tormasov's lead units reached Groitzsch. Yorck's I Corps followed Blücher's cavalry, filing by the monarchs from 8:00 to 9:30 A.M. Röder's brigade, which included the Prussian Guard, brought up the rear of the column; its parade lasted until 10:30, at which time the sovereigns departed. The actual march through Pegau and across the bridge (almost two miles west of Pegau) to Carsdorf commenced around 9:00. Tormasov's army, which marched in one column from Löbstedt to cover the nine miles to Groitzsch by 7:00 A.M., debouched from there in three columns. The Russian march through Pegau continued uninterrupted until 2:30 P.M.[3]

Fortunately for the Allies, the crossing of the Elster at Storkwitz by Blücher's two brigades and Berg's corps progressed smoothly. Berg led his corps south from Zwenkau, turning west at Löbschütz and halting at Döhlen until Blücher's right wing column crossed the Elster and reached Storkwitz on the western bank. The Russians then followed Klüx's brigade across the river so that altogether some 20,000 men completed the crossing in three hours and then proceded west to move across the Floßgraben at Werben.[4] This provided quite a contrast to the seven hours it took Blücher's left wing and Yorck's corps to march through Pegau and offers further proof of the inadequacies of Wittgenstein's battle orders.

North of the Allied army, Kleist prepared to execute Wittgenstein's orders, which required him not only to defend Leipzig, but also to take the offensive with his 5,000 men as soon as he heard the thunder of artillery to the southwest. Leading 36,000 imperial troops toward Leipzig, Lauriston's V Corps commenced its march from the region of Günthersdorf, halfway between Merseburg and Leipzig, around 8:00 A.M. Two hours later, the French approached Kleist's weak position just east of the Lindenau causeway that led to Leipzig. Having only 100 troopers, Lauriston unlimbered his artillery to drive off Kleist's 1,800 sabers. At the same time, he directed the left wing of his foremost division – General Nicholas-Joseph Maison's 16th – north through Leutzsch to envelop the enemy's right. Recognizing Lauriston's superior numbers, Kleist ordered a retreat. One Prussian and two Russian battalions supported by a half-battery held Lindenau as the rearguard. This tactic forced the French to deploy and demonstrate while awaiting the enveloping attack. In the meantime, Kleist's main body crossed the Elster and fell back on Leipzig. His rearguard then withdrew from Lindenau and prepared to make a stand at the bridge. By fording the Elster, the French cut short the struggle around the bridge that Kleist had neglected to mine. Maison's troops raced across as the Prussians retreated into the interior of Leipzig after some light combat that cost the Allies twenty casualties. Kleist took a new position at Paunsdorf, some four miles east of Leipzig. Inexplicably, he withdrew thirteen miles further east to Wurzen that evening. Just as Maison's division started to emerge on the eastern side of Leipzig to pursue the Allies, Lauriston received Eugene's order to halt and keep V Corps in readiness west of Leipzig because battle had commenced south of Lützen.

After crossing the Elster, Blücher's Reserve Cavalry – commanded on this day by the king's brother, Prince William – moved northwest of Pegau and then west to Werben and across the Floßgraben; the troopers led their horses along the side of the road so the hungry beasts could feed. Large dust clouds on the Weißenfels–Lützen–Leipzig highway marked the French march, convincing Wittgenstein that an advance through Starsiedel would allow him to launch a surprise flank attack and possibly turn the rear of the French army as it moved east to Leipzig. To reconnoiter, Major Grolman of Blücher's staff led one squadron of Guard cavalry toward the northern spur of a broad hill one and one-quarter miles south of Großgörschen around 9:00. After reaching this hill, later named the Monarchenhügel (Monarchs' Hill) because the tsar and king established their command post on it, Grolman observed the terrain to the north between the Elster and the Saale. He noted that west of the hill the ground descended to marshy lowlands bordered on the left by the Grünabach and a series of villages; thick woods on the Floßgraben limited the view to the right (east and northeast) of the Monarchenhügel. To the south extended a plateau; its northern rim formed by the Monarchenhügel. Immediately north of the hill stood four villages that did not appear on the map, yet the first great battle of 1813 would take place in and around them: Großgörschen, Kleingörschen, Rahna, and Kaja (see Map 4).[5]

Grolman noted that the terrain steadily but gently descended from the Monarchenhügel through Großgörschen to Lützen. According to Cathcart: "This part of the country is unenclosed but arable and under cultivation; its military features are tame but there is a considerable undulation of the surface which rises to a commanding elevation [the Monarchenhügel] toward the center of the Allied position, and there is a corresponding elevation opposite, sufficient to conceal the preparatory movements of both sides." In addition: "The country is uncovered and open, the soil dry and light but with a very considerable variety of hill and valley, and much intersected by hollow ways and mill streams, the former not discernible until closely approached." Thus, the trees, bushes, hedges, and trenches – not to mention Souham's 8th Division – that filled the two and one-half square miles of terrain that formed the interior of the quadrilateral between these four villages could not be observed from the Monarchenhügel. Conversely, from Großgörschen, the French could not view the Allied forces merely 100 yards beyond the edge of the plateau that began at the Monarchenhügel.[6]

Further afield, Grolman discerned heavy dust clouds in the distance rising from the Weißenfels–Lützen–Leipzig highway a little more than six miles distant. Smoke from artillery fire could be seen around Markranstädt, about halfway between Lützen and Leipzig, but the thunder of the guns could not be heard. Closer at hand, he could see what appeared to be a rearguard of the imperial army camped between the villages of Großgörschen, Kleingörschen, and Rahna. Müffling led a patrol close to the villages and found a bivouac for apparently 2,000 men but the troops had yet to stir, security measures were lax, and the closest village – Großgörschen – was not occupied. According to the statement of a prisoner brought in by the Cossacks these troops belonged to Souham's 8th Division. After receiving this news, Wittgenstein proceeded from Pegau to the Monarchenhügel around 11:00 to obtain an overview of the situation; Alexander and Frederick William joined him. From there they could see "the bivouac in question," reported Cathcart, "about a mile below them, still occupied and the fires still smoking but without any advanced posts. This did not appear to be any experienced or formidable body, and Wittgenstein evidently thought so, for the author heard him promise that he would put His Imperial Majesty in possession of the enemy's corps which he saw before him within an hour's time."[7]

In the meantime, the Allied army continued to make its general movement west through Werben to face Starsiedel (northwest) along the shallow ridge south of the Monarchenhügel that extended slightly northeast to southwest from Werben to Domsen. Wittgenstein's army moved into a position parallel to the Weißenfels–Lützen–Leipzig highway. Finding imperial forces in the villages on the Floßgraben so close to his position surprised Wittgenstein and disrupted his plans to march northwest. With the troops of Blücher, Yorck, Berg, and Wintzingerode on line and ready for battle, he faced his first decision: should he start the battle or wait for Tormasov to reach the field? The best estimate placed Tormasov's arrival at 3:00 P.M. Wittgenstein hoped to engage at least one of Napoleon's columns by sweeping west to gain the Weißenfels–Lützen–Leipzig road and possibly get his left behind the French army. The great cloud of dust rising in the vicinity of this road convinced him that an Allied advance through Starsiedel would enable him to launch a surprise flank attack and possibly turn Napoleon's rear as the French army marched east to Leipzig. Thus, he wanted to await Tormasov's arrival before commencing the movement that would lead to the main action. For the moment, the Allied commander in chief decided to attack the supposed rearguard found in the villages immediately in front of his army: Großgörschen, Kleingörschen, Rahna, and Kaja. According to Clausewitz: "The plan of attack consisted of taking and occupying these villages with an advance guard, then, with the front facing the enemy, whose position was observed in the area of Lützen, approximately parallel with the road to Weißenfels, advance so that the main forces were directed against his right wing but taking no further action against his left. The forces thus concentrated, the desire was, where possible, to force the right wing to retreat, thereby pushing the enemy army away from the road to the Saale and with the mass of the numerous cavalry to completely go around the right wing in order, where possible, to deliver the decisive attack against the enemy rear."[8]

To adjust, Wittgenstein issued a new disposition that included orders for the army to execute a difficult and time-consuming pivot or right wheel to the north so its front would be directly oriented on Großgörschen. "For almost one full hour, the troops moved forward and backward," complains Müffling, "and were exhausted needlessly."[9] Shortly after 11:00 A.M., the Allied soldiers received a much-needed rest of thirty minutes. Concealed behind the shallow ridge south of the Monarchenhügel, the army formed in the following order: between the hill and Werben stood Blücher's corps as the first echelon with Zieten on the left and Klüx on the right; Röder's brigade was left of center in the second wave. Prince William's cavalry, supported by Wintzingerode's sabers, advanced about one mile west of the Monarchenhügel, taking a position between it and Domsen. Behind Blücher in the second echelon stood Yorck's corps on the left and Berg's to the right. Wintzingerode's foot, the II Infantry Corps commanded by Duke Eugen of Württemberg, formed the third echelon. "Blücher was now at the head of his corps and already on the ground," noted Cathcart, "his troops were assembled *en masse*, and in high spirits."

According to the new disposition: "The villages of Kleingörschen and Großgörschen, Rahna, and Kaja should be attacked by Klüx's brigade, the enemy rearguard driven out, and the villages occupied; after this, the army will advance in battle order toward the enemy, who is believed to be posted in the region of Lützen, and in such a manner that the main force is especially directed against his right wing to prevent the enemy from regaining the road to Weißenfels. In particular, General Wintzingerode will seek to envelop the enemy's right wing with the Reserve Cavalry and endeavor to make a decisive attack on the rear of the enemy army." Bogdanovich harshly judges Wittgenstein's plan: "The Allies did not use the advantage of their position. The French corps of Marmont (VI), Bertrand (IV), and Jacques-Étienne Macdonald (XI) could not reach the battlefield for two or three hours. In the meantime, Napoleon had no more than 50,000 men (Ney's 35,000 and 15,000 Guard). Instead of overwhelming the enemy with superior forces, Wittgenstein ordered Klüx's Lower Silesian Brigade to take the village of Großgörschen and Dolffs's Reserve Cavalry to turn left upon Kaja to disorder the enemy through horse artillery and complete his defeat through cavalry attacks."

Blücher received orders to take the villages with Klüx's brigade: the salty Prussian replied that he would command the first wave himself. At 11:45, the old hussar "with hoary locks, but vigorous and fiery as a youth," galloped up to Wittgenstein, saluted, and with his sword drawn requested permission to open the struggle. "With God's help," responded Wittgenstein in German. Shortly before noon, Blücher led Klüx's 1st Brigade over the shallow ridge that concealed them and down the slope that led to Großgörschen. According to Wittgenstein's verbal instructions, as soon as Blücher's infantry engaged the front of the French position, the cavalry and light artillery would, according to Cathcart, "take ground to their left [west] and, supported by other columns of infantry, ascend the opposite rising ground and turn the villages: it was expected that the enemy, being engaged and entangled in them, would be easily cut off from their main columns, which were not supposed to be so near at hand as they proved to be."[10]

While Blücher advanced, Prince William led twenty-three squadrons and three horse batteries toward Starsiedel. Wintzingerode deployed his cavalry behind the Prussian troopers, somewhat echeloned to the southwest so that his left wing came close to the villages of Söhesten and Tornau. At this early stage of the battle and knowing that Tormasov remained two or even three hours away, Wittgenstein ordered his only reserve – Wintzingerode's infantry – to follow the Russian cavalry and likewise move up to the left wing. Eugen of Württemberg complied, swinging his II Infantry Corps northwest and into a position between Yorck's corps and the village of Domsen. Five Cossack regiments continued westward.

As the Prussians emerged on the horizon, Souham scrambled to occupy Großgörschen and push troops to the outskirts of the village. General Jean Chemineau's 1st Brigade moved into the village while the rest of 8th Division formed in the fields of the quadrilateral. At some 1,300 yards south of Großgörschen, Klüx's infantry halted while the artillery escorted by light cavalry moved closer to the village. One Russian twelve-pound battery as well as the batteries (six-pound foot) from both Klüx's and Zieten's brigades – altogether thirty-six guns – unlimbered 800 yards from the village and opened fire. Directed at the French infantry south of Großgörschen and between the four villages, the bombardment lasted some forty-five minutes. The Prussian attack took Souham completely by surprise in part because the French had neglected to establish a single forward post. The fact that Ney had failed to patrol toward Zwenkau and Pegau per the emperor's orders also contributed to the success of the Allied surprise. Equally important, the marshal had not complied with Napoleon's orders to assemble all five of his divisions at Kaja: only Souham's held the quadrilateral; General Jean-Baptiste Girard's 10th Division stood at Starsiedel and the remaining three near Lützen. Conversely, finding an entire division of 12,000 men camped on the quadrilateral surprised Blücher, who expected to face only 2,000 men per Müffling's report.

Although intense, the Prussian bombardment did more to raise the alarm in the French camp than to disable command and control. In fact, security measures around the French perimeter were so completely lacking that the Prussians might have been better served by simply charging with the infantry instead of waiting for the artillery. Souham quickly rallied his troops, who Jomini claims were all eighteen-year-old French conscripts, and placed them under arms while two batteries of light artillery responded from the southeast side of Großgörschen. He immediately sent forward light troops that took advantage of the sunken road that ran across the length of the village. Soon, the heads of six or seven battalions moved out from his position. This did little to slow the pace of the Prussian shelling. Very soon the French light foot fell back and the columns halted; Souham pulled them out of sight. After inflicting considerable casualties on the French infantry south of the village, the Allied gunners turned their attention to counter-battery fire. Russo-Prussian shells claimed three French guns. After a Prussian horse battery unlimbered to provide flanking fire from the west, the French guns went silent and fell back. As it became clear that the French would not advance in the open terrain, Blücher gave the order for Klüx's brigade to storm Großgörschen.[11]

Klüx's troops assaulted the village in three waves. All accounts indicate that both officers and soldiers attacked with determination, but the Prussians met strong resistance. Elements of Chemineau's brigade held the defile south of Großgörschen as a forward defensive position. Skirmishers and Jäger detachments from the two battalions of Klüx's first wave ousted the French, forcing the rest of the defenders to withdraw to the edge of the village. French resolve likewise crumbled there as the Prussians took some hundred prisoners and captured two damaged guns. Klüx's foremost battalions entered Großgörschen, but order quickly dissolved as a result of street fighting and the struggle to take each house. Per Wittgenstein's instructions, the light cavalry and light artillery posted on the right wing of Dolffs's Reserve Cavalry attempted to turn Souham's right but received withering grapeshot from the closest village to the west, Starsiedel. Commenting on the French grape, Professor Steffens, who served on Blücher's staff as a propaganda specialist, wrote: "it seemed to me as if the balls came in thick masses on every side – as if I was in a heavy shower of rain without getting wet. Gneisenau seemed quite joyful in his element."[12]

Klüx committed the battalions of his second wave. After sending in their skirmishers, the battalions closed ranks, formed tight columns, and drove from one end of Großgörschen to the other. Emerging on the opposite side, the Prussians observed strong French forces in the middle of the quadrilateral waiting to engage. Unlike the carefully manicured fields of today, in 1813 trees and marshy lowland covered both sides of the Floßgraben, similar to the natural arms of the Elster. The terrain and geographic features of the quadrilateral – millponds, willow-bordered streams, swamps, houses, gardens, hedges, intervening enclosures, tree-lines, foot

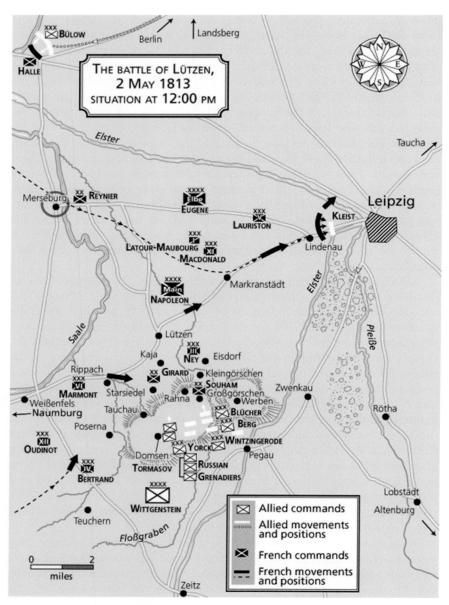

**15.** Battle of Lützen, 2 May 1813, situation at 12:00 P.M.

bridges, sunken paths, and villages close together – granted a defender the great advantage of being able to contest every step of an advancing foe. Throughout the day, French officers and noncommissioned officers made the most of these advantages. Their men, although mostly young conscripts trained on the march, quickly learned to seek and use cover, to fire from the houses and gardens, from behind trees and fences, and to conceal themselves in the undergrowth. "For the first time the Allied [Russian] troops encountered a fundamental difference between Saxon and Russian battlefields," explains Dominic Lieven. "On the latter, wooden villages offered no help to defenders. Solid Saxon stone walls and buildings were a very different matter and could sometimes be turned into small fortresses. Ney's troops were inexperienced but they were courageous and, in the nature of such soldiers, they drew strength from being able in part to fight behind fixed, stone defenses." Klüx's advance faltered and the French quickly turned the tables on him, driving his men back into the village, which the Prussians held with difficulty. Blücher possessed Großgörschen but the battle had just begun.[13]

Meanwhile, Prince William and the majority of the 3,000 troopers from Dolffs's Reserve Cavalry reached the vicinity of Starsiedel to find the troops of Girard's 10th Division likewise still in their bivouacs. In fact, the French had sent their artillery horses to water. Artillery support could be provided only by Étienne-Pierre Ricard's 11th or Antoine-François Brenier's 9th Division, both of which passed the night on the western bank of the Floßgraben between Starsiedel and Lützen. Instead of immediately attacking and overwhelming his surprised adversary, the Prussian prince first ordered his artillery to begin an intense bombardment and then issued reports to both Wittgenstein and Wintzingerode suggesting that the latter's infantry should advance and occupy the village. Wintzingerode considered having Eugen of Württemberg attack Starsiedel but could not make this decision on his own and accepted Wittgenstein's refusal. Until the Russian main army arrived, Wittgenstein wanted to commit the least amount of force possible to his left wing. He did not understand that an advance there would have facilitated the operations of his other wing. At the least, Wintzingerode corresponded to William's request by moving General Semyon Panchulidzev's cavalry brigade and one horse battery closer to Starsiedel. This did little good, for time quickly ran out for the Hohenzollern prince. His decision to bombard Starsiedel allowed Girard to shelter his men inside the village and prepare a stubborn defense until relieved by Marmont's corps moving east from Rippach. Girard's artillery gradually came on line so that an intense artillery duel ensued; William's horse was shot dead under him. A staff officer soon informed him of the approach of enemy troops in combat formation from the direction of Poserna: Marmont's VI Corps would soon arrive. Although a few squadrons from the prince's right wing supported Klüx's struggle at Großgörschen, the majority of the Prussian troopers simply sat waiting for orders from the grandnephew of Frederick the Great.

If Wittgenstein had ordered the rest of Blücher's corps to simultaneously advance on both sides of Klüx's 1st Brigade so that Kleingörschen and Rahna fell into Prussian hands immediately after Großgörschen, the French would have been hard pressed. In this case, the majority of Souham's division that waited in the quadrilateral would have been attacked on three sides. Doubtless the French would have been forced to retreat to the plain of Lützen, where the superior Allied cavalry would have decimated Napoleon's young troops despite their bravery. But at this early stage of the battle, Allied High Command concluded that Wittgenstein had not caught Napoleon's columns strung out on the march. This realization forced Wittgenstein to make another fundamental change to his battle plan. According to the statements of prisoners, the Allies stumbled into the 45,000 men of Ney's III Corps; Napoleon and the Guard passed the night at Lützen, only four miles north of Großgörschen. "This force together could not amount to less than 60,000 men," explains Cathcart, an eyewitness to these quick deliberations, "who had passed the night within a few miles of the ground, and were consequently fresh and ready for action. The three corps constituting the Allied force already in the field, might perhaps amount to 60,000 men, but certainly not more; and the corps under Miloradovich, whose infantry could not arrive until evening, would complete their strength to about 80,000, but their whole army, with the exception of Wintzingerode's corps ... had been marching all the previous night, and were much exhausted. A new disposition became necessary."[14]

Barely into the battle, Wittgenstein faced an almost insurmountable task. Retreat was out of the question for a variety of reasons, including the negative impact it would have on the troops, not to mention potential allies such as Austria. Closer at hand, the Allies feared having the army crushed at the Elster just as Napoleon had driven the Russians into the Alle River during the battle of Friedland in 1807. Committing all of Blücher's corps supported by Berg and Yorck at this moment likewise did not appear prudent, particularly because the Allies did not know the size of the enemy force beyond the quadrilateral. Consequently, with a tired army, Wittgenstein resolved to hold an enemy force equal in number to his own but commanded by the emperor himself until the Russian Guard and Reserve could reach the field. Also, the fact that additional French columns would probably arrive during the course of the battle could not be ignored. All of this ended any thoughts of continuing the army's westward movement to seek the right flank and rear of the imperial army as it marched east from Weißenfels to Leipzig. Hopes of seeing the Allied cavalry utilize the great plain of Lützen – just a few miles north of the Allied position – to rout

Napoleon's army faded. Until more troops arrived, Wittgenstein felt he could do little more than watch Blücher continue the struggle for the four villages.

Fortunately for Souham, this meant that his division faced only Klüx's brigade. The French general quickly counterattacked with superior numbers. Klüx's men held the village but the attack provided Souham with time to reorder the battalions shaken by the initial assault. Not only did Souham's counterattack gain time, but it sapped the strength of the Prussians. To support Klüx, Blücher directed Zieten's 2nd Brigade to Kleingörschen – one mile northeast of Großgörschen – around 1:00. Preceded by an artillery barrage, Zieten's battalions formed three waves and attacked. Unfortunately for the Prussians, they did not catch the French by surprise. Having had time to prepare their defense, Souham's troops obstinately resisted. Zieten countered with finesse, sending a single battalion around the east side of the village. With the Prussians behind them, the French broke: some fled but many fell into the hands of the Neumark Dragoons. After the Prussians gained Kleingörschen and thus started working toward Souham's rear by pursuing his battalions toward Kaja, the French general could no longer continue the struggle at Großgörschen with Klüx's 1st Brigade which held, despite being hard pressed and low on ammunition. Souham disengaged his battalions from the village, withdrawing the majority of the division to Rahna. Reinvigorated, Klüx's men pursued the French to Rahna, which fell to the Prussians after fierce street fighting. Souham then withdrew toward Starsiedel. According to Charles Lanrezac, a distinguished staff college lecturer and French general during the First World War, the fighting around Rahna and Kleingörschen erupted into "the fiercest battle; everywhere both sides fired at close range, attacked with the bayonet, and displayed the most brilliant bravery." Gneisenau adds: "The discharges of musketry raged with such indescribable destruction and the troops on both sides were so close to each other that the number of killed and wounded was incredible." Blücher controlled Rahna, Großgörschen, and Kleingörschen but inexplicably neither he nor his staff moved up sufficient artillery to secure the infantry's gains.[15]

As for Napoleon, accompanied by Ney and a detachment of Guard Cavalry, he left Lützen around 10:00 A.M. and rode five miles northeast to Markranstädt.[16] "On the morning of 2 May," explains Jomini, "the viceroy continued his movement on Leipzig. Napoleon wanted to join it by linking with the viceroy's right at Markranstädt. Eager to learn if the enemy would oppose him or would abandon without a fight the important strategic point of Leipzig, the center of all major communications of northern Germany, the emperor went there with the Guard." At Markranstädt, Napoleon reviewed XI Corps and observed Lauriston's progress with his glass. He reached Lindenau shortly after 11:30 just as Maison's division secured the town. Assuming that the road to Leipzig would be open, he prepared to issue orders for the army to march there. At this moment, news arrived that the Allied army had crossed the Elster at Pegau and attacked Souham's division. He initially did not believe it, especially because Ney vouched for the security of his sector, although he had not dispatched patrols to Pegau and Zwenkau. The emperor's doubts quickly faded after hearing a heavy cannonade to the southwest shortly after the noon hour. Napoleon immediately grasped the situation. He purportedly turned to Ney and said: "It looks as if while we have attacked their flank here, they have been turning us. But there is no harm done. They will find us everywhere prepared to meet them." He issued orders for Ney to return to III Corps – which he believed to be assembled at Kaja – and maintain his position at any cost. Marmont's VI Corps would link with Ney's right by reaching Starsiedel while Bertrand's IV Corps operated against the enemy's left flank by advancing on Söhesten; the Guard would march to the sound of the guns. As for Eugene's Army of the Elbe, Lauriston's V Corps would hold Leipzig with one division while the two others took a position echeloned south toward Zwenkau, ready to march either there or southwest to Kaja. Although some question exists as to when the emperor ordered the rest of Eugene's army – XI Corps and I Cavalry Corps – to advance against the enemy's right flank, the time of their arrival at Eisdorf (between 6:00 and 7:00 P.M.) clearly suggests that Napoleon had issued these orders at least two hours later, as Macdonald himself confirmed.[17]

Ney reached Kaja around 1:00 as columns of Prussian infantry approached shouting "*Vaterland! Vaterland!*"[18] His situation would not have been so bad had he complied with Napoleon's orders and assembled all five of his divisions at Kaja the night before. Instead, only two were present and he scrambled to move up the others. En route to Kaja, he had directed Marchand's 39th Division to Eisdorf, less than one mile east of Kleingörschen, and from there it was to march to the sound of the guns. Next, he ordered Brenier and Ricard to lead their divisions south to Kaja. As Ney approached the battlefield, he observed Zieten envelop Souham's left wing but counted on Marchand's approach to provide relief. At Kaja, Ney took charge of Girard's division and Souham's battalions from Kleingörschen. Increasing numbers of French artillery gradually came on line along a shallow rise southwest of Kaja that mastered the quadrilateral. Due to the failure of Blücher and his staff to move artillery into this square, the French shelled the Prussians without fear of receiving counterbattery fire. With artillery blazing, Ney ordered his thick attack columns to advance. After forming his 10th Division on the right wing to move against Rahna, Girard shouted to his men: "Soldiers, this is the day of France; we must avenge the insult of Moscow or die."[19] Souham's 8th advanced on the left to storm Kleingörschen while Brenier's 9th followed in reserve. Despite repeated flank attacks by the Prussian brigade cavalry, the French infantry remained steady. Three French divisions slammed into the two Prussian brigades with a manpower advantage of more than double. Blücher's soldiers fought bravely but the imperials took Rahna and Kleingörschen. From its position east and west of Großgörschen, the Allied artillery managed to prevent the French from reaching that village.

Blücher now summoned all of his artillery – 104 guns – as well as Röder's brigade to support Klüx and Zieten. Because Blücher needed support on all points, Röder did not launch a uniform assault in three waves like the previous Prussian attacks. The majority of his battalions moved on Rahna, which the Prussians recaptured after a simultaneous assault from several directions. Zieten's brigade regrouped and drove Souham's men from Kleingörschen before Röder's support arrived. Blücher sent two battalions to Eisdorf to contain Marchand's division, the head of which could be seen moving in that direction. A verbal order from Blücher sent two columns toward Kaja. The first, consisting of Major Karl Heinrich von Block's Guard Fusilier Battalion supported by the Leib Grenadier Battalion, advanced east of Kleingörschen before turning northwest. Major Ludolph August von Alvensleben led the second column – four battalions including two Guard and two Guard Jäger companies – straight through Kleingörschen toward Kaja. With the crown prince of Prussia, referred to as Fritz at this time, and his cousin, Prince Frederick, in their ranks, the Prussian Guard enveloped the right flank of the French forces in the interior of the four villages, repulsed a French battalion near the southern exit of Kaja, and occupied the key village shortly after 2:00. In the midst of this action, Frederick William, with his aide-de-camp, Henckel von Donnersmarck, in tow, left the Monarchenhügel and rode up on his white Arabian to join his men in the struggle: such was the monarch's desire to erase the memory of 1806 that the heat of battle mastered his reserved nature. Block informed the king that the entire battalion had dispersed in the village as skirmishers and that for the moment he had no reserve. Undaunted, Frederick William continued to the northern exit of Kaja to find his son. He arrived just as the Royal Guard drove the last French troops from the burning village. "As the sacred Guard was in full death throes with the French Guard," wrote the future Frederick William IV a few days later to his sister, "Papa emerged from the flames that were rising up on all sides of the village to join us just as we expelled the French for the fifth time. What a sight!!! The whole village, all the trenches, all the hedges, everything was full of the dead and dying." To retake Kaja, Ney committed some battalions from Ricard's 11th Division. According to Henckel, the king remained with the troops until the French came within eighty paces and then sought the protection of the nearby Brandenburg Hussars. Outnumbered, the Guard Fusiliers withdrew toward Kleingörschen. After returning to the Monarchenhügel, Frederick William sent Henckel along with another adjutant, Major

Konstantin von Stolberg, to retrieve Fritz and Frederick from the struggle. After the teenaged Hohenzollern princes returned, the king ordered his son to remain at his side with the praise "you have been in enough fire!"[20]

Meanwhile, Marmont's foremost divisions, the 20th under Jean-Dominique Compans and Jean-Pierre Bonet's 21st, marched east and approached Starsiedel around 2:00. Informed that he would face cavalry, the marshal organized his divisions into battalion columns one behind the other so they could quickly form squares. Marmont's troops reached Starsiedel and then turned southeast along both sides of the village seeking to continue the march along the Starsiedel–Pegau road. Compans's division formed the first wave, with Bonet's in reserve and echeloned to the left: Marmont arranged them in six large squares of one brigade each. As soon as Compans's foremost brigade moved away from the protection of Starsiedel and into the open, Prince William and Gneisenau charged with the Brandenburg Cuirassier Regiment, driving back the French. William repeated this scene several times, utilizing Wintzingerode's cavalry as well. Inexplicably, the prince never launched a general assault but instead employed only portions of the Allied cavalry. While assuring himself fresh horses and eager sabers, he failed to mount a numerically effective attack that could stop the gradual deployment of the French infantry south of Starsiedel.

Marmont, on the other hand, remained unduly cautious. Not only did he refrain from ordering the advance, but his idleness also allowed the Allies to move up between sixty and eighty guns. This indicated to the marshal an imminent infantry attack, which became all the more probable when he discerned infantry massing on the Allied left. For his part, Wittgenstein reconsidered Prince William's call for an infantry attack on Starsiedel. The Russian commander now believed a successful assault on this village could decide the day. He transferred Berg's infantry from the right wing of the second wave across Yorck's front to a position behind the Prussian Reserve Cavalry and moved Berg's guns as well as a portion of Yorck's heavy artillery into the Allied firing line. According to Yorck's after-action report, this decision "produced a negative impact on the movements that followed." Nevertheless, it prompted Marmont to yield his position south of Starsiedel. To create a defensive line, he withdrew his troops into and behind the village. Marmont brought his artillery on line and engaged in a duel that proved completely futile for the Allies. The number of bayonets at Berg's disposal did not justify the marshal's precautions. Without Wintzingerode's infantry, Berg faced a three-to-one disadvantage in foot soldiers. We will never know what the outcome of that struggle would have been because, before Berg could pass Rahna and commence his assault, Marshal Ney launched a powerful charge into the quadrilateral that took the fight out of Wittgenstein. Not only did Ney's counterattack induce Wittgenstein to hold

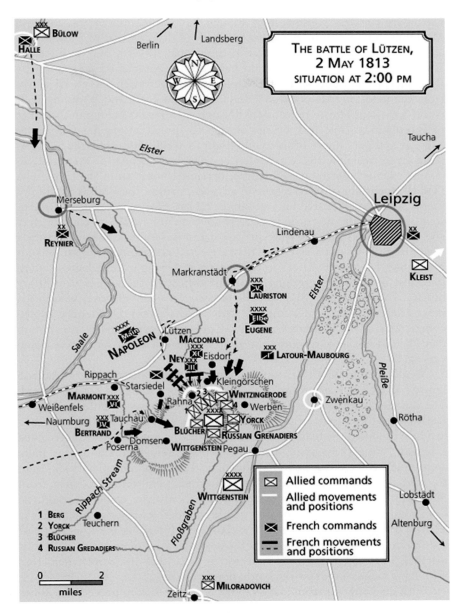

**16.** Battle of Lützen, 2 May 1813, situation at 2:00 P.M.

back Berg's troops southwest of Rahna, but Girard, under the cover of Marmont's guns, also marched his reorganized division east to Kaja.

Ney's foothold at Kaja pointed to additional Allied mistakes. First, the advance of Röder's brigade should have been accompanied on the left by Berg and on the right by Yorck. While these forces swept Ney's III Corps from the field, the Allied cavalry under Prince William and Wintzingerode could have kept Marmont at bay. Although such results belong in the realm of speculation, panic had already started to spread among III Corps; the baggage and park drove off in a wild flight to Weißenfels and large numbers of deserters made their way to the left bank of the Saale. As for Marmont, his closest support, Bertrand's IV Corps, remained hours from the battlefield. Had Wittgenstein ordered a general advance, neither the French III nor VI Corps could have resisted his vast numerical superiority in cavalry. Wittgenstein, however, did not order a general advance nor would he commit Berg and Yorck. News that the Russian Guard and Reserve had taken the wrong road and thus would arrive later than expected contributed mightily to his reluctance. Moreover, Klüx's initial success at Großgörschen led to one of the most irresponsible actions of a staff officer in the annals of military history. To reserve the Guard for the tsar to personally dispose, Volkonsky, most likely on his own authority, sent Mikhailovsky-Danilevsky to the commander of the Russian Grenadier Corps, Konovnitsyn, to inform him that "he did not have to hurry the approach march as the battle was going very well."[21]

While the tsar's elite troops remained a few hours away, Napoleon himself arrived at Kaja around 2:30 with his Imperial Guard not far behind. The thunder of almost 200 guns greeted the emperor as he galloped toward Kaja, passing hundreds of wounded as well as groups of soldiers who had lost heart and fled the field. Despite this disturbing scene, Napoleon received a hearty *"Vive l'empereur"* from the troops, reinvigorated by his mere appearance. Regardless, he found the tactical situation completely different from what he expected. Three of Ney's divisions were reeling in defeat; from Marmont came the request for support. As only the emperor could, he briefly examined the situation and quickly rendered his judgment. "This is a battle of Egypt," he purportedly exclaimed, referencing the 1798 battle of the Pyramids that he had waged with only a handful of cavalry. "Tell your marshal," he said turning to Marmont's aid, "that he is mistaken, that nothing is facing him, that the battle hinges on Kaja."[22]

With the battle far from lost, Napoleon first needed to prevent the Allies from advancing any further north and reaching the plain of Lützen, where they could unleash their superior cavalry. Moreover, control of Kaja did not promise victory. He recognized that Wittgenstein certainly had considerable forces en route; otherwise a battle would not have been sought. In addition, to achieve decisive results, the emperor needed time for IV Corps to arrive

12 Napoleon at the battle of Großgörschen, 2 May 1813

on the Allied left and XI Corps to envelop the Allied right. For the moment, he could only pour more men into the sausage grinder of the quadrilateral. Shortly before 3:00, Napoleon ordered six fresh battalions from General Jean-Joseph Tarayre's 1st Brigade of the 11th Division to advance through Kaja. Ney's last reserve, the division's 2nd Brigade under General Charles Dumoulin, followed at a close distance. As they surged forward, some thousand individuals from Ney's other divisions as well as numerous reorganized units from Souham's joined the advance. Rejuvenated by the presence of the emperor, the French tide swept through Kleingörschen and Rahna, reaching the outlying hamlets of Großgörschen.

Numerous attempts by the Prussian brigade cavalry to stem the French advance in the quadrilateral failed, partly due to the hedges and trenches that limited movement and partly because of the French artillery.[23] "I saw the Prussian cavalry exposed to the fire from the guns," recalls Steffens. "I saw how their ranks thinned, and how, as here one and there another was unhorsed with frightful wounds, the rest quietly closed up and filled the gaps." The Prussians gradually withdrew from the square but managed to hold Großgörschen thanks to the artillery posted south of the village. Blücher and Scharnhorst continuously rallied the men. By 3:00, 18,000 Prussian infantry faced approximately 36,000 French, of which Dumoulin's 4,000 men had yet to see action. Knowing that Tormasov would soon arrive, Blücher remained optimistic. More importantly, the morale of the soldiers remained high, with Yorck's men especially wanting to grapple with the French. Around this point of the battle, Wittgenstein learned that strong enemy forces (Bertrand and Macdonald) would soon threaten both flanks. Russian sources do not reveal the nature of the report that alerted Wittgenstein to this danger but the complexion of the battle now changed for the Allies. Impending threats to both flanks completely nullified the execution of Wittgenstein's original battle plan. Preventing defeat, which required extreme economy in the commitment of forces, became his sole objective.[24]

Since 3:00, Yorck's corps had stood about 1,300 yards south of Großgörschen at the spot where Klüx's brigade had commenced the first attack. Yorck initially supported Blücher's corps with two battalions from Hünerbein's 8th Brigade before committing the whole unit to the struggle at Kleingörschen. After an exhausting contest, Hünerbein's troops secured this village but could not continue the attack with vigor. Around 4:00, Tormasov's lead units started to arrive, providing the signal to commit Yorck's corps. Thirty minutes later, Yorck summoned General Heinrich Wilhelm von Horn's 7th Brigade to move into the battle line; the same instructions arrived from Volkonsky in the tsar's name. Horn designated two battalions for the reserve and led his remaining three west, passing Großgörschen for the attack on Rahna. His attack not only swept the French from the village, but it also triggered a surge by the entire Prussian line. "Yorck marched with his corps to the right of the village," recounts Gneisenau; "The entire army executed a clockwise rotation and soon the struggle became general along the entire line of Blücher's corps. The enemy deployed several guns, especially heavy caliber, and the small arms fire in the villages continued for many hours with a great ferocity."

Yorck himself attempted to direct the advance on Kaja and against the strong French artillery position southwest of the village. A light battery moved up to support his infantry followed by squadrons from the brigade cavalry. As Horn's battalions marched north on Kaja, Hünerbein's West Prussians advanced east from Kleingörschen. Blücher rode at the head of Horn's column as the Prussians stormed Kaja from the south and east. At Blücher's side, Prince Leopold of Hessen-Homburg received a mortal chest wound. At this point of the battle, Wittgenstein earned Yorck's censure for moving Berg's corps to the left wing. To the Prussians, it appeared that the French were beginning to retreat in the direction of Merseburg. "Now was time to commit the reserve and the glorious victory would have been decided," laments German historian Johann Gustav Droysen, echoing Yorck, "but Berg marched off and Volkonsky, the tsar's adjutant, told the infantry of the Russian Reserve not to hurry." "After the campaign," confirms Henckel, "many French assured me when I was assigned to the observations corps in France that not an insignificant portion of infantry

13 The charge of the West Prussian Infantry Regiment at Großgörschen

retreated in disorder toward Merseburg in the evening and that on the next morning they could not believe their eyes when they found us retreating."[25]

Death reaped a plentiful harvest during this part of the struggle. While not anti-Prussian, Wilson indicated in his 3 May journal entry that the relative inexperience of the Prussian officer corps took a bloody toll on the men: "I was quite unhappy to see the poor Prussians slaughtered from mismanagement. They are fine material, but they require exactly what has been done with the Portuguese – the loan of British leaders to train their own. The cavalry, however, are perfect. I never saw such steadfastness: it is quite incredible. I was obliged to ride up to several squadrons to express my admiration." According to the oft-quoted journal of the Prussian Guard Jäger Battalion: "The field between Großgörschen, Kleingörschen, Rahna, and Kaja looked like a bivouac where entire battalions had laid down." "The most severe and galling attacks of all arms took place in close contact with each other," continued Gneisenau, "and on which, it may be said, fell Slaughter in all his horrid terrors, crowned with desolation and, prodigal of death, reigned triumphant."

Followed by the monarchs, Wittgenstein rode to the entrance of the quadrilateral, helping and advising where they could. Scenes of general slaughter and chaos greeted them: burning houses, the maimed, dead and dying, shell-shocked men, and wounded blocking the path of the advancing troops. "Count Wittgenstein came down to the skirts of the village," wrote

Campbell, "followed by the emperor [tsar] and king, saw the state of affairs, but resolved to persevere." "The emperor, the king of Prussia, and all the Prussian princes were very frequently in heavy fire," stated Wilson in his after-action report. "Blücher, Scharnhorst, and Yorck labored in and around the villages providing order and leadership in the midst of constant fire."

Facing the renowned Marshal Ney – "the bravest of the brave" – Blücher and his suite demonstrated similar pluck, leading their troops in the blood-bath. "Since we could not exercise any decisive influence on the conduct of the battle," explains Clausewitz, "nothing else remained but to take up the sword and fight. Scharnhorst mainly led the battle on the right wing against the three villages. With his sword drawn, he drove into the enemy at the head of the cavalry and infantry several times; he encouraged the men, shouting: 'Long live the king!' Gneisenau was on the left wing and fought at the head of the cavalry. That old Blücher also was very brave, you can just imagine."[26]

"In unison with these [Yorck's] fresh battalions," comments historian Walther Görlitz, "Blücher's brigades stormed anew Kleingörschen and Rahna, blood-red flames and smoke pouring from their barns and houses ... and the attack continued to a hill beyond Rahna. There, when the advance again came to a standstill, Blücher himself sprang forward to entrain the infantry, with his blue general's coat and field cap upon his silver-white hair all widely recognized. The balls flew as thick as hail showers, and the bursting of shells incessantly ripped the air." Blücher's horse was shot out from under him and the general himself was hit by three musket balls. After he and Scharnhorst did everything possible to reform the battalions to hold Kaja until the Russian reserves could move up, the 71-year-old accepted his staff's exhortations to seek medical attention. Blücher sent them to Yorck, who now assumed command of all Prussian forces.

Casualties among the general officers of the French III Corps likewise mounted: Ney lost his horse and was slightly wounded in the right leg by a musket ball while leading a counterattack by the Badenese Dragoons. A musket ball to the abdomen mortally wounded his chief of staff, General Louis-Anne Gouré; Girard fell severely wounded after being pierced by several balls – he refused to leave the field, vowing: "the time has come when every Frenchman must either triumph or die"; a bullet shredded Brenier's right thigh; and several brigade commanders including Chemineau, who lost a leg, likewise sustained wounds. Napoleon himself remained at Kaja but constantly exposed himself to heavy fire – more than ever before, according to Marmont – while rallying Ney's men.

Despite the vicious French artillery fire from the flank position south-west of Kaja, the Prussian tide steadily approached the village. "The ground over which they marched was strewn with the dead and wounded, and blood and carnage paved the way," recounted Gneisenau. Clausewitz received a bayonet gash behind his right ear as more officers fell but the Prussians kept coming. "Each side fought with a fury worthy of admiration," comments the Saxon Ernst Otto von Odeleben, who served on Napoleon's staff, "and the brave Prussians found plenty of employment for the French. Their batteries near Großgörschen and Rahna played on the Imperial Guard and several balls and grenades fell near Napoleon: an *inspecteur des postes* lost a leg close by him, and even bullets were whistling around him. Several members of the emperor's suite became visibly unsettled." Nevertheless, Napoleon calmly watched the Prussians gain a foothold in Kaja after two failed attempts.[27]

Around 5:30 P.M., Napoleon ordered General Pierre Lanusse's 1st Brigade of Young Guard to secure Kaja. His bearskins ferociously charged with fixed bayonets, driving the Prussians from the village. Troops from III Corps followed Lanusse's men and kept going after the Guard halted. The imperial tide penetrated both Rahna and Kleingörschen but failed to break into the Prussian stronghold at Großgörschen. Fighting in the quadrilateral continued until the very end of the battle some four hours later. Details are sketchy: Rahna and Kleingörschen may have changed hands five or six times and the Allies may have reached Kaja three or four times. Blücher and Yorck led eight fresh Russian battalions in a final attack that came to naught after initial success. Aside from the human tragedy that unfolded in the quadrilateral, the stalemate there hardly influenced the actual result. Like so many of his past triumphs, the emperor's ability to maneuver his chess pieces proved to be the decisive factor at Großgörschen. Not the mighty Guard at Kaja, but the threat of a double envelopment decided the day.

Wittgenstein knew that time did not favor his army. As early as 3:00 P.M., he received reports of Bertrand's approach from Taucha. This movement threatened the Allied left south of Starsiedel. With plenty of time to prepare, Wintzingerode moved up his entire cavalry so that it came on line with the Prussian troopers, but held back his own left wing to form a defensive flank. Regardless, Wintzingerode handled his troopers little better than Prince William; by the end of the battle, the Russian had only managed to splinter this huge cavalry mass into small, completely useless packets. On the next day, Wittgenstein relieved him of command of the cavalry.

Berg's infantry remained in its position behind the Prussian infantry. Although fewer than 6,000 men, Berg's corps could have turned left to confront the threat posed by Bertrand, or Wittgenstein could have posted Wintzingerode's infantry at Domsen and Tornau to threaten Bertrand's extreme right flank. However, expanding the left wing another two miles appeared dangerous due to the French infantry's numerical superiority. By this time, shortly before 4:00, only two battalions of the Russian Guard and Reserve had reached the battlefield, so Wittgenstein did not dare squander Wintzingerode's infantry or Berg's corps. Instead, he posted the entire Cuirassier Corps of the Russian Reserve followed by the Russian Guard

14 The Allied left wing at Großgörschen

Light Cavalry and the Guard Artillery's horse guns on the left wing, thus increasing the strength of Wintzingerode's cavalry to 12,000 troopers and some 100 pieces of horse artillery. Facing Weißenfels, Gallitzin's Cuirassier Corps formed at a right angle to Wintzingerode's front to prevent Bertrand from enveloping Wittgenstein's left.

Meanwhile, Bertrand's IV Corps started marching east from Taucha around 3:00, only after the corps commander received the emperor's express order. Reports of an enemy force south of his position caused him concern. Indeed, the enemy force belonged to Miloradovich's corps. Around 4:00, Miloradovich personally reached Zeitz (thirteen miles south of Taucha) and learned of a battle in the vicinity of Lützen as well as the advance of strong French forces through Weißenfels en route to the battlefield. On this news, he forwarded Yuzefovich's vanguard of one cavalry brigade and one Jäger battalion northward. However, after the main body of his corps reached Zeitz between 4:00 and 5:00 P.M., Miloradovich did nothing. In his journal, "waited for orders" is expressly noted.[28]

During the days of planning prior to the battle, Gneisenau suggested that Miloradovich advance in the direction of Weißenfels, from where he could attack the enemy's flank and rear. According to Marmont's judgment, this movement inevitably would have brought the Allies victory by allowing Wittgenstein to execute the great flanking movement with his left wing.[29] Gneisenau's suggestion did not find support at Russian headquarters. In 1830, as commander of Prussian occupation forces in Poland, Gneisenau asked the commander of the Russian army, Diebitsch, why on 2 May 1813 Miloradovich did not receive orders to march to Großgörschen. Diebitsch replied that an incorrect assumption over where Miloradovich stood on that day caused the error. Wittgenstein's 27 April disposition had ordered Miloradovich to remain at Chemnitz until the arrival of confirmed reports over Napoleon's march on Leipzig. On receipt of this news, Miloradovich would march seventeen miles west to Waldenburg. On the 28th, Miloradovich advanced from Chemnitz to Penig rather than Waldenburg. The last report that Wittgenstein's headquarters received from Miloradovich, dated 1 May, contained "Altenburg" in the heading but a Cyrillic letter looking like a "W" (such as a **ш** or a **ш**) had been penned before the name of this town, making it appear as Waldenburg instead of Altenburg. Miloradovich indeed marched to Altenburg on the 1st but due to the mysterious "W," Wittgenstein assumed the Russian corps commander had gone to Waldenburg, some twelve miles south-southeast of Altenburg. Believing Miloradovich could not reach the battle in time, Wittgenstein ordered him to march presumably thirty miles northwest from Waldenburg to Zeitz. Wittgenstein himself told Mikhailovsky-Danilevsky "that they had advised him several times during the battle to send for the corps of Miloradovich but they could not understand why he did not want to do this, because he had intended to renew the battle on the following day and to place this corps in the first line. 'It is not possible to battle Napoleon', he added, 'without having a strong reserve behind you.'"[30]

Regardless of the reason for Miloradovich's inaction, it allowed Bertrand's corps to march to the sound of the guns unmolested. The lead division, General Charles-Antoine Morand's 12th, reached the edge of the Grünabach at Pobles; the Italians of General Luigi Gaspare Peyri's 15th Division remained a solid two miles behind. The sight that greeted Morand's 9,000 men could not have been very encouraging: more than 10,000 Allied cavalry including a huge mass of ironclad cuirassiers supported by scores of guns. Yet six and one-half years earlier, Morand had fought at Auerstedt under the great Davout against Prussian cavalry more numerous than the force that now faced his division. He pushed a vanguard of three battalions across the Grünabach and brought his artillery into action. Morand then formed the entire division into checkerboard squares and advanced. A strong nucleus of veteran soldiers held the vulnerable right wing. His men, many of whom were experiencing combat for the first time, repulsed several attacks by Wintzingerode's cavalry. Fortunately for the French, Wintzingerode never massed his cavalry for a general assault but instead attacked piecemeal. He later attempted to excuse his failure by erroneously claiming that bushes and shrubs had hindered the attack.

Observing Bertrand's approach, the tsar himself ordered General Aleksey Nikitin to form a battery of forty guns to stop the French march. Alexander rode forward with Nikitin, saying: "I will keep an eye on the effects of your guns." Approaching the battle line, the Russian monarch halted within musket range of the enemy. According to Henckel von Donnersmarck, on returning to the Monarchenhügel to report the arrival of the Russian grenadiers, he learned that Wittgenstein had ridden to the left wing in pursuit of Alexander. Likewise giving chase, he found both Wittgenstein and the tsar in heavy artillery fire; an equerry and an orderly from the imperial entourage fell. Henckel observed Wittgenstein beg the tsar to take cover but the monarch remained glued to his spot for some time. "There is no ball here for me," was his response to the pleas from his entourage to move away from the danger.

Nikitin's guns disordered the French. Taking advantage of the shell-shocked imperials, General Ivan Panchulidzev charged with the mounted Jäger attached to the Chernigovskii Regiment as well one dragoon regiment, capturing two guns. The constant threat of a flank attack by the Russian cavalry considerably slowed Bertrand's march. Nevertheless, Wittgenstein rescinded the order for Berg to exploit Panchulidzev's success. "In this way," laments the Russian historian Bogdanovich, "instead of a decisive attack as our objective, we limited ourselves to passive behavior toward the enemy who was immediately in front of the left flank of our position."[31]

Although slow and cautious, Bertrand's advance in the direction of Rahna impacted other parts of the battlefield. As his left wing emerged between Kölzen and Starsiedel, Marmont deployed VI Corps from the latter. With Compans's division as the right wing, Bonet's as the left, and Jean-Parfait Friederichs's 22nd Division in reserve behind them, the corps followed the Starsiedel–Pegau road in the general direction of Rahna to support Ney's extremely hard-pressed III Corps. Marmont soon encountered difficulties similar to Bertrand's. The massive Allied battery on the hills south of Starsiedel, Prince William's cavalry interspersed among the guns, and behind them the clearly discernible infantry line formed by Berg's corps intimidated Marmont. Thus, he squandered any decisive impact he could have had on the fighting in the quadrilateral in favor of extreme caution.

In the meantime, after the infantry of the Russian Guard and Reserve started to arrive around 4:00, Duke Eugen of Württemberg received orders to lead eight battalions of his II Infantry Corps to the quadrilateral and the right wing of the Allied line. Seeing General Karl Friedrich von Steinmetz's Prussian 1st Brigade still in reserve south of Großgörschen, the duke decided to envelop the enemy's left. While the strong 3rd Infantry Division under General Ivan Shakhovsky retook Kleingörschen and marched through the quadrilateral to attack Kaja from the south, Eugen led the 4th Infantry Division to Eisdorf from where it would proceed to Kaja along the right bank of the Floßgraben. South of Eisdorf, Eugen united six Prussian and three Russian squadrons, one Cossack regiment, and one Prussian horse battery as an ad hoc vanguard commanded by Russian General Ilya Alekseyev. Advancing through the meadows north of Kleingörschen in the direction of Meuchen, this Allied column soon encountered Marchand's 39th Division marching south. Ney had counted on the 39th reaching the battlefield no later than 3:00 but the threat posed by Cossacks swarming his flanks and rear froze Marchand, who did not continue his march until around 5:00. Regardless, Alekseyev withdrew eastward, citing no favorable opportunities to attack Marchand. To the east, the Russian general could also discern the advance of strong enemy forces – Macdonald's XI Corps – south from Markranstädt through Großschkorlopp. Closer at hand, Marchand continued south and reached the Floßgraben east of Kaja and north of Kleingörschen, prompting Alekseyev to evacuate the right bank of the Floßgraben. Around this time, Duke Eugen reached Eisdorf with the main body of his 4th Infantry Division. Observing the approach of Macdonald's corps, he occupied the village to defend the Allied right. His quick report to Alexander enabled Allied Headquarters to direct the arriving infantry of the Russian Reserve to the imperiled wing: the 2nd Grenadier Division marched to Eisdorf.

Along the Allied center, Shakhovsky's 3rd Infantry Division and elements from the two Prussian corps again came close to Kaja just as Marchand's division reached the Floßgraben. A furious firefight erupted along the steep banks of the narrow, muddy brook. Marchand's 1st Brigade, consisting exclusively of Badeners, reached the Floßgraben first. The Allies greeted the Germans with intense musketry. To their credit, the Badeners responded with equal passion, exhausting their ammunition in less than one hour. As XI Corps moved closer to his left flank, Marchand ordered his 2nd Brigade – Hessians from Hesse-Darmstadt – to storm Kleingörschen. Duke Emile of Hesse-Darmstadt led his men into the village but paid for his boldness with the lives of his subjects. After fierce fighting, the Allies repulsed the Hessians; Emile's losses are estimated to be around 400 killed and wounded with 500 missing. In the retreat from Kleingörschen, the Hessians carried away the Badenese battalions.[32]

French reinforcements soon arrived from Macdonald's XI Corps. Around 5:00 P.M., the marshal's artillery – sixty cannon and howitzers – opened fire; the infantry engaged thirty minutes later. The impact on Allied morale had to be crushing. Although the hour is wrong, Yorck's after-action report captures the Allied mindset at the end of the battle: "We were in the process of achieving a decisive victory when around 7:00 P.M. strong enemy columns, allegedly the corps of the viceroy of Italy coming from Leipzig, advanced on Eisdorf, thus threatening our right flank." Forming the right wing of General Henri-François Charpentier's 36th Division, the 2nd Brigade deployed against Kleingörschen while the 1st Brigade moved against Eisdorf. The right wing of General Philibert Fressinet's 31st Division likewise turned on Eisdorf as his left occupied Kitzen. To defend the line of the Floßgraben, Duke Eugen led numerous counterattacks on both sides of Eisdorf. After losing the village, the Russians returned several times but could not regain Eisdorf. Wittgenstein dispatched Frederick William's adjutant, Henckel von Donnersmarck, to the tsar's brother, Grand Duke Constantine, with orders to move up the Guard Infantry in support. If Constantine could not comply, Wittgenstein instructed Henckel to go to the Grenadier Corps. After the grand duke claimed his troops were not ready, Henckel found the commander of the grenadiers, Konovnitsyn, who personally led three regiments (six battalions) supported by fifty guns from the Russian Reserve into the struggle before receiving a serious leg wound. Wittgenstein thus described this period of the battle:

> At 7:00 P.M., a new enemy corps appeared between the villages of Großgörschen and Kleingörschen on our right wing, probably the troops of the viceroy, and made a determined attack against us, seeking to deprive us of all advantages we had gained so far. At this moment, part of the Russian infantry reserve entered the fight to reinforce General Yorck's corps, which suffered a rather fierce attack on the right wing. A violent battle, which the Russian artillery and the corps of Yorck, Blücher, and Wintzingerode fought with such great success during the entire day, resumed once again and continued until nightfall. The enemy also renewed his attacks against our center and the villages but was unable to gain ground on us.[33]

After Duke Eugen finally accepted the loss of Eisdorf, the rest of the Grenadier Corps helped form a new line of defense that extended from Hohenlohe to Großgörschen by 6:30. Numerous Russian guns from Tormasov's Reserve Artillery moved into the line. Prince William and the Prussian Reserve Cavalry anchored the left side of the line by forming just west of Großgörschen. Behind the infantry and artillery, Allied cavalry including more than twenty Prussian squadrons from the brigades, stood ready. Directly behind the cavalry, the Russian Guard infantry provided a final reserve. Viceroy Eugene, who had reached the field with I Cavalry Corps, felt his forces did not suffice to attack such a formidable line. Thus, the duke held the viceroy at Eisdorf and prevented him from enveloping the Allied right wing. "When hostilities ceased for the night," notes Cathcart, "the two armies remained in parallel position; though since the arrival of Viceroy Beauharnais, the French army considerably outflanked that of the Allies, and stood with its left thrown forward, menacing their right and their line of retreat by Pegau; but the day was far too spent, and the night was afterwards too dark for the viceroy to press his advantage."[34]

Napoleon recognized that the moment had arrived to deliver the *coup de grâce*. With the sun sinking, he snapped a simple command: "eighty guns." General Antoine Drouot responded by having the entire Guard Artillery – fifty-eight guns – unlimber next to the powerful French batteries southwest of Kaja. Together, line and Guard artillery spewed their roundshot and canister into the interior of the quadrilateral for thirty minutes. Both friend and foe feared and respected the astonishing rapidity with which the Guard Artillery fired. Gneisenau, allegedly "perfectly calm and cheerful," turned to the professor, who was now quite pale, saying: 'Steffens, is that not a grand cannonade? It is to celebrate your birthday.' "He had passed the last anniversary with me at my house," explains Steffens, "that he should remember and joke about it at such a moment struck me as wonderful." While the artillery pulverized the quadrilateral, sixteen battalions of Marshal Édouard Adolphe Mortier's Young Guard formed in four brigade columns of four battalions each between the grand battery and Kaja. Behind them, six battalions of Old Guard followed by the Guard Cavalry formed the last reserve. As the emperor rode past the Guard's position, he issued his order in classic form: "*La garde au feu!*"[35]

Mortier's left column advanced toward Kleingörschen, while the two middle columns took the direction of Großgörschen and the right column assailed Rahna. The spectacle of the Guard massing for attack attracted all who still had the strength to advance and cartridges to fire. Thus, survivors from Ney's corps preceded the Guard like a thick cloud of skirmishers; behind the bearskins the music corps blazed away. Allied artillery, which throughout the day had exerted hardly any influence on the fighting inside the quadrilateral, likewise had little effect on the march of the Guard. Yet Blücher and Scharnhorst ordered a charge by some dozen Prussian squadrons. During the fighting, Scharnhorst received a musket ball to the leg and had to be evacuated to Pegau. The wound, which Clausewitz described on 3 May as not serious, eventually claimed his life on 28 June.[36] Rahna, also threatened from the west by Marmont's lead division, fell first. The Allied defenders of Kleingörschen could not resist being stormed by the Guard coming from Kaja as well as by Macdonald's right wing under Charpentier. Only when the Guard approached Großgörschen did the Allied artillery have a devastating effect on the dense columns. Regardless, the fall of Rahna and Kleingörschen forced the Prussians to evacuate Großgörschen; only two Prussian Guard Jäger companies held the village center. A final counterattack managed to drive the French from Großgörschen. Gneisenau recounted this last Allied attack in a report jointly drafted with Scharnhorst that night:

> Toward evening, a large, superior force unexpectedly pressed our right wing and retook the conquered villages from us at the moment when no fresh

troops were available for us to call up. A cluster of the various battalions that fought on this place united to retake the villages. This was just a small force and nobody thought of numbers. "Forward brother, hurrah," cried the entire mass. They drove into the village, throwing down all before them, driving through the village; a murderous enemy fire rained upon them, many fell – the mass stopped short – then one heard "Forward, hurrah," and so one threw himself onto the enemy, following him to the exit of the village; meanwhile two guns followed by two more came up for support. We saw Russian and Prussian officers from the rearward corps fighting, as well as a couple of English officers. Together, soldiers and officers fought side by side. During this struggle we saw no wounded as long as a man still had a weapon. Nobody was ready to bring back the wounded; all were fighting. One saw no dead being carried off. A sacred, holy feeling seized the warriors. The inexperienced youths of the regiments and the volunteer Jäger detachments who had never experienced combat fought just like the brave Russian troops who already tasted victory; here, none enjoyed an advantage over the other. Thus, the victory of this day was fought on our right wing; what occurred on the left I do not know, but I saw that there also the battlefield was taken and the enemy was beaten back from his position.[37]

Darkness brought an end to the fighting sometime after 7:00; the groans of the dying replaced the thunder of the guns. Lacking sufficient cavalry, the French did not attempt to pursue from the quadrilateral. This greatly assisted the Allies in restoring command and control in their units. "The Prussian infantry," continues Wilson's critique, "from want of experienced officers, had been brought so loosely into action that great disorder prevailed, and the field was covered with the scattered wanderers of their battalions." Blücher's II Corps regrouped southwest of Großgörschen under the protection of the famed Kolberg Regiment from Steinmetz's brigade. In the darkness, a French column collided with Steinmetz's infantry, who had already stacked their arms and were resting. After gaining their composure, the Prussians repulsed the French. A bitter Blücher wanted to make the French pay for such audacity. Summoned to attend a council of war, he stormed off to propose a night attack.[38]

In the meantime, Yorck's I Corps and Shakhovsky's division formed behind Duke Eugen's front. Berg's corps, which had engaged Marmont's corps toward the end of the battle, withdrew slightly on the road to Pegau. On the left wing, Wintzingerode's cavalry mass remained one mile west of Großgörschen. Viewing the battle as a draw, the two monarchs left the field shortly before 9:00 P.M., expecting to continue the struggle the next day. "To move through and beyond the villages," continued Yorck in his after-action report, "and undertake a night attack did not appear advisable because it had already started to get dark, the strength and position of the enemy could no longer be discerned sufficiently, and [all] expected the battle to continue the next day." After being evacuated from the field, Scharnhorst wrote a report that captures the Prussian view of the battle's end: "It was between 6:00 and 7:00 when I was wounded in the leg and forced to leave the battlefield. I do not know what occurred on the left wing. I only saw that we had taken a significant amount of ground there as well. The battle was therefore won; I still do not know the further results. The enemy occupied Leipzig to his rear. Toward evening, reinforcements arrived from the [Russian] main army; also Miloradovich's corps was approaching. When the battle ended we maintained not only the battlefield, but all the terrain that we had won."[39]

Around 9:00, Wittgenstein assembled the corps commanders in the dark on the Monarchenhügel after the sovereigns had departed; he presented a very different picture. From all reports he received, the condition of the infantry did not appear favorable: confusion, dissolution, and extreme exhaustion reigned. Despite the unbroken fighting spirit of the troops, order could not be restored during the night. Moreover, the Russian ammunition parks did not follow the army across the Elster; thus little chance existed for timely resupply. The larger question concerned the real prospect of success on 3 May. Napoleon clearly enjoyed numerical superiority. While the Russian Guard and Reserve as well as the cavalry on the left wing offered relatively fresh forces, Wittgenstein's army contained only a handful of battalions that had not seen extensive combat that day. Could these in unison with Miloradovich's corps offset Napoleon's fresh forces? A sober assessment of the Allied situation on the evening of 2 May renders a resounding no. According to Gneisenau's estimates, about 38,000 Allied foot soldiers out of a total of 53,000 engaged that day, leaving only 15,000 fresh troops in reserve. Considering the forces that Eugene brought up, Gneisenau figured the Allies could face as many as 40,000 to 50,000 fresh imperial troops. Any thought to the contrary only revealed an underestimation of Napoleon's generalship. News that Kleist had retreated almost twenty miles east from Leipzig to Wurzen arrived during this debate. With the closest road leading to the rear of the Allied army now open to the French, few doubted that a strong imperial corps at Leipzig stood ready to sever its line of retreat. Wittgenstein made the preliminary arrangements for the retreat and then departed to report to the monarchs at Groitzsch.[40]

Before departing, Wittgenstein, urged by Cathcart, authorized Blücher to conduct his night attack to extract revenge for the attack on Steinmetz's brigade.[41] Dolffs assembled nine squadrons, including the Garde du Corps, the Brandenburg and East Prussian Cuirassier Regiments, and two squadrons of Brandenburg Hussars. With his wound still throbbing, Blücher led the cavalry toward the flames of Rahna. "Making as little noise as possible," the cavalry advanced "in close order up to the battalions formed in squares behind which stood Napoleon," reports Odeleben. Charging in two waves, the Prussians routed the light regiment of Bonet's division and came very close to another square behind which stood the emperor himself. "We could see only the flashes of the artillery firing without being able to judge their positions," continues Odeleben. "The burning villages illuminated the horizon in three places, when suddenly on the right flank of the French army a line of cavalry rushed forward with a dull rattle and came close to the square in which the emperor stood. I believe that had they advanced 200 paces further, Napoleon and his entire entourage would have been captured."

In the general confusion, the French fired on friend and foe alike. Marmont saved himself by diving into the midst of a square. Regardless, the attack broke on the large French infantry masses. Blücher could never have imagined the deadly game that had unfolded so close to him which the impenetrable darkness had concealed. After regaining their composure, the French poured heavy fire into the Prussian horsemen. "Although the villages," stated Wittgenstein in his after-action report, "located side by side from each other in this region, as well as the ravine and the enemy's precautions, did not allow our cavalry to charge the enemy line, the Prussian Guard and the Brandenburg Cuirassier Regiment nevertheless charged, even into the zone of crossfire between the villages, and cut down a great number of enemy infantry, thus sharing in the immortal glory that the Prussian soldiers earned in this bloody battle." Soon, the volley fire of the French squares drowned the battle cries of Blücher's cuirassiers and hussars. Dolffs finally signaled the retreat after losing several troopers, particularly in the sunken road and defiles south of Großgörschen. They did not sacrifice themselves in vain. The Prussian charge proved to the French that the Allies could continue the struggle. Moreover, the foray into the French camp kept the imperials on their guard throughout the night rather than allowing them to rest or prepare to exploit their gains. Many battalions passed the night under arms and formed in squares. Jomini notes that "the alarm spread to Weißenfels and Lützen, and was even greater in the rear, where the Cossacks on the other hand made a hurrah on the ambulances behind the line, from where some fugitives went as far as Naumburg to sow terror."[42]

Around 10:00 on the morning of 2 May, Eugene's troops found the road to Leipzig blocked by Kleist at Lindenau, where the battle of Lützen began. Napoleon's other corps – some 51,000 men – followed in intervals on the roads from Naumburg and Erfurt. Ney's III Corps and a portion of the Guard, more than 50,000 men, took positions by division along the hills that extended southeast from Lützen to the quadrilateral. Finding Ney in this dangerous position, Wittgenstein attacked. Although a comprehensive advance early in the battle would have swept "the bravest of the brave" from the field, Wittgenstein could not abandon his vision of enveloping Napoleon's army from the south and west. To be fair, the hills concealed Ney's divisions, and the troops that the Allies found at Großgörschen – Souham's 8th Division – appeared to be a rear- or flank guard of Napoleon's army, which Wittgenstein placed at Lützen. Rather than launch a general assault on Souham's position, Wittgenstein attacked piecemeal while he waited for Tormasov's reserves to implement the envelopment. Yet with each new hour, French forces arrived from Lützen, Weißenfels, and Leipzig to provide Napoleon with the key to so many of his victories: mass at the point of attack.

Emphasizing the benefits of a flank attack, Toll originally proposed the idea of advancing due north. The strategic relationship between the Allied line of operation and Napoleon's mainly interested him. Distinctive of this type of planning, the Russian staff officer placed little importance on the random tactical situations in which the Allies might encounter the imperial army. While a flank attack on a deep marching column appeared to offer the prospect of easier success than a head-on confrontation, such thinking suggests an ignorance of Napoleon's operations. As most famously illustrated by the *bataillon carré* of 1806, Napoleon strove to have his columns advance within mutual supporting distance in such a flexible manner that his highly mobile corps could easily change front to engage a threat. Moreover, instead of being the weaker side, the flank of a deep column is the stronger, because the flank can wheel and quickly produce a combat-ready front of considerable size. No other operational system better facilitated Napoleon's flexible employment of his superior forces. On 2 May, the emperor exploited this advantage as decisively as he could in view of his limited cavalry.

As for the issue of whether Wittgenstein's attack surprised Napoleon, Jomini maintained that "it was extremely important for the emperor to support at Lützen because possession of it would have given the enemy the ability to cut his army in half. On the morning of 2 May, Wittgenstein debouched on this town but instead of finding the extreme right [of Napoleon's army], he fell on its center, which as of yet had not moved. Although it did not achieve its goal, the Allied maneuver was commendable. Napoleon believed an attack from that side to be so unlikely that he had ordered Ney to accompany him [to Markranstädt], and his corps was now without its chief [and] little prepared for combat."[43] In the end, whether the attack on 2 May surprised Napoleon or not is immaterial: his *bataillon carré* of 1813 allowed him to rapidly adjust so that the right wing of his army (Ney's III and Marmont's VI Corps) became the center, the left wing (Lauriston's V Corps) became the rear, the rear (Bertrand's IV Corps) became the right wing, and the van (Macdonald's XI Corps) formed the left wing. Napoleon stood in the middle with his Grand Reserve: the Imperial Guard.

Souham's unsuspecting division – carelessly camped on the quadrilateral – provided an opportunity for the Allies to score a quick tactical success. This would have required Wittgenstein to dispense with the formalities of linear tactics, "which viewed the entire army as a strictly unitary organism that upon the order of the commander in chief would move in a completely uniform manner toward the objective. All rearward waves were to follow the movements of the first in a parallel direction." Caemmerer condemns the Russian high command for its dependence on linear tactics: "The disposition and order of battle prove in quite an astonishing way how backwards the Russian leadership still was at that time." He also remarks that "in the leadership of troops on the battlefield, the authoritative persons among the Allies unfortunately were hardly skilled, and they lacked the correct understanding for the exploitation of the favorable moment. Schematic battle scenes of the past floated in front of them as examples and prevented the realization of simple decisions. Added to this, the fact that the leadership was not even consistent, we must recognize that for them the game against Napoleon was too much."

On the other hand, Wittgenstein did embrace the modern or Napoleonic concept of deep columns by forming the army into consecutive infantry waves. In addition, he selected battalion columns as the basic formation of the infantry. Yet Wittgenstein should have known that the Prussian Regulations of 1812 theoretically preferred combined-arms brigades as the organization of troop units rather than the deployment of infantry in two or three waves with the cavalry in the rear. Thus, he should not have imposed a linear deployment that the Prussian army's new doctrine considered obsolete. At Großgörschen, the Prussian infantry brigades formed two waves of battalion columns. Maude found that Wittgenstein's determination to employ Tormasov's army as his reserve indicates a degree of acceptance of the rules of modern, Napoleonic warfare by the Russians. Maude provides an instructive explanation of the importance of reserves in Napoleonic warfare as opposed to eighteenth-century, Frederician warfare:

> The old Prussian army would have attacked *en masse* and overwhelmed III Corps in its first rush. This marks a very important difference between the guiding ideas of post-Revolutionary tactics and those of the Frederician era, and deserves more attention ... since it involves the whole theory of the use of reserves in battle. The fundamental conception underlying the old line tactics lay in the idea of *overwhelming the enemy by a single crushing blow*, in contradistinction to the plan of *wearing him down by attrition*. The same idea still underlies the employment of cavalry in action. Hence the necessity for heavy reserves became apparent, and in time this provision of reserves came to be regarded as the essential point, and *not the provision of an all-destroying "Line."*[44]

Known in Anglophone literature mainly by its French name, the battle of Lützen, the struggle – called the battle of Großgörschen by the Germans – proved extremely bloody. Scharnhorst's new army shouldered the weight of the engagement and paid dearly in its debut. At the start of the day, Blücher and Yorck together commanded approximately 33,000 officers and men. By evening, they had lost 8,400 men: 1,400 dead including 53 officers, 5,300 wounded including 244 officers; and more than 1,700 men and 6 officers captured or missing. Wittgenstein's report of 3 May mentions the loss "of many worthy" Prussian officers. Röder's brigade went into the battle with 159 officers: only 85 reported for duty after the battle. One fusilier battalion lost all of its officers: three dead and the rest wounded. Of the sixty officers who started the day in the Guard Regiment, twenty-two remained. In the fusilier battalion of that regiment, only two officers emerged unscathed. In a letter to his wife on 6 May, Gneisenau criticized the Russians and bemoaned the resulting carnage:

> The battle was indecisive. Much blood was spilled for nothing. The plan for it, rather the execution of the plan, was not extraordinary because troops were left out of the battle that one [Wittgenstein] could have easily moved up, for example the corps of Miloradovich, Kleist, and Bülow. The first named has 100 cannon, which we could have put to good use. At the end of the battle the enemy had a superiority of 50,000 infantry to the 20,000 that still remained to us or were not fatigued from combat, for death raged among several battalions and dissolved them. We have three battalions of which two have only two officers remaining while the third has only one officer. Mainly we had too few infantry. With such uncertainty, one wanted to avoid suffering a defeat and so did not want to commit the rest.[45]

Russian casualty figures do not exist: only Duke Eugen reported the loss of 1,632 men and 87 officers of 8,700 troops in less than three hours of combat. At the least, the Russians lost 3,000 total casualties, raising the estimate of Allied losses to 11,500 combatants and 2 guns. Bogdanovich defends the idea that the Prussians should have borne the brunt of the fighting: "Our allies reproached the Russian army for having weakly supported their efforts: indeed, Count Wittgenstein and many of our generals believed that after the Russians had fought for their independence without any foreign aid, they had the right to impose on the Prussians the greater share in the struggle for the liberation of Germany."[46]

Wittgenstein reported to the tsar that the Allies "retained the battlefield and captured 16 guns and 1,400 men, many of them officers. We did not lose a single cannon. The enemy lost up to 15,000 men. Our losses amount to some 10,000 men, most of them *lightly wounded.*" Written on the 7th, Campbell's account is one of the few Allied reports that claim the Allies lost more than the French: "I would estimate our loss at 12,000 or 15,000 men – the French infinitely less. I was in the villages at different times during the day and saw very few French while the Prussian killed and wounded were very numerous. A great number of the latter must have been left there."[47] In fact, few wounded Allied soldiers fell into imperial hands in part because no previous battle saw as many wagons allocated to ambulance service. Neither side lost a flag or standard.

For the French, Ney's III Corps suffered egregiously. Of the approximately 45,500 officers and men who started the battle on 2 May, the corps shrank to 18,050 combatants according to the muster of 5 May. "The day had been bloody without being decisive," explained Jomini. "Ney's sole corps had 12,000 men and 500 officers out of action, and obtained neither trophies nor results. Generals of Division Girard and Brenier were seriously wounded as was almost every other general and Ney himself was lightly ... the numbers of wounded were so considerable that one accused these young conscripts, frightened by the fatigue of war, of maiming themselves in the hope of escaping it. Maybe it was only due to their clumsiness. Regardless, although French honor refuted this accusation, it seemed serious enough to warrant an investigation." Losses among XI Corps's 31st and 36th Divisions as well as the Young Guard division averaged 850–1,050 men each. In total, the French lost some 22,000 combatants and 5 guns.[48]

Pleased and grateful for the sacrifices his army had made on the 2nd, Frederick William expressed to Wittgenstein his extreme displeasure over the decision to retreat. In fact, Alexander just barely managed to convince the Prussian king to endorse the retreat. Practically barging into the quarters of a sleeping Frederick William at Groitzsch, Alexander took a seat next to the king's bed and explained the need to retreat. Not having time to rise and dress, Frederick William simply remained in bed and listened to his ally. "This I know," responded the Prussian monarch, "if we start to retreat, we will not stop at the Elbe but will also cross the Vistula and in this way I again see myself at Memel." Alexander attempted to explain that a retreat would move the army closer to its reinforcements. Shocked at the prospect of sacrificing his kingdom after what he thought was a hard-fought victory, the king replied: "I give you my compliments; I must get up." Thus forcing the tsar to leave, Frederick William sprang from his bed shouting: "This is just as bad as Auerstedt." The discord persisted, especially after Frederick William received the after-action reports from his corps commanders. Blücher assured the monarch that the French had suffered extraordinarily in the battle and that Napoleon had actually prepared to retreat. Bülow and Kleist reported that they had reoccupied Halle and Leipzig respectively on the 3rd but had evacuated these cities as a result of Wittgenstein's retreat. Only after a meeting with Scharnhorst at Altenburg did Frederick William accept the Russian decision to retreat.[49]

Although "losing" the battle, the Allied soldiers marched from the battlefield refusing to believe they had been beaten. A report coauthored by Scharnhorst and Gneisenau on the night of 2/3 May confirmed this sentiment but stretched the truth concerning the events on the army's flanks: "After the victory on 2 May at Großgörschen, the Russo-Prussian army made a movement to the left [east] to resupply ammunition and to place itself in position to fight for a new victory. We were satisfied with taking the battlefield and leaving the enemy in possession of not a single piece of terrain that had been won. On both wings, we drove the enemy from the battlefield. A chivalrous spirit animated our warriors."[50] In an account Gneisenau provided for journalists, the gifted writer employed his propaganda skills, yet his conviction that the Allies actually won the battle is irrefutable:

> Around 7:00 P.M. a new enemy army corps appeared to our right of Großgörschen and Kleingörschen – probably part of the army of the viceroy – and for its part ferociously attacked, seeking one more time to rip from us the advantages we had won. Also, the enemy attacked the center and the villages one more time but our position held. In this situation, night brought an end to the battle. The enemy should have been attacked again on the following morning of 3 May. However, during the battle he had taken Leipzig, which forced us to maneuver with him. Only later we learned that because of the battle he had been forced to evacuate Leipzig; likewise because of the battle he lost Halle; 15,000 of his best troops were lost; many of his cannon were destroyed, a quantity of caissons were blown; our light detachments again have the freedom to inflict damage on him and to further increase the advantages we just won. Therefore, we held the battlefield, the victory is ours, and the objective achieved. And 50,000 of our best troops were not committed to the battle. We lost not a single gun, and the enemy must now be aware of what the combined national feeling of two very firmly allied peoples can do to generate resistance and fortitude and that the higher hand of Providence will protect the just cause of the powers, which want nothing but autonomy and a lasting peace based on the independence of every people. Thus was the struggle on 2 May in the vicinity of the plain of Lützen, where earlier in history the freedom of Germany had been fought.[51]

"The battle was essentially a draw," wrote Clausewitz on 3 May, "and it is still not certain whether we have done well to withdraw." Cathcart reported to London that "the Allies remained in possession of the field of battle and of the positions from which in the course of the day they had dislodged the enemy." Frederick William's congratulatory message to his corps commanders described the day of Großgörschen as a victory. According to Cathcart, Alexander also "spoke of the result as a victory gained on our side, and it was afterwards the fashion in the army to consider it as such." At Borna on the 3rd, Prince William delivered to Blücher the king's praise for the performance of the troops. A few days later, Blücher received Alexander's commendation accompanied by the Order of St. George, Second Class. On 6 May, he received another flattering letter from the tsar along with 300 St. George Crosses to be awarded to Blücher's officers and men.[52]

Despite any complaining from the Prussians about Russian leadership, the battle served to foster a sense of brotherhood between the Russian and Prussian troops. "Similarly," continued Cathcart, "the Russian soldiers have shown that in Germany they are fighting with the same spirit that gained them a victory in their homeland. In general, I cannot quite do justice to all the troops who fought on this memorable day in front of their sovereigns, their courage, and the order with which all the movements were executed under intense fire."[53] In his long account drafted solely for the newspapers, Gneisenau insisted that "the enemy witnessed at first hand the resoluteness and gallantry of the combined forces of two nations seized with ardent love for their Fatherlands and how mighty is the hand of Providence that protects the righteous cause of the great powers, which have no other intention than to deliver lasting peace and freedom to each nation."[54] The performance of both Allied contingents in the battle of Großgörschen raised the self-confidence of the Coalition, yet its outcome made it clear that a greater exertion of strength would be necessary to defeat Napoleon.[55]

## Notes

1 Holleben and Caemmerer, *Frühjahrsfeldzuges 1813*, II:49. In *Napoleon's Last Campaign*, 67–68, Petre unfairly criticizes Wittgenstein for omitting "all reference to the order of march of the columns before reaching and passing the Elster, the result of which was the crossing of columns and consequent delays." Wittgenstein's instructions for Yorck to be behind Blücher by 5:00 A.M. appear adequate; the slow march of Blücher's corps caused the collision. Droysen, in *Yorck*, II:57–58, criticizes Wittgenstein for ordering this march in the first place: "The disposition was completed only thirty minutes before midnight; it could not reach Blücher's headquarters at Rötha until around 1:00 A.M.; at least one more hour passed before the orders could be issued to the troops in the surrounding villages; the distances from Rötha to Storkwitz and Pegau are ten strong miles. Wittgenstein's headquarters should have known that 24,000 men cannot cover ten miles in three hours. Or did he calculate on Blücher, 'as a result of a preliminary notification', which was sent to him earlier in the evening, departing before receiving the disposition as was actually the case? Regardless, he had to know that a night march with 24,000 men, even if not rapid, was still doubly tiring and required halts." Caemmerer, in Holleben and Caemmerer, *Frühjahrsfeldzuges 1813*, II:48–49, asserts that, if Blücher had received the order to march in two columns while he was still at Rötha on the evening of 1 May, the collision and resulting delay could have been avoided, "but because Blücher received these instructions only in the Disposition and in the region of Pegau [on the morning of 2 May] this solution proved impossible; thus, the collision actually occurred." However, the author did find two copies of just such an order in Gneisenau's papers (GStA PK, VI HA Rep. 92 Nl. Gneisenau, Nr. 18, I, and Nr. 160), a rare oversight by the otherwise

thorough historians assigned to the Historical Section of the German General Staff. As for the Russians, the General Staff historian Bogdanovich, in *Geschichte des Krieges,* I:186 and 204–05, surprisingly follows Droysen verbatim, actually citing the German historian's account. Later, Bogdanovich castigates Wittgenstein: "The disposition was sent so late that its execution at the stated time was impossible and, moreover, the desire to place Blücher's corps in the front line gave such a direction to the Allied columns that they were bound to collide. This circumstance, combined with the late dispatch of the disposition, delayed the crossings of the Elster and the Floßgraben as well as the positioning of the troops in battle order for about four hours. Fortunately for the Allies, the French, because of the lack of good cavalry, remained in uncertainty over the [Allied] decision to attack." However, Mikhailovsky-Danilevsky, in *Denkwürdigkeiten,* 75, blames the blunder on the inefficiency of Blücher's headquarters: "The delay was caused when late on the previous evening the disposition was delivered to Blücher's headquarters where an official so deep in sleep received it and, although he registered the receipt of the dispatch, he put it under his pillow without first reading through it. Upon waking, he remembered that a dispatch had been delivered at night. He pulled out the envelope, found in it the disposition for the battle, and saw to his surprise that the commander in chief's appointed hour for departure had long since passed. This circumstance was the main reason why Count Wittgenstein's bold and well-established arrangements for the attack could not be executed with complete success." As for Mikhailovsky-Danilevsky's accusations, hindsight and the desire to exonerate Wittgenstein appear to be the motivation behind this account. Regarding the "official" who was so deep in slumber that he put the dispatch under his pillow, later in the war Gneisenau gained the reputation of sleep-working. Exhausted beyond description, he would often receive reports and issue instructions in the dead of night, having absolutely no recollection of his actions on the following morning. As for Blücher's headquarters being asleep on the night before the battle of Lützen, reports indicate that the general and his staff were on the road to Pegau by at least 1:00 A.M. on 2 May. Although this is a case of national pride with the Russian Mikhailovsky-Danilevsky basically blaming the defeat at Lützen on Blücher and the German Caemmerer countering with charges of faulty staff work on Wittgenstein's part, the story of the sleeping "official," while not completely impossible, is difficult to accept.

2 Campbell to Bunbury, Dresden, 7 May 1813, in Bunbury, *Memoir,* 320; Droysen, *Yorck,* II:57; Mikhailovsky-Danilevsky, *Denkwürdigkeiten,* 108; Bogdanovich, *Geschichte des Krieges,* I:173.

3 Tormasov's first column, commanded by the former chief of staff, Konovnitsyn, consisted of his own Grenadier Corps, General Nikolay Lavrov's Guard Infantry Corps, and the 136 guns of General Aleksandr Eyler's massive Reserve Artillery; this column would pass the Elster at Pegau and Stönsch. General Prince Dmitry Golitsyn V led the second, consisting of the cavalry (his own Cuirassier Corps and Light Guard Cavalry Division) to the bridge at Pegau. The third column, Gorchakov's, was to guard the Elster crossings at Werben, Storkwitz, Pegau, Stönsch, and Carsdorf. See Mikhailovsky-Danilevsky, *Denkwürdigkeiten,* 75–76; Henckel von Donnersmarck, *Erinnerungen,* 181; Plotho, *Der Krieg,* I:108–09.

4 Although Droysen utilized Yorck's *Tagebuch* (journal) in his research, he incorrectly claims that Berg had followed Yorck through Pegau. Caemmerer utilized the same *Tagebuch* to set the record straight.

5 Bogdanovich, *Geschichte des Krieges*, I:187–88; Plotho, *Der Krieg*, I:119; Beitzke, *Geschichte der deutschen Freiheitskriege*, I:367.

6 Add MSS, 20111, 22: Cathcart to Castlereagh, Dresden, 6 May 1813; Cathcart, *Commentaries*, 126; Petre, *Napoleon's Last Campaign*, 69–70.

7 Cathcart, *Commentaries*, 127.

8 Clausewitz, *Hinterlassene Werke*, VII:275.

9 Caemmerer states that evidence supporting Müffling's statement "can be found in the statements of various *Tagebücher*. The pedantry in this regard of our earlier army can hardly be imagined at the present. Yet, in 1866, we still saw the most remarkable cases of this kind": Holleben and Caemmerer, *Frühjahrsfeldzuges 1813*, II:336, n. 15.

10 The disposition is in Plotho, *Der Krieg*, I:113; Bogdanovich, *Geschichte des Krieges*, I:190–91; Mikhailovsky-Danilevsky, *Denkwürdigkeiten*, 76; Cathcart, *Commentaries*, 126–28.

11 Jomini, *Précis politique et militaire*, I:244. "It was evident from the first dispositions that the French army would not try their strength in the field which was sought for by their opponents": Campbell to Bunbury, Dresden, 7 May 1813, in Bunbury, *Memoir*, 321.

12 Steffens, *Adventures*, 96.

13 Lieven, *Russia Against Napoleon*, 315.

14 Cathcart, *Commentaries*, 129–30.

15 Lanrezac, *Lützen*, 149; Gneisenau, *Blücher*, 86.

16 Norvins, *Portefeuille de mil huit cent treize*, I:271; Odeleben, in *A Circumstantial Narrative*, I:45–47 incorrectly claims that Ney never left Kaja.

17 Jomini, *Précis politique et militaire*, I:242; Napoleon is quoted in Atteridge, *Ney*, 247; Macdonald, *Souvenirs*, 197. Around noon, the 31st and 36th Divisions of Macdonald's XI Corps stood between Gärnitz and Seebenisch, three miles south of Markranstädt. The 35th Division and the I Cavalry Corps had escorted Eugene to Schönau, which today is part of Leipzig's urban sprawl. Had Napoleon issued these orders immediately after the noon hour, Eugene and the cavalry could have reached the 31st and 36th Divisions in one hour, and then comfortably covered the five miles between Seebenisch and Eisdorf in two hours, placing the viceroy on the enemy's right wing between 3:30 or 4:00 – long before the Allies were prepared for such a measure – rather than between 6:00 and 7:00, the hour at which the viceroy actually arrived.

18 Atteridge, *Ney*, 247.

19 Quoted in Jomini, *Précis politique et militaire*, I:246.

20 "Tagebuch des Füsilierbataillons des 1. Garderegiment zu Fuß über die Feldzüge 1813 und 1813, geführt von Kommandeur M. von Block," GStA PK, IV Rep. 15a Nr. 359; Fritz to Charlotte, Dresden, 5 May 1813, Griewank, *Hohenzollernbriefe*, Nr. 26, 45–46; Natzmer, *Aus dem Leben*, 135; Henckel von Donnersmarck, *Erinnerungen*, 183–84.

21 Mikhailovsky-Danilevsky, *Denkwürdigkeiten*, 77.

22 Bulletin de la Grande Armée, Lützen, 2 May 1813, *CN*, No. 19951, XXV:260; Norvins, *Portefeuille de mil huit cent treize*, I:274; Lanrezac, *Lützen*, 150.

23 Parkinson's colorful and entertaining account of Lützen, particularly the sweeping cavalry charges led by Blücher, simply cannot be supported by the authoritative sources. Parkinson offers little documentation to support his interpretation of the battle. See Parkinson, *Hussar General*, 110–15.

24 Steffens, *Adventures*, 97; Hüser, *Aus dem Leben des Generals Hüser*, 112.

25 "Gneisenaus Bericht für den Korrespondenten," in Pertz and Delbrück, *Gneisenau*, II:718; Droysen, *Yorck*, II:61; Henckel von Donnersmarck, *Erinnerungen*, 183.

26 Wilson, *Private Diary*, I:355; Gneisenau, *Blücher*, 87; Pertz and Delbrück, *Gneisenau*, II:590; Campbell to Bunbury, Dresden, 7 May 1813, in Bunbury, *Memoir*, 320; "Memorandum of the Battle of Lützen, Fought on 2 May 1813," Rochlitz, 2 May 1813, in Wilson, *Private Diary*, I:360; Clausewitz to Marie, Proschwitz by Meißen, 3 and 8 May 1813, in Schwartz, *Clausewitz*, II:79–80.

27 Gneisenau, *Blücher*, 88; Clausewitz to Marie, 3 May 1813, in Schwartz, *Clausewitz*, II:79; Odeleben, *A Circumstantial Narrative*, I:54–55.

28 In addition, it is very likely that Miloradovich halted his march to Zeitz for some time. According to his journal, the corps departed Altenburg around 3:00 A.M. but took fourteen hours to cover fifteen miles. It is quite conceivable that Miloradovich, on receiving Yuzefovich's report from 1 May, halted at the fork in the road at Meuselwitz (halfway between Altenburg and Zeitz) and sent to Wittgenstein for final instructions as to whether he should march to Predel or Zeitz. See Holleben and Caemmerer, *Frühjahrsfeldzuges 1813*, II:51, 76.

29 Marmont, *Mémoires*, V:22–24. Lieven, *Russia Against Napoleon*, 316, disagrees, claiming that Miloradovich's presence "would not have altered the outcome." Regardless of hypothetical scenarios, it was the perception shared by the Prussians that counted the most in regards to the internal harmony of the Coalition.

30 On 3 May, Mikhailovsky-Danilevsky accompanied Volkonsky to Miloradovich's headquarters to deliver Wittgenstein's verbal instructions for his corps to form the rearguard of the Allied army. Mikhailovsky-Danilevsky claims that, when he was alone with Miloradovich, the Russian general revealed: "'Yesterday, I cried like a child, because for the first time in my life, upon hearing the sound of the guns, I did not participate in the battle. If I am not trusted with an army, then let me have a battalion or a company. Although Count Wittgenstein was always junior to me in rank and often was under my command, I am willing to serve not only under his command, but under that of anyone else.' These words, whose importance only military personnel can properly appreciate, sufficiently refute the rumors that were spreading in the army which, even until now, many still believe: that during the battle Miloradovich received the order to appear on the battlefield and did not follow it, but instead maintained that the presence of his corps at Zeitz was absolutely necessary": quoted in Mikhailovsky-Danilevsky, *Denkwürdigkeiten*, 82.

31 Bogdanovich, *Geschichte des Krieges*, I:194–95; Mikhailovsky-Danilevsky, *Denkwürdigkeiten*, 78; Henckel von Donnersmarck, *Erinnerungen*, 183.

32 Jomini, *Vie politique et militaire de Napoléon*, IV:283.

33 Wittgenstein to Alexander, 3 May 1813, RGVIA, f. VUA, op. 16, d. 3926, ll. 77–79b.

34  Cathcart, *Commentaries*, 132.

35  Steffens, *Adventures*, 97; Berthezène, *Souvenirs militaires*, II:237.

36  Much disagreement over when Scharnhorst received his wound can be found in the sources, with many historians incorrectly placing the time much earlier in the day. According to Scharnhorst's own report, written on the night of 2/3 May, he was wounded between 6:00 and 7:00: "Schreiben eines Officiers vom Blücherschen Korps über die Schlacht bei Großgörschen," Altenburg, 3 May 1813, in Pflugk-Harttung, *Das Befreiungsjahr 1813*, Nr. 98, 123. Scharnhorst and Gneisenau dictated this to the former's secretary, Feldjäger Greulich; Scharnhorst made the corrections. See Pertz and Delbrück, *Gneisenau*, II:715.

37  Clausewitz to Marie, 3 May 1813, in Schwartz, *Clausewitz*, II:79; "Schreiben eines Officiers vom Blücherschen Korps über die Schlacht bei Großgörschen," Altenburg, 3 May 1813, in Pflugk-Harttung, *Das Befreiungsjahr 1813*, Nr. 98, 123–24.

38  "Memorandum of the Battle of Lützen, Fought on 2 May 1813," Rochlitz, 2 May 1813, in Wilson, *Private Diaries*, I:359.

39  Yorck's report is quoted in Droysen, *Yorck*, II:62; "Schreiben eines Officiers vom Blücherschen Korps über die Schlacht bei Großgörschen," Altenburg, 3 May 1813, in Pflugk-Harttung, *Das Befreiungsjahr 1813*, Nr. 98, 123.

40  "If even an advantage could have been gained by the Allies in battle on the following day," judged Cathcart, "which under existing circumstances was a contingency scarcely possible against an enemy so superior in numbers, and in possession of Wittenberg, Torgau, and Magdeburg, it is certain that the French, having the shortest and most direct road through Leipzig to Dresden open before them, would, if they gained the start, have possessed themselves inevitably of the Allied line of operations, intercepted their reserves and supplies, and effected the complete discomfiture of the Allied army by a movement which, while it gave Napoleon possession of Saxony, left Prussia and Silesia at his mercy": Cathcart, *Commentaries*, 133.

41  Unger, in *Blücher*, II:26, and Görlitz, in *Fürst Blücher von Wahlstatt*, 244, claim that the Russian cavalry refused to participate without the tsar's permission, which could not be secured in time.

42  Sources for the battle of Lützen include: Wittgenstein to Alexander, 3 May 1813, RGVIA, f. VUA, op. 16, d. 3926, ll. 77–79b; Add MSS, 20111, 22: Cathcart to Castlereagh, Dresden, 6 May 1813; Gneisenau to Caroline, Meißen, 6 May 1813, GStA PK, VI HA Rep. 92 Nl. Gneisenau, Nr. 18; Clausewitz to Marie, 3 May 1813, in Schwartz, *Clausewitz*, II:80; Plotho, *Der Krieg*, I:114; Jomini, *Précis politique et militaire*, I:241–49; Holleben and Caemmerer, *Frühjahrsfeldzuges 1813*, II:51–76; Cathcart, *Commentaries*, 126–33; Odeleben, *A Circumstantial Narrative*, I:44–57; Petre, *Napoleon's Last Campaign*, 75–76; Mikhailovsky-Danilevsky, *Denkwürdigkeiten*, 76–82; Bogdanovich, *Geschichte des Krieges*, I:192–203; Henckel von Donnersmarck, *Erinnerungen*, 182–83; Beitzke, *Geschichte der deutschen Freiheitskriege*, I:375–82; Pertz and Delbrück, *Gneisenau*, II:584–87; Görlitz, *Fürst Blücher von Wahlstatt*, 243–45; Lanrezac, *Lützen*, 146–53; Vaudoncourt, *Histoire de la guerre*, 77–79; Marmont, *Mémoires*, V:26; Droysen, *Yorck*, II:60–67; Atteridge, *Ney*, 245–50.

43 Jomini, *Précis politique et militaire*, I:243.
44 Holleben and Caemmerer, *Frühjahrsfeldzuges 1813*, II:42, 47; Caemmerer, *Die Befreiungskriege*, 23; Maude, *Leipzig Campaign*, 109–10; Rahden, *Wanderungen eines alten Soldaten*, I:69.
45 Gneisenau to Caroline, Meißen, 6 May 1813, GStA PK, VI HA Rep. 92 Nl. Gneisenau, Nr. 21.
46 Bogdanovich, *Geschichte des Krieges*, I:206.
47 Wittgenstein to Alexander, 3 May 1813, RGVIA, f. VUA, op. 16, d. 3926, ll. 77–79b, emphasis added; Campbell to Bunbury, Dresden, 7 May 1813, in Bunbury, *Memoir*, 323.
48 Jomini, *Précis politique et militaire*, I:249.
49 Quoted in Henckel von Donnersmarck, *Erinnerungen*, 186–87.
50 Cathcart, *Commentaries*, 135; Scharnhorst and Gneisenau, "Nachricht von der Schlacht am 2 Mai auf der Straße von Weißenfels nach Leipzig" or "Schreiben eines Officiers vom Blücher'schen Corps," in Pertz and Delbrück, *Gneisenau*, II:716.
51 "Gneisenaus Bericht für den Korrespondenten," in Pertz and Delbrück, *Gneisenau*, II:719–20.
52 Clausewitz to Marie, 3 May 1813, in Schwartz, *Clausewitz*, II:80; Gneisenau to Merckel, Gumschütz, 13 May 1813, *Briefe des Generals Neidhardt von Gneisenau*, ed. Pflugk-Harttung, Nr. 93, 124; Add MSS, 20111, 21: Cathcart to Castlereagh, Dresden, 6 May 1813; Droysen, *Yorck*, II:66; Frederick William to Blücher, Groitzsch, 3 May 1813, *Blücher in Briefen*, ed. Colomb, 29; Alexander to Blücher, Dresden, 5 May 1813, in Blasendorff, *Blücher*, 192.
53 Add MSS, 20111, 21: Cathcart to Castlereagh, Dresden, 6 May 1813.
54 Gneisenau's report for the correspondents, in Pertz and Delbrück, *Gneisenau*, II:717–19.
55 Unger, *Blücher*, II:29.

# 6

## The Elbe

Around 2:00 A.M. on 3 May, Miloradovich received orders to march seven miles northeast along the right bank of the Elster from Zeitz to the village of Predel. There he would unite with Duke Eugen's II Infantry Corps to form the rearguard of the Allied army as it retreated from Lützen. After requisitioning several wagons from the nearby villages to use to transport his infantry and having kept his corps in a state of readiness throughout the night, Miloradovich immediately began the march. His main body reached Predel, less than five miles southwest of Pegau, at daybreak. For the retreat on the 3rd, Wittgenstein divided the Allied army into two columns based on nationality: on the left, the Prussians marched to Borna while the Russians withdrew to Frohburg on the right. After the French pulled out of Leipzig, Kleist's Cossacks reoccupied the city on the 3rd, but Wittgenstein's orders to retreat prompted them to follow the rest of the corps through Wurzen and across the Elbe by way of the pontoon bridge at Mühlberg. Bülow, who had driven the French from Halle on the 2nd, retreated across the Elbe to cover Berlin.

Numerous wagons carried the wounded from Pegau through Groitzsch on the road to Borna. Further east, the Russian parks and baggage proceeded along the Penig–Freiberg road to Dresden. Again, faulty Russian staff work plagued the operation. As for issuing instructions to the corps commanders, Volkonsky relied on Auvray to determine the direction of the retreat while Auvray believed Volkonsky would arrange the details of the march and so did nothing. This blunder and the overlooking of many details rendered an orderly retreat from the battlefield impossible. "At the very first step the instability of the duality of command was proven," judges Bogdanovich. "Had the bravery and perseverance of the Allies on 2 May not made such a deep impression on the enemy," explains Caemmerer, "the aimlessness of the departure certainly would have had evil consequences. As it was, they found time to gradually solve even this difficult task."[1]

To reach Borna, the Prussians should have crossed the Elster at Pegau while the Russians utilized the crossing further south at Predel (see Map 5). Instead, to move the Russian Guard and Reserve across the Elster as quickly as possible, the Russians crossed at Pegau and the Prussians at Predel. This arrangement would have sufficed had the Russians formed the left wing column and continued due east to Borna while the Prussians marched on the right likewise due east to Frohburg. As it stood, the columns would not be able to continue marching on the other side of the Elster without colliding. To further confound the situation, Wintzingerode led his cavalry to Zeitz apparently without orders. This act, combined with his inexplicable conduct in the battle, led to his removal from command of the cavalry.

Crossing the Elster at Pegau, the main mass of the Russian army trooped southeast through Groitzsch and Lucka to the vicinity of Altenburg and then curved north through Windischleuba to Frohburg, a stretch of twenty-seven miles. As a result of the Russians marching southeast, the Prussians likewise traversed the road through Windischleuba to Frohburg. Commanding all Prussian troops in place of the wounded Blücher, Yorck crossed the Floßgraben during the night, leaving behind a strong rearguard consisting of the Kolberg Infantry Regiment, sixteen squadrons, and part of Wintzingerode's cavalry. At dawn, this rearguard followed the road to Frohburg, where the last units did not arrive until early on the 4th. The Russian and Prussian columns collided several times, and the majority of the Prussians never reached Borna. During the course of the 3rd, Alexander ordered the Russian cavalry to follow the baggage on the Chemnitz–Freiberg road to Dresden. Rather than unite all Prussian and Russian cavalry for rearguard duty, only one cavalry brigade and General Vasily Ilovaysky XII's Cossacks received the task of attacking the right flank of any French force that crossed the Elster. The condition of the Allied army left much to be desired. Disordered throngs of soldiers sought to make their way east as best they could. To the great credit of the Russian and Prussian officers, they speedily reorganized their units, completely restoring the order of battle by the 4th.[2]

Napoleon's failure to harass the retreat – let alone his inability to launch a devastating pursuit – greatly aided the Allies. Russian and Prussian troops remained on the battlefield until as late as 9:00 A.M. on 3 May. Gneisenau reported seeing nothing of the enemy at this hour. Thus, the Russians completed their crossing at Pegau without encountering any French resistance other than isolated packets of skirmishers. Forming the rear of the Russian column, Eugen of Württemberg's II Infantry Corps took a position east of the defile at Groitzsch. He held this post until late afternoon, at which time he departed through Lucka after learning of the approach of Lauriston's V Corps from Zwenkau. Miloradovich likewise did not have to defend his position on the left bank of the Elster. Unmolested, he followed the army toward Frohburg, halting east of Lucka; his patrols found Leipzig free of the French. All Russian troops along with Yorck's I Corps and two of Blücher's brigades passed the night of 3/4 May at Frohburg; Blücher spent the night at Borna with his 2nd Brigade, Reserve Cavalry, and the parks.

While Blücher remained separated from the main mass of Prussian troops, Yorck retained command of both Prussian corps. Gneisenau joined Yorck's headquarters as the ranking officer of the General Staff. At Frohburg on the 4th, Yorck spent considerable time reorganizing the Prussian troops and then led the army to Colditz, where Blücher had already arrived with Zieten's 2nd Brigade and Dolffs's Reserve Cavalry. As a rearguard, Blücher posted Lieutenant-Colonel Andreas Georg von Katzler at Borna with six squadrons supported by one battalion and a half-battery. A competent cavalry commander, Katzler executed successful counterattacks at Löbstedt and Borna against the head of Macdonald's pursuing column.

Meanwhile, Napoleon returned to Lützen around 10:00 on the night of 2 May. One hour later, Berthier issued the emperor's instructions for Eugene. Napoleon specified that his stepson be on horseback by 3:00 on the morning of the 3rd to lead the 35th Division of XI Corps in "strong pursuit of the enemy" by 4:00 A.M. After Imperial Headquarters learned on the 3rd that neither friendly nor enemy forces held Leipzig, Berthier instructed Lauriston to occupy the city with one battalion until one of Ney's divisions arrived. Lauriston also received the task of obtaining news over Bülow and Kleist: "Please send me the news that you have of the enemy and anything you can find out at Leipzig. The emperor wants to know what became of the small corps that was at Halle, what became of the one at Dessau, and what is between Leipzig and Torgau." Ney's III Corps needed a day to rest and reorganize after the bashing it had sustained on the 2nd. Thus, Ney received the light tasks of transferring his headquarters to Lützen, guarding the defiles leading to Weißenfels, and dispatching patrols to Leipzig. Later in the day, Berthier changed this last directive, informing the marshal of the emperor's wish for him to dispatch one division to Leipzig. In addition, the staff chief communicated Napoleon's impatience over Ney's sloppy staff work: in this case, the failure to submit a requested status report concerning the condition of his corps.

Leaving Ney's battered corps to reorganize at Lützen, Napoleon departed at daybreak to inspect the battlefield. Finding his battalions still formed in squares hardly provided the picture of a victorious army. Odeleben notes that "the field hospitals were in a dreadful state of activity, and near the villages of Rahna and Kaja, almost the entire surface of the ground was strewn with dead ... the majority being French." Regardless, the emperor received "the lively acclamations of the troops ... He reviewed several brigades and minutely examined the position of the preceding day." For several hours, the emperor remained by the bivouac of the Old Guard near Großgörschen awaiting Eugene's report concerning Allied activity on the left wing near Leipzig. Wittgenstein's rearguard remained in sight on the hills near Pegau, and Miloradovich's troops could be seen to the south. Riding to the Monarchenhügel, Napoleon directed the army to move across the Elster at Zwenkau, Pegau, Predel, and Ostrau. Fatigue caused the pursuit to start late and proceed sluggishly. Thankful for what he later termed an "unexpected victory," the emperor sought to reenergize his troops, whose performance did earn his respect. "If victory raises the morale of the victor," explains Colonel Lanrezac, "it spreads among them at the same time an extreme desire to rest, which was echoed by officers of the highest rank. The commander in chief needs much character to go against popular opinion and force the army to resume its march immediately."[3]

Aside from some minor skirmishing with Miloradovich's rearguard, the French met no resistance. Yet, physically exhausted from days of marching and mentally drained by the battle on the previous day, they did not venture too far from the banks of the Elster. On the left wing, V Corps marched to Zwenkau while in the center Eugene led XI Corps and I Cavalry Corps across the Elster at Pegau, covering only five miles before halting at Podelwitz. Marmont just barely moved VI Corps across the Elster, reaching Löbnitz–Bennewitz, west-southwest of Macdonald's XI Corps. On the right wing, not only did Bertrand find Predel's bridge destroyed, but he also found the Russians. Delayed by Miloradovich's troops, IV Corps managed to get across the Elster at Ostrau but went no further. Behind the army, XII Corps reached Jena. During the course of the 3rd, Imperial Headquarters moved to Pegau, where Napoleon passed the night.[4]

After the horrors of the Russian campaign and the retreat from the Vistula to the Elbe in 1813, Napoleon needed to politically exploit his victory to the fullest extent. During the height of the struggle at Großgörschen, he dispatched messengers to Paris, Vienna, Kraków, and Constantinople with news of victory. To his brother Jerome, he wrote: "My brother, your aide found me on the battlefield, pursuing the enemy, whom my army completely defeated yesterday. The emperor of Russia and king of Prussia commanded in person: their Guards have been crushed." The language he employed in his 3 May "Proclamation to the Army" contains a clear political message concerning the fate of Europe should the Coalition triumph:

> Soldiers, I am pleased with you! You have fulfilled my expectations! You have furnished all of your goodwill and bravery. On the celebrated day of 2 May, you defeated and routed the Russian and Prussian army, commanded by Emperor Alexander and the king of Prussia. You have added fresh luster to the glory of my Eagles; you have shown everything that French blood is capable of achieving. The Battle of Lützen will rank above the battles of Austerlitz, Jena, Friedland, and the Moskova [Borodino]. In the previous

campaign, the enemy found refuge against our arms according to the methods of his fierce barbarian ancestors: the armies of the Tartars burned their countryside, their cities, and even holy Moscow itself. Preceded by all the bad subjects and deserters of Germany, France, and Italy, they have arrived in our region to preach rebellion, anarchy, civil war, and murder; they are the apostles of all crimes. It is clear that they want to start a fire between the Vistula and the Rhine for, according to the custom of their despotic governments, they will lay waste to the land between us and them. Fools! They know little of the attachment the Germans have to their sovereigns, of the wisdom, the spirit of order, and the common sense of the Germans. They know little of the power and bravery of the French.

In a single day, you have thwarted all of these parricidal plots. We will drive back the Tartars to their horrible climate; they should not have left it. They will remain in their frozen desert, living in slavery, barbarism, and corruption, where man is reduced to the level of beasts! You have earned the gratitude of civilized Europe. Soldiers: Italy, France, and Germany give you thanks![5]

The intelligence Napoleon received on the night of 3/4 May alleviated his uncertainty over his next move and the direction taken by the Allies. According to the reports, the enemy army retreated in two columns through Colditz and Rochlitz toward Dresden. Although they were marching in good order, the defeat impacted the spirit of the Coalition more than expected. A misunderstanding now arose between the Russians and the Prussians, who blamed each other for the loss of the battle. In view of this information, Napoleon decided to transfer his headquarters to Borna on the 4th to "strongly pursue the enemy." Writing to Ney at 4:00 on the morning of the 4th, he directed all of III Corps to Leipzig and placed Reynier's VII Corps, which at that time consisted only of the 32nd Division (3,000 men) at Merseburg, under the marshal's command. Ney also received command of Victor's II Corps, which reached Bernburg on the Saale. After Napoleon reached Borna, he would decide whether or not to proceed to Dresden. Should he go to the Saxon capital, Ney's army group would remain on his left. As for his tasks, Ney first would relieve Torgau, plucking between 6,000 and 7,000 Saxons from its garrison to form an additional division for VII Corps. From Torgau he would proceed to Wittenberg, where he would unite with General Horace-François Sébastiani, who was en route up the Elbe from Lüneburg with the 10,000 men of General Jacques-Pierre Puthod's 17th Division and the 4,000 sabers of II Cavalry Corps. According to the emperor, II, III, VII Corps and II Cavalry Corps would provide Ney with "a very fine army." Napoleon explained that the presence of this army at Wittenberg "will allow me, based on the subsequent information I receive, either to limit myself to the Elbe or to debouch through Wittenberg and move immediately on Berlin. But I cannot fix my thoughts on this because I do not know the exact status of your corps; send me precise information."[6]

At 4:00 A.M., on 4 May, Berthier likewise penned a letter to Ney, requesting the names of all generals and colonels killed or wounded in the battle, an update on the condition of his artillery, and a report on the overall status of the corps, which the marshal had still neglected to submit. He communicated the emperor's belief that the enemy army had retreated to the Elbe and that nothing stood in front of Ney except Cossacks. Thus, Napoleon wanted Ney to leave behind at Lützen the supplies necessary to care for the wounded and to enter Leipzig that day "with as many soldiers as possible in their full dress uniforms and with as much military pomp as possible." Berthier also summoned the reinforcements in the rear of the army, directing one cavalry division and one Bavarian brigade of Young Guard infantry from Naumburg to Pegau. He also ordered Oudinot's XII Corps and 37th Division, which consisted of Westphalians, to march from Naumburg to Zeitz. To the rest of the army, Berthier expressed Napoleon's desire for news of the Allies. Bertrand's IV Corps would push "strong" patrols east to Borna as well as south toward Zeitz and Altenburg to cover Oudinot's approach. Later in the day, Berthier directed IV Corps to Frohburg, six miles south of the emperor's headquarters at Borna. At the head of the army, Eugene led XI Corps and I Cavalry Corps to Borna while V Corps took a position seven miles to the north at Rötha to cover the viceroy's march. Marmont likewise received Borna as the destination for VI Corps. Ney led the rest of III Corps and the sole division of VII Corps to Leipzig, entering the city on the 4th with all the pomp that the shell-shocked survivors of Lützen could muster.[7]

Despite telling Ney that he would determine his next step from Borna, Napoleon made up his mind before departing Pegau. Eugene's 7:00 A.M. report from Borna that the Allies were retreating toward Rochlitz proved to be the catalyst. "The losses of the enemy have been enormous," wrote Napoleon to Ney at 9:00 A.M. "Here [Pegau] we found the body of the prince of Hessen-Homburg; I will have him buried with the honors his rank deserves. It is rumored that one of the Prussian princes was wounded. Despair is in the hearts of the Prussians. I march on Dresden. Because General Sébastiani has 4,000 cavalry, it is possible that I will have you march on Berlin to anticipate the enemy; but, of course, as soon as I have more specific information."[8]

On 4 May, Napoleon continued to laud his victory to reassure allies and intimidate any who considered betraying him. His father-in-law, Kaiser Francis, stood atop that list. Mindful not to offend his fellow emperor, Napoleon quaintly stated that Providence had granted the victory of his arms on the fields of Lützen. However, his tune changed in a letter to King Frederick of Württemberg: "the king of Prussia and the emperor of Russia, with Wittgenstein's Russian army of between 150,000 and 200,000 men, including 30,000 cavalry, attacked me at the village of Kaja at 6:00 on the morning of the 2nd. I defeated them completely with my infantry; I pursue with sword in hand and the viceroy has reached Borna. The Prussian Royal Guard was destroyed, that of the emperor of Russia suffered much; the Russian cuirassier regiments were crushed; I calculate the loss of the enemy at 25,000 to 30,000 men. It is said that many princes of the house of Prussia were wounded; I have just buried the prince of Hessen-Homburg." Although Napoleon was notorious for exaggerating his enemy's numbers and understating his own for numerous reasons ranging from political to psychological, the majority of these statements were outright lies. "With only a third of my army," he concluded, "I won this victory against all the enemy's armies. I am not surprised, given the current poor composition of the Russian infantry. The emperor of Russia and the king of Prussia head to Dresden, and I pursue them; this will lead to the Vistula. So many hopes of change and upheaval shattered!"[9]

Scharnhorst accompanied the king's headquarters to Dresden so he could draft measures to complete the Prussian army's mobilization and arrange for the strong defense of Berlin. With tireless energy, he proceeded with the business of acquiring military supplies, provisioning the troops, and advising the king. After a full day of work on the 7th devoted "to the completion of our combat forces," he informed Gneisenau that the British had at last delivered 10,000 muskets and artillery to Kolberg; 60,000 kilograms of powder had arrived from Austria as well as 20,000 muskets with an additional 10,000 en route. According to his calculations, the Silesian, Pomeranian, and Neumark Landwehr brigades would be completely armed. Only the Kurmark Landwehr required more than 10,000 muskets to complete its mobilization. Apparently, Frederick William refused to allow Silesia's surplus muskets to be sent to Berlin for use by the Kurmark militia. He decided that any British muskets that remained after arming the Pomeranian Landwehr would be forwarded to the capital. Artillery for the Kurmark Landwehr and defense of Berlin were to be *requested* from the fortress of Spandau.[10]

During meetings with Frederick William, Hardenberg, and Knesebeck on the 7th and 8th, Scharnhorst formally separated the defense of Berlin from the operations of Wittgenstein's army. Bülow's corps of 6,400 men and 24 guns would cover Berlin supported by the few combat-ready battalions of the Kurmark Landwehr, while the Berlin Landsturm guarded the inner city.[11] Moreover, the Prussian leadership decided that the Military Government between the Elbe and the Oder would determine how the Landwehr and Landsturm would cooperate with Bülow.[12] To assist and serve as a liaison between Bülow and the Military Government, Scharnhorst dispatched Colonel Boyen to Berlin. Finally, Frederick William issued a call for perseverance: "His Majesty is confident that the inhabitants of his capital will act with the greatest example of courage and sacrifice for the nation."

While not abandoning Berlin, this monumental decision to leave the capital to its own defenses would have a tremendous impact on both Allied and French operations. Napoleon in part based his plans on the belief that the Prussians would separate from the Russians to defend Berlin. Conversely, Frederick William's decision to continue to operate with the Russians provided a further sign that this coalition would be different from previous efforts against Napoleon, in which military strategy had fallen victim to politically motivated acts of national self-interest.[13]

Napoleon's weak pursuit, the French evacuation of Leipzig, and the numerous fugitives from Ney's III Corps who fell prey to the Cossacks sparked the rumor that the emperor had decided to retreat. Thus, on the afternoon of the 4th, Wittgenstein decided "to hold the position on the [Zwickauer] Mulde." The Allied commander in chief wanted the Prussians to make a stand at Colditz, and the Russians less than seven miles to the south at Rochlitz, with strong vanguards at Borna and Frohburg respectively. This came to naught after Wittgenstein changed his mind during the night of 4/5 May for reasons unknown. On the morning of the 5th, the Allied army continued its retreat. Wittgenstein's instinct served him well, as Napoleon finally launched his pursuit on 5 May. Had the Allies maintained the Colditz–Rochlitz line with their 55,000 men, they would have faced a French force of approximately 73,000 troops. It would have been extremely difficult for Wittgenstein to avoid a repetition of Friedland, particularly because his battle plans incorporated the use of the Zwickauer Mulde River.[14]

Napoleon began his work on 5 May with a severe tongue-lashing of his stepson at 2:00 A.M. "My cousin," starts Napoleon's instructions to Berthier, "write to the viceroy that he marches much too slow, that he takes up too much space, that he has compromised the march of the army, that he has too many wagons in his corps and there is no order, that the cavalry drags behind him, as usual, and that there is a lot of embarrassment and a lot of crippled men." The emperor wanted Eugene's troops to cover the eight miles between Bad Lausick and Colditz by noon, at which time Imperial Headquarters would reach the latter. In addition, he instructed Eugene to establish his headquarters as close as possible to Waldheim, some twenty miles east of Colditz. Unfortunately for Eugene, Berthier did not spare his feelings, repeating verbatim the emperor's harsh criticism. Napoleon sent IV Corps to Rochlitz and directed VI Corps to the Zwickauer Mulde between Colditz and Rochlitz. Should the Allies defend Colditz, Marmont would lead VI Corps across the Zwickauer Mulde to turn the enemy's position. Oudinot received instructions to march XII Corps to Altenburg. Berthier issued these orders at 3:00 A.M. on the 5th.

Two hours later, Imperial Headquarters dispatched directives for Sébastiani and Victor to unite with Ney as soon as possible. With "the bravest of the brave" being the more senior marshal, Victor received frank notice from Berthier that he now stood under Ney's command. To invigorate Victor, the staff chief informed him that the emperor had achieved "the most complete victory over the combined Russian and Prussian army commanded in person by the emperor of Russia and king of Prussia; overthrown at all points, the enemy left the battlefield covered with dead; he is in full retreat and we are exploiting our success." To further augment Ney's force, General Armand Philippon received instructions to post four battalions of his 1st Division at Magdeburg and join Sébastiani with his remaining twelve. In addition to moving up Victor and a reinforced Sébastiani on Ney's left, Napoleon pushed V Corps northeast toward Wurzen to investigate incorrect reports concerning the march of a large Prussian column on the Wurzen–Dresden road. As Ney's divisions commenced the 45-mile march northeast from Lützen to Torgau, Napoleon wanted V Corps in a position to protect the marshal's right flank. In the end, it was the retreat of Kleist's small Russo-Prussian corps that had given rise to this false alarm. Regardless, Napoleon expected the Russians and Prussians to separate sooner or later.[15]

Meanwhile, the Allied army continued to withdraw east in two masses: Blücher and the Prussians formed the northern columns with Wittgenstein and the Russians to the south. Blücher received orders to withdraw from Colditz to Döbeln, cross the Freiberger Mulde, and then proceed to the bridge over the Elbe at Meißen. Klüx's brigade held Colditz during the night of 4/5 May while Zieten's and Röder's brigades stood two and three miles respectively to the northeast at Collmen and Skoplau. Inexplicably, Blücher's Reserve Cavalry camped some seven miles east of Colditz at Leisnig. Two miles southeast of Colditz, Yorck's corps halted at Hausdorf. For the 5th, the army would continue east with Steinmetz's brigade forming Blücher's rearguard southeast of Colditz. The majority of Miloradovich's rearguard stood at Rochlitz on the left bank of the Zwickauer Mulde (see Map 5).

On the morning of 5 May, Eugene led XI Corps and I Cavalry Corps from Bad Lausick through Colditz toward Waldheim. East of him, Steinmetz's cavalry post withdrew through Colditz and burned the bridge over the Zwickauer Mulde. Eugene then turned north and forded the river one-half mile downstream. Steinmetz evacuated Colditz and attempted to reach Yorck's main body at Tautendorf but Eugene's rapid advance severed his column in two. While some battalions did reach Yorck at Tautendorf, the majority of Steinmetz's battalions withdrew through Schönerstädt under steady combat before being taken in at Gersdorf, two miles east of Schönerstädt, by the Russian 2nd Grenadier Division. South of Steinmetz, Miloradovich's superior handling of the Russian rearguard continued to intimidate and stymie Bertrand. Continuing his advance southeast from Colditz toward Waldheim, Eugene relieved the pressure on IV Corps by threatening to sever Miloradovich's line of retreat, thus forcing the Russians to fall back.[16]

Altogether, the Allies suffered approximately 550 casualties during this rearguard action, which nevertheless enabled the main columns to reach their objectives for 5 May. Steffens recalls:

> I remember once in the [Zwickauer] Mulde Valley, not far from Colditz, where the enemy had to cross the river, there was considerable confusion. Just when the confusion was the greatest, news arrived that the Russian general Miloradovich had been fiercely attacked. While I looked anxiously about, I perceived that Blücher and his suite were as calm as possible and that no movement was taking place, except that adjutants hastened backwards and forwards from him to the Russian general. It appeared to me that the heavy firing both of cannon and small arms was approaching fast, and I fancied every minute that the whole enemy army would burst upon us. I felt like a landsman in his first storm at sea looking with amazement at the composure of the sailors.[17]

With Eugene at Hartha, thirty-five miles west of Dresden, Napoleon moved to Colditz on the evening of the 5th and touted Eugene's engagement at Gersdorf as a victory over Miloradovich.[18] At the end of that day, IV Corps trooped into Rochlitz, VI Corps caught up with XI at the Zschopau River, a tributary of the Freiberger Mulde, while the Guard escorted Imperial Headquarters to Colditz. Reaching Altenburg behind the army, Oudinot drove his XII Corps to catch up with the rest of the army. Sending two divisions of III Corps to relieve Wittenberg, Ney continued the march to Torgau with his remaining divisions and VII Corps. Reports confirmed that the enemy column marching on Mühlberg belonged to Kleist and thus posed no threat. Based on this information, Berthier forwarded orders at 8:00 P.M. for Lauriston to force-march his soldiers along the highway that led through Wurzen to Dresden and for Oudinot to likewise continue his movement on Dresden.[19]

The reports that reached Napoleon during the 5th strongly suggested that the Allies had retreated toward Meißen and Dresden. He suspected they would stop running at Dresden and defend the right bank of the Elbe. With his bridge train two weeks behind at Erfurt, he feared a strong enemy stand that would prevent him from getting across the Elbe. Demonstrating his brilliant ability to adapt and master the situation, he speculated that he could fix the Allies at Dresden's *Neustadt* on the right bank and swing the majority of his forces fifty miles downstream to cross the river at Torgau.[20] For this reason, Ney received orders to reach Torgau "as soon as possible, because if the enemy wants to defend the right bank of the Elbe and be master of half of the city of Dresden [the *Neustadt*], His Majesty will take possession of the portion of the city on the left bank [the *Altstadt*] and maneuver to quickly cross at Torgau."[21]

Despite the favorable reports and Eugene's bold push, the situation made the emperor restless. He chastised his stepson for not doing more, especially because the hill country west of the Elbe negated the enemy's advantage in cavalry. His own lack of cavalry made it imperative that he remain in close contact with the Allies. If all their columns converged on Dresden, he feared they would escape unless his army could "rapidly arrive there at the same time." At 3:30 A.M. on 6 May, Napoleon directly expressed his anxiety to Ney. He complained about the marshal's apparent lack of progress and reiterated the importance of securing Torgau and Wittenberg "because the situation can change and make it very possible that I will immediately move on Berlin." Later on the 6th, he again wrote to Ney, urging him "to press the junction with Sébastiani" because the roads from the lower Elbe "should be open." He again reminded Ney that after uniting with Sébastiani and Victor, the marshal would command *une belle armée*, "which I want to see you lead to Torgau." To facilitate the "safe and fast" communication between Ney and Napoleon's eventual position at Dresden, the emperor instructed Ney to bridge the Zwickauer Mulde near Wurzen with boats.

For the present, Napoleon planned to continue pursuing the Russians. "I do not know if I can cross at Dresden," continues his letter to Ney. "I'm afraid if I try to cross I will encounter difficulties because I have *pontonniers* but no pontoons; they will not arrive for two weeks. If I don't have boats and if the enemy seriously defends the passage and exposes Dresden to the circumstances of war, I will have to go back to Torgau; but the presence of your army corps at Torgau should make an impression on the enemy and force him to renounce his plans to defend the Elbe." Certain that the Allies would defend the Elbe, Napoleon appeared convinced that he would not be able to cross at Dresden and thus would have to go to Torgau. Moreover, the emperor seemed torn between the idea of leading Ney's army to Berlin or having it maneuver his adversary away from the Elbe. With an estimated 135,000 men and 386 guns, Napoleon could fix the Allies in their suspected position on the Elbe while Ney's 65,000 men and 129 guns advanced east from Torgau to strategically envelop their right wing. At this point in his planning, the emperor did not reveal if he considered assigning this task to Ney.[22]

Early on the morning of the 6th, Napoleon executed the penultimate surge to the Elbe. At dawn, Eugene's men started marching "straight and rapidly" thirteen miles due east to Nossen. Marmont's VI Corps followed Eugene "without delay." Lauriston continued his sprint through Wurzen along the highway leading to Dresden. By marching "seven to eight leagues per day," Napoleon expected V Corps to reach Meißen – thirty-eight miles southeast of Wurzen – on the same day that the main body reached Wilsdruff. As for Bertrand, IV Corps marched in two columns from Rochlitz, with one moving across the Zschopau at Waldheim and the other further south between Waldheim and Mittweida. After crossing the river, it veered southeast toward Freiberg. As usual, Bertrand lagged behind and failed to make Freiberg.

Reports from spies informed Napoleon that, in addition to bickering, the Russians and Prussians had marched from the Zwickauer Mulde in *separate* columns. Bolstered by this news as well as various rumors, he hoped the Allies would split, as indicated by his statement to Ney that he would continue to pursue the Russians. As for the Prussians, he informed Ney "that the Prussian corps of 20,000 to 25,000 men appears to have retired on Meißen." Napoleon assumed the point of departure would occur on the right bank of the Elbe. As soon as the Allies crossed the river, he expected the Russians to continue their retreat on the great east–west highway that ran through Bautzen, Görlitz, and Breslau to Poland while the Prussians turned north with no more than 70,000 men to defend Berlin. Based on this assessment, he viewed Ney's presence at Torgau – eighty miles south of Berlin – as bait to lure the Prussians away from the Russians. As soon as they separated, Napoleon planned to mask the Russians and concentrate as much force as possible against the Prussians.[23]

That afternoon, Imperial Headquarters moved to Wurzen, where the intelligence reports arrived in the evening. These failed to confirm the separation of the Allies. As a result, Berthier instructed Lauriston to dispatch a local gendarme to investigate rumors that only 12,000 Prussians had retreated to Meißen while the remainder had accompanied the Russians to Dresden. Lauriston would follow with all of V Corps, seize Meißen, and force the enemy to cross the Elbe by 8 May. Purportedly, the Allies already had constructed several defensive works on the right bank but none on the left. "It is very important that you march rapidly," concluded Berthier's dispatch to Lauriston. Until further reports arrived, Napoleon decided that only Imperial Headquarters would proceed fifteen miles east to Nossen on the 7th.[24]

Returning to the Allies, the Prussian portion of the army continued the retreat to Meißen on 6 May. Morale remained high despite the fatigue. "The soldiers of the Prussian army," maintains Stewart, "had, at this crisis, a higher and more animated feeling [than the Russians]: they were fighting for their existence; and every mile, if in retreat, raised a murmur of discontent. Their state of discipline was good and their officers most efficient; their cavalry fine, and artillery excellent." Gneisenau reported to Hardenberg that "the soldiers do not believe they were defeated. Because of the poor supply situation, which arose through ignorance and lack of insight, a portion of the troops are exhausted. We will soon refresh them as much as we can. If you can do something about this situation it would have a good effect; perhaps send white bread, wine, etc. along the Elbe." Gneisenau also pushed for measures to reinforce the army: "If everyone works with effort to reorganize and increase combat power, I have no doubt whatsoever over the fate of this war." He mainly suggested that Prussian troops besieging French-held fortresses be relieved by Landwehr units. "The sieges must be raised and blockades established that can be assumed by the Landwehr. This would give us some twenty-four battalions. We found three battalions on the Elbe; we can now unite with General Kleist ... perhaps we will do the same with Bülow and Borstell. Altogether this would give us a force the same size as the one we possessed on the day of the battle while the enemy grows weaker. Under such circumstances, victory is certain. But all forces of the nation must be summoned and all must be employed."[25]

To cover the retreat of the Russians, Wittgenstein wanted both Prussian corps to remain in and around the portion of Meißen situated on the west bank of the Elbe. He believed their presence would give the appearance that the Allies intended to defend the river line. In such a dangerous position, Blücher withdrew his baggage and the majority of the infantry across the bridge. Two of Yorck's brigades (Steinmetz's and Klüx's) as well as the Reserve Cavalry of both corps remained in and west of Meißen. The Prussians hastily built redoubts to reinforce the weak position. On the morning of the 7th, Scharnhorst informed the king that the imperials would probably attack Blücher that day. He also took a swipe at Wittgenstein: "It is an unforgivable error of the commanding general to stand still for one day before the defile that he wants to cross on the next day. I fear that the Prussian corps is very exposed and has a defile behind it that is difficult to pass. In any case, the bridge at Meißen has to be crossed this night if we want to move behind the Elbe."[26]

After receiving this information, Frederick William immediately rode to Meißen but found Blücher in the process of evacuating the left bank after receiving instructions from Wittgenstein. The king inspected the defensive measures and issued a proclamation to reinvigorate the troops by assuring them of his satisfaction. He watched as the troops defiled across the bridge; their thinned ranks made a noticeable impression on the monarch. The crossing concluded early on the 8th, just as Lauriston's troops reached Meißen's suburbs. "When we halted on this side of the Elbe, near Meißen," explains Steffens, "the two armies were posted just out of reach of gun-shot but the outposts stationed on each bank of the river opposite each other frequently exchanged shots. We stood on a hill out of reach of the fire but near enough to observe how men on each side quietly leveled their pieces and took deliberate aim at individuals, and when a man fell we heard the shouts of joy. I felt firm while watching many fall in battle but this savage coolness filled me with horror."[27]

On the right bank, Blücher's main body camped on the hills north of Meißen at Proschwitz (see Map 5). After covering almost seventeen miles, Steinmetz's tired soldiers quartered in the portion of Meißen situated on the right bank of the Elbe. Food supplies ran low after the Russians confiscated several Prussian supply wagons. Southeast of Blücher, the Russian rearguard reached Dresden on the 8th, crossed the Elbe, and fortified Dresden's

*Neustadt*. Closely pursued but not pressed by the French, the Russians torched their two bridges and destroyed the wooden repairs made to the beautiful stone bridge damaged earlier in the year by Davout.[28] After Blücher wrecked the bridge at Meißen, the bridge at Mühlberg – guarded by Kleist – remained the only crossing available to the Allies. Thus, on 8 May, all Allied troops reached the right or eastern bank of the Elbe.[29]

At Meißen, Blücher and Scharnhorst parted ways for the last time. Despite his wound, Scharnhorst left for Vienna in the hope of accelerating Austria's declaration of war. Improper care of the wound led to his death in June. Frederick William appointed Gneisenau to replace Scharnhorst as Chief of the General Staff of the Prussian Army while Lieutenant-Colonel Müffling assumed Gneisenau's post as Blücher's quartermaster-general. Much more than Scharnhorst, Gneisenau stood close to Blücher in terms of attitude, aggressiveness, and temperament. For this reason alone, he never managed to provide the same service as his great predecessor.[30] For the Prussian General Staff to function properly, Scharnhorst proposed a military marriage of the seasoned, hard-hitting field commander and the erudite, conscientious chief of staff. In this way, Scharnhorst envisioned the relationship of commander and staff chief being governed by a system of checks and balances that would bring out the best of both for the leadership of the army. Yet the pairing of Blücher and Gneisenau represented the military marriage of two aggressive field commanders. Their relationship worked so well not because one's talents complemented the other's, but because of their similarities. Both fiercely hated Napoleon and both based success on battlefield results. A friendship based on mutual respect and support, the clear understanding of their respective roles, and intense patriotism characterized their working relationship. Blücher appreciated Gneisenau's superior abilities to plan and coordinate operations while the latter recognized the invaluable leadership qualities of the senior general. In this way, the pairing of Blücher and Gneisenau fulfilled Scharnhorst's vision of the military marriage between commander and staff chief. Gneisenau took the lead in planning and executing operations that Blücher either approved of on Gneisenau's suggestion or had himself demanded. For this reason, Blücher allowed Gneisenau a degree of autonomy, usually conferring his full support on the staff chief's ideas. Yet Gneisenau's rash, hot-headed, politically driven strategy could not compensate for the loss of Scharnhorst's exceptional grasp of operations, careful attention to every detail, and apolitical approach to coalition war fighting that earned him such high marks with allies. Gneisenau's shrill epistles to Allied Headquarters in 1813 and 1814, many of which Blücher signed, provided a marked contrast to Scharnhorst's careful considerations and superior understanding of operations. Conversely, lacking Scharnhorst's clout, acumen, and tact – not to mention Frederick William's trust – Gneisenau resorted to bullying to force the acceptance of "Blücher's" views by Allied Headquarters. Only the close relationship that Blücher eventually built with Tsar Alexander prevented disciplinary action from being taken against him and his rogue staff chief later in the war.

After crossing the Elbe, Wittgenstein possessed no clear idea of what to do next. Charles Stewart offers some explanation for this: "In addition to the celerity of movement that always distinguishes a French army, their possession of so many strong places [fortresses], both on the Elbe and on the Oder, gave them a peculiar facility and security of operations while the Allies were reduced to a state of fluctuating uncertainty and difficulty with respect to their communications, in whatever direction their movements might be carried on." Wittgenstein's uncertainty over whether Napoleon would advance through Dresden or on Berlin manifested itself in orders and counterorders. For example, Kleist received three different orders on the 5th followed by a fourth on the 6th.[31]

At Dresden on 7 May, Wittgenstein allotted considerable thought to basing the army on the lower Oder. "To be able to fall on the enemy with all forces" as soon as Napoleon had crossed the Elbe, he planned to take a position east of Torgau along a 25-mile line that ran southwest to northeast between Herzberg and Luckau.[32] This suggests that, unlike the late Kutuzov, Wittgenstein did not fear sacrificing the Russian main line of communication that ran through Silesia and Poland, nor did he worry about losing contact with Austria.[33] Underpinning the plan was his confidence in Saxony's continued neutrality and a certain naivety in thinking Napoleon would respect it, particularly the closure of Torgau. Moreover, from this flank position, the Allies could protect Berlin, which won the commander in chief support from some Prussians who did not want to see the tricolor again flying over their capital.

As for Blücher and his staff, they desired to operate along the great east–west highway that ran toward Silesia and the upper Oder. As long as the Oder fortresses north of Glogau remained in French hands, they felt the Allies could not abandon the highway nor allow Napoleon to maneuver them away from this vital artery. Should this occur, the Prussians predicted the army's destruction either on the banks of the Oder or along the Austrian frontier. Above all, the Prussians urged Wittgenstein to select a position that would allow the army to concentrate under any circumstances. Frederick William received requests to advocate these ideas at Allied Headquarters.

Wittgenstein's plan to defend the Elbe requires a brief explanation as it contributed to the growing discord between Blücher's headquarters and the Russians. Apparently, Wittgenstein hoped to catch the French army in the midst of crossing the river. Yet Herzberg – the southern end of Wittgenstein's proposed line – stood too far from the main points of passage, mainly fifty-five miles north of Dresden, forty-four miles north of Meißen, twenty miles north of Mühlberg, and fifteen miles northeast of Torgau.

To exploit the emperor's river passage, the Allied army needed to reach the crossing point before the main mass of the French army moved across. This would have been impossible based on the army's position along the Herzberg–Luckau line (see Map 5). To be fair to Wittgenstein, he may have wanted the majority of Napoleon's forces to get across the river to create the situation for a decisive encounter. However, the position between Herzberg and Luckau could prove fatal to the Allies if Napoleon crossed the Elbe at Dresden. From the Saxon capital, he would have uninhibited access to the closest road to the Oder. With Glogau, Küstrin, and Stettin all in French hands, the imperials could move down both banks of the Oder, threatening to envelop Wittgenstein's left while Ney's army closed on his right from Torgau. In this case, the Allied army would be forced to accept battle under conditions that favored Napoleon or to retreat north to the Baltic coast. "How he [Napoleon] would have sought and found the opportunity for his battle of annihilation," judges Caemmerer. "Had Wittgenstein moved north, then the decision would have come much faster; the struggle would have ended before Austria was ready."

Unfortunately for Napoleon, Wittgenstein's staff brought him to his senses in less than twenty-four hours. That same day, 7 May, he abandoned the Herzberg–Luckau plan and issued new instructions. Although supplemented and clarified on the 8th, they still raised eyebrows.[34] According to Wittgenstein, the Russians would defend the Elbe from Meißen upstream while the Prussians held the river from Meißen downstream. To execute this defense, the Russian main body marched ten and one-half miles northeast of Dresden to Radeberg while Blücher led the Prussians to Großenhain, ten and one-half miles north-northeast of Meißen. Kleist received orders to defend the bridge at Mühlberg so Allied patrols could still access the left bank of the Elbe. Wittgenstein instructed all Cossack regiments to carefully patrol the river line and immediately report any activity that appeared to indicate the enemy's attempt to cross the river. As Wittgenstein still intended to attack the French army while it crossed the Elbe, these arrangements made more sense but still contained inherent flaws. Admittedly, the Allies could easily reach the likely crossing points in their sectors as long as they received news of the French operation in a timely manner. However, what if Napoleon made numerous feints or attempted several crossings at once? What would prevent the Russians and Prussians from marching back and forth between their respective bases and the right bank of the Elbe each time imperial forces appeared on the left bank?

Gneisenau viewed the plan with even more skepticism, seeing it as the premature abandonment of a defensible river. In addition, one line in the disposition particularly irked Blücher and later drew Caemmerer's ire. Wittgenstein ordered the troops to collect large amounts of gabions and fascines for the construction of covered batteries at suspected crossing points along the Elbe. Extra teams of horses would be held ready to transport the gabions to the threatened point at a moment's notice. In his report to the king, Blücher calls these instructions "completely impracticable." Caemmerer, who shows no mercy in his evaluation of the Russian High Command, asserts that Wittgenstein's statement again clearly displays "the ambiguity of his tactical thinking. What could one expect of a counterattack on an enemy crossing a river when the field commander is concerned only with building batteries! This ambiguity corresponded to the leadership." In the end, Wittgenstein's growing awareness of Napoleon's numerical superiority caused him to lose heart, especially after the imperials drove Miloradovich from Dresden.[35]

As for the French on 7 May, Bertrand's IV Corps reached Freiberg on the right wing. In the center, Eugene with XI Infantry and I Cavalry Corps, closely followed by VI Corps, continued the march to Dresden after passing Nossen, where the emperor eventually arrived. Eugene's van reached Wilsdruff, thirteen miles west of the Saxon capital. On the left, Lauriston's V Corps continued to race toward Meißen. In the rear, Oudinot herded XII toward the Elbe. Reynier reached Torgau with VII Corps but Thielmann refused to admit the French without the express orders of Frederick Augustus. Before setting out for Nossen, the emperor again reminded Ney that the appearance of his *"belle armée"* on the other side of Wittenberg and Torgau would force the Allies to abandon the right bank of the Elbe.[36]

During the course of the day, locals informed the French that they had heard artillery from the direction of Meißen. Napoleon could not be sure what this meant or even if it was true. At the earliest, Lauriston's V Corps could not reach Meißen until that night.[37] However, reports again indicated that the majority of Prussian forces had retreated to Meißen, thus rekindling the hope that his adversaries had separated. Whatever the state of the Allies, Napoleon planned to enter Dresden's *Altstadt* on the following day. "Since the 2nd," he wrote to King Frederick of Württemberg, "we have pursued the enemy army, which burned all the bridges and did everything it could to delay my march. The Prussians have retreated on Meißen, the Russians on Dresden. There have been various rearguard combats at Gersdorf, Waldheim, Hartha, and Blankenstein where the enemy has lost many prisoners. All the villages along the road are filled with his dead and wounded. Tomorrow I plan to enter Dresden, at least the part of the city on this bank. The prince de la Moskova marches on Wittenberg to maneuver along the right bank."[38]

Napoleon planned to remain at Wilsdruff on the 8th. Odeleben recounts that, as the emperor approached that village, he learned that Eugene's vanguard had entered Dresden. To ensure a politically appropriate reception at the Saxon capital, Napoleon called for an adjutant to immediately go to Dresden and "bring the city's deputation to me; I have appointed General

[Antoine-Jean] Durosnel commandant of Dresden. Gallop all the way."
As Napoleon approached, black clouds rose on either side of the city,
marking the burning remains of the enemy's bridges. Not a single Allied
soldier could be found on the left bank and "the most profound tranquility
existed in the city." Alexander had purportedly left Dresden at 1:00 A.M.;
Frederick William sometime after sunrise. Meeting with the Saxon delegation about three miles east of Dresden, the emperor coldly demanded an
inordinate supply of bread, meat, and wine. One eyewitness claimed that
the scale "threatened to reduce to the worst extremities a city worthy of
compassion." After dismissing the Saxons, Napoleon rode toward the
"Pirna" suburb.[39] He traversed the ramparts of the city, making his way
to the smoldering remains of the Russian bridge. Driven downstream
by the wind and current, the burning and smoking bridge had settled
across the piers of Dresden's great stone bridge, which enabled the French
to save several of the boats.

At the Pirna suburb, Napoleon met with Eugene. The two solitary
figures standing in the open offered quite a target for the Russian posts on
the opposite heights. Concluding that the Elbe could not be crossed there,
Napoleon issued instructions for the procurement of boats, planks, and
laborers. He then left for Briesnitz, a village located three miles northwest
of Dresden on the left bank of the Elbe and opposite Übigau. There, he
found the burning remains of the Russian raft bridge. Although detached
from the left bank, it remained anchored to the right. As no enemy posts
could be detected, the French hopped into some small boats and extinguished the flames with the help of several Saxons. In this manner, they
saved approximately two-thirds of the bridge, which they towed to the left
bank. Napoleon immediately ordered the procurement of carpenters and
material to rebuild the bridge at that very spot.[40]

To cover the construction, VI and XI Corps and I Cavalry Corps moved
into Dresden's *Altstadt* along with the Guard and Imperial Headquarters.
On Napoleon's left wing, V Corps camped at Meißen while on the right, the
head of the slow-moving IV Corps reached Tharandt, ten miles southwest
of the Saxon capital. Always mindful of the threat posed by Austria,
the emperor issued orders for Bertrand to post one division twelve miles
southeast of Dresden at Pirna to observe the main highway to Bohemia.[41]
Napoleon also learned that Thielmann had refused to admit Reynier into
Torgau. Having no time for such nonsense, he decisively resolved the
situation. On the 8th, the emperor ordered the hapless Saxon king – now
at Prague – to immediately return to Dresden. Moreover, Frederick
Augustus would provide the Saxon troops assigned to Reynier's VII Corps
and order Thielmann to open the gates of Torgau. Should the king fail
to comply within forty-eight hours, Saxony would be removed from
the Rhinebund and treated as conquered territory. Just in case Frederick

Augustus secured Austrian support for Saxony's neutrality, Napoleon sent a member of the Saxon regency to Torgau with instructions for Thielmann to open the fortress to Reynier.[42]

At 11:00 P.M. on the 8th, Berthier notified the corps commanders that the army could remain in its current position for several days – only Lauriston should prepare for a possible march on 9 May. Consequently, the emperor expected them to rest their men in barracks and "above all provide good food." Berthier explained the need to obtain victuals from the countryside for several days but insisted that marauding be prevented. He advised the marshals and generals to keep their "troops well policed and well disciplined." Four hours later, at 3:00 A.M. on the 9th, Napoleon concluded his plan for the day's operation, which included crossing the Elbe at Dresden. He again lectured Ney on the importance of getting to Wittenberg and uniting his various corps. For the moment, VII Corps would remain at Torgau while the marshal crossed the thirty miles to Wittenberg. To support VII Corps, Lauriston left one division at Meißen and moved the rest of V Corps down the left bank of the Elbe to a position halfway to Torgau. He established communication with Ney and remained ready to march either to Torgau or Meißen.[43]

During the course of the 9th, Miloradovich attempted to hold Dresden's *Neustadt* but the French completed the raft bridge at Briesnitz. Two battalions covered by 100 guns crossed the Elbe in boats to drive off the Russians and establish a bridgehead at Übigau. French engineers also erected a *va-et-vient* (ferry pulled by cables) that transported cargos of 400 men across the river. The Russians responded with the furious cannonade of sixty guns firing from the wooded hills near Übigau. Napoleon established his command post near an abandoned powder magazine and personally directed the measures to drive the Russians from the right bank. He initially disapproved General Antoine Drouot's positioning of the guns north and south of Briesnitz, shaking his faithful servant by the ears. His anger gave way to a smile of satisfaction after he observed the effectiveness of the French artillery thanks to Drouot's knack for selecting battery positions. Several shots and shells fell by Napoleon; one shattered a plank of the powder magazine, sending a huge splinter whizzing by the emperor's head. Examining the shard, he told his suite that it easily could have put an end to him. A few minutes later, a shell exploded between the imperial entourage and an Italian regiment that stood twenty paces behind. After observing the Italians recoiling from the explosion, the emperor taunted them: "*Ha! Cujoni, non fa male* [Ha! Rascals, it will not hurt you]." With Russian shells falling too close, the imperial suite moved to a safer position.[44]

After sustaining 1,000 casualties, Miloradovich commenced his retreat on the road to Bautzen around 3:00 that afternoon. He had hoped to receive support from Blücher but the Prussian commenced his march to

Großenhain that same morning in accordance with Wittgenstein's orders. Around 5:30 P.M., a report from the Prussian officer attached to Miloradovich's staff reached Blücher, concerning French attempts to throw a bridge across the Elbe near Übigau. One hour later, a second Prussian officer arrived at Blücher's headquarters, now at Großenhain. He verbally reported that the French appeared to have the bridge at Übigau half completed. Miloradovich, whose manpower did not suffice to defend both the *Neustadt* and Übigau, requested that Blücher deploy his left wing to prevent the French from finishing their bridge at the latter. According to some sources, an actual order arrived from Wittgenstein to reverse the march and stop the French from crossing the Elbe at Übigau.[45]

On this day, Blücher's wound so pained and weakened him that the seventy-year-old needed rest. On the 9th and 10th, Blücher could be moved only in a carriage.[46] Signaling the start of a controversial expedient that frequently occurred at Blücher's headquarters during his bouts of illness, Gneisenau assumed command rather than the next senior general, Yorck. This breach of military protocol became known throughout the army, causing disgruntlement, but the otherwise pedantic king remained silent. Despite the king's apparent indifference, Gneisenau proceeded cautiously when issuing orders to the more senior Prussian corps commanders: Yorck, Kleist, and Bülow. In particular, Yorck expressed his dissatisfaction over this practice, not because he wanted to assume command of Blücher's army, but because he resented being commanded by a staff officer junior in rank to him. Gneisenau's assumption of army command during moments of Blücher's incapacity combined with the normal carte-blanche autonomy that the staff chief normally enjoyed became the source of severe internal problems in Blücher's armies, particularly in 1814 and 1815.

With the troops beginning to trickle into Großenhain, some twenty miles north of Dresden, Gneisenau could do little for Miloradovich other than put his quill to work. He reported to Wittgenstein that, although one Prussian brigade remained at Meißen, it could not cover the distance to Übigau in time to assist Miloradovich. Frustrated, he tersely noted that Wittgenstein ordered the Prussians to Großenhain. Now that they arrived there, it was "impossible" for them to support Miloradovich. He expressed his profound disgust that the Russians could not do more themselves. "Overall, I must judge that if Miloradovich, who is only thirty minutes from there [Übigau], and the Russian main army, which also is much closer than I, do not attempt to prevent this crossing, then nothing can be done to stop the passage." He informed the Allied commander in chief that to stop the French at Übigau, the Prussians would be forced to undertake a night march southeast to Radeburg. "If you intend to attack the enemy on the plain of Übigau immediately after his crossing, I will also march there and appear on your right wing in the battle. But if you do not intend to attack the enemy I will act according to circumstances."[47]

The tone of his letter clearly reveals the growing dissatisfaction in Blücher's headquarters over Wittgenstein's leadership. Undoubtedly, Blücher shared Gneisenau's thoughts on both the situation and the Russian execution of the war. To increase the pressure, Gneisenau tasked Natzmer with delivering the report and insisting on an answer as to whether Wittgenstein intended to seek battle on the 10th. Gneisenau also issued orders for the Prussian I and II Corps to commence the march to Radeberg at 2:00 A.M. on the 10th. He likewise took the initiative to send orders for Kleist to move closer to Blücher's main body. At 1:30 A.M. the Allied generalissimo's counterorder arrived; thirty minutes later came new orders sending the Prussians seventeen miles east to Königsbrück. Kleist's small corps would evacuate Mühlberg after destroying its bridge, form Blücher's rearguard, and proceed to Großenhain. From Radeberg, the Russians would withdraw thirteen miles east to Bischofswerda on the road to Bautzen (see Map 5). Wittgenstein decided to turn his back on the Elbe.

Miloradovich's inability to hold his ground or maintain Dresden's *Neustadt* on the right bank of the Elbe prevented Wittgenstein from launching a counterattack from Radeberg. Wittgenstein could have overcome the loss of Dresden had he possessed fortitude. Based on the load-carrying capacity of a pontoon bridge in 1813, no more than 40,000 imperial soldiers could have crossed the Elbe by the morning of the 11th. These in turn would have been obliged to radiate outward to allow the troops following them to deploy on the right bank. Based on this common knowledge of river crossings, Wittgenstein could have devised a plan in which the Prussians backtracked on the 10th to Moritzburg, nine miles north of Dresden, while the Russians held their position at Radeberg. Covered by a thick screen of cavalry, both Allied armies could have reached a position by that night to launch an attack on the 11th along the roads that converged on Napoleon's center.[48]

Instead, Wittgenstein suddenly decided to retreat toward Bautzen, which surprised and angered many.[49] "Since then [Lützen]," wrote an aggravated Gneisenau, "we often had rearguard combats that ensued up to the Elbe. We abandoned it without need, although one [Wittgenstein] had promised to remain behind this bulwark."[50] In fact, the monarchs transferred their quarters westward on the 9th to be closer to a possible battle north of Dresden. Regardless, numerous factors persuaded Wittgenstein. As late as noon on the 9th, he returned to the idea of abandoning his main line of communication and withdrawing north: the Prussians to Elsterwerda and the Russians through Königsbrück to Ruhland. However, Alexander put an end to all such thoughts. On the afternoon of the 9th, the tsar explicitly instructed Wittgenstein to maintain the Russian line of communication.

Alexander argued that all of his depots and hospitals stood on this line and that all reinforcements marched on this road to join the army.[51]

The reports that arrived on the 9th and 10th not only provided a more accurate assessment of the size of Napoleon's army, but also appeared to reveal the emperor's intentions.[52] From the Dresden area, Miloradovich reported that only a small French force lacking artillery had crossed the Elbe in boats. Allied outposts near Dresden's *Neustadt* monitored the roads leading from the capital to Königsbrück, Radeberg, Bautzen, Pillnitz, and the Bohemian frontier. Imperial forces occupied Dresden's *Neustadt* and the surrounding villages along the river bank. Intelligence led Wittgenstein to assume that Napoleon would cross the Elbe at Wittenberg as well as some forty-five miles downstream from Dresden at Belgern, where the French had started building a bridge under the protection of a battery of fifty twelve-pound guns. Based on this news, Wittgenstein concluded that Napoleon sought to envelop his right (northern) flank by moving the main mass of his army across the Elbe at Wittenberg and Belgern; the operation at Dresden was merely a feint to mask this maneuver. He decided to halt the Allied army one march west of Bautzen to "await a decisive movement by the enemy. Should he want to force me there, I will still have sufficient time to unite the entire army, take a position at Bautzen, and deliver a battle there. However, if the enemy crosses further downstream, which is likely, I will attack him in the flank with my entire force." Wittgenstein tasked Toll and Diebitsch with finding an advantageous position one march west of Bautzen.[53]

Thus, the Allied army continued to withdraw toward Bautzen on the 10th. Blücher, Yorck, and Kleist received orders to march from Großenhain to Königsbrück, while the main body of the Russian army moved from Radeberg to Bischofswerda. The sovereigns transferred their headquarters to Bautzen. To guard Berlin, Wittgenstein instructed Bülow "to take a central position observing Wittenberg, Roßlau, and Magdeburg." On the 11th, Blücher's Prussians fell back nine miles to Kamenz, itself seventeen miles slightly northwest of Bautzen. Blücher posted his rearguard at Königsbrück to remain level with the Russian main body at Bischofswerda. His headquarters informed the troops that they would join the Russians in an entrenched camp five miles west of Bautzen.[54]

Wittgenstein's continued retreat prompted another blazing assessment of the situation by Gneisenau. "The greatest evil from which we suffer is the leadership of the army," he grumbled to Hardenberg, counting on the chancellor to relay the message to Frederick William:

> Wittgenstein is not equal to the task and the trust that he once placed in Diebitsch has disappeared. On the other hand, this one has lost his head. Auvray, the chief of staff, is lazy and indolent. Three times I was in Borna on 1 May and three times I found these men in bed: afternoon, evening, morning.

From their mistakes come inexpedient, insensate, and impracticable orders. With them we do what we can or what is possible, but it takes much to avoid exposing ourselves to danger. Thus, we had to abandon the Elbe before the enemy forced us to do so. We are now in a region that will drive us off sooner than will the enemy.

After his rant against the Russians, Gneisenau explained to Hardenberg that the Allied defeat on the 2nd as well as Saxony's declaration for France would likely make Austria cautious and delay the kaiser's decision. "This cannot scare us," he insisted. In addition, he assured Hardenberg that Wittgenstein would not accept a second battle at Bautzen as promised but instead would continue the retreat. Exasperated by the Russian leadership, Gneisenau actually endorsed the retreat and suggested that the armies separate. Blücher's army, he advocated, "must fall back with order and gradually be reinforced by the forces in Silesia." Returning to his pet project of a Spanish-inspired people's war, Gneisenau explained that in Silesia "we have several strong positions. Three of them – Silberberg, Glatz, and Neiße – are protected by powerful fortresses. If these fortresses are supplied with provisions for 20,000 men for three months ... the Landwehr and field troops can fall back to there and the Landsturm can act accordingly."

As for the Russians, he suggested that they withdraw to Poland. "As soon as this occurs, the war will become balanced. Napoleon can only follow the Russians with a portion of his army while he must leave the other portion to face the Silesian fortresses. Will he attack these strong bulwarks or storm the strong entrenched positions? I doubt it. The portion of the French army left behind will always be weaker than our forces in the entrenched positions. These can then unite dispensable manpower and assume offensive operations." He suggested transferring the investment of Stettin to a portion of the Landwehr, while uniting the corps of Tauentzien, Bülow, and Borstell. This corps, augmented by the rest of the Landwehr, could take the offensive. In the worst case, it could fall back on the entrenched camp at Kolberg and await the arrival of the East and West Prussian Landwehr. Thus, Gneisenau's "Silesian Plan." "You can see from this," he concludes, "that I have really assumed the worst suppositions. Nevertheless, only from the most unfavorable suppositions can an ultimate positive result be construed only as long as one is steadfast. Therefore, only fortitude." His thoughts about separating from the Russians would change before month's end.[55]

Hardenberg supported a second battle for political reasons. In particular, he wanted to demonstrate to Austria and the rest of Europe that Napoleon had not crushed the Prussians at Großgörschen. Yet he secretly requested that Gneisenau provide him with a comprehensive report over the combat readiness and morale of the troops. Any decision for battle needed to be based on these factors. To ensure secrecy, he did not want the question presented to Blücher: the general's bellicosity made this expedient necessary in Hardenberg's opinion. Gneisenau entrusted the task to Clausewitz.[56]

On the evening of the 9th, Imperial Headquarters issued extensive instructions for XI Corps supported by the Guard's massive artillery train to lead the movement across the Elbe on the following day. Behind XI Corps, VI Corps moved up for close support, while XII Corps advanced to within six miles of Dresden and IV Corps took a position between Pirna and Dresden. Although the fighting on the 9th secured a bridgehead on the right bank for the raft bridge at Briesnitz, the imperials could not take immediate advantage of the crossing. With the Elbe being deep and swift at that spot and the French lacking sufficient cables and anchors, they deemed that the repair of Dresden's stone bridge would take less time than trying to secure the raft bridge. While the repair work ensued, the light infantry used long fire ladders to cross the damaged part of the bridge and reach the *Neustadt*. Napoleon followed to familiarize himself with the status of the bridge. Artillery crossed by way of old ferry boats the French stumbled upon. Thanks in part to Miloradovich's evacuation of the *Neustadt* as well as Napoleon's personal supervision for part of the day, imperial engineers finished the repairs of Dresden's stone bridge late on the evening of the 10th.[57]

15 Napoleon observing his troops crossing the Elbe at Dresden, 10 May 1813

Eugene assembled his corps to pursue the enemy at daybreak but the crossing did not begin until 10:00. Napoleon planned to have the entire army, including XII Corps, on the right bank the next day, the 11th. Moreover, he issued instructions for Lauriston to summon his division from Meißen so all of V Corps could cross the Elbe at Torgau. As soon as Napoleon received confirmation that Ney had crossed the Elbe at either Torgau or Wittenberg, he would send the marshal detailed orders. According to reports from spies, the Russians commenced the retreat to Silesia. Regarding the Prussians, Napoleon estimated that no more than 20,000 could have survived Lützen. Assuming they had received at least 10,000 reinforcements, the emperor placed their strength at 30,000 soldiers. Looking forward to serving a cold dish of revenge to his former ally, Frederick William, the emperor expressed the intention to place Joseph Fouché, his former police minister, at the head of the Prussian government as soon as the imperial army crossed into Prussian territory. "The celerity of this operation put Bonaparte in a good mood," relates Odeleben, "and he hardly left the bridge during the whole day, during which he observed the troops of the viceroy, of General Bertrand, and a part of Marmont's corps pass. He placed himself at his ease on a stone seat, casting his eyes toward his dear cannon, and his undisciplined children of the war, who rent the air with their acclamations, and were about to carry in their train misery and despair from the left to the right bank of the Elbe."[58]

Earlier on the 10th, at 4:00 A.M., Napoleon had received a letter from Frederick Augustus that placed Torgau at his disposal. After much brow-beating, the Saxon king formally renewed his allegiance to the French emperor. Thielmann frantically wrote to Yorck on 10 May to inform him that he probably would have to open the fortress to the French: "If there were time for you to arrive here, I would turn over the fortress to you, but they have tied my hands and I can do nothing more. If you cannot come, everything is lost, the generals are against me – I abandon my army, my Fatherland, everything, and fly to you in order to die with you." After thirty-two years of service, Thielmann resigned his commission in the Saxon army. He and his chief of staff left Torgau and journeyed to the tsar's headquarters, where both received appointments. On the orders of their king, who arrived at Dresden on the 12th, the Saxons opened the gates of Torgau to the French on 11 May. Ney, who had quartered eight miles southwest of Torgau at Langenreichenbach, sent III Corps across the Elbe. Reynier led his French division into the fortress and completed the formation of VII Corps by adding 9,000 Saxon infantry, 250 cavalry, and 3 batteries. Lauriston likewise marched to Torgau and crossed the Elbe. West of Ney, the troops under Victor, Sébastiani, and Puthod approached Köthen, thirty-five miles from Wittenberg.[59]

Events on 11 May quenched Wittgenstein's thirst for a tactical strike. Approximately 70,000 soldiers of Napoleon's army poured across the Elbe at Dresden. Led by Macdonald's XI Corps, the French smashed into Miloradovich at Weißig, prompting the Russians to withdraw step by step after bitter fighting. That evening, the lead elements of Bertrand's IV Corps surprised and crushed one of Kleist's outpost detachments seven miles southwest of Königsbrück. Kleist evacuated his position and moved closer to Blücher's main body at Kamenz. Also on the 11th, news arrived that Frederick Augustus had capitulated to Napoleon. Overwhelmed by these foreboding developments, Wittgenstein scrapped the idea of building an entrenched camp west of Bautzen at Göda. For 12 May, he directed the Allied army to withdraw across the Spree River. General Yegor Karlovich Sievers, chief engineer of the Russian army, received orders to fortify the position at Bautzen east of the Spree; Volkonsky promised to place thousands of laborers at his disposal. As noted, the tsar and the king had already lodged near Bautzen: Alexander took his headquarters "in a gentleman's house" at Wurschen, the king in a "farm-house" at Kumschütz, a small, cramped peasant village not far from the Bautzen–Görlitz road.[60]

Wittgenstein remained committed to his plan of accepting battle but, now that conjecture had transitioned to reality, a position needed to be chosen.[61] "Thus, we went as far back as behind Bautzen, where one [Wittgenstein] took a position," opined Gneisenau. "Long and detailed were the discussions of the manner it was to be taken. On the day of the enemy's attack, one chose the most awkward." With Scharnhorst en route to Vienna, the king's chief military advisor, Knesebeck, represented the Prussians in Allied planning sessions. He, too, would fail to fill Scharnhorst's shoes, in part because of their completely opposite views on the art of war. On this occasion, Knesebeck disagreed with Toll on the position to be taken. Recalling the great results of the formidable defensive position at Borodino, Toll suggested positioning the Allied army east of Bautzen in eleven consecutive waves. This did not appear feasible to Knesebeck, who rejected the proposal based on the small size of the Allied army. Unable to reach an agreement, Knesebeck accepted a compromise measure: Toll would arrange the general position while the Prussians managed the details of their own deployment.[62]

## Notes

1 Bogdanovich, *Geschichte des Krieges*, 1b:9; Holleben and Caemmerer, *Frühjahrsfeldzuges 1813*, II:93–94.
2 Droysen, *Yorck*, II:65; Unger, *Blücher*, II:29. Again comparing the new Prussian army's refusal to collapse like the army that had fought at Jena, Maude, in *Leipzig Campaign*, 108, notes that "in a surprisingly short time the stragglers had sorted

themselves out and were well on their way from the field, and when next morning dawned not a single gun or trophy of any kind remained as prizes for the victorious French. This was a most fatal blow to imperial prestige."

3　Odeleben, *A Circumstantial Narrative*, I:58–59, 60–62; SHAT, C¹⁷ 177: Berthier to Eugene, 2 May 1813; Berthier to Ney and Lauriston, 3 May 1813; *CN*, No. 20094, XXV:367; Lanrezac, *Lützen*, 172.

4　Lanrezac, *Lützen*, 172–73.

5　Norvins, *Portefeuille de mil huit cent treize*, I:282; *CN*, Nos. 19952 and 19953, XXV:262–63.

6　"The two French armies were not united," comments Lanrezac on Napoleon's decision to divide his forces, "but could be whenever Napoleon wanted ... the region between the Spree and the upper Elbe is easily passable for all large bodies of troops. That said, there are only benefits to leave a certain interval between the two armies, through which all would enjoy greater maneuverability": Lanrezac, *Lützen*, 191.

7　*CN*, Nos. 19956, 19958, and 19961, XXV:264–65, 268; SHAT, C¹⁷ 177: Berthier to Ney, Reynier, Oudinot, Hammerstein, Milhaud, Bertrand, Eugene, Lauriston, and Marmont, Pegau, 4 May 1813. Berthier's evening dispatches, issued at 6:00, conveyed the emperor's instructions for Eugene to move nine miles further east from Borna to Bad Lausick with VI Corps a few miles behind him at Flößberg and IV Corps remaining to their south at Frohburg. After reaching Zeitz, Oudinot received instructions to continue to Frohburg with XII Corps. Reminiscent of the *bataillon carré*, XI Corps and I Cavalry Corps stood at Bad Lausick, forming the advance guard of the army or tip of the diamond. Eight miles behind them, VI Corps, the Guard, and Imperial Headquarters reached Borna, while XII Corps reached Zeitz, twenty miles west of Borna, to form the rear point of the diamond. On the left, Lauriston's V Corps passed the night at Stockheim, six miles northwest of Bad Lausick, while on the right, IV Corps halted at Frohburg, eight miles southwest of Bad Lausick. See Lanrezac, *Lützen*, 173–74.

8　*CN*, No. 19958, XXV:265–66.

9　*CN*, Nos. 19963 and 19964, XXV:268–70.

10　Scharnhorst to Gneisenau, Dresden, 7 May 1813, GStA PK, VI HA Rep. 92 Nl. Gneisenau, Nr. 23.

11　A hesitant Frederick William decreed the formation of the Landsturm on 21 April 1813 for men between forty and sixty years of age. Similar to a national guard, the Landsturm would be called to arms when the enemy threatened a specific location. Units would then conduct scorched-earth operations to sabotage and disrupt enemy lines of communication. The Spanish guerrillas provided the philosophical inspiration for the Landsturm, but Frederick William never accepted the principle of a popular, insurrectionary force. In its original form, the Landsturm lasted only three months before conservative opposition prompted the king to sharply curtail its role. See Simon, *Prussian Reform Movement*, 168–80.

12　Thanks to Frederick William's 15 March 1813 decision to partition his kingdom into four autonomous Military Governments, Berlin did not serve as the central hub of Prussian mobilization on par with Paris. The main tasks of the Military

Governments included mobilizing the Landwehr and arranging both provincial and local defense measures. The four Military Governments were headquartered at Königsberg, Stargard, Berlin, and Breslau, corresponding to the following regions: between the Vistula and the Niemen; between the Oder and the Vistula; between the Elbe and the Oder; and Upper and Lower Silesia.

13 Pertz and Delbrück, *Gneisenau*, II:598–99.

14 Blücher to Bülow, 3 or 4 May 1813, GStA PK, IV HA Rep. 15a Nr. 248; Wittgenstein to Blücher, Rochlitz, 4 May 1813; *ibid.*, VI HA Rep. 92 Nl. Gneisenau, Nr. 18, I; *ibid.*, Disposition for 5 May 1813, Rochlitz, Auvray to Gneisenau.

15 *CN*, Nos. 19965 and 19966, XXV:270–71; SHAT, C$^{17}$ 177: Berthier to Eugene, Bertrand, Marmont, Oudinot, Victor, Sébastiani, Ney, and Lauriston, 5 May 1813.

16 Lanrezac, *Lützen*, 175; Holleben and Caemmerer, *Frühjahrsfeldzuges 1813*, II:100–01.

17 Steffens, *Adventures*, 99.

18 In *CN*, No. 19971, XXV:272–73, Napoleon instructed Berthier to convey his satisfaction to Eugene as well as his complaint that the latter had not captured more Allied prisoners. The emperor thought he should have taken between 2,000 and 3,000 prisoners: SHAT, C$^{17}$ 177: Berthier to Eugene, 6 May 1813.

19 SHAT, C$^{17}$ 177: Berthier to Lauriston and Oudinot, 5 May 1813; Berthier to Marmont, 6 May 1813.

20 Odeleben, in *A Circumstantial Narrative*, I:64, claims that Napoleon intended to cross the Elbe at Königstein, twenty miles upstream of Dresden.

21 *CN*, Nos. 19960, 19972, and 19975, XXV:267–68, 273–775; Lanrezac, *Lützen*, 175–76; SHAT, C$^{17}$ 177: Berthier to Ney, 5 May 1813. Berthier did not hesitate to scold Ney, showing why many of his fellow marshals detested him: "Having received no information from you since you reached Leipzig, the emperor cannot give you any specific orders." Early on the 6th, Napoleon finally received a 5 May status report from Ney.

22 *CN*, Nos. 19971, 19972, 19975, and 19976, XXV:273–75.

23 *CN*, No. 19971, XXV:273; SHAT, C$^{17}$ 177: Berthier to Eugene, Marmont, Lauriston, and Bertrand, 6 May 1813; Lanrezac, *Lützen*, 178–79.

24 SHAT, C$^{17}$ 177: Berthier to Lauriston, Waldheim, 6 May 1813.

25 Stewart, *Narrative*, 33; Gneisenau to Hardenberg, Meißen, 6 May 1813, GStA PK, VI HA Rep. 92 Nl. Gneisenau, Nr. 53a.

26 Wittgenstein to Blücher, Wilsdruff, 6 and 7 May 1813, GStA PK, VI HA Rep. 92 Nl. Gneisenau, Nr. 18, I; quoted in Droysen, *Yorck*, II:67.

27 Steffens, *Adventures*, 99.

28 Odeleben, in *A Circumstantial Narrative*, I:66, 69, describes these bridges as "one of timber-work near Uebigau, the other, at the upper part of Dresden, formed of well-pitched boats." Odeleben also refers to the bridge of "timber-work" as a "bridge of rafts." Lanrezac, *Lützen*, 179, refers to it as a bridge of rafts.

29 Pertz and Delbrück, *Gneisenau*, II:602; Unger, *Blücher*, II:31; Petre, *Napoleon's Last Campaign*, 96. For a thorough account of the Russian rearguard actions during the retreat from Lützen to Bautzen, for which Alexander made Miloradovich a count on 13 May, see Bogdanovich, *Geschichte des Krieges*, I:11–23, 29–39.

30 See the brusque character comparison in Müffling, *Aus meinem Leben*, 33–45.

31 Stewart, *Narrative*, 30–31; Pertz and Delbrück, *Gneisenau*, II:596.

32 Wittgenstein to Bülow, Wilsdruff, 7 May 1813, GStA PK, IV HA Rep. 15a Nr. 248.

33 Severing contact with Austria was not desired by the Prussians. "We hope for a strong diversion by the Austrians," wrote Clausewitz on the 8th, "which was even mentioned by the king in a letter to the army": Clausewitz to Marie, Proschwitz by Meißen, 8 May 1813, in Schwartz, *Clausewitz*, II:81.

34 Auvray to Gneisenau, 8 May 1813, GStA PK, VI HA Rep. 92 Nl. Gneisenau, Nr. 18, I.

35 Unger, *Blücher*, II:30–31; Holleben and Caemmerer, *Frühjahrsfeldzuges 1813*, II:116–17.

36 SHAT, C¹⁷ 177: Berthier to Bertrand, Marmont, Eugene, and Oudinot, 7 May 1813; *CN*, No. 19978, XXV:276. Berthier wrote to Thielmann on the 5th informing him that Reynier would arrive shortly to take command of the Saxons for his VII Corps. See SHAT, C¹⁷ 177: Berthier to Thielmann, 5 May 1813; Jomini, *Précis politique et militaire*, I:252.

37 *CN*, No. 19979, XXV:276. The letter is addressed to Lauriston at Lommatzsch, which is nine miles slightly northwest of Meißen.

38 *CN*, No. 19983, XXV:278.

39 Suburbs as well as city gates often received the name of the closest and largest population center that the main road from that gate or suburb led to. In this case, Dresden's Pirna suburb stood on the road leading to the town of Pirna.

40 Odeleben, *A Circumstantial Narrative*, I:65–70; Lanrezac, *Lützen*, 179–80.

41 *CN*, No. 19985, XXV:280. "Order General Bertrand to ... place pickets on the various roads that lead to Bohemia to see what is happening and to cover the rear": SHAT, C¹⁷ 177: Berthier to Bertrand, 9 May 1813.

42 *CN*, No. 19984, XXV:278–79; SHAT, C¹⁷ 177: Berthier to Ney, 9 May 1813; Jomini, *Précis politique et militaire*, I:252.

43 SHAT, C¹⁷ 177: Berthier to Bertrand, Oudinot, Mortier, Lauriston, and Eugene, 8 May 1813; Berthier to Ney and Lauriston, 9 May 1813; *CN*, No. 19986, XXV:280.

44 Odeleben, *A Circumstantial Narrative*, I:70–73.

45 *CN*, No. 19988, XXV:282; Bogdanovich, *Geschichte des Krieges*, I:20–21; Holleben and Caemmerer, *Frühjahrsfeldzuges 1813*, II:120.

46 Blücher to Amalie, Kumschütz, 15 May 1813, *Blüchers Briefe*, ed. Unger, 165; Natzmer to Frederick William, Königsbrück, 10 May 1813, in Pertz and Delbrück, *Gneisenau*, II:603. Unger, *Blücher*, II:32, also tells of "other old evils" that resurfaced. It is unclear whether these were mental or physical afflictions.

47 Gneisenau to Auvray, Großenhain, 6:30 P.M., 9 May 1813, in Holleben and Caemmerer, *Frühjahrsfeldzuges 1813*, II:121–22.

48 Holleben and Caemmerer, *Frühjahrsfeldzuges 1813*, II:121–22; Pertz and Delbrück, *Gneisenau*, II:604.

49 "The neighborhood of Bautzen is a '*point stratégique*,'" explains Cathcart, "which appeared favorable for the purpose of covering Silesia; the surrounding country, well known in the Seven Years War, offered a choice of good positions that rested their left on the Bohemian frontier. This frontier afforded a very efficient '*appui*,' not from its natural strength alone, but from political

circumstances that arose from the indecision of the court of Vienna and produced a virtual neutrality which neither of the belligerent parties could venture to disregard": Cathcart, *Commentaries*, 139.

50 Gneisenau to Münster, Puschkau by Striegau in Silesia, 29 May 1813, GStA PK, VI HA Rep. 92 Nl. Gneisenau, Nr. 20b. Cathcart, in *Commentaries*, 138–39, states that the monarchs "did not intend to dispute the passage of the Elbe in force."

51 Wittgenstein to Bülow, Radeberg, 9 May 1813, GStA, PK, IV HA Rep. 15A Nr. 248; Wittgenstein to Frederick William, Bischofswerda, 10 May 1813, in Holleben and Caemmerer, *Frühjahrsfeldzuges 1813*, II:124. In addition, Wilson contends that "the fear of displeasing Austria, who promises to make her declaration on the 1st of June," induced the Allies "to remain on a flank where we hazard our communications with the Vistula and expose ourselves to many inconveniences from want of provisions, stores, etc.": Wilson, *Private Diary*, I:361.

52 At the time, Wilson did not think Allied intelligence provided much. On 10 May he wrote: "It is strange but true that we have little good information of what is passing in the enemy's army, and as of yet there are very few deserters." See Wilson, *Private Diary*, I:363.

53 Wittgenstein to Alexander, Bischofswerda, 10 May 1813, in Mikhailovsky-Danilevsky, *Denkwürdigkeiten*, 96.

54 Wittgenstein to Bülow, Bischofswerda, 10 May 1813, GStA PK, IV HA Rep. 15A Nr. 248; Holleben and Caemmerer, *Frühjahrsfeldzuges 1813*, II:125–26; Bogdanovich, *Geschichte des Krieges*, I:30.

55 Gneisenau to Hardenberg, Kamenz, 11 May 1813, GStA PK, VI HA Rep. 92 Nl. Albrecht, Nr. 47.

56 Unger, *Blücher*, II:33.

57 CN, No. 19987, XXV:281–82; SHAT, C[17] 177: Berthier to Eugene, 9 May 1813; Odeleben, *A Circumstantial Narrative*, I:74–75.

58 Odeleben, *A Circumstantial Narrative*, I:75–76.

59 CN, No. 19987, XXV:281–82; SHAT, C[17] 177: Berthier to Lauriston, 10 May 1813; Thielmann to Yorck, Torgau, 10 May 1813, GStA PK, VI HA Rep. 92 Nl. Gneisenau, Nr. 18, I; Mikhailovsky-Danilevsky, *Denkwürdigkeiten*, 92; Jomini, *Précis politique et militaire*, I:252; Pertz and Delbrück, *Gneisenau*, II:607–08; Droysen, *Yorck*, II:69; Petre, *Napoleon's Last Campaign*, 96–98; Yorck von Wartenburg, *Napoleon as a General*, II:256; Lanrezac, *Lützen*, 182.

60 Wittgenstein to Blücher, 11 May 1813, GStA PK, VI HA Rep. 92 Nl. Gneisenau, Nr. 18, I; Plotho, *Der Krieg*, I:138–40; Bogdanovich, *Geschichte des Krieges*, I:30–31; Lanrezac, *Lützen*, 192; Cathcart, *Commentaries*, 145.

61 According to Caemmerer: "Wittgenstein would have acted correctly if he had held firm to his idea of 10 May to stand on the hills of Bischofswerda or at Göda west of Bautzen, where he already ordered a camp to be marked for the entire army. Then he would have been able to proceed to the counterattack on 14 or 15 May and certainly would have succeeded." See Holleben and Caemmerer, *Frühjahrsfeldzuges 1813*, II:177.

62 Gneisenau to Münster, Puschkau by Striegau in Silesia, 29 May 1813, GStA PK, VI HA Rep. 92 Nl. Gneisenau, Nr. 20b; Müffling, *Aus meinem Leben*, 36; Pertz and Delbrück, *Gneisenau*, II:612.

# 7

## Bautzen

The lack of experienced cavalry continued to hamper Napoleon after the Allies crossed the Elbe. With his mounted arm unable to maintain contact with the enemy, he could not determine the direction of Wittgenstein's retreat. Thus far, the Allies had proved two of Napoleon's assumptions wrong: they did not defend the Elbe and they did not separate, although he still counted on this happening at any moment. As of 12 May, he did not know where their main body stood. He so desired to see them separate that he convinced himself that it would happen despite lacking hard evidence. Certain that the Russians remained on the great east–west highway to Breslau, he did not know if the Prussians had followed or had moved north to defend Berlin, which appeared the natural response for them to make.

Napoleon's first step on 12 May officially dissolved Eugene's Army of the Elbe, summoning its staff to join the imperial *maison* and sending his stepson to Italy via Munich. To intimidate the Austrians, he would form a corps of observation on the Adige River consisting of all troops of the Kingdom of Italy and the Illyrian provinces. Napoleon directed Macdonald's XI Corps toward Bischofswerda on the highway to Bautzen. General Pierre-Joseph Bruyères's 1st Division of Light Cavalry would screen Macdonald's march east. Napoleon's orders to Macdonald explained that Eugene's departure signaled the marshal's complete control of XI Corps, meaning he should communicate directly with Berthier. In essence, Macdonald now commanded the vanguard of the Grande Armée, and with it came certain expectations.[1]

On the 12th, General Louis-Chrétien Beaumont led Marmont's vanguard of three battalions, one brigade of Westphalian cavalry, and one half-battery to Moritzburg. From there, he reconnoitered in the direction of Großenhain, twenty miles northwest of Dresden, to investigate reports of

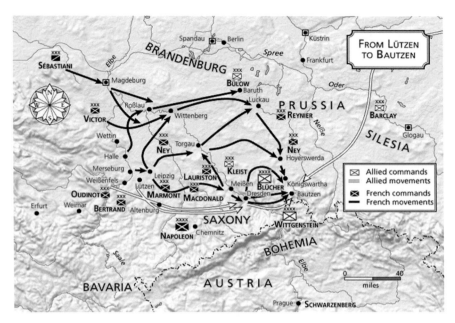

**17.** From Lützen to Bautzen

a large body of Allied cavalry. Napoleon craved information about the Allies: had they split, or did the Russians and Prussians march together? "The emperor wants to know," Berthier informed Marmont, "what has become of the Prussian army; General Bertrand claims that it took the road to Breslau, others claim that it retreated toward Berlin; clarification is necessary." Reports of the construction of fortifications at Bautzen made little impression on Napoleon, as he believed the Allies would continue to run from him.[2]

For the 13th, the imperial army fanned out from its base at Dresden. Beaumont remained at Moritzburg while Marmont's main body moved halfway to Bischofswerda so that VI Corps stood in second line behind XI Corps. Bertrand's IV Corps marched nineteen miles northeast from Dresden to Königsbrück, sending patrols in every direction and pushing its van to Kamenz. Oudinot's XII Corps crossed the Dresden bridge at noon and camped in the *Neustadt*. Macdonald pushed eastward to provide IV and VI Corps with room to maneuver. Although he drove Miloradovich east of Bischofswerda before Russian resistance stiffened, the marshal overextended XI Corps. An enterprising Allied commander could have exploited Macdonald's isolation to crush the marshal but Wittgenstein squandered the opportunity. Instead, Macdonald transferred his headquarters to Bischofswerda, twenty-two miles east of Dresden. There, he received a blistering lecture from Berthier after commanding the army's vanguard for one day. Napoleon did not have time for on-the-job training, which a marshal of France should not have needed:

> The emperor expects to receive several letters from you each day; you are his advance guard; it is up to you to provide news of the enemy, to question, to dispatch spies, to intercept letters in the post offices of the towns, and, finally, to use all means, all the ruses of war to find out what is happening. M. de Beaufremont, one of my aides-de-camp, arrived yesterday evening – I was hoping to receive a long report from you. His Majesty asked me twenty times if I had received news from you; M. de Beaufremont told me that you passed the night at Bischofswerda and that enemy infantry, cavalry, and thirty pieces of cannon executed a fighting withdrawal before you; that we would likely receive news from you during the night. I was not content with this officer's report, which left the emperor in painful uncertainty about your position; your silence prevents any disposition from being made. His Majesty has charged me with instructing you to write me several times each day and have your officers deliver the letters to me. These officers must give me detailed reports on the position of the enemy. I repeat, you are the vanguard and it is your responsibility to instruct His Majesty. Correspond with me several times each day.[3]

Turning to Ney, on the 11th he crossed the Elbe at Torgau with III, V, and VII Corps. For the 12th, the master only expected him to expedite his union with the 25,000 men approaching under Victor. The latest report from that marshal reached Imperial Headquarters early on the 13th. According to Victor, he would reach Köthen that day with his corps as well as the troops commanded by Sébastiani, Puthod, and Philippon. Napoleon responded on the 13th by ordering Victor to push these 25,000 men another thirty-five miles east to reach Wittenberg on the 15th and cross the Elbe. With Sébastiani's cavalry scouring all the roads, Victor would send part of the vanguard of II Corps toward Berlin and another part toward Luckau. For the 16th, the emperor wanted Victor to threaten Berlin by taking a position between Wittenberg and Luckau. Meanwhile, Napoleon instructed Ney to have V Corps at Doberlug by the 15th, III Corps at Luckau on the 16th, and VII Corps posted between II and III Corps. With his headquarters at Luckau, the marshal would be fifty-five miles from Berlin and sixty-seven miles from Dresden (see Map 5). Although not exactly a *bataillon carré*, this arrangement would allow Ney to march in any direction. This brilliant plan afforded Napoleon a huge flank force that could crush the Prussians if they split from Wittgenstein or envelop the right of a united Allied army as it retreated east. At the least, with some 85,000 men three marches from Berlin, the emperor hoped to scare the Prussians into separating from the Russians for the purpose of guarding their capital.[4]

That same evening, 13 May, Napoleon wrote directly to Ney. This document provides invaluable insight into the emperor's thinking as well as definitive proof that the "master plan" dominated his views. He described in detail the size of Victor's contingent as well as its role and the timetable for its movements. "He can be kept within range or form your vanguard if I order you to turn left on Berlin," wrote Napoleon, "or he can join you at Luckau if that becomes necessary." Still uncertain about Allied movements, Napoleon revealed to Ney that he "failed to see what the Prussians have done. It is quite certain that the Russians have retreated on Breslau, but are the Prussians withdrawing on Breslau as reported, or have they thrown themselves on Berlin, which seems natural, to protect their capital?" Napoleon hoped the report he expected to receive from Bertrand that night as well as any information Ney could provide would answer this question. He then made clear to Ney that with such a considerable force at his disposal, the marshal could not remain idle. Reflecting his recent experience at Lützen which, according to Lanrezac, demonstrated to him that he needed forces double those of his adversary to obtain a decisive victory, the emperor did not view Ney's command as an independent army but instead as a wing of his own. "For the position that I will have you take," wrote Napoleon, "we will always be united, [and] we can move to the right or to the left with as many troops as possible according to the reports." The relief of Glogau, the taking of Berlin while Davout's five divisions advanced into Pomerania after reoccupying Hamburg, and the capture of Breslau by Napoleon himself – all geographic objectives – formed the three goals the emperor wanted to achieve.[5]

Expecting to have Bertrand at Hoyerswerda and Macdonald at Bautzen by the 14th, Napoleon believed he would be able to make a definitive decision on the 15th on his next move. Based on the enemy's movements, the emperor would order Ney either to take Berlin or to attain another objective. Napoleon did not have to wait until 15 May to settle the issue. At 3:00 on the morning of the 14th, he informed Ney that reports had arrived confirming that "Blücher, Yorck, Kleist, the king of Prussia, and five or six princes of his house had passed through Königsbrück on the 10th and 11th coming from Großenhain and Dresden and en route to Bautzen on the highway to Breslau. There is no longer any doubt that Berlin is exposed and that this city is guarded only by some cavalry and Bülow's corps: this makes orderly movement all the more necessary."[6] Moreover, the enemy's rearguard – "30,000 men and many guns" – appeared to be guarding the small town of Bautzen. He wanted Lauriston to be ready to reinforce the Grande Armée should the Allies seek a second battle. "I impatiently await news of your army and the intelligence that you have obtained," concluded his letter to Ney; "but what I have received here regarding the passage of the majority of the Prussian army on the road to Silesia is certain."[7]

Napoleon remained at Dresden for several days, transforming the Saxon capital into an enormous forward depot to serve his operations in Lusatia. He accused the Allies of "burning the villages as in the last campaign," which further limited his soldiers' ability to live off the already exhausted Saxon countryside: "The enemy commits horrors, burns the villages, and does all that he did in Russia: it will be a good lesson for the Germans." In addition to logistical preparations, the emperor resurrected Frederick Augustus's government, reorganized the Grande Armée, and did all he could to continue the political exploitation of his victory at Lützen. Considerable reinforcements arrived, including several Guard battalions and 4,000 Guard Cavalry. Napoleon continued to rebuild his line cavalry, which now included 3,000 Saxon cuirassiers. "I am beginning to see cavalry," he informed Ney on the 13th. In particular, he boasted that the four divisions of General Marie-Victor Latour-Maubourg's I Cavalry Corps provided around 9,000 sabers. By the 15th, Napoleon expected to have some 203,000 men and 400 guns around the Saxon capital, while Ney commanded 84,000 men and 200 guns.[8]

Initial Allied plans focused on the French continuing their advance due east from Dresden. As the immediate position on the Spree did not suffice for a defensive, Allied Headquarters sought a position on the hills east of Bautzen that could dominate all approaches from the west.[9] The suburb of Nadelwitz, about one mile east of Bautzen, was nestled around the juncture of the main east–west highway (Dresden–Bautzen–Görlitz–Breslau) and a road running southeast through Hochkirch to Löbau, twelve miles from Bautzen (see Map 6). Wittgenstein chose a position straddling both roads halfway between Bautzen and Hochkirch. Six and one-half miles southeast of Bautzen, Hochkirch formed the highly visible center of a vast hilly region that extended from the northernmost mountain range of Lusatia. Hochkirch overlooked the heights along the banks of the Spree. Halfway between Bautzen and Hochkirch, the villages of Baschütz and Jenkwitz would form the center of the Allied position. The hills on which they stood, almost equal in elevation to those along the right bank of the Spree, offered a good field of fire for the artillery. If Napoleon granted the Allies time to fortify the villages and erect numerous batteries, a frontal assault would cost him dearly. Wittgenstein's right wing, spreading two miles north from Baschütz to Litten, cut across the east–west highway. A marsh formed by the Blösa stream that flowed across the Allied front adequately protected this flank from the west while the open country to the north boded well for Allied cavalry.[10] His left wing extended south, cutting across the Bautzen–Löbau road and through the village of Rieschen to the foot of a considerable hill chain. Not merely the protection by thick forest cover, but also the close proximity of the Austrian frontier (seven and one-half miles to the south of Rieschen) as well as the Lusatian mountains would hinder any flanking maneuver by large forces. According to Charles Stewart:

> The Allies determined to meet the attack in the position they have chosen; having weighed all the consequences likely to result from a retreat even to a more favorable one at Görlitz, together with the advantages they have here. I think they have decided wisely, *if they can allure the enemy to take the bull by the horns.* The ground that has been chosen is open and adapted for cavalry in the center; on our left flank, we have a range of mountains ... Some strong batteries have added to the security of this part of the position. It then extends through some villages which are strongly entrenched, and through the plain to three commanding hills on the right, which rise abruptly, and form strong points; but the ground again beyond is open, intersected by roads in all directions, and I can see no impediment to the enemy moving round us here, if their columns of infantry can cope against our masses of cavalry in the plain.

In the tradition of Austerlitz, Eylau, and Borodino, Wittgenstein and his staff believed that the position between Rieschen and Litten provided a strong bastion from which the mammoth Allied artillery could be employed with devastating results. Moreover, the position did not require a strong reserve, and the proximity of the Bohemian frontier provided an obstacle that secured the left wing. It appeared to the Allied leadership that the Rieschen–Litten line would allow their soldiers to wage an obstinate defense, just as the Russians had done so many times in the past.[11]

Allied intelligence improved noticeably after the French moved east. Wittgenstein received vital news as well as several reports from spies about the strength of the French army. Unlike in April, the Allies gained an accurate view of the situation. Nevertheless, Allied Headquarters did not want to fall victim to Napoleon's campaigns of misinformation and sought to guard against any exaggeration of the emperor's strength. Some simply could not believe that Napoleon had managed to field an army of 200,000 men after losing 500,000 in Russia less than one year earlier. In fact, reports that Napoleon had detached large forces to operate against Berlin increased hopes that parity would exist between the two opposing armies as soon as Barclay de Tolly arrived after taking Thorn. Partially because of these thoughts and hopes, Allied Headquarters decided on 13 May to extend north beyond the Rieschen–Litten line and position a flank force that could counterattack from the heights near the village of Kreckwitz.[12] Although the Blösa stream would separate this wing from the center of the Allied line, the Russians envisioned it executing a powerful attack against Napoleon's left flank while his main forces struggled before the Rieschen–Litten position. For this wing, Wittgenstein selected Yorck's I Corps and Kleist's Russo-Prussian corps. Early on the 13th, they moved into the new position on the Kreckwitz heights.[13]

While the army took positions along the Rieschen–Litten–Kreckwitz line on the 13th, Blücher's staff moved to Kumschütz, two miles east of Baschütz, where it just barely found accommodation even after royal head-quarters joined the tsar's at Wurschen. A few miles south of Kumschütz rose the white steeple of the church at Hochkirch, the site of Frederick the Great's mauling by a much larger Austrian army on 14 October 1758. To strengthen the conviction of the troops, officers reminded them of Frederick's greatness in adversity. Gneisenau immediately inspected the Kreckwitz position and determined the whole idea to be ridiculous based on the numbers discussed by the Russians. Together totaling only 11,000 troops, Yorck and Kleist in Gneisenau's opinion hardly sufficed for such an operation in which 80,000 men could be utilized. Complaining to Knesebeck, he judged that, unless Wittgenstein allocated 40,000 men for this attacking force, the Russian commander should scrap the plan. However, if Wittgenstein found this number, he could not leave the troops exposed on the hills in a large semicircle, where the French would easily see them. Instead, he had to pull them behind the hills to conceal their strength and his intent. Lastly, Gneisenau bluntly informed Knesebeck that it would be impossible for these troops to conduct a defensive on the hills because of their isolation from the rest of the army.[14] Gneisenau's letter to his wife, Caroline, likewise written on the 13th, provides valuable insight into the mood of the Prussian army:

> Yesterday we arrived here due to the retreat ordered by Russian headquar-ters, which our army is very discontent about. The enemy follows our fighting withdrawal. Tomorrow or the day after we will deliver a new battle. Tomorrow morning we will make the preparations for this. The war is moving closer to our borders through the fault of people who do not know what they want. We have abandoned the Elbe unnecessarily. The soldier is discontent with the constant retreat and I cannot blame him for this. Should we deliver a new battle and lose, the rumor of it will reach you quickly enough. In the meantime, do not be concerned. The fate of arms is sometimes quite odd but what I know comes from the spirit of the soldier, which provides great hope. He is full of fortitude. It is lively in the camp before us. Music and singing ring forth and everyone is cheerful because the retreat has stopped.[15]

On the 14th, Gneisenau received Knesebeck's support of his objections to the Kreckwitz position. Somewhat relieved but still skeptical of the Russians, he informed Hardenberg that "we prepare for battle. I am encour-aged that it will open favorably, yet I hope Barclay de Tolly, who stands at Spremberg, will arrive. If he does and if he is deployed where he should be and where he is needed, the battle could be decisive for the whole war." He continued by alerting the chancellor to the fact that, if Wittgenstein's leadership failed again, the battle would be in doubt. Getting to the real reason for the communiqué, Gneisenau again reminded Hardenberg that no one should despair if the Allies lost this battle. Instead, he suggested the implementation of his "Silesian Plan." "Please tell me if you have already done something for my plan. I wrote to [Friedrich Theodor] Merkel and requested that he arrange on paper the supply of the fortresses and camps. Please tell me if you agree with my ideas."[16]

That evening, Hardenberg's trusted aide, Hippel, arrived with a letter from the chancellor as well as verbal instructions for Gneisenau. Hardenberg had not lost courage. He assured Gneisenau that "one must double the efforts; I have omitted nothing that my sphere of influence allows me to do for our cause." However, in regards to the "Silesian Plan," he hoped for a better solution, especially the expansion of the coalition: "The fortresses and the entrenched camps by them must be our last recourse; I will always consider it a great misfortune if we are forced to resort to this. As a result of this, public opinion – especially in Silesia, where we will have difficulty creating guerrillas – will be very depressed. With the end of the month we will know where Austria stands. Scharnhorst is at Vienna. Our alliance with Sweden is concluded; that with England, which will give us subsidies and arms, is in the works. [Johann Philipp von] Stadion has been here since the day before yesterday. Tell Hippel everything you wish to say to me. Perhaps we will see each other soon." Gneisenau and Clausewitz met with Hippel in the attic of a farmhouse and talked long into the night of 14/15 May. Hippel provided an overview of Austria's combat-readiness as well as a strong assurance that Kaiser Francis would join the Coalition. In turn, Gneisenau answered his questions about the mood of the army.[17]

The presence of the Austrian envoy, Stadion, at the tsar's headquarters spurred the Allies toward a resolution, while at Dresden the Austrian general Ferdinand von Bubna pressed Napoleon to accept an armistice and peace congress under Austria's armed mediation. Stadion, the pro-war foreign minister during Austria's 1809 struggle with France, represented the Austrian war party. He rejected the notion that Austria's attempts to mediate between the belligerents – a policy implemented by his successor, Klemens von Metternich – would garner any success with the likes of Napoleon. Stadion hoped Austria would soon join the war but did not conceal from the Allies that only a powerful showing on their part would overcome the kaiser's fear of war. In his report to Castlereagh, Stewart stated that Stadion "regretted the necessity of the Allies having passed the Elbe; declared it his opinion they should now fight the enemy, and gave me the impression that he conceived that the more battles that were fought the better for Austria." Clausewitz explains that it was "part of the Allied plan to fight as much as possible for every bit of ground in order to show Europe that they had not suffered a defeat in the first battle [Großgörschen] and were neither morally nor physically unable to continue to defy the enemy. However, it was preferable to give the Austrians the impression that we were determined not to spare our forces and not to leave, in timid anticipation, the liberation of Europe to them. Moreover, from its feeling of moral superiority, the army nurtured the desire to test itself against the enemy once more as soon as possible. A further withdrawal without a battle would have destroyed this great spirit and weakened the confidence in the leadership. Therefore, it was decided to make another attempt at resisting the enemy's forces."[18]

Stadion reached Görlitz on 13 May and immediately met with Hardenberg and Nesselrode. He asked the two ministers to communicate their peace terms, thus emphasizing the difference between the purely Austrian issues and those of Europe. After they stated that the latter (Italy, Holland, and Spain) would be decided at a general peace conference, they sought his assurance that no delay, no excuse, and no ambiguity in the diplomatic language of France would delay the march of the Austrian army as soon as it was combat-ready. They also demanded a guarantee of Austria's participation in the war if Napoleon either rejected or refused to accept completely the Russo-Prussian conditions for peace by 1 June. Although he did his best to reassure them, Stadion countered by presenting Vienna's demand that the Allies refuse to allow any circumstance, either success or defeat, to undermine the unshakable strength of their political and especially their military posture. Stadion considerably impressed Nesselrode and Hardenberg by requesting proposals for a common plan of operations and declared himself ready, although he was not authorized to do so, to conclude a possible agreement concerning Austria's full participation should Napoleon reject the conditions for peace. On the morning of the 14th, at - Nesselrode's invitation Stadion traveled to Weißenberg to be closer to Allied Headquarters at Wurschen. From Weißenberg, he rode another thirty minutes to Wurschen, meeting first with Tsar Alexander and then Frederick William. After returning to Weißenberg that same day, he drafted memos to Hardenberg and Nesselrode seeking the respective peace terms of the two states.[19]

A 16 May meeting between Hardenberg and Nesselrode expanded the war aims established by the Treaties of Kalisch and Breslau. According to the Wurschen Convention, the Allies would seek the complete dissolution of Napoleon's Confederation of the Rhine and the total independence of all of Germany, including the vital 32nd Military Division. To entice the Austrians, the first of the seven articles called for the full material, territorial, and demographic restoration of Austria to its 1805 extent. Nothing is explicitly stated concerning the Polish–Saxon exchange. Article two states only that Prussia would be restored materially to its 1806 extent while article four stipulates that the Grand Duchy of Warsaw had ceased to exist in its present form. In addition, they pledged their respective states to fight for the liberation of Spain, Holland, and Italy.[20]

Stadion communicated the provisions of the Wurschen Convention to Metternich, who agreed in principle with the terms but feared Napoleon would exploit the harsh conditions to rally the French people. Moreover, Metternich wanted to direct any peace negotiations to ensure maximum benefit for Austria and to undermine the cornerstone of the Kalisch and Breslau treaties: the exchange of Saxony for Prussian Poland, which would go to a new Polish state controlled by the Russians. Although the Wurschen Convention contained no language regarding the Polish–Saxon exchange, such a swap of territory would challenge Austrian national security by increasing Prussia's influence in Germany and extending Russia into the heart of Central Europe. Lastly, knowing Napoleon as well as he did, Metternich insisted that the Allies would have to propose a minimum set of peace terms just to attract the French emperor to the negotiating table. Metternich's own peace plan called for Russia and France to retire behind their respective frontiers of the Vistula and the Rhine, to remain separated by an independent and strengthened Central Europe. Over the next six weeks, he worked diligently to convince the Allies to offer Napoleon a minimum set of conditions as the basis for a peace conference. Success would come in late June.[21]

Not only did Stadion answer questions regarding Austria's proposed mediation, and claim that Francis would make a declaration one way or the other by 1 June, but he also came prepared to engage in serious military planning. He provided information on the strength, condition, and position of the Austrian forces in Bohemia and Galicia. Stadion also shared a memo drafted in Vienna on 10 May by Count Jan Josef Václav Radetzky von Radetz, the chief of staff of the Austrian army assembling in Bohemia. According to Radetzky's "Memorandum Regarding the Purpose of the Operations and Their Presumed Course, as Well as the Resources to Be Applied," the 120,000-man Austrian army would not be combat-ready and assembled on the northwestern frontier until "the last days of June," ostensibly to support the Allies in a theater of war west of the Elbe. However, should the Allies fall back to the Oder, the Austrian army could be available on the northeastern frontier by mid June.[22] Regardless of the whereabouts of the Russo-Prussian army, Radetzky declared that Napoleon would fall on the Austrian army with his main force as soon as Kaiser Francis declared war on him. In this case, noted Radetzky, the Austrians would resist Napoleon with all their forces while "the efforts of the Allies are to be regarded as merely ancillary and to facilitate our operations." According to Radetzky:

> It appears beyond doubt that, at the moment when an Austrian army seeks to inhibit Napoleon's further advance, he will turn his main force against it in order to repulse his most dangerous opponent and perhaps drive it into its

own country, therefore onto its source for the war effort. Therefore, we may assume with reason that our army will have to contend with the enemy's main force, while the Russo-Prussian army is merely occupied by several French army corps. If the above circumstances are to be accepted along with the understanding that in reciprocal operations a unity of will and activity exists, then certainly the strength of the 120,000-man [Austrian] army would suffice for the purpose of combined operations. However, because this cannot be presupposed and until Austria declares war on France the Allies will be even further weakened and unable to contain the enemy forces facing them, so arises our imperative necessity to resist with all of our forces the enemy's advances and to view the efforts of the Allies as merely ancillary and as support for our operations.

Thus, the Austrian General Staff viewed a defensive strategy as the best for the Austrian army to be employed against Napoleon. This opinion would not change despite progressive thinking on the part of the Russians and Prussians in June.[23]

Pleased by Stadion's report over the progress of the Austrian army, the Allies responded that they needed the support of an immediate Austrian offensive. Some began to doubt Austria's intentions. While Cathcart remained confident that Kaiser Francis would join the Coalition, Stewart wrote a scathing report to Castlereagh on 18 May:

> The 1st of June is the time fixed for the Austrians moving. Still the fate of the armies may be decided before that period. It is a curious game for a great nation to play – to procrastinate, I fear, by futile negotiations, which, to judge from the past, will never avail, and thus lose the only opportunity ever afforded her of acting with effect. If her troops were to *débouch* now – and why should they not, for it is absurd to suppose a *large force* must not be ready – the French dare not advance. What policy but a deep game can keep her from acting instantaneously, if she really desires to be effectual? It is troops in the field that will procure peace, and not Stadion with the gout at our headquarters, and Count Bubna in Bonaparte's camp. (I understand he arrived at Dresden on the 15th with a similar mission to Stadion's.) I may calculate all this erroneously, and those behind the curtain may know more. But it is so like the game Austria played before it is difficult not to have doubts.[24]

In the hope that Austrian troops would appear in the field sooner rather than later, Knesebeck, Volksonky, and Toll drafted guiding principles – the Wurschen Plan – for future Allied operations.[25] Due to Scharnhorst's absence, Toll and Knesebeck vied for the leading voice on military matters at Allied Headquarters. Knesebeck argued the centrality of Austria to the fate of the Coalition, maintaining that as long as the Allies could not count on the Austrians, "one could risk nothing and must resign himself to retreating before the enemy even if this retreat continued east of the Oder." Accordingly, the Russians accepted his proposal to hug the Bohemian frontier if forced to retreat further. The Allies chose this direction to remain close to the Austrians and to lean on the Riesengebirge (Karkonosze), part of the Sudetes Mountain system, which could provide coverage and support. If pressed by Napoleon, the Allied army could move into one of the entrenched positions such as Schweidnitz (Świdnica) that Frederick II had made famous during the Seven Years War. The Prussians had already started restoring the works at Schweidnitz and other points in Upper Silesia. By finally agreeing at least to reroute their main line of communication, the Russians acknowledged that unreserved, close collaboration with Austria would be the primary objective of future operations.

Nevertheless, the Russians would not allow their line of operation to be completely cut by an advance of the French army to Breslau and Glogau. They remained willing to have their reinforcements and supplies make detours as long as their light cavalry could harass the imperials from every direction and secure the freedom of movement for the reinforcements approaching the field army. However, the Prussians feared Alexander would lose his nerve if Napoleon pushed his main force between the Russian army and its homeland. Caemmerer reminds us that "of course he who outflanks is himself outflanked, and Napoleon would have quickly realized that basing himself on Glogau would be good for the moment to replenish his scanty ammunition and secure temporary asylum for the sick, but that he could not be deprived of continuous communication with the regions of the Confederation of the Rhine and with France."[26]

Detailed in a memo titled "Proposals Regarding the Campaign Plan," which both Knesebeck and Volkonsky signed, the Wurschen Plan sought to exploit Austria's physical location. The first of the memo's seven articles states that "the plan of campaign is based on the geographic position of the Austrian states in relation to the theater of war in North Germany." Article two declares that "because the Austrian states are situated in the flank of the enemy's line of operation and the Allied army is likewise in his flank, the latter would follow the enemy closely and throw itself on his communications should he drive into Bohemia or turn against the Austrian army." If Napoleon continued to pursue the Allies along his current line of operation, the Austrians would closely follow and do the same. Thus, the Austrians would take a position opposite Napoleon's flank. As soon as he turned toward Austria, the Russo-Prussian army would threaten his opposite flank. Whichever Allied army Napoleon did not attack would immediately take the offensive. If the Russo-Prussian army advanced against the flank and rear of Napoleon's army, it would press the French hard, but not seek a geographic objective. In the opposite case, the Austrian army would likewise pressure the French, but seek to attain geographic objectives. If the Allied army stood between the Elbe and the Oder when Austria issued its declaration of war against France, the Austrians would commence an offensive from Bohemia. If the French army held a position on the Elbe, the Austrian army would advance through Komotau (Chomutov) and Chemnitz to Leipzig. On the other hand, if the French army stood east of the Elbe, the Austrians would march from Theresienstadt (Terezín) to Dresden. Combined with Radetzky's ideas, the Wurschen Plan later became the core of the Reichenbach Plan that brought the Allies so much success in the upcoming Fall Campaign.[27]

Although a favorable development, the Allies still could not agree on a plan for their current situation. Knesebeck did not help the situation by offering staunch opposition to another battle. After convincing Frederick William to likewise oppose battle, the Prussians reversed their position and accepted a Russian proposal during a 16 May council of war attended by Stadion. Other than agreeing to wage another battle, the Allies decided nothing further. Vacillating between an offensive and a defensive, Wittgenstein finally announced on the 17th his intention to attack in two days but then postponed the operation.[28]

Per Hardenberg's promise to Gneisenau, the Prussian chancellor pressed Stewart for an offensive and defensive "treaty of alliance." He also mentioned the need for the Prussians to be reimbursed for the merchant ships seized by the British since 1806. "To all I replied I had no authority," reported Stewart to Castlereagh on 18 May. "Our subsidiary convention proceeds slowly. I have the points with Prussia chiefly to fight myself as Lord Cathcart thinks them less momentous; indeed, the whole of this has been very dilatory, and I see no end to it; but this is not my fault." On the previous day, Stewart presented the Prussians with a convention consisting of nine articles concerning various methods of funding their war effort; presumably, Cathcart likewise submitted a contract to the Russians. The Allies sought to distinguish between alliance and subsidy treaties, and expected to negotiate and conclude these issues separately.[29]

On the evening of the 19th, Cathcart met with Nesselrode while Stewart received an audience with Hardenberg to discuss numerous points of contention. First, the Prussians accepted the number of troops (100,000) requested by the British in return for the subsidy. However, Alexander still wished to set the Russian quota at 150,000 men. Stewart remained at a loss as to how Cathcart could convince the tsar to accept the figure of 200,000. "Lord Cathcart with every exertion will not get it up, I fear, to more than 170,000 or 180,000. Prussia will then only agree to be pledged to the half. They both wished to take the numbers of the Treaty of Kalisch [80,000 Prussians and 150,000 Russians] as their mark." Second, the British specified that the £2,000,000 be payable in London to avoid losses to the exchange rate. However, the Russians and Prussians urged payment on the continent and insisted on "knowing how and where they are to be paid, whether in *pièces sonnantes* [coin], or in paper." Third, the Russians requested a special issue of paper money called "federative paper" for the Russians and Prussians to pay their military expenses. The basic principles of this plan called for the British to issue the federative paper to the Russians and Prussians each month with two-thirds going to the former and the remainder to the latter. Once in circulation, the paper would accrue no interest but at the conclusion of the war it would do so at a specified rate until redeemed. After the peace settlement, Great Britain, Prussia, and Russia would jointly redeem all federative paper in circulation. In short, Great Britain, Russia, and Prussia would merge their credit to bankroll the latter two. Despite concerns about hyperinflation and counterfeiting, London agreed, especially because the plan enabled the British to fund the Allies without having to provide specie upfront and deferred payment of the debt until after the war ended.[30]

Although accepting the Russian plan, the British proposed limiting the issue to £5,000,000 redeemable at 5 percent interest six months after the peace or on 1 July 1815, whichever came first. All federative paper had to be used exclusively to cover the cost of military expenditure. Moreover, Great Britain would assume responsibility for half the capital and interest, Russia one-third and Prussia one-sixth. Finally, London would never be asked to assume responsibility for more than one-half the total issue. The Allies countered this offer by insisting that the British assume the capital and interest for the full amount. Negotiations continued after the June armistice concluded the Spring Campaign. In September, the British government accepted an Allied proposal that reduced the issue of federative paper to £2,500,000 with London accepting responsibility for the full amount.[31]

Returning to Blücher, Gneisenau confided to him that the Russian generals understood "half" of his concerns over the Kreckwitz position. Allied Headquarters accepted the principle of concealing the troops behind the hills but Gneisenau continued to negotiate with the Russians over the size of the attacking force. To actually reach the figure of 40,000 men, Gneisenau proposed uniting Miloradovich and Barclay with Yorck and Kleist. After Wittgenstein decided to post Miloradovich south of Bautzen, Gneisenau suggested joining Blücher's corps with Barclay's to provide a total of 35,000 men. Indecision prevailed. Days passed as the Russians debated and Wittgenstein vacillated between the merits of attacking or defending. In the end, the Russo-Prussian plan for a flank counterattack from Kreckwitz was both brilliant and shortsighted. By occupying the villages north of Kreckwitz (Doberschütz, Pließkowitz, Malschwitz, Salga, and Klix) with small battalion-sized garrisons and using the Cossacks to hinder French reconnaissance, the Allies could have deceived Napoleon over their force distribution (see Map 6). As his army engaged the Allies along the

Rieschen–Litten front, the flanking force from Kreckwitz could have slammed into his left wing. Yet in their planning, the Russians and Prussians persisted in assuming that Napoleon's attack would come from the west only. Despite knowing that he had detached a large force to Torgau, the Allies never considered the possibility that this force could envelop their right. In this scenario, not only would an offensive strike across the Kreckwitz hills in the direction of Bautzen become impossible but, as Gneisenau himself observed, the defense of the hills would be extremely risky. Attacked from both the west and the north, the Allies would have to fight with their backs to the Bohemian mountains and their line of retreat on the highway through Weißenberg to Görlitz would be compromised. In such a scenario, they would need nothing short of a miracle to prevent a disaster.

On the French side, Bertrand led IV Corps to Kamenz, twelve miles north of Bischofswerda, on 14 May. He pushed one division to Panschwitz, the halfway point between Kamenz and Bautzen (see Map 5). With Beaumont remaining at Moritzburg, Marmont moved VI Corps to Frankenthal, slightly northwest of Macdonald's XI Corps, which Napoleon initially ordered to remain at Bischofswerda. To support Macdonald if necessary, Oudinot forwarded the lead division of XII Corps to Fischbach, eight miles west of Bischofswerda, and echeloned the remainder of his corps along the great east–west highway. The Guard and I Cavalry Corps remained at Dresden. Further reports convinced Napoleon that the Allies had stopped work on their defensive position at Bautzen and renounced plans to offer strong resistance on the right bank of the Spree. In fact, several reports indicated that the enemy had evacuated Bautzen. In a letter to Macdonald, he insisted that his vanguard commander should have some evidence of this, advising that the marshal's occupation of Bautzen would be advantageous "if it came to a simple advance guard affair." He left the matter to Macdonald's judgment: "If you go to Bautzen, tell the duc de Raguse [Marmont], so he can move into Bischofswerda."[32]

Macdonald declined another encounter with Miloradovich after the Russians stopped his advance on the 12th. Nor did the marshal attack Miloradovich on the 13th or 14th, but instead waited for Bertrand and Marmont to flank the Russians. This allowed Macdonald to surge forward on the 15th. After a violent engagement with Miloradovich's rearguard at Göda, XI Corps forced the Russians to withdraw across the Spree to Bautzen. By that evening, Macdonald faced Bautzen with IV and VI Corps in line on his left for close support and XII Corps in reserve. The French could clearly see the Allied camps on the opposite bank of the river: the enemy had not evacuated Bautzen. Napoleon still hoped the Allies would leave but instructed Macdonald to take a good position secured by fleches "if the enemy continues to remain there in force."[33]

16 The Grande Armée crossing the Elbe at Dresden, 14 May 1813

Wittgenstein knew that at least one French corps and at most three had moved out of Dresden. Miloradovich's rearguard still held the left bank of the Spree. Had Wittgenstein counterattacked on the 16th, Macdonald, Marmont, and Bertrand would have been hard pressed without the decisive leadership of the emperor. The Allies did not need to await Barclay's reinforcements to launch such an attack. With Barclay's troops arriving that day, the 16th, Wittgenstein could have postponed the attack until the 17th if he had wanted to include the additional bayonets. Admittedly, French support would have been closer but their forward position still would have been vulnerable. On that day, a Prussian captain led a patrol of twenty hussars to the hill of Merka, five miles north of Bautzen. He correctly estimated the size of the imperial force to be three army corps. This news made no impression on Wittgenstein.[34]

The overall direction of Allied operations began to drift, marred by uncertainty, a lack of energy, and the failure to establish a clear plan. Debates ensued as Wittgenstein experienced even more adversity exerting his will at Allied Headquarters. "There appeared some difficulty in the interior arrangements of the Russian army," notes Stewart, "between the emperor [tsar] and his general-in-chief." To Castlereagh he wrote: "The tsar should do one thing or another – either command or keep entirely out of the way. As it is, both his Imperial Majesty and the King mar and confound the arrangements, and this is visible. Wittgenstein, having failed in carrying this as triumphantly as was expected when he assumed the command, has a strong party against him, being so junior an officer to others serving under him." The German historian Droysen, who at times is just as morose as his biographical subject, Yorck, claims that, although "possessing the noblest characteristics and fullest of devotion to the general cause, Wittgenstein lacked the hardness and strength that was required for him to meet all the objections and unwillingness that only grew more intense with every retrograde march. That the Prussians were not satisfied with his leadership could not escape him. And neither Blücher, nor Gneisenau, nor Yorck hid it; they felt the embarrassing lack of a firm and unwavering will, [and] of precision in the service. 'Rarely do we get a decision from Russian headquarters on the important matters,' complained Gneisenau."

Barclay's arrival complicated the situation. Senior to Wittgenstein, he had held an independent command since 1812. "Barclay de Tolly, who commanded at Borodino, and under whom Wittgenstein served, arrived yesterday," continued Stewart in his letter to Castlereagh, "and is placed *en second*. This is a strong case, and cabal is not surprising." An exasperated Wittgenstein submitted his resignation as commander in chief but Alexander provided no clear answer, thus perpetuating the uncertainty in the chain of command. It is possible that Wittgenstein retained command because he favored another battle with Napoleon, which the Austrians clearly wanted before they made their decision. A Prussian memorandum dated 14 May discusses the impact of Barclay's arrival:

> Unfortunately, this general is senior to Wittgenstein and either must receive overall command of the army, in which case a proposal to retreat all the way to Moscow for a second time can be expected, or be removed. If not, the disunity of the generals, which unfortunately we already have so much to thank for, will be even more out of hand. Today, Wittgenstein informed the tsar of this situation and said that he would gladly serve under his [Barclay's] command because the tsar must give the entire command to one person to prevent envy and disunity from doing damage to the general cause. The tsar has decided nothing over this, saying that he must consult with the king because it will affect the entire army.[35]

Meanwhile, for the stand at Bautzen, Wittgenstein considerably reorganized the Russian army. Miloradovich received command of the advance guard of the army's left wing consisting of a portion of his own corps but mainly Wintzingerode's corps to total 14,550 men and 54 guns, Wittgenstein placed this vanguard in a forward position along the Spree extending south from Bautzen to Doberschau. Miloradovich's light troops (2,300 men) took posts along the left bank of the Spree to engage the enemy's flank. Berg's corps and the main body of Miloradovich's former corps formed a new corps of 13,700 men and 64 guns commanded by General Gorchakov. Supported by the heavy batteries of the Russian Reserve Artillery, Gorchakov's troops occupied the Rieschen–Jenkwitz–Baschütz line (see Map 6). After Wintzingerode's poor leadership of the cavalry at Lützen, Wittgenstein considered placing all Allied cavalry under Blücher's command. However, because the Russians expected Napoleon to attempt to turn the left of the Allied position and because the terrain on the left wing did not suit cavalry operations, Blücher instead received "chief command of the several corps of the Prussian army forming the right wing of the Allies."[36]

Blücher's army stood north of Gorchakov's corps and echeloned along the road to Weißenberg. Yorck, who did not care for Blücher or Gneisenau and would have preferred to remain on the Kreckwitz hills with Kleist, found his small I Corps next to Blücher's II Corps. Grand Duke Constantine, the new commander of the Russian Guard and Reserve (19,900 men with 252 guns), placed his artillery and horse behind Blücher and on both sides of the road to Weißenberg; the infantry of the Russian Guard and Reserve camped south of Canitz-Christina. Finally, Barclay de Tolly's corps of 13,590 men and 84 guns moved into a concealed position along the northeast foot of the Kreckwitz hills. On the hills stood Kleist's 2,550 Russians and their 16 guns. In total the Russians provided 64,290 men; the Prussians another 31,900 men. Of this figure, Blücher's II Corps numbered 23,300 men supported by 90 guns; Yorck's I Corps, 5,670 men and 36 guns; and the Prussian portion of Kleist's corps, 2,930 men with 24 guns. Altogether, Wittgenstein possessed 96,190 combatants: 64,610 infantry; 19,220 cavalry; 3,920 Cossacks; and 8,440 gunners and pioneers with 622 guns. Including the 5,940 men and 20 guns of the various *Streifkorps* operating against the flanks and rear of the French army, the total figure of Allied forces in eastern Saxony exceeded 100,000 soldiers. Sitting east of the Spree for one week allowed the men to rest and recover after having campaigned continuously since 1 May. They would need the rest, for Napoleon would assail them with more than 140,000 men.[37]

Returning to the French, Ney's army marched northeast from Torgau in compliance with the emperor's orders from 13 May. Two days later, III and VII Corps reached Herzberg while V Corps moved into Doberlug, eighteen miles east of Herzberg (see Map 5). Victor's contingent arrived at Wittenberg. On the night of 15 May, Napoleon decided to have Victor, Reynier, and Sébastiani march on the Prussian capital while Ney and Lauriston "turned Bautzen." "The arrival of these two corps, which number 60,000 men, will provide us with a great superiority," he assured Macdonald. "At the same time, 40,000 men will march on Berlin." Berthier's orders to Ney and Lauriston on the night of 15 May called for the former to march almost sixty miles east from Herzberg to Spremberg on the Spree, and the latter to cover the forty miles between Doberlug and Hoyerswerda. Berthier provided both with a short explanation: the enemy appeared to be concentrating his forces to hold the position at Bautzen. The couriers departed Dresden around 11:00 on the night of the 15th but did not find the recipients until the evening of the 16th. Although V Corps remained at Doberlug, III Corps advanced from Herzberg to Luckau during the course of the 16th per the emperor's orders to march there on the 15th and 16th. Nevertheless, Berthier sent his courier to Herzberg. "It cannot be explained how the major-general could assume his message would reach Ney at Herzberg," comments Lanrezac.[38]

Although Ney received Berthier's order from the night of 15 May on the evening of the 16th, he still needed to comply but could not do so until the 17th, twenty-four hours later than Napoleon expected. Moreover, Ney received a copy of the orders sent to Lauriston but Berthier's instructions did not specify whether Ney should lead his entire army or just III Corps to Spremberg. Failing to understand Napoleon's intentions, he ordered the whole army to march on Spremberg. Lanrezac commends this decision, which he attributes to the influence of Ney's chief of staff, General Henri Jomini: "We recognize that on this occasion, the marshal proved wiser than Napoleon, because the situation demanded that the imperious officer act with the most resources possible against the main army of the Allies."[39]

Back at Dresden, Imperial Headquarters realized that Berthier's couriers had experienced difficulty in finding Ney. This prompted the major-general to reissue the orders for Ney's recall at 10:00 on the morning of the 16th as well as at 1:00 that afternoon. In addition, Napoleon became convinced that the Allied army would hold its position and accept battle. He thus shortened the marshal's objective to Hoyerswerda and had Berthier instruct Ney to march with "all diligence." Thus, at noon on the 16th, the major-general informed Macdonald that he expected Ney's 60,000 men to reach Hoyerswerda on the 18th, at which time the emperor would "force the enemy position." Until then, he advised Macdonald "to take a good position and link with Bertrand, who is between Kamenz and Bautzen, and do all that is required to avoid exposing yourself to an enemy attack."[40]

In a third letter to Ney, written at 5:00 P.M. on the 16th, Berthier provided the marshal with clear and precise instructions concerning Victor, Sébastiani, and Reynier.[41] Accordingly, the emperor wanted Ney to place Reynier and Sébastiani under Victor's leadership. Thus commanding II and VII Corps and II Cavalry Corps, around 25,000 men, Victor received the task of taking Berlin. Berthier used painstaking detail to explain Victor's mission to Ney: gain possession of Berlin, reoccupy Spandau, pursue Bülow if circumstances allowed, and communicate with Davout, whom Napoleon instructed to march from Hamburg to Mecklenburg. Victor's *première opération* involved driving Bülow across the Oder and burning the bridge over that river at Schwedt as well as destroying its bridgehead. From Berlin, Victor would establish communication with Stettin, Küstrin, and Glogau. Should the Allies attempt to take these fortresses, he would rush to the one that had the greatest need. If the Allies did not besiege the Oder fortresses, the emperor authorized Victor to proceed according to circumstances but in a manner to make a diversion by crossing the Oder at Stettin, Küstrin, or Glogau. After crossing the river, he would establish an entrenched camp on its right bank to threaten the entire region between the Oder and the Vistula. So confident of Victor's success was Imperial Headquarters that Berthier even discussed the manner in which the troops should be quartered around the Prussian capital.[42]

Ney received this letter at Calau, fifty miles north-northwest of Bautzen, on the evening of the 17th. On that day, VII Corps reached Luckau, III Corps Calau, V Corps Senftenberg, and II Corps and II Cavalry Corps Dahme. Ney communicated Berthier's instructions for the Berlin offensive to Victor, who received them on the 18th. He also instructed VII Corps to remain at Luckau on the 18th. Meanwhile, at 10:00 on the morning of the 17th, Berthier again issued orders to Ney, instructing the marshal to proceed from Hoyerswerda toward Bautzen. "Our whole army is converging on Bautzen," wrote the staff chief; "the enemy army is in the presence of ours." This, however, is all the detail that Berthier provided. Although previous notes spoke of Ney turning the enemy position at Bautzen, Berthier makes no mention of III and V Corps enveloping Wittgenstein's right while Napoleon fixed the Allied army at Bautzen. It may have been implied or expected that a marshal of France would understand his role but, for a headquarters accustomed to issuing precise instructions, this omission is striking. Instead of exact directions, Berthier requested that Ney inform him of the direction the marshal planned to take to reach Bautzen and the day he could expect III and V Corps to arrive. "The intention of the emperor," concludes his short note, "is that the prince de la Moskova and General Lauriston march on Bautzen from Hoyerswerda." Moreover, as we know, Napoleon intended for Victor, Reynier, and Sébastiani to advance on Berlin. Yet in this letter, Berthier advised Ney to direct these three commanders *according to what you have learned of the enemy and what you consider the most appropriate in the circumstances; every indication is that we will have a battle.*"[43]

That Ney ordered his entire army to march to Bautzen based on this letter should come as no surprise. Probably departing Dresden between 10:00 and 11:00 on the morning of the 17th, Berthier's courier rode fifty-five miles due north to reach Calau. Arriving late during the night of 17/18 May, this dispatch definitively clarified the situation for Ney. With the emperor poised to give battle, "the bravest of the brave" did what he considered to be "the most appropriate in the circumstances" in regard to Victor, Reynier, and Sébastiani. On the 18th, Ney issued his orders: VII Corps would remain at Luckau on the 18th and then follow III Corps to Hoyerswerda on the 19th. Victor, who had already commenced the march to Berlin with II Corps and II Cavalry Corps, received instructions to turn around and follow VII Corps to Hoyerswerda. "We repeat: he [Ney] was right," maintains Lanrezac, "unfortunately, II and VII Corps lost twenty-four hours: because of this delay they arrived too late to participate in the battle." In partial fulfillment of Napoleon's expectations, III Corps reached Sabrodt on the 18th, ten miles north of Hoyerswerda, where V Corps arrived.[44]

As for the Grande Armée, it did little on 16 May: only XII moved closer to Bautzen. Bertrand continued to loiter around Kamenz, neglecting to effect his junction with Macdonald. This earned a sharp rebuke and snide comment from Berthier in the emperor's name: "This movement is very urgent because the enemy has his whole army at Bautzen." For the 17th, Macdonald received the task of collecting as much intelligence as possible; Bertrand finally closed the gap between IV and XI Corps, and Oudinot's light infantry cleared the woods both before and behind the army, driving off the Cossacks to secure communication. All of the Young Guard and I Cavalry Corps commenced the march east with orders to reach the camp before Bautzen on the 18th, the day that Napoleon planned to join the army.[45]

Despite Wittgenstein's statements early on the 17th about attacking the enemy, the disposition that his headquarters issued that same evening prepared for a defensive battle. Because the disposition placed Barclay's corps one march away from the battlefield, Wittgenstein apparently drafted the battle plan on 15 May, but let it sit during the debates at Allied Head-quarters. Gneisenau relayed the corresponding orders to the troops early on the 18th; the Prussians prepared for battle. Late that morning, the imperials probed Miloradovich's security perimeter; the Allies believed this signaled the opening of the battle. After assembling the troops, the Russians dispatched several combined-arms detachments to reconnoiter the southern wing of the French position. The monarchs and their staffs ascended the church steeple at Bautzen from where they could see the entire French position. The patrols found nothing noteworthy and so the alarm ended.

Although the Russian reconnaissance found little to report, news streamed into the Allied camp from various directions. According to a Bohemian spy, the French army advancing to Bautzen consisted of 75,000 men and 120 guns. Most likely, Marshal Ney had already crossed the Elbe at Torgau with almost 80,000 men and over 150 guns probably to advance on Berlin. Napoleon left Dresden at noon on the 16th to join the army. In addition, the commander of one of Blücher's *Streifkorps*, Major Karl

Ludwig von Hellwig, incorrectly reported that Napoleon was at Torgau on 15 May and would march to Magdeburg and Berlin with a considerable army. Prisoners told the Prussians that "he [would] distract you before Bautzen and move everything to Berlin."[46] That same day, 18 May, Wittgenstein received the papers of a captured French staff officer. According to a letter from Berthier to Bertrand, Lauriston's V Corps would reach Senftenberg on the evening of the 17th and Hoyerswerda – twenty-one miles slightly northeast of Bautzen – on the 18th; the major-general directed Bertrand to establish communication with V Corps.

Piecing together the reports, the Allies concluded that Lauriston's corps of approximately 12,000 men would curve through Luckau and Hoyerswerda toward their right wing. With 18,000 men, Ney appeared to be following one march behind Lauriston. Reynier's VII Corps had purportedly reached Luckau and Lübben. Although this news shed light on the operations of Ney and Lauriston, some incorrectly assumed that these French commanders would continue to curve south to unite with Napoleon in a frontal attack on Bautzen from the west. Others, including those close to Frederick William, believed a report that Napoleon had united with Victor and was marching on Berlin, while an officer captured on the 17th stated that Napoleon's main army had taken roads leading northeast to Küstrin and Frankfurt on the Oder. Regarding Napoleon's supposed march on Berlin, Stewart informed Castlereagh that "if this intelligence is correct, and it came from the King of Prussia's *aide-de-camp*, I do not comprehend our remaining long here."[47]

Anxiety mounted in the Allied camp but morale remained solid. "More than a week we had been in daily expectation of a battle," recalled Cathcart, "sleeping in our clothes and with our horses saddled." "For eight days we have stood here and awaited the enemy," wrote Clausewitz on the 18th, "who has been facing us likewise for eight days but up to now still has not attacked. Most likely tomorrow, maybe the day after tomorrow, will be a great battle. Our troops are full of courage and we have received some reinforcements, although not considerable. We hope that, after what the enemy lost in battle and detached following the battle, we can be a match for him." "It was generally known that we were to take up a position and offer battle," reminisces Steffens. "Many jokes passed regarding this movement, and it was asked whether it was to be made in fact, or in a Fichtian sense – in a positive or a transcendental mode. There seemed no expectation of a real, important battle." Bogdanovich explains that an Allied advance against Ney's army would have occurred with the Spree behind them and the thick forest of Bischofswerda in front of them, where Allied cavalry superiority would have had no effect, while the imperials would have benefited from their considerable number of infantry. "This explains the inactivity of the Russo-Prussian army," notes the Russian historian, "which facilitated

Napoleon's concentration of his troops. It is incomprehensible that the Allies did not properly detect the position of the enemy before them through their vast number of light cavalry and Cossacks, which proved completely useless."[48]

Early on the 18th, Napoleon issued his final orders to move Imperial Headquarters, the bridging equipment, and the engineers and sappers, as well as the Old Guard and Guard Artillery, from Dresden to the camp facing Bautzen. Before dawn, Oudinot received orders to clear the woods around Neukirch to the south with a flying column of infantry and cavalry while Bertrand sought communication with Ney at Hoyerswerda. The emperor tasked I Cavalry Corps with scouring the gap between the army's right and the Bohemian frontier as well as driving the Cossacks from all the main roads. Later in the day, at 10:00 A.M., Napoleon showed mounting concern for the Cossacks on his right. Writing directly to Oudinot, he reiterated instructions for the marshal to "chase the enemy from Neustadt in Sachsen and Neukirch, and from all the positions on the right in such a manner that your right leans on Bohemia; I assume you have done this. If you have not, do so immediately. This position of the enemy on our right is embarrassing and contrary to the principles of war. From Bautzen and Bischofswerda it is only three to four leagues to Bohemia; drive the enemy from there. You will occupy it immediately and report to me . . . that you have done so." Berthier, who had probably received a tongue-lashing over Oudinot's negligence, added: "I have written you three times to inform you of the importance the emperor places on your pursuing and driving off the Cossacks that infest your right. His Majesty thinks that you have not taken any measures because there are still many [Cossacks]. As I wrote earlier, send strong columns; this is of the highest importance."[49]

Napoleon planned for Ney to be in position to turn the enemy's position at Bautzen. Writing to the marshal in code at 10:00 A.M. on the 18th, Berthier relayed Napoleon's thoughts and instructions: "We are a cannon shot from the small town of Bautzen, which the enemy occupies as the head of his position and where he has made entrenchments; the Prussians are on the right and the Russians on the left." From Hoyerswerda, III and V Corps would march twenty-two miles southeast to Drehsa. "The emperor desires that you and Lauriston unite all your forces and march on Drehsa," continued the major-general, "crossing the Spree near Gottamelde.[50] After crossing the Spree, you will find that you have turned the enemy's position. You will take a good position. His Majesty assumes that in any event you can easily reach Hoyerswerda by the 19th. You will approach us on the 19th and 20th, and on the 21st you will take a position that will have the effect of either forcing the enemy to evacuate [his position] and retire further or placing us in an advantageous position to attack him." General Emmanuel Grouchy received the task of delivering one of the copies of these orders.

Both Napoleon's letter to Berthier containing the instructions for Ney as well as the major-general's orders to the marshal identify Drehsa but the name of the village on modern German maps is Brösa (see Map 6). Another Drehsa is located further south between the Bautzen–Weißenberg and Bautzen–Löbau roads, and would have been directly in the rear of the Allied position. Not surprisingly, some contemporaries and historians disagree over which Drehsa Napoleon meant and question if Berthier bungled the orders because of Drehsa-Weißenberg's location immediately east of the Allied army. Based on the timetable and wording in the instructions for Ney that Napoleon wrote to Berthier it is clear that he meant Brösa. He explained to Berthier that having reached Drehsa (Brösa), Ney would then cross the Spree and turn the enemy's position. If he meant Drehsa-Weißenberg, then the marshal would first need to cross the Spree and then turn the enemy's position before reaching the village. Yet Napoleon's letter to Berthier makes no mention of Ney crossing the Spree at Drehsa "near Gottamelde." Moreover, he wrote that Ney should "approach us on the 19th, and on the 20th he will be able to move against the position [of the enemy]." According to Lanrezac, Berthier informed the emperor that the 20th was not feasible and that Ney would not be in position until the 21st. Regardless, it is clear Napoleon wanted the battle of Bautzen to take place on the 20th. In the end, Ney did not reach his position until the 21st, which forced the emperor to distract the Allies for twenty-four hours.[51]

The emperor departed Dresden late on the afternoon of 18 May and made for Großharthau, just west of Bischofswerda (see Map 5). On horseback, Napoleon rode alone with his entourage slightly behind, per his custom. In excessive heat and stifling dust, the master remained deep in thought. After some time he summoned the grand equerry, General Armand de Caulaincourt, and conversed with him privately for the duration of the ride to Großharthau. Undoubtedly they discussed the contents of a letter the emperor had addressed to Caulaincourt prior to leaving the Saxon capital:

> Being committed to employing all means to restore the peace, general or continental, we propose the convening of a congress, either at Prague, or in any other neutral place determined by the belligerent powers. We hope that this conference will quickly lead to the restoration of peace, which so many people desire. Therefore, we are determined to conclude an armistice or ceasefire with the Russian and Prussian armies for the duration of the congress. Wishing to prevent the battle that appears imminent based on the position taken by the enemy and wishing to spare humanity a useless effusion of blood, my intention is that you go to the outpost, where you will request an audience with Tsar Alexander to make this proposal to him and negotiate, conclude, and sign any military agreement designed to suspend hostilities.

The master knew how to manipulate his opponents: diplomatic issues would now befuddle military planning as the Allies considered, discussed, and debated the proposal. In addition, Napoleon wanted to negotiate directly with Alexander and hoped this proposal would trump Metternich's offer to mediate between the warring parties.[52]

Caulaincourt appeared at the Allied forward posts that same night. Alexander shelved the issue until convening a conference on the morning of the 20th. With battle at hand, Caulaincourt's mission took on larger proportions. Should the Allies agree, or reject and hold their ground, or reject and withdraw to another position? Frederick William and Hardenberg voiced the sentiment of the Prussian army when they urged Alexander to stand and fight. Fortunately for the Prussians, the tsar still did not understand the emperor. Napoleon's armistice proposal caused the Russian sovereign to doubt that the French would attack. In fact, this apparent confession of weakness reinforced Alexander's belief that victory was certain.[53]

Turning to Ney, the marshal instructed V Corps to depart Hoyerswerda at daybreak on the 19th and march through Wittichenau to Neschwitz with its right seeking communication with the Grande Armée through Panschwitz. As for his own III Corps, Ney intended for it to continue its march from Sabrodt through Hoyerswerda to Königswartha (see Map 5). Victor, Reynier, and Sébastiani received orders to advance to Hoyerswerda with the utmost diligence. Based on his directives to Lauriston, it is obvious that Ney had placed the enemy on the left bank of the Spree west of Bautzen. Knowing that the Grande Armée faced it, he sought communication with Napoleon's left, which he figured to be at Panschwitz. "It was impossible for him to be more incorrectly oriented," notes Lanrezac. Again, blame falls on Berthier for failing to provide Ney with precise information on the army's position. Had the marshal executed his movements as planned, III and V Corps would have moved into a position between Zerna and Neudorf facing south and much too far west to operate in accordance with the emperor's wishes. Fortunately for the imperials, Grouchy encountered V Corps and met with Lauriston very early on the 19th. En route, he learned – and no one knows how – that an enemy corps had marched from Bautzen in the direction of Königswartha. Grouchy notified Lauriston, who in turn warned Ney, informing the marshal that he would assemble his corps at Wittichenau and Maukendorf and await further orders.

Reaching Hoyerswerda around 11:00 A.M. on the 19th with the lead elements of III Corps, Ney received the orders directing him to Drehsa-Brösa as well as Lauriston's report. He immediately replied to Berthier: "Tomorrow I will maneuver on the position of Drehsa but I think it is very important to support my movement so that in case the enemy decides to await battle on the hills of Bautzen I am able to contain him if he marches on me through Kleinbautzen. Today my headquarters will be at Königswartha, and tomorrow probably Klix." The marshal also learned of the approach of an Allied force, possibly Yorck or Kleist. Ney responded by directing V Corps fifteen miles southwest to Lippitsch and Oppitz, the latter being four miles east of Königswartha. For III Corps, the marshal planned to continue the march on the Hoyerswerda–Königswartha road. He directed his van – Souham's division and one cavalry brigade – to Neudorf. Behind Souham, two divisions would halt at Niesendorf, just south of Königswartha, while corps headquarters escorted by two divisions occupied Königswartha itself. Unfortunately for Ney, V Corps did not march, meaning its baggage and trains blocked the roads. Thus, III Corps could not proceed to Königswartha until V Corps cleared Hoyerswerda around 3:00 P.M.[54]

Meanwhile, eleven miles south of Hoyerswerda, Peyri's Italian division (8,000 men), "a small number of French troops, and a few artillery pieces" from Bertrand's IV Corps reached Königswartha around noon. Increasingly apprehensive about Ney's approach, Napoleon wrote directly to Bertrand on the 18th ordering him to send a strong reconnaissance of infantry and cavalry in the direction of Hoyerswerda. "It is indispensable for you to establish communication with them on your left," exclaimed Napoleon. Bertrand delegated this task to Peyri's conscripts. Upon reaching Königswartha without any cavalry, the green Italians failed to take adequate security measures.[55]

As noted, no general Allied attack occurred on 19 May despite the intentions Wittgenstein had expressed on the 17th. The Allied commander in chief merely ordered the troops to remain ready to march but planned to counterattack as soon as Napoleon commenced his attack. For this reason, the Allies diligently completed the transformation of the Kreckwitz–Jenkwitz–Rieschen line into a formidable bastion (see Map 6). Directed by Sievers, hundreds of pioneers, civilian laborers, and troops erected one dozen batteries with strong profiles along the line. Infantry positions on the Baschütz and Jenkwitz hills placed the troops behind the artillery for maximum protection against enemy guns. The left of the Allied position leaned south toward the northern spur of the Bohemian mountains that pushed the Spree westward in a deeply cut valley upstream of Bautzen and along an eastern hill chain downstream of the city. Along this stretch, the Spree flowed in a narrow, craggy valley through the hill country that formed the intersection of the Lusatian hill chain and the wooded plain of Lower Lusatia. Two miles downstream from the village of Burk, the valley widened. With its rocky overhangs, woods, and ravines, the mountainous sector favored a tenacious defense. The numerous villages provided good points of support, especially after the Allies had fortified them with redoubts and abattis.[56]

Wittgenstein decided to post troops on both banks of the Spree. He positioned the vanguard on the left bank and in the town of Bautzen, with the main position on the hills and in the villages slightly east of the right bank; all could be defended by the row of entrenched artillery. Although earlier Wittgenstein had expressed willingness to exchange his communications with Bohemia for a position on the lower Oder, Stadion's news reoriented the Allies toward the importance of keeping open the road to Austria. In addition, they assumed Napoleon would probably direct his main attack against their left to sever communication between the Allied monarchs and Vienna. For these reasons, Wittgenstein planned to place the bulk of the Russian army on the left wing. Despite its strength, the Allied front extended 15,000 yards, making it too large for the army to hold. Moreover, Wittgenstein's overextension of his right wing considerably weakened the Allied position: a weakness that the master would exploit.[57]

Late on the morning of the 19th, Wittgenstein issued a new version of his disposition for battle. It contained the main points of the 15 May disposition, including the belief that a French attack would come from the west only. Like his earlier instructions, the twelve articles of the disposition of 19 May attempted to provide a response for every scenario that Wittgenstein could conceive, except the one that actually arose. With one exception, which will be noted below, and one omission – the failure to provide instructions regarding how the battle should unfold in general – his arrangements are adequate responses to the scenarios he foresaw. First and foremost, if the French crossed the Spree with superior forces either north or south of Bautzen, Miloradovich would hold his position for as long as possible. If forced, he would slowly withdraw and take a position in reserve behind Gorchakov's corps, with his infantry committed to the defense of Rieschen. Second, if the French crossed the Spree to attack Wittgenstein's right (Kleist and Barclay), the commander in chief first wanted to make sure that the right wing was indeed the French objective. After confirming that "all main movements of the enemy are directed on this point," the army would "reinforce the right wing through a typical right flank march." Third, if Napoleon attacked Blücher in the center of the Allied position, Barclay and Kleist would attack his left flank while the Allied left wing and reserve supported Blücher. Fourth, if Napoleon committed his main strength against the Allied left wing, Barclay and Kleist would attack his left flank and rear. Blücher would follow Barclay's attack accordingly. "By this turn of all our lines," wrote Wittgenstein, "the enemy must be driven against the mountains." Sixth, should Napoleon attack both Allied wings, Barclay, supported by the Russian Guard and Reserve, would reverse the situation as soon as possible and take the offensive while Blücher held his ground to provide time for Barclay to envelop the French left wing and "drive him into the mountains." By far, the response to this last scenario is the weakest; Wittgenstein provided no explanation of how Barclay would manage such a difficult task. Finally, in case the French left wing advanced through Gottamelde/Guttau to envelop the Allied right, Barclay would extend the right wing north to prevent this movement while the rest of the army followed.[58]

Wittgenstein's remaining articles addressed important house-keeping issues. For example, he instructed "the officers of the General Staff, the regimental adjutants, and the battalion adjutants to examine their system of communication and improve them where necessary ... for the better execution of these movements." He "earnestly" encouraged the corps commanders "to perpetually maintain communication with each other and inform each other of the enemy's precise movements and their own." All baggage would be sent to Reichenbach as soon as the battle began; all wounded and prisoners would be directed there as well. Wittgenstein planned to observe the battle from the hills behind the left wing; the tsar would accompany him. In case of a retreat, Barclay and Blücher would take the road to Weißenberg while Gorchakov, Miloradovich, and Grand Duke Constantine withdrew along the road to Löbau. The two columns would unite at Reichenbach.[59]

Reports had alerted Wittgenstein to the approach of Lauriston's presumably isolated corps. Not knowing that III and VII Corps followed so closely, the Russian commander saw an opportunity to crush one French corps with little risk due to the ability of Allied cavalry to mask the operation. To execute this surprise attack, Barclay received command of Yorck's I Corps and the Russian Grenadier Corps – altogether 23,700 men. Assuming Lauriston would strike the highway that ran from Hoyerswerda through Königswartha, Wittgenstein assured Barclay that he would find the French at the latter. As soon as Wittgenstein heard the sound of Barclay's guns, Miloradovich's forward posts would demonstrate against the French center to prevent it from supporting Lauriston.

From their bivouacs, the Allies marched in two columns at 12:00 A.M. on 19 May. On the left, Barclay's 13,000 men crossed the Spree at Niedergurig and turned directly northwest toward Johnsdorf, three miles east of Königswartha. Around 1:00 in the afternoon, Barclay's vanguard reached Johnsdorf and his scouts moved very close to Peyri's outposts without being detected. "It appears they [the Italians] had neglected their advance posts," explains Odeleben, "and as is their manner thought more of resting and refreshing themselves than guarding against an attack." Barclay sent one division around the north side of Königswartha and a second to the south side to cut the road to Bautzen. The Russians pounced, smashing the Italians, who fled north to Wartha, where Souham's division took them in around 3:00 P.M. Peyri, whom the Russians captured along with three brigadier generals, lost 2,860 men and 7 guns. Sustaining 1,000 casualties,

Barclay remained at Königswartha until 9:00 that night while the Cossacks continued to terrorize the poor Italian youths. According to Barclay's report to the tsar:

> Having discovered the enemy, I ordered General [Aleksandr] Rudzevich to engage the enemy outposts from the direction of Johnsdorf. In a vigorous attack, our Jäger swept the enemy outposts, who then retreated into the town while a dense forest and swampy terrain constrained our further attacks; this offensive allowed us only to reconnoiter the area. Having discovered another, more advantageous road that merged with the main route coming from Bautzen, I ordered the 18th and 9th Divisions ... to attack the village from the direction of Bautzen. The former division [the 18th], advancing at the head of the column ... encountered the enemy inside the woods near the town; despite his resolute resistance and fierce musket and cannon fire, the enemy was ejected from the woods and forced to retreat into the town, where he desperately fought in the streets and inside the houses but was driven out by the resolution and valor of Your Imperial Majesty's troops, who also captured seven cannon (two of which were damaged) and four enemy generals, including the Italian division commander Pecheri [Peyri], the brigade commanders Belottier and [Pietro] San Andreas, both of whom were wounded; of these, the first two soon died [of wounds], the third remains in captivity while the fourth was left on the battlefield with the gravely wounded. In addition, we captured 14 staff and junior officers and 740 rank-and-file.

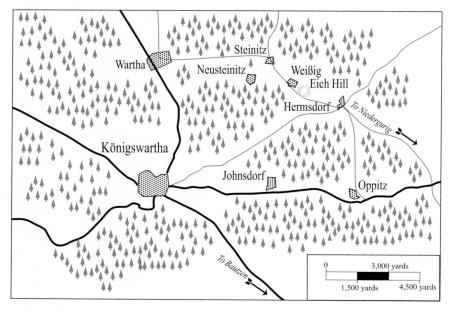

**18.** Combat of Königswartha, 19 May 1813

Forming the right Allied column, Yorck's corps moved northwest through Gleina and Gottamelde/Guttau in accordance with Barclay's orders, halting around 3:00 P.M. at Hermsdorf, four miles northeast of Königswartha. There, Yorck received Barclay's order to hasten his march to Wartha. At the same time, Lauriston's vanguard pushed south through Steinitz – two miles northwest of Hermsdorf – on the road coming from Spremberg. After French scouts emerged from the village of Weißig, halfway between Steinitz and Hermsdorf, Yorck's van drove them back through Weißig. From the Eich hill just south of the village, Yorck could see the head of a large column debouching from Steinitz. He immediately ordered Steinmetz's 1st Brigade to occupy Weißig, the Eich, and the surrounding woods; one horse battery unlimbered on the Eich hill to sweep the clearing between Steinitz and Weißig. Yorck placed his 2nd Brigade, Reserve Cavalry, and the rest of the artillery behind the Eich. Lauriston's vanguard deployed at the exit of Steinitz and started to gain ground in the woods between Neusteinitz and the Eich hill. As the engagement intensified, Yorck realized that he faced Lauriston's V Corps, which headquarters had mistakenly placed at Königswartha. Although outnumbered, Yorck's troops stubbornly held their position until 5:00 P.M. At that time, he received Barclay's request for support at Königswartha. Hard pressed, Yorck did not have to comply but felt obligated to do so and therefore dispatched his 2nd Brigade and Reserve Cavalry through the woods toward Johnsdorf. Yorck then withdrew his 1st Brigade from Weißig, the woods, and the Eich. Maison's division immediately occupied the positions abandoned by the Prussians.

Between 5:00 and 6:00, the Prussian 2nd Brigade reached Johnsdorf but by now Barclay had realized that Souham did not intend to advance from Wartha. Consequently, the Russian commander ordered Yorck to retake Weißig and establish his position for the night. One Russian division moved east to directly support the Prussians while a second marched northeast through the woods toward Neusteinitz to envelop the French right. Steinmetz counterattacked and a bloody struggle ensued for possession of the Eich hill, which changed hands several times. The French finally mastered the height and the woods near Hermsdorf but the Prussians did not allow them to enter that village. Fighting continued until 11:00 P.M.; Yorck did not leave Hermsdorf until midnight. Odeleben claims that "the Prussians fought like Spartans and thrice repulsed the French." According to Barclay's after-action report:

> A ferocious firefight quickly erupted and time and again the battle became rather bloody, which prompted me, after occupying the town [Königswartha] and observing that the enemy received reinforcements hourly, to order 9th Infantry Division and several battalions of the Grenadier Corps to support General Yorck. During this bloody engagement, our forces

and the troops of His Majesty the King of Prussia remained in intense fire for about seven hours, distinguishing themselves through their customary resolution and gallantry, and forcing the enemy to fall back a bit. The battle ended around 10:00 P.M. I have the pleasure of informing Your Imperial Majesty that success in this battle was achieved largely because of the bravery of the Allied forces that are entrusted to my command, as well as the prudent leadership of Generals Yorck and Prince [Aleksey] Shcherbatov.

Indicative of the "fog of war," Lauriston reported that his 13,000 men had defeated an enemy corps of 32,000 men in a glorious struggle. According to German sources, Lauriston's units sustained 1,500 casualties while the Prussians lost 1,883 men, more than 25 percent of Yorck's effectives. Steinmetz's brigade particularly suffered: of 2,000 combatants, only 950 could muster the following morning. The attrition of Prussian officers also continued: seventy-seven numbered among the casualties with thirteen killed, sixty-two wounded, and two missing. Together, the Russians and Prussians brought back 1,500 prisoners. Barclay, who received the Order of St. Andreas for his actions, raved about the performance of the Prussians, claiming that they endured murderous fire in difficult terrain yet always attacked. "General Yorck is beyond all praise," he boasted to Frederick William. "One cannot surpass the deliberate courage, sustained resistance, and the penetrating wisdom that he demonstrated during the course of this struggle."[60]

Earlier on the 19th, Napoleon had climbed the hills on the left bank of the Spree to reconnoiter the enemy's positions just after dawn. He then conducted reconnaissance throughout the northern sector of his line. He returned to his headquarters at Kleinförstchen around 7:00 that evening. The intensity of the cannonade, which had been heard from the direction of Königswartha since lunch, seemed to increase each minute. At 8:00, Napoleon mounted and rode to Kleinwelka. The burning villages in the distance and the thunder of the guns convinced him that considerable enemy forces were attacking Ney and Lauriston. Aside from remaining at Kleinwelka until midnight, the emperor did nothing. Yet he severely reproached Bertrand for not marching to the aid of his Italian division. Bertrand's deplorable conduct becomes all the more shameful when we consider that his outposts must have informed him of the march of an enemy corps through Niedergurig early that morning.

Although the Allies did not achieve Wittgenstein's objective of crushing V Corps, Peyri's destruction made an impression on Ney, who made no attempt to pursue Barclay. The events of the day persuaded him to keep III Corps north of Königswartha: three divisions remained at Hoyerswerda while two escorted the marshal's headquarters to Maukendorf. In an after-action report to Berthier written at 9:00 P.M., Ney stated that "one prisoner said that the enemy army is marching on Hoyerswerda. If this is true, I will receive a battle tomorrow. General Bertrand must have heard the firing today. I believe it is essential that somebody order him to move left [north] to facilitate my deployment. If the enemy attacks me tomorrow, I will accept battle at Neubuchwalde." Considering the position of the two armies on the night of the 19th, it is difficult to understand Ney's idea of accepting battle at Neubuchwalde, six miles south of Hoyerswerda, where the bulk of his corps had passed the night (see Map 5). Moreover, it is surprising that fewer than 20,000 Russians and Prussians stopped Ney cold and put him on the defensive, especially considering the numerous reinforcements moving up behind him. Lanrezac simply states that Ney did not understand the role assigned to him. While this is true, his conduct is likewise indicative of the problems of the aging marshalate. By 1813 warfare had changed. Multiple armies operating in multiple theaters both heralded the future and rendered obsolete the eighteenth-century concept of the sole omnipotent captain waging war. At a time when Napoleon desperately needed his marshals to take the reins of armies operating independently of his direct control, each would fail him.[61]

Among the many reports that reached either Russian or Prussian head-quarters on any given day, one in particular caught Gneisenau's attention. Written around 11:00 A.M. on the 19th by Prussian Captain Schöning, it established that Lauriston's corps had marched from Hoyerswerda south to Caminau earlier that morning. Also, imperial forces supposedly moving north from the French position west of the Spree had occupied Königswartha. Schöning's report alerted Gneisenau to the possibility of the French attempting "to proceed from Hoyerswerda toward Klix or another crossing over the Spree in order to envelop our right flank." He immediately notified Auvray that, instead of reinforcing the emperor's main army, Lauriston and Ney would execute a bold envelopment of the Allied army.[62]

This news left little doubt about Napoleon's intentions. Hopes that Ney's command would be insignificant in number quickly faded: such an independent operation required a considerable force to be effective. Conse-quently, the plan to launch a counterattack from the Kreckwitz hills likewise evaporated. Opposing Ney with sufficient forces would dangerously extend and thus thin the Allied line. Already trumped operationally, Wittgenstein could not seek a decisive battle at Bautzen. Instead, he needed to arrange the army's retreat from along a broad front. If Napoleon attempted to cross the Spree before Ney arrived, the opportunity to execute tactical strikes and perhaps cause considerable damage to the French army would arise, but only for a short window. To be able to exploit this opportunity, should Napoleon present it, the Allied army would maintain its current position for as long as possible until Ney's approach necessitated the retreat.[63]

By nightfall on the 19th, the entire imperial army stood along the left bank of the Spree. Oudinot's XII Corps held the right wing. In the center,

Macdonald's XI Corps faced Bautzen astride the great east–west highway. To its left stood VI Corps with IV Corps further north on the extreme left. North of the main army, Ney's lead corps – Lauriston's V – passed the night at Weißig, fifteen miles from Bautzen; III Corps camped at Maukendorf, eight miles further north, while VII Corps only made Calau, a full thirty-five miles north of Ney's position. Napoleon issued orders to attack the Allied left wing and center on the 20th. This would fix the Allies as Ney circled around their right wing to deliver the *coup de grâce* on the 21st. Thus, Napoleon needed twenty-four hours for Ney to be at full strength so he could slam the Allies like a hammer on an anvil. Remembering his experiences in Russia, the emperor could not allow the Allies to slip away during the night. Thus, he needed to tease them without entangling himself in a full frontal assault on the formidable Allied position. He planned to spend the morning of the 20th moving his pieces around the board to attract Wittgenstein's attention. Marmont and Macdonald received instructions to advance north and south of Bautzen respectively around noon on the 20th. On the right wing of the army, Oudinot's XII Corps would advance on Sinkwitz. To manipulate Wittgenstein into throwing all of his reserves onto his left, Napoleon wanted to give the appearance that he sought to turn the left wing of the Allied army. Despite Wittgenstein's objections, Alexander transferred to the left wing the precious few reserves that remained available. Having had enough of being ignored, Wittgenstein napped under a tree.[64]

## Notes

1  *CN*, Nos. 19996, 19998, and 20006, XXV:286–87, 293; SHAT, C$^{17}$ 177: Berthier to Macdonald, 12 May 1813. Chandler, in *Campaigns of Napoleon*, 889, clearly errs by referring to Napoleon's "single army" as "the new French Army of the Elbe" and claiming that Macdonald was its "deputy." Nothing exists in the correspondence to support these assertions.

2  SHAT, C$^{17}$ 177: Berthier to Marmont, 12 May 1813.

3  *CN*, No. 20000, XXV:288; SHAT, C$^{17}$ 177: Berthier to Marmont, Bertrand, and Oudinot, 13 May 1813.

4  *CN*, No. 20001, XXV:289; SHAT, C$^{17}$ 177: Berthier to Ney, Victor, Lauriston, and Reynier, 13 May 1813.

5  Despite these geographic objectives, Lanrezac maintains that the enemy army remained Napoleon's principal objective: Lanrezac, *Lützen*, 191–92.

6  By this time, Bülow's corps had doubled in size. His Prussian contingent included thirteen battalions, two Jäger companies, four volunteer detachments, thirteen squadrons, and six batteries. Russian units amounted to five battalions, four squadrons, three and one-half Cossack regiments, and two batteries. See Prittwitz, *Beiträge*, II:435.

7  *CN*, Nos. 20001, 20006, and 20007, XXV:289, 292–94.

8 *CN*, Nos. 20005–20007 and 20009, XXV:291–95; Petre, *Napoleon's Last Campaign*, 102; Lanrezac, *Lützen*, 185–86.

9 According to Cathcart, in *Commentaries*, 143: "A defensive position entirely on the right bank of the Spree, with Bautzen in the center, was objectionable, since, from the course the river takes below the town, the right wing must have been thrown far back. Bautzen is surrounded by an old wall, and favored by the steep bank of the Spree, yet it is a bad post, being much commanded, and it would have been a very salient point in the center of the line, not easily supported, though it must have been the key of the position."

10 Cathcart, *Commentaries*, 142–43. According to Clausewitz: "Jenkwitz lies on a stream that springs from the high mountain ridge where Hochkirch is located. This mountain ridge, therefore, went past the left flank of the position. The stream flows from Jenkwitz via Nadelwitz, Niederkaina, and Basankwitz toward Kreckwitz, where it turns to the right and flows through Kleinbautzen and Preititz toward Gleina. This stream curved ahead of the front, which at the center was about 1,500 yards away and formed a completely even segment of a circle. At Kreckwitz, the stream bisected the position in that the right wing occupied the section of ground between the stream and the Spree. This river, namely, runs for one mile completely parallel to the stream. At Gleina, the stream again came in contact with the extreme right flank of the position from the rear, because this flank ran diagonally between the Spree and the stream from Niedergurig towards Gleina. Just as the stream covered the front line up to Kreckwitz, the Spree covered the line of the flank from Niedergurig to Gleina. The space between Kreckwitz and Niedergurkau is approximately 1,500 yards wide and open. Ahead of it lie the heights that, at the village of Burk, form the edge of the Spree valley. All of the ground from Jenkwitz to Kreckwitz can be considered completely even, despite the left wing standing somewhat higher. Behind the position, however, the ground rises." See Clausewitz, *Hinterlassene Werke*, VII:287–88.

11 Stewart to Castlereagh, Wurschen, 18 May 1813, *CVC*, IX:11–12; Bogdanovich, *Geschichte des Krieges*, I:50–51; Holleben and Caemmerer, *Frühjahrsfeldzuges 1813*, II:125, 174.

12 The idea of a counterattack from the wing, uncommon at that time, could probably be traced to Toll, who had expressed similar views in the campaign of 1812. See Clausewitz, *Feldzug 1812*, 127.

13 Holleben and Caemmerer, *Frühjahrsfeldzuges 1813*, II:173, 175.

14 Plotho, *Der Krieg*, I:141–42; Bogdanovich, *Geschichte des Krieges*, I:33; Unger, *Blücher*, II:34; Gneisenau to Knesebeck, Kumschütz, 13 May 1813, in Droysen, *Yorck*, II:220.

15 Gneisenau to Caroline, Kumschütz, 13 May 1813, GStA PK, VI HA Rep. 92 Nl. Gneisenau, Nr. 21.

16 Gneisenau to Hardenberg, Kumschütz, 13 May 1813, GStA PK, VI HA Rep. 92 Nl. Gneisenau, Nr. 20b.

17 Pertz and Delbrück, *Gneisenau*, II:615.

18 Clausewitz, *Hinterlassene Werke*, VII:285–86; Stewart to Castlereagh, Wurschen, 18 May 1813, *CVC*, IX:13; Mikhailovsky-Danilevsky, *Denkwürdigkeiten*, 93. See Lieven, *Russia Against Napoleon*, 317–20, for an account of the diplomatic

negotiations between Austria and the warring powers. For Metternich's instructions to Stadion, see Oncken, *Österreich und Preußen*, II:305–06.

19  Oncken, *Österreich und Preußen*, II:316.

20  The seven articles of the Wurschen Convention can be found in Oncken, *Österreich und Preußen*, II:318. For the sake of simplicity, I refer to these agreements as a "convention" but the Allies did not draft a new treaty to replace those of Breslau and Kalisch. Instead, this seven-point program is spelled out in two very similar notes from Nesselrode and Hardenberg in response to Stadion's request for an explanation of Allied war aims. In fact, in articles one, two, and four it is only the wording that differs slightly in the two responses.

21  Ross, *European Diplomatic History*, 332; Kissinger, *A World Restored*, 73; Nicolson, *The Congress of Vienna*, 53; Kraehe, *Metternich's German Policy*, I:174; Schroeder, *European Politics*, 460–61. For Metternich's maximum and minimum proposals, see Oncken, *Österreich und Preußen*, II:306–07.

22  On the advice of Schwarzenberg and Radetzky, the Austrian cabinet changed plans. Per their earlier decision, Austrian forces in Bohemia would assemble on the Eger, from where they could penetrate the Upper Palatinate. However, now that the Allies had withdrawn east of the Elbe, the Austrians assumed the retreat would continue to the Oder. Subsequently, the Austrian cabinet decided to post the army on the Elbe close to the Saxon frontier: Oncken, *Österreich und Preußen*, II:307.

23  Radetzky to Schwarzenberg, "Memoire über den Zweck der Operationen und deren muthmaßlichen Gang, so wie die anzuwendenden Mittel," Vienna, 10 May 1813, reproduced in full in Radetzky, *Denkschriften*, 101–04. The key paragraphs are located on pages 103–04.

24  Stewart to Castlereagh, Wurschen, 18 May 1813, *CVC*, IX:13.

25  The term "Wurschen Plan" is used to reference military operations while "Wurschen Convention" is used to denote the revised Allied war aims.

26  Oncken, *Österreich und Preußen*, II:320–21; Pertz and Delbrück, *Gneisenau*, II:635; Holleben and Caemmerer, *Frühjahrsfeldzuges 1813*, II:252, 262.

27  No date is stated on the document but it was signed in time for Stadion to include a copy in his 16 May report to Metternich. The plan, "Vorschläge über den Feldzugsplan," is reproduced in Oncken, *Österreich und Preußen*, II:321–22 in German and 658–59 in French.

28  Wittgenstein to Bülow, Purschwitz, 17 May 1813, GStA PK, IV HA Rep. 15A Nr. 248.

29  Stewart to Castlereagh, Wurschen, 17 and 18 May 1813, *CVC*, VIII:390–91, IX:13–14.

30  The actual Russian proposal submitted to Cathcart by Nesselrode can be found in Stewart to Castlereagh, Wurschen, 17 May 1813, *CVC*, VIII:391–97; Stewart to Castlereagh, Wurschen, 18 May 1813, *ibid.*, IX:16; Sherwig, *Guineas and Gunpowder*, 289–90. See "Suggestions Respecting the Proposed Federative Paper," by N. Vansittart, *CVC*, VIII:404–05. Cathcart took offense to Stewart's description of his travails and, as the senior diplomat demanded that Stewart first read his reports for London to him, prompting Stewart's comment: "Lord C[athcart] takes two days to consider a dispatch, and two to write one, and he never

begins to think till other people have done. Now this may send you the wisest results, but certainly not the most expeditious details. If I were to send a dispatch unknown to him, and he were to discover it, there would be an end to our harmony." See Stewart to Castlereagh, Reichenbach, 19 June 1813, *ibid.*, IX:28–29.

31 Castlereagh to Stewart, London, 22 June 1813, *CVC*, VIII:406–08; Muir, *Britain and the Defeat of Napoleon*, 253–54. In June, the British conceded to Alexander's figure and consequently reduced the Prussian contribution to 80,000 men. Although the Prussians eventually fielded double this number, they still received only one-third of the £2,000,000.

32 SHAT, C[17] 177: Berthier to Macdonald, Bertrand, Marmont, and Oudinot, 14 May 1813; *CN*, Nos. 20008 and 20009, XXV:294–95; Lanrezac, *Lützen*, 193.

33 SHAT, C[17] 178: Berthier to Macdonald, 15 and 16 May 1813; Lanrezac, *Lützen*, 193; Mikhailovsky-Danilevsky, *Denkwürdigkeiten*, 97; Bogdanovich, *Geschichte des Krieges*, I:33–36.

34 Holleben and Caemmerer, *Frühjahrsfeldzuges 1813*, II:177–78; Foucart, *Bautzen*, I:221, 258–60; Droysen, *Yorck*, II:73. According to Stewart, in *Narrative*, 43: "At this period, reports of the enemy's movements were very contradictory. Some affirmed that Bonaparte was in person at the camp opposite Bautzen ... and that he meditated an immediate attack: others conjectured that not more than 30,000 men were immediately in our front."

35 Quoted in Droysen, *Yorck*, II:71; Stewart, *Narrative*, 43; Droysen, *Yorck*, II:70; Stewart to Castlereagh, Wurschen, 18 May 1813, *CVC*, IX:12–13; Mikhailovsky-Danilevsky, *Denkwürdigkeiten*, 107, claims Wittgenstein submitted his request to resign shortly after the battle of Bautzen rather than before it.

36 Cathcart, *Commentaries*, 148.

37 Prittwitz, *Beiträge*, II:142; Holleben and Caemmerer, *Frühjahrsfeldzuges 1813*, II:181–82. Bogdanovich, *Geschichte des Krieges*, I:39, 53, states that there were 93,000 men at Bautzen (65,000 Russians and 28,000 Prussians) with 610 guns.

38 Jomini notes that Lützow's *Freikorps* disrupted communication between Ney and Napoleon and that "several important orders had been intercepted": Jomini, *Précis politique et militaire*, I:266.

39 SHAT, C[17] 178: Berthier to Ney and Lauriston, 15 May 1813; *CN*, Nos. 20001 and 20011, XXV:295–96, 299; Lanrezac, *Lützen*, 195. Jomini of course claims full credit: "Attaching too much importance to the movement on Berlin, Ney was prepared to go there in person; fortunately, he was prevented by the news received from Lübben that informed him of Barclay's arrival near Bautzen. This incident gave General Jomini the opportunity to perform an outstanding service. After the marshal prescribed to him an eccentric order to move in the direction of Berlin without telling him the goal, his chief of staff presented to him the disadvantages of leaving the emperor alone to struggle with the Allied army toward Bautzen, and instead he proposed following Lauriston to Hoyerswerda with III Corps." Jomini maintains that Ney refused to accept the argument, and so Jomini drafted the orders as if Ney himself had written them and thus had to sign the document. "Surprised at this unusual form, the marshal demanded an explanation and Jomini observed to him that this movement was absolutely in

opposition to the principles he had outlined in all his works on strategy, and he could not bring himself to compromise at the same time both the army and his own military reputation: he preferred to resign as chief of staff and go, if necessary, to Berlin, with one brigade that he [Ney] would entrust to his command, but that his conscience would not allow him to sign the order that would direct all the marshal's forces there. Enjoying the firmness of conviction and perhaps having individual orders, Ney also refused to sign. Jomini said to him: 'So we'll stay where we are, which is always better than pushing ourselves to our left when all the rules of war and the salvation of the army demand that we push ourselves to the right.' The marshal accepted these accurate reasons, and the two corps marched on the 17th toward Senftenberg and Hoyerswerda, following Lauriston. General Jomini advised to move the duc de Bellune [Victor] and Sébastiani's cavalry to Spremberg to complete the maneuver that was intended to seize the only line of retreat of the Allies. This movement was not executed either because Ney was too afraid to isolate the corps or Bellune did not march fast enough to arrive on time." See Jomini, *Précis politique et militaire*, I:264–65.

40  SHAT, C¹⁷ 178: Berthier to Ney and Macdonald, 16 May 1813.

41  Puthod's 17th Division received orders to rejoin V Corps but remained with Victor while Napoleon transferred Philippon's 1st Division to II Corps.

42  SHAT, C¹⁷ 178: Berthier to Ney, 16 May 1813.

43  Lanrezac, *Lützen*, 198; SHAT, C¹⁷ 178: Berthier to Ney and Lauriston, 17 May 1813, emphasis added.

44  Lanrezac, *Lützen*, 198; Weinzierl, "Victor," 348; Finley, "Jean Reynier," 387–88.

45  *CN*, No. 20016, XXV:299; SHAT, C¹⁷ 178: Berthier to Oudinot, 16 May 1813; Berthier to Mortier, Bertrand, Macdonald, and Oudinot, 17 May 1813.

46  Wittgenstein to Blücher, Purschwitz, 17 May 1813, GStA PK, VI HA Rep. 92 Nl. Gneisenau, Nr. 18, I; Hellwig to Blücher, Hoyerswerda, 17 May 1813, 10:00 P.M., *ibid.*, Nr. 18; Holleben and Caemmerer, *Frühjahrsfeldzuges 1813*, II:183–86. In *Private Diary*, II:13–14, Wilson notes that "nothing is known of the movements of the enemy except that a large column [Ney] is advancing from Kamenz, as I think, to Hoyerswerda, to turn our right; while the corps now opposite to us will march through the mountains on our left, as [Leopold Joseph von] Daun did when he turned Frederick the Great."

47  Stewart to Castlereagh, Wurschen, 18 and 19 May 1813, *CVC*, IX:14; SHAT, C¹⁷ 178: Berthier to Bertrand, 10:00 P.M., Dresden, 17 May 1813; Foucart, *Bautzen*, I:233; Plotho, *Der Krieg*, I:146–47; Petre, *Napoleon's Last Campaign*, 112; Knesebeck's report on the battle of Bautzen, Wurschen, 20 May 1813, in Pflugk-Harttung, *Das Befreiungsjahr 1813*, 159.

48  Cathcart, *Commentaries*, 154; Clausewitz to Marie, Kumschütz, 18 May 1813, in Schwartz, *Clausewitz*, II:82; Steffens, *Adventures*, 100; Bogdanovich, in *Geschichte des Krieges*, I:40.

49  *CN*, Nos. 20020–20023, XXV:302–04; SHAT, C¹⁷ 178: Berthier to Oudinot, 18 May 1813.

50  Gottamelde is Guttau on modern German maps.

51  *CN*, No. 20024, XXV:304; SHAT, C¹⁷ 178: Berthier to Ney, Dresden, 10:00 A.M., 18 May 1813; Lanrezac, *Lützen*, 199.

52 Odeleben, *A Circumstantial Narrative*, I:85; *CN*, No. 20031, XXV:309–10; Chandler, *Campaigns of Napoleon*, 889–90.

53 Unger, *Blücher*, II:39; Pertz and Delbrück, *Gneisenau*, II:620–21; Droysen, *Yorck*, II:72.

54 Jomini, *Précis politique et militaire*, I:266.

55 SHAT, C² 145: Ney to Berthier, Hoyerswerda, noon, 19 May 1813; *CN*, No. 20027, XXV:306; Lanrezac, *Lützen*, 202–03.

56 Holleben and Caemmerer, *Frühjahrsfeldzuges 1813*, II:180, 186–88; Unger, *Yorck*, II:36.

57 Maude, *Leipzig Campaign*, 135; Pertz and Delbrück, *Gneisenau*, II:618; Foucart, *Bautzen*, I:259–60.

58 In *Commentaries*, 148, Cathcart makes an interesting observation: "In the Allied army, Wittgenstein was to retain ostensibly the chief command during the battle, although he was junior to Barclay de Tolly; ostensibly, because the Emperor Alexander in fact assumed the supreme direction of affairs." According to Cathcart, Barclay "was to act independently with his corps, and employ it as a *colonne mobile* according to circumstances, for the security of the right."

59 Wittgenstein to Blücher, Purschwitz, 19 May 1813, GStA PK, VI HA Rep. 92 Nl. Gneisenau, Nr. 18, I; Maude, *Leipzig Campaign*, 135.

60 Sources for the engagements on 19 May: Odeleben, *A Circumstantial Narrative*, I:91; Barclay to Frederick William, Först, 20 May 1813, in Droysen, *Yorck*, II:88; Barclay to Alexander, "Report ego imperatorskomu velichestvu," Först, 20 May 1813, in *Voyna 1813 goda*, I/1:94–95; Jomini, *Précis politique et militaire*, I:266–67; Bogdanovich, *Geschichte des Krieges*, I:40–48; Mikhailovsky-Danilevsky, *Denkwürdigkeiten*, 97–98; Lanrezac, *Lützen*, 203–06; Plotho, *Der Krieg*, I:148–52; Holleben and Caemmerer, *Frühjahrsfeldzuges 1813*, II:197–206; Vaudoncourt, *Histoire de la guerre*, 91–92. Droysen, in *Yorck*, II:74–89, offers incredible detail on this little-known combat. He also provides Yorck's after-action report, written on 7 June 1813. See also Knesebeck's report on the battle of Bautzen, Wurschen, 20 May 1813, in Pflugk-Harttung, *Das Befreiungsjahr 1813*, 159–60. Lanrezac, who cites Lauriston's losses at 2,000 and Yorck's at 2,300, defends Lauriston against the accusation that he committed his troops haphazardly by arguing that an encounter battle on unfamiliar terrain limits the commander's ability to direct the action.

61 *CN*, No. 20090, XXV:363; SHAT, C² 145: Ney to Berthier, Maukendorf, 9:00 P.M., 19 May 1813; Odeleben, *A Circumstantial Narrative*, I:90–91; Lanrezac, *Lützen*, 208.

62 Gneisenau to Auvray, 19 May 1813, GStA PK, VI HA Rep. 92 Nl. Gneisenau, Nr. 18.

63 Holleben and Caemmerer, *Frühjahrsfeldzuges 1813*, II:207–08.

64 SHAT, C¹⁷ 178: Berthier to Macdonald, Oudinot, Bertrand, and Marmont, 20 May 1813; Yorck von Wartenburg, *Napoleon as a General*, II:258; Maude, *Leipzig Campaign*, 135–36.

# 8

# The Prussian Thermopylae

All remained quiet in the French camp on the "lovely May morning" of the 20th, giving the appearance that Napoleon would not attempt to cross the Spree on this day. From one of Bautzen's church steeples, Prussian staff officers noted at 9:15 the march of two imperial infantry divisions northeast from the plateau of Welka as well as the massing of cavalry on the French left. Napoleon himself could be seen reconnoitering the Bautzen position. Along with the reports from the previous day, this news prompted Wittgenstein to continue the measures already started by the corps commanders that corresponded to his instructions for countering a movement through Guttau (Gottamelde) by the French left wing to envelop the Allied right. Accordingly, Barclay would extend the right wing north, leaving Kleist's corps on the hills at Burk to cover his movement; the army then would follow Barclay.

Earlier that morning, Barclay posted his main body between Klix and Brösa; Yorck's corps remained in reserve on the hill of Guttau; and Blücher pushed forward an entire brigade to the Kreckwitz heights (see Map 6). Around noon, he received final instructions from Wittgenstein to move II Corps from Baschütz north to a position between Kreckwitz and Brösa. Grand Duke Constantine's two cuirassier divisions would combine with Blücher's Reserve Cavalry to extend the right wing to Brösa and serve as an intermediate line between Blücher and Barclay. Unsure of the number of villages on the right bank of the Spree between Kreckwitz and Brösa, Wittgenstein directed Blücher to occupy as many as he found. Gorchakov's infantry would form the second line by marching north and assuming the position vacated by II Corps at Baschütz. Kleist would remain at Burk; the infantry of the Russian Guard and Reserve would likewise maintain their positions south of the Bautzen–Weißenberg road. These measures did not achieve fruition. Wittgenstein recalled the cuirassiers to cover the batteries south of Litten. Next, Barclay reported that he could not maintain the Klix–Brösa line and so fell back to the Malschwitz–Gleina line. Under these circumstances Blücher posted Zieten's brigade between Kreckwitz and Doberschütz, concealing his other two brigades as well as Dolffs's Reserve Cavalry along the eastern foot of the Kreckwitz heights.

Around noon, French artillery blasted the Allied positions while IV, VI, XI, and XII Corps and I Cavalry Corps advanced toward the Spree. "At Wurschen on 20 May," recalls Mikhailovsky-Danilevsky, "we heard artillery fire around 11:00 AM and initially thought nothing of it, believing that a rearguard combat, which took place daily, had started; but soon the cannonade grew stronger, and around noon the tsar went to the troops. He remained on the hills at Niederkaina, from where the French attack on Miloradovich's vanguard and the Prussian general Kleist could be clearly seen; from the great number of troops that Napoleon led in waves one concluded that he would reach our redoubts, just like at the battle of Borodino." Building trestle bridges, the French speedily crossed the Spree. Macdonald's XI and Oudinot's XII Corps slammed into Miloradovich's center and left respectively. In a last gasp, Miloradovich repulsed the French through a counterattack by six battalions of Russian Guard. Regardless, Marmont's VI Corps crossed the Spree north of Bautzen, prompting the Russians to fall back. Fearing that his garrison at Bautzen would be cut off, Miloradovich ordered the strongly entrenched post to retreat. After the Russian garrison evacuated Bautzen, Miloradovich ordered a general retreat of the Allied left around 4:00 P.M. By 6:00, the imperials controlled Bautzen.

Earlier in the day, Blücher's corps had trooped north from the center of the Allied position as the thunder of the guns resounded from Bautzen to the Kreckwitz heights. To confront the French, the Prussians took a position between Malschwitz and the village of Kreckwitz. Zieten's 2nd Brigade formed the front while Klüx's 1st Brigade and Röder's reserve stood at Kleinbautzen. Just west of the right wing, the Prussians occupied the villages of Pließkowitz and Doberschütz with one battalion each. One mile west of Doberschütz, the right wing of Kleist's truncated corps held the village and height of Niedergurig as well as the bridge over the Spree 1,000 yards upstream. Forming Blücher's vanguard, Kleist's small corps inexplicably stretched almost three miles from Niedergurig along the hills to Burk and Niederkaina.

Around 1:00 P.M., Bertrand's IV Corps and Latour-Maubourg's I Cavalry Corps, both commanded by Marshal Nicolas Soult, reached the region of Quatitz, five miles north of Bautzen and less than two miles west of the bridge over the Spree near Niedergurig. A Russo-Prussian cavalry detachment from Kleist's corps supported by one Russian horse battery slowly yielded before Soult's superior numbers as Blücher's corps approached in support. After crossing the Niedergurig defile, the Fusilier

17  Napoleon directing the crossing of the Spree at Bautzen, 20 May 1813

Battalion of the 2nd East Prussian Infantry Regiment took position on the right bank to cover the further retreat of Kleist's troopers and protect the bridge. From Doberschütz, Zieten sent the Fusilier and 3rd Battalions of the 1st Silesian Infantry Regiment to occupy the village of Niedergurig. Soult deployed Morand's division opposite Niedergurig; three columns followed by General Friedrich von Franquemont's Württemberger division converged on the Spree. Morand's left column moved north toward the village of Briesing, and the middle column made for Niedergurig itself, while the right column marched toward the Gottlobs hill on the left bank south of Niedergurig. Blücher's batteries enfiladed Morand's middle and left columns from the Weißestein, Galgen, Kiefern, and Bölau hills, all of which formed a semicircle around the Niedergurig defile and the Gottlobs. At the village of Niedergurig, two Prussian battalions held for three hours against numerous attacks by Morand's middle column. Finally, an assault by four imperial battalions (three French and one Württemberger) managed to expel the Prussians, who withdrew to Doberschütz.

The three-hour struggle for Niedergurig mattered little because earlier the imperials had bypassed the village and won the bridge but had failed to get across the Spree. According to Blücher's after-action report, "the defile through which the enemy was forced to move was completely surrounded by artillery ... a semicircle of fire was concentrated on this sole exit." After taking the Gottlobs, the French quickly unlimbered heavy artillery and responded to the Allied battery directly across the Spree on the Bölau,

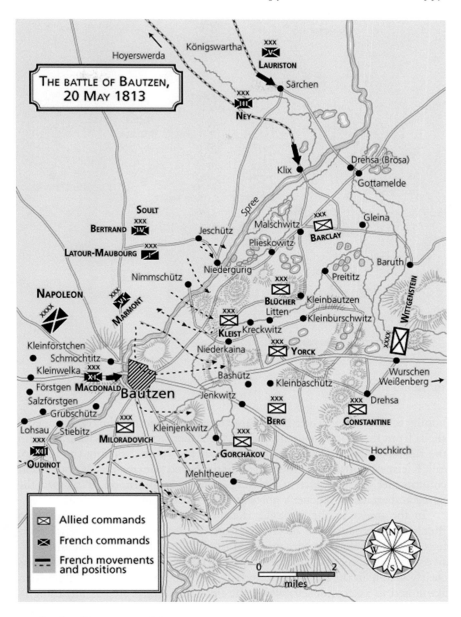

**19.** Battle of Bautzen, 20 May 1813

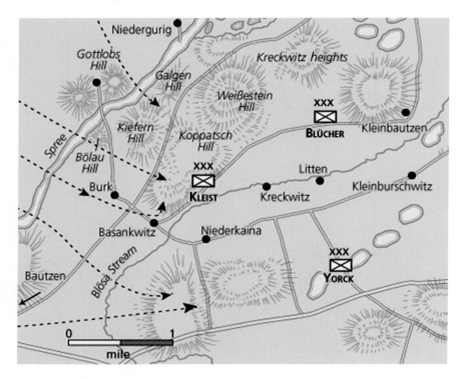

**19.** (*cont.*) Inset.

hoping to silence it so the right column could move across the river. Imperial shells from the Gottlobs finally forced the Allied artillery to withdraw from the Bölau; French infantry swarmed across the Spree, reaching the Kiefern hill. Kleist's cavalry drove them back to the Spree. Meanwhile, Morand's left column met no resistance at Briesing. Later that afternoon, it crossed the Spree and attacked Blücher's posts at Doberschütz and Pließkowitz.

In the midst of the struggle, the monarchs and Wittgenstein rode to Blücher's command post on the Kiefern hill. According to Professor Steffens, "a bare rock of granite crowned the hill, and it commanded an extensive view, including the widespread field of battle. Every part of the field was clearly visible in the dazzling noonday." With the tsar present, Wittgenstein attempted to assert himself, which the Prussians interpreted as meddling in Blücher's arrangements. According to one of Blücher's adjutants, August Ludwig von Nostitz, Wittgenstein pontificated "about the advantages of the position and the preparations that had been made." Turning to Blücher, the Allied commander in chief stated that, "if today you hold this position, tomorrow's battle will be won for us." Blücher blew up over the implied meaning of the statement. "I will hold the position today – I give you my word of honor – tomorrow *you* win the battle," he barked. A French shell that exploded at the foot of the hill ended the conference. Crown Prince Fritz informed his brother that, leaving Blücher behind, "the two rulers and all of us, an enormous suite, retired through flying cannonballs and grenades that began to fall among us to a higher, rather distant hill, but here they followed us, and so we went to the left wing."[1]

Around 5:00 P.M., Kleist's situation became critical after Miloradovich's men withdrew from their positions south of him. Bonet's division from Marmont's VI corps attacked his position at Burk while Friederichs's division emerged from Bautzen and began working around Kleist's left wing at Niederkaina. Burk fell but Kleist led a successful counterattack to retake the village with his last reserve: the Kolberg Infantry Regiment. The monarchs instructed Blücher to commit three battalions to support Kleist but Burk again fell before the reinforcements arrived. Attacked by ever increasing numbers, Kleist's small corps fought with noteworthy bravery and endurance until the onset of darkness. As imperial forces moved southeast to take Niederkaina and envelop his position, Kleist recognized that time had run out. With his ammunition completely exhausted, he ordered the retreat around 7:00. Saved by Dolffs's cavalry from being encircled, Kleist's exhausted warriors retreated eastward through Basankwitz to Litten.

Meanwhile at Niedergurig, Blücher's guns lambasted the French. Addressing the effectiveness of his artillery, the general noted in his after-action report that "the enemy advanced with scattered infantry, establishing a battery on this side of the Spree that was silenced in a few hours by superior fire, and his skirmishers were driven back across the Spree before sunset." Despite the artillery's deadly work, the Prussians could not hold the Niedergurig bridge. "After Kleist abandoned the hills of Burk at sunset," continues Blücher's report, "the artillery, which had prevented the debouching from the Spree, also had to fall back, and the enemy was allowed to advance against General Blücher's center. The corps passed the night in its position." Around 8:30 P.M. the firing ceased in Blücher's sector. With the burning remains of eighteen villages providing the only light, the Fusilier Battalion of the 2nd East Prussian Infantry Regiment fell back from the right bank of the Spree to the Kiefern hill, being joined by Zieten's main body. His troops camped in complete darkness only 200 yards from the French. Later that night, Blücher's battalions at Doberschütz and Pließkowitz rejected French probes. Nevertheless, the combat that unfolded in the evening hours north of Blücher around the crossing of the Spree at Klix (eight miles downstream of Bautzen) proved that Ney's army could be expected to join the battle in the morning. Altogether, the Allies lost around 2,000 men: 800 from Miloradovich's corps and 600 Russians and 500 Prussians from Kleist's corps. French losses are not known.[2]

That night, the Prussians met at Wurschen in the headquarters of their king while the Russians convened with the tsar at Purschwitz. Gneisenau vociferously blamed Miloradovich for abandoning Bautzen without firing a shot and for failing to attack in the afternoon. He argued that, with Bautzen in French hands, the Allies could not maintain their position with any advantage. In his view, Miloradovich's failure placed Napoleon in a position to completely encircle the Allied army. Although Gneisenau later stated that Miloradovich had based his decision to retreat on a misunderstanding, such outbursts – as well as the fact that the leading figures of both powers met separately – reveal the tenuous nature of coalition warfare.[3] Despite Gneisenau's rants, the Prussian soldiers believed they had repulsed the enemy. "The troops passed the night on the battlefield with the soothing feeling of a successful defense," wrote Gneisenau, "and if ever an example is needed to know what the victorious success of a day could bring, it was the order and calm that reigned among the troops, which one seldom or never encounters after such a bloody engagement."[4]

Napoleon now held the keys to Wittgenstein's forward position: the town of Bautzen and the crossings over the Spree to the south and north. By pinning the Allies and deceiving them over his true point of attack, the emperor attained basic objectives through the simplest of means. As with most of Napoleon's operations, the battle of Bautzen entailed a degree of risk. Executing a river crossing so close to the Allied front should have cost him dearly. If the tsar or Wittgenstein had arranged a counterattack around 5:00 P.M. with the almost 60,000 men that remained at their disposal, the French VI, XI, and XII Corps could have been thrown back across the river with considerable loss. Yet, due to the conditions that reigned at Allied Headquarters, rapid decisions could not be made. As soon as the battle commenced, Alexander completely ignored Wittgenstein. As questions arose, the tsar did not hesitate to consult Diebitsch and Toll, and even Knesebeck and Frederick William, but not the Allied commander in chief. Undoubtedly Wittgenstein felt slighted, but had he felt the need for a counterattack he would not have hesitated to make the suggestion. Although hypothetical situations cannot escape the realm of speculation, one point remained clear: the rest of Ney's army would arrive from Hoyerswerda on the following day, utilize the crossing at Klix, and provide the emperor with even greater numbers.

Sometime after midnight a summons arrived for all commanders to meet at the tsar's headquarters for a council of war. Indicative of the amount of autonomy Gneisenau held, he and Müffling went while Blücher rested; Frederick William likewise did not attend. Backed by Wittgenstein and Diebitsch, Alexander presided over the meeting but Barclay was not present, a circumstance that would have profound implications. Relishing his role as Allied generalissimo, the tsar declared that Napoleon would direct his main attack against the Allied left to drive them away from the Austrian frontier. In his opinion, Oudinot's attack on Miloradovich's left confirmed this assumption. The Prussians immediately retorted that the real threat would come from the north and be directed against the right wing. Müffling particularly argued that Ney would have the opportunity to advance all the way to Weißenberg, thus severing the line of retreat for the Allied right and center. To avoid this fatal scenario, he suggested extending the right wing to the windmill hill at Gleina, where at least one heavy battery should be positioned. Alexander turned to Wittgenstein, wanting to know the strength of Barclay's corps. After receiving the answer of 15,000 men, the tsar expressed his belief that Barclay's corps would suffice to hold Ney while Napoleon's attacks would shatter on the strong Allied front. For verification, he turned to Müffling, who stated that Barclay's numbers would suffice to extend the right wing and occupy Gleina. Gneisenau secured the tsar's promise to assign several batteries from the Russian Reserve to Blücher. According to Bogdanovich:

> Many Russian generals were of the opinion that no second battle should be delivered; on the contrary, the Prussians, and most of all Knesebeck, who enjoyed the particular confidence of the tsar, wished to renew the battle; they believed that the retreat would not only weaken the spirit of the army and the devotion of the people, but also destroy Austrian confidence in the Coalition and cause them to join Napoleon. Under the influence of excessive fears in regard to Berlin, some even advised taking the offensive; but Tsar Alexander did not give his approval to this. Therefore, they would accept a defensive battle. The strength of the entrenched position, the bravery of the troops, and the superiority in artillery and cavalry – the latter especially could repulse the efforts of the pursuing enemy – seemed to provide a secure guarantee of success.

After dismissing the officers, Alexander instructed Nesselrode to reject Napoleon's armistice proposal and inform him that further offers would be accepted only through Austria's mediation; Nesselrode relayed the response to Caulaincourt early on the morning of the 21st.[5]

Gneisenau and Müffling did not return to the bivouac on the Kreckwitz heights until after dawn. Around 4:00 A.M., the French resumed the attack with a heavy cannonade in almost every direction. Bright flashes to the west marked where the sun's first rays tapped the helmet, cuirass, or bayonet of an imperial soldier. As it climbed higher in the east, the extent of the French position could be clearly seen; only the Spree lowland remained concealed by thick fog. According to Cathcart:

> It was a fine summer morning on the 21st of May, all was still and even the sound of an occasional musket-shot, discharged along the distant line of advanced sentries, was scarcely to be heard. At daybreak we were in the

field, and the Tsar of Russia and King of Prussia were already on a height in front of the center. However, the enemy was in motion, and appeared to be assembling in force on the ground immediately rising in front of Bautzen, menacing our left or center. Napoleon himself was very distinctly to be seen, accompanied by his staff, and apparently superintending the assembly of his troops. While his preparations were in progress, he dismounted and walked about with his hands behind his back in conversation with officers of his suite.

The thunder of the artillery soon echoed in the hills as both sides exchanged shells at the wide distance of over 2,100 yards. On the French right, legions of skirmishers opened the battle. Cathcart's insightful account continues:

> Although the two hostile staffs were not out of the range of each other's artillery, and though Napoleon himself was quite within reach of the Russian batteries, the Allies were too courteous to disturb his meditations by shot. Berthier and others were recognized, but one person in the group with whom Napoleon seemed to have much conversation, and while discoursing with he frequently consulted his map, puzzled Allied Headquarters very much; he was in a bright yellow uniform, and after various conjectures it was agreed that it could be no other than Murat, who delighted in dress, and was occasionally to be seen in all sorts of costumes. This was important ... because the presence of Murat argued that the Italian levies were in a state of forwardness; besides that, the personal exertions to be expected from his well-known activity and skill as a cavalry officer would require increased vigilance on our side.

All the leading figures knew each other or knew well the reputations of their adversaries. Almost six years prior, Napoleon and Alexander had showered each other's generals with medals at Tilsit. The belief that the individual was Murat, concludes Cathcart, "was entertained till much later in the day, when it was ascertained from prisoners and deserters that the man in yellow was no other than a Saxon postillion employed as a guide, of whom Napoleon was asking the names of the different villages."[6]

Oudinot attacked the left wing of the Allied position at daybreak; Macdonald's corps prepared to support. North of them, Marmont and Soult stood ready to exploit Ney's breakthrough. Yet Soult informed Imperial Headquarters that Zieten's position on the Kiefern prevented him from crossing the Spree. At this late stage, Napoleon believed Ney would comply with his most recent orders to reach Brösa and march "on Weißenberg in a manner to turn the enemy," which would settle the fate of the Allies on the Kiefern. However, after receiving Napoleon's dispatch at 4:00 A.M., Ney again became confused – for good reason – and requested clarification over whether he should march southeast to Weißenberg or south toward the sound of the guns. His staff officer arrived at Imperial Headquarters shortly after 7:00 A.M. to explain the marshal's dilemma. Napoleon decided to have Ney advance four miles south from Klix to Preititz, itself one mile north of the Bautzen–Weißenberg road. To avoid further confusion, the emperor did not risk verbal orders. His instructions required Ney to reach Preititz at 11:00 A.M. As soon as the marshal engaged the enemy there, Napoleon would "attack along all points." He also ordered Ney to have Lauriston advance on his left to ensure the success of the envelopment.[7]

Although Ney's vanguard had secured Klix on the 20th, the main body of his army did not cross the Spree. Instead, the five divisions of III Corps passed the night one mile west of Klix at Sdier with Lauriston's V Corps one mile north of Klix at Särchen. Reynier's VII Corps camped at Hoyerswerda with Victor's II Corps far to the west at Senftenberg. To his credit, the marshal did not allow his confusion to hinder the advance; his operation to cross the Spree at Klix commenced sometime between 4:00 and 5:00 on the morning of the 21st. Two of Lauriston's divisions led the way by driving the Russians east through Brösa and Guttau. After commandeering Maison's 16th Division from Lauriston's corps to protect his right by advancing on Malschwitz, Ney led three columns toward Barclay's position on the windmill hill at Gleina around 6:00 A.M.[8]

Observing Ney's columns debouch, Alexander sent an order to Blücher for Müffling to inform Barclay "of the circumstances on the ground." Müffling met Barclay on the windmill hill at Gleina, where a Russian heavy battery opened fire on the approaching French. Müffling conveyed the substance of the previous night's discussion at the tsar's headquarters and how Alexander expected Barclay to hold the extreme right with his 15,000 men. According to Müffling, "Barclay remained silent." They estimated that Ney would reach Gleina with 40,000 men (actually 23,000) in about twenty-five minutes. The two officers retired to the miller's house where, to Müffling's horror, Barclay revealed that he commanded only 5,000 men at Gleina after having distributed the remainder in small groups along his front.[9] With Alexander fixated on the combat along the Allied left, reinforcements from this sector could not be expected. In addition, Müffling did not believe the reserves closer at hand – Yorck and Kleist in the Allied center at Litten – could arrive in time to save Barclay. With no other option, Barclay sent Müffling rushing to Blücher with an urgent plea for support.[10]

During Müffling's absence, Blücher's troops moved into their positions. Blücher harangued the battalions as they passed with fiery words; spirited shouts of "Hurrah" resounded in the hills in response. He exhorted the troops to fight to the last man, calling the numerous hilltops of their position on the Kreckwitz "the Prussian Thermopylae." "The front of Blücher's corps," explains Gneisenau, "which might be rated at 18,000 strong, extended from Kreckwitz to Niedergurig and from thence by Doberschütz to Pließkowitz. Blücher's position was on the advantageous heights near Kreckwitz ... having the valley of the Spree, full of meadows, intersected with ditches, before him; his front was, without doubt, difficult to access, but the extension of his line ... might be considered as much too great for a body of only 18,000 men. Marshy ground full of pools connected with each other and having but few passages between them, formed a line of defense from Pließkowitz on the Spree to Preititz on the [Blösa] rivulet in front." Zieten moved his 2nd Brigade from the Kiefern to concentrate it along the Doberschütz–Pließkowitz line. Klüx's 1st Brigade held the stretch from the Weißenstein across the Koppatsch hill to Kreckwitz. Forty-eight Russian cannon arrived: twelve-pound guns accounted for half of them, six-pound pieces the other half. Gneisenau positioned some of the heavy guns facing the bridge at Niedergurig with the remainder at Kreckwitz; he held the six-pounders in reserve. At the northern foot of the Kreckwitz heights extended a chain of ponds north from Doberschütz to Malschwitz, east of which, in the right rear of Blücher's position, the terrain rose from Preititz to Barclay's position on the windmill at Gleina. South of II Corps, Yorck's I Corps plugged the gap between the Russians in the center of the Allied line and Blücher by taking a position at Litten. Kleist's corps stood in reserve at Purschwitz.[11]

With Blücher's closest battery west of Weißenberg and less than 700 yards from the Kiefern, Soult determined that the Niedergurig defile still remained closed to his troops until Ney's envelopment could facilitate their passage. Soult's artillery on the Gottlobs remained silent while the Allied artillery limited itself to firing howitzers at the concealed portion of the terrain along the banks of the Spree and the points where the French would most likely attempt to throw a bridge. Thus, most of the morning passed without Blücher's front experiencing serious combat. "A light attack in the early morning was repulsed in part through artillery fire, in part through the fire of the battalions in the villages of Pließkowitz and Doberschütz," is all that Blücher's after-action report states concerning combat during the morning hours. "General Blücher," recalled Gneisenau, "having before him the wood on the side of the Spree, could form no judgment of the strength of his adversary, and only some trifling affairs between the Jäger and light troops occurred in the valley. This was the state of the battle [until] about noon."[12]

In the midst of battle, Blücher always insisted on having every report read aloud in front of his staff. He and Gneisenau placed considerable emphasis on inspiring the officers around them by responding to the reports with positive energy and optimism. Through this, they hoped the naysayers of his suite, whom Blücher referred to as the "*Trübsals-spritzen* [trouble-squirts]," would be marginalized and restrained from spreading gloom and doom. Gneisenau in particular liked to see Blücher's talents employed for this task. According to Müffling, the old hussar possessed "the unique talent for reducing exaggerated statements to the right track by a bon-mot." With "the sound of the hurrahs catching my ear on the way," Müffling returned to the Kreckwitz heights with the terrible news that Barclay could not hold the Gleina windmill hill. As customary at Blücher's headquarters, all the curious of his entourage pressed close to Blücher and Gneisenau – to whom Müffling derisively referred as "the defenders of public discussion" – to hear Müffling's report. He informed Blücher of Barclay's inability to maintain the Gleina hill but with so many ears hanging on his every word he refrained from mentioning that Barclay's 5,000 men faced around 40,000 imperials. Instead, he relayed Barclay's intention to withdraw to Preititz. Although this movement would keep open the road to Weißenberg, it would expose the right and rear of Blücher's position. Blücher at first did not believe that Barclay planned to abandon Gleina. Müffling then implied that Blücher should order an immediate retreat. Gneisenau snapped at Müffling for having too little confidence in Russian bravery. He rejected Müffling's suggestion and the three went to work planning countermeasures. After Gneisenau issued the orders, Blücher gave an inspiring speech to the troops.[13]

Jomini maintains that, as of 7:00 A.M., Ney still had not received instructions from Napoleon. Nevertheless, the marshal continued his advance. Armed with a map of Frederick the Great's devastating defeat at the 14 October 1758 Battle of Hochkirch, Jomini "knew the importance of Hochkirch, whose name alone (high church) indicated that it dominated the chessboard on which we would operate. He therefore proposed to direct all available forces there and modify the instructions for Generals Lauriston, Souham, [Joseph-Jean] Albert, [Antoine-Guillaume] Delmas, Ricard, and Marchand to that effect. That the bell tower of this church, which seemed to be lost in the clouds and that one discovered to be ten leagues away, would be assigned to them as their objective." Around 9:30 A.M., the troops of Ney's III Corps took the Gleina windmill hill. Thirty minutes later, Maison overran Malschwitz, west of Gleina, while Lauriston reached Buchenwalde to the east. To protect the Bautzen–Weißenberg road, Barclay fell back to Baruth, one mile southeast of Buchenwalde. At this juncture, Ney received Napoleon's instructions from earlier that morning to be at Preititz by 11:00. Jomini describes Ney's operation up to that point as "perfect; its results should have been incalculable; but numerous unfortunate circumstances led to failure." It must be noted that Jomini felt that Berthier and probably Napoleon blamed him for Ney's mistakes that day. Thus, his account of the proceedings is suspect, yet still interesting and worthy of consideration. To begin, Jomini accused Napoleon of waiting too long "to give Ney instructions on the role reserved for him in the battle. These same instructions were inadequate, because one was limited to sending him at 8:00 A.M. a note in pencil, bearing the laconic order to be at the village

of Preititz around noon and attack the enemy's right. The officer who
delivered the order had to make the long detour through Klix; he arrived
at 10:00 on the heights of Gleina, which Ney had just taken much sooner
than one expected." Jomini relates that because Preititz stood on their path,
the columns on Ney's left wing could continue the march toward the spire
of Hochkirch. But it was only 10:00 and not noon," he continues; "this
village [Preititz] was located only 600 or 700 yards from the heights of
Gleina, the marshal feared committing to the affair too soon, as he did at
Jena, and, instead of continuing his victorious march, he formed his divisions
between Gleina and the windmill height."[14]

For the advance on Preititz, Ney possessed 23,000 men with four
additional divisions moving up behind him. However, as the noon hour
approached, the marshal no longer viewed the situation as Napoleon wished.
Seeing the Kreckwitz hills to the southwest, he became enthralled with the
idea that they were the key to the Allied position. Dismissing Jomini's
advice, he disregarded the emperor's directive. Rather than march his massive corps to Preititz, the marshal decided to await the arrival of his rearward
divisions and then storm the Kreckwitz heights.[15] He summoned Lauriston
to join his attack on the hills but the general ignored the call, recognizing
that such a flank march would only waste precious time. For the time being,
Ney sent only one division – Souham's 8th – to Preititz in compliance
with the master's order. Weakly occupied by the Russians, Souham's troops
seized the village around 11:00. Souham now stood immediately east of
Blücher's position. Nostitz explains the significance of Preititz: "this village
lay between our corps and that of Barclay de Tolly, close to Kleinbautzen,
therefore behind our right wing. Possession of Preititz was extremely
important for our retreat because only through Preititz could it be executed
without considerable losses." "This village," added Gneisenau, "lay between
General Blücher and General Barclay de Tolly ... consequently behind the
right wing of General Blücher. Nothing could be of more importance to
this general than the occupation of this village."[16]

As a first step to support Barclay, Blücher positioned the twenty-four
Russian six-pound guns and directed them to shell the approach to Preititz
at 10:00. Escorted by a cavalry brigade, the Russian cannon crowned the
northeastern edge of the Kreckwitz heights. As noted, Preititz fell before
the Allies completed this laborious task. Blücher then ordered the Guard
Regiment of Röder's brigade to Preititz. Led by Alvensleben, the three
Guard battalions supported by two squadrons proceeded from their position northwest of Kleinbautzen along the left bank of the Blösa stream until
the Prussians learned that Preititz had already fallen to the French. While
awaiting the four horse guns assigned to him, Alvensleben observed the
French emerge from Preititz; the Prussians attacked and forced their
way into the village. Around 10:30 A.M., the remainder of Röder's brigade

(four battalions, four squadrons, and three batteries) marched toward Preititz. "General Blücher," states his after-action report, "sent three battalions from his reserve brigade to retake it [Preititz]. He then received news that the enemy pressed very strongly, so he detached the entire Reserve Brigade [Röder] with orders to take the village at any cost, hand it over to Barclay, and quickly return to its position."[17]

Around the same time, Blücher sent a detachment from Dolffs's Reserve Cavalry north toward Klix to threaten Ney's right flank. Blücher himself joined Röder to observe the course of the combat. He also ordered Kleist, whose small corps stood in reserve east of Purschwitz, to likewise march on Preititz from the opposite direction. Faulty staff work caused Kleist and Röder to collide at Kleinbautzen, which ruined Blücher's plan to double-envelop Souham's position. Fierce combat erupted in Preititz, which now blazed thanks to Allied grenades. Led by the Guard Regiment and Kleist's Kolberg Infantry Regiment, the Prussians inflicted and sustained considerable casualties. The struggle swayed back and forth while Ney incomprehensibly remained glued to the Gleina windmill hill, from where he could see in the distance the backsides of the troops of the Allied center, whose cartridge bag fittings glistened in the sun. Much to his anxiety, the marshal could also see that the Allied center remained solid. Thus, "the bravest of the brave" decided to delay his assault until Napoleon attacked, completely contradicting the emperor's orders.

After intense combat, the Prussians drove Souham's division from Preititz around 1:00. After sustaining 4,000 casualties, the French withdrew to Ney's position at the Gleina windmill hill. Blücher dispatched Nostitz to implore Barclay "to support the retaking of this village with all forces because this was the only means to avoid a total defeat," but Nostitz failed to persuade the Russian commander.[18] Even after Kleist suggested that they jointly retake the Gleina hill Barclay refused to advance. Admittedly, a pursuit would have been risky; Ney's 9th and 10th Divisions had received Souham's spent warriors. To reorganize, all withdrew to the Gleina windmill hill where 11th Division joined them; Marchand's 39th Division soon arrived after being relieved at Klix by Puthod's 17th Division. Ney ordered Reynier to accelerate his march and repeated the instructions for Lauriston to turn toward Preititz and link directly with III Corps. In the meantime, Lauriston made short work of Barclay, driving him south to a position on the hills between Briesnitz and Rackel, dangerously close to the Bautzen–Weißenberg road. To his credit, Barclay managed to reunite most of his corps while retreating. Recalled by Ney, Lauriston left General Donatien Rochambeau's 19th Division along with a few cavalry squadrons at Baruth. He then commenced the hour-long march north through Buchwalde and then west toward Preititz with General Joseph Lagrange's 18th Division and the rest of his cavalry.

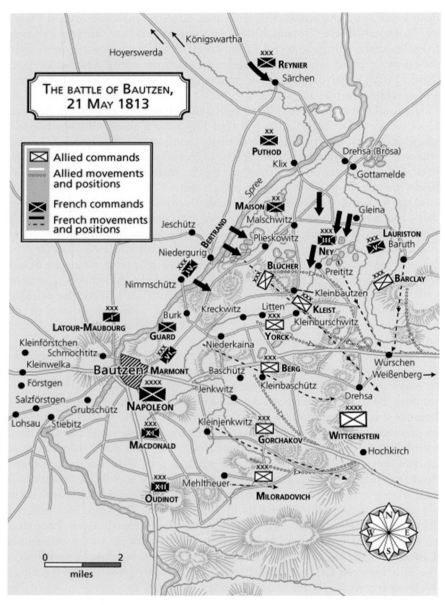

**20.** Battle of Bautzen, 21 May 1813

18 The Kolberg Infantry Regiment at the battle of Bautzen, 21 May 1813

Earlier in the day, Oudinot's attack had proceeded smoothly with the taking of Rieschen on the left of the Allied position. French success served to reinforce the conviction Alexander shared with almost all the Russian generals that Napoleon sought to drive the Allies away from the Austrian frontier. From his command post at the flèche east of the village of Baschütz between the center and the left wing, Alexander committed more reserves to support Miloradovich. According to Mikhailovsky-Danilevsky, Wittgenstein exclaimed: "'I'll wager my head that this is only a feint: Napoleon intends to envelop our right and drive us into Bohemia!' Events would shortly justify this comment, which no one except Wittgenstein's chief of staff, Auvray, supported." Alexander steadily committed troops to reinforce Miloradovich. "But in a short time," continues Mikhailovsky-Danilevsky, "the horizon to our right was almost obscured by enemy columns deploying from the villages of Klix, Gottamelde [Guttau], and Baruth."[19]

Despite the scene to the north and Barclay's reports, the tsar remained focused on his left. By 11:00 A.M., Miloradovich recovered and drove back Oudinot's outnumbered corps. On Oudinot's left, Macdonald moved onto the hills at Rabitz, southwest of Jenkwitz, intensely exchanging withering artillery fire with the Russians. Observing Oudinot's retreat, Macdonald demonstrated toward Binnewitz, itself southwest of Reischen. The ploy

worked and Miloradovich halted. Although Oudinot begged for reinforcements, the progress of XI and XII Corps satisfied the emperor. By 1:00 P.M.,
Macdonald and Oudinot had succeeded in fixing the Allied left and
prompting the gullible tsar to commit the majority of his reserves. Not
much else occurred on Napoleon's right for the rest of the battle. Instead,
focus shifted to his center and left. Hearing Souham's first attack on Preititz
unfold around 11:00, Napoleon sent Marmont across the Blösa stream to
move against the Allied center. One hour later, Mortier received instructions
to move the entire Guard corps onto the hills of Burk and Basankwitz.
Mortier unlimbered a portion of his artillery to face the Kreckwitz hills
to the northeast but oriented his infantry to the east.

Unnoticed by the Prussians, Soult pushed an entire brigade across the
Spree by way of a ford and moved it onto the Kiefern. Under its protection
and concealed by the height, the French completed work on a bridge around
1:00 P.M. Within one hour, two divisions of IV Corps had crossed the river
and prepared to assault the Kreckwitz heights. Blücher attempted but
failed to prevent the crossing through a counterattack by Klüx's foremost
battalions. "It drove the enemy infantry into the defile, from where,
reinforced by a reserve positioned in battalion columns, he forced our
infantry to yield." Around 2:00, Franquemont received the order to attack.
A French battery of twenty-two guns opened fire from the Gottlobs hill.
Under their cover, thirty more rumbled onto the western edge of the Kiefern
hill. Due to the batteries of Mortier, Soult, and Ney, the Prussian position on
the Kreckwitz heights smoldered from a three-way crossfire. By 2:30,
Maison's 16th Division achieved its next objective: Pließkowitz, which the
Prussians set ablaze and evacuated. "The enemy ... attacked Blücher's
corps," states the general's after-action report, "between Malschwitz and
the windmill hill of Gleina with artillery, the villages of Plieskowitz and
Doberschütz with infantry, and he also moved through the defile at
Niedergurig with infantry and artillery and fiercely attacked the front."
"A most heavy and destructive fire of musketry was maintained without
interruption," noted Gneisenau, "and with his second line of infantry
coming into action, General Blücher began to discover, with that quickness
of foresight so unique to this military hero, how unsafe it was to maintain his
extended lines, and issued prompt orders for the reserve brigade [Röder's]
to return."[20]

Soult moved the cavalry of IV Corps south to link with the Guard.
Franquemont's eight infantry battalions turned north, formed a deep
column, and marched on Kreckwitz. Following a shallow depression that
offered little cover, the column curved sharply north toward the Koppatsch
hill. Blücher's artillery roared, mowing down the Württembergers. To the
great credit of Franquemont's conscripts, the momentum of their march
carried them forward in fairly good order; they charged the Allied guns at

150 yards. Already running low on ammunition, the Russian battery on the Koppatsch increased its fire to maximum capacity and then withdrew, covered by Prussian Jäger. Klüx again countered with his foremost battalions but the Württembergers repulsed the attack. Before the main strength of Klüx's brigade could arrive, Franquemont deftly switched from column to line; the batteries on the edge of the Kiefern moved into the gaps between the battalions. General Joseph-Victorien Sicard's 2nd Brigade from Morand's 12th Division took a position behind Franquemont's left wing, forming two closed squares and slowly advancing. Klüx charged and the Germans engaged in an intense struggle. Franquemont, his most senior brigade commander, Karl August von Neuffer, and Sicard all fell, the last mortally. "This bloody engagement," recounts Odeleben, "the most obstinate of the day, consisted therefore almost solely of charges with the bayonet; the infantry advanced to the charge with furious shouts; the Württemberger troops took a considerable share in the affair." The Prussians failed to punch through the Württemberger line. Fighting was bitter as the Germans took no mercy on each other, epitomizing Gneisenau's statement a few days earlier that "the blood of the men of the Thirty Years War runs in our veins." "Too much cannot be said in praise of General Blücher's corps on this occasion," comments Stewart, "and the Prussians on this eventful day, as at the battle of Lützen, again evinced that ardor and prowess which never will fail them." Suffering hideous casualties from the caseshot of the French batteries that had moved up, Klüx withdrew to the Doberschütz–Kreckwitz hill line after losing 1,073 casualties out of 3,700 combatants.[21]

While advancing toward the Koppatsch, the Württembergers received deadly fire from an Allied battery positioned north of the village of Kreckwitz. To silence it, Franquemont instructed the last battalion of his column to advance toward Kreckwitz. Although the Württembergers forced the battery to withdraw and moved into Kreckwitz, Yorck sent the East Prussian Fusilier Battalion and one horse battery from Litten to retake the village; Blücher likewise committed one battalion. Thanks to Yorck's timely intervention, the Prussians captured nearly the entire Württemberger battalion. More importantly, by retaining Kreckwitz, Klüx's brigade could maintain its new position on the Doberschütz–Kreckwitz hills. However, success would be short-lived, as Soult implemented a two-pronged attack on Doberschütz from Niedergurig and Briesing. Under increasing pressure himself, Zieten could spare no reinforcements for Klüx.

After losing Pließkowitz and the Koppatsch, Blücher's position considerably narrowed. Around this time, 3:00 P.M., two massive Guard batteries under Napoleon's personal supervision opened fire from the hills of Burk, spewing destruction on Kreckwitz and the adjacent Prussian infantry.[22] Under this protection, General Pierre Barrois's Young Guard division of sixteen battalions advanced toward Kreckwitz from the hills of Bautzen.

According to Blücher's after-action report, the twenty-four Russian twelve-pound guns "performed extraordinary service and earned the greatest commendation" for slowing the Guard's advance. Other sources state that, thanks to Alexander's intervention, enfilading artillery fire managed to halt this attack. Regardless, Barrois still menaced Blücher's position from the south while Maison pressed from the north. Northeast of Blücher, Ney ordered 9th Division, now commanded by General Antoine-Guillaume Delmas, supported by 10th and 11th Divisions, to retake Preititz. Marchand and Souham remained at the windmill hill, where Puthod's 17th Division arrived. Delmas formed his veterans of Lützen in two brigade masses and marched toward Preititz. As noted, Blücher redirected Röder's brigade – his only reserve – to Purschwitz, hoping the tsar could send reinforcements to Preititz. This "hope" did little for Kleist, who could not hold his position against three French divisions. To make matters worse, Kleist learned of Lauriston's approach from Buchwalde. As Ney personally led his three divisions against Preititz, Kleist abandoned the village around 3:00 P.M. and withdrew toward Belgern. With 32,000 men, the marshal turned west to storm the Kreckwitz heights.

Fighting on three fronts, Blücher requested reinforcements from Yorck, who held the position around Litten. For an instant, Blücher hoped that with Röder and Yorck he could restore the situation. Unfortunately for him, Röder pulled out of Preititz very late and his column again succumbed to confusion.[23] Yorck could not leave his place in the line until a replacement moved into his position from the left wing. From his command post, Yorck could easily see the threat to the Allied center at Baschütz and Jenkwitz posed by Marmont's masses. Closer at hand, he observed the French Guard preparing to rumble through Basankwitz to strike Litten. Yorck's troops occupied the three redoubts south of Litten while the main body of his two brigades waited in columns east of the redoubts; his Reserve Cavalry under General Karl Friederich von Corswant took a position southeast of the infantry. On Yorck's request, three regiments of Russian cuirassiers moved close behind Corswant. During this time, Blücher's plea for support reached Yorck, who ordered Steinmetz's brigade to march through Litten. Yorck sent an adjutant to the monarchs in the hope of accelerating the process of moving up Russian forces to take his place. Frederick William already had made this request. Shortly afterward, Yorck received word from Allied Headquarters that a Russian detachment under General Aleksey Yermolov would relieve him so he could assist Blücher with all his infantry. After posting one battalion on each wing of the artillery, Yorck led Horn's brigade to the Kreckwitz heights.[24]

Müffling provides an interesting explanation as to why the Russians at Allied Headquarters refused to support the right wing sooner: "The Russians, entrenched up to their teeth, would not leave their impregnable position. The pretext for this was easily found. Blücher, they said, with Yorck, Kleist, and Barclay will hold the right wing as we have held the left because it is not at all certain that Napoleon will not attempt to draw us out of our strong position in order to turn his reserve and fall upon our left wing with a superior force." As noted, the monarchs released Yorck followed by Yermolov to support Blücher but time had run out. With imperial forces closing on his position from the west, north, and east, Blücher became convinced that the hills could no longer be held. As the imperials began climbing the Kreckwitz heights, Müffling pulled out his watch and said to Blücher that within fifteen minutes they would not be able escape the closing net. Gneisenau, who stood near, purportedly stated: "Müffling is right, and due to the change in circumstances not only has all bloodshed been in vain, but the preservation of our forces for a better opportunity is now our duty. Blücher consented and the retreat was executed boldly and successfully through Purschwitz."[25]

Thus, sometime between 3:00 and 4:00 on the afternoon of 21 May, Blücher chose "a well-ordered retreat over the danger of being completely destroyed by continuing the struggle against such superior numbers." Klüx retired through Purschwitz followed by Zieten while units from Röder's brigade held the hills at Purschwitz and Kleinbautzen. Katzler assembled the brigade cavalry into a large body of troopers to cover the retreat in unison with Dolffs's Reserve Cavalry. Steinmetz's brigade deployed at the foot of the Kreckwitz heights, allowing Blücher's men to file past and then followed. Horn's brigade also fell in; the Prussians withdrew along both sides of Purschwitz in exemplary order. Dolffs held his troopers close to the imperials to cover the retreat of the other arms. Yorck's West Prussian Musketeer Battalion took post at Litten with orders to defend the village to the last man. After all the troops safely retreated, the musketeers fired the village and followed. "The order to retreat was duly executed," continues Blücher's after-action report; "the horse artillery of the rearguard held the enemy at a respectful distance, yet a detachment of enemy cavalry ... did manage to sneak toward Purschwitz and was in the process of taking several cannon when the Neumark Dragoon Regiment and the 1st Silesian Hussar Regiment spotted it, counterattacked, and cut down all of them."[26]

After Ney took Preititz the second time, Knesebeck, whom the tsar looked to for advice rather than Wittgenstein, suggested breaking off the battle. Alexander refused. "The tsar seemed to wish for an offensive movement," Wilson recorded in his diary. "While the matter was under discussion, Blücher sent word that he was overpowered and had ordered a retreat."[27] As reports of Blücher's retreat arrived, Alexander reluctantly turned to Wittgenstein around 4:00, stating: "*Commandez la retraite, je ne veux pas être le témoin de ce désordre* [order the retreat, I don't want to watch this mess]."[28] "Around this time," recalls Mikhailovsky-Danilevsky, "considerable enemy forces turned toward Baschütz. We did not have any troops except some Guard regiments to send to reinforce Barclay and Blücher. The enemy columns facing our center appeared only to be waiting for Wittgenstein to weaken himself by sending these troops to reinforce the threatened points. Wittgenstein later said to me that he could have held the position at Bautzen if one [Alexander] had not, against his view, which he expressed many times, sent so many troops to the hills on our left wing."[29] Wittgenstein issued the necessary orders according to his original disposition. Three main columns formed. The northern consisted of Barclay's troops; the center of Prussian troops and Yermolov's detachment; and the southern column of all remaining Russian troops. Barclay received instructions to maintain his position south of Rackel and Briesnitz until all troops of the middle column cleared Wurschen. He would then follow and unite with this column at Weißenberg while the southern all-Russian column marched to Löbau. To cover the retreat of the southern column, Russian troops remained at Jenkwitz; the cavalry and horse artillery maintained close contact with the imperials to slow their pursuit.

Although it was not an easy task, the Allies executed this retreat in a noteworthy manner. Barclay's strong position neutralized the most immediate threat: Rochambeau's 19th Division. Kleist's corps held the hill at Belgern while Horn's brigade took post on the shallow hill west of Wurschen. The combined Prussian cavalry of Corswant, Dolffs, and Katzler along with all horse artillery and initially numerous foot batteries reinforced by half of the Russian Cuirassier Corps mastered the plain that extended south from Purschwitz to Neupurschwitz. Fortunately for Blücher, the French troops at Preititz did little. Moreover, while facing the Russians of the Allied center, Napoleon hesitated to launch a costly attack, still hoping Ney's envelopment would achieve the desired effect. Consequently, Blücher's retreat through the hilly terrain went unnoticed by the French for some time. Yorck executed a brief counterattack to keep them off balance but the imperials easily repulsed him. Regardless, it provided just enough time for Blücher to slip away. Bursting upon the Kreckwitz heights from three sides, the imperials found that Blücher had escaped. Now jammed together in a narrow space, their columns became mingled and their tired men less responsive to orders. The need to reorganize hindered them from pursuing Blücher over the broken terrain, although Stewart claimed that "the enemy immediately opened a tremendous fire from the heights of Kreckwitz and the village of Cannewitz on the retiring columns." "It is surprising that the enemy did not attempt to molest the march," wrote Wilson on the 23rd, "but they were satisfied with cheers of victory and a furious discharge of artillery. This was not permitted to pass altogether with impunity, for we opened a heavy fire, particularly from one battery of forty guns, and checked their cannon for half an hour."

We did not lose a single gun or tumbrel. Above 600 pieces and 1,800 caissons, exclusive of the regimental caissons, withdrew in the presence of the enemy."[30]

The other half of the Cuirassier Corps remained south of the Bautzen–Weißenberg road to maintain communication with the southern column, which received the bulk of the punishment during the retreat. Advancing in six brigade masses, Marmont drove Berg's corps and the garrisons of Jenkwitz and Baschütz from their positions. Eight Russian Guard battalions – all that remained of the Allied reserve – took them in and slowed Marmont. Duke Eugen of Württemberg held Macdonald to enable the Russian left wing to withdraw. Napoleon ordered Latour-Maubourg and his 4,000 troopers to drive the Russians south and into the mountains. The combination of Duke Eugen's staunch resistance and the presence of considerable Russian cavalry on the Bautzen–Löbau road as well as the other half of the Cuirassier Corps made it difficult for Latour-Maubourg's relatively inexperienced troopers to attain success in the broken terrain on the Allied left wing. At the end of the day, a "hurricane-like" downpour starting around 6:00 drenched the men.

Blücher fully expected to receive orders to continue the struggle at Purschwitz despite the low-lying terrain that poorly suited a defensive position. Ney's presence at Preitwitz ruled out any ideas of reforming the Allied line. Moreover, the monarchs refused to linger west of Weißenberg any longer than necessary. East of Purschwitz, Blücher awaited orders that never came. Instead, he received word that Allied Headquarters had decided to retreat. "It was truly a sad sight," notes one of Yorck's staff officers, "when we found Blücher, dismounted from his horse, sitting on a rock in despondency."[31] Fortunately for the Allies, the retreat ensued along a broad front on two solid highways. This minimized French pressure and allowed the soldiers to again feel that they had not lost the battle.

That they had not lost the battle and could disengage was indeed fortunate, because Napoleon's plan should have resulted in their complete destruction. By evening, the emperor commanded 144,000 combatants facing 96,000 Allied soldiers. If Ney had advanced according to his orders, two complete army corps rather than one division would have reached a position directly in the rear of the Allied army before noon. Was Napoleon's star setting? Why were the best-laid plans going awry? The answers to these questions mattered little to the Allies as they marched east fully expecting to fight another day: "The army is together and determined to perform new deeds," Gneisenau assured Hardenberg on the morning of the 22nd. Not doubt over the spirit of the troops, but instead suspicion of Russian leadership prompted Gneisenau to give verbal instructions to the courier who delivered this letter to Hardenberg. If the Allied retreat continued, Gneisenau predicted Wittgenstein would direct the army to Silesia, in which case the staff chief requested that Hardenberg see to the provisioning of the entrenched camps as the first step in implementing the "Silesian Plan."[32]

During the evening, Barclay moved into a position north of Weißenberg with his rearguard and Dolffs's Reserve Cavalry two and one-half miles northwest at Gröditz. Blücher stood east and southeast of Weißenberg with the main mass of Prussian troops. Yermolov's detachment and Katzler's cavalry brigade held Niederkotitz two miles southwest of Weißenberg. The main body of the southern column reached Löbau, eight miles south of Weißenberg. Alexander and Frederick William left the battlefield around 5:00, making for Reichenbach, some eighteen miles east of Bautzen. For a long time they rode next to each other in silence. Finally, the king exclaimed: "I had expected something different. We hoped to be riding west but now we go east." To comfort his ally, Alexander replied that not a single Allied battalion had been routed and that, although retreat was unavoidable, nothing was lost and with God's help the situation would get better. "If God gives his blessing to our labors," responded Frederick William, "we will have to confess to the whole world that we owe the glory of our success to him alone." Alexander grasped his hand in friendship.[33]

Allied losses on the second day of the battle of Bautzen are estimated to be 10,850 men, including 2,790 casualties from Blücher's corps, which Stewart claimed "was very much cut up." Bogdanovich cites 6,400 Russian and 5,600 Prussian casualties. One destroyed Prussian gun remained on the battlefield. Again the Allies fought hard. "I see nothing as yet in what has happened," reported Lowe, "to make me alter the sentiments expressed in my last [letter] regarding the Russians and the Prussians, whose valor has been most conspicuous and whose patriotism entitles them to every praise ... the bravery and firmness of the Russian soldier are beyond all praise. Among thousands of wounded whom I either saw on the field, or passed on the march from it, I never heard a sigh of pain, or complaint uttered; nor did I ever see a wounded man without his arms and accoutrements." On 24 May, Lowe reported that "the Russian Bulletins state the loss of the combined army to have been only 6,000 men, whilst that of the French is estimated at 14,000. I have been told, however, by a person whose authority ought to be unquestionable, that the number of Russian wounded, of whom reports had been received, as having been brought off from the field, was 4,300 and the same person supposed the real loss of the Russians alone to have been nearly treble that number, as the reports did not come in a regular way, and as several must have been left in the field. The loss of the Prussians could not have been so great, though they must have suffered severely in the night."[34]

By comparison, French losses reached 22,500 men including 3,700 missing. Odeleben places the number of imperials killed on the battlefield between 5,000 and 6,000. Based on reports that reached Imperial

Headquarters, the Saxon officer claims that Bautzen provided refuge for 20,000 wounded imperial soldiers, most of whom would not survive their wounds or be fit for service if they did. Ney's III Corps suffered the greatest loss, with estimates ranging between 7,600 and 10,300 men.[35] Macdonald's XII Corps lost 6,100 men in fierce fighting with the Russians on the Allied left while the French IV Corps suffered 4,100 casualties, including 1,270 Württembergers. Although a victory, the results of Bautzen fell far short of satisfying Napoleon. He knew the reasons why his great envelopment had failed but he could not admit it without causing serious harm to the prestige of his subordinates and the army itself.[36]

As the battle closed on the evening of the 21st, the outposts of both armies became intertwined as the fighting ended. At first light, around 3:00 A.M. on the 22nd, skirmishing resumed. Allied posts still held the heights that ran southwest to northeast from Niederkotitz to Weißenberg. East of this line, the main body of the Allied army approached the long defile between Reichenbach and Görlitz. Retreating along a broad front on several roads helped speed the Allied withdrawal on 22 May. Protected by their rearguards, the two Allied columns withdrew toward Reichenbach: eight miles southeast of Weißenberg and seven miles northeast of Löbau. Just west of Reichenbach, the northern group (Barclay and Blücher) left the main highway and proceeded east along side roads in three columns. Its heavy guns and some of the larger trains still found among the troops took a detour through Mengelsdorf with an appropriate escort. Scouts also found a road through Dobschütz to Königshain for infantry and the light artillery. Both roads merged at the latter and continued through Ebersbach to the bridges over the Neiße downstream of Görlitz. For the cavalry, a northern detour through Niederseifersdorf and Ullersdorf offered the best position from which to threaten the pursuing enemy's flank.

Napoleon's right wing (XI and XII Corps) passed the night of 21/22 May south of the Bautzen–Löbau road at Meschwitz, Soritz, and Blösa, the foremost village being one and one-half miles west of Hochkirch. His center camped at Drehsa (IV Corps), Waditz (VI Corps), and Canitz-Christina (I Cavalry Corps). On the left, Ney's army (III, V, and VII Corps) reached Wurschen and Belgern; the marshal took quarters at the former. Napoleon passed the night near the inn at Neupurschwitz with his Guard. Early on the 22nd, Berthier issued preliminary orders for the pursuit. Continuing to lead the army, Macdonald received instructions for XI Corps to drive the enemy from Hochkirch. He would be supported by VI Corps, which Berthier directed to Wurschen, and IV Corps, which would march from Drehsa to Nostitz. Napoleon tasked Oudinot's XII Corps with securing Bautzen and the battlefield, clearing the woods to the south, finding the wounded, and organizing the local authorities to bury the dead. The emperor issued verbal orders for Ney to form a huge mass of infantry (55,000 men) by stacking VII, V, and III Corps one behind the other and to pursue the Allies eastward from Wurschen in the direction of Weißenberg–Reichenbach. This movement came to naught for various reasons. First, Lauriston had already led the main body of his corps across the Löbau stream, thus moving V Corps out of the prescribed order. Second, for unknown reasons, Ney's own III Corps remained behind on the battlefield. As a result, the Guard passed III Corps and moved immediately behind VII Corps while Puthod's division of V Corps followed the Guard. Reynier's VII Corps and I Cavalry Corps led Ney's pursuit.[37]

Wittgenstein expected the mass of the French left wing to follow his northern column on the same roads. For this reason, he wanted the troops of his southern wing to occupy the Töpferberg height at Reichenbach in a timely manner. At Reichenbach, the Russians would be in position to dominate the highways coming from Löbau and Weißenberg, and be less than one mile from the road running through Mengelsdorf. By deploying large cavalry forces on both sides of the height, the position on the Töpferberg, some forty to fifty yards above the east–west highway, would be so strong that even with a substantial numerical superiority Wittgenstein did not think the French would achieve much success disrupting the further retreat of the Allied army. As the Russian rearguard took a position on the height, the southern column coming from Löbau continued east on the main highway as well as the closest side roads to the area upstream of Görlitz to cross the Neiße. With the most northern point of the Austrian frontier some eight miles south of Görlitz, sufficient space existed for the Allies to maneuver.[38]

West of the Allied army, Reynier's VII Corps, which the emperor considered fresh because it had missed the battle, led the march of the army's left wing around 7:00 A.M. despite having made consecutive forced marches since 17 May. Supported by I Cavalry Corps, the exhausted Franco-Saxon troops of VII Corps followed by the Guard and VI Corps trudged east from Nechern toward Weißenberg. On Reynier's left, V Corps kept pace while III Corps brought up the rear. On the right wing, XI Corps supported by IV Corps marched east through Löbau. Escorted by the Guard Cavalry, the emperor accompanied the march of VII Corps. West of Weißenberg, the French encountered Barclay's Russo-Prussian rearguard commanded by Yermelov and Katzler. After Reynier dislodged the Allies from the heights between Niederkotitz and Weißenberg, they conducted a fighting withdrawal to another ridge at Rotkretscham upstream from Weißenberg on the Löbau stream. Napoleon directed the entire Guard Cavalry and I Cavalry Corps – together 6,500 sabers – to cross the rivulet further upstream at Lautitz. By rapidly executing the master's order, the French horse not only prompted the Allied rearguard to retreat but also threatened the march of both Barclay and Blücher. The latter deployed his Reserve

Cavalry to support Katzler. Observing the large body of Prussian cavalry, the French troopers halted, which allowed Yermelov's infantry to retreat unmolested. At Schöps on the eastern bank of the Schwarze Schöps stream, Allied artillery slowed Reynier's advance. A few miles east of Schöps, Katzler's cavalry linked with the Russian 2nd Cuirassier Division near Mengelsdorf. For the moment, Reynier could go no further.

Meanwhile, the Russian Guard and Reserve with its massive artillery train cleared Reichenbach but Miloradovich's corps had yet to arrive. In fact, its rearguard, commanded by a native Frenchman, General Guillaume Emmanuel de St.-Priest, had just evacuated Löbau. Pressed by Macdonald, St.-Priest's Russians methodically conducted a fighting withdrawal toward Reichenbach. Yet this took time, giving Reynier's corps the opportunity to reach Reichenbach first. Consequently, when Duke Eugen of Württemberg arrived with the Russian II Infantry Corps, he recognized the need to secure Reichenbach before it fell into Reynier's hands. Two Russian Jäger battalions occupied the town while Eugen posted his main body east of Reichenbach on the plateau of the Töpferberg. Around 9:00 that morning, Barclay's rearguard followed the northern column, thus opening the road to Reichenbach. One hour later, Reynier's VII Corps arrived. Emerging on the eastern side of Reichenbach, the imperials observed Duke Eugen's 7,000 Russians supported by eighteen guns provided by Yermelov. Drawn up on the Töpferberg, the Russians received orders to hold their position long enough to allow the southern column to retreat across the Neiße River.

Reynier's lead division halted to reconnoiter the strong enemy position anchored on the Töpferberg height. Napoleon arrived and ordered a frontal attack while V Corps maneuvered from the north to envelop the Russian right. Despite the emperor's presence, his troops achieved little against the enemy's strong position. "The Allies had chosen very prudently as an essential point for covering their retreat," comments Odeleben, "the height that rises at an angle of eight or ten degrees immediately behind Reichenbach. Their numerous artillery hurled death and destruction among the ranks of the French and swept all the approaches to the town and its environs. Covered by these pieces, their light infantry occupied Reichenbach and the terrain around the town. The numerous cavalry, posted in battle order to the right of the Russian batteries, for some time prevented the French cavalry from advancing." As the fighting dragged on, the emperor's impatience mounted as he realized that with every hour more of his prey slipped through Görlitz and into Silesia. He finally decided to commit the 4,000 troopers of his Guard Cavalry division. About one mile south of Reichenbach, the cavalry crossed through the small valley in which the village stood and moved toward the road leading to the Töpferberg. As the imperial squadrons began to climb toward the hills, fire from two Russian horse batteries tore through their ranks, devastating man and horse.

"The cannon caused considerable loss to the French," describes Odeleben, "and the ground was covered with the dead and wounded. The French and Saxon cavalry suffered most on this occasion; the Mamelukes and Lancers of the Guard participated in several charges."

Immediately following this brutal greeting, the imperials observed a large body of Russian cavalry bearing down on them. The horsemen of Latour-Maubourg's I Cavalry Corps moved up to support the Guard as quickly as their beasts could carry them. To enable the Russian Guard and Reserve to reach Görlitz, the cavalry of the Russian rearguard engaged in a massive, two-hour combat with the pursuing French: 6,800 Russians against 6,500 French. "It was the first time since the beginning of the campaign that the French cavalry engaged *en masse*," comments Lanrezac, "and the result was far from brilliant." Cathcart described the action:

> About noon, their [French] cavalry and artillery commenced a most vigorous attempt to force the position of Reichenbach; but two Russian light battalions [Jäger] held the entrance of the defile. A powerful Russian battery on the high ground, supported by a strong force of cavalry and well posted infantry, was not easily to be forced or turned, and continued in the meantime to deal destruction on every French column that presented itself. In one of the attacks, a regiment of cavalry consisting of the lancers of the Dutch Guard ... was cut off and nearly every man and horse killed or taken. The French cavalry of the Guard was engaged and at length prevailed.

During the cavalry melee, Reynier's Saxons gained Niederreichenbach, thus flanking the right of the Russian position on the Töpferberg. The Russians met their charge up the height with a storm of lead that sent the Saxons scrambling down the slope. Nevertheless, Eugen observed the approach of Lauriston's V Corps and realized that his line of retreat would soon be cut. Knowing that Miloradovich would have a fallback position prepared to receive him, he ordered the retreat to continue east toward Markersdorf. "The dispositions made for the defense of the height confer the highest honor on the commander of the Russian rearguard," continues Odeleben. "The Russian general took advantage of the position until the last moment, and his troops did not withdraw until the French came up in such strong masses that resistance became totally impossible." Just before departing, the Russian artillery released a final volley. Several balls fell close to Napoleon; one mowed down several Saxon soldiers just ten yards away from the emperor. Exact casualty figures for the engagement at Reichenbach are difficult to obtain; Lanrezac states that the Guard cavalry lost 300 killed, wounded, and captured while the combat cost I Cavalry Corps 100 troopers. In addition, Reynier's losses are estimated at 400 men. Russian and German historians claim both sides sustained around 1,000 casualties.

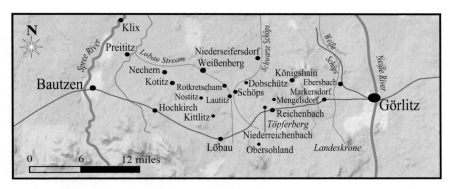

**21.** Region between the Spree and the Neiße Rivers

As V Corps approached to threaten the Russian right, Napoleon observed the Allies abandon the Töpferberg around 3:00, but they did not go far. Quickly retreating to another hill two miles east of Markersdorf, Eugen's Russians again turned to defend their position. After the imperial infantry and cavalry consumed nearly an hour to reorganize, they finally debouched from Reichenbach. Again the onslaught forced Eugen to abandon his position. Retreating in good order, the Russians won the Landeskrone, a height southwest of Görlitz that formed the highest terrain feature in the region. A 45-minute pause ensued during which not a single gun unleashed its frightful contents. With his men on the verge of collapsing from fatigue, Reynier requested permission to halt but Napoleon replied firmly by ordering the march to continue four additional miles to Görlitz. Two columns of infantry and one of cavalry – approximately 50,000 men – surged forward at the emperor's command, making each step at significant cost.

After crossing the Markersdorf stream on both sides of the village, VII Corps proceeded toward the Russian position on the Landeskrone. Napoleon exited Markersdorf on the main highway, riding well ahead of his entourage according to his custom, when the Russian cannon resumed their deadly work. The first salvos screamed over his head, falling fifty yards behind him. A few minutes later an aide-de-camp rode up to inform him that one ball had ricocheted off a tree-trunk into the midst of the imperial staff, instantly killing General François-Joseph Kirgener of the engineers and mortally wounding General Géraud Christophe Duroc, Napoleon's close friend and Grand Marshal of the Palace. Moved by this tragic event, the emperor suddenly ordered the fighting to stop. Duroc, whose abdomen was ripped open and guts were strewn over his uniform, saddle, and horse, agonized for twenty-four hours until death ended his suffering. Moved by

19 The death of General Géraud Christophe Michel Duroc, 22 May 1813

the incident, Napoleon left the highway, rode north among the corn to a small farm, and then gazed at the Russian position as if trying to determine which gun had claimed his friend. After contemplating for several minutes, he skirted Markersdorf's gardens, halting just west of the village on a rise where the infantry of the Old Guard formed an oblong square. In the midst of his bearskins, the emperor's servants pitched his five household tents. Napoleon sat on a stool alone, considering his next move. Around him, the fire of burning villages illuminated the sky.

Napoleon's left wing (I Cavalry Corps, and V, VI, and VII Corps) passed the night of 22 May around Markersdorf while the right (IV and XI Corps) reached Obersohland, four miles south of Reichenbach. Ney's III Corps remained at Weißenberg; Victor and Sébastiani reached Baruth just east of the killing fields around Gleina and Preititz. Despite stubborn Russian resistance, the left wing of the Grande Armée – personally led by the emperor – covered thirty miles on this day. Regardless, 22 May brought Napoleon another huge disappointment. Like Lützen, the victory at Bautzen could not be exploited. Without cavalry, he could not unleash a pursuit that would rout the enemy army and make his victory decisive. No matter how fast his men marched, infantry simply could not replace cavalry.[39]

Having no appetite for a general engagement, Wittgenstein did not utilize the favorable positions at Reichenbach or on the Landeskrone. Instead, he continued the retreat east to Görlitz, seeking to use the four bridges that spanned the Neiße in its vicinity to slip into Silesia. After departing Görlitz on the 23rd, the Allies again divided their army into two columns. Barclay led the northern wing, consisting of his own corps as well as those of Kleist, Yorck, and Blücher. This group planned to reach Liegnitz on the Katzbach River by 26 May based on achieving the following march objectives: Oberwaldau on 23 May, Bunzlau on the 24th, and Haynau on the 25th. The southern wing under Wittgenstein's direct command and composed of the Russian main body sought to reach Goldberg (Złotoryja) on the 25th by marching through Lauban (Lubań) on the 23rd and Löwenberg (Lwówek Śląski) on the 25th. Throughout the retreat, the tenacious Russian rearguard, supported by legions of Cossacks and other irregular light cavalry, maintained steady contact with the imperials. Systematically destroying bridges as they crossed them, the Russians forced Napoleon's soldiers to fight for each yard they gained.[40]

Mikhailovsky-Danilevsky claims that, while at Reichenbach, Allied Headquarters had decided to withdraw to Schweidnitz in Silesia. Such a retreat would allow them to move closer to reinforcements coming from Russia.[41] Moreover, he maintains that the Allies did not want to distance themselves from the Austrian frontier. "The concern was raised," he adds, "that by marching to Schweidnitz the army would be cut off from the Oder. That also, in the case of a movement by the enemy's left wing to the Oder, it would be cut off from its communication." Thus began the debate in the Allied camp whether to comply with the Wurschen Plan and hug the Austrian frontier, which would force the Russians to abandon their direct line of communication through Kalisch and Warsaw. Should the Russians drop the Wurschen Plan and follow their direct line of communication, the Prussians would be forced to evacuate Silesia or part ways with their liberators. By following the Russians, the Prussians would leave Napoleon free to dispatch numerous corps to overrun Brandenburg, take Berlin, and proceed through Pomerania and West Prussia to the Vistula. Yet adherence to the Wurschen Plan appeared feasible only if the Austrians were ready to enter the war. If not, turning southeast and hugging the mountains that separated Silesia and Bohemia could be perilous. Napoleon could easily reach the Oder, outflank the Allies to the east, sever Russian communications, and either drive the Allied army into the mountains or watch it slowly starve. Momentous questions loomed on the horizon for the Sixth Coalition.[42]

On 23 May, Blücher and the Prussians, all under Barclay's command, joined the Russian corps as it trooped eight miles from Mengelsdorf just north of Reichenbach to the bridges over the Neiße downstream of Görlitz.

East of the Neiße, Gneisenau wrote a bitter epistle to Hardenberg on the morning of the 23rd concerning Wittgenstein's leadership:

> We arrived here yesterday to take a position and to give the troops a much-needed rest. At this very moment, we received an order from Wittgenstein to retreat behind the Queis at Naumburg [Nowogrodziec]. As of yesterday, the troops, who are so very tired and for the most part have fought for three days straight, still maintained good order, but this continued retreat will dissolve them. Wittgenstein is completely incompetent for command. Misfortune can be the only result of his leadership of the army. During the engagement the day before yesterday, he supported neither Barclay de Tolly nor Blücher. The reinforcements moved up only after Blücher's corps yielded its position to avoid being completely routed or captured. The retreat was made in the best order. The adjoining report, which we have made for the public, contains nothing but the pure truth ... but not the whole truth, which is embarrassing for our allies and so must be kept a secret.

Predicting Wittgenstein would continue to retreat "until political developments force the enemy to halt," Gneisenau again raised the idea of parting ways with the Russians. Believing that the Russians would disregard the Wurschen Plan in favor of retreating across the Oder and along their line of communication, he suggested that the Prussians fall back to the fortress of Silberberg in far Upper Silesia close to the Bohemian border. "The camps at Glatz and Neiße are now important and must be supplied with provisions. Landwehr and other troops not mobilized for the [field] army can go there. For the present we must depend on our own steadfastness and with it alone we can persevere for a long time. Your advice must not become timid. If we lose our heads at this moment, Austria will not trust us and we will then fall to despondency. Steadfastness and tenacity will save us."[43]

Returning to the French, Berthier issued the disposition for VII Corps to spearhead the attack on the Allied position at Görlitz on the morning of 23 May. Bertrand received orders for IV Corps to turn the village from the south while V Corps reciprocated from the north. Macdonald would lead XI Corps to Schönberg (Sulików), eight miles southeast of Görlitz, pursuing any enemy forces he encountered. Berthier issued these orders at 6:30 A.M. but French patrols reported that the Allies had evacuated Görlitz around dawn. From his bivouac at Markersdorf, Napoleon could see the flames rising from Görlitz's wooden bridge, which the enemy had torched, around 8:00. Hoping to catch the Allies on the other side of Görlitz, Napoleon issued new orders to narrow the distance between his wings by moving his corps closer to the great east–west highway. On the right wing, Macdonald received orders to march in the direction that he thought "would cause the enemy the most trouble." If he could not determine this, the emperor wanted him to march to Schönberg, occupying Seidenberg (Zawidów) on the Bohemian frontier and not allowing a soul to cross the border. On the left wing, Imperial Headquarters tasked Marmont with leading VI Corps sixteen miles to Hermsdorf (Jerzmanki), some five miles east of Görlitz. If he heard the sound of the guns coming from the latter, Berthier instructed the general to march on Görlitz "to contribute to the pursuit of the enemy." Napoleon ordered Lauriston to position V Corps on the great east–west highway at Hennersdorf (Jędrzychowice), five miles northeast of Görlitz. Reynier and Latour-Maubourg supported by the rest of the right wing would continue east on the road to Lauban. Based on news that Bülow's Prussian corps trailed Ney's army as it marched to Bautzen, the emperor assigned Victor and Sébastiani the task of "marching against Bülow," whose corps appeared to be at Luckau "or against anything that follows our rear." Napoleon reached Görlitz around noon and planned to pass the night there.[44]

After destroying the bridges over the Neiße around Görlitz, Barclay left a rearguard of 7,600 men on the eastern bank to cover the retreat of his column. South of them, Wittgenstein posted Duke Eugen of Württemberg with 12,800 soldiers to secure his retreat: both rearguards received the task of preventing the imperials from restoring the bridges or building new ones. Regardless, the availability of several fords allowed the French to get across the Neiße and drive them off. By the end of the day, the imperials had constructed no fewer than seven bridges in and around Görlitz. Fortunately for the Allies, their rearguards destroyed the bridges that spanned an unnamed marshy stream east of Görlitz. Restoring these crossings delayed the march of the French considerably. During the course of the 24th, V Corps crossed the Neiße in two columns. Its vanguard remained engaged with Barclay's rearguard as the Allies withdrew on Bunzlau. At Schützenhain (Strzelno), eighteen miles west of Bunzlau, the Allies turned against their pursuers. After

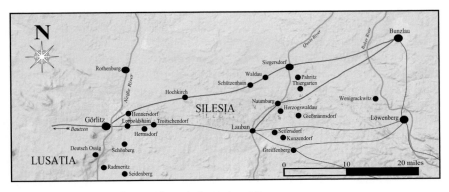

**22.** Region between the Neiße and the Bober Rivers

a short engagement, the rearguard followed Barclay's column to Oberwaldau. Maintaining contact with the enemy's forward posts, Lauriston's vanguard camped at Schützenhain; his main body camped several miles behind at Hochkirch (Przesieczany).

South of Lauriston, VII Corps and I Cavalry Corps crossed the Neiße at Görlitz and upstream of the town, pushing east on the road that gradually turned southeast to Lauban. After advancing only three miles, they again encountered Eugen's II Infantry Corps. Early that afternoon at Leopoldshain (Łagów), the imperials found the Russians positioned behind a swampy stream that favored the defenders. After more hard fighting, by 4:00 P.M. Reynier had finally managed to secure Leopoldshain only to find the Russians entrenched in another position. Overcoming this obstacle by evening, the march continued but Reynier reached only Troitschendorf (Trójca), six miles east of Görlitz. His footsore soldiers could only be grateful the emperor turned in early to his headquarters at Görlitz and did not accompany their march. Four miles south of Reynier, VI Corps moved into Hermsdorf. The Guard remained at Görlitz with the emperor while III Corps loitered about Weißenberg.

On the right wing, Macdonald planned for XI Corps to reach Schönberg in accordance with the emperor's recommendation. To get across the Neiße, the marshal found one downed bridge at Deutsch Ossig and a second further upstream at Radmeritz (Radomierzyce). While the French quickly restored the bridge at Deutsch Ossig to such an extent that artillery could cross, they experienced considerable delays at Radmeritz that lasted until sunset. In addition, Cossacks besieged the units of XI Corps waiting to cross the river. On the eastern side, the situation hardly improved. The portion of Wittgenstein's rearguard commanded by General Yegor Emmanuel drove west between XI and IV Corps, causing panic among both. As a result of the bridging difficulties and Russian harassment, only Macdonald's vanguard reached Schönberg. Meanwhile, hearing the sound of the guns to the north that signaled Reynier's running combat with the Russians, Bertrand led IV Corps north toward Troitschendorf before halting near Hermsdorf.[45]

That afternoon at 4:00, Berthier communicated the emperor's instructions for Marshal Ney to take command of the left wing of the army, consisting of V, VI, and VII Corps as well as I Cavalry Corps. Ney received the task of briskly pursuing Barclay through Bunzlau along the great east–west highway toward Breslau or wherever "it appears that the enemy marches." Napoleon and the Guard would follow Ney while III Corps, temporarily commanded by Souham, moved up to Görlitz to serve as the general reserve. On the right wing, XI Corps supported by 3rd Heavy Cavalry Division from I Cavalry Corps and IV Corps received orders to reach Lauban on the 24th.[46]

The reconnaissance reports that arrived during the night of 23/24 May did not indicate that the Allies had divided their forces for the retreat. Thus, Imperial Headquarters suspected that the bulk of the enemy's army would retreat through Bunzlau to Breslau along the Russian line of communication. To beat the Allies to the Oder, Napoleon decided to make for Glogau. For flank protection during this march, he changed Victor's assignment. Instead of sending him to seek Bülow, Berthier directed the marshal to Rothenburg, fifteen miles north of Görlitz. From there, the emperor wanted II Corps and II Cavalry Corps to follow the army eastward by always marching on its left several miles north of the great east–west highway but on parallel roads. Instead of II Corps, a reinforced XII Corps received the task of contending with Bülow, operating against Berlin, and protecting the left flank of the emperor's line of operation. Oudinot's orders called for XII Corps to reach Hoyerswerda on the 25th and then proceed northwest to Luckau and Lübben. To be clear, Napoleon emphasized as Oudinot's main goal: "to contain Bülow and drive him beyond the Oder." To Ney, the major-general offered more detailed instructions in his 3:00 orders on the morning of the 24th than simply pursuing the enemy. He charged the marshal with commencing the march of Lauriston's V Corps to Bunzlau at 6:00 A.M. followed directly by VII Corps, I Cavalry Corps, and VI Corps to provide Ney with "the resources to force the enemy rearguard." If necessary, XI and IV Corps would also be directed to Bunzlau. Although these directives indicate that Napoleon expected a battle, his own actions prove otherwise. According to Berthier, the emperor planned "to remain at Görlitz for the majority of the day but could arrive at Bunzlau during the night if necessary." Napoleon instructed Berthier to inform Davout that "we take prisoners, we collect the wounded: all is well here."[47]

Napoleon's orders for 24 May did not achieve fruition mainly due to enemy resistance and the difficulties of crossing the Neiße and the Queis. In addition, Ney missed a golden opportunity to inflict considerable losses on Kleist, who now commanded Barclay's rearguard. At Siegersdorf (Zebrzydowa), Lauriston's vanguard waded across the Queis. Unable to hold the river, Kleist ordered a retreat but numerous wagons clogged the highway to Bunzlau. If Ney had pushed V Corps, Kleist would have been hard pressed. Yet inhabitants informed the marshal that large Allied forces stood at Bunzlau. Consequently, Ney remained content with getting across the Queis. At the end of the day's march, the head of V Corps and I Cavalry Corps reached Thiergarten (Zabłocie), seven miles southwest of Bunzlau; the main bodies of both corps remained at Siegersdorf and Pahritz (Parzyce) respectively. Three miles behind them, VII Corps camped at Naumburg; two divisions of VI Corps halted just south of Naumburg, while Marmont's third division stood further rearward. Imperial Headquarters and the

Guard remained at Görlitz, outside of which arrived III Corps. Meanwhile, confusion reigned on the right wing as IV and XI Corps collided en route to Lauban because the latter had taken the wrong road. Cossacks beset Bertrand's lead division consisting of Franquemont's Württembergers. Completely swarmed, the Württembergers resorted to unlimbering their artillery in a futile attempt to blast the Russian warriors. Eventually, Bertrand's patrols found that the Allies had evacuated Lauban. Fording the Queis, the Württembergers entered the town. Macdonald's corps reached Lauban late that evening.

During the course of this day, 24 May, a Russian *Streifkorps* commanded by General Paisi Kaysarov and operating on the left bank of the Neiße between Görlitz and Reichenbach intercepted the baggage of Imperial Headquarters. His Cossacks made short work of the escort: one company of Westphalian infantry, twenty elite gendarmes, and two guns from V Corps. Between thirty and fifty Cossacks swarmed each gun and rode off with the prizes. Had not two Guard companies arrived to escort Duroc's corpse to Dresden, the Cossacks would have seized even more loot. The arrival of the Guard sent the Cossacks fleeing, yet this small incident made a deep impression on Napoleon by demonstrating how vulnerable his communications had become. Napoleon's first order on the 25th placed Soult in command of the Old Guard and Guard Cavalry as well as all of the Guard's administration, equipment, and artillery that did not fall in the jurisdiction of Mortier's Young Guard. He tasked Soult with arranging the Guard Cavalry's protection of Imperial Headquarters, the emperor's baggage, and convoys of military equipment and artillery. On the following day, he ordered all transports operating east of Erfurt to be escorted by at least 1,000 soldiers, including 300–400 infantry.[48]

After clearing the Queis, Blücher moved to Herzogswaldau (Milików), just east of Naumburg between 3:00 and 4:00 P.M. on the 23rd without being pursued. "We heard around six or seven cannon shots in the distance," Gneisenau wrote to Hardenberg. "I tell you this intentionally because I hear that one has told His Majesty that the enemy presses strongly and in force, which is a mistake that I ask you to inform the king as such." He also mentioned that Blücher had just received a letter from Frederick William concerning the battle. According to the king, "the battle on the 21st was broken off because preponderant reasons demanded that on this day no more strength should be sacrificed that could later achieve victory. Perseverance is the watchword in this war; only through it will the destruction of the enemy be possible. I have confidence that my brave army will show further perseverance in the highest extent, exhibit fortitude, and guarantee the outcome." Although certain that the royal letter would calm Blücher's headquarters, Gneisenau insisted that "we must nevertheless complain over such an insult that is truly undeserved."[49]

On the 24th, both columns of the Russo-Prussian army reached the Bober River at Bunzlau and Löwenberg respectively. "After two days we arrived in Silesia," recounts Mikhailovsky-Danilevsky, "where during our march through from Russia, we had been received with the greatest joy; at that time triumphant arches were raised for us in each city and in each village; but now our return heralded the approach of the hated enemy. The prosperous inhabitants abandoned their homes and fled with their families to the mountains and to the Silesian interior. It was very sad to see the depression of our hosts when we checked into the same quarters that we occupied just four weeks earlier when we marched to Dresden." "Berlin was threatened as well as Breslau," adds Steffens, "and the old men, women, and children hastened towards the Austrian frontier; all the young men were with the army."[50]

As the Allies crossed the Bober at Bunzlau and Löwenberg, they posted rearguards on the western bank and in contact with French forces. Wittgenstein continued his eastward trek a further sixteen miles to the Katzbach on 25 May: Barclay's northern column reached Haynau while his southern column attained Goldberg. Alexander announced his desire to hold the line of the Katzbach for at least the day of the 25th. Blücher received instructions to prepare to stop the pursuing enemy without engaging in serious combat; the rearguard should withdraw from Bunzlau "step by step and only before superior forces." In addition, to honor the Wurschen Plan and withdraw along the Riesengebirge, the Russians agreed to pivot southeast on the Goldberg–Liegnitz line. Thus, the left wing of the army under Wittgenstein would rest at Goldberg on the 26th, while Barclay's right wing turned southeast to Liegnitz.[51]

Berthier issued the emperor's initial wave of instructions for operations on the 25th at 3:30 that morning. Hoping to pin the Allies at Breslau, Napoleon wanted his right wing – IV and XI Corps – to continue its movement from Lauban toward Liegnitz by crossing the Bober and reaching Löwenberg (see Map 7). On the left wing, he expected V Corps and I Cavalry Corps to lead the advance by legging twenty-four miles through Bunzlau to the hills of Kreibau (Krzywa) and pushing their vanguard beyond Haynau. Reynier's VII Corps would cross the Bober at Kroischwitz (Kraszowice) just south of Bunzlau and proceed on a road parallel to the east–west highway so its van could reach Modelsdorf (Modlikowice) and its main body Mittlau (Iwiny).[52] Marmont's VI Corps would likewise cross the Bober further south at Ottendorf (Ocice) to occupy Altjäschwitz (Stare Jaroszowice) with its main body and Großhartmannsdorf (Raciborowice Górne) with the vanguard. On the far left, orders called for Victor and Sébastiani to march east toward Bunzlau on the road that ran parallel with the army. Behind the left wing, Mortier received instructions to have the Young Guard marching east toward Bunzlau on the main highway by 5:00 A.M. One hour later the Old Guard and Guard Cavalry would follow; Souham would bring up the rear with III Corps, leaving the Hessians and Badenese of Marchand's 39th - Division to hold the vital post at Görlitz. The Guard would utilize the bridges south of Görlitz to pass the Neiße while III Corps used those to the north.[53]

For the same reasons as the previous days, the corps of the Grande Armée failed to achieve Napoleon's march objectives. The vanguard division of V Corps reached Bunzlau to find the bridge over the Bober ablaze. On the opposite bank, a Prussian rearguard prevented the imperials from dousing the flames. After artillery fire forced the Prussians to withdraw, the French extinguished the fire and repaired the bridge. Meanwhile, Lauriston forded the Bober three miles upstream with his other divisions and I Cavalry Corps. The two columns reunited east of Bunzlau. Lauriston's van then trooped ten miles along the east–west highway to Wolfshain (Wilczy Las); the rear of the column halted at Thomaswaldau (Tomaszów Bolesławiecki). As for VII Corps, after crossing both arms of the Bober, the only road for Reynier to take ran north to the southern suburbs of Bunzlau and then turned south to circumvent a steep, thickly wooded hill chain that stretched south from Bunzlau. After heading south for three miles, a road running east could be struck at Neujäschwitz (Nowe Jaroszowice), which proved to be as far as Reynier could push his exhausted soldiers on the 25th. By marching south of Reynier and thus avoiding the loop around Bunzlau's southern hills, Marmont fared somewhat better. He managed to move one division to Altjäschwitz but the rest of the corps remained on the Bober at Ottendorf.

Further south on the right wing, XI Corps marched in three columns northeast from Lauban to Seifersdorf (Mściszów) before turning southeast to clear the road for IV Corps. West of Kunzendorf (Niwnice), Macdonald ran into Wittgenstein's rearguard. Commanded by General Pyotr Pahlen, the 10,000 Russians resisted so fiercely in the wooded, hilly terrain between Lauban and Löwenberg that the marshal believed he faced triple his own forces. Beginning around 10:00 that morning, the engagement lasted for twelve long hours as Pahlen's warriors slowly yielded step by step. Russian resistance stiffened a few miles west of Löwenberg on a flat ridge east of the elongated village of Kunzendorf. After XI Corps defiled, Bertrand's IV Corps followed to Seifersdorf and then through Gießmannsdorf (Gościszów) to Wenigrackwitz (Rakowice Małe), six miles south of VI Corps at Ottendorf, to secure communication between Macdonald and the left wing of the army. At the sound of Macdonald's cannon, Bertrand moved south to support but arrived too late to participate in the engagement. The Russian rearguard, commanded by St.-Priest after a head wound had incapacitated Pahlen, broke off the engagement at dark, withdrawing unmolested through Löwenberg and across the Bober, destroying the bridge in the process. St.-Priest remained on the hills of the eastern bank facing Löwenberg until the following afternoon when Bertrand's crossing of the Bober threatened to cut his line of retreat.[54]

In the aftermath of Bautzen, Wittgenstein's position as Allied commander in chief became completely untenable and the tsar decided to make a change. At Jauer (Jawor) on the 25th, Alexander interviewed Barclay de Tolly, who used this opportunity to express the need to continue the retreat all the way to Poland. He viewed the spring of 1813 as a crusade to care for his men after the rigors of 1812. On reaching the German front on the eve of Bautzen, he found the Russian field army weakened and short of provisions, arms, uniforms, and ammunition. What a sight for Barclay, Alexander's former minister of war! Nothing could persuade him from viewing the internal condition of the Russian field army as desperate and its military efficiency as sapped. The representatives of the British crown appear to have agreed. In a report to Cathcart dated 8 May 1813, Wilson warned "that the Russian force is rapidly diminishing daily. The battalions are too weak for duty, and they waste away without extraordinary casualties. The general spirit, I am very much grieved to note, is not favorable to those exertions and sacrifices that the exigency of the time requires." Prior to Bautzen on 18 May, Stewart expressed concern over the state of the Russian army: "Every retrograde march, in the present position of affairs, prejudices public opinions, and the soldiers have begun to lose their *morale*; and I cannot conceive, from what I have seen of a Russian army, that they can support a retreat in the immediate presence of the enemy pursuing vigorously, with order, or without great loss." In his *Narrative*, Stewart commented that "it was impossible not to observe that the state of the Russian army was, at this period, somewhat on the decline from the incredible fatigues and hardships it experienced during two campaigns. The battalions were so weak that three or four scarcely formed a regiment and seldom exceeded 250 or 300 men. The general tone prevalent throughout the military officers of the Russian army was of a desponding nature. They thought they had done enough, especially as Austria had not declared herself, and Saxony continued to oppose them. To them, the tide of their success seemed to be arrested, and they eagerly looked to their own frontiers. A deficiency of ammunition existed."[55]

Barclay argued that no worthwhile improvements could be made while the army remained in daily contact with the enemy. To provide the troops with the proper rest and steady supply that they needed, he advised falling back and trading space for time. This would allow the army to recover through the ample replenishment of men, horses, uniforms, equipment, and weapons. Battles should not be sought in Silesia, but instead rest and reorganization would be the objective of a retreat beyond the Vistula. Barclay advocated having the Russian army exit the theater for six weeks, returning only after it had rested and received reinforcements and supplies. Many officers who enjoyed the tsar's confidence agreed with Barclay's assessment. "In May," recalls one Russian commander, "our munitions were so exhausted that we had nothing left to fight a third battle. Our soldiers were fatigued by eleven months of consecutive campaigning and by marches in unprecedented heat during the summer and one of the most rigorous winters that was ever seen, even in Russia; their clothes and coats were in tatters, their shoes completely worn out, and their weapons in poor condition."[56]

After having spent the previous winter quartered at Warsaw, many Russian officers longed to return to the comforts of the Polish capital. On a more practical note, the Russians could spare no forces should the Poles rise up to support their former master. "In the present situation of the Allies," wrote Wilson, "I look with terror to the renovation of the Polish insurrection. Russia would be able to send no succor ... the Allies would then have only Silesia and, if Austria joined, Bohemia as the base of operations; but if Austria did not join, we would be cooped up in Silesia, or be obliged to fight our way through Poland under every disadvantage." On 19 May, Stewart had informed Castlereagh that according to rumors: "General Sacken has had an action with the Poles, and it would argue that that country is in insurrection and would join France."[57]

On the other hand, the Russians knew that the Prussian army could not follow them to Poland. A province rich in resources such as Silesia could not be sacrificed to imperial plunder similar to East Prussia in 1812. Thus, if he appointed Barclay the new Allied commander in chief, Alexander either would be at odds with him or would be forced to endorse his proposal to withdraw from the German theater. The latter would certainly require the tsar to part ways at least temporarily with Frederick William. Alexander slept on the issue but rendered his decision the next day to appoint Barclay. According to Müffling, the Russian monarch imposed his will on Barclay during their meeting. Instead of allowing his new commander to continue the retreat due east to cross the Oder at Breslau, the tsar ordered him to follow Knesebeck's recommendation to turn southeast, hug the mountains, and march to Schweidnitz. Later, Barclay bitterly lamented having abandoned the shortest route through Breslau, which forced him to make considerable detours. Barclay also abandoned his main line of communication and rerouting took time, as Stewart explains: "Reinforcements were no doubt arriving, but many might be intercepted: and the enemy captured 800 men, 10 pieces of artillery, and a large number of tumbrils that were moving toward Liegnitz, ignorant of present events. The great line of communication being abandoned, much exertion was necessary to turn the reinforcements in the new direction."[58]

Michael Andreas Barclay de Tolly, the 51-year-old descendent of Scottish immigrants who had settled in Livonia (Estonia) in the 1600s, had seen action in his early years against the Turks, Swedes, and Poles, attaining the rank of general by 1799. Minister of war since 1810, the German-speaking non-ethnic Russian commanded Russia's main army in 1812 until the tsar buckled under xenophobic pressure to replace him with Kutuzov, an ethnic Russian. One of Barclay's subordinates during the 1812 campaign, Yermolov, described him at that time: "He had only few competent men around him and so rarely thought of sharing his work with them and wanted to accomplish everything through personal hard work. Thus, matters initially proceeded very slowly; gradually, actions became so uncoordinated that they eventually led to an unavoidable mess." A French émigré in Russian service, General Louis Alexandre de Langeron, provides a lengthier description:

> In the War of 1807 against the French, [Levin August von] Bennigsen, who was commander in chief of the Russian armies, fell ill in the middle of the campaign and the tsar asked him to whom he should entrust command of the army if he was forced to leave it; Bennigsen designated Barclay de Tolly, who was not yet a major-general: he made the right decision. According to many, Barclay was, after Bennigsen, the best general in the Russian army. He was well educated and displayed excellent *coup d'oeil* and bravery ... and knew how to maneuver well on a battlefield. No one possessed a higher degree of talent than him for the details of the internal administration of an army: it is to him that we must attribute in this war the perfect organization of the reserve armies and the recruit depots, which ceaselessly maintained the field armies and replaced their losses. His unbending severity, his cold harshness, which extended to all under his orders, rendered each man attentive to fulfilling his duties. He knew how to inspire such salutary terror among the staff in charge of provisions, uniforms, and hospitals that these miserable men, the shame and scourge of Russian armies, no longer dared commit their customary depredations and the troops never knew want for any necessity, even 2,000 leagues from their frontier.
>
> General Barclay maintained his integrity intact; but unfortunately he was married and was too often dominated by his wife, who was not as scrupulous. One can reproach Barclay for his constant and often unjust predilection for his compatriots: a predilection that was humiliating for Russians. His headquarters was composed solely of Germans, of relatives and protégés of his wife, for whom advancement was often as fast as it was unmerited. One only spoke German there, and one only saw two Russians, General [Ivan Vasiliyevich] Sabaneyev, and one other, both of whom were referred to as "the

foreigners." This fault in general was shared by all Germans: the heaviness, formal stiffness, and slow imagination of the people of this country as well as their coarseness rendered them disagreeable to others and, as they were only well understood amongst themselves, they sought each other out.

According to Müffling, the story that reached the Prussians concerning the reason for Wittgenstein's demotion concerned accusations that he "bestowed too little care on the internal order of the troops." Müffling claims that, prior to Bautzen, Russian convalescents coming from Poland had reached the army in march battalions of 1,000 men led by few officers:

> Instead of immediately dissolving these march battalions, which contained soldiers from all regiments of the Russian army and assigning the men to their organic regiments, these march battalions were used in the battle of Bautzen where, unorganized, without officers or noncommissioned officers, they performed unreliably, and were poorly supplied and if they wandered from their march battalion could not find it again. Thus, on the retreat from Bautzen, large groups of Russian soldiers, just out of the hospital, still weak, badly armed and clothed, were roaming about; they often did not even know the numbers of their battalions and when they did, the Russian officers were unable to help them to find their battalions because numbers were quite unknown in the Russian army.

As for the Prussian perception of Barclay in May 1813, Gneisenau sounds a sour note:

> The new commander in chief, General Barclay de Tolly, is an industrious man in the cabinet who loves order. Although a German, he is nevertheless not free of Russian hoodwinking and intrigue. He is very jealous of his authority. He has an ongoing feud with Volkonsky because of the latter's influence on orders and promotions. He is a completely well-experienced minister of war. As a field commander he is an unenterprising moral coward who listens to no advice. In battle he is very brave, although at Bautzen he withdrew too quickly and thus could not advance any more although Kleist offered to retake the hills of Gleina with him. He is mastered by his wife, who is one of his adjutants.

Müffling adds: "For us Prussians, his nomination was anything but agreeable."[59] Blücher did not express his thoughts on Barclay in writing. Although agreeing with Gneisenau's description of Barclay as "a pedantic detailer" who "was poor in ideas" and lacked the ability to see the big picture, General Caemmerer's assessment of him is quite favorable: "His firm, direct, and kind character, his will power, his bravery, and humbleness, and not least his concern for the soldiers secured for him the respect and love of his subordinates." Maude adds that "Barclay ... took a very cool and level-headed view of the situation, and refused altogether to satisfy the patriotic but impracticable longings of the Prussians for another battle. The troops were far too spent for there to be any prospect of success were they allowed to fight, and a thorough reorganization was essential." Stating the obvious, Bogdanovich comments that Blücher "was very pleased" by Wittgenstein's demotion. "In general, there reigned at this time no friendly feelings between the Allies, which is typically the case in unfavorable circumstances." Bogdanovich suggests that the reason for the disharmony were Prussian complaints over "the carelessness of the Russian intendants in obtaining food supplies for the troops who, according to Prussian administrators, because of this desolated the land like stragglers."[60] With a new commander in chief who advocated abandoning Prussian territory, what hope did the Prussians have of liberating their Fatherland?

## Notes

1  Nostitz, *Tagebuch*, I:49; Fritz to Wilhelm, Liegnitz, 25 May 1813, Griewank, *Hohenzollernbriefe*, Nr. 40, 57–58.
2  The account of 20 May is based on Wittgenstein to Blücher, 20 May 1813, GStA PK, VI HA Rep. 92 Nl. Gneisenau, Nr. 160; Bogdanovich, *Geschichte des Krieges*, I:57–60; Mikhailovsky-Danilevsky, *Denkwürdigkeiten*, 98; Nostitz, *Tagebuch*, I:49; Steffens, *Adventures*, 101–03; Unger, *Blücher*, II:38; Blücher's after-action report, "Angaben über den Antheil des Blücher'schen Corps an der Bautzener Schlacht am 20. und 21. Mai," 31 May 1813, which Müffling drafted, Gneisenau approved, and Blücher signed. The original Russian version is in RGVIA, f. VUA, op. 2, d. 3902, ll. 73–74b. The report is reproduced in full by Pertz and Delbrück, *Gneisenau*, II:619–20, and in part by Unger, *Blücher*, II:37–39. See also Gneisenau to Münster, Puschkau by Striegau in Silesia, 29 May 1813, GStA PK, VI HA Rep. 92 Nl. Gneisenau, Nr. 20b; Plotho, *Der Krieg*, I:160–63; Vaudoncourt, *Histoire de la guerre*, 93–95; Holleben and Caemmerer, *Frühjahrsfeldzuges 1813*, II:212–16.
3  "Unfortunately, General Miloradovich, supposedly through a misunderstanding, evacuated the town of Bautzen without firing a shot and only by holding Bautzen could this new position be maintained with any advantage": Gneisenau to Münster, Puschkau by Striegau in Silesia, 29 May 1813, GStA PK, VI HA Rep. 92 Nl. Gneisenau, Nr. 20b.
4  Quoted in Unger, *Blücher*, II:39.
5  Bogdanovich, *Geschichte des Krieges*, I:62; Holleben and Caemmerer, *Frühjahrsfeldzuges 1813*, II:216–17; Müffling, *Aus meinem Leben*, 36–37; Droysen, *Yorck*, II:91; Pertz and Delbrück, *Gneisenau*, II:621–22.
6  Cathcart, *Commentaries*, 159–60.
7  SHAT, C$^{17}$ 178: Berthier to Ney, 20 and 21 May 1813.
8  Jomini claims that Ney waited in vain throughout the night of 20/21 May for orders that he requested from Napoleon. According to Jomini, Blücher's "salient position on the hills of Niedergurig and the many troopers of his cavalry forced the

French officers to make great detours": Jomini, *Précis politique et militaire*, 268. For details of the action during this part of the battle, see Bogdanovich, *Geschichte des Krieges*, I:67–68; Vaudoncourt, *Histoire de la guerre*, 96.

9 On 22 May, Barclay commanded a total of 17 battalions totaling some 8,000 bayonets. Two battalions held Guttau, two stood in the woods between Brösa and Gleina, and three occupied Malschwitz, while 2,400 cavalry held Lömischau (one mile north of Guttau) to threaten Lauriston's left and the crossing at Klix: Holleben and Caemmerer, *Frühjahrsfeldzuges 1813*, II:226. See also Stewart, *Narrative*, 49.

10 The conversation between Müffling and Barclay is reproduced in Müffling, *Aus meinem Leben*, 37–38. Citing Müffling, Bogdanovich, *Geschichte des Krieges*, I:68, likewise reproduces this account.

11 Müffling, *Aus meinem Leben*, 40; Pertz and Delbrück, *Gneisenau*, II:623; Gneisenau, *Blücher*, 112–14; "Angaben über den Antheil des Blücher'schen Corps an der Bautzener Schlacht am 20. und 21. Mai," 31 May 1813, RGVIA, f. VUA, op. 2, d. 3902, ll. 73–74b.

12 Gneisenau, *Blücher*, 119.

13 According to Müffling, he did not suggest an immediate retreat, only that "speedy measures" be taken: Müffling, *Aus meinem Leben*, 39–41.

14 Jomini, *Précis politique et militaire*, 269–70.

15 In his sympathetic account of Ney's career, Atteridge lamely speculates on why the marshal did not conform with Napoleon's orders: "it is very likely that if Ney had had under his command the war-worn veterans he had led at Friedland and Borodino he would not have minded much having a gap between his advance and the nearest corps of the main attack, and would have concentrated all his efforts on the turning movement. But with his young and inexperienced troops he saw a risk in plunging boldly into the Allied positions and leaving his own right for a while 'in air' and exposed." After Lützen, referring to Ney's troops as inexperienced is not accurate. See Atteridge, *Ney*, 254.

16 Nostitz, *Tagebuch*, I:50; Gneisenau, *Blücher*, 120.

17 "Angaben über den Antheil des Blücher'schen Corps an der Bautzener Schlacht am 20. und 21. Mai," 31 May 1813, RGVIA, f. VUA, op. 2, d. 3902, ll. 73–74b.

18 Nostitz, *Tagebuch*, I:50.

19 Mikhailovsky-Danilevsky, *Denkwurdigkeiten*, 101.

20 Gneisenau, *Blücher*, 121.

21 Gneisenau's quote is in Steffens, *Adventures*, 100; Stewart, *Narrative*, 46; Odeleben, *A Circumstantial Narrative*, I:97.

22 Mikhailovsky-Danilevsky, *Opisanie voiny 1813 goda*, I:210. The Russian eyewitness states that the Guard Artillery opened fire at 2:00.

23 Gneisenau's assessment offers a biased yet insightful account: "the expected support [Yorck] came too late; the two brigades of General Blücher's front gradually withdrew from their convex position to the high ground around Kreckwitz, but could not find a position there suitable for the further defense and, as a result, the only measure that remained [to Blücher] was to keep himself master of the terrain. To do this, he needed to unite the weakened battalions of the brigades with the rest of the reserve and, waiving all other considerations, to take

the offensive with impetuous firmness. No doubts can be entertained that, by this very rapid movement, he would have again penetrated to the valley of the Spree, but at this point the brigade reserves had not yet returned. If Blücher had retaken this ground, still that battle would not have been won; the less so, as the terrain already lost on the extreme right wing was so decisive an event." See Gneisenau, *Blücher*, 122–23.

24 Bogdanovich, *Geschichte des Krieges*, I:73–74. Yermolov received command of the 2nd Guard Division of the Russian Reserve after having been demoted earlier in the month. The detachment that he brought up to relieve Yorck consisted of two battalions of the Life Guard Jäger Regiment, the Pernovskii and Kexholmskii Grenadier Regiments, two battalions of Guard Ekipazh (Marines), the Glukhovskii Cuirassier Regiment, and one horse battery.

25 Mikhailovsky-Danilevsky, *Opisanie voiny 1813 goda*, I:210; Müffling, *Aus meinem Leben*, 42–44; Pertz and Delbrück, *Gneisenau*, II:624–25, follow Müffling's account verbatim.

26 "Angaben über den Antheil des Blücher'schen Corps an der Bautzener Schlacht am 20. und 21. Mai," 31 May 1813, RGVIA, f. VUA, op. 2, d. 3902, ll. 73–74b.

27 Wilson, *Private Diary*, II:19–20.

28 In an annotation on the bottom of page 76, the Russian officer who translated Bogdanovich's volumes into German, "A.S., a retired colonel of the Russian General Staff," claims to have heard Alexander utter these words at 4:00 P.M. See Bogdanovich, *Geschichte des Krieges*, I:76–77.

29 Mikhailovsky-Danilevsky, *Denkwürdigkeiten*, 104.

30 Stewart, *Narrative*, 48; Wilson, *Private Diary*, II:20–21. The eyewitness Nauck claims that, as the French bore down on the last battery to leave the field, Frederick William "placed himself at its head and thus led it from the combat": Pertz and Delbrück, *Gneisenau*, III:679.

31 Reiche, *Memoiren*, I:283.

32 Gneisenau to Hardenberg, Reichenbach, 22 May 1813, *Gneisenau*, ed. Griewank, Nr. 117, 228.

33 Quoted in Bogdanovich, *Geschichte des Krieges*, I:80–81.

34 Stewart, *Narrative*, 49; Add MSS, 20111, 29: Lowe to Bunbury, Löwenberg, 24 May 1813. The account of 21 May is based on "Angaben über den Antheil des Blücher'schen Corps an der Bautzener Schlacht am 20. und 21. Mai," 31 May 1813, RGVIA, f. VUA, op. 2, d. 3902, ll. 73–74b; Jomini, *Précis politique et militaire*, I:267–76; Clausewitz, *Hinterlassene Werke*, VII:293–99; Holleben and Caemmerer, *Frühjahrsfeldzuges 1813*, II:207–40; Bogdanovich, *Geschichte des Krieges*, I:49–81; Plotho, *Der Krieg*, I:164–72; Vaudoncourt, *Histoire de la guerre*, 95–98; Beitzke, *Geschichte der deutschen Freiheitskriege*, I:433–48; Droysen, *Yorck*, II:88–94; Gneisenau, *Blücher*, 120–21; Pertz and Delbrück, *Gneisenau*, II:627–29; Nostitz, *Tagebuch*, I:51; Unger, *Blücher*, II:41; Maude, *Leipzig Campaign*, 137; Atteridge, *Ney*, 252–55.

35 Odeleben, *A Circumstantial Narrative*, I:100. He also reports that at this time the French started the practice of transporting the wounded in wheel-barrows.

36 Maude, in *Leipzig Campaign*, 138–39, contends that, politically, Napoleon's "second failure to reap the rewards of a crushing success was almost as disastrous

as an actual defeat. With 200,000 men at his disposal – 170,000 of whom had actually appeared on the field – he failed to capture a single gun or stand of colors."

37  SHAT, C$^{17}$ 178: Berthier to Macdonald, Marmont, and Oudinot, 22 May 1813.

38  Holleben and Caemmerer, *Frühjahrsfeldzuges 1813*, II:242–43.

39  Sources for the combat at Reichenbach include: SHAT, C$^2$ 144: Reynier to Marmont, 24 May 1813; Odeleben, *A Circumstantial Narrative*, I:101–06; Lanrezac, *Lützen*, 246–49; Holleben and Caemmerer, *Frühjahrsfeldzuges 1813*, II:244–47; Bogdanovich, *Geschichte des Krieges*, I:84–88; Beitzke, *Geschichte der deutschen Freiheitskriege*, I:457–59.

40  Lanrezac, *Lützen*, 245.

41  After praising the Russians for their performance at Bautzen, Lowe added: "thirty or forty battalions more of them (and it is confidently said large reinforcements are on their road) would still turn the tide in our favor, even independent of the active aid of Austria." See Add MSS, 20111, 30: Lowe to Bunbury, Löwenberg, 24 May 1813.

42  Mikhailovsky-Danilevsky, *Denkwürdigkeiten*, 104; Lieven, *Russia Against Napoleon*, 323–25. According to Lieven, even in peacetime Upper Silesia depended on Poland for food supplies and could not suddenly accommodate the Allied army. Also part of the problem was Stein's failure to establish the magazines in eastern Saxony that Kutuzov had requested in April.

43  Gneisenau to Hardenberg, Hennersdorf, 23 May 1813, GStA PK, VI HA Rep. 92 Nl. Albrecht, Nr. 47.

44  SHAT, C$^{17}$ 178: Berthier to Macdonald, Bertrand, Lauriston, Victor, and Reynier, 23 May 1813; Odeleben, *A Circumstantial Narrative*, I:110.

45  Lanrezac, *Lützen*, 247–48; Holleben and Caemmerer, *Frühjahrsfeldzuges 1813*, II:249–50.

46  SHAT, C$^{17}$ 178: Berthier to Ney, Reynier, Latour-Maubourg, Lauriston, Marmont, and Macdonald, 23 May 1813.

47  CN, No. 20037, XXV:312–13; SHAT, C$^{17}$ 178: Berthier to Victor, Ney, Marmont, Oudinot, and Davout, 24 May 1813. Oudinot would be supported by an ad hoc brigade composed of eight battalions spread between Magdeburg and Torgau as well as a battery of eight guns that had been earmarked for II Corps, all of which Berthier directed to Wittenberg to await Oudinot's orders. To cover Oudinot's left flank, Napoleon ordered Davout to dispatch General Vandamme with the 2nd and 5th Divisions in the direction of Mecklenburg and Berlin.

48  SHAT, C$^{17}$ 178: Berthier to Soult, 25 May 1813; Lanrezac, *Lützen*, 249–50; Holleben and Caemmerer, *Frühjahrsfeldzuges 1813*, II:250–51.

49  Quoted in Unger, *Blücher*, II:44; Gneisenau to Hardenberg, bivouac at Günthersdorf near Herzogswaldau, 23 May 1813, GStA PK, VI HA Rep. 92 Nl. Albrecht, Nr. 47.

50  Mikhailovsky-Danilevsky, *Denkwürdigkeiten*, 105; Steffens, *Adventures*, 107.

51  Barclay to Blücher, 25 May 1813, and Volkonsky to Blücher, 26 and 27 May 1813, GStA PK, VI HA Rep. 92 Nl. Gneisenau, Nr. 160.

52  The actual order states "Schlimmer," which German sources correct as Schlemmer (Sieroniów), a tiny hamlet east of Ocice. The town of Kraszowice is the nearest population center on the east bank.

53 SHAT, C¹⁷ 178: Berthier to Bertrand, Macdonald, Victor, Mortier, Souham, and Soult, Görlitz, 4:00 A.M., 25 May 1813; Lanrezac, *Lützen*, 250.

54 Mikaberidze, *The Russian Officer Corps*, 292; Lanrezac, *Lützen*, 250–51; Holleben and Caemmerer, *Frühjahrsfeldzuges 1813*, II:251–52.

55 Wilson, *Private Diary*, II:5; Stewart to Castlereagh, Wurschen, 18 May 1813, *CVC*, IX:11; Stewart, *Narrative*, 31, 33, 56. In *Russia Against Napoleon*, 324, Lieven claims that by late May the Russians "were also beginning to go hungry." Bogdanovich, in *Geschichte des Krieges*, I:102, adds that "the majority of Russian infantry regiments consisted only of a single battalion; several regiments were barely 150–200 men strong. Captains commanded brigades. Instead of eight, cavalry regiments consisted of two or three or at the most four squadrons. The artillery, which participated in two battles and many rearguard engagements, lacked ammunition." See also Bernhardi, *Toll*, II:455.

56 Langeron, *Mémoires*, 201; Osten-Sacken, *Militärische-politische Geschichte des Befreiungskrieges*, II:343.

57 Wilson, *Private Diary*, I:362; Stewart to Castlereagh, Wurschen, 19 May 1813, *CVC*, IX:14.

58 Müffling, *Aus meinem Leben*, 47–48, 52; Pertz and Delbrück, *Gneisenau*, II:644–45; Stewart, *Narrative*, 55.

59 Ermolov, *The Czar's General*, 128–29; Langeron, *Mémoires*, 205; Müffling, *Aus meinem Leben*, 45; Gneisenau is quoted in Pertz and Delbrück, *Gneisenau*, II:644.

60 Holleben and Caemmerer, *Frühjahrsfeldzuges 1813*, II:265; Maude, *Leipzig Campaign*, 140–41; Bogdanovich, *Geschichte des Krieges*, I:94.

# 9

# Silesia

During the course of 25 May, Napoleon wrote to Durosnel, the commandant of Dresden. This letter stated that the emperor planned to go to Bunzlau that day and from there to Glogau and Frankfurt-am-Oder. This intention accounted for the orders early that morning for his right wing to march northeast toward Liegnitz. Assuming that the Allied army would retreat to Breslau along the Russian main line of communication, Napoleon returned to the idea of a great strategic envelopment and combined it with the core tenet of his master plan: the taking of Berlin. While he fixed the Allies at the Silesian capital presumably with his right, he would swing north with his left, cross the Oder at Glogau and then swoop south to fall on the rear of the Allies at Breslau. Meanwhile, the advance of the Grande Armée downstream the Oder probably would force the Prussians to evacuate Berlin. If not, a reinforced Oudinot would dispatch Bülow and take the capital.[1]

Yet rumors reached Imperial Headquarters that a portion of the Allied army had marched north to unite with Bülow. Did this mark the long anticipated split between the Prussians and Russians? If, as Napoleon expected, the Allied army continued the retreat from Bunzlau through Breslau along the Russian line of communication, the Prussians certainly would recognize that they could not follow their allies into Poland. If the Prussians indeed separated from the Russians, he could return to the idea of defeating each in detail. If they did not separate and did not detach any forces to support Bülow, he could pursue his plan of a strategic envelopment on the Oder. Thus, to determine his next move, he needed accurate intelligence. Consequently, Napoleon ordered II Corps, which stood seven miles northwest of Bunzlau at Thommendorf (Tomisław), to march twenty-five miles further north to Sprottau (Szprotawa) on the Bober. Hoping Victor would arrive there that same day, the emperor instructed him to dispatch patrols in every direction and pursue any Allied forces that he found marching in the direction of Berlin. In particular, he wanted the marshal to find Bülow: had the Prussian moved closer to Berlin or the Oder, or had he continued his movement toward Luckau? Returning to the master plan, Napoleon informed Victor that II Corps needed to remain ready to march on Berlin to support Oudinot's XII Corps as it advanced to the Prussian capital. Assuming Bülow would retreat to defend Berlin, Victor would fall on the rear of the Prussian corps.

Shortly after Berthier dictated his version of the emperor's instructions to Victor at 6:00 A.M., he received a second letter from the master. Its contents provide additional insight into the French system of command. Napoleon's directives for Victor demonstrate his need to receive daily reports from his corps commanders. "Write to the duc de Bellune [Victor]" he snapped, "that it pains me to see that he has not corresponded [with us]; that if he encountered enemy posts he should have sent a local man to cross through them on the promise of a large reward; that at Sprottau he must collect intelligence and send it to me at Bunzlau; because, if nothing is found on the road to Berlin and if Bülow is closer to Berlin and the Oder, the duc de Bellune will be ordered tomorrow to move on Glogau to lift the siege of this place."[2]

Meanwhile, Berthier already had issued the first round of the emperor's orders for the 26th at 9:00 the previous evening. Napoleon wanted III Corps and all Guard units (Young, Old, and Cavalry) marching east by 5:00 A.M. Marmont received orders to maintain communication with IV Corps as it marched with XI Corps from Lauban toward Löwenberg. Demonstrating the extent to which a commander of a pre-industrial age army could be uncertain of the events unfolding around him, the major-general expressed Napoleon's concern that "for two hours we have heard a lively cannonade from your direction. Tell us what you know." Stirring later than usual on the 26th, the master did not issue orders for the rest of the army until 6:00 A.M. For now, Napoleon sought to destroy the enemy rearguard at Liegnitz on the great east–west highway by pinning it with his left and smashing it with his right. With V and VII Corps, Ney would advance on Haynau, pushing one column toward Liegnitz and another toward Glogau to set the stage for the strategic envelopment. Behind Ney, Mortier and Soult would follow with all Guard units. Napoleon placed I Cavalry Corps under the command of Marmont with orders to proceed toward Goldberg, to "maneuver to cut off the enemy rearguard and fall on its right flank ... and to strongly pressure the enemy in unison with Bertrand and Macdonald." Souham would move III Corps one league east of Bunzlau and await Ney's orders.[3]

In a second letter to Marmont written only thirty minutes later, Napoleon both expands the marshal's assignment and clearly explains his intentions so his subordinate would understand the task. Some background is required to explain this second communiqué. Being placed under Ney's command outraged the junior marshal, who could hardly conceal his extreme jealousy of "the bravest of the brave." According to intelligence he received from various sources and influenced by his desire to avoid Ney, Marmont became convinced by the 25th that the enemy had posted only a small rearguard on the great east–west highway. Instead of withdrawing along this vital artery, he believed Wittgenstein's main body had retreated through Löwenberg to Goldberg. Consequently, early on the morning of the 26th, he requested authorization from Ney to march southeast to Löwenberg. Based on his instructions from the emperor to drive east through Haynau toward Liegnitz, Ney refused to grant Marmont permission. Marmont's report must have reached Napoleon sometime between 6:00 and 6:30 – the times of Berthier's two letters to the marshal. Marmont stated his case so persuasively that Napoleon considered the possibility that he did not have the enemy's main force directly in front of him on the east–west highway. Consequently, the emperor overrode Ney and granted Marmont's request.

"Not expecting to find a large amount of cavalry on his flanks, the enemy could experience great difficulty," explained the emperor in his second letter to Marmont. He informed the corps commander that Ney would lead the army's left wing to Haynau that day while Bertrand and Macdonald "must reach Goldberg today" with the right. Wittgenstein's main body would be withdrawing to Breslau on one of two roads: the Bunzlau–Haynau–Liegnitz stretch of the east–west highway or the Lauban–Löwenberg–Goldberg–Liegnitz road. With Goldberg eleven miles due south of Haynau, Napoleon instructed Marmont to take a position between the army's two wings to be able to march to Liegnitz in three columns the following day, 27 May. Liegnitz, the next major population hub on the great east–west highway, stood eleven miles east of Haynau and twelve miles northeast of Goldberg. Planning for his respective wings to drive the enemy forces that opposed them on Liegnitz, Napoleon instructed the marshal to either turn south to strike the left flank of any enemy force marching on the Goldberg–Liegnitz–Breslau road, or curve north to hit the right flank of an enemy withdrawing along the Haynau–Liegnitz–Breslau portion of the east–west highway. According to the emperor, the reconnaissance conducted by Marmont's troops would enable the marshal to decide which direction to take. Their reports would reveal which of the two roads "the majority of the enemy army" had taken so that the marshal could launch his flank attack against Wittgenstein's main body.[4]

On the Allied side, Barclay's promotion caused changes in the command structure: Wittgenstein retained command of the southern column while Blücher assumed leadership of all the troops of the northern column (Prussian I and II Corps as well as Barclay's corps) with command of II Corps going to Kleist and that of Barclay's to Langeron. During the 26th, the Allies retreated across the Katzbach: Blücher went to Liegnitz with the right wing while Wittgenstein directed the left to Goldberg. Napoleon held back the advance of his own left wing until Marmont gained enough ground to cover its right flank. Thus, V and VII corps commenced the march to Haynau at 11:00 A.M. Lauriston's vanguard, consisting of Maison's 16th Division of 4,000 men and one division of I Cavalry Corps, reached Haynau sometime after 2:00 that afternoon. By 3:00, Maison's infantry had crossed through Haynau and moved onto the heights east of Michelsdorf (Michów). Due to a misunderstanding, the cavalry division halted west of Haynau, believing the day's toils to be over. Maison's men camped covered by skirmishers, who had remained in continuous contact with those of the enemy since morning. About fifty troopers received security detail but performed this duty with inexcusable negligence and did not bother to climb the hills that obscured the view at close range. After learning that the cavalry division had not followed Maison through Haynau, Lauriston ordered one of its brigades to move up and join 16th Division. The dispatch rider had just dug his spurs into the sides of his steed when a windmill south of the highway burst into flame: it was a signal.[5]

After Barclay had departed for his meeting with Alexander at Jauer on the 25th, Blücher immediately took advantage of his absence to launch a bold cavalry strike at Haynau against the pursuing French. Perturbed by the continuous retreat, Blücher wanted to attack simply to reinvigorate the troops. "Long have General Blücher and I wished to deliver such a combat," Gneisenau informed Hardenberg.[6] To Münster he wrote: "Since then [Bautzen], we have retreated. The leadership of the army comes from Russian headquarters. We have no part in it. The Russians do not listen to us. We are merely tools. Finally, Barclay de Tolly, who commanded us, was summoned to Imperial Headquarters. We immediately used this emancipation. The march went through a wide plain. The enemy followed our rearguard day in and day out. We wanted to punish him for this."

Under Gneisenau's supervision, staff officers Rühle von Lilienstern and Müffling made the preparations to attack the French. They designated the plain east of Haynau on the great east–west highway for an ambush; Blücher approved with gusto. While Klüx and Röder proceeded twelve miles east to Liegnitz in accordance with Barclay's orders, Zieten's 2nd Brigade moved five miles southeast of Haynau to Pohlsdorf (Pątnów) to serve as support for the cavalry operation. Meanwhile, Dolffs's Reserve Cavalry – twenty-two squadrons and two batteries – lay in ambush four miles south of Haynau at Brockendorf (Brochocin) and Schellendorf (Strupice). They would await Zieten's signal – the firing of the windmill at Baudmannsdorf (Budziwojów) – and then move north on the Goldberg–Haynau road to strike the east–west highway. Yorck's Reserve Cavalry under Corswant – eight squadrons – took a position five miles east of Haynau at Siegendorf (Siedliska).

Langeron's rearguard under General Yefim Chaplits, consisting of three battalions, ten squadrons, four Cossack regiments, and one battery, stood five miles southeast of Haynau between Doberschau (Dobroszów) and Steudnitz (Studnica). As bait, Colonel Johann Karl von Mutius remained on the west side of Haynau with three battalions, nine squadrons, and two horse batteries to slowly draw the enemy into the trap. Zieten, who was commanding the operation, took post at the Baudmannsdorf windmill, two miles south of Haynau and three miles west of his infantry at Pohlsdorf, with two squadrons and one horse battery. Blücher and his staff took a position "somewhat further back." The undulating terrain covered by high corn fields particularly favored a surprise.

As noted, Ney did not commence his march to Haynau until 11:00 that morning, thus forcing the Prussians to exercise patience. By noon, Mutius had fallen back to a position southwest of Haynau on the southern bank of the Schnelle Deichsel (Skora) River. Maison's 16th Division – eight battalions, eight squadrons, and three batteries – pursued almost grudgingly. The opposing forces exchanged artillery at ineffectual ranges until Mutius learned that a strong enemy column – Reynier's VII Corps – was approaching his left by advancing toward Modelsdorf. Assuming that this news accounted for Maison's lethargy, Mutius sought to lure him across the Schnelle Deichsel. He withdrew southeast, passing Michelsdorf and halting east of Doberschau, where he again made front next to Chaplits. After stopping for quite some time at Haynau, Maison followed very cautiously

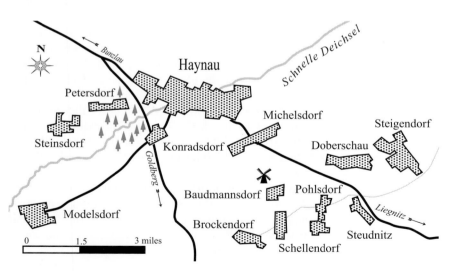

**23.** Combat at Haynau, 25 May 1813

around 2:00. At Michelsdorf he again halted. Finally, around 4:30, the column deployed to take a position for the night east of this village. His cavalry remained west of Haynau except for a weak detachment; one battalion occupied Michelsdorf, while a second remained at Haynau with the park. Around 5:00, the French artillery fired on Mutius's withdrawing rearguard. Zieten decided to signal the advance by torching the Baudmannsdorf windmill.

Before Dolffs saw the signal, he had also received news of the enemy column approaching Baudmannsdorf from Modelsdorf. This news prompted him to leave behind two cuirassier regiments and one battery to cover his rear. With the remainder of his cavalry – fourteen squadrons – he joined four of Mutius's squadrons and the horse guns to attack Maison. Aside from a few Cossack regiments, none of the other units arrived in time to participate. Dolffs himself led the Guard Light Cavalry Regiment as well as the East Prussian and Silesian Cuirassier against Maison's right wing, which immediately formed squares. The Prussian horse guns opened fire at a distance of 500 paces. With the West Prussian Uhlans, Mutius moved onto the highway and turned against the French left wing. Despite brave resistance, the squares on both wings broke while the squares in the middle of the French position were already crumbling when the 3,000 Prussians charged. All six battalions were swept away and the artillery captured. The Prussians pursued the fugitives into Michelsdorf but the French found cover in the houses. A Prussian horse battery shelled the length of the village as five squadrons moved west in order to circumnavigate the village. This detachment apparently caught up with and scattered the French battalion that had occupied Michelsdorf. Maison's men fled toward Haynau, pursued for one and one-half miles by the Prussian troopers. His last battalion emerged to take in the survivors, while one infantry regiment from Puthod's 17th Division with several batteries moved up in haste. Blücher had just caught up to the action.

After engaging for one hour, Zieten ordered the retreat around 7:00 under the cover of his horse batteries. French losses amounted to 1,363 men, one-third of Maison's division. Prussian losses totaled 226 men including 19 officers and 205 horses. Of the 19 officer casualties 15 were fatal, and 70 of the 226 men likewise died of their wounds. Struck by a ball during the charge on Michelsdorf, Dolffs numbered among the missing; his troopers later found his dead body. Stewart regarded the affair at Haynau as "one of the most distinguished cavalry attacks against solid squares of infantry that has been recorded during this war." Gneisenau wrote:

> We concealed a portion of our cavalry in overgrown terrain. Our rearguard enticed the enemy over the plain. The signal for the attack was given by igniting a windmill. Without hesitation, our cavalry hurled themselves on the

enemy infantry, which quickly sought to form squares. Many were formed but ridden down. Our cavalry granted no quarter; because of this, few prisoners were taken, perhaps 300–400; eighteen guns were taken, but owing to the speed with which such an operation is conducted and must be completed, only half of them could be brought back because of the lack of horses. The entire field was littered with dead and wounded. After this, the enemy has followed us very cautiously because we showed him our teeth.[7]

That evening, Zieten's brigade and Blücher's Reserve Cavalry withdrew to Lobendau (Lubiatów), six miles west of Liegnitz, while Chaplits and Mutius remained at Steudnitz and Pohlsdorf respectively. Maison reorganized his men and resumed his position east of Michelsdorf supported by one brigade from Lagrange's division. The rest of Lauriston's V Corps halted at Haynau while the VII Corps passed the night five miles to the southwest at Steinsdorf (Jadwisin). Fear of Allied cavalry increased French caution substantially thanks to Blücher. From the 26th until the armistice, Ney's army group moved only in battle order with cavalry guarding the front, flanks, and rear with particular diligence. More importantly, Haynau added to the list of battles and engagements where the imperials suffered greater losses than the Allies. According to Odeleben, Imperial Headquarters fully recognized that, until the affair at Haynau on the 26th, the last serious engagement before the signing of the armistice, "the Allies had invariably lost less artillery and fewer men than the French; they had obtained the advantage in some minor affairs by turning the French with the assistance of their cavalry; and they had intercepted their couriers and orders. At Rippach, Lützen, Königswartha, Bautzen, Reichenbach, in short, everywhere, Napoleon lost more men than the Allies, nor could he boast of captured artillery or other trophies, nor of the death of general officers belonging to the enemy."[8]

Indicative of the manner in which the new Prussian General Staff functioned as the nerve center of the army, Blücher had left the details of the surprise attack to his staff. Although present, he did not assume personal leadership of the operation. Regardless, the disposition and its execution remained his responsibility. For that reason, he received criticism from Barclay, who prohibited such operations in the future "because they unnecessarily weaken the forces." Of course the general completely ignored Barclay's criticism for dividing his forces. The king defended him in his candid manner, remarking to Blücher during the armistice: "You had a very favorable combat at Haynau but it also caused great losses in my Guard." Blücher answered: "Your Majesty, I sincerely regret the loss of so many brave lads but on such an occasion the head of the Guardsman is worth no more than that of the militiaman."[9]

Elsewhere on the 26th, Reynier received additional instructions requiring VII Corps to take a position north of V Corps on the road to Glogau.

However, after Victor reported that his patrols had not encountered any enemy forces west of Glogau, Napoleon rescinded this order and directed VII Corps to Steinsdorf, thus south of V Corps, which accounts for the appearance of Reynier's columns near the engagement at Haynau. Imperial Headquarters remained at Bunzlau with the Old Guard while the Young Guard halted at Thomaswaldau. Heading to Sprottau on the army's extreme left, Sébastiani's II Cavalry Corps reached Puschkau (Puszków) and Loos (Łozy) on the Queis while the infantry of Victor's II Corps ended the day's march further upstream at Neuhammer (Świętoszów).

Between the two wings of the army, Marmont found his bold plans foiled by the Bober, whose waters delayed the crossing of his artillery and the two divisions he had left at Ottendorf the day before. In addition, he could not establish communication with IV or XI Corps to coordinate operations. That evening, Macdonald, Bertrand, and Marmont reported that they could not make contact with each other for most of the day, thus indicating the Cossacks' proficiency at intercepting imperial couriers.[10] After Marmont assembled VI corps at Altjäschwitz quite late, he directed it through Großhartmannsdorf to Wilhelmsdorf (Sędzimirów), where it rendezvoused with I Cavalry Corps. Around 7:00 P.M., just when Marmont had decided to continue the march southeast toward Goldberg, the marshal heard artillery to the south and observed thick clouds of dust indicating the march of a large column on the Löwenberg–Goldberg road: Wittgenstein's rearguard commanded by St.-Priest in place of the wounded Pahlen. He immediately directed I Cavalry Corps to Pilgramsdorf (Pielgrzymka) on the Löwenberg–Goldberg road, six miles west of the latter. Unfortunately for the French, the cavalry could not cross the seven miles that separated Wilhelmsdorf from Pilgramsdorf before night fell. On arriving, they found no sign of the Russians but on the hills to the east they spotted Eugen's II Infantry Corps in a strong position to take in St.-Priest's haggard soldiers. With his infantry scrambling to catch up, Marmont thought it prudent to have it take a position southeast of Wilhelmsdorf at Neudorf-am-Gröditzberg (Nowa Wieś Grodziska). As for St.-Priest, he left the highway to avoid the French and safely brought his troops to Goldberg that night (see Map 7).

Meanwhile, the emperor insisted that XI and IV Corps reach Goldberg that day: he would be disappointed. After crossing the Bober at Großrackwitz (Rakowice Wielkie), IV Corps reached Deutmannsdorf (Zbylutów), six miles west of Marmont's position at Neudorf-am-Gröditzberg and fourteen miles west of Goldberg, at 7:30 P.M. after a march of four miles. Macdonald started the march of XI Corps very late. After advancing nine miles, the corps halted with its vanguard at Lauterseiffen (Nowe Łąki) on the Löwenberg–Goldberg road, seven miles west of the latter. Having failed to meet the master's expectations, Macdonald – who had a habit of being quite frank – informed Berthier that his men were simply exhausted: "they do nothing but march and fight." The laborious march and twelve-hour combat on the previous day had shattered the bonds of discipline in XI Corps. Before resuming the advance on 26 May, Macdonald dispatched flying columns to collect thousands of marauders and stragglers.[11]

Napoleon could not ignore these ugly indicators, which could be found in every one of his army corps. Marauding and straggling marked an army that had been pushed beyond exhaustion. This growing problem as well as the admission that he could not substitute infantry for cavalry to make his victories decisive prompted the emperor to reconsider an armistice. Napoleon also revealed that Austria's "hostile position" could no longer be ignored. Lastly, driving almost 250 miles from the Saale to the Oder in less than one month presented a logistical nightmare. Most corps lacked ammunition for a third major battle. Smaller rations had led to malnourishment, which compounded the normal physical exhaustion of the troops. To remedy all these problems, Napoleon authorized Caulaincourt on 26 May to begin negotiations just south of Liegnitz at the small village of Neudorf (Nowa Wieś Legnicka) with General Pierre Dumoustier and Napoleon's aide-de-camp, General Charles-Auguste-Joseph de Flahaut, representing the French army, Kleist and Lieutenant-Colonel Georg Wilhelm von Valentini the Prussian, and Alexander's adjutant-general, Pavel Shuvalov, as well as his aide-de-camp, Colonel Mikhail Orlov, the Russian. Napoleon instructed Caulaincourt to negotiate an armistice that would last at least two and one-half months so he would have time to rebuild his cavalry but not to agree to a peace congress while hostilities continued. Meanwhile French foreign minister Maret held talks with Bubna in the rear of the Grande Armée. Napoleon proposed the Oder as the line of demarcation. On 27 May, the Allies received his proposal to negotiate an armistice.[12]

A steady flow of reinforcements strengthened the Prussian resolve to face Napoleon a third time. Blücher received the first wave of reinforcements on 23 May in the form of four Reserve battalions from the blockade corps of Glogau and more than 1,000 replacements from Silesia. According to the schedule, another Reserve battalion, some squadrons that had recently received mounts, and 2,300 replacements would reach him on 2 June for an increase of 6,200 infantry. General Schuler von Senden received orders dated 23 May to lift the siege of Glogau and transfer his 5,870 men to Breslau.[13] Russian reinforcements likewise arrived in the form of 9,100 replacements that reached Schweidnitz on 26 May; seventeen Reserve battalions were scheduled to arrive on the 31st. Coming from Kraków, General Sacken would reach Wernersdorf (Wojnarowice) between Schweidnitz and Breslau with 9,110 men on the 29th with fourteen battalions, seventeen squadrons, five Cossack regiments, and four batteries. A column of two battalions, eight squadrons, and one battery (2,510 men) coming from Warsaw was scheduled to arrive in early June. Finally, the siege corps of Danzig, the garrison of Warsaw, and the Russian troops from the siege of Glogau all joined the field army, adding eight battalions, six squadrons, four Cossack regiments, and one and one-third batteries totaling 6,280 men. In total, the Allies expected to have 40,000 reinforcements in the region of Schweidnitz or Breslau by 1 June; a further 22,000 Russian soldiers were expected to reach the theater by the middle of June. The Allies retreated from Bautzen with approximately 86,000 men; losses up to 1 June amounted to 1,050 Prussians and 2,500 Russians. These reinforcements would provide a 45 percent increase in the Coalition's combat power. Regardless, Stewart felt that the number of reinforcements did not suffice: "These were the principal great bodies of troops that were reckoned upon: of course there were other detachments, which would do little more than supply casualties. Good as were the materials, and great as was the spirit observable in the army, it was very much outnumbered by the enemy."[14]

With the Russians committed to following the Wurschen Plan, the Prussians fully expected Barclay to utilize the entrenched camp at Schweidnitz. Frederick William assigned Müffling to Barclay's headquarters with the task "of providing all that was needed for the Russian army ... and with the secret order to dissuade the general from the idea of retreating across the Oder. In the Seven Years War, Frederick II had established his famous camp at Bunzelwitz [Bolesławice] protected by the fortress [Schweidnitz], and the combined Austro-Russian army did not dare attack him. Therefore, we assumed that we could occupy the same camp and Napoleon likewise would not attack us. We would thus gain six weeks' time, which Vienna needed to complete its mobilization." Although the French destroyed Schweidnitz in 1807, the Prussians started rebuilding it after receiving the news of Napoleon's retreat from Moscow. Valentini planned the fortifications and prepared the camp to receive the army.[15]

Inspecting the works on 26 May, Rühle found them nowhere near completion but strong enough to enable the army to offer solid resistance. Rühle returned that same day accompanied by Valentini. As the two Prussian officers approached Jauer, they observed the tsar's large entourage meeting on a hill next to the road. After moving toward the Russians and being ordered to halt, the Prussians heard Alexander declare that the army would withdraw across the Oder. According to Delbrück, Major Rühle urged Lieutenant-Colonel Valentini to protest. He refused and the two started to argue so loudly that the tsar heard them. He asked them to explain their problem. Rühle purportedly blurted out that a retreat behind the Oder was completely unnecessary. Alexander countered that Schweidnitz could not be held. Rühle retorted that not only would the Allies hold Schweidnitz against any attack, but also the strength of the position would appear so formidable that Napoleon would not risk a battle. The Russian monarch challenged Rühle to prove that Schweidnitz was as strong as he claimed. Rühle answered that he had just inspected the camp. Alexander responded that he would "consider the situation" and ordered his engineer chief, General Sievers, to inspect Schweidnitz.

That same day, the 26th, Sievers reported that although the Prussians had not finished restoring the fortifications at Schweidnitz, they appeared better than many of the Turkish fortresses that had caused the Russians so many difficulties in the past.[16] Thanks to Sievers's report, the march to Schweidnitz continued on the 27th. Although the Prussians believed that the fortifications would suffice, the Russians – with the possible exception of their tsar – looked longingly to the Vistula. The moment was fast approaching when the Russians would be forced either to disregard the Wurschen Plan and retreat due east across the Oder or continue southeast hugging the Austrian frontier.[17]

With armistice talks underway, the Allied army continued to operate according to the Wurschen Plan to maintain communication with the Austrians. Bogdanovich maintains that Alexander forced the issue with Barclay after the monarch conceded to Frederick William's desire to terminate the direct march to the Oder and turn southeast to take a flank position in the vicinity of Schweidnitz.[18] Thus, the Allied army abandoned the great east–west highway and commenced the march southeast from Liegnitz to Schweidnitz. The retrograde movement continued for the next three days. Not an indifferent observer, Stewart captured the significance of this decision:

> It is difficult to give an adequate idea of the anxiety that prevailed at this eventful crisis with respect to the decision of Austria. The Allied armies had thrown themselves on her frontier: they had abandoned their main line of communication by Kalisch; they had placed themselves absolutely in a *cul de sac*; and had Austria not declared for them, it would be easy to calculate what the consequences might have been: on the other hand, if she declared in their favor, Bonaparte's position was equally critical. The Austrian declaration, on the point of coming forth, was deferred from one day to another. It was first fixed for the 24th of May, then for the 1st of June, and was now postponed until the 10th.

Although Napoleon pursued and narrowed the gap between the two armies, the Allied decision to abandon the Russian main line of communication thwarted his efforts to engage the Allies in a third battle. Cathcart speculated on what appeared to be hesitation on the part of the French emperor:

> Napoleon's forbearance in refraining from an attack on the Allied army [arose from a] disinclination to hasten the decision of Austria, whose

neutrality must have been brought at once to an end if he had fought the army of the Allies and forced it back upon the Austrian frontier under cover of Glatz; for this would evidently have been its only base, and with reference to apparent political circumstances it was an insulated base. He may well have supposed that the Allies would not have abandoned their regular line of operations, the direct road through Breslau to the Russian frontier and, as it were, have placed their backs to a wall, unless there already existed a secret understanding with Austria, that a door should be opened to receive them in case of defeat.[19]

On the evening of the 26th, Napoleon started planning the final push to Liegnitz on the following day. Until the daily reports from his corps commanders arrived during the course of the night to reveal how much progress they made, the emperor could arrange only the dispositions of his reserves. At 9:00 P.M., Berthier issued instructions for Mortier to have the Young Guard marching on the road to Liegnitz at 4:00 the next morning; Soult would follow with the Old Guard and Guard Cavalry at 5:00 A.M. Behind the Grand Reserve, III Corps would commence its march at 6:00. The reports from the corps commanders did not induce Napoleon to deviate from the general plan. For the 27th, the emperor wanted Ney to reach Liegnitz with the left wing while the right continued its movement to Goldberg. In the center, Marmont again received the freedom to direct his march on either Liegnitz or Goldberg.[20]

On the left wing, Napoleon joined Ney at Haynau to examine the battlefield. By the time he arrived, the French had buried their dead and only bloated Prussian corpses remained to cook in the spring sun. Nevertheless, the emperor's irreconcilable mood prompted his lieutenants to humor him by leading the master to a corpse purported to be that of Dolffs. Napoleon then proceeded to Michelsdorf, which Russian cavalry occupied. With Russian infantry in the distance and his own infantry too far west to be a factor, the emperor coolly turned his back to the Russian troopers and ordered two batteries to advance. Berthier called his attention to the Russians, who moved increasingly closer to the imperial entourage. Napoleon jokingly responded: "if they advance, we will also advance." Instead of attacking, the Russians offered a flag of truce as they came within 100 paces of the French forward cavalry post. Designed to slow the French advance, obtain information on the imperial forces that faced them, and provide time for their own infantry to retreat, the Russian ploy earned an immediate refusal. In the meantime, Ney's infantry moved up, prompting the Russians to withdraw through Liegnitz.

The emperor then led the advance. He rode from one hill to the next, reconnoitering, touring each town and village, and taking full advantage of every terrain feature. Columns and batteries moved hither and thither, taking possession of a wood, a village, or a hill, all orchestrated to perfection by the Corsican maestro. Napoleon rode into Liegnitz at 9:00 that night after inspecting the surrounding region and all of the town's exits. Lauriston's V Corps advanced from Haynau, halting three miles east of Liegnitz at Großbeckern (Piekary Wielkie) while VII Corps kept pace by marching on a parallel road slightly south of the highway. The Guard escorted Imperial Headquarters to Liegnitz as III Corps advanced to Haynau and Marchand's 39th Division occupied Bunzlau. North of the army on the far left wing, II Corps reached Sprottau, capturing a Russian artillery convoy that had taken the wrong road.[21]

Meanwhile, in the center, Marmont led VI Corps and I Cavalry Corps from Neudorf-am-Gröditzberg fifteen miles east to Kroitsch (Krotoszyce), taking a position between the road running northeast to Liegnitz and one that led southeast to Jauer. On the right, IV and XI Corps continued their movement east. Macdonald needed to confront the Russians of Eugen's II Infantry Corps if he hoped to reach Goldberg and cross the Katzbach. Both sides fought tenaciously; Macdonald ordered numerous charges by 3rd Heavy Cavalry Division. Although the marshal led the last charge in person, the French horse failed to dislodge the Russians. Finally, the weight of Macdonald's infantry forced the Russians to yield their strong position, retreat through Goldberg, and cross the Katzbach. Macdonald moved into Goldberg with most of XI Corps but only its vanguard emerged on the eastern side of the town. From Deutmannsdorf, IV Corps crossed the Schnelle Deichsel at Ulbersdorf (Wojcieszyn) and passed north of Goldberg before running into the rear of VI Corps. As a result, Bertrand halted at Hohendorf (Wysocko), two miles west of Kroitsch and four miles northeast of Goldberg (see Map 7).

On the 28th, Marmont directed VI Corps and I Cavalry Corps across the Katzbach at Kroitsch but Russian resistance held them close to the eastern bank. Shielded by Marmont, XI Corps trooped fourteen miles southeast from Goldberg to Jauer. Bertrand, notorious for his slow marches, covered half of the fourteen miles between Hohendorf and Jauer before halting at Schlaup (Słup). Napoleon's left wing remained at Liegnitz; Ney received instructions to have Lauriston and Reynier collect their stragglers and rest the men after taking the proper security measures. Berthier likewise ordered Souham to rally and rest III Corps at Haynau. No doubt Napoleon knew of the talk in Prussia to conduct a guerrilla war based on the Landsturm should the French invade. Now, moving deep into Silesia, the emperor did not want to antagonize the population. Nor did he want to see a recurrence of the horrors his soldiers had suffered at the hands of Spanish and Calabrian guerrillas. "Maintain proper order among the troops and do not let any man travel alone," advised Berthier in his dispatch to Souham. To the north, Victor and Sébastiani reached Primkenau (Przemków) and established communication with Glogau less than twenty miles to the northeast. On this day, the 28th, their van drove off the Allied forces blockading the fortress. Victor informed Berthier that Allied detachments appeared to be headed for Breslau rather than northwest to support Bülow. To the marshal, all signs indicated an Allied concentration at Breslau in anticipation of a third battle.

With the armistice negotiations ensuing, two interconnected considerations shaped Napoleon's next step. Numerous reports clearly indicated that the Allies had abandoned the great east–west highway and with it Breslau as well as the Russian main line of communication in favor of a retreat south to Schweidnitz. To Napoleon, only one development could explain this extremely uncharacteristic behavior: Austria had decided to join the Coalition and would soon enter the war. More than any other reason, this assumption pushed the master to quickly conclude an armistice that would provide more time for him to woo his father-in-law as well as to prepare in case Francis did throw his weight behind the Coalition. Wanting to negotiate from the best position possible and on the basis of *uti possidetis*, Napoleon needed to secure Breslau immediately. Moreover, the urgency he attached to concluding the armistice to freeze Austria conflicted with the time he needed to execute the strategic envelopment on the Oder. Not only did he have to consider time, but the emperor certainly recognized that an Allied retreat south to Schweidnitz would completely neutralize the effects of this plan. In addition, if he did not advance downstream along the Oder with a considerable portion of the Grande Armée, Berlin most likely would remain in Prussian hands. To somewhat offset this disappointment and still score a moral victory over the Prussians, he wanted to see the tricolor flying above the city that had done so much for Prussia's initial war effort: Breslau. Thus, Napoleon scrapped the idea of the strategic envelopment and decided to send Ney to take Breslau with the left wing of the army.

Returning to the Allies, Blücher fell back thirteen miles southeast from Liegnitz to Mertschütz (Mierczyce) in two columns on 27 May; General Sergey Lanskoy's Russian cavalry division covered the road to Breslau. Wittgenstein started the march from Goldberg to Jauer at dawn on 27 May. After Macdonald crossed the Katzbach south of Goldberg, XI Corps threatened to envelop Wittgenstein's rearguard under St.-Priest. The Russians managed to outdistance their pursuers, reaching Hennersdorf (Chroślice), halfway between Goldberg and Jauer (see Map 7). On 28 May, Blücher continued to slide southeast, marching twelve miles from Mertschütz to a position east of Rauske (Rusko), about six miles northeast of Striegau (Strzegom). His rearguard took a position halfway between Mertschütz and Rauske. Meanwhile, Wittgenstein withdrew south of Striegau, with St.-Priest holding Macdonald at Jauer until Marmont threatened his flank. After sustaining some losses, St.-Priest withdrew to Großrosen (Rogoźnica), halfway between Jauer and Striegau. On the extreme left wing of the army, *Streifkorps* commanded by Emmanuel, Kaysarov, and Colonel Osip Ilovaysky X assembled 2,000 sabers at Schönau (Świerzawa), fifteen miles west of Jauer. On the extreme right wing, Lanskoy lingered on the Breslau highway halfway between Liegnitz and Neumarkt (Środa Śląska).[22]

On the 28th, Barclay instructed Blücher to submit plans by the 31st for his wing to withdraw across the Oder in two columns. According to Müffling, this order left the Prussians "thunderstruck." Desperate to see it countermanded, Blücher sent two staff officers, Rühle and Krauseneck, to brow-beat Knesebeck at Breslau. Knesebeck bluntly responded to their admonitions: "The disposition has been changed; we will march behind the Oder and the works of Schweidnitz will be destroyed." Both officers protested against the latter measure, especially since the field guns needed the powder that would now be used to raze the fortifications. Knesebeck purportedly shrugged his shoulders and refused to do anything further. Just before departing, they noticed Frederick William at the window of his residence. Knowing the king personally, Krauseneck gambled and requested an audience. Frederick William received the officers and patiently listened to their grievances, declaring his agreement. At the end of the interview, he claimed to have approved the march across the Oder only after having become convinced that the Russians would do nothing else. He dismissed Krauseneck with the words: "My dear Krauseneck, the situation likely will not change; the Russians want it no other way."[23]

This being the case, Frederick William took steps to reestablish a Prussian field army separate from that of the Russians. In a letter from Breslau dated the 28th, the king appointed Blücher commander of the Army of Silesia. "The current situation of the army and the need to provide unity of command as long as the [Prussian] army is designated to fight as one body as well as the measures already taken by the Russian High Command induce me to temporarily assign to you command over all of my troops stationed in Silesia with the exception of the garrison troops and depots." Blücher received direct command over the operations and supply of the troops in Silesia: Yorck's I Corps, Kleist's II Corps, and the Silesian Landwehr Corps. He also received command of Bülow's corps, which eventually became the Prussian III Corps. In a move that later would cause headaches for Blücher and Gneisenau, Frederick William granted Yorck a special independent status in the chain of command that permitted him to report directly to the king. Although the king authorized Yorck to exercise this privilege only when conducting operations independent of Blücher's army, the cantankerous hero of Tauroggen later took advantage of this to lambast Blücher.[24]

Barclay's retreat southeast continued on the 29th. Blücher's wing withdrew to a position east of Striegau, establishing contact with Wittgenstein's main body. A French advance from Liegnitz drove Lanskoy's cavalry into Blücher's rearguard at Järischau (Jaroszów). Blücher ordered Mutius to move north with nine squadrons. At Rackschütz (Rakoszyce), five miles south of Neumarkt, Mutius established contact with the Silesian Uhlans patrolling from Breslau, Schuler's cavalry retreating from Glogau, and the *Streifkorps* of Prince Byron of Kurland, which operated west of Glogau. Blücher's headquarters moved through Jauer, halting at Puschkau (Pastuchów) east of Striegau and seven miles north of Schweidnitz (see Map 7). He gave the troops some rest that day while patrols reestablished contact with the French to monitor their movements. Gneisenau took advantage of the lull to provide his friend, Münster, with an update on the status of the Prussian army and the hopes of Blücher's headquarters:

> The campaign that recently commenced appeared to be a war which, as far as I know history, will not be rivaled in the fierceness in which it would be conducted. In four weeks, we have had more than twenty heavy engagements and three days of battle. Death has tremendously emptied our officer corps. Many battalions have only two officers remaining; cavalry regiments the same. The latter has lost more than a third in general. Nevertheless, this war appears to provide the most peculiar results. We have now captured fifty-one pieces of artillery but have yet to lose a single gun. Despite the constant retreat, the army is determined and unbroken in its courage – although discontent with the retrograde movements – and is completely ready to accept a new battle at any moment. In a few days we will deliver a new battle if our allies are still true and confident. The fate of the continent will depend on it. If it is lost, Austria will prefer to negotiate rather than fight. Nevertheless, we hope for the best. The worst element is the faint-heartedness of the leading persons. Right at the moment when their energy would provide the greatest use, they seem deprived of it. We are really in a far better frame of mind than on the day of the battle of Lützen and we can proceed with confidence to a new battle; but I observe some signs that I do not like. Nevertheless, I freely admit that many times I see black.[25]

With both wings of the Allied army approaching Schweidnitz, Barclay rejected the Prussian proposal to utilize the entrenched camp for a third battle. Pointing to the Russian army's shortage of ammunition, he declined Frederick William's offer to cover its needs. The fact that strategic consumption and combat casualties had steadily eroded the massive numerical superiority Napoleon enjoyed at Bautzen made little impact on Barclay. Moreover, the 38,000 reinforcements that had already arrived or would reach the Allies within days failed to make an impression on him. Unlike their allies, the Russians did not view Silesia as a rich utopia. "In all of Silesia not a single magazine had been established," complains Bogdanovich, "it lacked supplies of clothing and footgear." The Russian general claims that "nothing had been prepared" and that "the whole Prussian effort appeared to lack the insight, strength of will, and administrative talents of Scharnhorst, whom no one could replace. All of Chancellor Hardenberg's efforts were directed at diplomacy with foreign powers; internal affairs interested him little." However, Stewart argued that, "as far as the means of subsistence, there was an improvident waste among the Russians. A deficiency of ammunition existed; and the army could ill afford the loss of the supplies that were forthcoming."[26]

Northwest of the Grande Armée, General Michel-Marie Pacthod's 13th Division led Oudinot's XII Corps toward Berlin. On 26 May, the French drove Bülow's Cossack outpost from Hoyerswerda, less than 100 miles south of the Prussian capital. Bülow decided to probe southward with two of his brigades and hold his main body in reserve. On the following day, he ordered his brigades to attack the French force at Hoyerswerda. Around 9:00 A.M. on the 28th, two separate combats erupted as the Prussian brigades converged on Hoyerswerda. The Prussians had bitten off more than they could chew as Oudinot's corps doubled their number. Just as the French unlimbered their heavy artillery, the Prussian brigades withdrew northward after losing 360 men. Without proper cavalry, Oudinot could not capitalize on the minor victory that cost XII Corps 450 casualties.[27]

At Liegnitz, approximately 100 miles east-southeast of Oudinot's position at Hoyerswerda, Berthier's correspondence on the evening of the 28th gives the impression that uncertainty plagued Napoleon. Throughout that day numerous reports arrived indicating that the Allies had turned south instead of continuing their eastward retreat to Breslau. By 9:00 P.M. on the 28th, the only decision made at Imperial Headquarters involved moving the rearward echelons east on the following day: Marchand's 39th Division from Bunzlau to Haynau and III Corps from Haynau to Liegnitz. To Victor, whom Napoleon wanted to reach Glogau and send patrols down the Oder as well as to Posen and Kalisch, Berthier expressed the emperor's intention to proceed "from Liegnitz in the direction of Breslau." However, as for Ney, Soult, and Mortier, Berthier advised that they be ready to march the following morning "to execute the orders that you will receive this night." Not signing such orders until 6:45 on the morning of the 29th, the major-general instructed Ney to direct V and VII Corps to Neumarkt, twenty miles west of Breslau. "I think the emperor will follow your movement with his Guard," he added somewhat lamely. A little later, he issued orders for Mortier to follow Lauriston toward Neumarkt. Thus, the march to Breslau would continue.[28]

Odeleben recounts that on the morning of the 29th "a great bustle was observed at Imperial Headquarters. By 8:00, everything was prepared to march. The Guard was under arms, yet the hours passed and no departure took place." Not until 2:00 on the afternoon of the 29th did Napoleon make a decision concerning the operations of his right wing. He ordered Marmont to assume a central position between the two wings of the army by moving

VI Corps and I Cavalry Corps through Jauer and then four miles northeast to Eisendorf (Snowidza) on the road to Neumarkt. Macdonald and Bertrand would march to Jauer, with XI Corps pushing a vanguard southeast toward Striegau. Again, Berthier indicated that Napoleon and the Guard would probably be at Neumarkt that evening.[29]

After "a very visible degree of indecision," Napoleon left Liegnitz at 3:00 that afternoon and rode south toward Neudorf, where Caulaincourt negotiated with Kleist and Shuvalov. Appearing "much agitated," the emperor waited for his envoy's report. At length, he turned east to Wahlstatt (Legnickie Pole), thinking Caulaincourt would not have success. Napoleon "had left Liegnitz as much to be prepared for all events as to give the enemy no reason to doubt how greatly he desired an armistice," comments Odeleben. Not wanting to raise suspicion about his sincerity by going direct to Breslau, the emperor rode northeast to the dilapidated farmhouse in the village of Rosenig (Rogoźnik), just south of the east–west highway and halfway between Liegnitz and Neumarkt (see Map 7). It had already been pillaged and considerably damaged, so he found only one room and a closet suitable for his use; Berthier established his bureau in a servant's apartment. Napoleon joked that they could pretend they were in Poland. The rest of the Imperial Staff lodged in cottages or barns, with the less important bivouacking in the gardens alongside the Guard.[30]

Around 6:00 that evening, Lauriston's V Corps halted a few miles east of Neumarkt at Kammendorf (Komorniki), less Maison's weak division, which took post slightly to the north. In accordance with Napoleon's instructions, Ney ordered Reynier to keep pace with Lauriston. However, later in the day, the emperor halted the main body of VII Corps at Wahlstatt, just east of Neudorf. Reynier occupied Neudorf itself with one Saxon division and two guns. Ney, whom Berthier had neglected to warn in time, did nothing to hide his dissatisfaction over the units of his wing receiving orders unbeknownst to him. He wrote Berthier asking "to be replaced at the head of the vanguard, because my wounds are very tiring and do not allow me to ride." "It was not without trouble that he [Berthier] barely managed to calm his irritation. This incident has a certain importance because it was a symptom of the depression that had started to invade our generals," comments Lanrezac.[31]

Regarding the armistice talks, Caulaincourt's first report arrived that night: it proved far from satisfactory. In particular, the Prussians balked at Napoleon's proposal for the Oder to form the line of demarcation. The emperor responded on the 30th:

It seems from your letter that these gentlemen would argue that I have to evacuate all of Upper Silesia, and even my communication with Glogau; there is so much nonsense in this that it is inconceivable ... give the news to the plenipotentiaries that General Bülow was defeated on the 28th, north of Hoyerswerda, that the day before a unit of 12 officers and 100 Cossacks was surprised and captured, and that this army was strongly pursued; that, concerning Hamburg, we entered on the 24th, that the Danes make common cause with us, and that 18,000 men of their troops have assembled under the prince d'Eckmühl [Davout]. The principle of all negotiations for a ceasefire is that each one remains in the position where he is; the lines of demarcation are then determined based on this principle. Yet if the conditions are as absurd as you explain in your letter, there is no need to argue, and it is pointless to continue the conference. In this case, return as soon as possible.[32]

Despite his insistence on *uti possidetis*, Napoleon continued to take half-measures with the army, which in part may have been due to its exhaustion, although the emperor makes little mention of this situation in his correspondence. More likely, he wanted hostilities to cease before Austria could enter the war and while he still maintained a good position from which he could resume the war. Napoleon hesitated to pursue the Russians and Prussians deeper into Silesia and thus closer to the Austrian frontier, where his communication with Dresden would be extremely vulnerable. He also considered the limitations of his drive east. With the Allied army somewhere between Striegau and Schweidnitz, his right wing needed to take a central position to shield his rear. Thus, the further southeast he pushed his right wing, the more isolated and exposed became his left.

Marmont maintained his intermediate position between the two wings on the 30th. His vanguard proceeded thirteen miles east to Obermois (Ujazd Górny) but his main body stretched back to Eisendorf. North of him, V Corps did not move, thus enabling VII Corps to catch up with it; the Guard pressed to Neumarkt, where Imperial Headquarters arrived very late in the evening. Orders for the right wing did not go out until 12:30 that afternoon: Berthier instructed Macdonald to determine whether an enemy rearguard held Striegau. If so, the emperor wanted him to "pursue and dislodge it." Bertrand received instructions to support XI Corps, cover the road to Jauer, and maintain communication with Marmont, who in turn remained in communication with the rest of the army. Berthier also issued the call for news of the enemy and the ceaseless demand that the corps commanders honor the crucial requisite of maintaining communication with neighboring friendly forces. The manner in which Napoleon and Berthier clearly and concisely explained to each corps commander the operations and goals of the neighboring corps as well as the emperor's intentions for each corps and the army in general remained unparalleled.[33]

Learning that the majority of the Allied army had retreated through Striegau toward Schweidnitz, Macdonald cautiously limited his movement on the 30th to pushing through Jauer with XI and IV Corps. Thus, by nightfall, the 90,000 men of the Grande Armée stood on a southwest to northeast axis extending twenty-three miles from Jauer through Eisendorf to Neumarkt. At 10:00 A.M. on 31 May, Macdonald and Bertrand conducted a reconnaissance in force: 20,000 men advanced southeast from Jauer in five columns. Warned by his patrols of their approach, St.-Priest positioned 6,700 infantry, 2,600 cavalry, and 48 guns between Herzogswaldau (Niedaszów) and Großrosen, four miles southeast of Jauer on the road to Striegau; Eugen's II Infantry Corps stood three miles southeast of him (see Map 7). Macdonald found the Russian position at Herzogswaldau too formidable for a frontal assault and so awaited IV Corps to envelop the enemy's right. Bertrand pushed his Württembergers through Profen (Mściwojów) to Großrosen but likewise overestimated the strength of the Russian position. Blücher's rearguard – 10,000 Prussians and Russians under the sole command of Zieten – stood at Järischau, less than eight miles to the east. Zieten desired to march to the sound of the guns but his request for permission went unanswered for reasons unknown.

Proceeding with undue caution, Bertrand committed his battalions successively rather than as part of a general advance. This enabled the Russians to repulse the Württembergers with relative ease. Finally, around 4:00 P.M., Macdonald rode to Bertrand's command post and ordered the general to attack Großrosen. A bloody six-hour struggle ensued between the Württembergers and the Russians. Württemberger after-action reports attest to the intrepid Russian defense of the village: further evidence that refuted Barclay's claims of Russian exhaustion. That night, Bertrand moved up his French and Italian brigades to facilitate the Württemberger withdrawal. Macdonald held back his own corps due to the Allied *Streifkorps* in his right flank that denied him an overview of the situation. Bertrand returned to Jauer around midnight after losing 900 men; the Russian claim of having sustained only 300 casualties appears too low. Bertrand's withdrawal forced Macdonald to likewise conduct a retrograde march to Jauer on the morning of 1 June. In their after-action reports, the two French commanders blame each other for their mistakes but each deserves an equal share of the responsibility.[34]

Elsewhere along the French line on 31 May, III Corps continued moving east toward Liegnitz on the great highway. Late that morning, Ney finally received orders to take Breslau with V Corps while VII Corps halted seven miles to the west at Deutschlissa (Leśnica) to guard communication and stand ready to support Marmont in the center. In an interesting move that some contemporaries referred to as Napoleon's gesture to Frederick William, the emperor decreed that Lauriston's troops camp at the gates of Breslau and enter the city only if a police force needed to be established and to restore the bridges over the Oder if necessary. Thirty minutes after Berthier dispatched these orders, he penned another communiqué stating that V and VII Corps could be called on the following day to maneuver against the enemy. "Do not make them march too much today because it is already late," wrote the major-general at 10:00 that morning. He advised both corps to cover only the thirteen miles that separated Neumarkt and Deutschlissa, suggesting that they send deputies to Breslau to announce the city's imminent capture. Berthier insisted that Reynier and Lauriston conduct an orderly march and have a rearguard collect stragglers. Even more perplexing is the order sent to Marmont at 3:00 that afternoon instructing the marshal not to make any movement that day.

The explanation for the baby steps toward Breslau and the freezing of Marmont appears to have been Napoleon's final, reluctant acceptance of the fact that the Allies had indeed turned south rather than east to Breslau. Now he needed to address the threat posed by the Allied concentration between Striegau and Schweidnitz. Allied cavalry became very active on this day, harassing the French across their entire line. Fearing Macdonald would be attacked, Napoleon warned Marmont to be ready to march southeast to his support; the emperor also ordered bread and ammunition be sent to Marmont and Macdonald. A road running north from Striegau to Leubus (Lubiąż) on the Oder downstream of Breslau concerned the master: "this road intersects the Jauer–Neumarkt road not far from Eisendorf, where you are: we must watch this road; it is also necessary for you to take a position on the Neumarkt–Striegau road to intercept everything." Marmont complied, remaining around Eisendorf throughout the day and establishing cavalry posts all along his perimeter.

During the course of the 31st, V Corps, which started its march at 11:00 A.M., encountered Schuler's Landwehr detachment coming from Glogau to cover Breslau. Lauriston drove the Prussians across the Schweidnitz stream (Bystrzyca) that cut the east–west highway eight miles west of Breslau. He ordered a halt and allowed his men to prepare their evening meal. At 7:00, he received urgent orders from the emperor to continue the march immediately. Schuler's Prussians resisted until darkness brought an end to the fighting in Breslau's far eastern suburbs. South of Lauriston, Reynier's VII Corps took a position at Arnoldsmühl (Jarnołtów). Imperial Headquarters and the Guard remained at Neumarkt, where III Corps arrived; Marchand's division moved into Liegnitz.[35]

Napoleon prepared to change his army's orientation from the east to the south and southwest. Although the possibility of a third battle loomed, Odeleben claims that the emperor's "temper daily became more agreeable and he appeared free from anxiety. All this signaled how well pleased he was with the expectation of seeing the armistice shortly concluded." During his eight-day stay at Neumarkt, he attended to various military, diplomatic, and political affairs. Contrary to his norm, the emperor relaxed in the evening by riding about the region. He visited the bivouacs of his troops, talked with the

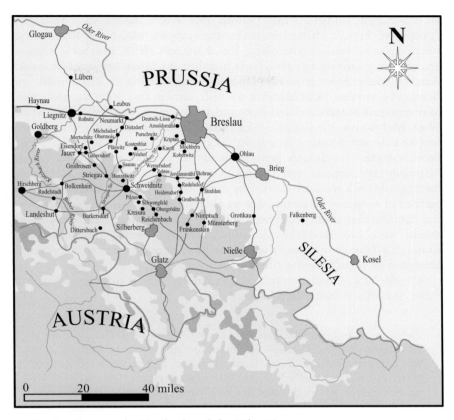

**24.** Region between the Katzbach and the Oder Rivers

locals, and could often be heard humming or singing bits of French and Italian songs. Against this setting his troops transformed Neumarkt's pleasing environs into a desert. "A single nightingale remained alone in the desolate churchyard," recalls Odeleben, "and seemed nightly to deplore in her melancholy strains the calamities of the land."[36]

As for the Allies, inspections by Barclay and Müffling eliminated the regions around Bunzelwitz and Burkersdorf (Burkatów) – north and southwest of Schweidnitz respectively – as potential battlefields. On the 30th, Barclay selected a position on the hills of Pilzen (Boleścin) and Kreisau (Krzyżowa) southeast of Schweidnitz, where the terrain along the western foothills of the Riesengebirge offered several advantages. According to his plan, the army would move into this position on the 31st. Not that the new Allied commander in chief sought an opportunity to strike the emperor, but he nevertheless missed one. On the morning of 31 May, approximately

96,000 Allied soldiers stood within one day's march of Großrosen. A captured French officer stated that the emperor would not advance any further out of fear of provoking the Austrians. With Blücher's wing of 40,000 men guarding against a flank attack from Eisendorf and Neumarkt, Barclay could have crushed Napoleon's right wing – Macdonald and Bertrand – at Jauer. A bold attack by Wittgenstein's wing on the 31st could have engaged Macdonald and Bertrand with a high probability of success. With Marmont's VI Corps at Eisendorf, Blücher likewise would have received the opportunity to triumph if given the latitude to do more than provide flank coverage. A general attack on 31 May would have caught Napoleon by surprise and the result would have weakened his forces, barring a French miracle. It must be noted that with Ney reaching Breslau on the 1st, a pitched battle that day would have been too risky. Nevertheless, the damage that could have been inflicted on imperial forces on 31 May would have increased the Coalition's prestige among potential allies. Bloodying Napoleon's nose during armistice negotiations certainly would have paid dividends for the Allies.[37]

On the 31st, Gneisenau felt certain Barclay would turn and fight. The Prussian staff chief informed his wife that:

> Today we go to Schweidnitz to fight a new battle there. The army is in the best condition ever. Courage and order are still unbroken and we have received reinforcements. If one [Barclay] does not lose his nerve and strength everything will turn out well. Never have so many elements been at hand for victory. Even if we are defeated, we will retreat a few miles into an almost insurmountable position and through this bring the war into balance. But if he [Napoleon] who has brought so much misfortune to the world is defeated, his entire army will collapse. Little of it will ever see their native countries again. The Austrians will then immediately advance to the Elbe and sever the retreat. Also, our General Bülow stands in the rear of the enemy with 25,000 men and has already advanced to Spremberg. Thus, a victory will rid the world of a great plague.[38]

Barclay shattered this optimism by refusing to exploit the situation. Regardless of the merits of the Pilzen–Kreisau position, plans for a third battle fizzled under his concern for the debilitated condition of the Russian army. He believed the retrograde march should continue until the Swedes commenced an offensive on the lower Elbe and Austria joined the alliance. "The object, at present," explained Stewart, "was to gain time; to delay the enemy, by making a demonstration of fighting, but still not to give him battle. A camp was taken up in front of Schweidnitz; but if the enemy showed a disposition to attack it, the intention was to move to the entrenched camp at Neiße, which had been preparing for some time, and to have assembled all the Landwehr and irregular forces at Glatz, and there, if pressed, to make a stand." Thus, instead of an attack on the 31st, the army moved into the position southeast of Schweidnitz to engage in unit reorganization. Barclay transferred all Russian troops assigned to Yorck and Kleist to Russian units while the Prussian Guard left the II Corps to be part of Grand Duke Constantine's Guard Corps.[39]

Although not as severe as Wittgenstein's problems, Barclay also encountered difficulties at Allied Headquarters. According to a letter written by Hardenberg to Gneisenau on the 31st, the relationship between the Russians and Prussians reached its breaking point. Not only does Hardenberg provide invaluable insight into the Prussian perception of Russian headquarters, but he reveals the difficult position that Frederick William now found himself in after hitching his wagon to the Russian horse:

Tsar Alexander has the best will but absolutely no strength to control the cabal. Prince Volkonsky is absolutely no match for the situation and has a very adverse influence. No decision stands firm. From one hour to the next different measures that are the most pernicious are adopted. Now the Russians are so lacking in ammunition that we, who still have our own needs, must help them and we must go without. It is completely inconceivable how one can bring 800 cannon into the field and not take care to bring supplies so they can be used. From Barclay de Tolly more order is promised but won't he also be limited by the *Faiseurs* [show-offs]? Already, as everyone knows, Toll and Volkonsky are very much against him. Everyone insists that the main intention of the Russians is to go back over the Oder, indeed completely across the Vistula. It is certain that much is spoken of this. What shall we do if our allies really go across the Oder? Follow them and let the country fall into enemy hands? This would be horrible, completely smothering the good spirit and depriving us of all resources; our fortresses would hold for a while but would fall rather sooner than later. Should we separate from the Russians, stand alone, relying only on ourselves? To this I am most inclined but what measure should be taken?

My decision depends very much on whether Austria declares and acts for us. Our retreat already caused some apprehension at the Vienna court. It has of course mobilized its entire army but it has too much faith in negotiations, from which only Napoleon gains an advantage. If we were completely certain that the Austrians still would unite with us if the Russians withdrew across the Oder, I would not hesitate to advise [Frederick William] to follow your idea of placing ourselves in our fortresses and remaining there until the Austrians arrived in Napoleon's rear and cooperated with our corps in the north and east according to circumstances. He would also send something after the Russians and we could then resist him more forcibly. Since you do not have time to write I send you Hippel. He will tell you many things over the internal state of our affairs and in my name request your counsel. It is truly a calamity that Scharnhorst is not here and is inactive in Bohemia. According to his last letter he was at Iglau; thus, do not count on him for another two to three weeks. His wound has become worse. I request that you speak with no one other than Hippel.[40]

On 1 June, Gneisenau took up his quill, drafting identical letters to Frederick William and Barclay that urged an attack. Signed by Blücher, the missive notes that Napoleon had divided his forces, sending a portion to Breslau. "This is the moment," asserts Gneisenau, "that we must fall on the throat of the enemy forces that he has left behind. Perhaps it will be possible to destroy this portion. At the least, we hope to succeed in driving back his right wing so that we can create an opportunity to unite with Bülow." To silence the naysayers who would base their opposition on the Russians being short of ammunition, Gneisenau noted that 150 wagons filled with Prussian ammunition had arrived on the 31st for use by the tsar's soldiers: more would be provided. He also responded to concerns about waiting until the Russian reinforcements arrived from Poland. He argued that the approaching units were not as large as the forces Napoleon dispatched to Breslau. By postponing an offensive until the reinforcements arrived, Barclay would grant Napoleon time to unite his army, which likewise would receive reinforcements and thus considerably outnumber the Allies. Gneisenau urged Barclay to attack immediately and exploit Napoleon's momentary weakness. Moreover, if they seized the offensive and managed to link with Bülow, his numbers would more than compensate for the expected reinforcements.

Gneisenau also offered a very sober assessment of the overall situation in regard to retreating across the Oder: "At this moment, the Russian army is already cut off from most of the Oder crossings while the enemy corps [Ney] advancing toward the Oder stands closer to these crossings than we do. If the Russian army marches toward the crossings of the upper Oder, it will depart from its direct line of communication with Warsaw and throw itself toward Kraków in southern Poland. Therefore, in order for one to win the Oder crossings that are threatened, one must make a forward movement." Gneisenau again suggested an immediate operation against Napoleon's right, which would have the added benefit of forcing him to recall the troops he detached to Breslau. Of all Gneisenau's conjectures, his recognition of the blockage of direct Russian communication caused by the French force at Breslau indicates that he understood at least somewhat the reasons behind Barclay's anxiety.

Indeed, the presence of two imperial corps at Breslau exponentially increased Russian apprehension over their line of communication through Kalisch and Warsaw – a concern that had dominated Russian headquarters since March. The difference between the Prussians and Russians lay in their approaches to solving this problem. While the Russians – fretting over the combat-effectiveness of their soldiers – demanded the immediate march to Poland to reopen their direct line, Gneisenau argued that this situation provided the appropriate moment to assume the offensive:

> The approaching reinforcements ... must assemble on the right bank of the Oder and remain ready to fall on the heels of the French forces withdrawing from Breslau and seeking to unite with the main French army as a result of our movement against the enemy's right flank. Avoiding a decisive battle is always in our power. Our superior cavalry guarantees us this freedom. It is extremely likely that such a maneuver will succeed because the enemy certainly will not expect it. With each day that we continue our retreat, we will separate ourselves from our resources, morale will plummet, and moroseness – caused by all the negative symptoms associated with long, continuous retreats – will set in. To count on Austria's help is illusory if the retreat continues. Only our success can secure us this support. Everything said here is based on the assumption that the enemy has detached considerable forces against Breslau. If he has done so, there is no reason for us to withdraw from our current position. In every regard, it is better to await further developments here.

In his cover letter to the king, Blücher expressed his belief that Barclay would ignore this proposal:

> I submit to you the letter that I wrote today to the Russian general Barclay de Tolly about the current situation of the war. I do not expect the Russian general to agree with my suggestion; instead, I foresee that he will make the army retreat as soon as the enemy shows troops in the vicinity of our front. If this occurs and we remain united with the Russian army, the discontent of the army will increase even more. In this case, I must request that your army separate from the Russian and withdraw from position to position toward the feet of the mountains that surround the county of Glatz to the north while the Landwehr temporarily occupy the entrenched camps at Glatz and Neiße. The Russians can then withdraw toward their reinforcements and later rejoin the offensive. The French emperor will then face the dilemma of having to divide his army and this will perhaps provide us the opportunity to unite with Bülow.

"We proceed burdened with heavy chains and have little hope that things will be better, because no one wishes to seize the keys to victory," laments Gneisenau to Hardenberg in a second letter written on 1 June. "I can boldly say that in no period of this war have we been in such a combat-ready state as we are at this moment." Clausewitz wrote:

The army is in very good shape and probably is already stronger than the enemy. The enemy's situation is desperate and miserable, only the timidity of the commander [Barclay] could see the matter differently. Later, someone will make this clearly visible and everyone will be indignant. I myself want nothing more than for someone to now summon the courage to deliver another battle; this time there is more of a chance for victory than before and, even if it fails like the previous two, it still would bring us closer to our goal. He has been weakened by the battles and considerable desertions; the emperor Napoleon has never played such a desperate game. Why should we fear him? It is truly childish.

Stewart provided the following analysis in his 31 May report to Castlereagh:

Our operations have been conducted counting with implicit faith on Austria: we have fallen back concentrated, and have committed ourselves to a narrow strip of country, where subsistence for 120,000 horses and an army becomes very doubtful. We have abandoned Breslau, the direct communication with Kalisch, and have thus given Poland over to Bonaparte's influence, and all for Austria; and still she does not declare. Bonaparte's force, still maneuvering on us on our right, forces us back. He is playing with us with armistice and negotiations at the same time, and there is no head here that is able to cope with his subtlety and military proceedings. This is a true picture. We made a show here, but we retreat again to Strehlen and Neiße tonight. An offensive movement on Bonaparte's flank in the plains with all our force, when we consider our superior cavalry, might possibly arrest him in his march on Breslau, and certainly should be attempted. Nevertheless, if we do not act boldly now, all will be lost. You will find fault with me, very likely, when I say in confidence I am by no means pleased with the manner things are going, both in the councils and in the field.[41]

Gneisenau frantically urged Hardenberg to do everything possible to prevent the Prussians from retreating across the Oder. To the Prussians, following the Russians east of the Oder meant continuing the retreat across the Vistula. Not only would this sacrifice the core of Prussia's resources to Napoleon, it also would abruptly end the mobilization and with it the possibility of Blücher receiving further reinforcements. Hardenberg responded that a council of war had already taken place and that he had not received an invitation. "I am completely disheartened by the military measures that we take but will use everything to avoid going across the Oder. I wish to be able to speak with you. Can you come here tomorrow by the shortest route?"

Rejecting all Prussian arguments, Barclay continued the retrograde march south of Schweidnitz on 1 June. Blücher's Prussians took a position north and west of Pilzen to form the army's right wing, Langeron's corps moved south of Blücher to form the center, and Wittgenstein posted the main mass of the Russian army as the left wing four miles southeast of Schweidnitz around Schwengfeld (Makowice) and Kreisau. Constantine's Guard and Reserve escorted Allied Headquarters to Obergröditz (Grodziszcze). After being chased from Breslau, Schuler withdrew sixteen miles southeast to Ohlau (Oława) while Mutius led his detachment south toward Strehlen (Strzelin); Sacken likewise reached Ohlau. Schuler, Mutius, and Sacken, a combined force of 15,000 men, covered the march of Russian reinforcements from the Vistula and also received the task of guarding the Prussian siege park that had sailed up the Oder from Glogau on eighty boats and reached the region between Ohlau and Brieg (Brzeg) on the 1st.[42]

For 31 May, Macdonald and Bertrand received orders to reach Striegau. As noted, the two commanders ran into the Russians four miles southeast of Jauer. Deeming the enemy position to be too strong, they retreated to Jauer. They did not make their daily reports to the major-general on the evening of the 31st, which left Napoleon uncertain over the status of his right wing. On the other hand, Marmont did, writing to Berthier at 4:30 P.M. In a passage written in code, we see an example of the panic that sometimes seized commanders, especially a marshal who had learned a hard lesson in Spain about overextending his forces:

> I beg you to inform the emperor that I am in a region that is completely open, without any kind of point of support, without a fixed position in range, and unless I receive quite a few reinforcements I am very far from any support. If I am attacked by large forces, it would be difficult for Bertrand and Macdonald to arrive in time to help me, because their march would encounter many obstacles before they could arrive. Finally, we are very close to the enemy and we are divided when he is concentrated and *en masse*. The enemy has moved his troops from Striegau against my entire front. The dust I see constantly during the day indicates this. It is difficult, rather impossible, to remain in direct communication with Macdonald due to the numerous cavalry that the enemy employs and the distance from here [Eisendorf] to Jauer; if I had to march to his aid, my progress would be slow and difficult, as it was yesterday, or I would lose many soldiers to combat.[43]

Napoleon gave little sympathy to this cry for help yet he purposefully ensured that his reply could be used as a learning tool by one of France's newest marshals. In addition, we see the *sang-froid* and *coup d'oeil* that made him the master of war. At 11:30 on the night of 31 May he dictated his response in a letter to Berthier:

> Write immediately to the duc de Raguse [Marmont] that you received his letter from 4:30 P.M. today in which there are several sentences in code,

that III Corps is at Dietzdorf [Ciechów] and Latour-Maubourg at Obermois, that Dietzdorf to Mois is only 3,300 toises [4.10 miles]; that you cannot conceive how he finds himself in the air with three divisions and one cavalry corps, and 3,000 toises from the army. Tell him that in this kind of war we must avoid being too close together, and that the Russians have a lot of cavalry, so their situation is quite different. From Dietzdorf, only one road goes to Schweidnitz ... that he has not paid attention to the road that you mentioned to him yesterday, the one that runs from Striegau to the Oder. This road is wide and good; I have reconnoitered to the point where it meets the Oder.

Tell him not to worry about the details of the infantry in front of him, that all the reconnaissance made near his camp have seen cavalry only far off in the distance, that we are certain artillery was heard today between the Zobtenberg and Schweidnitz or Striegau, and we do not know if he heard anything. Tell him to let you know tomorrow, at daybreak, what he has before him and repeat that we must avoid the inconvenience of taking a position that is too tight, that prevents our arms from deploying, and that gives great advantage to the enemy cavalry.

Tell him that everything in the villages of Neumarkt and Dietzdorf can come quickly to his support; to try to establish contact with the duc de Tarente [Macdonald] and send you news of him; that with Latour-Maubourg's cavalry, supported by a few battalions and artillery, he could have pushed his reconnaissance very far today so that he would know positively what is in front of him; that it appears he has not done this because he is concerned about what is in front of him. Tell him that spies claim the enemy is moving from Schweidnitz on Zobten. This would be the dust that he has seen on a line six leagues from him. If this is correct, it means that the enemy is trying to get closer to Breslau with his right. Tell him to dispatch strong reconnaissance tomorrow and inform you of the results; that the duc de Tarente was summoned yesterday, the 30th, to march to Striegau on the 31st; that the artillery fire that was heard must be his movement on Striegau. Tell him that, if the duc de Tarente has reached Striegau, he [Marmont] should move forward, on the road from Schweidnitz to the Striegau stream [Strzegomka] on the side, for example, of Kostenblut [Kostomłoty] or Neuhof [Bogdanów], taking there a good position. Let him know that we will enter Breslau today.

Finally convinced that the Allied army stood at Schweidnitz, Napoleon reoriented his army south-southwest on 1 June. After receiving at 6:00 that morning Ney's report on the successful occupation of Breslau, Berthier instructed the marshal to guarantee its inhabitants the emperor's protection. Moreover, Napoleon wanted the *garde bourgeoise* of the city to perform all police duties. According to Odeleben, "the burgesses sent a deputation to Bonaparte at the head of which was the mayor, von Kospoth. It was received with extreme affability, for Napoleon was much interested in winning over the inhabitants of Silesia; indeed he said to them: 'I am well aware that the king has been misled.' This expression had no other purpose than to alienate the Silesians from the Prussian monarch."

As for the enemy, Berthier alerted Ney that the Allies appeared to be concentrated at Schweidnitz. If Caulaincourt did not inform Imperial Headquarters of a ceasefire by 3:00 that afternoon, Ney would turn V and VII Corps southwest and make for Schweidnitz in unison with the rest of the army. To better support Marmont, Berthier directed Souham to position all of III Corps between Dietzdorf and Michelsdorf, the latter being two miles northeast of Latour-Maubourg's position at Obermois and fifteen miles northeast of Marmont's at Eisendorf. Macdonald received orders to establish his right at Jauer and spread his left toward Eisendorf, placing IV Corps between XI and VI Corps.[44]

During the course of the day, II Corps reached Steinau (Ścinawa) on the Oder, forty miles downstream from Breslau. Imperial Headquarters and the Guard remained at Neumarkt while V Corps left a detachment at Breslau and moved seven miles southwest to Kriptau (Krzeptów) and Mochbern (Muchobór). Lauriston's vanguard division joined VII Corps at Purschwitz (Bogdaszowice), twenty-eight miles northeast of Schweidnitz. In accordance with Berthier's orders, III Corps took the position between Dietzdorf and

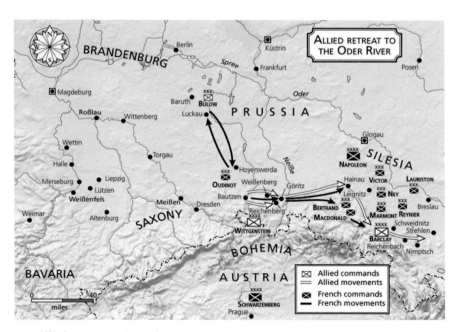

**25.** Allied retreat to the Oder River

Michelsdorf while Marmont maintained VI Corps and I Cavalry Corps at Eisendorf and Obermois respectively; IV and XI Corps loitered around Jauer.

It is difficult to view Napoleon's position in any other way but extremely advantageous. Barclay's army stood concentrated south of Schweidnitz only twenty-five miles from Imperial Headquarters. The front of the Grande Armée extended forty miles from Jauer to Breslau; Ney's turn south immediately threatened Barclay's line of retreat. In less than thirty-six hours, the emperor could have united his entire army, including Marchand's division and II Corps, between the Katzbach and the Schweidnitz stream. This would have forced the Allies to either accept battle in the Schweidnitz area or retreat across the Oder as they could not move any deeper into Silesia without running the risk of being driven into the mountains of Austria. Assuming they accepted a third battle at Schweidnitz and Napoleon won, he could then pin them against the Austrian frontier. Although the master did not fear being defeated, he let this opportunity slip through his hands in favor of an armistice. "Who would have thought," laments Lanrezac, "that a bout of weakness would prevent Napoleon from pursuing such a great opportunity to deal a decisive blow to his enemies?"[45]

East of Jauer, at the tiny village of Gäbersdorf (Grzegorzów), Caulaincourt, Kleist, and Shuvalov met a second time. Napoleon relented on his insistence that the Oder form the line of demarcation, thus clearing the final obstacle to a truce. Yet the envoys agreed that further operations could alter the situation at any moment and thus render the task of concluding an armistice impossible. Consequently, they agreed that both sides would halt operations and hostilities for thirty-six hours at 3:00 P.M. on 1 June, effective immediately. All concerned believed this preliminary measure would provide time to reach a more comprehensive agreement, which initially appeared to be a difficult task. French forces remained in the same position until the signing of the actual armistice on 4 June with one exception: on 3 June Victor received orders to march to Sagan on the lower Bober to join Oudinot in a joint attack on Bülow.[46] Although Victor received new orders as a result of the armistice, word did not reach either Oudinot or Bülow in time to prevent them from engaging at Luckau on the 4th. In gruesome combat amid the flaming village, the Prussians repulsed Oudinot's XII Corps.[47]

Allied forces maintained their positions on 2 June but continued the retreat on the 3rd. Barclay feared that Napoleon had agreed to negotiations only to buy time to execute his infamous *manoeuvre sur les derrières* by marching to Nimptsch (Niemcza) and Strehlen – thirty-five miles southwest of Schweidnitz – in Upper Silesia. To prevent this, he insisted on withdrawing to Strehlen. At a council of war held on the 2nd, Blücher and Yorck hotly insisted that the Prussians separate from the Russians if Barclay crossed the

Oder. Barclay overcame all resistance with such determination that he received the approval of both monarchs. Volkonsky had already sent the army's treasury to Kalisch and made preparations to destroy the Oder bridges after the army crossed. Alexander spoke of the possibility of seizing the offensive and Barclay agreed but Gneisenau gained the impression that the Russian commander "would not fight until all reinforcements reached him and he forced them into a parade ground formation."[48]

As soon as the meeting ended around 3:00 P.M., Volkonsky issued instructions for Blücher's wing as well as the Russian Guard and Reserve to march immediately. However, orders soon reached the corps commanders postponing the march for twelve hours until dawn on 3 June. That morning, this portion of the army formed three columns and marched fifteen miles southeast to reach the Breslau–Frankenstein (Ząbkowice Śląskie) highway. The northern column, commanded by Yorck and consisting of the Prussian I Corps as well as Langeron's cavalry, marched east to Rudelsdorf (Radzików). Blücher led the middle column (Prussian II Corps and Langeron's infantry and artillery) to Heidersdorf (Łagiewniki), less than two miles south of Rudelsdorf. Commanding the southern column in place of the ill Constantine, Miloradovich directed the Russo-Prussian Guard and Reserve to Großwilkau (Wilków Wielki), three miles south of Blücher's position at Heidersdorf. All three columns formed a line approximately eleven miles west of Strehlen. South of Schweidnitz, Allied Headquarters remained at Obergröditz, guarded by the rest of the Russian army under Wittgenstein. Rearguards under Zieten and St.-Priest maintained positions north of Schweidnitz at Saarau (Żarów) and Großrosen. Lieutenant-Colonel Wilhelm Ernst von Zastrow already had led the majority of the Silesian Landwehr Corps from Schweidnitz to the fortress of Glatz; six battalions deemed combat-ready remained behind to occupy the town. During the reorganization of 31 May, the king assigned four of these battalions to Yorck's I Corps and the other two to Kleist's II Corps. As a result, all Prussian forces evacuated Schweidnitz.[49]

Although Barclay wanted the columns to continue to Strehlen on the 3rd, they halted for the night after reaching their march objectives on the Breslau–Frankenstein highway. Not only Blücher, Gneisenau, and Müffling but Yorck as well – one of the few times he ever agreed with Gneisenau – anxiously sought to prevent the further march east. Having reached their breaking point, the Prussians believed the time had come to make Barclay stand and fight. If not, the Russians could withdraw across the Oder without them. In a letter to Knesebeck, Yorck urgently lectured that even without the Russians duty demanded that they defend the land with their last drop of blood. According to his own account, Müffling pleaded with Barclay to listen to reason. Müffling claims that he told Barclay outright that Frederick William could not follow the Russians to Poland. "Of the 80,000 men he has in Silesia, 10,000 will be deposited in the fortresses, and 70,000 will remain available. If he follows the Russian army with all of these forces, he will lose all the resources to feed and pay his army: who knows where that will lead." Purportedly, "General Barclay shrugged his shoulders: 'I cannot sacrifice the armies of my emperor as they are not in fighting condition. In six weeks I will return here: the Prussian army must help itself as best it can.'"[50]

Establishing a pattern that would persist throughout their military marriage, Blücher entrusted Gneisenau with waging a fervent letter campaign on the 3rd and 4th. Gneisenau wrote with the complete understanding that Blücher endorsed his views absolutely. In the absence of Blücher's own words, Gneisenau's letters offer the best insight into the ideas discussed and approved by Blücher. In Gneisenau's correspondence, Blücher's desperation sometimes emerges, as in the case of an idealistic memo to the king that bluntly begins with the statement: "No significant enemy forces stand at Jauer. Nothing stands at Liegnitz." According to the reports Blücher had received, Napoleon had positioned his main force at Neumarkt and his left wing held Breslau. Gneisenau emphasized the benefits of remaining in Silesia rather than following the Russians across the Oder. In his opinion, nothing could prevent the Prussian army from executing its own *manoeuvre sur les derrières* by marching through Schweidnitz and Striegau to Jauer. Napoleon could not allow Blücher to threaten his main line of communication along the east–west highway to Dresden. Yet Gneisenau asserts that Napoleon could alter this situation only by turning with superior forces against either the Prussians or the Russians. If he drove toward the Prussians, Blücher could withdraw south from Jauer toward Bolkenhain (Bolków Śląskie) in the mountains and even further from there. While he retreated, Gneisenau – ignoring the fact that the Russians were committed to withdrawing across the Oder – speculated that Barclay could advance west to Neumarkt, "taking the entire territory without having to attack Breslau itself." If Napoleon ignored Blücher and continued his offensive against the Russians, then Barclay could withdraw as far as he felt necessary. In case Blücher did not want to risk a battle, he could simply "remain quiet" at Jauer. By merely threatening Napoleon's line of communication, Gneisenau believed Blücher would force the emperor to return to Silesia rather than pursue Barclay. Aside from overestimating the value Napoleon placed on his line of communication, Gneisenau failed to explain how Blücher and his 34,000 men would defeat Napoleon without Russian support. Instead, he maintained that "no danger exists because both armies can withdraw for a time." He even suggested that Blücher could liberate Silesia "quickly and without a great battle. The advance of the French army absolutely bears the character of its audacious leader. Audacity can be defeated only with calm level-headedness. Thus, one cannot order a retreat that surrenders all of the unique advantages of his position. The prudent swordsman exploits the opening that his opponent gives without placing himself at risk."[51]

Gneisenau forwarded a copy of this letter to Hardenberg on the 4th. Carping that Frederick William probably would ignore it, he hoped the chancellor would share its contents with Alexander. He advised Hardenberg to argue that this plan granted the Russians the freedom to fall back on their reinforcements and supplies if they did indeed lack sufficient ammunition, which Gneisenau refused to believe. In addition, reports indicated that Oudinot led XII Corps against Bülow. "If this is the case," explains Gneisenau, "it proves that Napoleon will not receive reinforcements in the near future; that he is very sensitive to the disruption of his communications; and that the army facing us cannot be very strong." Another point the staff officer wanted Hardenberg to make involved the considerable increase of desertion in the French army, which "allows one to conclude [that there is] discontentment and dissolution." Finally, he raised another point of contention: Russian deceit. "The Russians demanded that we provide ammunition for 840 pieces of artillery but the total number of guns, both Prussian and Russian, is only some 600 pieces. Obviously, according to this, they made a false statement. Then, they demanded fifty kilograms of powder. This quantity can produce some 160,000 cartridges. During the battle of Großgörschen, Blücher's corps fired over 5,000 [musket] balls. Here again you can easily see a deliberate exaggeration. I suspect premeditation and intrigue."

Although Gneisenau's letter to Frederick William offers no explanation of how Blücher could take a position at Jauer with only 34,000 Prussians, the staff officer had already formulated an idea to quickly increase combat power. He submitted plans to Knesebeck and the king for arming Silesia. According to the figures he received, the Military Government at Breslau had raised a Landwehr force of 32,000 infantry and 3,000 cavalry. Of the latter, 1,700 had received sabers and could be considered armed. Applying the same ratio to the infantry, Gneisenau determined that only half had received serviceable muskets. "Nothing prevents us," he concludes, "from taking the two most service-ready companies from each battalion of four companies and combining them with the two most service-ready companies of another battalion to form a thoroughly service-ready battalion. In this way, we will perhaps assemble more than 25,000 men who can reinforce the army. Such an operation will provide us with numerical superiority." Gneisenau himself volunteered to take control of the mobilization of the Landwehr, a process he labeled a "failed venture" thus far. He noted that, in order for this plan to succeed, "the king must drop all scruples regarding rank and place the men suggested by me in their appropriate place. For example, Grolman must be Blücher's chief of staff."

Two momentous developments emerged from Gneisenau's proposal. First, Frederick William decided to amend the Landwehr's original auxiliary function and combine it with the army for frontline combat duty. Second, to make the Landwehr combat-ready, he transferred responsibility for its training from the Military Governments to the army. These adjustments, which enabled the Prussians to field an army of 279,000 soldiers by mid August, are at the forefront of explaining Prussia's paramount success in 1813 and 1814.

News that Hardenberg had gone to Reichenbach presumably for peace negotiations prompted Gneisenau to fire a second frantic missive: "Do not be led astray by the poor army command. Concerning the army, we have never been in a better condition. The spirit of the army is not broken and its men have gained experience. The Russians can now receive reinforcements daily and we can provide some order to the state of our Landwehr. If the negotiations aim at something other than gaining a few days of time they are mistaken. We Prussians are battle-ready every hour. The loss of a battle can cause no great result. We have the freedom to move to our fortresses, the Russians to Poland. But one must not lose one's head."

Gneisenau urged Hardenberg to consider Napoleon's situation. A defeat would immediately bring the Austrians to the Elbe. "Except for his last campaign in Russia, never has he been in such a dangerous situation. Only our inactivity entices him to risk such danger." Again Gneisenau returned to the idea that Allied numerical superiority in cavalry would always prevent Napoleon from achieving a decisive victory. "Due to our better and more numerous cavalry, we retain the ability to break off any battle that turns disadvantageous for us at any moment."[52]

Steffens insists that "at Blücher's headquarters the determination was fixed and strong that he [Napoleon] should be treated with only on the other side of the Rhine. The two battles that had been fought rather raised than depressed the hope of future victories; and it was loudly proclaimed that the war must be carried forward in the spirit that gave rise to it, and that it would remain a deep national disgrace if it were abandoned without a signal triumph that would cripple Napoleon's power forever. I was too much behind the scenes not to be aware of the doubtful and dangerous point upon which our deepest interests hinged." The fact that the Russians as well as Knesebeck did not sufficiently appreciate this advantage infuriated Gneisenau. "I beseech you to make the negotiators aware of this," Gneisenau begged Hardenberg. "I have nothing against negotiating to gain time for the Russians to receive reinforcements and to gain time for the Austrians – thus to gain a few days – but any other objective of the negotiations is pernicious." Immediately after writing this letter, a frantic Gneisenau sent a second warning to Hardenberg: "I want to inform you that the French may have offered an armistice with this army in order to detach against Bülow and destroy him with superiority. One must take care to prevent this."[53]

Still that same day, 4 June, the Prussians received Barclay's orders to cross the Oder. Rather than proceed to Strehlen with the other two columns, the Allied commander instructed Yorck to lead his column three miles north to Jordansmühl (Jordanów Śląski) and then turn east toward the fortress of Brieg on the Oder. At Bohrau (Borów), he would establish communication with Sacken, who had reached the right bank of the Oder. Lanskoy's cavalry would take a position at Koberwitz (Kobierzyce), twelve miles southwest of Breslau. Barclay hoped Yorck and Sacken would prevent imperial forces from reaching Brieg before the Allied army.[54]

Again Gneisenau turned to Frederick William and Hardenberg. To the king he stated that the Prussians could not follow the Russians beyond Strehlen. "If we go even a little further, we will run the risk of being cut off from our strong positions. A march to Poland would dissolve the army and turn public opinion against us. Silesia will be completely empty of troops, and the mountains, where we are now in the process of organizing a very useful *kleinen Krieg*, will be abandoned to the enemy. The fortress of Neiße will fall in his hands unless it is protected by a troop position in its vicinity. For all of these important reasons I beseech you not to agree to a march further than Strehlen. The security of Your Majesty's throne, dynasty, and people compel me to make this solemn appeal."

Gneisenau cannot be faulted for lacking persistence. Again he urged Frederick William to have confidence in his army. He recommended taking a strong position at the foot of the Riesengebirge and reinforcing Blücher with Landwehr. In this way, the Prussians would "win public opinion and conduct an active mountain war, which can easily lead to a union with Bülow, a situation that alone can have a decisive influence on the turn of the war. In any case, a mountain position will facilitate the reappearance of the Russians on this bank as soon as they have been reinforced with their replacements. The choice lies in Your Majesty's hands. Here our army corps is 34,000 strong. It appears that we can speedily increase to 54,000 men if we receive 20,000 of the best Landwehr. This significant force can hold the Silesian mountains and master most of the plain while the enemy is forced to send a considerable force across the Oder to follow the Russians." To Hardenberg he pleaded: "I send you a copy of what I was just forced to submit to the king. Earlier you promised us that we would not follow the Russians across the Oder. Please use all of your influence to avoid this pernicious step."[55]

Gneisenau's haranguing worked, yet we will never know the full extent of his success. His tenacity stemmed from Knesebeck's influence on Frederick William, a situation that would both benefit and hinder the Blücher/Gneisenau team throughout the war. Rather than Gneisenau, Knesebeck replaced

Scharnhorst as the king's principal advisor. As such, Knesebeck believed nothing could stop Barclay from carrying out his plan to reorganize in Poland. From a purely military point of view, Knesebeck supported the idea of regrouping but recognized that a retreat to Poland would end all hopes of an alliance with Austria. "I have known Barclay from 1806/07: he is firm as a rock," Knesebeck assured Müffling, "and he will be less likely to relinquish his notion of a retreat on Poland which, from a military point of view, has much to offer. However, if we do this, the alliance with Austria is lost; as soon as we cross the Oder, the Viennese cabinet must maintain its neutrality."

Knesebeck argued that an armistice provided the only means to freeze the Russian army in Silesia where it could spend six weeks reorganizing while at the same time furnishing the Austrians with six weeks to finish their mobilization and commence military operations in close proximity to the Russians and Prussians.[56] Moreover, Müffling claims that Barclay viewed the extension of the armistice "as the only means to avoid the separation of the two armies." Thus, Knesebeck and Müffling persuaded Frederick William to discount Gneisenau's opposition to negotiations. Furthermore, Gneisenau's numerous epistles stressing the combat-ready status of the Allied army, the sinking morale of the imperial army, and the extremely dangerous situation in which Napoleon would be placed as soon as Austria declared war provided Hardenberg with powerful ammunition. Based on Gneisenau's ideas, the chancellor made proposals to Alexander, which the tsar accepted. According to some sources, it was the Russian monarch who firmly decided to remain in Silesia.[57] Despite the speculation, it is clear that it was Barclay who decided to retreat further from Strehlen to Brieg on the 5th. Unless Alexander intervened, Frederick William would be faced with a decision of profound importance and unfathomable difficulty. News that an Austrian proposal to extend the armistice to 20 July followed by an eight-day suspension of hostilities was signed at Pläswitz (Pielaszkowice) on 4 June spared the king from having to choose between his army and his benefactor.

According to the armistice agreement, the imperial army would withdraw behind (west of) the Katzbach while the Allies would maintain their current position from Streigau to Ohlau; Breslau would remain neutral. Imperial garrisons holding the Oder and Vistula fortresses would be victualized every five days by the surrounding communities. Berlin remained in Prussian hands while Hamburg would "rest with whatever Power that may occupy it on the 8th of this month." The armistice would last for six weeks and six days with both sides being bound to give notice before commencing hostilities. "Such are the terms that well-informed persons have agreed on," Lowe informed Bunbury; "but you may possibly find some variations when the exact conditions are made known. An abundant subject for reflection they will give rise to!"[58]

After receiving confirmation of the armistice, Barclay ordered the Allied army to move into tight cantonments with the respective vanguard formations camping in bivouacs. Some feared a French trick. According to Langeron:

> As of 2:00 A.M., I was considering the dislocation of the troops when Prince Aleksey Menshikov, the tsar's adjutant, arrived; he was looking for a village in which to camp a Guard regiment. He appeared surprised that I had not received the counterorders and informed me that an armistice had been signed and that we were to remain in our positions; this seemed so extraordinary to me that I had trouble believing it. A moment later, another adjutant arrived to confirm the order; my disbelief was such that I still thought it was a feint by Napoleon to keep us in place and attack us. I ran to my advance posts, where I witnessed French officers returning all the posts that they occupied on the right bank of the Schweidnitz stream to my Cossacks and withdrawing to the left bank.[59]

Awarding western Germany as far as the mouth of the Elbe, all of Saxony, and the majority of Lower Silesia to the imperials, the armistice created a neutral zone ranging from fourteen to twenty-eight miles in length to separate the opposing armies in Silesia. On the French side, the line of demarcation extended north from the Bohemian frontier through Schreiberhau (Szklarska Poręba) to the Bober just east of Berthelsdorf (Barcinek) and along this river to Lähn (Wleń). From there it followed the Katzbach to the Oder. Imperial forces could occupy the towns of Lähn, Goldberg, Liegnitz, and Parchwitz (Parszowice). Hungry imperial soldiers eventually exhausted the territory on their side of the neutral zone in addition to Saxony and Lower Lusatia. On the Allied side, the demarcation line likewise started at the Bohemian frontier, running northeast through Landeshut (Kamienna Góra), Bolkenhain, Striegau, then along the Striegau stream to Kanth (Kąty Wrocławskie), and from there along the Schweidnitz stream to the Oder slightly downstream of Breslau. Allied troops could occupy these towns but neither side could enter Breslau or the neutral zone. North of the neutral zone, Allied forces retained possession of Mecklenburg, Brandenburg, and Pomerania.[60]

To prevent a surprise attack and stifle communication between the inhabitants of the Allied zone and their neighbors in the neutral and French zones, Allied commanders staffed their outpost chains with units commanded by officers skilled in security measures. On the left, Wittgenstein's wing quartered at Pilzen, with the vanguard between Striegau and Schweidnitz. His forward posts extended across the front of the Allied army: from Dittersbach on the Bohemian frontier along the upper Bober to Rudelstadt, and from there sharply northeast along the Striegau stream from Bolkenhain through Striegau to Kostenblut. East of Wittgenstein, Langeron's corps took a position with its van posted at Wernersdorf and

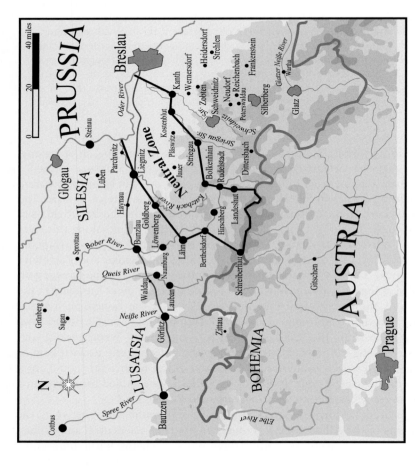

26. The neutral zone in Silesia

main body around Heidersdorf; its outposts linked with Wittgenstein's to the left and extended on the right along the Striegau stream up to Kanth, which Jäger and cavalry occupied in force.[61]

For the signal service along the outpost line and between the outposts and the main formations in the rear, the Allies positioned beacons with lookouts on prominent heights. Upon the beacons being lit, the troops would move to designated assembly areas and take positions assigned to them. Flying posts would maintain communication between Allied Headquarters and those of Blücher and Sacken. All troops had to be behind their lines of demarcation by 12 June. Alexander established his headquarters at the Peterswaldau (Pieszyce) Schloß approximately four miles from Reichenbach; Frederick William formed his at Neudorf on the road to Schweidnitz, three miles from Reichenbach and one from Peterswaldau. Barclay de Tolly based himself at Reichenbach. Kaiser Francis arrived at the Bohemian town of Gitschin (Jičín), on the Prague–Breslau highway eighty miles southwest of Reichenbach.

After approving the agreement, Napoleon sent the Old Guard to Dresden, where Imperial Headquarters would be established.[62] Leaving Neumarkt on the night of the 5th, Napoleon rode west for a while before stopping to sleep not far from Liegnitz in the small village of Roßnitz (Rogoźnik), where a blazing watch-fire caused his headquarters to go up in flames, destroying a portion of the imperial baggage and coffer. This being perhaps an omen, hindsight and reflection later prompted Napoleon to regret his decision to accept the armistice. A French émigré in Russian service, Langeron, comments on the issue of blame, reflecting on an interesting conversation he had with Berthier after the war. "One can reproach Napoleon for numerous mistakes ... At the same time, many have judged him too harshly, yet many have not seriously considered the gravest of his errors, especially this armistice that he concluded after the battle of Bautzen, an unpardonable military and political error for which he alone is culpable. In 1814, while I was speaking to General Berthier in Paris, he replied: 'You would be unjust if you accused us of all the faults that brought you here, we were not responsible. Napoleon alone did everything; he was no longer the same man who had fought in Italy and Germany before 1812.'" After learning of the armistice, Langeron made his way to Barclay's headquarters. On arriving, the Allied commander in chief "received me with thunderous laughter: this explosion of gaiety was not at all normal for him. Barclay was always cold, serious, and inclined toward a stiff spirit and language. We rejoiced at the expense of Napoleon. Barclay, all of the generals, and our sovereigns were drunk with joy, and with good reason."[63]

We can easily agree with Langeron's judgment of an unpardonable military and political error, yet the situation of the Grande Armée in early June provided sufficient reason for a temporary cessation of hostilities. History supported the decision: during his career, Napoleon had signed many armistices that had led directly to peace treaties that he dictated.

In addition to the army's exhaustion, this reason may well account for the fact that none of his military or political subordinates advised him to reject the armistice. Moreover, the battles of Lützen and Bautzen had thinned his ranks; deprivation had exhausted his young soldiers, exponentially increased the sick list, and dissolved the bonds of discipline. Just as the Allies hoped to gain time for the Prussians to complete the mobilization of the Landwehr and for the Russians to replenish their depleted ranks, Napoleon urgently needed to rest and reorganize his army. Five weeks of campaigning had reduced Ney's III Corps from its 25 April muster of 49,189 men to 24,581 on 31 May, despite its having received reinforcements prior to Bautzen. Having numbered 26,194 men on 25 April, Oudinot's XII Corps contained a mere 13,818 men under arms by 4 June. A few days after the armistice halted operations, a paralyzing phenomenon struck the imperial army: tens of thousands of soldiers flooded the hospitals. Finally granted rest after enduring privations, physical and mental exhaustion, and combat fatigue for several weeks, the men suffered the collapse of their immune systems. For some the sudden halt ushered in latent illnesses, for others the ailments could be attributed more to psychosomatic factors, while still others, especially the younger soldiers, resorted to voluntary mutilations in the hope of escaping the horrors of Napoleonic warfare. Sick lists for each army corps averaged between 33 and 50 percent of the effectives.[64]

Thus, Napoleon's agreement to a cessation of hostilities appears to have been a calculated gamble. Completely aware that he desperately needed time to rebuild the Grande Armée, he firmly believed that in two or three months he would again be at the head of the most effective fighting force Europe had seen since the Romans. For this reason, he eventually agreed to extend the armistice to 10 August followed by a six-day suspension of hostilities. In a letter to Clarke on 2 June, Napoleon expressed his willingness to wait until the month of September if it meant his army would be ready to "deliver great blows."[65] To his credit, the emperor applied his superhuman work ethic to improving the army. The imperial legions that he fielded in August 1813 for the Fall Campaign were far superior to those that had waged the Spring Campaign. Yet the Allies utilized the armistice to create armies of unprecedented size and quality. The Fall Campaign would pit a much improved Grande Armée against 600,000 Russians, Prussians, and Austrians. Would Napoleon's genius be enough to overcome such numbers?

## Notes

1  *CN*, No. 20043, XXV:323. See also SHAT, C$^{17}$ 178: Berthier to Oudinot, 24 May 1813: "The army will move on Glogau"; and Berthier to Durosnel, 26 May 1813: "The army, arriving at Glogau, will make a movement to occupy Berlin, which is likely to make General Bülow retire quickly."

2 *CN*, Nos. 20047 and 20048, XXV:326–27; SHAT, C$^{17}$ 178: Berthier to Victor and Ney, 24 May 1813; Berthier to Victor, 26 May 1813; Lanrezac, *Lützen*, 255.

3 *CN*, No. 20046, XXV:326; SHAT, C$^{17}$ 178: Berthier to Souham, Mortier, Soult, and Marmont, 25 May 1813; Berthier to Ney, Marmont, and Latour-Maubourg, 26 May 1813.

4 *CN*, No. 20048, XXV:327; SHAT, C$^{17}$ 178: Berthier to Marmont, 26 May 1813.

5 Lanrezac, *Lützen*, 254–56.

6 Gneisenau to Hardenberg, Poischwitz (Paszowice), 27 May 1813, GStA PK, VI HA Rep. 92 Nl. Albrecht, Nr. 47.

7 Gneisenau to Münster, Puschkau, 29 May 1813, GStA PK, VI HA Rep. 92 Nl. Gneisenau, Nr. 20b; Stewart, *Narrative*, 51; Clausewitz to Marie, by Schweidnitz, 28 May 1813, in Schwartz, *Clausewitz*, II:84; Fritz to Wilhelm, Koschwitz (Koszowice), 27 May 1813, Griewank, *Hohenzollernbriefe*, Nr. 40, 60. Fritz mentions the names of numerous junior officers of the Prussian Guard who had fallen at Haynau but was generally excited by Blücher's success: "600 prisoners have been brought in ... more than 1,000 were cut down!" In *Commentaries*, 170, Cathcart described the engagement as "one of the most brilliant cavalry affairs of modern days." In *Campagne de 1813*, 62, Commandant Maurice-Henri Weil of the French General Staff likewise refers to Haynau as a brilliant cavalry affair. "In this engagement," wrote Clausewitz, "the cavalry won the glory that in later times would be difficult to attain due to the superior tactics of the infantry. This shows that there are circumstances where this superiority does not prevail, where the cavalry can do great things. Colonel Dolffs, who lay dead among the enemy, could justifiably be compared with Seydlitz." According to Clausewitz, the Prussians captured eighteen cannon but had enough horses to haul away only eleven guns: Clausewitz, *Hinterlassene Werke*, VII:304.

8 Odeleben, *A Circumstantial Narrative*, I:112–13. The account of Haynau is derived from Zieten's after-action report, reproduced in full in Henckel von Donnersmarck, *Erinnerungen*, 197–98; Clausewitz, *Hinterlassene Werke*, VII:302–04; Bogdanovich, *Geschichte des Krieges*, I:95–101, and Weil, *Campagne de 1813*, 57–62, provide the most extensive coverage. See also Plotho, *Der Krieg*, I:187–88; Beitzke, *Geschichte der deutschen Freiheitskriege*, I:470–75; Gneisenau, *Blücher*, 130–34; Unger, *Blücher*, II:46–48; Blasendorff, *Blücher*, 196–97; Petre, *Napoleon's Last Campaign*, 147–48; Cathcart, *Commentaries*, 170–71; and Holleben and Caemmerer, *Frühjahrsfeldzuges 1813*, II:258.

9 Quoted in Blasendorff, *Blücher*, 197; Barclay to Blücher, 27 May 1813, GStA PK, VI HA Rep. 92 Nl. Gneisenau, Nr. 160; Bogdanovich, *Geschichte des Krieges*, I:101.

10 SHAT, C$^2$ 145: Macdonald to Berthier; Bertrand to Berthier; and Marmont to Berthier, 26 May 1813. Lowe later reported that "the Cossacks and detached parties have been uniformly successful in their attacks on the rear and flanks of the French armies, and since the affair of Reichenbach in Saxony [22 May], where Duroc was killed ... have captured about 1,500 prisoners and taken four couriers." See Add MSS, 20111, 35: Lowe to Bunbury, Reichenbach, 6 June 1813.

11 SHAT, C$^2$ 145: Macdonald to Berthier, 26 May 1813; *CN*, No. 20048, XXV:327; Lanrezac, *Lützen*, 257–58; Holleben and Caemmerer, *Frühjahrsfeldzuges 1813*, II:253–54.

12 *CN*, Nos. 20052 and 20070, XXV:329–30, 346; Bowden, *Napoleon's Grande Armée of 1813*, 111–12.

13 Schuler's troops consisted of seven battalions, one Jäger company, seven squadrons, and one and one-half batteries; his five and one-half Landwehr battalions went to the entrenched camp at Schweidnitz.

14 Osten-Sacken, *Militärische-politische Geschichte des Befreiungskrieges*, II:561; Holleben and Caemmerer, *Frühjahrsfeldzuges 1813*, II:259, 62, 67; Stewart, *Narrative*, 56.

15 Müffling, *Aus meinem Leben*, 47.

16 Sievers's findings are called into question by Wilson's testimony of 29 May 1813: "Schweidnitz was once a strong fortress. The French have partly destroyed the works, but the Prussians are working to restore them. Why and wherefore I know not, as there are no guns to place on the fortifications and there cannot be time for the ramparts to be restored sufficiently for any defense. If the work had begun six weeks earlier we might have derived some advantage from the position ... but it now appears to me to be labor ill applied." See Wilson, *Private Diary*, II:35–36.

17 Pertz and Delbrück, *Gneisenau*, II:645–46. In *Aus meinem Leben*, 49, Müffling also claims to have inspected Schweidnitz on behalf of Barclay. "Here I found a ruin; that is, the walls in the same condition as when they were blown up." Pertz and Delbrück follow Müffling very closely but make no mention of this passage. Lowe reported on 31 May from Schweidnitz that "by the place from which this letter is dated, you will observe that the army has still continued its retrograde movement. The town, however, which was dismantled after the peace of Tilsit, is being put into a state of repair, and a position has been taken up in its rear": Add MSS, 20111, 30: Lowe to Bunbury, Schweidnitz, 31 May 1813.

18 In *Geschichte des Krieges*, I:104, Bogdanovich agrees with this decision, judging that it allowed the Allies to remain in Silesia longer without basing the fate of the army on the uncertainty of a battle and without distancing them from the Austrian frontier.

19 Barclay to Blücher, 27 May 1813, GStA PK, VI HA Rep. 92 Nl. Gneisenau, Nr. 160; Stewart, *Narrative*, 54–55; Cathcart, *Commentaries*, 174–75.

20 *CN*, No. 20049, XXV:327; SHAT, C$^{17}$ 178: Berthier to Mortier, Soult, and Souham, 26 May 1813.

21 Odeleben, *A Circumstantial Narrative*, I:112, 117–19. The French claim to have captured 22 guns, 80 caissons, and 500 men. The Russians contend that the convoy consisted of only 13 guns and 200 men. See Plotho, *Der Krieg*, I:192.

22 *CN*, No. 20053, XXV:331; SHAT, C$^{17}$ 178: Berthier to Ney and Souham, 28 May 1813; Plotho, *Der Krieg*, I:192–95; Lanrezac, *Lützen*, 258–59; Holleben and Caemmerer, *Frühjahrsfeldzuges 1813*, II:267–70; Weinzierl, "Victor," 351; Foucart, *Bautzen*, II:177.

23 Barclay de Tolly to Blücher, 28 May 1813, GStA PK, VI HA Rep. 92 Nl. Gneisenau, Nr. 160; Pertz and Delbrück, *Gneisenau*, II:646–47; Müffling, *Aus meinem Leben*, 46.

24 Frederick William to Blücher, Breslau, 28 May 1813, in Pflugk-Harttung, *Das Befreiungsjahr*, Nr. 132, 163–64.

25 Gneisenau to Münster, Puschkau by Striegau in Silesia, 29 May, GStA PK, VI HA Rep. 92 Nl. Gneisenau, Nr. 20b; Barclay de Tolly to Blücher and Volkonsky to Blücher, 28 May 1813, *ibid.*, Nr. 160.

26 Prince August received a cabinet order dated 29 May to provide the Russians with as much shot and power as possible without shorting the needs of the Prussian fortresses and army. On 30 May the amount of powder was set at 25,000 kg. See Holleben and Caemmerer, *Frühjahrsfeldzuges 1813*, II:347; Barclay to Blücher, 30 May 1813, GStA PK, VI HA Rep. 92 Nl. Gneisenau, Nr. 160; Bogdanovich, *Geschichte des Krieges*, I:103; Stewart, *Narrative*, 56.

27 SHAT, C² 146: Oudinot to Berthier, 28 May 1813; Leggiere, *Napoleon and Berlin*, 75–78.

28 SHAT, C¹⁷ 178: Berthier to Marchand, Souham, and Victor, 28 May 1813; Berthier to Ney, 29 May 1813.

29 *CN*, No. 20048, XXV:327; SHAT, C¹⁷ 178: Berthier to Marmont, Macdonald, and Bertrand, 29 May 1813.

30 Odeleben, *A Circumstantial Narrative*, I:122–23.

31 SHAT, C¹⁷ 178: Berthier to Reynier, 29 May 1813; SHAT, C² 145: Ney to Berthier, 29 May 1813; Lanrezac, *Lützen*, 259–60.

32 *CN*, No. 20057, XXV:333–34.

33 SHAT, C¹⁷ 178: Berthier to Lauriston, Ney, Macdonald, and Bertrand, 30 May 1813.

34 Osten-Sacken, *Militärische-politische Geschichte des Befreiungskrieges*, II:326; Holleben and Caemmerer, *Frühjahrsfeldzuges 1813*, II:262–66; Lanrezac, *Lützen*, 261.

35 SHAT, C¹⁷ 178: Berthier to Ney and Marmont, 31 May 1813; Lanrezac, *Lützen*, 260; Plotho, *Der Krieg*, I:200–02.

36 Odeleben, *A Circumstantial Narrative*, I:125–26.

37 Barclay de Tolly to Blücher, 30 May 1813, GStA PK, VI HA Rep. 92 Nl. Gneisenau, Nr. 160. On this day, Barclay wrote to Blücher three times; the Prussian commander also received letters from Wittgenstein, Auvray, and Volkonsky: Pertz and Delbrück, *Gneisenau*, II:639. Defending Barclay, Bogdanovich, in *Geschichte des Krieges*, I:104, insists that a third battle with Napoleon would have exhausted the Allies and led to the loss of Silesia anyway.

38 Gneisenau to Caroline, 31 May 1813, GStA PK, VI HA Rep. 92 Nl. Gneisenau, Nr. 21. "Lord Cathcart says General Bülow is hanging on the rear of the enemy and is not too distant from Bautzen. This is well, and with the hope it may be the forerunner of a regular system of attack on the line of his communication, which appears to offer the best prospect of success in the operations against him": Add MSS, 20111, 30: Lowe to Bunbury, Löwenberg, 24 May 1813.

39 Wittgenstein to Bülow, Löwenberg, 25 May 1813, GStA PK, IV HA Rep. 15a Nr. 248; Stewart, *Narrative*, 56–57; Unger, *Blücher*, II:48.

40 Hardenberg to Gneisenau, Langenbielau (Bielawa), 31 May 1813, GStA PK, VI HA Rep. 92 Nl. Albrecht, Nr. 47.

41 Blücher to Frederick William, Kreisau, 1 June 1813, in Pertz and Delbrück, *Gneisenau*, II:650–51; Gneisenau to Hardenberg, Kreisau, 1 June 1813, GStA PK, VI HA Rep. 92 Nl. Albrecht, Nr. 47; Clausewitz to Marie, by Schweidnitz, 31 May 1813 in Schwartz, *Clausewitz*, II:85; Stewart to Castlereagh, Schweidnitz, 31 May 1813, *CVC*, IX:21.

42 Hardenberg to Gneisenau, Langenbielau, 2 June 1813, GStA PK, VI HA Rep. 92
Nl. Albrecht, Nr. 47; Barclay to Blücher, 31 May 1813, *ibid.*, Nl. Gneisenau, 160;
Holleben and Caemmerer, *Frühjahrsfeldzuges 1813*, II:277–78. Lieven, in *Russia
Against Napoleon*, 325–26, claims that, aside from finding the position at
Schweidnitz unacceptable, Barclay de Tolly's difficulties in feeding the troops
had become acute. Even in times of peace, Upper Silesia depended on food
supplies from Poland. Kutuzov had implored Stein to establish food magazines
in eastern Saxony, but nothing had been done. Lieven maintains that "this was
just part of Stein's overall failure to efficiently mobilize Saxon resources while the
Allies occupied the kingdom." In addition, the Russians could not requisition
food in Prussian territory and the Russian intendant-general informed Barclay
that the Prussians had provided next to nothing.

43 SHAT, C² 145: Marmont to Berthier, 31 May 1813. According to Lanrezac in
*Lützen*, 263, this incident shows "the degree of moral lassitude that had overcome
our generals, forced to operate continuously with a small cavalry of poor quality
against an enemy with a good horse, twice as large, [and] ready to swoop down
unexpectedly on our troops. The war in the dark was calculated to cause nervous-
ness among commanders of large units."

44 *CN*, No. 20066, XXV:337–38; SHAT, C¹⁷ 178: Berthier to Marmont, Ney, Souham, and Macdonald, 1 June 1813; Odeleben, *A Circumstantial Narrative*,
I:126–27.

45 Lanrezac, *Lützen*, 263–64.

46 SHAT, C¹⁷ 178: Berthier to Victor, Neumarkt, 3 June 1813.

47 See Leggiere, *Napoleon and Berlin*, 78–88.

48 Bogdanovich, *Geschichte des Krieges*, I:107; Lieven, *Russia Against Napoleon*,
326; Gneisenau to Hardenberg, Rothschloß, 3 June 1813, Stadt- und Landes-
bibliothek Dortmund, Nr. 12241.

49 Volkonsky to Blücher, 2 June 1813, GStA PK, VI HA Rep. 92 Nl. Gneisenau,
Nr. 160; Disposition signed by Diebitsch, 3 June 1813, *ibid.*; Holleben and
Caemmerer, *Frühjahrsfeldzuges 1813*, II:279–80. According to Müffling, *Aus
meinem Leben*, 49–50, these Landwehr troops received some of the 20,000
Austrian muskets that lacked touchholes. Until the touchholes could be bored,
a process that would take four weeks, Yorck's militia battalions received pikes.

50 Yorck to Knesebeck, Jordansmühle, 4 June 1813, quoted in Droysen, *Yorck*,
II:98–100; Müffling, *Aus meinem Leben*, 51.

51 Quoted in Pertz and Delbrück, *Gneisenau*, II:652.

52 Gneisenau to Hardenberg, Rothschloß (Piotrowice), in Pertz and Delbrück,
*Gneisenau*, II:652.

53 Knesebeck to Blücher, 28 May 1813 and Knesebeck to Gneisenau, 29 May and
17 June 1813, GStA PK, VI HA Rep. 92 Nl. Gneisenau, Nrs. 18 and 23; Steffens,
*Adventures*, 107–08; Pertz and Delbrück, *Gneisenau*, II:654–55.

54 Diebitsch to Blücher, 3 June 1813, GStA PK, VI HA Rep. 92 Nl. Gneisenau, Nr. 160.

55 Gneisenau to Frederick William, Rothschloß, 4 June 1813, GStA PK, VI HA
Rep. 92 Nl. Gneisenau, Nr. 16; Pertz and Delbrück, *Gneisenau*, II:659.

56 Cathcart explained why the Austrians needed so much time to mobilize: "The
Austrian army had been suffered, perhaps from necessity, perhaps from policy, to

decline at this time to the lowest and most inefficient condition. From the peculiar fiscal system of its component states, as well as from their geographical position which permits little foreign commerce at any time, and none in time of war, the Austrian empire had not the means possessed by commercial nations of raising those necessary supplies that are required for the instant organization of an army. It was found that an army of 60,000 men could not be brought into the field before the end of July, if indeed it could be organized so soon." See Cathcart, *Commentaries*, 177.

57 Dominic Lieven lauds the tsar's conduct: "In this week of supreme crisis, as his whole strategy threatened to fall apart, Alexander showed outstanding leadership. Amidst Austrian prevarication, Prussian hysteria, and the griping of his own generals he remained admirably calm, reasonable, and optimistic about final victory." Although the German sources offer no confirmation, Stewart claims that Alexander agreed to remain in Silesia: "The object, at present, was to gain time; to delay the enemy, by making a demonstration of fighting, but still not to give him battle. A camp was taken up in front of Schweidnitz; but if the enemy showed a disposition to attack it, the intention had been to move to the entrenched camp at Neiße, which had been some time preparing, and to have assembled all the Landwehr and irregular forces at Glatz, and there, if pressed, to have made a stand." Wilson wrote on 29 May that "the army is to fall back upon Neiße in case of the enemy's advance with his whole army. At Neiße we shall have a strong corps and the aid of the Landwehr, etc., which is now assembled at Glatz." See Müffling, *Aus meinem Leben*, 52–53; Pertz and Delbrück, *Gneisenau*, II:661; Lieven, *Russia Against Napoleon*, 326; Stewart, *Narrative*, 56–57; Wilson, *Private Diary*, II:36.

58 Add MSS, 20111, 31: Lowe to Bunbury, Reichenbach, 6 June 1813.

59 Langeron, *Mémoires*, 198.

60 Freytag-Loringhoven, *Aufklärung und Armeeführung*, 1–2. Müffling, in *Aus meinem Leben*, 54, claims credit for suggesting to the sovereigns that the imperials be forced to evacuate Breslau. The text of the armistice can be found in Höpfner, "Darstellung," 1843:26.

61 On the right wing, Blücher posted his main body at Strehlen, the vanguard between Wiltschau (Wilkszyn) and Peltschütz (Pełczyce), and outposts from Kanth east to Oltaschin (Ołtaszyn), south of Breslau. East of Blücher, Sacken's 9,000 men and Schuler's 6,000 Prussians camped at Ohlau on the Oder; the former's advance guard reached Kattern with forward posts extending from Oltaschin to the Oder. East of the Oder, one detachment held Hundsfeld (Psie Pole) and a second north of Breslau at Wohlau (Wołów); forward posts followed the Oder downstream from Breslau to Steinau. Thirty miles east of Glogau, Wintzingerode's detachment of 9,000 men held Leschnau (Leszno) with garrisons at Fraustadt (Wschowa), Schlichtingsheim (Szlichtyngowa), Herrnstadt (Wąsosz), and Trachenberg (Żmigród); an outpost chain continued north along the Oder from Steinau to Crossen (Krosno Odrzańskie). South of the army, the infantry of the Russo-Prussian Guard and Reserve accompanied the monarchs to Reichenbach (Dzierżoniów); the cavalry and Guard Horse Guns quartered between Grottkau (Grodków) and Falkenberg (Niemodlin), and the Reserve Artillery between Frankenstein and Münsterberg (Ziębice).

62  The rest of the Grande Armée took the following positions: in Silesia, Mortier's Young Guard cantoned at Polkwitz (Polkowice) south of Glogau; II Corps northwest of Glogau at Grüneberg (Wilkanowko); III at Liegnitz; IV at Sprottau (Szprotawa); V at Goldberg; VI at Thomaswaldau; XI at Friedeberg (Mirsk) and Greiffenberg (Gryfów Śląski); and Sébastiani's II Cavalry Corps at Niedersiegersdorf (Podbrzezie Dolne). Elsewhere, Davout's I Corps held Hamburg; Reynier's VII camped at Görlitz; Poniatowski's VIII was en route to Zittau through Austria; Rapp's X garrisoned Danzig; Oudinot's XII held Cottbus; and Latour-Maubourg's I Cavalry Corps quartered at Sagan, fifty miles west of Cottbus and forty miles north of Görlitz. See Plotho, *Der Krieg*, I:252–55; Mikhailovsky-Danilevsky, *Denkwürdigkeiten*, 115; Gneisenau, *Blücher*, 140; Bogdanovich, *Geschichte des Krieges*, I:186–89; Fain, *Manuscrit de mil huit cent treize*, II:4.

63  Langeron, *Mémoires*, 198–99.

64  Bowden, *Napoleon's Grande Armée of 1813*, 112.

65  *CN*, No. 20070, XXV:347.

# Assessment

Including Prussia among the five great powers is misleading. Based on its paltry resources, small population, and indefensible frontiers, the kingdom legitimately stood as the most powerful of the second-tier states such as Spain, Portugal, Naples, Bavaria, and the Ottoman Empire. The Prussians themselves recognized this fact. After Frederick the Great's War of Bavarian Succession (1778–1779) against Austria, Prussia did not want to risk a unilateral conflict against another great power. Prussia's deference to Great Britain, Austria, Russia, and France became quite apparent just two years after Frederick's death. In 1788, his nephew and successor, Frederick William II, assumed the status of junior partner in the Anglo-Prussian effort to end the Patriot Revolt in the Netherlands. In 1792, the alliance with Austria during the War of the First Coalition again relegated Prussia to junior status, as did Russia's orchestration of the Second and Third Partitions of Poland in 1793 and 1795 respectively. The situation did not change under Frederick William III. During the 1803 reorganization of Germany, the Prussians were quite content to have Napoleon to take the lead. In 1805, Alexander goaded Frederick William toward war with Napoleon but within the security of a multipower coalition. Prussian participation in the War of the Third Coalition did not come to pass, yet the War of the Fourth Coalition in the following year clearly demonstrated to the Prussians that they could not stand alone against another great power. Alexander did come to Frederick William's aid, but not in time. This became the crucial question of Prussia's pro-Russian party in 1811: could and would the tsar arrive in time to save Prussia from total annihilation? How much trust could the Prussians place in the timely support of Great Britain – which had committed its small army to Iberia – and Austria, now bound to Napoleon through marriage? Scharnhorst believed that only a miracle could save Prussia.

Yet miracles did occur. According to Gneisenau, when Prussia went to war with France in 1806, "there was no Spain, no victorious English general, and no vengeful Austria. Now the Russians are formidably armed, Prussia is in position to field an army larger and better than that which started the [previous] war, if we only have the will to do so; fermentation is brewing among the warlike nations, the morale of the French army is foundering." In the end, Frederick William refused "to attempt something without too cautiously computing the probability of success," as Gneisenau explained. Blücher, Gneisenau, and other anti-French war hawks who lobbied for a national revolt in 1811 failed to consider the estimated 165,000 imperial troops that ringed Prussia. From bases along the lower Elbe and the Oder, in Saxony, Westphalia, the Grand Duchy of Warsaw, and at Magdeburg and Danzig, French forces could have taken advantage of the imperial military highways to inundate Prussia and converge on Berlin within seventy-two hours. Prussian communication throughout the truncated kingdom could easily have been severed by the numerous French garrisons. Imperial forces in the Grand Duchy of Warsaw needed only one short march to cut Prussia in half by separating Silesia from Brandenburg, while the forces at Stettin could master the Oder crossings to separate Brandenburg from West Prussia. With Davout "the Terrible" at Hamburg, I have to agree with William Shanahan's observation that "under these circumstances it was fortunate that the plans for a national uprising were never carried out." Moreover, in 1811, many observers believed Napoleon would eventually invade Russia with no more than 200,000 men. Considering the size of the army that Napoleon assembled in East Prussia and Poland in June of 1812 for the invasion – almost triple this size – Frederick William's caution was justified.[1]

Like people in most of Europe, Frederick William did not believe Napoleon would lose in Russia. This made his decision to placate the French emperor at the expense of his own relationship with the tsar more palatable. Fortunately for the king, Alexander did not hold him accountable for his double-dealing in 1811. Perhaps Alexander placed little hope in winning the upcoming war to such an extent that his troops actually would reach Central Europe by the end of 1812. Claims of a secret agreement between Alexander and Frederick William that allowed the Prussians "to do in Russia only what honor required of them" fall short as an explanation for the tsar's beneficent treatment of the Prussian monarch. On a personal level, Alexander liked Frederick William and showed him more respect than his actions warranted. On a geopolitical level, Alexander needed the Prussian army to assist his exhausted survivors of the harsh 1812 campaign; otherwise the Russian effort to defeat Napoleon would have ended at the Vistula. Wise enough to recognize that merely driving Napoleon from Russia would do little for the state's long-term national security, Alexander committed himself to liberating Central Europe from French control. Just as Napoleon believed that defending the Rhine required France to control first the Elbe and then the Vistula, Alexander wished to guarantee the Niemen by pushing the French back to the Rhine.[2]

Although Alexander's vision and foresight boded well for Frederick William, no Prussian statesman or military official could assure the king that the Russians would persevere until the complete restoration of Prussia. Alexander's well-known desire for Polish territory added to the king's uncertainty. Very similar to 1805, the Prussians hoped to mediate between France and Russia in late 1812. We again see Frederick William engaged in diplomatic maneuvering that led to double-dealing and, ultimately, desperation. Caught between Russia and France and with Austria flippantly noncommittal, the king did not know where to turn. Napoleon's refusal to offer the Prussians an attractive alliance package certainly strengthened the voices of the pro-Russian party but Alexander's designs on Poland gave equal strength to the pro-French party. After failing to gain an advantageous diplomatic settlement with either France or Russia, Frederick William gradually realized that mere negotiations would not restore Prussia to its pre-1806 status nor liberate the kingdom from French control. As it became clear that he would have to fight for either restoration or liberation or both, Frederick William returned to the issue of deciding between France and Russia. At that point, the Prussian army took matters into its own hands when Yorck signed the Convention of Tauroggen, which "became a symbol of national independence and freedom from foreign bondage."[3] Thus, the resurrected Prussian military establishment forced a patriotic war on the king and determined that it would be more than a war of liberation: it would be a war of revenge.

Alexander's concessions to Prussia regarding Polish territory cleared the way for the Russo-Prussian alliance. Scharnhorst's intervention and excellent rapport with the Russians facilitated both the political accord and the military arrangements that followed. Although the attitude that reigned at Kutuzov's headquarters proved detrimental to Prussian hopes of a powerful offensive in April 1813, Scharnhorst worked ceaselessly to keep the alliance together and coordinate strategy and operations suitable for defeating Napoleon. In the latter regard, Napoleon's continued numerical superiority over the Allies combined with Kutuzov's lethargy to paralyze Allied operations in April. Moreover, Nesselrode decisively persuaded Alexander to reject calls by Stein and other Russian advisors to ignite a people's war in Germany against French rule.

Old and ill, Kutuzov impeded the march of the Russian army with every means available to him. Although believing that the Russians should play only an auxiliary role, he found himself forced to orchestrate a Russian-led war for the liberation of Central Europe. In this case, he viewed the contest as a Russian war and as a favor to the conquered peoples living under French tyranny. Consequently, all resources, including Prussia and its army, should be placed at the disposal of the Russians. Kutuzov also clearly recognized the exhausted condition of the Russian army. In addition to the great exertions of the previous year, the Russians overran most of the Grand Duchy of Warsaw and liberated Prussia by mid February 1813, but the cost was high. Of the main army at Kalisch, barely 15,000 men mustered on 2 April to be reviewed by the visiting Frederick William.

Regardless of their individual attitudes toward the war, all Russian planners acknowledged the extreme distance that separated the army from its heartland. An extended Russian line of communication could be threatened from numerous directions. To secure it, the French-occupied fortresses on the Vistula and the Oder needed to be blockaded, which in turn caused valid concerns over the effect of strategic consumption on frontline combat strength. Eugene's strong position at the Elbe posed an indirect threat, as did Poniatowski's corps in the southern reaches of the Grand Duchy of Warsaw. Ongoing negotiations with Vienna misled the Allies into thinking that they would soon be joined by legions of Austrian soldiers, thus eliminating a sense of urgency. For all of these reasons, weeks passed while Kutuzov remained at Kalisch. By the time of the king's visit on 2 April, illness prevented the field-marshal from mounting his horse. Frederick William awarded him the order of the Black Eagle and presented the Russian commander a cigarette case valued at 20,000 rubles. He sent Hardenberg to thank him as the savior of Prussia.[4]

Meanwhile, dissatisfaction with Kutuzov's leadership mounted at Blücher's and Wittgenstein's respective headquarters. From Dessau, Wittgenstein wanted to take the narrow passes of the Harz to prevent Eugene from uniting with Napoleon. "I was convinced of a victory," Wittgenstein later said to Mikhailovsky-Danilevsky, "because such a spirit animated my troops that nothing appeared impossible for them to achieve."[5] The inability to commence offensive operations against Eugene at the beginning of April lay solely in Kutuzov's failure to keep the Russian main army three marches behind Blücher and Wittgenstein: one of the chief tenets of the "Arrangement." Although the viceroy would probably have avoided the attack, an operation against him could have been attempted in early April with the combined forces of Blücher and Wittgenstein had Tormasov been closer. Boyen suggests that, had Tormasov gone to Dresden with Blücher and then pushed a division to Chemnitz, the operations of Blücher and Wittgenstein could have achieved a much wider scope. According to Boyen, they could have united and exploited their numerical superiority to over-whelm Eugene on the battlefield if he stood his ground or forced him to retreat miles from the theater. With this victory, Blücher and Wittgenstein could have disrupted the imperial mobilization at Erfurt, through which passed a considerable part of Napoleon's new army. Finally, the future

Prussian field-marshal and war minister speculates that the extension of operations by conventional Allied forces west of the Saale would have significantly rallied German public opinion in favor of resisting the French.[6]

At the battle of Lützen, the new Prussian army proved to be a worthy opponent in terms of combat-effectiveness. However, Allied leadership at the top fell just short of miserable on this day. Not only did the monarchs join Wittgenstein, but they also followed him wherever he went. They remained with him the entire day, adversely impacting his demeanor and independence. Stewart justified this behavior: "at this moment the emperor of Russia's presence in the field was a matter of no ordinary importance, as it served to allay certain feelings of annoyance that appeared among some of the older officers of the Russian army, in consequence of the nomination of Count Wittgenstein as commander in chief upon the death of Kutuzov." Yet Campbell explained in his report to Bunbury that "the emperor and king were in every part of the field of battle ... It might animate the troops, but this was not wanting, and their constant attendance near General Wittgenstein, questions, and messages, must have embarrassed any commander in chief. They at first posted themselves with him on the heights but half an hour after the action commenced he rode away, and they continued to follow him." Alexander, who received the reports and issued the orders, assumed his coveted role as Allied generalissimo during the course of the battle, and thus eclipsed Wittgenstein. Moreover, without warning, Alexander suddenly would ride into the heaviest fire – either to show his courage or to give the appearance of the omniscient field commander – compelling Wittgenstein to drop everything, give chase, and bring him back to safety. At times, no one commanded or everyone commanded: the tsar, Auvray, or Diebitsch, although Müffling asserts that Wittgenstein exerted the least influence. The Prussian crown prince related to his sister that, as night fell, "neither the tsar, nor Wittgenstein, nor Blücher could be found."[7]

Regardless of whether Alexander or Wittgenstein issued the orders at Lützen, the steps taken by Allied Headquarters bore the stamp of half-measures. Several historians of the various General Staffs, such as Bogdanovich, Lanrezac, Maude, Caemmerer, Friederich, and Unger, tend to be more forgiving of Wittgenstein because of his difficult position at Allied Headquarters. Yet other writers, especially German civilians, were not as lenient. "Wittgenstein did not know how to use the superiority of 438 cannon against 350," moans Droysen, "of 15,000 excellent cavalry troopers against the 5,000 nags of postillions and gendarmes. He allowed the valor of the Prussian youth to be bled to death in those struggles for the villages, which only gave the enemy time to concentrate for the decisive blows." Delbrück contends that the "flower of the land died in the quadrilateral." In their view, the army should have conducted a general operation instead of being divided for small actions and then being completely absorbed in attacking and defending villages. To give the cavalry a chance to play a greater role, Wittgenstein should have chosen a more open stretch of terrain with fewer obstacles. Not only did Wittgenstein allow himself to be consumed by gaining possession of the four villages, but he completely lost sight of his options. In addition, he became distracted with business, mainly staff work, rather than the leadership of the battle, and the tsar's antics did not help.[8]

Accepting the argument that Souham's presence at Großgörschen prevented Wittgenstein from implementing his envelopment, he should have at least attempted to exploit the tactical advantage that favored the Allies on 2 May. Blücher's entire corps should have been committed in the first attack at noon to take the quadrilateral, while Yorck and Berg simultaneously advanced on Starsiedel. Prince William's and Wintzingerode's cavalry should have formed the first reserve; the Russian Guard and Reserve should have advanced in extreme haste: cavalry and horse artillery at a trot. Had this occurred, Ney's individual divisions could have been smashed while Yorck and Berg ensured that Marmont and Bertrand contributed nothing substantial to the battle. Odeleben contends that, "if the Prussians had succeeded in penetrating for half an hour longer, the whole line of the French army on its march between Weißenfels and Leipzig would have been broken, and their [the Russo-Prussian] cavalry might have acted with great success on its rear, in the direction of Weißenfels." Bogdanovich essentially agrees:

> Around noon, when the Allies were in complete readiness for battle in the vicinity of Ney's corps, they should have attacked the four villages that were situated south of Lützen and occupied by the enemy with the entire infantry of Blücher, Berg, Yorck, and Eugen of Württemberg, numbering more than 40,000 men, and the entire cavalry, around 10,000 strong, should have advanced on Starsiedel to envelop the enemy. This cavalry would have made the defense of the villages difficult for Ney's corps and would have delayed the approach of French reinforcements, which could not arrive before 2:00 or 3:00 P.M.; by then, the fate of the battle would have been decided by Ney's defeat. Instead of this, the Allies limited themselves to a gradual attack and utilized insufficient forces while they fed one brigade after another into the engagement; the cavalry stood as if on the parade ground and opened a cannonade that did nothing but exhaust the ammunition. Even after Napoleon had received time to unite superior forces, the Allied cavalry, which was very superior to that of the enemy, could have delayed and impeded the march of the French infantry. Instead, it remained in a defensive posture that did not at all correspond to the spirit of this branch of the service.

With the seven fresh infantry divisions of the Guard, XI, and V Corps – almost 40,000 men – still at his disposal, Napoleon possessed formidable combat power. For the Allies, determining the right moment to disengage and end the battle would have been the greatest challenge if Wittgenstein had ordered a general attack. Faced by an opponent such as the emperor, this may have been too much to expect from Wittgenstein; it was certainly too much to expect from Alexander, who according to all accounts made the major decisions on this day.[9]

Wintzingerode's inexplicable conduct warranted the strongest censure: the continuous exposure of his and Dolffs's cavalry to French artillery while remaining completely inactive led to the loss of one-third of that arm. "The Allied cavalry, particularly the Prussians," reported Campbell, "remained in situations quite open to shot and shells, without any apparent necessity for it." "The king was on the field," commented Wilson, "and behaved very well. I had two or three opportunities of seeing him, and I lamented to him the unnecessary exposure of his brave horsemen, which he also regretted." A few days later, the tsar explained to Cathcart that his refusal to order a general advance with the cavalry early in the battle "had arisen from reluctance to engage that valuable body of heavy cavalry so early in the campaign; and though the attack could not have failed to produce important results at that time, he thought it might have been attended with severe losses that could not easily have been repaired."[10]

Although written at the end of the month, Gneisenau's assessment of the failures at Großgörschen provides a succinct enumeration of the mistakes made on 2 May. Obviously biased, his evaluation nevertheless sheds important light on the feelings and perceptions that reigned at Blücher's headquarters:

> Regarding our retreat from the battle of Lützen, you will be astonished. The French likewise withdrew in the night. The battle was indecisive. The causes for this lack of success were: (1) the idea of a battle was good, the plan was poor.[11] Instead of charging the surprised enemy with columns, we delayed too long with formalities and troop deployments. (2) Due to personal circumstances, Miloradovich was not summoned to move up.[12] I had suggested directing his 12,000 men and 100 guns in the direction of Weißenfels, where he would have appeared directly in the enemy's left flank. They did not follow my advice. (3) We had only half as much infantry as the enemy, thus we could only renew the combat with slighter numbers and not as often as the enemy. Bravery had to replace numbers; but the battle cost us Prussians alone more than 8,000 men. (4) There was a shortage of ammunition – not on our part, but the Russians'. At least that is what Prince Jachmil [Iashvili], commander of the Russian artillery, claimed and because of this urged the order to retreat, an order that nobody wanted to give![13] (5) Our line of retreat was on our right wing. They [the Russians] feared being cut off and because of this did not want to fight to the last extreme. These are the reasons for our retreat. I was on the battlefield around 8:00 A.M. on the following morning at our outermost cavalry posts. The deepest quiet reigned. Not one man of the

enemy was to be seen; but our infantry, Russian and Prussian, including the majority of the cavalry, was ready.[14]

In the end, the battle of Lützen/Großgörschen must be viewed in terms similar to the dichotomy created by the French and German names of the struggle, which in turn allows the rendering of operational and tactical judgments. Operationally, the battle of Lützen again demonstrated Napoleon's supremacy. His ability to move units to the battlefield to deliver maximum combat power remained unrivaled. The experience of the Russians and the zeal of the Prussians serve only to accentuate the brilliance of Napoleon's victory. Not the inexperienced Austrians of 1796 or 1801 overwhelmed by Bonaparte's highly mobile, destructive form of warfare, the Allies of 1813 had few excuses for falling victim to Napoleon's proficient generalship. Indeed on 2 May, the Sixth Coalition came within hours of being destroyed by a double envelopment that would have been so crushing in terms of numbers that it would have mattered little that Napoleon did not have Murat at the head of a potent cavalry to pursue. No pursuit would have been needed. Perhaps it was a stroke of good luck that Blücher and Yorck had collided that morning. Had the columns marched smoothly and Wittgenstein started the attack five hours earlier, Napoleon would have had a full day to move Macdonald and Bertrand to the battlefield.[15]

Tactically, the battle of Großgörschen provides further proof of parity in terms of combat-effectiveness between the imperial soldiers of the Grande Armée and their adversaries. Without doubt, Lützen proved that the young imperial soldiers, who in no way rivaled the *grognards* of 1805–1807, provided a capable instrument in the hands of their master. Yet Maude maintains that the emperor had no reason "to be pleased with the fighting quality which his men had shown. He actually engaged three corps, about 60,000 men, and had expended one [Ney's III] completely and, but for his arrival in person on the scene with the Guard, there could be no doubt that both VI and III Corps, together with any other corps in the army except the Guard, would have been completely defeated under any of his marshals." Conversely, the Allies in general, but the Prussians specifically, impressed Napoleon with their tactical and organizational improvements. His oft quoted statement that "the animals have learned something" indicates the emperor's reluctant admission that his adversaries had closed the gap in terms of tactical proficiency. More importantly for the Prussians, the self-sacrificing courage with which they fought provided the true significance of the battle. In the protracted street fighting, the Prussian army recovered its confidence, pride, and perhaps even its hubris. In his after-action report to the tsar, Wittgenstein attests that "the villages of Kleingörschen and Rahna, as well as Großgörschen, were captured in remarkable feats of gallantry." "No troops could show more impetuous courage or more ready good-will altogether," noted Wilson, "but no troops could have to contend with greater disadvantages from the want of proper direction."[16]

In this regard, Blücher did not escape criticism. According to Boyen, he earned a reproach for his direct attack on Großgörschen at the opening of the struggle instead of seeking to envelop the village. Had Blücher combined a flank attack with his frontal assault, the Prussians would have sustained far fewer casualties. Nevertheless, Souham still would have been able to regroup at Kleingörschen and Rahna. Moreover, the Floßgraben and Kleingörschen prevented Blücher from making an attempt to move around Souham's left. Of course, decisive results could have been achieved if William and Wintzingerode had also advanced to the hill north of Starsiedel – where the French eventually formed their grand battery – with Yorck following in reserve. This move would probably have forced Souham to abandon the quadrilateral altogether and withdraw to Lützen, thus opening the plain to the Allied cavalry. In any event, Wittgenstein should have pushed William and Wintzingerode to exert a more decisive role. According to Cathcart:

> The plan of operation determined from our view of the enemy was to attack the village of Großgörschen with artillery and infantry and in the meanwhile to pierce the line to the enemy's right of the villages, with a strong column of cavalry in order to cut off the troops in the villages from support. The remainder of the enemy's line was to be engaged according to circumstances by the corps opposed to it. The cavalry of the Prussian reserve, to whose lot this attack fell, presented themselves and supported their movements with great gallantry but the shower of grape shot and musketry to which they were exposed on reaching the hollow way made it [impossible].[17]

Thus, we return to Wittgenstein, whom Boyen does not paint very favorably as a battlefield commander on this day. Commenting on Wittgenstein's failure to be more aggressive in the opening stages of the battle, particularly with regard to utilizing Wintzingerode's cavalry, Boyen insists that the Allied commander in chief failed to grasp the importance of such a movement:

> He bravely rode around on a bold horse, was pleased to the very bottom of his heart that the soldiers were fighting so bravely and said (literally) with a cheerful face that, when the battle was won he, as the commanding general, had the right according to the statutes of the Order of St. George to nominate the number of knights to the tsar and that the latter would surely award the first class of that order. These adverse circumstances must be permanently kept in view to get a true picture of the course of the battle and the conduct of the troops. There was in fact no general *Schlachtlenkung* [battle leadership].

In his report to Bunbury, Campbell hit on this key question of Allied leadership not only during the battle of Lützen but for the entire campaign up to that point:

> It is difficult to imagine the plan in passing the Elbe, or in the attack on the enemy's force, unless we were determined to go on. To go as far as the Elster, and when concentrated near them, to make an attack on a small party in advance of their center, and then retreat, seems unaccountable. There was no disposition for a general battle, or a decided trial of strength; and I do not believe there was any preparation for following them if they had been forced from their position, or had chosen to retire from it. Why persevere in the unequal contest for the villages? Why expose the cavalry the whole day to a cannonade? Why not retire them out of reach of the cannon, or attack the enemy's right with them, and try to turn it?[18]

Boyen penned this passage twenty-five years after the fact on 22 July 1838. However, in May 1813, the Prussians felt no different. For the sake of Allied unity, they pushed their derogatory judgment on Wittgenstein's management of the battle into the background. Although accepting that the situation had demanded a retreat, the circumstances behind it did not sit well with the Prussians. Muted for the sake of unity, Prussian anger and resentment festered over Russian leadership of the war. Wittgenstein and his confidants suffered bitter censure within the Russian army as well. Neither Wittgenstein nor his chief assistants, Auvray and Diebitsch, were ethnic Russians – a fact that their detractors aired in the tsar's presence. According to Stewart, "Count Wittgenstein ... did not possess the general confidence of the Russian army, perhaps because he was not a Russian. They have [the] most confidence in their own native good fortune and ability."

Conversely, it mattered little to the Prussians that Diebitsch, the son of a Prussian general, had been born in Silesia or that Auvray, while of French descent, had been born in Dresden and was considered a Saxon nobleman, or that Wittgenstein's father also had been a Prussian general. To them, the faulty leadership of Wittgenstein's "Russian" regime was part of a larger problem posed by an alliance that rendered Prussia a junior partner. Bound by the king's acceptance of Russia's superior status in the relationship, the Prussians felt the sting of their subservience even more deeply as they perceived the Russians taking full advantage of the situation. Droysen claims the confidential sources that were made available to him on this subject "do not allow me to provide more than these general views that were expressed at that time." Mikhailovsky-Danilevsky offers a Russian perspective on the relationship between king and tsar that sheds light on Prussian frustration: "The exalted patriotism that inspired the Prussians can be compared only with the steadfast coolness of their king, who never gave the slightest impression that he doubted the favorable outcome of the campaign, and although his troops made up almost half of the active army he left them at the unrestricted disposal of his crowned friend; in everything he trusted Alexander's view." "The Prussians were in much the same relation to their allies," observes Stewart, "as the Portuguese in the Peninsula were to the British; and the king, depressed both from public and private misfortune, lived much secluded with his aides-de-camp and staff."[19]

Gneisenau bluntly informed Hardenberg that "the preparations for the battle were not good. One [Wittgenstein] did not direct General Miloradovich to the battlefield, but instead to Zeitz. Many troop units did not see action or were not committed at the right time. We wanted to envelop the enemy but since our attack misfired we found ourselves enveloped and our line of retreat threatened. Therefore, one [Wittgenstein] retreated across the Elster, Pleiße, and Mulde." According to Campbell: "The Prussians are extremely enraged against Wittgenstein for sacrificing so many of them." Nostitz provides poignant insight to Blücher's thoughts over the situation:

> Since the beginning of the campaign, Blücher had no favorable opinion of Wittgenstein's talents as a commander but he, the senior general, was placed under his orders. The battle of Lützen, in which the Prussian army did everything that courage and perseverance demanded to achieve a victory, had been lost and of course, as the general maintained, only because of the poor dispositions of the commander in chief and the inconsiderate inactivity on this day of entire units of the Russian army, namely the great majority of the cavalry. The general himself had been wounded, likewise his friend General Scharnhorst, who just saw himself forced to leave the army. The beautiful hopes to baptize the War of Liberation with a glorious deed were frustrated and the Fatherland again had to pay the price of all the horrors and devastations that are the inseparable companion of every theater of war.
>
> All of this filled the general with anger and vexation. The conviction that better leadership and better utilization of the available combat power would have made the defeat of the enemy unavoidable led to even more bitterness in his relationship with General Wittgenstein. Under his leadership, Blücher saw no salvation for the Allied cause and would have loudly expressed this conviction had he not been restrained by the concern of maintaining internal harmony at such a critical moment. Colonel Both of the Prussian General Staff was assigned to Wittgenstein's headquarters: an officer who had neither the confidence nor the favor of that general and thus had no influence. The situation continued along with the circumstances that could cause the open break that all painstakingly sought to avoid.[20]

Prussian dissatisfaction mounted after Wittgenstein decided to abandon the Elbe. However, his plan to combine a strong defense with a powerful counterattack should have brought the Allies success at Bautzen.

The general position corresponded well to other Russian battles: Austerlitz, Eylau, and Borodino, where the Russian troops performed just as well if not better than their adversaries. Russian commanders preferred strong, fortified positions from which they could effectively employ massive numbers of guns. "At Bautzen," comments Müffling, "busy preparations were being made for choosing a strong position ... and here the differences of principles between the Russian and Prussian armies first came to light. In contending with Napoleon, the Russians trusted not only in the system of masses, but also in lumping together all their corps and armies to form such masses. At Borodino they stood ten echelons deep, but did not attribute the inglorious outcome of the battle to this disposition." Thus, Wittgenstein chose a formidable position and based his battle plan on the conviction that only one enemy army would attack his front. A more discerning eye will notice that his disposition extended the various corps in a long line that lacked cohesion and fatally minimized the opportunity for mutual support. Moreover, the extension of the right wing robbed the Allies of a substantial reserve while Alexander squandered the remaining reserves on the left wing.[21]

Yet again a faulty disposition combined with Russian desires to recreate Borodino to undermine the Coalition's effort at Bauzten. Although bastion-like, the Allied position left much to be desired in two critical areas: overextension and unit placement. Understanding that his army was overextended, Wittgenstein hoped to overcome this disadvantage by employing either the Russian Cuirassier Corps or the flanking movement of neighboring corps to support any threatened point. However, the corps in the main position remained separated from each other: Gorchakov and Yorck by a considerable gap; Yorck and Blücher by a stretch of water and a wide, swampy marsh; and Blücher and Barclay by ponds. As Gneisenau explains:

> General Blücher's position was on the heights near Kreckwitz and Niedergurig, having before him the valley of the Spree, full of meadows [and] intersected with ponds; his front was, without doubt, difficult to access, but the extension of his line to three miles from Kreckwitz by Niedergurig to Malschwitz, can be considered much too large for only 18,000 men; and being a mile and a half from the main army, if he met with a repulse, he would be obliged to retreat through two defiles over the boggy sides of the stream to reach the main body; therefore, he could not spare any considerable reserve, nor, in arranging his dispositions, post fewer than 12,000 men in his front. General Barclay de Tolly had to defend a point of the general position that afforded some good natural bulwarks of defense but he was surrounded by woods, and at a greater distance from the center than General Blücher.[22]

With the interior movements of the troops obstructed, the various Allied corps that were thinly stretched along the front line had to rely on themselves instead of mutual support. In actuality, Wittgenstein's disposition limited his corps commanders to repulsing enemy attacks through tactical strikes or waging an almost exclusively passive defensive. Again, Wittgenstein appeared to at least recognize or even embrace this outcome and relied on the Borodino stratagem, building numerous redoubts, fleches, and entrenched batteries. According to Hudson Lowe, "The battle was not general and very few columns or lines of troops were opposed to each other's fire for a considerable time in any direction. On the whole, Bonaparte may be said to have rather maneuvered the combined armies out of their position than to have fought them out of it. Had he made his advance in the center, he would probably have been defeated, but the position he assumed baffled the designs that were laid for him and made all the movements of his opponents subservient to his own."[23]

The intelligence that revealed the approach of Ney's task force required quick and drastic measures. Wittgenstein made a bold attempt to meet this threat head on, allocating almost 25 percent of his combat power. Yet as Mikhailovsky-Danilevsky notes: "the engagement of Königswartha ended without having any decisive influence on the situation of the two opposing armies." After the tsar hijacked command of the Allied army, decision-making foundered at the decisive moment, and Müffling shares some of the blame. As much as Blücher and Gneisenau would have protested, the order to retreat should have been issued on the night of the 20th. "But since the Russo-Prussian army had allowed the majority of the enemy troops to cross the Spree and deploy in battle order," comments Bogdanovich, "while Ney threatened to envelop the Allied right wing with three corps, nothing else remained for them to do except either withdraw or accept battle in a very unfavorable situation. Barclay advised withdrawing to Görlitz, taking a position there, and then withdrawing further under the appearance of a renewed battle. In this way, they could have won two days and spared the lives of several thousand brave warriors who were sacrificed on the second day of the battle of Bautzen."[24]

Admittedly, hindsight is perfect, but Ney's approach eliminated the component of the powerful counterattack from Wittgenstein's plan, leaving only a strong defense. No one in the Allied camp should have assumed that Napoleon would break himself in frontal assaults on Bautzen to achieve a tactical victory as he did at Borodino. Convinced that the danger posed by Ney to the right wing would be contained by Barclay's "15,000 men," Alexander remained fixated on the threat to his left. With few reserves remaining because of overextension, Allied Headquarters could do little to influence the outcome of the battle. Although inaccurate concerning Napoleon, Mikhailovsky-Danilevsky's comments hold true for the Allies: "Of all the battles in which I found myself, I know not one in which the main leaders of the contending armies were so little active and less exposed to danger than Bautzen. Napoleon and Wittgenstein even left for a time to sleep. All arrangements had been communicated to the commanders of the various sectors, who acted as they saw fit, in part, because of the very prolonged position that extended ten miles on which the battle took place."[25]

Like Lützen, the idea for a battle at Bautzen corresponded to Allied military and political needs. "The Allies determined to meet the attack in the position they had chosen," explains Stewart; "having weighed the consequences likely to result from a retreat, even to a more favorable one at Görlitz, against the advantages they now possessed: and they decided wisely, for every retrograde movement, in the present posture of affairs, prejudiced public opinion; and the soldiers had already begun to lose something of their morale." Mikhailovsky-Danilevsky contends that the Allies "waged the battle with the intent of slowing the enemy somewhat and winning time to negotiate with the Austrians, who already favored us. The Prussians particularly sought battle because they wanted to again try fortune before the alliance with Austria and while the theater of war still remained outside Prussian territory."

Although yielding the field, the Allies did not panic after the right wing folded under the weight of Ney's advance. According to Caemmerer, "this preserved the moral superiority of the army even in retreat." "It is just to state that the spirit of the army was unbroken," continues Stewart; "its conduct and firmness continued unaltered and unabated; and more was done for the common cause by fighting the battle than if the Allies had retired from the presence of the enemy without awaiting his onset." Wilson offers a slightly different appraisal: "For very many reasons this battle ought never to have been fought; but it has proved the worth of the troops and, although unsuccessful in its issue, has added a wreath of military glory to the renown of the Allies."[26]

Moral victory aside, the defeat at Bautzen worked against the shaky unity of the Russians and Prussians. "We have much frustration," Gneisenau confided to Münster. "We see our land plundered by our friends no less than by our enemy. One [the Russians] robs our soldier of the supply transports that we procured with care and trouble. Yet I will not complain, only fight. But it is disgusting to see our own wounded being plundered on the battlefield by our friends." He likewise carped about Wittgenstein's incompetence, declaring the hapless Russian general completely unfit to be commander in chief. Blücher became more forceful; many times he informed Allied Headquarters of the threat to his position on the Kreckwitz heights. But from his command post at Jenkwitz, Alexander remained obsessed with the threat he perceived to the Allied left. Wittgenstein begged him to listen to reason. As the French advanced, Frederick William suggested that the left wing send some support to the Kreckwitz. By the time Alexander approved the sending of Yermolov's detachment to support Blücher, the situation had become untenable. "The right wing of the uncommonly long position was enveloped and Barclay de Tolly defeated," recounts Gneisenau. "Now the line of retreat for us Prussians through the village of Preititz was taken. After committing all of our reserves in battle, we were attacked on three sides. We fought in a square, whose only way out was through a single corner. We made the mistake of leaving our troops in this dangerous position for too long. We hovered in this crisis for two hours. The promised help did not come."[27]

The promised help did come but it appeared too late. In his history of the 1813 campaign, Mikhailovsky-Danilevsky claims that "Yermolov arrived just as Blücher, already having twice repulsed the French and defending every inch of ground like a lion, was forced to retreat beyond Kleinbautzen."[28] Mikhailovsky-Danilevsky's memoir of the 1813 campaign differs slightly and does not mention Yermolov by name, yet the Russian eyewitness exonerates Blücher all the same:

> After the most stubborn resistance, Blücher, who had twice repulsed the attacking French, was forced to abandon these hills and withdraw to Purschwitz. He still could have held his position for some time, if General _____, who had been sent to reinforce him had not made a mistake, which one can neither blame on his military experience nor on his courage, which he displayed on many occasions. After receiving the order to rush to Blücher's support, this general approached the Kreckwitz heights during the French attack upon them and remained standing at their feet without informing the Prussian commander of his arrival; when he retreated, the Prussian commander was very surprised to run into his reserve behind him, of whose presence he had not been notified.[29]

Although Blücher blamed the failures of Bautzen on the Russians, his leadership came under fire. Some blamed him for the retreat on the 21st, pointing to the slight number of casualties in his corps among field-grade officers and none among the general officers. Worst yet, Blücher's corps had retreated. Criticism that purportedly found a receptive ear with the tsar labeled Blücher a brave man but not a general. Extremely dissatisfied about Blücher's evacuation of the Kreckwitz hills, Alexander shared the discontent felt by his generals who noted that Miloradovich had not only maintained his position but had even advanced somewhat. Müffling explains that Blücher's "abandonment of the Kreckwitz heights met with severe censure from all around the sovereigns, in which the tsar joined to a degree. Only our king, who tried but failed to get Wittgenstein to shift his left wing toward the center ... fully approved our retreat."[30]

According to Nostitz, "the loss of this second battle of course deeply and powerfully affected the disposition of the general." To make matters worse, "Colonel Both stated his opinion at Allied Headquarters that the premature retreat of the Prussian corps caused the loss of the battle. Both's statement was communicated to Blücher by the staff officer Major Oppen. This allegation angered the general even more because he was convinced that the corps was saved for the king only by using the sole favorable moment for the retreat. He always spoke with the greatest bitterness about this accusation directed against him and at every opportunity conveyed his displeasure to its author." Nostitz contends that "this accusation aroused in the general's heart the suspicion that someone was working to remove him from the command of the army. With pleasure, Count Wittgenstein heard from the mouth of a Prussian officer [Both] that not he and not the Russian army, but Blücher and his corps bore the guilt for the loss of the battle. The tsar felt likewise." Blücher's detractors demanded that the Prussian army be placed in more capable hands. "Even General Yorck expressed this sentiment: that he would harbor no misgivings obeying orders from the much more junior General Kleist and through this he designated the one whom he held to be the worthiest for the command of the army. Blücher heard and knew all of this; it increased his anger, but it did not worry him; he did not think it was possible to lose command."[31]

Blücher's supporters, led by Gneisenau and those who spent the day of the 21st with the general, steadfastly rejected the accusations. "The Allies were not in a condition to assume the offensive against an enemy who had an advantage in numbers of nearly two to one," judges Cathcart, "and whose principal columns were now concentrated toward a focus and brought to bear simultaneously on the corps of General Blücher in his salient and exposed position, with six hours of daylight still remaining. To prolong the affair would only have occasioned an increased loss on both sides in killed and wounded, which the enemy could afford better than the Allies." Müffling recalled that "Blücher with Gneisenau and the officers of the staff remained where the cannon fire was the heaviest and calmly oversaw that we could not prevent ourselves from becoming gradually surrounded. No one doubted that, if we remained there, we would have to defend ourselves to the last man or surrender if the enemy did not attack us because it was impossible to fight our way through." The Russian heavy artillery exhausted its ammunition after engaging at too great a distance. Gradually, "battery after battery dropped off to our rear." Blücher reported his situation to the monarchs and requested help many times. "I shall never forget Blücher's rage," claims Steffens, "when he called furiously for his horse, intending to lead a cavalry charge. The generals, however, surrounded him with entreaties to abstain from such a desperate measure that would risk everything by sacrificing his own life. They restrained the veteran with the utmost difficulty, and a general retreat was ordered." Muffling explains that "after their recent harangues, neither General Blücher nor Gneisenau could order a retreat: at most they could consent to it."

Cathcart disparagingly claims that Blücher delayed executing the order to retreat and "his troops suffered severely in consequence." Yet, by holding out to the last minute, Blücher fixed Napoleon, forcing the emperor to direct his Guard against the Kreckwitz heights rather than pressure the Russians. Had Blücher retreated after Ney took Preititz at 11:00, the marshal would have driven deep into the Allied rear, severing the line of retreat to Weißenberg and fulfilling Napoleon's expectations. The war quite conceivably could have ended with both Alexander and Frederick William being taken prisoner. Fortunately for the Allies, the compulsive Ney could not look away from the Kreckwitz heights. Instead of advancing south and east from Preititz, he turned west between Malschwitz and Preititz to attack Blücher. Never could a mistake have been more fortuitous for an army.[32]

"Yesterday, the troops fought with much stubbornness," wrote Gneisenau in a brief and simple explanation of the battle to Hardenberg, "the position which the Russians wanted to defend was very bad. Barclay de Tolly was defeated and routed in our right flank at Gleina's windmill hill. As a result of this, we Prussians were attacked according to the figure." In the right-hand margin of Gneisenau's letter is a sketch of three sides of a square with thick black lines facing dots on all sides. "The dots are enemy troops. In the end we had to begin the retreat."[33] On the 23rd, he communicated the sentiments of Blücher's headquarters to Hardenberg: "One officer said that the king and the tsar were furious that Blücher's corps had retreated. This news has disgusted the officers of the General Staff and of the headquarters very much. They see themselves harshly treated for their exertions and are in an uproar."[34] A few days later, Gneisenau further developed his defense of Blücher, which likewise served as justification for his own actions:

> Blücher sent various officers to inform [Allied Headquarters] of these circumstances and to request assistance; because he sent a third of his corps to support the right wing [Barclay] it was impossible for him to hold the villages and the Kreckwitz heights with so little infantry for any length of time. But, because Blücher knew that the commanding general had few disposable troops in this engagement and he recognized that in this position he could not receive support from the left wing in a timely manner, he thus preferred a good, orderly retreat over the danger that would have led to complete dissolution in a continued struggle with such superior numbers.[35]

The controversy strained the relationship between Gneisenau and Müffling, a condition that would affect Blücher's headquarters throughout the war. According to the king's adjutant, Henckel von Donnersmarck, during the fierce struggle on the Kreckwitz hills "a junior adjutant made a very heated report [at Allied Headquarters] that another commander must be sent to the Kreckwitz heights because the one currently there had lost his head! This impetuous statement was ignored."[36] Delbrück contends that the young adjutant had been influenced by hearing Müffling's report. Gneisenau's emotional admission that Müffling's initial suggestion to retreat had been correct earned him the latter's praise "because he [Gneisenau] rescinded the decision to hold the hills that he had so strongly expressed earlier and thus sacrificed his vanity."[37] "This judgment by the staff officer and future field-marshal is not accurate," retorts Delbrück. "He praises individual action because he did not recognize the greatness of the man for whom duty was the highest guiding principle, behind which any personal consideration unconditionally receded. On the contrary, Blücher judged correctly. In the conclusion of the report in which Blücher described for the king the performance of the troops on this day, he wrote: 'The chief of my General Staff, Gneisenau, again on this occasion exhibited the correct view, the sound judgment, and uncommon composure that makes him a distinguished general.'" Müffling later admitted that what appeared to him to be a mistake – the death-defying stand on the Kreckwitz heights – had fixed the enemy's attention and as a result had made possible the orderly, successful retreat of the entire Allied army. Thus, if Blücher had accepted his recommendation for a hasty, premature retreat, Napoleon would have won his decisive battle and ended the Sixth Coalition on 21 May 1813. "In this episode," continues Delbrück, "emerges for the first time the difference of the character of [Blücher's] headquarters, which we can often discern during the course of the campaign and at significant moments. The boldest decisiveness and heroic perseverance that only increased with each situation – the highest attributes of the field commander – were Gneisenau's as well as Blücher's innate characteristics while Müffling ... quickly recoiled in the face of difficulties; being eclipsed by Gneisenau's great character made him uneasy. It is not apparent in his *Aus meinem Leben* that he overcame the vanity that he alleges controlled Gneisenau but according to his claims he himself had surmounted."[38]

Regarding the cavalry combat at Haynau amidst the controversy that swirled around Blücher's alleged culpability for the defeat at Bautzen, Nostitz wrote:

> He seized with joy the opportunity for an engagement to put to shame the detractors and to reinvigorate the spirit of the corps through its favorable outcome. The surprise attack at Haynau met this expectation; [because it had been] arranged with prudence and executed with decisiveness, he led the cavalry to great honor. The trophies won during it came at the cost of many distinguished officers but after lost battles and a long retreat, the first victorious engagement exercised a magical effect on all persons ... If the question actually had been asked whether the general should or should not give up command of the army, the engagement at Haynau essentially helped to decide it in Blücher's favor and to restore firm confidence in his leadership.[39]

In his report of 27 May, Wilson provides a glimpse of the effect that Blücher and the Prussians later would have on the Coalition: "The Prussian advantage is of great moral importance. The enemy, the people, the troops, Austria, and Europe will all recognize it as of high interest at this moment, and especially so soon after the enemy's vaunt of a victory that ruined the Allies. England may believe that we are a formidable hydra; we may be hacked and reduced, but the *Vis Vitæ* is immortal against the power of France."[40] Stewart's 6 June report to Castlereagh also lauds the Prussians: "The disorder in the Russian army is great; [the] Prussians are infinitely better. They have everywhere greatly distinguished themselves, and will do much more in a little time. You cannot send them too much ammunition and arms. Russia rides the bear over them, but they are obedient and patient, and I will pledge my faith for theirs; although the Germans will not burn *their Moscow,* and lay waste their country, still they will be true; and Prussia will not be the first power that will withdraw from English alliance."[41]

Estimates by various German historians agree that, as of 1 June, the Allies had achieved a numerical superiority over Napoleon's army by approximately 10,000 soldiers and 200 guns.[42] If Barclay had been able to provide the decisive leadership that Wittgenstein – in part due to Alexander's meddling – could not, the Allies had little to fear from a third battle.[43] Barclay did indeed provide decisive leadership, but not for the delivery of a battle. Instead, his concern over the Russian army made him irreconcilable. Even if he resolved to fight, we can only speculate if his numerical advantage could have overcome Napoleon's superior generalship. Regardless, Russian High Command did not believe they could win because it had lost confidence in the troops. Russian commanders such as Langeron viewed the situation as grim. In his memoirs, Langeron rejected the notion of Allied numerical superiority. Instead, he claims that Napoleon commanded 130,000 men to only 80,000 Coalition soldiers. Langeron explains:

> Had he continued the war, he would have forced us to occupy the entrenched camp of Schweidnitz, where we could have locked ourselves in or could have marched out to fight with worse chances of success than at Lützen and Bautzen, or to risk another battle on the spot in which the enemy's numerical superiority could have rendered them another victory for which in any case we had no more munitions, or finally to retire behind the Oder, which was the alternative accepted at the council of war held at Schweidnitz. Having withdrawn behind the Oder, we could have maintained our position only with difficulty. Napoleon, by his possession of different points along the river, principally at Glogau, could easily have crossed it and pushed us back to the Vistula, at which point he would have had an excellent chance to conclude a peace; it would have been impossible for Austria to come out against him; the prince royal of Sweden could not have and would not have dared to join us; Berlin would have been threatened at the least and would

likely have been occupied, and the conscription in Silesia and the Mark of Brandenburg, which were so useful, would have been paralyzed.[44]

Cathcart returns to the Allied decision to move southeast into Silesia as the reason for Napoleon's decision: "The Allies could not fail to derive strategic advantages from a new line of operations opened to them within the Bohemian frontier, besides an actual increase of force from an Austrian contingent, and this in addition to the moral effect which an Austrian declaration of war would have upon all the disjointed members of the old Germanic empire, whose spirit of nationality had not been extinguished by subjugation, and whose contingents were a large part of Napoleon's force. These were strong inducements for him to pause before striking a blow that might have reversed the fortunes of Europe ... and may explain his preference for an armistice, which prolonged the hope of bribing or cajoling the emperor Francis to persevere in his neutrality." Müffling adds his opinion that Napoleon did not "establish his headquarters at Breslau because he feared such a solemn step ... would impede the armistice, and consequently he cared more for its conclusion than for Breslau." Maude likewise provides an interesting argument. Rightly asserting that strategy is "the servant of national policy" and that policy rendered the armistice inevitable, the British staff officer and historian claims that Napoleon already knew that Austria would betray him and that the "large" Austrian army concentrating in Bohemia would not serve his needs. If the Allies accepted a third battle, Napoleon recognized that he no longer enjoyed numerical superiority. Had he lost a conjectural third battle, which Maude doubted was possible, the defeat would have precipitated an Austrian declaration against him. If the Allies retreated across the Oder and continued eastward, "the danger of the presence of the Austrian army on the flank of his long unguarded line of communication would become greater with every march in pursuit." Successful raids by Russian *Streifkorps* near Halle and Halberstadt at the end of May and Bülow's victory over Oudinot at Luckau on 4 June demonstrated the danger of Napoleon's overextended line of communication.[45]

Unfortunately for Napoleon, the strong rearguard actions fought by Miloradovich as well as Blücher's exploits at Haynau concealed from him the gaping internal conflict in the Allied camp. If Napoleon had continued across the Oder, he would have separated the Allies, defeated them in detail, and ended all Austrian thoughts of intervention. That the Prussians and Russians remained committed to their alliance in the short Spring Campaign of 1813 marks a true triumph for the Coalition. Had the Russians and Prussians separated, the Sixth Coalition would have ended much like the Fourth, only much worse for Frederick William. Regardless, the emperor of the French accepted the Armistice of Pläswitz despite winning two battles and driving the Allies 250 miles from the Saale to the Oder in four weeks.

The armistice did not sit well with all members of the Coalition. The British goal of forming and orchestrating a grand alliance against Napoleon appeared to become even more elusive thanks to the conduct of the Eastern powers. Neither the Russians nor the Prussians consulted the British envoys at Allied Headquarters regarding the negotiations with the French or the signing of the armistice. "The news we send home is not the best," stated Stewart in his 6 June report to Castlereagh, "and, from what I see, I fear political treachery and the machinations that are in the wind more than any evils from Bonaparte's myrmidons. We must keep a sharp look-out, especially since our refusal of Austrian mediation. I cannot help thinking that ... Metternich will attempt some family alliances to aid the object of peace."[46] Hudson Lowe's report from Russian headquarters at Reichenbach on 6 June in particular sounds the alarm. Addressed to Undersecretary of State for War and the Colonies Bunbury, it enumerates his concerns that the Allies intended to ignore British interests. He identifies the short duration of the armistice – six weeks – "as almost to prevent the possibility of any communication with England" during any negotiations that may ensue. While the British envoys could send information to Britain regarding any negotiations and even receive a response within the six weeks, Lowe still considered that "deliberation and discussion must, I fear, be confined to the actual managers on the spot, who will need now more than ever to cast a watchful eye over what is now passing."

It remained difficult for the British to determine what was passing, and the thought of another Tilsit between Alexander and Napoleon could not be ruled out. Austria had already placed its demands on the table. Kaiser Francis "made his conditions with France that the Littoral, Dalmatia, Trieste, Fiume, etc., are to be restored to him," reported Lowe. "He has a very large army assembled in Bohemia and I am inclined to imagine he must have presented very strong language to Bonaparte to have induced proposals for a suspension of hostilities." Not much could be done to protest the absence of any British interests from the kaiser's laundry list of demands. However, Lowe concluded that, should Austria negotiate a settlement with Napoleon, the Russians and Prussians could be influenced to follow suit. He speculated that, if Napoleon abandoned Poland to the three Eastern powers, "the principal obstacle" to negotiations between the Allies (Russia and Prussia) and France would be removed. Moreover, if Austria had already secured the concessions Metternich demanded, Lowe believed that the three eastern powers "will consider their cause to be gained and leave England with the south of Europe to its fate." Conversely, should Napoleon insist on restoring the Grand Duchy of Warsaw, Lowe predicted that the armistice would soon rupture "unless Austria absolutely sides with France." As for Napoleon insisting on the return of Poland, Lowe maintains that such a concession by Russia and Prussia would imply a degree of weakness on their part "beyond [that which] any present appearance indicates."

By diagnosing Poland as the point of contention between the three Eastern powers, Lowe demonstrates incredible insight into the complex politics of the Coalition. "How far the affairs of Poland have attracted the attention of our government at home as to what degree they may have been attended to by His Majesty's ministers abroad I am wholly uninformed," he concluded. For most of 1813, Castlereagh did not understand these dynamics. The foreign secretary simply hoped to mesh Anglo-Russian-Prussian interests into the general goals of a grand coalition: Russian domination of Poland, Prussian compensation in Saxony, and a free hand for Great Britain in Iberia, the Low Countries, Sicily, and the colonies, and on the high seas. However, Metternich could not accept these objectives and sought to undermine the cornerstone of the Kalisch–Breslau treaties – the exchange of Prussian Poland for Saxony – which challenged traditional Habsburg national security objectives of limiting Prussia's influence in Germany and restraining Russian expansion in Central Europe. He believed that Austria's main goals – containing Russia and preventing future revolutions – could best be achieved by maintaining a Napoleonic France that included its natural frontiers. Conversely, the Austrian statesman had no interest in the issues that concerned Great Britain most: the Low Countries, Iberia, and maritime trading rights. Thus, Metternich disregarded British interests to concentrate on peace for Eastern, Central, and Southern Europe. To achieve his goal, he sought to isolate London and exclude the British from negotiations, just as Lowe had predicted.[47]

Speculating on Napoleon's reasons for agreeing to an armistice, we know that with a sick list containing 90,000 names his soldiers desperately needed rest and reorganization. He left Dresden with ammunition for only one day of battle and marched so rapidly after Bautzen that he considerably outdistanced his trains. Moreover, two major battles within a full month of campaigning demonstrated to the emperor the tremendous disadvantages he faced without sufficient cavalry. Not only did the army lack eyes and ears, but it also lacked the shock power that would render a victory decisive and provide Napoleon with the tools to implement a successful strategy of annihilation. All of his engagements with the enemy thus far had proved that they would accept the death that his artillery rained down on them but his infantry could do little to exploit the butchery without adequate cavalry support. As soon as his troops appeared to gain the advantage, Allied cavalry forced his advancing columns to form squares. Shielded by their cavalry, the Allies broke off the fighting and escaped. He needed at least six weeks for his functionaries to finish rebuilding his cavalry. Even if Austria joined the Allies, he believed he could still regain the numerical advantage by moving up fresh troops and forming new corps. With numerical superiority and sufficient cavalry, he could destroy the Coalition in one decisive battle.[48]

As for other reasons that explain Napoleon's willingness to halt hostilities, feeding his masses must be considered. Both armies had completely drained Saxony of resources. While the imperials found more in Silesia, the Grande Armée could not remain in a fixed position for long before it exhausted the local resources. With the provinces in the rear of the army depleted, the army faced starvation. Moreover, from the French point of view according to Odeleben, the move south to Schweidnitz instead of east across the Oder meant that the Russians and Prussians could supply themselves for a much longer time by drawing on the resources of Upper Silesia. In addition, Odeleben remarks on Napoleon's expectation of receiving "very considerable reinforcements from France." Odeleben concludes that the armistice, which left Napoleon little hope of a successful outcome of the war, is "certain proof of how much he wanted time to recruit the strength of his army."[49]

Napoleon opened the campaign with many preconceived notions that proved to be illusory. First, he counted on a decisive victory that would render one and possibly both of the coalition partners incapable of continuing the war in Central Europe. Lützen and Bautzen counted as victories but they fell far short of decisive. Second, despite the tsar's refusal to treat with him after the capture of Moscow in 1812, Napoleon fooled himself into believing Alexander would accept a separate peace as soon as he offered to negotiate. Not only did the emperor's ploy on the eve of Bautzen crush this illusion, but the tsar's insistence that all negotiations be mediated by the Austrians also shattered his third assumption. Although he probably never thought victory or defeat would depend on Austria uniting with France in this war, he did depend on Austrian neutrality.[50] Alexander's demand that negotiations be orchestrated by the Austrians meant that Habsburg interests would be placed on the table alongside those of Russia and Prussia. Austrian involvement would bring a much louder voice to the table, demanding changes to Napoleonic Germany, not to mention Napoleonic Italy – changes that Napoleon could not accept, especially after winning two battles. In short, Napoleon's inability to destroy the Coalition in May opened the door to Austrian intervention through mediation and then through arms – either way, Napoleon had crossed his Rubicon. From the moment he agreed to Austrian mediation, the full extent of the empire he created could never be saved at the peace table. Napoleon's inability or refusal to see this and his insistence on waging war to keep his empire intact led to the human tragedy that accompanied the final year of his reign.

In 1813, the Prussians hampered Napoleon's plans on several levels, all of which fall into two general categories. First, the Prussians utilized all their resources, even nature, for the direct defense of their capital. Three of the four French offensives against Berlin in 1813 resulted in French defeats.

Second, the self-sacrifice the Prussians were willing to accept by not making the defense of Berlin their priority saved the Russo-Prussian alliance and with it the Coalition. A local determination to protect the capital emerged that featured a joint civil–military homeland defense network, the damming of rivers to flood the surrounding countryside, and the volunteer enlistment of the educated youth. However, in the aftermath of Lützen, the civilian and military leadership decided against making the defense of Berlin the army's priority. By casting his lot in with the Russians, Frederick William accepted that the struggle in 1813 would be a war to the death. Its result would bring about either the end of Napoleon's domination of Central Europe or the end of Hohenzollern Prussia. His acceptance of this situation can be seen in his willingness to subordinate himself and his state to the Russians. As the Russians sacrificed Moscow in 1812, so should the Prussians sacrifice Berlin in 1813. Unaffected by the prospect of losing Berlin, Frederick William made the Russo-Prussian army the Coalition's center of gravity.[51] Should the Russian army suffer a decisive defeat, the war would be lost, just as in 1807. Very early in the 1813 campaign, the Prussians demonstrated that they would not pursue national interests that could jeopardize the Coalition's community of interest. Although he came very close in early June 1813, Napoleon failed to drive a wedge between the Prussians and Russians. This more than any other factor served as the Coalition's greatest victory in the Spring Campaign of 1813.

## Notes

1 Gneisenau is quoted in Unger, *Blücher*, I:373; Shanahan, *Prussian Military Reforms*, 188; Boyen, *Erinnerungen*, ed. Nippold, II:101–02, 115–16, 374–79, 480–83.

2 Nesselrode's early February memorandum on Russian grand strategy says nothing of pursuing the French to Paris and effecting regime change in France: Lieven, *Russia Against Napoleon*, 289–91.

3 Kissinger, *A World Restored*, 47

4 Mikhailovsky-Danilevsky, *Denkwürdigkeiten*, 49.

5 Quoted in Mikhailovsky-Danilevsky, *Denkwürdigkeiten*, 64.

6 Boyen, *Erinnerungen*, ed. Nippold, III:21.

7 Stewart, *Narrative*, 21; Campbell to Bunbury, Dresden, 7 May 1813, in Bunbury, *Memoir*, 323; Pertz and Delbrück, *Gneisenau*, II:586–87; Scheer, *Blücher*, III:114; Müffling, *Betrachtungen*, 19; Fritz to Charlotte, Dresden, 5 May 1813, Griewank, *Hohenzollernbriefe*, Nr. 26, 46.

8 Droysen, *Yorck*, II:64; Pertz and Delbrück, *Gneisenau*, II:592.

9 Odeleben, *A Circumstantial Narrative*, I:51; Bogdanovich, *Geschichte des Krieges*, I:204–05; Holleben and Caemmerer, *Frühjahrsfeldzuges 1813*, II:64, 85.

10 Wilson, *Private Diary*, I:355; Campbell to Bunbury, Dresden, 7 May 1813, in Bunbury, *Memoir*, 322; Cathcart, *Commentaries*, 138.

11 "We cannot help but agree with Gneisenau's opinion that the idea for the battle of Lützen was just as good as its execution was poor," explains Bogdanovich in *Geschichte des Krieges*, I:204. "Indeed, what could have been more advantageous for the Allies? The enemy army was unexpectedly attacked by forces superior in number and character. The Allies possessed the means not only to achieve victory, but also to exploit the victory: their cavalry was incomparably more numerous and better than the enemy's. Instead of this, the Allies were forced to retreat and to some extent temporarily relinquish their role as liberators of Germany, although they maintained the portion of the battlefield they had initially occupied and the enemy could boast of no trophies. The main reason for such unexpected results was the slowness of the action."

12 In *Geschichte des Krieges*, I:206, Bogdanovich also rejects Gneisenau's assertion of "personal circumstances." According to Bogdanovich, "Wittgenstein earned the reproach for having ordered Miloradovich to Zeitz, which denied the army the cooperation of around 12,000 men. Some believe this situation must be attributed to the rivalry between Wittgenstein and Miloradovich, but it is much more likely that the memory of Napoleon's maneuver before the battle of Jena was influential here and that the Allies wanted to be secured against an envelopment of their left wing."

13 "During the night," recalled Cathcart in *Commentaries*, 133, "the commandant of the Allied artillery reported that the corps that had been engaged during the day had expended all their ammunition, and that the reserve was so far in the rear, that it could not be replaced by the ensuing morning." Lieven, in *Russia Against Napoleon*, 314, explains that on the eve of the battle, Wittgenstein removed General Yermolov from his post as chief of the army's artillery because of his failure to move up the ammunition supplies with sufficient speed. In Yermolov's place, Wittgenstein appointed the artillery chief of his own corps, General Leo Yashvili, who did not even know where the available ammunition could be found. Mikhailovsky-Danilevsky, in *Denkwürdigkeiten*, 81, claims that on learning that the parks were too distant to resupply the troops, Wittgenstein chastised Yashvili for personally failing the tsar.

14 Gneisenau to Hardenberg, Wohl, 3 May 1813, in Pflugk-Harttung, *Das Befreiungsjahr 1813*, Nr. 95, 120.

15 Lieven, *Russia Against Napoleon*, 315. Lieven disagrees with Bogdanovich's assertion that if Wittgenstein had "started the attack around 8:00 A.M., Bertrand and Marmont, who at the time were a considerable distance from Lützen, would have taken no part in the battle. Aside from Ney's corps and the Guard, only a part of the viceroy's troops could have participated" so that Wittgenstein would have faced "no more than 70,000 or 80,000 men." See Bogdanovich, *Geschichte des Krieges*, I:205.

16 Maude, *Leipzig Campaign*, 108–09; Wittgenstein to Alexander, 3 May 1813, RGVIA, f. VUA, op. 16, d. 3926, ll. 77–79b; Holleben and Caemmerer, *Frühjahrsfeldzuges 1813*, II:86; "Memorandum of the Battle of Lützen, Fought on 2 May 1813," Rochlitz, 2 May 1813, in Wilson, *Private Diary*, I:359.

17 Add MSS, 20111, 22: Cathcart to Castlereagh, Dresden, 6 May 1813.

18 Boyen, *Erinnerungen*, ed. Schmidt, II:570; Campbell to Bunbury, Dresden, 7 May 1813, in Bunbury, *Memoir*, 323.

19 Mikhailovsky-Danilevsky, *Denkwürdigkeiten*, 105; Droysen, *Yorck*, II:64–65; Stewart, *Narrative*, 43, 48.

20 Gneisenau to Hardenberg, Meißen, 6 May 1813, GStA PK, VI HA Rep. 92 Nl. Gneisenau, Nr. 53a; Campbell to Bunbury, Dresden, 7 May 1813, in Bunbury, *Memoir*, 324; Nostitz, *Tagebuch*, 48–49.

21 Müffling, *Aus meinem Leben*, 35.

22 Gneisenau, *Blücher*, 114–15.

23 Plotho, *Der Krieg*, I:159; Bogdanovich, *Geschichte des Krieges*, I:54–56; Add MSS, 20111, 29: Lowe to Bunbury, Löwenberg, 24 May 1813.

24 Mikhailovsky-Danilevsky, *Denkwürdigkeiten*, 98; Bogdanovich, *Geschichte des Krieges*, I:62. It is unclear when Barclay made this suggestion as he did not attend the council of war on the night of 20 May.

25 Mikhailovsky-Danilevsky, *Denkwürdigkeiten*, 100–01.

26 Stewart, *Narrative*, 42, 49; Mikhailovsky-Danilevsky, *Denkwürdigkeiten*, 104; Holleben and Caemmerer, *Frühjahrsfeldzuges 1813*, II:125, 239; "Memorandum of the Battle of Bautzen, fought May 21st, 1813," 3 May 1813, in Wilson, *Private Diary*, II:31.

27 Gneisenau to Münster, Puschkau by Striegau in Silesia, 29 May 1813, GStA PK, VI HA Rep. 92 Nl. Gneisenau Nr. 20b; Pertz and Delbrück, *Gneisenau*, II:626.

28 Mikhailovsky-Danilevsky, *Opisanie voiny 1813 goda*, I:210. Müffling, *Aus meinem Leben*, 44, somewhat validates this story: "Finally, the king resolved to support Blücher with a part of the left wing. It was then too late. The adjutant who delivered the news arrived just after we had evacuated the Kreckwitz heights."

29 Mikhailovsky-Danilevsky, *Denkwürdigkeiten*, 103.

30 Bogdanovich, *Geschichte des Krieges*, I:76; Droysen, *Yorck*, II:94–95; Müffling, *Aus meinem Leben*, 44.

31 Nostitz, *Tagebuch*, 51–52.

32 Cathcart, *Commentaries*, 164–65; Steffens, *Adventures*, 104–05; Müffling, *Aus meinem Leben*, 41–44.

33 Gneisenau to Hardenberg, Reichenbach, 22 May 1813, *Gneisenau*, ed. Griewank, Nr. 117, 228.

34 Gneisenau to Hardenberg, bivouac at Günthersdorf near Herzogswaldau, 23 May 1813, GStA PK, VI HA Rep. 92 Nl. Albrecht, Nr. 47.

35 "Angaben über den Antheil des Blücher'schen Corps an der Bautzener Schlacht am 20. und 21. Mai," 31 May 1813, RGVIA, f. VUA, op. 2, d. 3902, ll. 73–74b; Pertz and Delbrück, *Gneisenau*, II:628.

36 Henckel von Donnersmarck, *Erinnerungen*, 196.

37 Müffling, *Aus meinem Leben*, 43.

38 Pertz and Delbrück, *Gneisenau*, II:625–26. According to Müffling, *Aus meinem Leben*, 41, after assuring Blücher and Gneisenau that the Gleina windmill would be in Ney's hands in fifteen minutes, "Gneisenau did not consider my statement worthy of attention, and Blücher made another inspiring harangue, which was received with great applause, and had the effect of postponing my proposed measures. When a little later I found an opportunity of explaining the circumstances in detail to Gneisenau alone, he fell into a gloomy silence and assumed the role of an unbeliever." Later he states: "I saw in the speeches that had been made,

and in the declaration that the Kreckwitz heights should be Prussia's Thermopylae, an inconsiderate forestalling of events and thus an unwarranted misuse of
power." See Müffling, *Aus meinem Leben*, 43.

39 Nostitz, *Tagebuch*, 52.
40 Wilson, *Private Diary*, II:32.
41 Stewart to Castlereagh, Reichenbach, 6 June 1813, *CVC*, IX:22–23.
42 According to the reports made to Barclay's headquarters on 1 June 1813 that are
contained in the Russian archives, Wittgenstein's "army" numbered 32,370 men
and 90 guns; Langeron's corps totaled 12,265 men and 96 guns; Blücher's army
provided another 34,562 men with 146 guns; Sacken's corps, 9,116 men and 48
guns; and the Russian Guard and Reserve, 20,094 men and 114 guns. A 10 June
report states Wintzingerode's "detachment" at 9,170 men and 48 guns; and the
personnel and guns of the Russian Reserve Artillery at 4,859 men and 305 guns.
These figures produce a total of 122,436 men and 847 guns. See Bogdanovich,
*Geschichte des Krieges*, I:lxvi–lxx.
43 Maude, in *Leipzig Campaign*, 141, disagrees: "The indomitable energy of the
emperor had again triumphed over all obstacles, and if the Allies stood their
ground ... it would seem, from the map, that their doom was certain. The French
stood on a front of thirty miles from Jauer to Breslau, and in thirty-six hours
would have penned them against the Austrian frontier."
44 Langeron, *Mémoires*, 198–99.
45 Cathcart, *Commentaries*, 175. Müffling, *Aus meinem Leben*, 53; Maude, *Leipzig
Campaign*, 141–42, 144.
46 Stewart to Castlereagh, Reichenbach, 6 June 1813, *CVC*, IX:22–23.
47 Add MSS, 20111, 31: Lowe to Bunbury, Reichenbach, 6 June 1813; Nicolson, *The
Congress of Vienna*, 42, 52–53; Nipperdey, *Germany from Napoleon to Bismarck*,
70; Muir, *Britain and the Defeat of Napoleon*, 281; Kissinger, *A World Restored*, 30.
48 See Yorck von Wartenburg, *Napoleon as a General*, II:267–70. Maude takes issue
with Yorck von Wartenburg for criticizing Napoleon for accepting the armistice
based on his want of cavalry. Maude claims that Yorck and other German
historians "have systematically viewed this cavalry question from the standpoint
of its reconnoitering value and not from that of its 'victory completing' power."
See Maude, *Leipzig Campaign*, 142–43.
49 Odeleben, *A Circumstantial Narrative*, I:120, 129.
50 Kissinger, *A World Restored*, 71.
51 By signing of the Treaty of Kalisch, Prussia became Russia's junior partner. This
was logical in view of Frederick William's vulnerable position, financial weakness,
and poor foreign policy record. In return for Russia's pledge to restore his state,
the great-nephew of Frederick II accepted a subordinate role. "To be safe in the
arms of the strong power," explains historian Enno Kraehe, "the weak one must
be absolutely unswerving and devoted in its loyalty." More importantly, the
treaty did not enslave the Prussians as Napoleon had the previous year, nor did
it diminish the state to a Russian satellite. Tsar Alexander pledged to fight for
Prussia's restoration in terms of territory and population. See Muir, *Britain and
the Defeat of Napoleon*, 247–48; Kraehe, *Metternich's German Policy*, I:157.

# Bibliography

## ARCHIVES

### Baden-Baden, Germany

Ehemals Mitteilungen aus dem Gräflichen Bülow Familien-Archiv zu Grünhoff. Friedrich Wilhelm Graf Bülow von Dennewitz. Dokumentation in Briefen-Befehlen-Berichten. Gesammelt Übertragen und mit Anmerkungen Versehen von Joachim-Albrecht Graf Bülow von Dennewitz

### Berlin, Germany

Geheimes Staatsarchiv Preußischer Kulturbesitz zu Berlin

### London, United Kingdom

British Manuscript Collection

### Moscow, Russia

Rossiiskii Gosudarstvennyi Voenno-Istoricheskii Arkhiv

### Paris, France

Service Historique de l'Armée de Terre

## PUBLISHED PRIMARY SOURCES

Bailleu, Paul, ed. *Briefwechsel König Friedrich Wilhelms III und der Königin Luise mit Kaiser Alexander I nebst ergänzenden fürstlichen Korrespondenzen.* Publicationen aus den königlischen preußischen Archiven, vol. 75. Leipzig, 1900.
Berthezène, Pierre. *Souvenirs militaires de la république et de l'empire.* Paris, 1855.
Bieske, Carl Ludwig. *Der Feldmarschall Fürst Gebhard Leberecht Blücher von Wahlstatt.* Berlin, 1862.

Blaise, Jean François and Édouard Lapène. *Campagnes de 1813 et de 1814: sur l'Ébre, les Pyrénées et la Garonne, précédées de considérations sur la dernière guerre d'Espagne*. Paris, 1823.

Blücher, Gebhard Leberecht von. "Aus Blüchers Korrespondenz." Edited by Herman Granier. *Forschungen zur brandenburgischen-preußischen Geschichte* 26 (1913): 149–78.

*Blücher in Briefen aus den Feldzügen, 1813–1815*. Edited by Wilhelm Günter Enno von Colomb. Stuttgart, 1876.

*Blüchers Briefe*. Edited by Wilhelm Capelle. Leipzig, 1915.

*Blüchers Briefe: Vervollständigte Sammlung des Generals E. v. Colomb*. Edited by Wolfgang von Unger. Stuttgart, 1912.

"Zwölf Blücherbriefe." Edited by Herman Granier. *Forschungen zur brandenburgischen-preußischen Geschichte* 12 (1900): 479–96.

Bourrienne, Louis Antoine Fauvelet de. *Memoirs of Napoleon Bonaparte*. Edited by R. W. Phipps. 3 vols. London, 1885.

Boyen, Hermann von. *Erinnerungen aus dem Leben des General-Feldmarschalls Hermann von Boyen*. Edited by Friedrich Nippold. 3 vols. Leipzig, 1889–90.

*Erinnerungen aus dem Leben des General-Feldmarschalls Hermann von Boyen*. Edited by Dorothea Schmidt. 2 vols. Berlin, 1990.

Bunbury, Sir Henry Edward, 7th bart. *Memoir and Literary Remains of Lieutenant-General Sir Henry Edward Bunbury, bart.* London, 1868.

Burckhardt, Wilhelm. *Gebhard Leberecht von Blücher preußischer Feldmarschall und Fürst von Wahlstatt: nach Leben, Reden und Thaten geschildert*. Stuttgart, 1835.

Castlereagh, Viscount, Robert Stewart. *The Correspondence, Dispatches and Other Papers of Viscount Castlereagh*. Edited by Charles William Vane. 12 vols. London, 1848–53.

Cathcart, George. *Commentaries on the War in Russia and Germany in 1812 and 1813*. London, 1850.

Chotterel, François Frédéric. *Précis historique de la vie et du procès du marechal Ney, duc d'Elchingen, prince de la Moskowa, ex-pair de France: avec des notes et particularités curieuses sur sa carrière politique, militaire, ses derniers momens, et les campagnes de Portugal et de Russie*. Paris, 1816.

Clausewitz, C. *La campagne de 1813 et la campagne de 1814*. Paris, 1900.

*Der Feldzug 1812 in Rußland und die Befreiungskriege von 1812–1815*. Berlin, 1906.

*Hinterlassene Werke des Generals Carl von Clausewitz über Krieg und Kriegführung*. 10 vols. Berlin, 1832–37.

*Historical and Political Writings*. Translated and edited by P. Paret and D. Moran. Princeton, NJ, 1992.

Ermolov, A. P. *The Czar's General: The Memoirs of a Russian General in the Napoleonic Wars*. Welwyn Garden City, UK, 2005.

Fain, Agathon-Jean-François. *Manuscrit de mil huit cent treize, contenant le précis de cette année, pour servir à l'histoire de l'empereur Napoléon; par le baron Fain …*. 3rd edn., 2 vols. Paris, 1829.

Fezansac, Raymond. *Souvenirs militaires de 1804 à 1814*. Paris, 1870.

Gneisenau, August von. *Briefe August Neidhardts von Gneisenau: eine Auswahl.* Edited by Koehler & Amelang Verlagsgesellschaft mbH München. Munich, 2000.

*Briefe des Generals Neidhardt von Gneisenau, 1809–1815.* Edited by Julius von Pflugk-Harttung. Gotha, 1913.

*Gneisenau: ein Leben in Briefen.* Edited by Karl Griewank. Leipzig, 1939.

*The Life and Campaigns of Field Marshal Prince Blücher.* London, 1815.

*Neithardt von Gneisenau: Schriften von und über Gneisenau.* Edited by Fritz Lange. Berlin, 1954.

Hellwald, F. J. H. and Karl Schönhals. *Der k.k. österreichische Feldmarschall Graf Radetzky: eine biographische Skizze nach den eigenen Dictaten und der Correspondenz des Feldmarschalls von einem österreichischen Veteranen.* Stuttgart, 1858.

Henckel von Donnersmarck, W. L. von. *Erinnerungen aus meinem Leben.* Leipzig, 1846.

Höpfner, Eduard von. "Darstellung der Ereignisse bei der schlesischen Armee." *Militair-Wochenblatt,* 1843–47.

Hüser, Heinrich von. *Denkwürdigkeiten aus dem Leben des Generals der Infanterie von Hüser.* Berlin, 1877.

Jaguin, Louis Ozé. *Historique du 137e régiment d'infanterie.* Fontenay-le-Comte, 1890.

Jomini, Antoine Henri de. *Précis politique et militaire des campagnes de 1812 à 1814.* 2 vols. Lausanne, 1886.

*Vie politique et militaire de Napoléon.* 4 vols. Paris, 1827.

Koch, Frédéric. *Mémoires pour servir à l'histoire de la campagne de 1814.* Paris, 1819.

Körner, Theodor. *Leyer und Schwert.* Berlin, 1814.

Langeron, Alexandre Louis Andrault. *Mémoires de Langeron, général d'infanterie dans l'armée russe: campagnes de 1812, 1813, 1814.* Paris, 1902.

Linnebach, Karl, ed. *Scharnhorsts Briefe.* Vol. I of *Privatbriefe.* Leipzig, 1914. Reprint, with commentary by Heinz Stübig, Munich, 1980.

Macdonald, Étienne-Jacques-Joseph-Alexandre, duc de Tarente, and Camille Rousset. *Souvenirs du Maréchal Macdonald, duc de Tarente.* Paris, 1892.

Marmont, A. de. *Mémoires du duc de Raguse.* 9 vols. Paris, 1857.

Martens, F. F. *Recueil des traités et conventions, conclus par la Russie avec les puissances étrangères.* 15 vols. St. Petersburg, 1874–1909.

Martens, G. F. *Recueil des traités et conventions d'alliance, de paix, de trêve, de neutralité, de commerce, de limites, déchange, etc., et plusieurs autres actes servant à la connoissance des relations étrangères des puissances et états de l'Europe depuis 1761 jusqu'à présent.* 16 vols. Göttingen, 1817–42.

Metternich, C. L. W. *Memoirs of Prince Metternich, 1773–1815.* 5 vols. Edited by R. Metternich. Translated by A. Napier. New York, 1970.

Mikhailovsky-Danilevsky, Aleksandr Ivanovich. *Denkwürdigkeiten aus dem Kriege von 1813.* Translated by Karl Goldhammer. Dorpat, 1837.

*Opisanie voiny 1813 goda.* 2 vols. St. Petersburg, 1840.

Müffling, Friedrich Karl Ferdinand von. *Aus meinem Leben.* Berlin, 1851.

*Betrachtungen über die großen Operationen und Schlachten der Feldzüge von 1813 und 1814.* Berlin, 1825.

*Passages from My Life; Together with Memoirs of the Campaign of 1813 and 1814.* Translated and edited by Philip Yorke. London, 1853.

*Zur Kriegsgeschichte der Jahre 1813 und 1814: die Feldzüge der schlesischen Armee unter dem Feldmarschall Blücher von der Beendigung des Waffenstillstandes bis zur Eroberung von Paris.* Berlin, 1827.

Napoléon I, Emperor of the French. *La correspondance de Napoléon Ier: publiée par ordre de l'empereur Napoléon III.* 32 vols. Paris, 1858–69.

Natzmer, Gneomar Ernst von. *Aus dem Leben des Generals Oldwig von Natzmer: ein Beitrag zur preußischen Geschichte.* Berlin, 1876.

Norvins, Jacques Marquet de. *Portefeuille de mil huit cent treize, ou tableau politique et militaire renfermant: avec le récit des événemens de cette epoque, un choix de la correspondance inéd. de l'empereur Napoléon.* 2 vols. Paris, 1825.

Nostitz, August Ludwig Ferdinand von. *Das Tagebuch des Generals der Kavallerie, Grafen von Nostitz.* 2 vols. Pt. 1 of *Kriegsgeschichtliche Einzelschriften.* 6 vols. Berlin, 1885.

Odeleben, E. O. von. *A Circumstantial Narrative of the Campaign in Saxony, in the Year 1813.* 2 vols. London, 1820.

*Napoleons Feldzug im Sachsen im Jahre 1813.* Dresden, 1816.

Osten-Sacken und Rhein, Ottomar von. *Militärisch-politische Geschichte des Befreiungskrieges im Jahre 1813.* 2 vols. Berlin, 1813.

Pelet, Jean-Jacques. *Des principales opérations de la campagne de 1813.* Paris, 1826.

Plotho, Carl von. *Der Krieg in Deutschland und Frankreich in den Jahren 1813 und 1814.* 3 vols. Berlin, 1817.

Prittwitz, Karl Heinrich. *Beiträge zur Geschichte des Jahres 1813: von einem höheren Offizier der preußischen Armee.* 2 vols. Potsdam, 1843.

Radetzky von Radetz, J. J. W. A. F. K. *Denkschriften militärisch-politischen Inhalts aus dem handschriftlichen Nachlaß des k.k. österreichischen Feldmarschalls Grafen Radetzky.* Stuttgart and Augsburg, 1858.

Rahden, Wilhelm. *Wanderungen eines alten Soldaten.* 3 vols. Berlin, 1846–59.

Reiche, Ludwig von. *Memoiren des königlichen preußischen Generals der Infanterie Ludwig von Reiche.* Edited by Louis von Weltzien. Leipzig, 1857.

Rochechouart, Louis Victor Léon. *Souvenirs sur la révolution, l'empire et la restauration.* Paris, 1933.

Russian General Staff, Main Directorate. *Voina 1813 goda: iskhodyashaya perepiska glavnokomanduyushago Zapadnoi armiei s 1 yanvarya po 31 dekabrya 1813 goda.* 3 vols. St. Petersburg, 1914–16.

Scharnhorst, Gerhard von. *Private und dienstliche Schriften.* Edited by Johannes Kunisch and Michael Sikora. 6 vols. Cologne, 2002–12.

*Scharnhorsts Briefe.* Edited by Karl Linnebach. Münich, 1914.

Scherbening, R. K. von and K. W. Willisen, eds. *Die Reorganisation der preußischen Armee nach dem Tilsiter Frieden.* 2 vols. Berlin, 1862–66.

Schwarzenberg, K. zu. *Briefe des Feldmarschalls Fürsten Schwarzenberg an seine Frau, 1799–1816.* Leipzig, 1913.

Seydlitz, August von. *Tagebuch des Königlich Preußischen Armee Korps unter Befehl des General-Lieutenants von Yorck im Feldzuge von 1812.* 2 vols. Berlin, 1812.

Steffens, H. *Adventures on the Road to Paris, During the Campaigns of 1813–1814.* London, 1848.

Stewart, Lieutenant General Sir Charles William Vane, Lord Londonderry. *Narrative of the War in Germany and France in 1813 and 1814.* London, 1830.

St.-Cyr, Laurent de Gouvion. *Mémoires sur les campagnes des armées du Rhin et de Rhin-et-Moselle. Atlas des cartes et plans relatifs aux campagnes du Maréchal Gouvion St. Cyr aux armées du Rhin et de Rhin et Moselle pendant les années 1792, 1793, 1794, 1795, 1796 et 1797.* 4 vols. Paris, 1828.

Valentini, Georg von. *Der grosse Krieg.* 2 vols. Berlin, 1833.

*Lehre vom Kriege.* 2 vols. Berlin, 1835.

Varnhagen von Ense, Karl August. *Das Leben der Generals Gräfen Bülow von Dennewitz.* Berlin, 1853.

*Leben des Fürsten Blücher von Wahlstatt.* Berlin, 1933.

Vaudoncourt, Guillaume. *Histoire de la guerre soutenue par le Français en Allemagne en 1813.* Paris, 1819.

*Histoire des campagnes de 1814 et 1815 en France.* 5 vols. Paris, 1826.

Venturini, Carl. *Rußlands und Deutschlands Befreiungskriege von der Franzosen-Herrschaft unter Napoleon Buonaparte in den Jahren 1812–1815.* 4 vols. Altenburg, 1816–18.

Wagner, Johann Christian August. *Plane der Schlachten und Treffen, welche von der preussischen Armee in den Feldzügen 1813, 1814 und 1815 geliefert worden.* 4 vols. Berlin, 1821–25.

Wilson, Robert. *General Wilson's Journal, 1812–1814.* Edited by Antony Brett-James. London, 1964.

*Private Diary of Travels, Personal Services, and Public Events: During the Mission Employed with the European Armies in the Campaigns of 1812, 1813, 1814.* 2 vols. London, 1861.


### SECONDARY SOURCES

Anon. *Précis militaire de la campagne de 1813 en Allemagne.* Leipzig, 1881.

Atkinson, C. T. *A History of Germany, 1715–1815.* London, 1908.

Atteridge, A. Hilliard. *The Bravest of the Brave, Michel Ney, Marshal of France, Duke of Elchingen, Prince of the Moskowa 1769–1815.* London, 1912.

Bach, Theodor. *Theodor Gottlieb von Hippel, der Verfasser des Aufrufs: "An mein Volk." Ein Gedenkblatt zur fünfzigjährigen Feier der Erhebung Preussens.* Breslau, 1863.

Barton, D. Plunket. *Bernadotte: Prince and King, 1810–1844.* London, 1925.

Beitzke, Heinrich. *Geschichte der deutschen Freiheitskriege in den Jahren 1813 und 1814.* 3 vols. Berlin, 1854–55.

Bernhardi, T. *Denkwürdigkeiten aus dem Leben des Kaiserlich Russischen Generals von der Infanterie Carl Friedrich Grafen von Toll.* 4 vols. Leipzig, 1856–66.

Blasendorff, Carl. *Gebhard Leberecht von Blücher: mit Bild und Nachbild eines eigenhändigen Briefes.* Berlin, 1887.

Bleck, Otto. *Marschall Blücher: ein Lebensbild.* Berlin, 1939.

Bogdanovich, Modest Ivanovich. *Geschichte des Krieges 1814 in Frankreich und des Sturzes Napoleon's I: nach den zuverläßigsten Quellen.* Translated by G. Baumgarten. Leipzig, 1866.

*Geschichte des Krieges im Jahre 1813 für Deutschlands Unabhängigkeit: nach den zuverläßigsten Quellen.* 2 vols. St. Petersburg, 1863–68.

Bowden, Scott. *Napoleon's Grande Armée of 1813.* Chicago, 1990.

Brett-James, Anthony. *Europe Against Napoleon: The Leipzig Campaign, 1813, from Eyewitness Accounts.* London, 1970.

Caemmerer, Rudolf von. *Die Befreiungskriege, 1813–1815: ein Strategischer Überblick.* Berlin, 1907.

Chandler, David G. *The Campaigns of Napoleon.* New York, 1966.

Charras, Jean Baptiste Adolphe. *Histoire de la guerre de 1813 en Allemagne: derniers jours de la retraite, insurrection de l'Allemagne, armements, diplomatie, entrée en campagne.* 2nd edn. Paris, 1870.

Clark, Christopher. *Iron Kingdom: The Rise and Downfall of Prussia, 1600–1947.* Cambridge, MA, 2006.

Clercq, Jules de and Alexandre J. H. de Clercq. *Recueil des traités de la France.* 23 vols. Paris, 1864–1917.

Conrady, Emil von. *Leben und Wirken des Generals Carl von Grolman.* 3 vols. Berlin, 1933.

Craig, Gordon A. *The Politics of the Prussian Army: 1640–1945.* Oxford, 1956.

"Problems of Coalition Warfare: The Military Alliance Against Napoleon, 1813–1814." In *War, Politics, and Diplomacy: Selected Essays by Gordon Craig.* London, 1966, 22–45.

Droysen, Johann. *Das Leben des Feldmarschalls Grafen Yorck von Wartenburg.* 2 vols. Leipzig, 1851.

Duncker, Max. *Aus der Zeit Friedrichs des Großen und Friedrich Wilhelms III.* Leipzig, 1876.

D'Ussel, Jean. *Études sur l'année 1813: la défection de la Prusse, décembre 1812–mars 1813.* Paris, 1907.

Elting, John and Vincent Esposito. *A Military History and Atlas of the Napoleonic Wars.* New York, 1964.

Fabry, Gabriel Joseph. *Étude sur les opérations de l'empereur, 5 septembre au 21 septembre 1813.* Paris, 1910.

*Étude sur les opérations du maréchal Macdonald du 22 août au 4 septembre 1813: La Katzbach.* Paris, 1910.

*Étude sur les opérations du maréchal Oudinot du 15 août au 4 septembre: Groß Beeren.* Paris, 1910.

Finley, Milton. "The Career of Count Jean Reynier, 1792–1814." Ph.D. dissertation, Florida State University, 1972.

Fisher, H. A. L. *Napoleonic Statesmanship in Germany.* Oxford, 1903.

Ford, G. S. *Hanover and Prussia: A Study in Neutrality, 1795–1803.* New York, 1903.

*Stein and the Era of Reform in Prussia, 1807–1815.* Princeton, NJ, 1922. Reprint, Gloucester, 1965.

Foucart, P. J. *Bautzen: 20–21 mai 1813.* 2 vols. Paris, 1897.

Freytag-Loringhoven, Hugo Friedrich Philipp Johann von. *Aufklärung und Armeeführung dargestellt an den Ereignissen bei der Schlesischen Armee im Herbst 1813: eine Studie.* Berlin, 1900.

*Kriegslehren nach Clausewitz aus den Feldzügen 1813 und 1814.* Berlin, 1908.

Friederich, Rudolf. "Die Aufassung der strategischen Lage seitens der Verbündeten am Schlusse des Waffenstillstandes von Poischwitz 1813." *Militair-Wochenblatt* (1902): 1–36.

    *Die Befreiungskriege, 1813–1815.* 4 vols. Berlin, 1911–13.

    *Geschichte des Herbstfeldzuges 1813.* 3 vols. Berlin, 1903–06. In *Geschichte der Befreiungskriege, 1813–1815.* 9 vols. Berlin, 1903–09.

    "Die strategische Lage Napoleons am Schlusse des Waffenstillstandes von Poischwitz." *Militair-Wochenblatt* (1901): 1–36.

Gallaher, John. *The Iron Marshal: A Biography of Louis N. Davout.* Carbondale, IL, 1976.

Gérôme, Auguste Clementé. *Campagne de 1813.* Paris, 1904.

Görlitz, Walter. *Fürst Blücher von Wahlstatt.* Rostock, 1940.

    *History of the German General Staff, 1657–1945.* Translated by Brian Battershaw. New York, 1954.

Griewank, Karl. *Hohenzollernbriefe aus den Freiheitskriegen 1813–1815.* Leipzig, 1913.

Grunwald, Constantin de. *The Life of Baron Stein: Napoleon's Nemesis.* Translated by C. F. Atkinson. New York, 1936.

Henderson, Ernest F. *Blücher and the Uprising of Prussia Against Napoleon, 1806–1815.* London, 1911.

Hochedlinger, Michael. *Austria's Wars of Emergence: War, State, and Society in the Habsburg Monarchy, 1683–1797.* Harlow, 2003.

Holleben, A. von and R. von Caemmerer. *Geschichte des Frühjahrsfeldzuges 1813 und seine Vorgeschichte.* 2 vols. Berlin, 1904–09. In *Geschichte der Befreiungskriege, 1813–1815.* 9 vols. Berlin, 1903–09.

Holzhausen, Paul. *Davout in Hamburg.* Mülheim, 1892.

Hourtoulle, François Guy. *Ney, le braves.* Paris, 1981.

Jany, Curt. *Geschichte der königlichen preußischen Armee.* 4 vols. Berlin, 1929.

Josselson, Michael and Diana Josselson. *The Commander: A Life of Barclay de Tolly.* Oxford, 1980.

Kissinger, Henry. *A World Restored: Metternich, Castlereagh, and the Problems of Peace, 1812–1822.* Boston, 1990.

Kitchen, Martin. *A Military History of Germany.* London, 1954.

Klippel, Georg Heinrich. *Das Leben des Generals von Scharnhorst: nach grösstentheils bisher unbenutzten Quellen.* Leipzig, 1869–71.

Koch, H. W. *A History of Prussia.* New York, 1987.

Kraehe, Enno. *Metternich's German Policy.* 2 vols. Princeton, NJ, 1963.

Lanrezac, Charles Louis Marie. *La manoeuvre de Lützen 1813.* Paris, 1904.

Leggiere, Michael V. *Blücher: Scourge of Napoleon.* Norman, OK, 2014.

    *The Fall of Napoleon,* vol. I, *The Allied Invasion of France.* Cambridge, 2007.

    *Napoleon and Berlin: The Franco-Prussian War in North Germany, 1813.* Norman, OK, 2002.

Lehmann, Max. *Freiherr vom Stein.* 3 vols. Leipzig, 1902–05.

    *Scharnhorst.* 2 vols. Leipzig, 1886–87.

Lieven, Dominic. *Russia Against Napoleon: The True Story of the Campaigns of War and Peace.* New York, 2010.

Lindemann, Mary. *Patriots and Paupers: Hamburg, 1712–1830.* New York, 1990.

Maude, F. N. *The Leipzig Campaign, 1813.* London, 1908.

Meinecke, Friedrich. *Das Leben des Generalfeldmarschalls Hermann von Boyen.* 2 vols. Stuttgart, 1896–99.

Mikaberidze, Alexander. *The Battle of Borodino: Napoleon Against Kutuzov.* Barnsley, UK, 2010.

*The Russian Officer Corps in the Revolutionary and Napoleonic Wars, 1792–1815.* New York, 2005.

Muir, Rory. *Britain and the Defeat of Napoleon, 1807–1815.* London, 1996.

Nafziger, George. *Imperial Bayonets: Tactics of the Napoleonic Battery, Battalion and Brigade as Found in Contemporary Regulations.* London, 1996.

*Lutzen and Bautzen: Napoleon's Spring Campaign of 1813.* Chicago, 1992.

Nicolson, Harold. *The Congress of Vienna: A Study in Allied Unity.* New York, 1946.

Nipperdey, Thomas. *Germany from Napoleon to Bismarck, 1800–1866.* Translated by Daniel Nolan. Princeton, NJ, 1996.

Oncken, Wilhelm. *Österreich und Preußen im Befreiungskrieg: urkundliche Aufschlüsse über die politische Geschichte des Jahres 1813.* 2 vols. Berlin, 1876–79.

Pajol, Charles Pierre Victor. *Pajol, général en chef.* Paris, 1874.

Paret, Peter. *Clausewitz and the State.* Oxford, 1976.

*Yorck and the Era of Prussian Reform, 1807–1815.* Princeton, NJ, 1966.

Parkinson, Roger. *The Hussar General: The Life of Blücher, Man of Waterloo.* London, 1975.

Pertz, G. H. *Das Leben des Ministers Freiherrn vom Stein.* 6 vols. Berlin, 1849–55.

Pertz, G. H. and Hans Delbrück. *Das Leben des Feldmarschalls Grafen Neithardt von Gneisenau.* 5 vols. Berlin, 1864–80.

Petre, F. L. *Napoleon's Last Campaign in Germany, 1813.* London, 1912. Reprint, London, 1992.

Pflugk-Harttung, Julius von, ed. *Das Befreiungsjahr 1813: aus den Akten des Geheimen Staatsarchivs.* Berlin, 1913.

Quintin, D. and B. Quintin. *Dictionnaire des colonels de Napoléon.* Paris, 1996.

Ranke, Leopold von. *Denkwürdigkeiten des Staatskanzlers Fürsten von Hardenberg.* 5 vols. Leipzig, 1877.

Richie, Alexandra. *Faust's Metropolis: A History of Berlin.* New York, 1998.

Rivollet, Georges. *Général de bataille Charles Antoine Louis Morand, comte d'Empire, 1771–1835: généraux Friant et Gudin du 3e corps de la Grande Armée.* Paris, 1963.

Rosenberg, Hans. *Bureaucracy, Aristocracy, and Autocracy; The Prussian Experience, 1660–1815.* Cambridge, 1958.

Ross, S. *European Diplomatic History, 1789–1815: France Against Europe.* New York, 1969.

Scherr, Johannes. *Blücher: seine Zeit und sein Leben.* 3 vols. Leipzig, 1887.

Schroeder, Paul. *The Transformation of European Politics, 1763–1848.* Oxford, 1994.

Schwartz, Karl. *Leben des Generals Carl von Clausewitz und der Frau Marie von Clausewitz geb. Gräfin von Brühl.* Berlin, 1878.

Scott, Franklin D. *Bernadotte and the Fall of Napoleon.* Cambridge, 1934.

Seeley, J. R. *Life and Times of Stein, or Germany and Prussia in the Napoleonic Age.* 3 vols. New York, 1969.

Shanahan, William. *Prussian Military Reforms, 1786–1813*. New York, 1945.

Sherwig, John. *Guineas and Gunpowder: British Foreign Aid in the Wars with France, 1793–1815*. Cambridge, 1969.

Showalter, Dennis E. "Hubertusberg to Auerstädt: The Prussian Army in Decline?" *German History* 12 (1994): 308–33.

"The Prussian Landwehr and Its Critics, 1813–1819." *Central European History* 4 (1971): 3–33.

Simon, Walter. *The Failure of the Prussian Reform Movement, 1807–1819*. Ithaca, NY, 1955.

Six, Georges. *Dictionnaire biographique des généraux et amiraux français de la révolution et de l'empire*. 2 vols. Paris, 1934.

Stamm-Kuhlmann, Thomas. *König in Preußens großer Zeit: Friedrich Wilhelm III, der Melancholiker auf dem Thron*. Berlin, 1992.

Telp, Claus. *The Evolution of Operational Art, 1740–1813: From Frederick the Great to Napoleon*. New York, 2005.

Tranié, J. and Juan Carlos Carmigniani. *Napoléon: 1813, la campagne d'Allemagne*. Paris, 1987.

Unger, Wolfgang von. *Blücher*. 2 vols. Berlin, 1907–08.

Vaupel, Rudolf, ed. *Die Reorganisation des Preußischen Staates unter Stein und Hardenberg*, part 2, *Das Preußische Heer vom Tilsiter Frieden bis zur Befreiung: 1807–1814*. Publicationen aus den königlischen preußischen Archiven, vol. 94. Leipzig, 1938.

Webster, Charles. *The Foreign Policy of Castlereagh*. 2 vols. London, 1931–34.

Weil, Maurice-Henri. *Campagne de 1813: la cavalerie des armées alliées*. Paris, 1886.

Weinzierl, J. "The Military and Political Career of Claude-Victor Perrin." Ph.D. dissertation, Florida State University, 1997.

White, Charles E. *The Enlightened Soldier: Scharnhorst and the Militärische Gesellschaft in Berlin, 1801–1805*. Westport, CT, 1989.

Wigger, Friedrich. *Feldmarschall Fürst Blücher von Wahlstatt*. Schwerin, 1878.

Yorck von Wartenburg, Hans Ludwig David Maximilian Graf. *Napoleon as a General*. 2 vols. Edited by Walter H. James. London, 1897–98.

# Index

32nd Military Division, 111–13, 141–43, 170, 306

Abendroth, Amandus Augustus, 140
Aken, 167
Alekseyev, Ilya, 251
Alexander I (tsar), 30–31, 62, 71, 73, 81, 83–84, 90, 94, 97, 100, 200, 373, 390, 418, 421, 429–31, 439, 447, 455
  accepts Toll's plan for concentration, 191
  adheres to Wurschen Plan, 392
  advises Frederick William on defense of Prussia, 44
  after Bautzen, 358
  alliance overtures to Francis I in 1811, 36
  alliance with Prussia, 67
  appoints Wittgenstein as Allied commander in chief, 199
  arrives at Breslau, 105
  as Allied generalissimo, 200
  at Bautzen, 191, 293, 330, 335, 342–43, 345, 351, 354–56, 379, 440–42, 445
  at Bunzlau, 190
  at Congress of Erfurt, 30
  at Dresden, 196
  at Lützen, 227, 230, 250, 433, 435
    formally appoints Wittgenstein, 227
  at Schweidnitz, 391
  comments by Hardenberg, 405
  considers Frederick William III his best friend, 37
  council of war at Bautzen, 191
  courts Swedes, 61
  critical of Blücher, 443
  determination to continue the war, 72–73, 114
  indifference to British gold, 65
  instructions to Wittgenstein, 288
  leadership in 1813, 427
  meets with Bernadotte, 61
  meets with Frederick William in 1805, 21
  meets with Scharnhorst, 49
  meets with Stadion, 306
  negotiates with British, 310
  negotiates with British and Swedes, 198–99
  negotiates with Napoleon in 1807, 2
  opposes German popular revolt, 131
  opposes Napoleon, 3
  plans to defend Russia in 1812, 36
  pleased by Scharnhorst's mission, 46
  praises Scharnhorst, 122
  reaction to Lützen, 260–61
  rejects armistice proposal, 322
  rejects Wittgenstein's resignation, 314
  relations with Napoleon sour, 32–33, 36
  relieves Wittgenstein, 373–74
  resolves to accept battle, 191
  respect for Scharnhorst, 201
  retreat after Lützen, 269
  secretly negotiates with Poles, 36
  seeks Prussian alliance
    in 1811, 37, 39, 43, 48–49, 55
    in 1813, 75, 78, 80
  supports Bernadotte, 64
  supports Swedes, 61
  surprised by Napoleon's rapid advance, 197
  wants to hold Katzbach, 371
Alps, 73, 188
Alsleben, 157
Altenburg, 148–49, 153, 159, 162–63, 179–80, 184–85, 191, 193, 196, 202–3, 207–9, 212–13, 215–16, 220, 249, 260, 269, 273, 275, 277
  affection for Blücher, 166
Altenstein, Karl vom Stein zu, 29

Altjäschwitz, 371–72, 389
Alvensleben, Ludolph August von, 239, 348
Amsterdam, 142
"An mein Kriegsheer," 107
"An mein Volk," 105
ancient Rome, 1, 4
Ancillon, Johann Peter , 37, 55, 58, 84, 105
Angermünde, 124
Ansbach, 160–61, 185, 187
Anstedt, Johann von, 94
Antwerp, 142
*Aquila*, 1
Arakcheyev, Aleksey, 48
Armistice of Pläswitz, 6, 388, 418, 448
Armistice of Zniam, 31
Arnoldsmühl, 402
Arrangement with the Russians over the
    Operations of General Scharnhorst,
    102, 124, 137, 145, 432
Aschaffenburg, 161
Aschersleben, 161, 177
Aspern-Essling (battle), 31, 189
Audigast, 214, 226
Auerstedt, 196
Auerstedt (battle), 249, 260
Augereau, Pierre , 93, 205
Augsburg, 137, 155, 161
August (prince of Prussia), 120, 166, 425
August Ferdinand (prince of Prussia), 166
Austerlitz (battle), 2, 21, 188, 271, 303, 440
Austria, 2, 5, 18, 21, 26–27, 29–32, 36, 39–40,
    54–55, 59–60, 64, 69, 79, 82, 85, 88, 100,
    103, 115, 120, 147–48, 162, 174, 178,
    181, 184, 189, 191, 195–96, 198, 223,
    236, 281–83, 285, 290, 296–97, 305–9,
    324, 332, 343, 366, 373–74, 380, 390,
    392, 395, 397, 400, 404–5, 407–8, 412,
    418, 428–29, 431, 442, 447–51
    1809 war of liberation, 30
    anti-French sentiment, 207
    armistice proposal, 418
    arms the Prussians, 274
    exploits Napoleon's reversals in Iberia, 30
    forced into Continental System, 32
    war with France in 1809, 27
    looks to Prussia, 30
Austrian army
    reorganization of, 30
Austrian Galicia, 32
Auvray, Frédéric Anton d', 76, 133, 155, 202,
    223, 268, 289, 295–96, 329, 335, 351,
    433, 438

Bachelu, Gilbert-Désiré, 82
Bad Düben, 220
Bad Kösen, 191
Bad Langensalza, 154, 163, 186, 205

Bad Lausick, 275–76, 294
Baltic Sea, 25, 47, 52, 60, 64–65, 72, 77, 86–88,
    97, 108, 140, 199, 283
Baltiysk, *see* Pillau
Bamberg, 147, 160, 175
Barcinek, *see* Berthelsdorf
Barclay de Tolly, Michael Andreas, 159, 206,
    303–4, 311, 313
    as Allied commander in chief, 373–76,
        384, 391–92, 396–97, 401, 403, 419,
        421, 447
    criticizes Blücher, 388
    difficulties as, 405–6
    missed opportunity, 404, 406
    orders retreat across Oder, 408, 412–13,
        417–18
    Prussian view of, 376
    wants to retreat to Poland, 373–74
    at Bautzen, 314–15, 318, 336, 345–47,
        355–56, 440–41, 443, 445
    commands northern wing of Allied army,
        365, 367–69, 371
    engagement at Königswartha, 325–26
    praises Yorck, 328
    meets with Scharnhorst in 1811, 49
    plans defense of Russia, 36, 43
    Prussian view of, 314
    retreats from Bautzen, 358–60
Barendorf, 143
Barrois, Pierre, 353
Baruth, 347, 349, 351, 364
Basankwitz, 331, 341, 352, 354
Baschütz, 302, 304, 323, 336, 351, 354, 356–57
battle of Großgörschen, *see* Lützen (battle)
Baudmannsdorf, 385, 387
Bautzen, 7, 122, 134, 185, 191, 279, 286,
    288–90, 293, 295–98, 301–2, 311–20,
    322–25, 330–31, 336–37, 341–42, 344,
    353, 358–59, 367, 377, 425, 441
    terrain features, 331
Bautzen (battle), 8, 314, 321, 329, 342, 359,
    364, 373, 376, 385, 388, 391, 397,
    421–22, 446–47, 451
    assessment, 439–43
    French losses, 358
    losses, 358
    results for Napoleon, 359
Bavaria, 160–61, 207, 429
    France's ally in 1809, 32
Bayreuth, 149–50, 160–61, 187–88
Beauharnais, Eugene de (viceroy of Italy), 5,
    82, 89, 119, 139, 167, 170, 211, 221, 224,
    264, 298, 432
    commands Army of the Elbe, 90, 99,
        110–13, 124–25, 133, 139–40, 142–43,
        152–53, 159–61, 175, 187, 205–6, 208,
        210–11, 271

after Lützen, 270, 273, 275–78, 284–85
at Lützen, 229, 238, 252, 256
crosses Elbe, 292
engagement at Möckern, 152
returns to Italy, 298
Beaumont, Louis-Chrétien, 298, 312
*Befreiungskrieg, see* Prussia: war of liberation
Belgern, 289, 354, 356, 359
Belzig, 139, 145–46, 148–49
Benckendorff, Alexander, 99, 124, 143
Berg, Grigory, 101, 133, 172, 176, 202–3, 207,
    209, 212, 214–15, 220, 222, 226, 228,
    230–31, 240, 244, 247, 250, 254, 315,
    357, 434
Bergedorf, 141, 169
Bernadotte, Jean-Baptiste (crown prince of
    Sweden), 61, 64, 85–89, 95–98, 122,
    145, 170, 198
  meets with Alexander, 61
  seeks British support, 61, 63
Bernburg, 272
Berthelsdorf, 419
Berthier, Louis-Alexandre , 71, 175, 186–88,
    205, 211, 270, 273, 275, 277, 279, 286,
    298, 300, 315–22, 328, 347, 359,
    366–69, 371, 383–84, 390, 393–94,
    398–402, 409–11, 421
Bertrand, Henri-Gatien, 161, 175, 185,
    187–88, 205, 211, 221, 224, 231, 238,
    242, 244, 247, 250, 257, 271, 273,
    276, 278, 284–85, 292–93, 299, 301,
    312–13, 316, 318–20, 323, 328, 337,
    366, 368, 370, 372–73, 383–84, 389,
    394, 399–401, 404, 409, 425, 434,
    436, 453
Bessières, Jean-Baptiste, 161, 175–76, 210
*Beurlaubten* , 35
Beuthen, 117
Białystock, 74
Białystok, *see* Bialystock
Bienenbüttel, 143
Binnewitz, 351
Bischofswerda, 288–89, 297–300, 312, 319–20
Blankenburg, 165
Block, Karl Heinrich von, 239
Blösa, 359
Blösa (stream), 302–3, 346, 348, 352
Blücher, Franz von, 179, 223
Blücher, Gebhard Leberecht von
  accepts Wittgenstein's authority, 201
  anti-French sentiment, 52
  Army of Silesia, 396
  at Dresden, 135
  candidate for Allied commander in chief,
    199
  cashiered, 57
  claims Cottbus District for Prussia, 125–27

commands all-Prussian units of Allied
    army, 315
commands Allied right wing, 384, 397, 401,
    404, 413, 421
  dissatisfaction with Barclay, 407
  expects third battle, 406
  opposes retreat across Oder, 412–14
  retreats to Oder, 396, 408
commands Allied southern army, 101–2,
    133, 136, 145, 149, 152, 172, 179, 186,
    197, 207, 220, 222
  dissatisfaction with Kutuzov, 432
commands Prussian II Corps, 98, 104, 120,
    123, 125, 202–3, 209, 212, 218, 340, 415
  after Lützen, 270, 276, 283
  ambush at Haynau, 385–88, 446, 448
  battle of Bautzen, 336–38, 340–43,
    345–49, 352–56, 379, 440, 443–44, 446,
    454
  battle of Lützen, 214, 226, 228–33, 235,
    237–38, 243–44, 247, 253–54, 260, 434,
    436
  bravery at Lützen, 246
  cavalry charge at Lützen, 254–56
  criticism of, 437, 443–45
  dissatisfaction with Wittgenstein, 283,
    314, 439, 442
  losses at Bautzen, 358
  praise for Lützen, 261
  prepares for Bautzen, 304, 311
  receives reinforcements, 390
  retreat to Oder, 370–71, 395
  retreats across Elbe, 280–81
  retreats from Bautzen, 355–60
  retreats from Elbe, 286
  retreats to Bautzen, 289
  retreats to Silesia, 365
  strategy after Lützen, 282
  wounded at Lützen, 246
complains about Russians, 145
concentrates Allied southern army, 180
confidence in army, 150, 209
confused over Napoleon's intentions, 155
crosses Elbe, 134
dissatisfaction with Russians, 182, 185
dissatisfaction with Wittgenstein, 282, 288
favors national revolt, 44
favourable reception at Dresden, 135
goes to Breslau, 58
ideally suited for dual command, 181
illness, 166
incapacitated by wound, 287
meets with Toll, 197
opposes Prussian pro-French party, 37
opposes retreat across Oder, 416
opposition to his command, 98
plans for war in 1809, 31

Blücher, Gebhard Leberecht von (cont.)
  pleased by Wittgenstein's demotion, 377
  proclamations in 1813, 125, 127–28, 130–32, 135, 168
  proposes offensive, 177
  rapport with Kutuzov, 123
  rapport with Wittgenstein, 123
  reaches Dresden, 134
  reaction to criticism, 132
  reacts to French drive to Saale, 191
  ready to face Napoleon, 207
  receives intercepted dispatches, 176
  reinstated in army, 98
  relationship with Gneisenau, 281, 414
  retreats to Oder, 413
  seeks to influence Kutuzov, 189
  seeks union with Wittgenstein, 154
  strategy in 1813, 158, 180
  supports Gneisenau's *Angriffskrieg*, 181
Bober (River), 8, 203, 371–73, 382, 389, 419
Bóbr, *see* Bober
Bogdanów, *see* Neuhof
Bogdaszowice, *see* Purschwitz
Bohemia, 19, 21, 48, 205, 285, 296, 307, 309, 320, 324, 332, 351, 365, 374, 406, 448–49
Bohrau, 417
Bölau hill, 338
Boleścin, *see* Pilzen
Bolesławice, *see* Bunzelwitz
Bolesławiec, *see* Bunzlau
Bolkenhain, 414, 419
Bolków Śląskie, *see* Bolkenhain
Bonaparte, Jerome, 25, 31
Bonaparte, Joseph, 24, 29, 32, 35
Bonaparte, Napoleon François Charles Joseph, 32
Bonet, Jean-Pierre, 240, 250, 255
Borcke, Karl August von, 144
Borna, 150, 152, 165, 172, 176, 185, 190–91, 202, 204, 207–9, 211–12, 215, 218, 220, 227, 261, 268–70, 272–75, 289, 294
Borodino (battle), 70, 197, 217, 271, 293, 303, 314, 337, 378, 440–41
Borów, *see* Bohrau
Borstell, Karl Ludwig von, 99, 101, 124, 133, 149, 155, 184, 280, 290
Bouches-de-l'Elbe Department, 140
Bourbons,
  of Naples, 23, 52
  of Spain, 27, 35, 38, 52
Boyen, Hermann von, 437
  adjutant to Frederick William III, 44
  as reformer, 3
  at Russian headquarters, 122, 189
  coordinates defense of Berlin, 274

  goes to Russia, 58
  liaison to Russians, 80
  measures to expand army, 47
  meets with Alexander, 59–60
  on Convention of Taurrogen, 78–79
  opposes Blücher as commander, 98
Braganza, 52
Brandenburg, 2, 21, 31, 35, 50, 117, 120–21, 124, 133, 149, 152–53, 159–60, 163, 172–73, 206, 239–40, 255–56, 365, 419, 430, 448
Brandenburg Gate, 2
Bremen, 32, 113, 141, 143, 168, 170
Brenier, Antoine-François, 235, 238, 246, 260
Breslau, 7, 20, 58, 83–84, 94, 98–99, 105, 120, 130, 147, 190, 279, 298–99, 301, 309, 368–69, 371, 374, 382, 384, 390, 393, 395–97, 399, 401–2, 404, 406–14, 417–18, 427, 448, 455
Brieg, 409, 417–18
Briesing, 338, 340, 353
Briesnitz, 285–86, 291, 349, 356
Britain,
  commits army to Iberia, 60
  declares war on Prussia in 1806, 23
  diplomacy in 1812, 60–65
  military supplies to Allies, 36, 53, 64, 118, 274
  needs allies to defeat Napoleon, 61
  negotiations with Russians, 63
  offers to evacuate Prussian royal family, 52
  opens dialogue with Prussia, 47
  subsidies to allies, 311
  subsidy for Swedes, 63
  supplies for Allies, 108
Brochocin, *see* Brockendorf
Brockendorf, 385
Brockhausen, Karl Christian von, 28
Brösa, 321, 336, 344–45, 378
Brunswick, 31, 145, 161, 167–68
Bruyères, Pierre-Joseph, 298
Brzeg, *see* Brieg
Bubna, Ferdinand von, 305, 308, 390
Budziwojów, *see* Baudmannsdorf
Bug (River), 72, 75
Bülow, Friedrich Wilhelm von, 66, 71–72, 80, 93, 99, 101, 122, 124, 133, 138, 155–56, 184, 204, 222, 260, 268, 270, 274, 280, 287, 289–90, 301, 316, 330, 367, 369, 382–83, 395–96, 398, 400, 404, 406–7, 412, 415, 417, 422, 425, 448
Bunbury, Henry, 86, 218, 418, 433, 438, 449
Bunzelwitz, 391, 403
Bunzlau, 122, 125, 127, 154, 190, 199, 365, 367–69, 371–72, 382–83, 389, 394, 398
Burk, 323, 331, 336–37, 341, 352–53
Burkatów, *see* Burkersdorf

Burkersdorf, 403
Byron of Kurland, 397
Bystrzyca, *see* Schweidnitz (stream)
Bytom, *see* Beuthen

Calabria, 4, 24
Calau, 317, 330
Camburg, 191, 197
Campbell, Neil, 218, 227, 433, 435, 438–39
Canitz-Christina, 315, 359
Cannewitz, 356
Carsdorf, 214, 227–28, 263
Castlereagh, Viscount (Robert Stewart),
       61–64, 85–86, 88, 97–98, 108, 119, 145,
       198–99, 305, 310, 313, 319, 374, 450
Cathcart, William, 64, 68, 97, 105, 108–9, 198,
       255, 308, 310, 373, 392, 435, 437,
       444–45, 448
Caulaincourt, Armand de, 321–22, 343, 390,
       399, 411–12
Central Commission for the Occupied
       German Territories, 131, 135, 150
Champ de Mars, 1
Champagny, Jean-Baptiste de, 28, 33, 39–40
Chaplits, Yefim, 386, 388
Charlemagne, 2
Charles (archduke of Austria), 19, 30–31
Charles IV (king), 35
Charles John, *see* Bernadotte, Jean-Baptiste
Charles William Ferdinand of Brunswick, 181
Charles XIII (king), 61, 95
Charpentier, Henri-François, 252–53
Chemineau, Jean, 232–33, 246, 260
Chemnitz, 152–53, 162, 184, 190, 196–97,
       203–4, 207, 220, 249, 310, 432
Chernishev, Alexander, 82, 93, 99, 101, 133,
       143, 161, 168, 184
Chichagov, Pavel, 73, 82
Chojnice, *see* Konitz
Chojnów, *see* Haynau
Chomutov, *see* Komotau
Chroślice, *see* Hennersdorf
Ciechów, *see* Dietzdorf
Clarke, Henri, 141, 422
Clausewitz, Carl von, 19, 58, 60, 75–76, 81,
       120, 122, 150, 164, 219, 246, 253, 291,
       305, 407
Coburg, 161, 175, 179, 185, 187, 205
Colditz, 172, 176, 203, 270, 272, 275–77
Compans, Jean-Dominique, 205, 240, 250
Confederation of the Rhine, 23, 26, 34, 54,
       125, 306, 309
Congress of Erfurt, 30, 32
Constantine (grand duke of Russia), 252, 315,
       336, 405, 409, 413
Continental System, 33, 35, 39, 54, 57, 60–61,
       63, 115, 140, 142

Convention of Åbo, 61–64, 71, 199
Convention of Tauroggen, 75, 77, 80–81, 431
Copenhagen, 63–64, 69, 98
Corswant, Karl Friedrich von, 354, 356, 385
Cöthen, 222
Cottbus, 125, 428
Cottbus District, 126–27, 132, 168
Crossen, 93, 108, 427
Cuxhaven, 142
Czartoryski, Adam, 36

Dahme, 136, 139, 317
Dalmatia, 449
Danzig, 5, 18, 25, 43, 50, 72, 79, 81, 91, 93, 112,
       159, 391, 428, 430
Davout, Louis-Nicolas, 34, 37, 51, 57, 66,
       113, 124, 140, 142–44, 161, 167, 221,
       249, 281, 301, 316, 369, 380, 400,
       428, 430
Dehlitz, 225
Delitzsch, 220
Delmas, Antoine-Guillaume, 347, 354
Denmark, 61–64, 85–88, 96, 98, 141–42,
       145–46, 184, 198
Dessau, 90, 153, 156–57, 182, 220, 222, 270,
       432
Deutmannsdorf, 389, 394
Deutsch Ossig, 368
Deutschlissa, 401–2
Diebitsch, Johann von, 75–76, 124, 213–14,
       217, 249, 289, 342, 426, 433, 438
Dietzdorf, 410–11
Dirschau, 82
Dittersbach, 419
Döbeln, 276
Döbeln, Georg Carl von, 145, 170
Doberlug, 300, 315
Doberschau, 314, 386
Doberschütz, 311, 337, 340–41, 345–46, 352
Dobroszów, *see* Doberschau
Dobschütz, 359
Döhlen, 228
Dohna-Schlobitten, Friedrich Ferdinand zu,
       29
Dohna-Schlobitten, Karl Friedrich zu, 58, 60,
       75–76
Dolffs, Florenz Ludwig von, 152, 162, 226,
       231, 233, 235, 255–56, 270, 337, 341,
       349, 355–56, 358, 385, 387
Dollstädt, 48
Domsen, 230–32, 247
Donauworth, 155
Dörnberg, Wilhelm Kasper von, 47, 52, 101,
       133, 143, 161, 168, 184
Dornburg, 191, 197, 205–6
*Dos de Mayo* uprising, 27
Drehsa, 320–22, 359

Dresden, 5–6, 101–2, 111–12, 120, 124–25, 131, 133, 139, 147, 149–50, 153–54, 158, 167, 185, 190, 277, 280, 282–88, 291–93, 298, 301, 310, 370, 438
  Allied Headquarters, 108, 191, 198
  *Altstadt*, 134, 277, 284–85
  bridge, 124, 127, 129, 134, 285, 291
  *Neustadt*, 125, 134, 277, 281, 286–89, 291, 299
Drezdenko, *see* Driesen
Driesen, 94
Drouot, Antoine, 253, 286
Droyßig, 212, 215
Dubreton, Jean-Louis, 170
duc de Bellune, *see* Victor, Claude
duc de Raguse, *see* Marmont, Auguste Frédéric
duc de Tarente, *see* Macdonald, Jacques-Étienne
Duchy of Oldenburg, 33, 49
Dufour, François-Marie, 170
duke of Wellington, *see* Wellesley, Arthur
Dumonceau, Jean-Baptiste, 170
Dumoulin, Charles, 243
Dumoustier, Pierre, 390
Duroc, Géraud Christophe, 363, 370, 423
Durosnel, Antoine-Jean, 285, 382
Durutte, Pierre-François, 167
Düsseldorf, 18
Dutch Revolt of 1787, 68
Dzierżoniów, *see* Reichenbach

East Prussia, 24–25, 35, 40, 49–50, 71–72, 77, 80–81, 99, 115, 374, 430
  French exploitation, 5, 70, 81
  Landtag, 84
École Militaire, 1
Eich hill, 327
Eilenburg, 172, 215, 220
Eisdorf, 238–39, 251–52, 264
Eisenach, 147, 161, 175, 177, 179, 183
Eisendorf, 399–400, 402, 404, 409, 411–12
Elbe (River) 5, 7–8, 51, 79, 99, 111, 121, 152, 167, 184, 193, 276–80, 282–88, 290–93, 298, 300, 307, 310, 438–39
Elbing, 48, 71, 81
Elbląg, *see* Elbing
Electorate of Salzburg, 27
Ełk, *see* Lyck
Ellrich, 165
Elster (River), 147, 157, 159, 193, 204, 208, 212, 225–28, 238, 263, 269, 438–39
Elsterwerda, 136, 139, 288
Emile of Hesse-Darmstadt, 251
Emmanuel, Yegor, 368, 396
Ems (River), 170

Erfurt, 111, 113, 125, 136, 146–48, 150–55, 157, 160–63, 175–77, 179–80, 185, 187, 190, 193, 197, 205–6, 219, 256, 277, 370, 432
Escheburg, 141, 169
Essen III, Peter, 75
Estonia, 375
Eugen of Württemberg, 215, 231–32, 235, 250–52, 254, 259, 269, 357, 361–63, 367–68, 389, 394, 401, 434
Ewald, Johann, 141
Eylau (battle), 24, 303, 440
Eyler, Aleksandr, 263

Falkenberg, 427
Fall Campaign of 1813, 112, 138, 142, 310, 422
federative paper, 311
Ferdinand (crown prince of Spain), 35
Ferdinand IV (king), 24
Finland, 61, 86–87, 96, 98
First Italian Campaign, 6, 208
Fischbach, 312
Fiume, 449
Flahaut, Charles-Auguste-Joseph de, 390
Flößberg, 294
Floßgraben, 210, 213–15, 228–30, 233, 235, 251–52, 269, 437
Francis I (emperor/kaiser), 2, 5, 27, 30, 32, 36, 65, 178, 189, 195, 273, 290, 305, 307–8, 395, 421, 448–49
Francis II (Holy Roman Emperor), *see* Francis I
Franco-Austrian alliance, 5
Franco-Austrian War of 1809, *see* War of the Fifth Coalition
Franco-Danish alliance, 145, 170
Franconia, 148, 151–53, 158, 161, 163–64, 177–78
Franco-Prussian Treaty of Paris
  1806, 23
  1808, 28–29, 31, 51, 53
  1812, 53, 58
Frankenstein, 413, 427
Frankenthal, 312
Frankfurt, 146–47, 150, 154, 177, 185
Frankfurt-am-Oder, 89, 93–94, 319, 382
Franquemont, Friedrich von, 338, 352–53, 370
Frauenprießnitz, 197
Fraustadt, 427
Frederick (prince of Prussia), 120
Frederick Augustus I (king), 39, 124–26, 128, 131, 134–36, 149, 153, 158, 163, 284–85, 292–93, 302
Frederick I (king), 187–88, 273, 284
Frederick II (king), 2, 106, 126, 166, 174, 199, 236, 304, 309, 334, 347, 391, 429, 455
Frederick VI (king), 85, 198

Frederick William (crown prince of Prussia),
    83, 120, 239, 341, 433
    at Lützen, 239
Frederick William ("Black Duke of
    Brunswick"), 31
Frederick William III (king), 2, 30–32, 81,
    84–85, 90–91, 94–95, 98, 103, 106, 120,
    122, 134, 306, 415, 421, 429–32, 448,
    452
    accepts French alliance, 52, 56
    after Bautzen, 358
    after Lützen, 274, 280
    Alexander's junior partner, 429, 455
    alliance proposals to Napoleon, 42
    alliance with Napoleon, 3, 60
    at Bautzen, 342, 354, 379, 442, 445
    at Lützen, 227, 230, 239
    awards first Iron Cross, 144
    between Britain and France, 23–24, 35, 39
    between Russia and France, 33–34, 36–38,
        41–43, 45–46, 48, 51, 55
    breaks alliance with Napoleon, 6
    changes role of Landwehr, 416
    creates Iron Cross, 4
    criticized by Russian ambassador, 57
    declares war on France, 105
    delines British offer to flee, 52
    difficult decisions in 1813, 4, 6, 8, 71, 79,
        418
    difficult position in June, 405
    discharges Blücher, 58
    disciplines Blücher, 132
    embraces people's war, 4
    establishes Silesian Army, 396
    flees to Breslau, 82
    Franco-Prussian Treaty of 1808, 29
    in 1807, 2
    instructions to Blücher, 105
    issues "An mein Kriegsheer", 107
    issues "An mein Volk", 105–6
    issues punishments for crimes against army,
        108
    letters to Alexander, 40, 45, 58
    measures to defend Prussia, 35, 39
    measures to expand army, 47
    meets with Alexander in 1805, 21
    meets with Stewart, 199
    negotiates with British and Swedes, 198–99
    on retreating to Oder, 396
    opposed to second battle, 310
    opposes Blücher as commander, 98
    opposes popular insurrection, 294
    passive role in foreign affairs, 429
    public opinion, 60
    reaction to Convention of Tauroggen,
        77–78, 80
    reaction to Lützen, 260–61

    reacts to Napoleon's ultimatum, 51
    reasons against Russo-Prussian alliance in
        1811, 56
    reasons for Russian alliance in 1813, 80
    reinstates Blücher, 98
    rejects alliance with Russia, 55
    rejects Gneisenau's advice, 418
    rejects retreat to Oder, 392
    rejects war with France in 1809, 27, 30–31
    relationship with Gneisenau, 281
    resolves to break alliance with Napoleon,
        78
    seeks Austrian alliance in 1813, 79
    seeks Russian alliance, 46
    ultimatums to Napoleon, 21, 24
    wants to give battle at Bautzen, 322
    withdraws from Continental System, 108
Frederick William IV (king), 2
Frederick William, ("Great Elector"), 106
Freiberg, 153–54, 196–97, 203, 207, 278, 284
*Freikorps* (paramilitary partisans), 101–2, 333
French Eagles, 1–2, 4, 6, 113, 140
French Imperator, *see* Napoleon, as new
    Caesar
French Revolution, 3, 29, 140
Fressinet, Philibert, 252
Friedeberg, 428
Friederichs, Jean-Parfait, 250, 341
Friedland (battle), 25, 217, 236, 271, 275, 378
Frohburg, 153, 185, 197, 209, 215, 268–70,
    273, 275, 294
Fulda, 155, 160, 185

Gäbersdorf, 412
Galgen hill, 338
Galicia, 40, 65, 307
*Garnisonkirch*, 2
Gärnitz, 264
Gdańsk, *see* Danzig
George (duke of Oldenburg), 33
George III (king), 24, 31
Gera, 148–49, 152–53, 159, 203
Geringswalde, 197
German Empire, 4
German Legion, 89, 96
Germany, 2, 37, 64, 88, 95, 98, 111, 198
Gersdorf, 276–77, 284
Gießmannsdorf, 372
Girard, Jean-Baptiste, 232, 235, 238, 242, 246,
    260
Gitschin, 421
Glatz, 25, 290, 366, 393, 405, 407, 413, 427
Gleina, 327, 331, 337, 343, 345–47, 349, 352,
    364, 376, 378, 445, 454
Gleisberg, 211
Gleiwitz, 117
Gliwice, *see* Gleiwitz

Glogau, 7–8, 25, 29, 34, 42–43, 46, 54, 57, 71,
    82, 90–91, 93–94, 99, 105, 112, 121, 124,
    136, 192, 282–83, 301, 309, 317, 369,
    382–83, 388–91, 395, 397–99, 402, 409,
    422, 427, 447
Glogów, *see* Glogau
Gneisenau, August von
    anti-French sentiment, 38, 52
    as Blücher's chief of staff, 281, 283, 288,
      305, 310, 396–97, 414, 417
    after Bautzen, 357
    ambush at Haynau, 385, 387
    assumes command, 287
    at Bautzen, 342–43, 346–47, 355, 444,
      446, 454
    complains over Barclay, 407
    complains about king's letter, 370
    defends Blücher, 444–45
    dissatisfaction with Barclay, 413
    dissatisfaction with Wittgenstein, 289–90,
      293, 314, 366, 442–43
    expects third battle, 404, 406
    instructions from Hardenberg, 305
    lobbies for third battle, 414–16
    mobilization of Landwehr, 415–16
    mood of the army, 304
    on Thirty Years War, 353
    opposes armistice, 416, 418
    opposes retreat across Elbe, 413
    opposes retreat across Oder, 406–8, 414,
      417
    prepares for Bautzen, 304, 311–12, 318,
      329
    retreats to Oder, 370
    Silesian Plan, 405, 417
    wants to separate from Russians, 366
    as leader of anti-French movement, 36
    as reformer, 3
    assistant chief of staff, 149, 248
    after Lützen, 274
    assessment of Lützen, 435
    at Lützen, 233, 240, 246, 253, 255
    complains about Central Commission,
      150
    criticizes Russians, 259
    dissatisfaction with Wittgenstein, 439
    on army after Lützen, 279
    retreat after Lützen, 269
    becomes assistant chief of staff, 122
    becomes chief of staff, 122
    communicates with British, 47, 53
    concern over Russian ammunition, 185–86
    critical of Barclay, 376
    evaluates Napoleon's options, 147
    excuses Russians for pillaging, 127
    favors national revolt, 44
    justifies Blücher's proclamations, 130

justifies Blücher's actions at Cottbus, 127
    measures to expand army, 47
    mood of the Saxons, 129
    opinion on "An mein Volk," 105
    petitions British for support, 47
    proclamations in 1813, 125, 127–28
    proposes *Angriffskrieg*, 180–81
    secret assignment from Hardenberg, 291
    Silesian Plan, 290, 305
    unimpressed with Toll, 197
    wants field command, 122
Gnesen, 82
Gniezno, *see* Gnesen
Göda, 293, 297, 312
Gohlis, 220
Goldberg, 365, 371, 383–85, 389, 393–95, 419,
    428
Golitsyn, Dmitry, 263
Goltz, Friedrich von der, 37, 41, 45, 54
Gommern, 152
Gorchakov, Andrey, 215, 263, 315, 324, 336, 440
Görlitz, 122–23, 125, 133, 190, 279, 303, 306,
    312, 359–61, 365–68, 370, 372, 428,
    441–42
Gorzów Wielkopolski, *see* Landsberg
Gościszów, *see* Gießmannsdorf
Gotha, 113, 150–51, 155, 157, 160, 163, 165,
    176–77, 179, 185, 187, 205
Gottamelde, 320–21, 325, 327, 334, 336, 351
Gottlobs hill, 338, 346, 352
Gouré, Louis-Anné, 246
Gräfenthal, 161, 187
Grand Duchy of Berg, 25
Grand Duchy of Warsaw, 5, 25, 32, 36–37, 39–
    40, 50–51, 65, 73, 82, 99, 117, 190, 306,
    430, 432, 449
grand duke of Warsaw, *see* Frederick
    Augustus I (king)
Grand Marshal of the Palace, *see* Duroc,
    Géraud Christophe
Grande Armée, 1
    1st Division, 143, 170, 276
    152nd Line, 140
    34th Division, 139, 167
    37th Division, 273
    I Cavalry Corps, 110, 167, 224, 238, 252,
      264, 271, 273, 276, 284–85, 294, 302,
      312, 318, 320, 337, 359–60, 362, 364,
      368–69, 371–72, 383, 385, 389, 394,
      399, 412, 428
    1st Light Cavalry Division, 298
    3rd Heavy Cavalry Division, 368, 394
    I Corps, 71, 82, 110, 167, 170, 428
    2nd Division, 170
    5th Division, 170
    II Cavalry Corps, 110, 167, 272, 316–18,
      369, 389, 428

II Corps, 8, 71, 82, 110, 167, 170, 272, 300, 316–18, 369, 382, 411–12, 428
  1st Division, 334
  4th Division, 170
III Corps, 8, 71, 82, 110, 119, 160–61, 175, 187, 205, 209–10, 221, 224, 236, 238, 242, 246–47, 250, 256–58, 260, 270, 272–73, 275, 277, 292, 300, 315–18, 320, 322–23, 325, 328, 330, 333, 345, 347, 349, 359–60, 364, 368, 370, 372, 383, 393–94, 398, 401–2, 410–11, 422, 428, 436
  8th Division, 209–10, 224, 229–30, 232, 238, 256
  9the Division, 224, 235, 238, 349, 354
  10th Division, 224, 232, 235, 238, 349, 354
  11th Division, 224, 235, 239, 243, 349, 354
  39th Division, 224, 238, 251, 349, 372, 394, 398
  losses at Bautzen, 359
IV Corps, 71, 82, 110, 160–61, 175, 185, 187, 205, 211, 224, 231, 238, 242, 248, 257, 271, 273, 275–78, 284–85, 291, 293–94, 299, 312, 318, 323, 330, 337, 352, 359–60, 364, 366, 368–72, 383, 389, 394, 400–1, 411–12, 428
  12th Division, 205, 224, 249, 353
  15th Division, 205, 249
  29th Division, 205
  38th Division, 205
V Corps, 8, 71, 74, 167, 207, 211–12, 224, 228–29, 238, 257, 269, 271, 273, 276, 278–79, 284–86, 292, 294, 300, 315–20, 322–23, 327–28, 334, 345, 359–64, 366–67, 369–72, 383, 385, 388, 394, 398–402, 411, 428, 434
  16th Division, 228, 345, 352, 385–86
  17th Division, 272, 334, 349, 354, 387
  18th Division, 349
  19th Division, 349, 356
VI Corps, 71, 82, 85, 110, 160–61, 175, 179, 187, 205, 211, 224, 231, 235, 238, 242, 250, 257, 271, 273, 275, 277–78, 284–85, 291, 294, 299, 312, 330, 337, 341–42, 359–60, 364, 367–69, 371–72, 389, 394, 399, 404, 411–12, 428, 436
  20th Division, 205, 224, 240
  21st Division, 224, 240
  22nd Division, 224, 250
VII Corps, 8, 75, 82, 90, 110, 167, 272–73, 277, 284–85, 292, 296, 300, 315–19, 325, 330, 345, 359–61, 363–64, 366, 368–69, 371–72, 383, 385–86, 388, 394, 398–402, 411, 428
  32nd Division, 272

VIII Corps, 71, 82, 428
IX Corps, 82
X Corps, 70, 81–82, 428
XI Corps, 71, 110, 167, 205, 208, 211–12, 224, 231, 237–38, 243, 251, 257, 260, 264, 270–71, 273, 276–77, 284–85, 291, 293–94, 298–99, 312, 318, 330, 337, 342, 352, 359–60, 366, 368–72, 383, 389, 394–95, 399–400, 411–12, 428, 434
  31st Division, 252, 260, 264
  35th Division, 264, 270
  36th Division, 252, 260, 264
XII Corps, 8, 110, 161, 187, 205, 210, 271, 273, 275, 277, 284, 291–92, 294, 299, 312, 318, 329–30, 337, 342, 352, 359, 369, 383, 398, 412, 415, 422, 428
  13th Division, 205
  14th Division, 205
Army of Germany, 34, 37
Army of Portugal, 35
Army of the Elbe, 89, 110, 119, 161, 175, 191, 197, 207, 238, 298
Army of the Main, 90, 110, 112, 119, 153, 160–61, 175, 179, 187, 191, 197, 209–10, 224
Austrian Auxiliary Corps, 74
Badenese troops, 185, 246, 251, 372
Bavarian troops, 125, 137, 148, 151, 161, 163, 167, 179, 185–87, 205, 221, 273
combat-effectiveness in 1813, 436
condition after Lützen, 271
defeated in Russia, 3
Dutch troops, 362
exhaustion in 1813, 421
*Grognards*, 436
Hessian troops, 251, 372
Imperial Guard, 71, 81–82, 139, 160–61, 167, 175, 185, 187, 205–6, 210–11, 221, 224, 231, 236–39, 242, 247, 253, 255–57, 260, 270, 273, 277, 285, 291, 294, 302, 312, 318, 320, 352–54, 359–62, 364, 368, 370–71, 383, 389, 393–94, 398–400, 402, 411, 421, 428, 434, 436, 445
in Fall Campaign of 1813, 422
inexperienced infantry in 1813, 7, 188, 235
invades Russia, 3, 70
Italian troops, 36, 73, 81, 137, 146, 155, 158, 161, 163–65, 175–76, 179, 182, 185, 189, 191, 205, 210–11, 221, 249, 286, 323, 325–26, 328, 344, 401, 403
  of 1806, 155
  of 1812, 70, 116, 207
  of 1813, 90, 109

Italian troops (cont.)
  personnel at Königsberg on 21 December
    1812, 72
  Prussian troops, 70
  retreats from Russia, 71
  Rheinbund troops, 163, 185, 189
  Saxon troops, 75, 125, 139, 158, 167, 272,
    292, 296, 302, 360, 362, 399
  weak cavalry in 1813, 7, 188, 364
  Westphalian troops, 186, 273, 298, 370
  Württemberger troops, 161, 185, 205,
    210–11, 338, 352–53, 370, 401
Graudenz, 25, 48, 50, 71–72, 75, 80, 112
Grawert, Julius August von, 70
Greiffenberg, 428
Greiz, 152
Grenier, Paul, 167
Grimma, 149, 161, 172
Grodków, *see* Grottkau
Grodziszcze, *see* Obergröditz
Groitzsch, 227–28, 255, 260, 268–69
Grolman, Karl Wilhelm von, 120, 166,
    229–30, 415
Großbeckern, 394
Großenhain, 136, 139, 283, 287–89, 298, 301
Großgörschen, ,210, 212–13, 217, 224, 229–33,
    236–37, 239, 242–45, 247, 249–50,
    252–54, 256, 258, 261, 271, 434, 436–37
  *see also* Lützen (battle)
Großgrimma, 225
Großharthau, 321
Großhartmannsdorf, 371, 389
Großrackwitz, 389
Großrosen, 395, 401, 404, 413
Großrosen (engagement), 401
Großschkorlopp, 227, 251
Großwilkau, 413
Grottkau, 427
Grouchy, Emmanuel, 320, 322
Grudziądz, *see* Graudenz
Grünabach, 213–14, 225, 229, 249
Grüneberg, 428
Gryfów Śląski, *see* Greiffenberg
Grzegorzów, *see* Gäbersdorf
Gumbinnen, 71
Günthersdorf, 228
Gusev, *see* Gumbinnen
Guttau, 325, 327, 334, 336, 345, 351, 378

Habsburgs, 2, 450–51
Hake, Georg Ernst Karl, 47
Halberstadt, 149, 151, 154, 165, 177, 448
Halle, 150, 156, 179, 183, 187–88, 191, 202–3,
    206–9, 212, 222, 224, 260, 268, 270, 448
Hamburg, 32, 66, 90, 99, 101, 112, 119, 125,
    139–45, 147, 169–70, 206, 301, 316,
    400, 418, 428, 430

Altona Gate, 139
Prefecture Guard, 139
Hanau, 161
Hanover, 21, 23–24, 33, 95, 101, 111, 113, 145,
    161, 168
  occupied by French, 21
Hanoverian Legion, 141
Hanseatic cities, 32, 140, 198
  Legion, 141
Harburg, 144
Hardenberg, Karl von, 29, 37–43, 45–48,
    51–57, 66–67, 83–84, 94, 105–6, 108,
    122, 126–29, 132–35, 138, 145, 149–50,
    162, 167–72, 180, 184, 192, 196–97,
    199, 220–22, 274, 279, 289, 291, 295,
    297, 304, 306, 310, 332, 357, 366, 370,
    385, 398, 407–8, 415–16, 418, 432, 439,
    445
  accepts French alliance, 52
  advises king to flee to Breslau, 83
  as reformer, 3
  as Stein's successor, 29
  criticizes Blücher, 130
  criticizes Blücher's action at Cottbus, 127
  discord between Russians and Prussians,
    405
  discussions with Russians, 40–41, 43, 57
  expands Prussia's war aims, 306
  fails to persuade king, 55–56
  forced to accept French demands, 54
  meets with Stadion, 306
  negotiates with Stewart, 198, 310
  opposes alliance with Russia, 40
  petitions British for support, 47
  responds to Silesian Plan, 305
  seeks French alliance, 39–43
  supports idea of a second battle, 290
  supports pro-French party, 38–39
  supports war against France, 80
  wants to give battle at Bautzen, 322
  wants to work with Napoleon, 79
Hartmannsdorf, 180
Harz Mountains, 111, 154, 158, 161, 165, 175,
    177, 179, 183, 186–87, 220, 432
Hatzfeld, Franz Ludwig von, 39, 42
Haugwitz, Christian von, 21
Hausdorf, 276
Havelberg, 5, 112
Haynau, 365, 371, 383–86, 388, 393–94, 398,
    448
Haynau (ambush), 385–88, 423, 446
Heidersdorf, 413, 421
Heister, Levin Karl von, 134, 169
Helfreich, Gothard August von, 220
Henckel von Donnersmarck, Wilhelm
    Ludwig Viktor, 77, 239, 252, 263, 445
Hennersdorf, 367, 380, 395

Hermsdorf, 327, 367–68
Herrnstadt, 427
Herzberg, 282–83, 315–16
Herzogswaldau, 370, 401
Hesse, 28, 31
Hippel, Theodor Gottlieb von, 105–6, 114, 305, 405
Hobe, Karl Friedrich von, 163, 223
Hochkirch, 302, 304, 331, 359
Hochkirch (battle), 304, 347
Hochkirch (Silesia), 368
Hof, 137, 147–54, 158–59, 161–62, 179, 181, 190, 196
Hohendorf, 394
Hohenlohe, 210, 226, 252
Hohenzollerns, 2, 4, 31, 34, 38, 41, 52, 240
Holland, 32, 55, 60, 106, 143, 306–7, 429
Patriot Revolt, 429
Holy Roman Empire, 2
Hope, Alexander, 89
Horn, Heinrich Wilhelm von, 244, 354–56
Hoyerswerda, 301, 316–20, 322–23, 325, 328–29, 333–34, 342, 345, 369, 398, 400
Hoyerswerda (engagement), 398
Humboldt, Wilhelm von, 195
Hundsfeld, 427
Hünerbein, Friedrich Heinrich von, 226, 244

Iberia, 28–29, 32, 56–57, 60, 63, 68, 118, 189, 192, 198, 429, 450
Ilovaysky XII, Vasily, 269
Iron Cross, 4, 105, 144
Iron Marshal, *see* Davout, Louis-Nicolas
Italy, 2, 23, 26, 56–57, 97, 137, 221, 298, 306–7, 451
Ivernois, Francis d', 65
Iwiny, *see* Mittlau

Jacobin general, *see* Scharnhorst
Jadwisin, *see* Steinsdorf
Jarnołtów, *see* Arnoldsmühl
Jauer, 373, 385, 391, 394–95, 397, 399–401, 404, 409, 411–12, 414–15, 455
Jawor, *see* Jauer
Jędrzychowice, *see* Hennersdorf
Jena, 2, 24, 112, 114, 149, 158, 180, 187–88, 191, 196–97, 202, 205–6, 271
Jena (battle), ,271, 293, 348, 453
*see also* Jena–Auerstedt
Jena–Auerstedt (battle), 2, 24
Jenkwitz, 302, 315, 323, 331, 351, 354, 356–57, 442
Jerzmanki, *see* Hermsdorf
Jičín, *see* Gitschen
Johnsdorf, 325–27
Jomini, Henri, 114, 119, 171, 174, 191, 316, 333, 347–48, 377

Jordan, Johann Ludwig von, 105
Jordanów Śląski, *see* Jordansmühl
Jordansmühl, 417

Kaysarov, Paisi, 370, 396
Kaja, 211–13, 224, 229–32, 237–39, 242, 244–46, 251, 253, 264, 270, 273
Kalckreuth, Friedrich Adolph von, 37
Kaliningrad, *see* Königsberg
Kalisch, 82, 91, 94, 98–99, 101, 103, 111, 115, 122, 124–25, 136–37, 151, 190, 206, 365, 392, 398, 406, 408, 413, 432
Russian headquarters, 137, 154, 201
Kalisch (engagement), 90, 93
Kalisch–Breslau Agreements, 127
Kamenski stratagem, 199, 222
Kamensky (Kamenski), Mikhail, 222
Kamenz, 289, 293, 299, 312, 316, 318, 334
Kamienna Góra, *see* Landeshut
Kammendorf, 399
Kanth, 419, 421, 427
Karkonosze, *see* Riesengebirge
Karl August of Weimar, 166
Karl of Mecklenburg-Strelitz, 120
Kassel, 31, 101, 111, 177, 180
Kattern, 427
Katzbach (River), 365, 371, 385, 394–95, 412, 418–19
Katzler, Andreas Georg von, 355–56, 358, 360–61
rearguard actions after Lützen, 270
Kaunus, *see* Kovno
Kėdainiai, *see* Keidany
Keidany, 73
Kiefern hill, 338, 340–41, 344, 346, 352–53
King's German Legion, 144
Kingdom of Naples, 23, 52, 89
Kingdom of Westphalia, 25, 28, 31, 101, 143, 430
Kirgener, François-Joseph, 363
Kitzen, 252
Kladau, 91
Klaipėda, *see* Memel
Kleinbautzen, 323, 331, 337, 348–49, 355, 443
*kleinen Krieg*, 157, 417
Kleinförstchen, 328
Kleingörschen, 210, 212–13, 224, 229–31, 236–39, 243–47, 250–53, 261, 436–37
Kleinschkorlopp, 227
Kleinwelka, 328
Kleist, Friedrich Heinrich von, 80, 172, 202–3, 207–9, 215, 220, 222–23, 228, 255–56, 260, 268, 270, 276–77, 280–83, 287–89, 293, 303–4, 315, 336–37, 340–41, 345–46, 349, 354–56, 365, 369, 376, 384, 390, 396, 399, 405, 412–13, 444

Klix, 311, 323, 329, 336, 341–42, 345, 348–49, 351, 378
Kłodawa, *see* Kladau
Kłodzko, *see* Glatz
Klüx, Joseph Friedrich Karl von, 172–73, 180, 276
  at Bautzen, 337, 346, 353, 355
  at Lützen, 226, 228, 231–33, 235–37, 239, 242, 244, 280, 352
  operations in Silesia, 385
Knesebeck, Karl Friedrich von dem, 84, 182, 190, 274, 304, 413, 415
  at Austrian headquarters in 1809, 30
  at Bautzen, 342, 355
  disagrees with Gneisenau, 416
  disagrees with Toll, 293
  influence over king, 417
  mission to Austria, 79–80
  mission to Russia, 56
  negotiates with Russians, 84, 91, 94–95
  opposes Blücher, 98
  opposes third battle, 310
  recommends war with France in 1809, 30
  reputation as strategist, 101
  respected by Russians, 343
  suggests march to Schweidnitz, 374
  supports armistice, 418
  supports retreat across Oder, 396
  Wurschen Plan, 308–9
Koberwitz, 417
Kobierzyce, *see* Koberwitz
Koblenz, 18
Köckritz, Karl Leopold von, 37
Kohren, 153, 173, 185, 197, 209
Kolberg, 25, 35, 37, 44, 47–48, 50, 52, 54, 112, 186, 274, 290
Kolo, 93
Koło, *see* Kolo
Kołobrzeg, *see* Kolberg
Komorniki, *see* Kammendorf
Komotau, 310
Königsberg, 2, 6, 24, 26–27, 30, 50, 58, 71–72, 77, 79–81, 97, 115
Königsbrück, 288–89, 293, 299, 301
Königshain, 359
Königswartha, 322–23, 325, 327–29
Königswartha (engagement), 323, 388, 441
Konitz, 82
Konovnitsyn, Pyotr, 72–73, 242, 252, 263
Koppatsch hill, 352
Körner, Theodore, 20
Kosel, 25
Kostenblut, 410, 419
Kostomłoty, *see* Kostenblut
Köthen, 156, 158, 220, 292, 300
Kovno, 73
Koźle, *see* Kosel

Kraków, 82, 206, 390, 406
Krasnoznamenskoye, *see* Dollstädt
Kraszowice, 380
  *see also* Kroischwitz
Krauseneck, Johann Wilhelm von, 120, 166, 396
Kreckwitz, 311, 337, 345–46, 352–53
Kreckwitz heights, 303, 312, 315, 329, 336–37, 343, 346–48, 352–56, 442–43, 445, 454–55
Kreibau, 371
Kreisau, 403–4, 409
Kriptau, 411
Kroischwitz, 371
Kroitsch, 394
Krosno Odrzańskie, *see* Crossen
Krotoszyce, *see* Kroitsch
Krümper, 35, 47, 53, 104
Krusemarck, Friedrich Wilhelm von, 42, 45–46, 57, 60, 80, 91–92
Krzeptów, *see* Kriptau
Krzywa, *see* Kreibau
Krzyżowa, *see* Kreisau
Kumschütz, 293, 304
Kunzendorf, 372
Kurakin, Aleksandr, 46
Küstrin, 18, 25, 29, 82, 91, 93, 99, 139, 283, 317, 319
Kutuzov, Mikhail, 72–73, 75, 82, 89–91, 93–94, 99–103, 105, 122–23, 282, 375, 426, 431–33
  advises against advancing beyond Elster, 147
  advises Wittgenstein not to cross Elbe, 156
  Allied commander in chief, 101, 131, 133, 136–37, 139, 147
  criticizes Blücher, 131
  rules for issuing proclamations, 132
  at Bunzlau, 190
  *"Aufruf an die Deutschen,"* 130
  Central Commission, 135
  concentrates Allied armies, 190
  death, 199
  disagrees with Wittgenstein, 133
  dissatisfaction with Wittgenstein, 139
  falls ill, 191
  justifies his caution, 156
  opposes continuing the war, 73
  proclamations, 135
  resists combined attack on Eugene, 147
  strategic views, 159
  strategy in 1813, 190
Kwidzyn, *see* Marienwerder
Kwisa, *see* Queis

Laboissière, François Garnier de, 221
Łagiewniki, *see* Heidersdorf

łagów, *see* Leopoldshain
Lagrange, Joseph, 349, 388
Lähn, 419
Landeshut, 419
Landeskrone, 363, 365
Landsberg, 93, 222
Landsturm, 4, 81, 115, 274, 290, 294, 394
Landtag, 81
Landwehr, 4, 30, 80–81, 99, 107, 115, 121,
    150, 274, 279, 290, 295, 366, 396,
    402, 405, 407, 413, 416–17, 422,
    424, 426–27
Langenreichenbach, 292
Langeron, Louis Alexandre de, 375, 384, 386,
    408, 413, 419, 421, 447
Lanskoy, Sergey, 122, 395–96, 417
Lanusse, Pierre, 247
Latour-Maubourg, Marie-Victor, 167,
    302, 337, 357, 362, 367, 410–11,
    428
Lauban, 125, 365, 367–68, 370–72, 383
Lauenburg, 141
Lauriston, Jacques-Alexandre, 141, 167,
    207, 228, 237–38, 257, 269–70,
    277–80, 284, 286, 292, 294, 301,
    315–17, 319–20, 322, 325, 327–30,
    333–35, 345, 347–49, 354, 360, 362,
    367–69, 372, 378, 385, 388, 394,
    398–99, 401–2, 411
Lauterseiffen, 389
Lautitz, 360
Lavrov, Nikolay, 263
Lecoq, Karl von, 125, 134
Legnica, *see* Liegnitz
Legnickie Pole, *see* Wahlstatt
Leipzig, 6–7, 113, 147–50, 188, 193, 204,
    208, 210, 228, 237, 270, 273, 310,
    434
Leopold of Hessen-Homburg, 244
Leopoldshain, 368
Leschnau, 427
Leśnica, *see* Deutschlissa
Leszno, *see* Leschnau
Leubus, 402
Leutzsch, 228
Lichtenstein, 162
Liegnitz, 123, 365, 371, 374, 382–85, 388, 390,
    392–96, 398–99, 401–2, 414, 419, 421,
    428
Lieven, Christoph, 36–41, 45–48, 50, 52,
    54–55, 57, 59, 198
Lindenau, 209, 213, 228, 237, 256
linear tactics, 202, 217, 227, 257
Lines of Torres Vedras, 36
Lippitsch, 323
Lisbon, 52
Lithuania, 24

Litten, 302–3, 337, 341, 345–46, 353–55
Littoral, 449
Livonia, 375
Löbau, 133, 302, 325, 356, 358–61
Löbau (stream), 360
Lobendau, 388
Löbstedt, 228, 270
Loos, 389
Louis Ferdinand (prince of Prussia), 166
Louisa (queen), 34, 37
Low Countries, 68, 450
Lowe, Hudson, 67, 81, 86–88, 95–96, 104, 358,
    418, 441, 449–50
Löwenberg, 125, 365, 371–72, 383–84
Löwenhjelm, Karl, 61
Łozy, *see* Loos
Lubań, *see* Lauban
Lübben, 319, 333, 369
Lübeck, 32, 35, 140, 143, 145
Lubiatów, *see* Lobendau
Lubiąż, *see* Leubus
Lucka, 269
Luckau, 7, 282, 300–1, 316–19, 367, 369, 383
Luckau (engagement), 412, 448
Ludwigslust, 141
Lüneburg, 140, 143, 272
Lüneburg (engagement), 143–44
Lusatia, 102, 302, 323, 419
Lützen, 8, 198, 202–3, 207–10, 212–13, 218,
    224, 229, 231–32, 235–37, 242, 248,
    256–57, 261, 270, 273, 276, 434, 437,
    453
Lützen (battle), 6–7, 200, 256, 258, 268, 271,
    273, 292, 295, 301–2, 315, 353–54, 364,
    378, 388, 397, 415, 422, 433, 435,
    438–39, 442, 447, 451, 453
    assessment, 436
    casualties, 259–60
    condition of Allied army after, 279
    disorder of Allied army after, 269
    opposing armies, 217
    terrain features, 213, 229, 233
Lützow Freikorps, 20
Lwówek Śląski, *see* Löwenberg
Lyck, 84

Macdonald, Jacques-Étienne, 70, 75–79,
    81–83, 231, 238, 244, 251, 253,
    257, 264, 270–71, 293, 298–99,
    301, 312–13, 315–16, 318, 330, 337,
    344, 351, 357, 359, 361, 368, 383,
    410, 436
    commands right wing of Grande Armée,
        366, 368, 370, 372, 384, 389, 394–95,
        399–400, 402, 404, 409, 411
    at Großrosen, 401
    at Herzogswaldau, 401

Madrid, 27, 29, 35, 68

Magdeburg, 5, 18, 48, 93, 97, 99, 101, 111, 113, 124, 139, 142, 145–46, 148–49, 151–52, 154–56, 161, 167, 178, 180, 184, 205–6, 221, 276, 289, 319, 380, 430

Main (River), 5, 147, 155, 158, 161

Mainz, 111, 125, 160–61, 175, 179, 187, 205

Maison, Nicolas-Joseph, 228, 237, 327, 345, 347, 352, 354, 385–88, 399

Makowice, *see* Schwengfeld

Malbork, *see* Marienburg

Malschwitz, 311, 337, 345–47, 352, 378, 440, 445

Marchand, Jean-Gabriel, 188, 238–39, 251, 347, 349, 354, 372, 394, 398, 402, 412

Maret, Hughes-Bernard, 42, 57, 390

Marienburg, 71

Marienwerder, 71, 82

Markersdorf, 362–64, 366

Markranstädt, 211, 213, 224, 230, 237, 251, 257, 264

Marmont, Auguste Frédéric, 161, 175, 179, 187, 205, 211, 224, 231, 235, 238, 240, 242, 246, 248, 250, 253–54, 256–57, 271, 275, 278, 292, 298, 312–13, 330, 337, 341, 344, 352, 354, 357, 367, 369, 371–72, 383–84, 389, 393–95, 398, 400–2, 404, 409–12, 425, 434, 453

Massena, André, 20

Maukendorf, 322, 328, 330

Mecklenburg, 120, 144, 316, 380, 419

Mecklenburg-Schwerin, 141, 145

Mecklenburg-Strelitz, 141, 145

Mediterranean Sea, 60, 87

Meiningen, 155, 160, 177, 179

Meißen, 134, 136, 139, 149, 151, 153, 167, 208, 219, 276–87, 292, 296

Memel, 24, 51, 73, 77, 81, 260

Menar, Friedrich Löwis von, 82

Mengelsdorf, 359–61, 365

Meretsch, 82

Merka, 313

Merkel, Friedrich Theodor, 305

Merkine, *see* Meretsch

Merseburg, 187–88, 191, 197, 202, 206, 208–10, 220, 224, 228, 244, 272

Mertschütz, 395

Meschwitz, 359

Metternich, Klemens von, 18, 80, 85, 305, 307, 322, 332, 449–50, 458

Meuchen, 213, 251

Meuselwitz, 265

Meyhen, 213

Michelsdorf, 385–88, 393, 411–12

Michów, *see* Michelsdorf

Mierczyce, *see* Mertschütz

Mikhailovsky-Danilevsky, Aleksandr, 242

Milików, *see* Herzogswaldau

Miloradovich, Mikhail, 74, 82, 91, 124, 134, 136, 154, 158, 161–62, 176–77, 181, 183–85, 190, 196–97, 200, 203, 207, 209, 211–12, 215–16, 220, 222, 236, 248–49, 255, 268–69, 271, 276–77, 284, 286–89, 291, 293, 295, 299, 311–12, 314, 318, 324–25, 337, 341, 343, 351, 361–62, 377, 413, 435, 439, 443, 448, 453

Mirsk, *see* Friedeberg

Mittlau, 371

Mittweida, 152, 163, 165, 180, 197, 207, 278

Mochbern, 411

Möckern, 145, 152

Modelsdorf, 371, 386–87

Modlikowice, *see* Modelsdorf

Modlin, 82, 89, 124, 159

Moldavia and Wallachia, 36, 40

*Monarchenhügel*, 229–31, 239, 250, 255, 271

Morand, Joseph, 139–41, 143, 167, 170, 249, 338, 353

Moritzburg, 288, 298, 312

Mortier, Édouard Adolphe, 253, 352, 383, 398

Moscow, 6, 20, 65, 70, 238, 314, 391, 447, 451–52

Mściszów, *see* Seifersdorf

Mściwojów, *see* Profen

Muchobór, *see* Mochbern

Müffling, Karl Ferdinand von, 120, 166, 184, 230, 232, 281, 342–43, 345–47, 354, 374, 376, 385, 391, 396, 403, 413, 418, 433, 440–41, 443–46, 448

Mühlberg, 148–49, 190, 208, 219, 268, 277, 281–83, 288

Mulde (River), 145, 149–51, 159, 187, 190, 193, 204, 275–79, 439

Münchberg, 179

Münster, Ernst Friedrich zu, 67, 150, 166, 385, 397, 442

Münsterberg, 427

Murat, Joachim, 25, 27, 29
    commands Grande Armée in 1812/13, 72, 81, 89

Mutius, Johann Karl von, 386–88, 396, 409

Myslowice, *see* Myslowitz

Myslowitz, 117

Nadelwitz, 302, 331

Napoleon,
    Proclamation to the Army, 271
    1803 reorganization of Germany, 429
    1812 Campaign, 36
    1813 Spring Campaign, 31–32, 64, 86, 97–98, 211, 306, 311, 402, 430
        achieves first goals, 206
        crosses Saale, 209

losses, 388
prepares to cross Saale, 206
stakes of, 189
surprised by Allied attack at Lützen, 211
uncertainty, hesitation, frustration, 188
accepts armistice, 6, 8, 421–22
  reasons why, 450–51
advises Eugene, 89
alliance with Prussia, 57
alliance with Prussia in 1812, 39, 54, 57
and Alexander I in 1808, 30
appoints Davout commander of Army of
  Germany, 34
as new Caesar, 1–3, 21, 27
at Dresden, 285–86, 302
at Lützen, 7
at the tomb of Frederick the Great, 2
*bataillon carré*, 103, 257, 294
battle of Bautzen, 8, 342, 344, 347, 352–53,
  356–57, 441
battle of Lützen, 226–62, 434
  impressed by Prussians, 436
berates Russian ambassador, 46
cashiers Blücher, 57
collapse of alliance with Russia, 32–33, 36
concerns over Austria, 189, 207, 390, 448
concludes peace with Britain, 21
conditions for armistice, 395, 399, 412
controls Central Europe, 32–33, 35
creates Confederation of the Rhine, 23
crosses Elbe, 291–92
dangerous position in Silesia, 412
defeated in Russia, 3, 5, 71
defeats Austria in 1809, 31–32
departs Mainz, 205
dichotomy of emperor and general, 189
disadvantages in Spring Campaign, 450
dissolves Army of the Elbe, 298
engagement at Reichenbach, 361–64
forces Prussia into alliance, 51
forces Spanish Bourbons to abdicate, 35
Franco-Prussian treaty of 1812, 58
French god of war, 2
from Elbe to Spree, 298–99
gives Prussia ultimatum in 1811, 51
Habsburg marriage, 32
hopes after Lützen, 279
inspects battlefield after Lützen, 270
instructs Eugene, 111–13, 140, 142–43,
  189
invades Russia, 3, 70
*manoeuvre sur les derrières*, 412
marries Marie Louise of Austria, 32
master plan, 5–8, 113, 301, 315, 382–83
meets with Hatzfeldt, 42
mobilization for Russian campaign, 68
mobilization in 1813, 90, 109

negotiates with Alexander in 1807, 3
occupation of Breslau, 410
offers armistice to tsar, 322
opens armistice talks, 390
operational mastery, 436
operations in Silesia, 372, 389, 393–94, 400,
  402, 409
  uncertainty, 398–400
oppresses Prussia, 3, 34–36, 38, 43, 53–54
plans to partition Prussia, 39–40
political exploitation of Lützen, 271,
  273–74
preconceived misperceptions of war, 451
prepares for Bautzen, 302, 312, 316, 320–21,
  328, 330
pressure from Austrians, 305
principle of mass, 189
pursuit after Bautzen, 276, 359–60, 364,
  366–68
pursuit after Lützen, 269–72, 275, 277–79,
  284
pushes forces to Saale, 186–88
reaches Dresden, 284–85
reaches Lützen, 210
reacts to evacuation of Hamburg, 141–42
rear-area security measures, 370
refuses to return Glogau, 46
rejects Prussian alliance proposal, 42–43
reorganizes Germany, 21
results of Bautzen, 364
Romanov marriage, 32
secret negotiations with British in 1806,
  24
spares Breslau, 401
strategy after Bautzen, 369, 371, 382–85,
  395, 402, 410, 412
strategy after Lützen, 272–73, 278–79,
  300–1
strategy in 1813, 5, 7, 112–13, 159–60, 175,
  188–89, 206
suspicious of Prussia, 48, 51
unaware of Russo-Prussian discord, 448
uncertain over Allied movements, 186–87
underestimates Prussian losses, 292
views on Austria, 5
wants Swedish support, 61
war in Iberia, 32
wounding of Duroc, 363–64
Narva, 96–97
Natzmer, Oldwig Anton von, 78, 288
Naumburg, 149, 154, 158, 179, 187–88, 191,
  197, 202–3, 205–8, 210–11, 213, 216,
  224–25, 256, 273, 366
Naumburg (Silesia), 369–70
Nechern, 360
Neiße (Prussian fortress), 37, 44, 290, 366,
  404, 407–8, 417, 427

Neiße (River), 8, 359–61, 365, 367–70, 372
Nemenčinė, *see* Niemenzin
Nesselrode, Karl, 94, 108, 131, 168, 198, 306,
   310, 332, 343, 431, 452
Neubuchwalde, 329
Neudorf, 322–23, 390, 399, 421
Neudorf-am-Gröditzberg, 389, 394
Neuhammer, 389
Neuhof, 410
Neujäschwitz, 372
Neukirch, 320
Neumarkt, 396–400, 402, 404, 410–11, 414,
   421
Neupurschwitz, 356, 359
Neustadt in Sachsen, 320
Neusteinitz, 327
Neustettin, 91
New East Prussia, 25
Ney, Michel, 206
   commands Army of the Main, 110, 159–60,
      163, 175–77, 179, 186–87
   criticism of, 187–88
   commands III Corps, 119, 161, 205–6,
      210–12, 221
   after Bautzen, 270
   at Lützen, 231–32, 235–40, 243, 250, 256,
      434, 436
   wounded at Lützen, 246
   commands left wing of Grande Armée
   after Bautzen, 276, 302, 359, 364, 367–69,
      383–84, 386, 388, 393–95, 398–99, 401,
      404, 406, 410–12
   after Lützen, 272–73, 275–79, 284, 286,
      292
   at Bautzen, 8, 341–49, 352, 354–57, 378,
      441–42, 445, 454
   Bautzen campaign, 7–8, 20, 315–17,
      321–23, 328, 330, 333, 377
   crosses Elbe, 292, 300–1
   instructions from Napoleon, 300–1
Niedaszów, *see* Herzogswaldau
Niedergurig, 325, 328, 331, 337–38, 341,
   345–46, 352–53, 377, 440
Niederkaina, 331, 337, 341
Niederkotitz, 358–60
Niederreichenbach, 362
Niederseifersdorf, 359
Niedersiegersdorf, 428
Niemcza, *see* Nimptsch
Niemen (River), 3, 34, 73
Niemenzin, 73
Niemodlin, *see* Niemodlin
Nikitin, Aleksey, 250
Nimptsch, 412
Niwnice, *see* Kunzendorf
Nordhausen, 149, 154
North Sea, 140

Norway, 61–63, 69, 85–89, 95–98, 198
Nossen, 152–53, 163, 172, 173, 203, 207,
   278–79, 284
Nostitz, 359
Nostitz, August Ludwig von, 340, 348–49,
   439, 443, 446
Nova Wieś Grodziska, *see* Neudorf-am-
   Gröditzberg
Nowa Wieś Legnicka, *see* Neudorf
Nowe Jaroszowice, *see* Neujäschwitz
Nowe Łąki, *see* Lauterseiffen
Nowogrodziec, *see* Naumburg
Nowy Dwór Mazowiecki, *see* Modlin
Nugent, Laval, 53
Nürnberg, 161, 185
Nysa, *see* Neiße

Obergröditz, 409, 413
Obermois, 400, 410–12
Obersohland, 364
Oberwaldau, 122, 365
Ocice, 371, 380
Odeleben, 398–99, 402, 410, 434, 451
Oder (River), 5, 7–8, 25, 45, 50, 56, 78, 82, 89,
   91, 93–94, 99, 111–12, 124, 159, 184,
   219, 283, 307, 309–10, 317, 369, 374,
   382–83, 391–92, 395–96, 398–99, 401–2,
   405–10, 412, 414, 417, 447–48, 451
Odra, *see* Oder
Ohlau, 409, 418, 427
Oława, *see* Ohlau
Oltaschin, 427
Ołtaszyn, *see* Oltaschin
Ompteda, Christian Friedrich Wilhelm von,
   53
Ompteda, Ludwig von, 70
Oppitz, 323
Orlov, Mikhail, 390
Osnabrück, 170
Osten-Sacken, Fabien Gottlieb von der, 75,
   374, 390, 409, 427, 455
Osterfeld, 202
Ostrau, 271
Ostrów Wielkopolski, *see* Ostrowo
Ostrowo, 90
Ötsch, 224
Ottendorf, 371, 389
Öttingen, 155
Ottoman Empire, 32, 41, 49, 57, 429
Oudinot, Nicolas-Charles, 8, 161, 187, 205,
   210, 273, 275, 277, 284, 299, 312, 318,
   320, 329–30, 337, 343–44, 351, 359,
   369, 380, 382–83, 398, 412, 415, 422,
   428, 448

Pahlen, Pyotr, 372–73, 389
Palczewo, *see* Palschau

Palschau, 82
Panchulidzev, Semen, 235
Panchulidzev, Aleksandr, 250
Panschwitz, 312, 322
Parchwitz, 419
Paris, 1–2, 28, 39, 46, 51, 71, 463
Parszowice, *see* Parchwitz
Pasłęka, *see* Passarge River
Passarge (River), 50
Pastuchów, *see* Puschkau
Pątnów, *see* Pohlsdorf
Paul I (tsar), 6
Paulucci, Philippe, 73
Paunsdorf, 228
Peace of Posen, 163
Pegau, 211–16, 218, 226–30, 232, 238, 240,
    253–54, 263, 268–69, 271, 273
Pełczyce, *see* Peltschütz
Peltschütz, 427
Penig, 145, 149, 152–53, 163, 165–66, 171–72,
    180, 207, 209, 249
Perleberg, 141
Peter (duke of Oldenburg), 33
Peter Frederick Louis of Holstein-Gottorp,
    115
Peterswaldau, 421
Peyri, Luigi Gaspare, 249, 323, 325–26, 328
Philippon, Armand, 276, 300, 334
Phull, Karl Ludwig von, 43, 45–46
Piekary Wielkie, *see* Großbeckern
Pielaszkowice, *see* Pläswitz
Pielgrzymka, *see* Pilgramsdorf
Pieszyce, *see* Peterswaldau
Piła, *see* Schneidemühl
Pilgramsdorf, 389
Pillau, 25, 35, 44, 48, 51, 82, 112
Pillnitz, 289
Pilzen, 403, 408, 419
Pirna, 285, 291
Pius VI (pope), 52
Platov, Matvei, 73, 81
Plauen, 125–26, 147–49, 151–53, 155, 158, 165,
    175, 203–4, 220
Pleiße (River), 162, 220, 225, 439
Pließkowitz, 311, 337, 340–41, 346, 352–53
Plock, 71, 82, 91
Płock, *see* Plock
Pobles, 249
Podbrzezie Dolne, *see* Niedersiegersdorf
Podelwitz, 271
Pohlsdorf, 385, 388
Poland, 5–8, 26, 32, 34, 40, 49, 65, 88, 90,
    93–94, 103, 147, 219, 223, 249, 279, 282,
    290, 307, 373–74, 376, 380, 382, 399,
    406, 408, 413, 416–18, 430–31, 449–50
  Austrian, 40
  Prussian, 40

Second Partition, 429
  Third Partition, 429
Polkowice, *see* Polkwitz
Polkwitz, 428
Pomerania, 5, 25, 35, 47, 96, 143, 170, 301, 365,
    419
Poniatowski, Jozef, 36, 74, 82, 120, 207, 428,
    432
Portugal, 27, 32, 36, 41, 44, 52, 55, 68–69, 198,
    429
Poscherun, 76
Posen, 82, 89–91, 93, 398
Potsdam, 21
Požerūnai, *see* Poscherun
Predel, 213, 216, 265, 268–69, 271
Preititz, 331, 345–49, 352, 354–56, 364, 445
Prendel, Victor, 154
Pretzsch, 224
Primkenau, 394
prince d'Eckmühl, *see* Davout, Louis-Nicolas
prince of Hessen-Homburg, 273–74
prince royal of Sweden, *see* Bernadotte, Jean-
    Baptiste
prince-regent of Britain, 52
Pripet Marshes, 75
Profen, 401
Proposed Plan of Action Beyond the Elbe,
    136–37, 147
Prussia, 2
  "*franzosenfreundliche*" (pro-French)
      period, 45
  after Tilsit, 3, 25–26
  annexes Hanover, 23
  anti-French sentiment, 4, 27, 31, 34, 71
  Armaments Commission, 84
  as great power, 2, 429
  declaration of war against France, 4
  French oppression, 3–4, 26, 35
  leadership of anti-French parties in
      Germany, 41
  Military Governments, 274, 294, 415
  Napoleon's Continental System, 23, 26
  neutral policy, 21
  patriotism, 4, 123
  popular revolt in 1813, 4
  pro-French party, 37–38, 43, 48, 55, 79
  pro-Russian party, 429
  reform after 1807, 3
    meritocracy, 3
  relations with France before 1806, 21
  war hawks want war in 1809, 30
  war of liberation, 3–4
Prussian army
  "blood and iron" of, 4
  1st Silesian Infantry Regiment, 338
  2nd East Prussian Infantry Regiment, 338,
      341

Prussian army (cont.)
  I Corps, 228, 254, 270, 288, 315, 325, 346, 413
    1st Brigade, 250, 327
    2nd Brigade, 327
    7th Brigade, 244
    8th Brigade, 226, 244
    Reserve Cavalry, 327, 354, 385
  II Corps, 104, 172, 288, 315, 336, 413
    1st Brigade, 180, 226, 232, 236–37, 337, 346
    2nd Brigade, 180, 209, 226, 237, 270, 337, 346
    Reserve Brigade, 180, 185, 207, 226, 349
    Reserve Cavalry, 125, 152–53, 162–63, 165, 173, 179–80, 185, 197, 214–15, 226, 228–29, 231, 233, 235, 240, 252, 270, 276, 280, 336, 349, 355, 358, 361, 385, 388
  III Corps, 122, 396
  Army of Silesia, 8, 50, 396
  Brandenburg Brigade, 35, 120–21, 149, 152–53, 163, 172–73, 180
  Brandenburg Cuirassier Regiment, 240, 255–56
  Brandenburg Hussar Regiment, 239, 255
    2nd Regiment, 31
  complaints over Russians, 6
  East Prussian Brigade, 50, 99
  East Prussian Cuirassier Regiment, 255, 387
  expansion, 47
  General Staff, 3, 121, 182, 281, 445
    success at Haynau, 388
    in 1810, 35
  Kleist's corps, 223
  Kolberg Infantry Regiment, 254, 269, 341, 349
  Lower Silesian Brigade, 153, 162–63, 172–73, 180, 231
  mobilization, 4, 98, 104
  needs British supplies, 166
  Neumark Dragoon Regiment, 105, 237, 355
  officer resignations in 1812, 3, 60
  partial mobilization in 1811, 39
  Pomeranian Brigade, 35, 50, 99, 101
  pushes Prussia to war in 1813, 4
  rearguard actions, 360
  Regulations of 1812, 258
  reputation, 2
  Reserve Brigade, 180
  Royal Guard, 158, 162, 228–29, 239, 245, 253, 255–56, 259, 274, 348–49, 388, 405, 413, 423, 427
    Guard Light Cavalry Regiment, 387
  Silesian Cuirassier Regiment, 387
  Silesian Hussar Regiment
    1st Regiment, 355
  Silesian Landwehr Corps, 396, 413

  Silesian Uhlan Regiment, 397
  troops in Silesia, 117
  Upper Silesian Brigade, 65, 153, 163, 172–73, 180
  West Prussian Brigade, 50, 99
  West Prussian Musketeer Battalion, 355
  West Prussian Uhlan Regiment, 387
Prussian patriotism in 1813, 4
Prypiackija baloty, *see* Pripet Marshes
Przemków, *see* Primkenau
Przesieczany, *see* Hochkirch (Silesia)
Psie Pole, *see* Hundsfeld
Purschwitz, 342, 346, 349, 354–57, 411, 443
Puschkau, 389, 397
Puszków, *see* Puschkau
Puthod, Jacques-Pierre, 272, 292, 300, 349, 354, 360, 387
Pyrenees, 32, 35, 73, 79

Quadriga, 2
quadrilateral, 212, 224, 229, 232–33, 236, 238, 240, 243, 245, 247, 250, 253–54, 256–57, 433–34, 437
Quatitz, 337
Quedlinburg, 177
Queis (River), 8, 203, 366, 369–70, 389
Querfurt, 205
Quesitz, 224

Rackel, 349, 356
Rackschütz, 397
Radeberg, 283, 288–89
Radetzky von Radetz, Jan Josef Václav, 307, 310
Radmeritz, 368
Radomierzyce, *see* Radmeritz
Radzików, *see* Rudelsdorf
Raglowich, Clemens von, 187
Rahna, 212–13, 224, 229–31, 236–40, 243–47, 250, 253, 255, 270, 436–37
Rakoszyce, *see* Rackschütz
Rakowice Małe, *see* Winigrackwitz
Rakowice Wielkie, *see* Großrackwitz
Rapp, Jean, 18, 428
Rauske, 395
Rawicz, *see* Rawitsch
Rawitsch, 99, 122
Rechberg, Joseph von, 167
Regensburg, 30, 125, 134, 136, 169
Reichenbach, 152, 325, 358–65, 370, 416, 421, 427, 449
Reichenbach (engagement), 361–62, 364, 379, 388, 423
Reichenbach Plan, 310
Republic of Venice, 26
Reynier, Jean-Louis, 74, 82, 89–91, 93, 124, 167, 272, 284–85, 292, 296, 315–17,

319, 322, 345, 349, 360–62, 367–68,
    371–72, 386, 388, 394, 399, 402, 428
Rheinbund, 285
    *see also* Confederation of the Rhine
Rhine (River), 21, 73, 79, 307
Ribbentrop, Wilhelm, 135, 150, 166, 169, 171
Ricard, Étienne-Pierre, 235, 238–39
Rieschen, 302–3, 324, 351
Riesengebirge, 309, 371, 403, 417
Riga, 64, 70, 73, 75
Rippach, 213, 224, 235
Rippach (engagement), 210, 388
Rippach (rivulet), 214, 225
Rochambeau, Donatien, 349, 356
Rochlitz, 153, 180, 185, 203–4, 207, 211, 215,
    272–73, 275–78
Röder, Friedrich Erhard von, 120, 172–73,
    180, 226, 228, 231, 239, 242, 259, 276,
    337, 348–49, 352, 354–55, 385
Rogoźnica, *see* Großrosen
Rogoźnik, *see* Roßnitz; Rosenig
Roguet, François, 167
Romanovs, 2
    Anna Pavlovna (grand duchess), 65
    Catherine Pavlovna (grand duchess), 115
    Yekaterina Pavlovna (grand duchess), 33
    rejects marriage with Napoleon, 32, 65
Rome, 142
Rosenig, 399
Roßlau, 148, 156–59, 167, 208, 220, 222,
    289
Roßlau-Dessau, 176, 187
Roßnitz, 421
Rötha, 209, 212, 218, 226, 273
Rothenburg, 369
Rotkretscham, 360
Rudelsdorf, 413
Rudzevich, Aleksandr, 326
Rügen, 61, 87–88, 97, 122
Ruhland, 288
Rühle von Lilienstern, Otto August, 120, 385
Rumiantsev, Nikolai, 41, 45, 47, 49, 57, 61, 64,
    94
Rusko, *see* Rauske
Russia,
    Continental System, 32
    negotiations with British, 63
    Order of St. George, 261, 437
    people's war, 4
    sacrifices in 1812, 6
Russian army,
    9th Division, 326
    18th Division, 326
    II Infantry Corps, 231–32, 250, 268–69, 361,
        368, 389, 394, 401
    3rd Infantry Division, 250–51
    4th Infantry Division, 251

Chernigovskii Regiment, 250
communications in 1813, 8
crosses Prussian frontier, 82
Cuirassier Corps, 247, 263, 354, 356–57, 440
    2nd Cuirassier Division, 361
    defeated in 1805, 23
    Glukhovskii Cuirassier Regiment, 379
Grenadier Corps, 242, 252, 263, 325, 327
    2nd Grenadier Division, 251, 276
Imperial Guard, 242, 247, 250, 252, 269,
    315, 336–37, 357, 361–62, 379, 405,
    409, 413, 419, 427, 434, 455
    Guard Infantry Corps, 263
in 1807, 2
Kexholmskii Grenadier Regiment,
    379
Kleist's corps, 223
Life Guard Jäger Regiment, 379
line of communication, 147, 190, 206, 282,
    288, 365, 382, 406
march to Kaluga, 195
Pernovskii Grenadier Regiment, 379
rearguard actions, 7, 276, 280, 286, 288, 293,
    295, 312, 360–63, 365, 368, 372, 389,
    394–95, 401
Reserve, 242, 244, 247, 251–52, 269, 315,
    343, 361–62, 379, 409, 413, 455
    Third Western Army, 73
Russian steppes, 3–4, 48
Russo-Prussian alliance, 6, 40, 50, 80, 84, 94,
    120, 431, 452
Russo-Swedish alliance, 61

Saalburg-Ebersdorf, 175
Saale, 6, 149–50, 157–61, 179, 181, 186–91,
    193, 205, 209
Saalfeld, 150, 155, 163, 175, 179, 185, 187, 191,
    193, 197, 205, 209, 221
Saalfeld (engagement), 166
Saarau, 413
Sabaneyev, Ivan, 375
Sabrodt, 318, 322
Sack, Johann August, 47
Sagan, 83, 412, 428
Salga, 311
Salzburg, 32
Sandersleben, 158
Särchen, 345
Saxon Immediate Commission, 164
Saxony, 6–7, 39, 79, 94–95, 100, 102–3, 125,
    127–35, 145, 149–51, 155, 158, 162–63,
    165, 170, 173–74, 182, 188, 195, 198,
    207, 218, 221, 266, 282, 285, 290, 307,
    315, 373, 380, 419, 423, 426, 430,
    450–51
Sayn-Wittgenstein, Wilhelm Ludwig Georg
    zu, 28, 37

Scharnhorst, Gerhard von, 429, 431, 439
  advises advancing beyond the Elbe, 148
  advises cautious operations, 151
  appointed chief of staff, 105
  Arrangement with the Russians over the
    Operations of General Scharnhorst,
    102
  as reformer, 3
  at Breslau, 58
  at Russian headquarters, 122, 136
  chief of staff, 120–21, 158, 176, 182, 418
    after Lützen, 274, 280
    at Lützen, 243, 246, 253
    wounded at Lützen, 253
  communicates with Russians in 1811,
    36–38
  complains over Russians, 154
  criticizes Blücher's requisitions, 135
  criticizes Wittgenstein's Instructions, 204
  directs mobilization, 104
  disagreement with Blücher, 148
  dissatisfaction with Russians, 184
  evaluates Napoleon's options, 147
  favors national revolt, 44
  General Staff system, 181
  good rapport with Wintzingerode, 122
  insists Blücher commands Prussian army,
    98
  leaves army, 58
  lobbies against Toll, 196
  lobbies for Russian alliance in 1813, 79
  measures to defend Prussia, 35
  meets with Wittgenstein, 146, 148–49, 184
  mission to Dresden, 192, 195–96
  mission to Kalisch, 98–100
  mission to Russia, 37–38, 45–49, 51, 55, 84,
    95, 459
  mission to Vienna, 281, 293, 305, 406
  objects to Wittgenstein's plans for Lützen,
    215, 217–18
  on system of dual command, 281
  on war in 1809, 27
  opposed to *Angriffskrieg*, 182
  opposes pro-French party, 38
  paralyzed by Kutuzov, 164
  pessimism over Russians, 154
  plans for offensive operations, 192–96
  proposes Spanish-style insurrection, 44
  respected by Russians, 117, 122, 207
  responds to criticism, 164
  rival to Wittgenstein, 201
  Russo-Prussian military convention, 49
  strategy in 1813, 182–84
  thoughts on French operations, 151
  tutors crown prince, 166
  unexpected death, 122
Scheldt (River), 73

Schellendorf, 385
Schill, Ferdinand von, 31
Schkeuditz, 202, 207, 209
Schkorlopp, 212, 227
*Schlachtlenkung*, 437
Schladebach, 224
Schlaup, 394
Schleiz, 158, 175, 179, 193, 203
Schlemmer, 380
*Schlesische privilegirte Zeitung*, 106
Schlichtingsheim, 427
Schlimmer, *see* Schlemmer
Schneidemühl, 91
Schnelle Deichsel (River), 386, 394
Schöler, Reinhold Otto von, 37, 39, 41, 45–46,
    48–49, 55, 67
Schönau, 264, 396
Schönberg, 366, 368
Schönerstädt, 276
Schöps, 361
Schreiberhau, 419
Schrottau, 428
Schuler von Senden, Ernst Julius, 105, 124,
    136, 390, 397, 402, 409, 424, 427
Schützenhain, 367
Schwarze Schöps (stream), 361
Schwarzenberg, Karl zu, 18, 74, 82, 159, 332
Schwedt, 35, 317
Schweidnitz, 309, 365, 374, 390–92, 395–97,
    400, 402–4, 408, 410–14, 419, 424,
    426–27, 447, 451
Schweidnitz (stream), 402, 412, 419
Schweinfurt, 155, 160–61
Schwengfeld, 409
Scinawa, *see* Steinau; Wohlau–Steinau District
Sdier, 345
Sébastiani, Horace-François, 272–73, 275–76,
    278, 292, 300, 315–17, 322, 364, 367,
    371, 389, 394, 428
Second Reich, 4
Second World War, 4
Sędzimirów, *see* Wilhelmsdorf
Seebenisch, 264
Seesen, 165
Seidenberg, 366
Seifersdorf, 372
Senftenberg, 317, 319, 334, 345
Serbia, 36
Seven Years War, 2, 80, 135, 296, 309, 391
Seydlitz, Anton Friedrich von, 75–77
Shakhovsky, Ivan, 250–51, 254
Shuvalov, Pavel, 390, 399, 412
Sicard, Joseph-Victorien, 353
*Sicherheitskommissare*, 37
Sicily, 24, 450
Siedliska, *see* Siegendorf
Siegendorf, 385

Siegersdorf, 369, 370
Sieroniów, *see* Schlemmer
Sievers, Yegor, 293, 323, 392, 424
Sieyès, Emmanuel Joseph, 140
Silberberg, 25, 290, 366
Silesia, 5, 7–8, 20, 25, 29, 39, 42, 48, 50, 54,
    57–58, 71, 82, 90–91, 93, 95, 98, 101,
    104–5, 112, 125, 160, 163, 223, 282, 290,
    292, 296, 301, 305, 309, 357, 361, 365,
    373–74, 390, 394, 397, 400, 411–12,
    414–15, 417–18, 424–25, 428, 430, 438,
    448, 451
  neutral zone, 419
Sitteln, 213–14, 216
Sixth Coalition, 6, 153, 165, 191, 195, 262, 308,
    365, 395, 440, 446
  community of interest, 6
  crisis, 8, 405, 418, 436, 448
Skora, *see* Schnelle Deichsel (River)
Słup, *see* Schlaup
Snowidza, *see* Eisendorf
Söhesten, 232, 238
Sondershausen, 154
Sophie Marie, Countess von Voss, 37
Soritz, 359
Souham, Joseph, 179, 210, 229–30, 232–33,
    236–39, 243, 256–57, 323, 325, 327,
    347–49, 352, 354, 368, 372, 383, 394,
    411, 434, 437
Soult, Nicolas, 337, 344, 346, 352–53, 370, 383,
    393, 398
South Prussia, 25
Sovetsk, *see* Tilsit
Spain, 4, 26–30, 32, 35, 41, 44, 55–56, 60,
    67–68, 90, 97, 198, 306–7, 429–30
  people's war, 27
Spandau, 35, 139, 146, 148, 274, 316
Spree (River), 7, 293, 302, 312, 314–15,
    319–25, 328–29, 331, 337–38, 343–45,
    352, 379, 440–41
Spremberg, 304, 316, 327, 334, 404
Spring Campaign of 1813, 97–98, 122, 133,
    138, 198, 311, 422, 448, 452
Sprottau, 382–83, 389, 394
Srebrna Górna, *see* Silberberg
Środa Śląska, *see* Neumarkt
St. Petersburg, 30, 36, 41, 45–46, 48, 56, 65, 96
St.-Cyr, Claude Carra, 139–41, 143
St.-Marsan, Antoine, 51, 53–57, 83, 107,
    120
St.-Priest, Guillaume Emmanuel de, 361, 372,
    389, 395, 401, 413
Stade, 140
St-Aignan, Nicolas-Auguste, 163
Stare Jaroszowice, *see* Altjäschwitz
Stargardt, 82
Starogard, *see* Stargardt

Starsiedel, 212–13, 224, 229–30, 232–33, 235,
    237–38, 240, 247, 250, 434, 437
Steffens, Henrik, 105, 117, 253, 416, 444
Stein, Heinrich Friedrich Karl vom und zum.
  as reformer, 3, 29
  at Königsberg, 81, 115
  chairman of Central Commission, 135
  encounters Saxon resistance, 136
  Prussia's Chief Minister of Domestic and
    Foreign Affairs
    ousted by Napoleon, 28
  Russian official, 65
    illness, 94
    negotiates with Prussians, 84, 94
  summons East Prussian Landtag, 81
  works with Yorck, 81
Steinau, 126–27, 411, 427
Steinitz, 327
Steinmetz, Karl Friedrich von, 250, 254–55,
    276, 280, 327–28, 354–55
Steinsdorf, 388–89
Stettin, 5, 18, 25, 29, 82, 91, 93, 97, 99, 101,
    105, 112, 124, 139, 283, 290, 317, 430
Steudnitz, 386, 388
Stewart, Charles, 61, 85–86, 108, 118, 145, 195,
    198–99, 222, 305, 308, 310, 313–14,
    319, 353, 358, 373–74, 387, 391–92,
    398, 404, 427, 433, 438–39, 442, 447,
    449
Stockholm, 60–64, 86, 88, 95–98
Stolberg, Konstantin von, 240
Stönsch, 215, 263
Storkwitz, 214–15, 226–28, 263
Stößen, 211, 216, 224
Stralsund, 97–98, 101, 118, 139–41, 145, 147,
    198
Straußfurt, 165
Strehla, 148–49
Strehlen, 408–9, 412–13, 417–18, 427
*Streifkorps*, 94, 99, 101–2, 116, 138–39, 143,
    149, 161, 168, 197, 315, 318, 370,
    396–97, 401, 448
Striegau, 395–96, 399–400, 402, 409–10, 414,
    419
Striegau (stream), 410, 419
Strupice, *see* Schellendorf
Strzegom, *see* Striegau
Strzegomka, *see* Striegau (stream)
Strzelin, *see* Strehlen
Strzelno, *see* Schützenhain
Studnica, *see* Steudnitz
Sudetes Mountains, 309
Sulików, *see* Schönberg
Suvorov, A. V., 20
Sweden
  as Baltic power, 60
  relations with France, 61

Swedish Pomerania, 61, 87–88, 127, 143
Świdnica, *see* Schweidnitz
Świerzawa, *see* Schönau
Świętoszów, *see* Neuhammer
Szczecin, *see* Stettin
Szczecinek, *see* Neustettin
Szklarska Poręba, *see* Schreiberhau
Szlichtyngowa, *see* Schlichtingsheim
Szprotawa, *see* Schrottau; Sprottau

Tarayre, Jean-Joseph, 243
Tarnowitz, 117, 120
Tarnowskie Gory, *see* Tarnowitz
Taucha, 211, 247–48
Tauentzien, Bogislav Friedrich von, 98, 101, 105, 116, 290
Tauragė, *see* Tauroggen
Tautendorf, 276
Tczew, *see* Dirschau
Tennstädt, 186
Teplice, *see* Teplitz
Teplitz, 197
Terezín, *see* Theresienstadt
Tettenborn, Friedrich Karl von, 73, 99, 101, 133, 141, 145, 168, 184
Teutonic Knights, 4
Tharandt, 285
Theresienstadt, 310
Thermopylae, Prussian, *see* Bautzen (battle)
Thesau, 210
Thielmann, Johann von, 125, 146, 163–64, 284–85, 292, 296
Thiergarten, 369
Thile, Ludwig Gustav von, 78, 105
Thirty Years War, 70, 353
Thomaswaldau, 372, 389, 428
Thommendorf, 382
Thorn, 71, 81, 89, 159, 206, 303
Thornton, Edward, 62–64, 85, 89, 97–98, 109
Thuringia, 102, 152–53, 164–65, 177–78
Thuringia Forest, 152–53, 155–56, 158, 165, 178–80, 183, 185–86
Tiedemann, Karl Ludwig von, 58
Tilsit, 3, 73, 76–77, 79, 344
Toll, Karl von, 72–73, 156, 159, 191, 196–97, 201, 207, 209, 257, 289, 293, 308, 331, 342, 405
Tomisław, *see* Thommendorf
Töpferberg, 360–63
Topographic-Military Map of Teutschland, 213
Torgau, 7, 90, 111, 125, 133, 136, 138, 146–49, 153, 158, 163, 167, 178, 183, 202–3, 270, 272, 276–79, 282, 284–86, 292, 300, 315, 380

Tormasov, Aleksandr, 73, 82, 101–3, 136–37, 148, 158, 161, 163, 177, 181, 189, 194, 196–98, 200, 203, 207, 209, 213, 215, 227–28, 230, 232, 243, 252, 257–58, 263, 432
Tornau, 232, 247
Toruń, *see* Thorn
Trachenberg, 427
Treaty of Amiens, 26
Treaty of Breslau, 108, 306, 450
Treaty of Campo Formio, 26
Treaty of Kalisch, 95, 108, 306, 310, 450, 455
Treaty of Lunéville, 26
Treaty of Orebro, 63
Treaty of Pressburg, 27
Treaty of Schönbrunn, 32
Treaty of Tilsit, 3, 25–26, 29, 34, 37, 39, 49, 55, 92, 95, 108, 112, 114, 125–26, 129, 424, 449
   Prussian indemnity, 28
Trieste, 32, 449
Troitschendorf, 368
Trójca, *see* Troitschendorf
*Trübsals-spritzen*, 346
Truce of Gäbersdorf, 412
Tsarskoye Seol, 48–49
Turks, 34, 36, 375
Tyrol, 4, 32

Übigau, 285–87, 295
Übigau (engagement), 286
Ujazd Górny, *see* Obermois
Ulbersdorf, 394
Ullersdorf, 359

Vacha, 179, 187
Valentini, Georg Wilhelm von, 390–91
Vandamme, Dominique-Joseph, 141, 143–44, 167, 170, 380
viceroy of Italy, *see* Beauharnais, Eugene de
Victor, Claude, 8, 82, 158, 167, 170, 221, 272, 275–76, 278, 292, 300–2, 315–19, 322, 334, 345, 364, 367, 369, 371, 382, 389, 394, 398, 412
Vienna, 27, 30, 39–40, 61, 64, 84–85, 165, 178, 281, 297, 305–7, 324, 391, 405, 432
Vilna, 71–73, 83–85
Vilnius, *see* Vilna
Vistula (River), 5, 7, 18, 49–50, 55–56, 71, 78–79, 89–91, 93, 99, 112–13, 188, 271, 297, 307, 365, 374, 392, 405, 409, 447
Volkonsky, Pyotr, 73, 133, 151–52, 154–55, 183–84, 191, 197, 200–1, 208–9, 213, 215, 242, 244, 268, 309, 376, 405, 413
Vorontsov, Mikhail, 159

Waditz, 359
Wagram (Battle), 31
Wahlstatt, 168, 173, 221, 266, 399
Waldenburg, 203, 249
Waldheim, 275–76, 278, 284
Wallmoden, Ludwig Georg, 144–45, 173
War of Bavarian Succession, 429
War of the Fifth Coalition, 30–32
War of the First Coalition, 21, 26, 429
War of the Fourth Coalition, 24, 27, 31, 33, 100, 191, 203, 429
War of the Second Coalition, 6, 21, 26
War of the Third Coalition, 21, 109, 178, 429
  Pitt Plan, 109
Warsaw, 20, 71, 82, 89, 102, 112, 124, 159, 365, 374, 390, 406
Wartenburg, 19, 148, 157
Wartha, 325, 327
Wąsosz, *see* Herrnstadt
Weimar, 154, 159, 165, 179–80, 185, 187, 191, 197, 205–6, 219, 221
  Geographic Institute of, 213
Weißenberg, 306, 312, 315, 325, 343–44, 346–47, 356–60, 364, 368, 445
Weißenfels, 180, 191, 197, 202, 206, 208, 210–16, 218, 224–25, 229, 231, 236, 242, 248, 256–57, 270, 434–35
Weißensee, 154, 205
Weißestein hill, 338
Weißig, 293, 327, 330
Wellesley, Arthur, 36, 56, 68, 118
Wellesley, Richard, 61
Wenigrackwitz, 372
Werben, 213–15, 227–31, 263
Wernersdorf, 390, 419
Werra (River), 158, 164
Weser (River), 111, 140, 149, 170, 180
West Prussia, 5, 35, 40, 72, 95, 365, 430
Wettin, 187, 207, 222
Wilczy Las, *see* Wolfshain
Wilhelmsdorf, 389
Wilkanowko, *see* Grüneberg
Wilków Wielki, *see* Großwilkau
Wilkszyn, *see* Wiltschau
William (prince of Prussia), 28, 120, 229, 231–32, 235, 240, 242, 247, 250, 252, 261, 434
William I (Elector), 31
William I (emperor), 2
William I (king), 77
William I of Hesse, 40
Wilson, Robert, 100, 103, 108, 117, 124, 157, 181, 192, 199, 297, 355, 373–74, 435, 437, 442, 447
Wiltschau, 427
Windischleuba, 269

Wintzingerode, Ferdinand von, 20, 74, 82, 90, 93, 99, 101, 122–23, 125–26, 131, 133, 149–50, 152–53, 156, 158, 165, 172–73, 176, 186, 191, 202–3, 207, 209–12, 214–15, 218, 220, 222, 227, 230–32, 235, 240, 242, 247, 249, 254, 269, 314–15, 434–35, 437, 455
Wisła, *see* Vistula
Wittenberg, 7, 90, 99, 111, 124–25, 146–49, 161, 167, 178, 182, 192, 208, 220, 272, 277–78, 284, 286, 289, 292, 300, 315, 380
Wittgenstein, Ludwig Adolph zu,
  Allied commander in chief, 199, 201, 207, 217, 223, 227, 247, 282, 288, 318–19, 376, 447
  after Lützen, 275
  attempts to resign, 314
  battle of Bautzen, 336, 340, 342–43, 351, 355–56, 440–41
  battle of Lützen, 211, 226–27, 230–33, 235–36, 240, 244–45, 247, 250, 252, 255, 257–58, 433, 435–36, 453
  concentrates army, 209
  criticized by Scharnhorst, 280
  crosses Spree, 293
  decides to attack Napoleon at Lützen, 208, 212
  difficulties as, 200–1, 207, 215, 288, 313–14, 366, 373, 433, 438
  disposition for Bautzen, 324–25
  disposition rejected by tsar, 208
  doubts Prussian combat effectiveness, 201–2
  instructions for offensive operations, 202–4
  meets with Blücher, 209
  mistakes at Bautzen, 299, 313
  mistakes at Lützen, 226–28, 236, 242, 262, 434, 437, 453
  plans to defend Elbe, 282–83
  prepares for Bautzen, 302–3, 310, 311, 313–15, 323–24, 325, 329
  prepares for Lützen, 198, 214–17, 227, 229, 231, 236
  Prussian criticism of, 438–39
  resolves to accept second battle, 293
  retreats from Bautzen, 360
  retreats from Elbe, 282, 287–89, 293, 439
  retreats from Lützen, 268, 280
  retreats to Bautzen, 288, 289
  retreats to Oder, 371–72
  retreats to Silesia, 365–68, 371
  strategy after Lützen, 282
  surprises Napoleon at Lützen, 212, 257
  uncertainty after Lützen, 282

Wittgenstein, Ludwig Adolph zu, (cont.)
  candidate for Allied commander in chief, 199
  commands Allied left wing, 384, 395–96,
    404, 408, 413, 419
  commands Allied northern army, 101–2,
    124, 133, 136, 138, 145, 156, 161, 168,
    176–77, 198, 220, 222
  dissatisfaction with Kutuzov, 432
  commands Russian right wing, 71, 73, 76,
    79, 81–82, 90–91, 93, 99
  crosses Oder, 124
  disagrees with Kutuzov, 138, 190
  disregards Kutuzov's orders, 139
  engagement at Möckern, 152
  feels threatened by Scharnhorst, 201
  meets with Scharnhorst, 184
  meets with Toll, 197
  plans for joint operations with Blücher, 162
  proclamation to Prussians, 71
  proclamations to Germans, 168
  rapport with Blücher, 123
  reaches Berlin, 124
  responds to Kutuzov's caution, 157
Wittichenau, 322
Wleń, *see* Lähn
Wohlau, 126, 427
Wohlau–Steinau District, 127
Wojcieszyn, *see* Ulbersdorf
Wojnarowice, *see* Wernersdorf
Wolfshain, 372
Wołów, *see* Wohlau; Wohlau–Steinau District
Wrangel, August Friedrich von, 37–38, 75, 77
Wrocław, *see* Breslau
Wschowa, *see* Fraustadt
Wurschen, 293, 304, 306, 337, 342, 356, 359
Wurschen Convention, 306–7, 332
Wurschen Plan, 308–10, 332, 365–66, 371,
  391–92
Würzburg, 137, 146–47, 150, 152–55, 158,
  162–63, 180, 185, 205
Wurzen, 152, 202–3, 208, 215, 223, 229, 255,
  268, 276–79
Wykróty, *see* Oberwaldau
Wysocko, *see* Hohendorf

Yashvili, Leo, 453
Yermolov, Aleksey, 354–56, 358, 360, 375, 379,
  442, 453
Yorck, Hans David von
  advises defending Silesia, 412
  agrees to cooperate with Russians, 99
  at Königsberg, 81
  commands Prussian I and II Corps, 269–70
  commands Prussian I Corps, 91, 93–94,
    101, 124, 133, 136, 138, 202–3, 207–9,
    212, 220, 222, 396
    after Bautzen, 385, 405
    after Lützen, 276, 280

  at Bautzen, 303, 315, 336, 345–46,
    353–56, 440
  at Lützen, 214–15, 226, 228, 230, 240,
    242, 244, 246–47, 254, 434, 436–37
  dissatisfaction with Wittgenstein, 314
  engagement at Königswartha, 325,
    327–28
  opposes retreat across Oder, 413
  retreats to Bautzen, 289
  retreats to Oder, 417
  retreats to Silesia, 365
  commands Prussians in Russia, 70
  crosses the Elbe, 156
  military governor of East Prussia, 50, 56, 80
  opposed to Blücher, 444
  parades through Berlin, 124
  resents Gneisenau, 287
  signs Convention of Tauroggen, 75–79,
    83–84, 95, 114, 431
  orders for dismissal, 77
  summons East Prussian Landtag, 81
Yuzefovich, Dmitri, 216, 248, 265

Ząbkowice Śląskie, *see* Frankenstein
Zabłocie, *see* Thiergarten
Żagań, *see* Sagan
Zamość, 124
Żarów, *see* Saarau
Zastrow, Wilhelm Ernst von, 413
Zawidów, *see* Seidenberg
Zbylutów, *see* Deutmannsdorf
Zealand, 64, 87
Zebrzydowa, *see* Siegersdorf
Zeitz, 153, 204, 211–12, 216, 248–49, 269, 273,
  294, 439, 453
Zerna, 322
Zezschwitz, Joachim Friedrich Gotthelf von,
  131
Ziębice, *see* Münsterberg
Zieten, Wieprecht Hans Karl von, 172–73,
  180, 270, 276, 401, 413, 423
  ambush at Haynau, 385, 387–88
  at Bautzen, 337–38, 341, 344, 346, 353, 355
  at Lützen, 226, 231–32, 237–39
Zittau, 428
Złotoryja, *see* Goldberg
Żmigród, *see* Trachenberg
Zobten, 410
Zobtenberg, 410
Zollenspieker, 141, 169
Zörbig, 184, 220, 222
Zschopau, 277–78
Zschopau River, 277
Zurich (battle), 6
Zurich (second battle of), 19
Zwenkau, 226, 269
Zwickau, 153, 162–63, 165, 172–74, 180, 187,
  193, 196, 203–4, 207, 227